# Eastern Caribbean

## a Lonely Planet travel survival kit

### Glenda Bendure
### Ned Friary

**Eastern Caribbean**

**1st edition**

**Published by**
**Lonely Planet Publications**
Head Office:   PO Box 617, Hawthorn, Vic 3122, Australia
Branches:      PO Box 2001A, Berkeley, CA 94702, USA
                 10 Barley Mow Passage, Chiswick, London W4 4PH, UK
                 71 bis rue du Cardinal Lemoine, 75005 Paris, France

**Printed by**
McPherson's Printing Group Ltd, Australia

**Photographs by**
Glenda Bendure (GB), Ned Friary (NF), Tony Wheeler (TW)
Front cover: Dancer in bright carnival dress, Guadelope, Sylvain Grandadam,
            The Photo Library – Sydney

**This Edition**
October 1994

National Library of Australia Cataloguing in Publication Data

Bendure, Glenda
    Eastern Caribbean – a travel survival kit.

    1st ed.
    Includes index.
    ISBN 0 86442 235 0.

    1. Antilles, Lesser – Guidebooks.
    I. Friary, Ned. II. Title.
    (Series: Lonely Planet travel survival kit).

917.2904

text & maps © Lonely Planet 1994
photos © photographers as indicated 1994
climate charts compiled from information supplied by Patrick J Tyson, © Patrick J Tyson, 1994

### Glenda Bendure & Ned Friary

Glenda grew up in California's Mojave Desert and first travelled overseas as a high school AFS exchange student to India.

Ned grew up near Boston, studied Social Thought & Political Economy at the University of Massachusetts in Amherst and upon graduating headed west.

They met in Santa Cruz, California, where Glenda was completing her university studies. In 1978, with Lonely Planet's first book *Across Asia on the Cheap* in hand, they hit the overland trail across southern Europe, through Iran and Afghanistan, and on to trains in India and treks in Nepal. The next six years were spent exploring Asia and the Pacific, with a home base in Japan where Ned taught at a prep school and Glenda edited *Kansai Time Out*, an English-language monthly.

They now live on Cape Cod in Massachusetts – at least when they're not on the road. Glenda has a travel column in the *Cape Cod Times*.

Ned and Glenda have a particular fondness for islands and tropical climes and are the authors of Lonely Planet's *Hawaii – a travel survival kit* and *Micronesia – a travel survival kit*. They also wrote the Norway and Denmark chapters of LP's *Scandinavian & Baltic Europe on a shoestring*.

### From the Authors

A hearty thanks to the many island tourist offices and their representatives in the USA, especially those of the French West Indies, Barbados, and the Netherlands Antilles. Thanks also to those friends and travellers who shared insights and experiences with us along the way.

### From the Publisher

Mapping, design, illustration and layout of this first edition of *Eastern Caribbean – a travel survival kit* were coordinated by the incomparable Tamsin Wilson. Illustrations were also contributed by Ann Jeffree, Trudi Canavan, Greg Herriman, Michelle Stamp, Sally Woodward, Jacqui Saunders, Jane Hart, Margaret Jung and Peter Morris. Jane Hart also designed the cover. Michelle Coxall, Rowan McKinnon and Kristin Odijk edited this book. Proofing was done by Diana Saad and Adrienne Costanzo. Special thanks to Adrienne for damage control.

### Warning & Request

Things change – prices go up, schedules

change, good places go bad and bad places go bankrupt, nothing stays the same. So if you find things better or worse, recently opened or long since closed, please write and tell us and help make the next edition better. Your letters will be used to help update future editions and, where possible, important changes will be included in a Stop Press section in reprints.

We greatly appreciate all information that is sent to us by travellers. Back at Lonely Planet we employ a hard-working readers' letters team to sort through the many letters we receive. The best ones will be rewarded with a free copy of the next edition or another Lonely Planet guide if you prefer. We give away lots of books, but, unfortunately, not every letter or postcard receives one.

# Contents

# TRINIDAD & TOBAGO ........................................................................ 502

# GLOSSARY .................................................................................... 542

# INDEX .......................................................................................... 543

# Map Legend

## BOUNDARIES

........International Boundary
........Internal Boundary
........District Boundary
........Tropics

## ROUTES

........Freeway
........Highway
........Major Road
........Unsealed Road or Track
........City Road
........City Street
........Railway
........Walking Track
........Walking Tour
........Ferry Route
........Cable Car or Chairlift

## AREA FEATURES

........Park, Gardens
........National Park
........Built-Up Area
........Pedestrian Mall
........Market
........Cemetery
........Reef
........Beach
........Rocks

## HYDROGRAPHIC FEATURES

........Coastline
........River, Creek
........Intermittent River or Creek
........Lake, Salt Lake
........Canal
........Swamp

## SYMBOLS

| | | | |
|---|---|---|---|
| ✪ CAPITAL | National Capital | ✪ ★ | Hospital, Police Station |
| ◉ Capital | State Capital | ✈ ✝ | Airport, Airfield |
| ⬤ CITY | Major City | ▱ ✿ | Swimming Pool, Gardens |
| ● City | City | ❖ 🦛 | Shopping Centre, Zoo |
| ● Town | Town | ↑ 🛱 | Golf Course, Picnic Site |
| ● Village | Village | ← 4B | One Way Street, Route Number |
| ■ | Place to Stay | ∴ | Archaeological Site or Ruins |
| ▼ | Place to Eat | ⛫ 🗼 | Stately Home, Monument |
| ☗ | Pub, Bar | ♨ ◫ | Castle, Tomb |
| ✉ ☎ | Post Office, Telephone | ⌒ ⌂ | Cave, Hut or Chalet |
| ❶ ⑤ | Tourist Information, Bank | ▲ ❊ | Mountain or Hill, Lookout |
| ⊖ 🅿 | Transport, Parking | ☖ ⩗ | Lighthouse, Shipwreck |
| 🏛 ⛺ | Museum, Youth Hostel | )( ∿ | Pass, Spring |
| 🏕 ⚑ | Caravan Park, Camping Ground | | Ancient or City Wall |
| ✝ ⊟ ✝ | Church, Cathedral | | Rapids, Waterfalls |
| ☪ ✡ | Mosque, Synagogue | | Cliff or Escarpment, Tunnel |
| ⚏ ⚎ | Buddhist Temple, Hindu Temple | | Railway Station |

Note: not all symbols displayed above appear in this book

# Introduction

Collectively, the islands of the Eastern Caribbean fit all of the tropical images: powdery white sands, clear turquoise waters, lush jungle rainforests, balmy weather and an unhurried pace.

Taken individually the islands vary widely. Some places are picture-perfect coral islands, nearly flat and fringed with palm-lined beaches, while other islands are high and mountainous with a terrain dominated by waterfalls and steaming volcanoes. Culturally, the islands are a hybrid – largely of African, English and French heritage but with a notable measure of Dutch and East Indian influences as well. Politically, the islands make up eight independent nations, two British colonies, two French *départements* and an affiliated state of the Netherlands.

From Anguilla in the north to Trinidad in the south, these islands make a 1000-km-long sweep that forms the eastern boundary of the Caribbean. Although it's certainly possible – with an open schedule and a fair bit of time – to island hop from one end of the Eastern Caribbean to the other, most visitors opt for a smaller slice.

Certainly if you're looking for specific activities or a certain ambience, you'll need to select destinations accordingly. In Martinique, you can have croissants and espresso at a sidewalk café and shop for French fashions in trendy boutiques. In Trinidad, don't expect to find croissants – the bakeries sell Indian curry rotis and English meat pies – and instead of boutiques you can pass the afternoon visiting back-street *mas camps* (workshops), where artisans design and sell elaborate Carnival costumes.

Divers can find a good variety of underwater attractions off most islands, including lesser known spots such as Saba, Dominica and Tobago which all offer pristine dive sites and a nice range of marine life and geological features.

Many of the islands have splendid

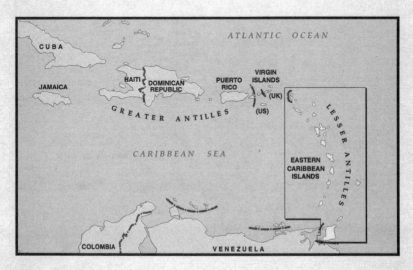

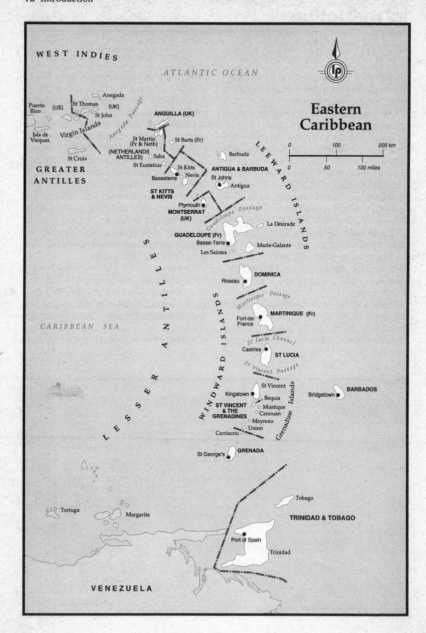

WEST INDIES

ATLANTIC OCEAN

Eastern
Caribbean

Puerto
Rico (US)
Isla de
Vieques
St Thomas
St John
Anegada
(UK)
Virgin Islands
St Croix
ANGUILLA (UK)
St Martin
(Fr & Neth)
(NETHERLANDS
ANTILLES)
Saba
St Eustatius
St Barts (Fr)
Barbuda
ANTIGUA & BARBUDA
St Johns
Antigua
LEEWARD ISLANDS

GREATER
ANTILLES
St Kitts
Nevis
Basseterre
ST KITTS
& NEVIS
Plymouth
MONTSERRAT
(UK)
Guadeloupe Passage
GUADELOUPE (Fr)
Basse-Terre
Les Saintes
La Désirade
Marie-Galante

DOMINICA
Roseau

CARIBBEAN SEA
Martinique Passage
MARTINIQUE (Fr)
Fort-de-
France
St Lucia Channel
Castries
ST LUCIA
St Vincent Passage

LESSER ANTILLES
WINDWARD ISLANDS
St Vincent
Kingstown
ST VINCENT
& THE
GRENADINES
Bequia
Mustique
Canouan
Mayreau
Union
Carriacou
St George's
GRENADA
Grenadine Islands
Bridgetown
BARBADOS

Tortuga
Margarita
TRINIDAD & TOBAGO
Tobago
Port of Spain
Trinidad

VENEZUELA

0        100        200 km
0     50     100 miles

Anegada Passage

beaches, but particularly notable as beach destinations are St Martin, Anguilla, St Barts, Antigua, Barbados, Tobago and some of the smaller Grenadine islands.

For hiking, Dominica and Guadeloupe are special places, with extensive tracks leading to unspoiled rainforests, steamy craters and towering waterfalls. If you're a birder, Trinidad and Tobago offer the greatest variety of birdlife in the Caribbean and both have small rainforest retreats catering to naturalists.

For colonial history buffs, there are notable fort ruins at Brimstone Hill on St Kitts, Pigeon Island on St Lucia and Fort Shirley and Nelson's Dockyard on Antigua. To absorb even more colonial character, you can stay in former soldiers' quarters at Nelson's Dockyard or in old sugar plantation estate houses that have been converted into country inns on St Kitts, Nevis and Martinique.

For a look at the unhurried Caribbean with a rural West Indian character, there's Irish-influenced Montserrat, the Dutch island of St Eustatius or the sleepy French island of Marie-Galante. On Saba you can easily imagine yourself to be in an Alpine village, while St Barts has much the feel of a Mediterranean isle. Other off-the-beaten-path charmers include Tobago, Bequia and Terre-de-Haut.

If you don't want to budget much money for travelling around but want to see a number of islands, a few destinations can become a multi-island combination without much effort or cost. From Guadeloupe, high-speed ferries run day trippers to the nearby islands of Terre-de-Haut, Marie-Galante and La Désirade, and from both St Vincent and Grenada there are mailboats to the nearby Grenadine islands. From St Martin, there are frequent boats to Anguilla and St Barts, and it's but a 15-minute flight to Saba or St Eustatius.

Part of the charm of the Eastern Caribbean lies in its diversity and the opportunity to experience a variety of cultures and environments in a single trip. This book will help you decide which of the Eastern Caribbean islands to visit and includes all the details of inter-island travel – be it by ship, private yacht or prop plane.

# Facts about the Region

## HISTORY

The Caribbean islands were originally inhabited by Amerindians who migrated from the American mainland.

For the most part, early European explorers were intent on ridding the islands of their native inhabitants and in the end enslaved, killed or exiled the majority of Amerindians in the Caribbean. The Europeans recorded precious little about these societies and the native islanders had no written languages of their own. Much of what is now known about their cultures comes from archaeological explorations; the discovery of stone tools, shellwork, pottery shards and petroglyphs is the main means for piecing together the history of the pre-Columbian period.

Not all islands in the Eastern Caribbean were populated by the same peoples at the same time. Archaeological research is still ongoing in the region; dates of migration are debated and occasionally revised by new discoveries.

### Ciboneys

The first people to the Eastern Caribbean were wandering Stone Age hunters and gatherers from the Archaic (pre-pottery) Period. Usually called Ciboneys, or Siboneys, they may have been present on some islands as early as 4000 BC. Their existence is mainly known through carbon dating of midden piles, crude stone axes and scraping tools.

### Arawaks

The Arawak Period in the Eastern Caribbean is generally thought to have begun about 2000 years ago, near the beginning of the Christian era.

The Arawaks were not a single tribe, but rather a group of South American tribes that all spoke the Arawak language and shared cultural similarities. They were a gentle, peaceful people who fished, hunted and farmed. They grew tobacco, cotton, corn, sweet potatoes and pineapples. Their main crop was cassava, also called manioc or yuca, from whose tuberous roots comes cassareep, a bitter juice used as a preservative, and tapioca, a nutritious starch which the Arawaks used to make cassava bread, their main food staple.

The Arawaks were very artistic. Women made pottery of red clay which was often engraved, painted with white designs or decorated with figurines called *adornos*.

The society was well organised. Villages consisted of a grouping of round houses, each of which housed several families. Like the natives of the American mainland, the people had bronze-coloured skin and long black hair. They wore little or no clothing.

In the Arawak religion, Yocahu, or Jocahu, was the God of Creation, also known as 'The Giver of Cassava'. The Arawaks carved anthropomorphic objects of stone or shell, called *zemis*, which they kept near places of worship.

It is believed that there were no Arawaks remaining in the Eastern Caribbean at the end of the 15th century when Europeans appeared on the scene.

There were, however, Arawak-speaking people living in the northern Caribbean in regions the Caribs had not yet conquered. One tribe of Arawaks, the Taino, were the people that Columbus first encountered and documented. It is from the Taino that much of the early knowledge of the Arawak culture was obtained.

### Caribs

Sometime around 1200 AD the Caribs, a group of warring tribes from South America, invaded the Eastern Caribbean, migrating in a northerly direction through the islands. They drove off or killed all of the Arawak men, apparently eating the flesh of some of their victims (the word 'cannibal' is derived from 'caribal' or 'Carib'). Some of the Arawak women were spared to be slaves for

Carib men and for a while these women kept some remnants of the Arawak culture alive.

The Caribs did not farm much, obtaining most of their food from hunting and gathering. They were not as sophisticated or artistic as the Arawaks and their pottery was of inferior quality. They were, however, ferocious defenders of their land and on many islands managed to keep the Europeans at bay for more than a century.

### Christopher Columbus

The first European to explore the Caribbean was Christopher Columbus, who reached the islands in 1492 while looking for a westward route to Asia. Over the course of a decade, Columbus made four voyages to the New World, opening the region to exploitation and colonisation. In his first voyage, which took him to the Caribbean's northerly islands, he left a party of soldiers on Hispaniola, establishing Spain's first settlement in the Americas.

On 25 September 1493, just six months after returning to Portugal from his initial voyage, Columbus set sail with a flotilla of 17 ships. He took a more southerly course this time, hoping to find new territory on his way back to Hispaniola. It was during this second voyage that he 'discovered' most of the islands of the Eastern Caribbean. The first island sighted was on 3 November 1493, a Sunday, and was thus christened Dominica. From Dominica, Columbus sailed north, landing at Marie-Galante, an island he named after his ship, the 'gallant' *Santa Maria*. He next touched land on Guadeloupe's Basse-Terre and then sailed north-west up the chain, discovering and naming the islands of Montserrat, Antigua, Redonda, Nevis, St Kitts, St Eustatius and Saba, before heading to the Virgin Islands and points west.

On Columbus' third voyage, in 1498, he sailed farther south still, making his first landfall at Trinidad. From there he sailed west along the coast of Venezuela and then sighted Tobago and Grenada before heading north once again to Hispaniola.

Despite the significance of his journeys,

Christopher Columbus

Columbus never fully realised that what he had discovered was indeed a new world and not islands off the coast of east Asia. It is as a consequence of his geographic disorientation that the native peoples of the Americas are still known as 'Indians'.

### Colonialism

The Spanish explorers, in pursuit of gold, concentrated their attention on the larger islands of the northern Caribbean and on the American mainland, paying scant notice to the smaller islands that comprise the Eastern Caribbean. They did, however, settle on Trinidad, just off the coast of mineral-rich Venezuela.

A flurry of colonial activity was set off in 1623, when the English became the first Europeans to establish a permanent settlement in the Eastern Caribbean (with the exception of Trinidad), founding a colony on the island of St Kitts. In 1625 Captain John Powell landed a party of settlers on Barbados, and other British colonies were soon established on Nevis, Antigua and Montserrat. In the 1630s the French settled Martinique and Guadeloupe while the Dutch settled Saba, St Eustatius and St Martin.

The Dutch, French and English all laid claims and counter-claims throughout the Eastern Caribbean. In some instances, such as on St Martin and St Kitts, different colonial powers established settlements on opposite sides of the same island. Sometimes the European powers coexisted peacefully, especially when jointly battling the native Caribs, but more often than not they were involved in a tug-of-war, each trying to gain control of the other's colonies. Over the next two centuries most islands of the Eastern Caribbean changed hands so many times that they developed societies with an almost hybrid culture, most commonly a British-French mix.

## Sugar Cane Plantations
The Dutch were largely concerned with establishing military and trade stations on the islands that they held. The French and British, on the other hand, saw the primary value of their Caribbean possessions in terms of agricultural production and quickly went about clearing the forests and planting crops. The original fields were largely in tobacco, cotton and indigo, but by the mid-1600s sugar had proven itself the most profitable crop and larger islands like Barbados and Martinique were heavily planted in sugar cane.

Unlike tobacco, which was cultivated in small plots, sugar production was large-scale and labour-intensive. Sugar cane must be crushed almost immediately after cutting or it will spoil, and as the mills that crushed the cane were expensive to build and operate, the plantations needed to be large enough to justify the expense.

To meet the increased demand for labour the planters began to import great numbers of slaves from Africa. By the end of the 17th century the islands had a firmly established plantation society comprised of a minority of free Whites and a majority of Black slaves.

On the British islands many of the plantations were owned by absentee planters, who returned to England leaving the plantation operation in the hands of managers. The absentee owners were among the wealthiest members of British society and had a powerful influence in enacting protectionist legislation that guaranteed British markets for their sugar. There were similar parallels in the French West Indies.

By the early 1800s, sugar's heyday had passed. Merchants who were tired of the interruption of supplies during British-French military skirmishes began to replace Caribbean cane with European-grown beet sugar. As the market for Caribbean sugar waned, so too did the influence of the planters. At the same time the abolitionist movement was gaining momentum.

In 1807 British legislation abolished the slave trade, although planters were allowed to keep the slaves they already had until 1833. On the French islands emancipation was enacted in 1848. In the two centuries prior to emancipation an estimated three million African slaves were brought to the British and French Caribbean.

Even after its decline, sugar cane continued to be grown on most islands and played a formative role in the shaping of island society. As Blacks left the plantations, indentured servants, mostly from India, were brought to replace them. Sizeable East Indian minorities were established on Trinidad, Martinique and Guadeloupe, and their culture has become an integral part of these islands' identity.

## The 20th Century
During the world depression of the 1930s most of the Caribbean was torn by high unemployment, labor unrest and civil strife. On many islands a concerted labour movement developed with demands for both economic and political independence. The British responded by enacting the first meaningful measures of internal self-government, the French by incorporating the islands more thoroughly with mainland France and the Dutch by allowing heightened domestic rule under association with the Netherlands.

**The British Islands** In the post WW II period Britain moved to divest itself of its Caribbean colonies by attempting to create a single federated state that would incorporate all of the British-held Caribbean. One advantage of the federation was that it could provide a mechanism for decolonising smaller islands that the British felt would otherwise be too small to stand as separate entities.

After a decade of negotiation, Britain convinced its Caribbean colonies – the British Windward and Leeward islands, Jamaica, Barbados and Trinidad – to join together as the West Indies Federation. The new association came into effect in 1958, with the intent that the federation work out the intricacies of self governing during a four-year probationary period before the islands emerged as a single new independent nation in 1962.

Although the West Indies Federation represented dozens of islands scattered across more than 3000 km of ocean, the British established Trinidad, at the southernmost end of the chain, to be the governing 'centre' of the federation.

For centuries the islanders had related to each other via their British administrators and the political and economic intercourse between the islands had been quite limited. In the end, the lack of a united identity amongst the islands, coupled with each island's desire for autonomy, proved stronger than any perceived advantage in union.

Jamaica was the first to develop a rift with the new association and opted to leave the federation in 1961. Trinidad itself soon followed suit. Both islands felt they were large enough, and rich enough in resources, to stand on their own. They were also wary of getting stuck in a position where they would have to subsidise the federation's smaller islands which were heavily dependant upon British aid. Thus in 1962, Jamaica and Trinidad became independent nations. The concept of a smaller federation limped along for a few more years but after Barbados broke rank and became an independent nation in 1966, the British were forced to go back to the drawing board.

The remaining islands continued to splinter. Dominica and St Lucia gained independence as single-island nations. Antigua, St Vincent, Grenada and St Kitts were each linked with smaller neighbouring islands to form new nations.

Anguilla, which was linked with St Kitts and Nevis, rebelled three months after the new state's inauguration in 1967 and negotiated with the British to be reinstated as a Crown Colony. Montserrat also refused to be dispensed with so readily by the British, and is also a Crown Colony.

During the same period, Barbuda made a bid to secede from its union with Antigua, but with barely 1000 inhabitants its independence movement failed.

The islands linked to both St Vincent and Grenada also initially grumbled, but have managed to work out their differences.

**The French Islands** In the French West Indies the policy has been one of assimilation rather than independence. Since 1946 Guadeloupe (whose administration includes St Barts and the French side of St Martin) and Martinique have been separate, if somewhat hesitant, departments of France, with representation in the Senate and National Assembly in Paris.

Separatist sentiments have long existed in the French islands, particularly on Guadeloupe, although the reliance upon economic aid from France has tempered the movement in recent years. Still, many islanders think it's but a matter of time before the islands achieve some measure of greater internal autonomy.

**The Dutch Islands** The Dutch, like the British, also hoped to create a single federation of all their Caribbean possessions – Curacao, Aruba, Bonaire, St Martin, St Eustatius and Saba – collectively known as the Netherlands Antilles. In 1954 a charter was enacted that made these six islands an autonomous part of the Netherlands, with its central administration in the southerly island of Curacao. Under the charter, island affairs were largely administered by elected officials, although the Dutch continued to hold the purse strings and maintained other controls. The islands were expected to develop the mechanisms for self rule and move gradually, as a unit, towards full independence from the Netherlands.

The islands, however, have not looked

| | Main Languages Spoken | Official Currency | Population | Sq Km | Number of People per Sq Km |
|---|---|---|---|---|---|
| **ANGUILLA** | English | Eastern Caribbean Dollar | 8000 | 155 | 52 |
| **ANTIGUA & BARBUDA** | English | Eastern Caribbean Dollar | 65,000 | 442 | 147 |
| **BARBADOS** | English | Barbados Dollar | 254,000 | 430 | 591 |
| **DOMINICA** | English | Eastern Caribbean Dollar | 73,000 | 750 | 97 |
| **GRENADA** | English | Eastern Caribbean Dollar | 97,600 | 344 | 284 |
| **GUADELOUPE** | French | French Franc | 351,600 | 1628 | 216 |
| **MARTINIQUE** | French | French Franc | 359,600 | 1080 | 333 |
| **MONTSERRAT** | English | Eastern Caribbean Dollar | 11,000 | 106 | 104 |
| **SABA** | English/ Dutch | Netherlands Antilles Guilder | 1100 | 13 | 85 |
| **ST BARTS** | French | French Franc | 5000 | 21 | 238 |
| **ST EUSTATIUS** | English/ Dutch | Netherlands Antilles Guilder | 1600 | 21 | 76 |
| **ST KITTS & NEVIS** | English | Eastern Caribbean Dollar | 45,000 | 261 | 172 |
| **ST LUCIA** | English | Eastern Caribbean Dollar | 157,000 | 616 | 255 |
| **ST MARTIN** | English/ Dutch | Netherlands Antilles Guilder/ French Franc | 79,000 | 88 | 898 |
| **ST VINCENT & THE GRENADINES** | English | Eastern Caribbean Dollar | 108,000 | 389 | 278 |
| **TRINIDAD & TOBAGO** | English | Trinidad & Tobago Dollar | 1,253,000 | 5128 | 244 |

| | Political Status | Geography | Notable Characteristics |
|---|---|---|---|
| **ANGUILLA** | UK Dependency | relatively flat dry, sandy | beautiful beaches; popular with wealthy travellers |
| **ANTIGUA & BARBUDA** | independent | both islands are largely dry and scrubby | Antigua has a wealth of colonial ruins; Barbuda has largest frigate-bird colony in the Caribbean |
| **BARBADOS** | independent | low hills in the interior, white-sand beaches along the coast | a leading tourist destination with good-value accommodation, British flavour, plantation-era homes |
| **DOMINICA** | independent | ruggedly mountainous with rainforests and waterfalls | ecotourist destination, good hiking and diving, the Eastern Caribbean's highest mountains |
| **GRENADA** | independent | high mountainous Islands with deeply indented coastlines | renowned for its nutmeg and other spices; scenic capital town and harbour; relaxed outer islands |
| **GUADELOUPE** | Overseas Department of France | two main adjoining islands and several offshore islands; largely mountainous | Creole culture, expansive national park, region's highest waterfalls, active volcano |
| **MARTINIQUE** | Overseas Department of France | mountainous interior topped by 1379-meter Mount Pelée | cosmopolitan capital, pre-dominantly French ambience; ruins of Saint-Pierre, destroyed by Pelée's 1902 eruption |
| **MONTSERRAT** | UK Dependency | central mountains, hot springs; steaming sulphur vents and black-sand beaches | rural, friendly and delightfully unspoiled and untouristed |
| **SABA** | part of the Netherlands Antilles | small but disproportionately high and mountainous | quaint alpine-like character, good hiking and diving |
| **ST BARTS** | part of Guadeloupe | hilly terrain with deeply indented bays | fashionable destination with nice white-sand beaches and a distinctly French flavour |
| **ST EUSTATIUS** | part of the Netherlands Antilles | largely dry island dominated by an extinct crater | peaceful one-town island with an intriguing history and colonial-period buildings |
| **ST KITTS & NEVIS** | independent | both islands are high with central volcanic peaks | both islands are rural and quiet and offer accommodation in plantation-era homes |
| **ST LUCIA** | independent | mountainous rainforested interior, bubbling sulphur springs | scenic landscapes, up-and-coming package tour destination |
| **ST MARTIN** | north side is part of Guadeloupe; south side is part of Netherlands Antilles | hilly interior; shoreline dotted with bays, coves and salt ponds | lovely beaches, unique dual-nation status, duty-free shopping, good, reasonably priced French food |
| **ST VINCENT & THE GRENADINES** | independent | St Vincent is mountainous; the Grenadines are a mix of hilly islands and sandy cays | multi-island nation; the scenic Grenadines are a haven for yachters and offer good sailing, diving and snorkelling |
| **TRINIDAD & TOBAGO** | independent | both islands have mountain ranges, rainforests and lowlands | both islands have abundant bird life; low-keyed Tobago has nice beaches and affordable prices; Trinidad has the Caribbean's top Carnival |

favourably towards the concept of union as a single nation. In the late 1970s Aruba moved to secede from the federation and in 1986 became a single island state. It is due to gain full independence in 1996. The remaining five islands have also grown weary of the concept of independence as a single federation; St Martin politics have centred as much upon independence from its union with Curacao as independence from the Netherlands.

## GEOGRAPHY

Geographically, the islands in this book make up the easternmost slice of the Caribbean, or West Indies. Included are all of the Leeward Islands (from Anguilla to Dominica) and the Windward Islands (from Martinique to Grenada) plus Barbados, Trinidad and Tobago. All except Trinidad and Tobago are part of the Lesser Antilles.

Geologically, most of the Eastern Caribbean is part of a double arc of islands running north to south. The islands on the inner arc, which extends from Saba to Grenada, are volcanic in origin. While most of the volcanic activity has long ceased, there are still steaming craters, bubbling hot water springs and pungent sulphur vents on some of the higher islands, and during the past century there have been major eruptions from Mt Pelée (1902) in Martinique and the Soufrière volcano (1979) in St Vincent.

The outer arc of islands, which extends from Anguilla to Barbados, is of marine origin, comprised of uplifted coral limestone built upon a base of rock.

Trinidad and Tobago are geologically unique, having broken off from the South American continent. Trinidad's southern plains were created from deposits from Venezuela's Orinoco River and its Northern Range is an extension of the Andes.

## CLIMATE

The entire Eastern Caribbean lies in the tropics. Consequently, the islands have near-equable temperatures year-round and only slight seasonable variations in the number of hours of daylight. Though it's hot and humid most of the time, tradewinds blowing from the north-east temper the humidity; they are prevalent most of the year, but are strongest from January to April.

### Hurricanes

The hurricane season in the Caribbean, like that of the eastern USA, is from June to November, with most activity occurring in August and September. Hurricanes can also appear outside the official season, but are much less frequent. While the annual average is only about five hurricanes per year, a few of the islands of the Eastern Caribbean have been walloped head-on by a 'Big One' in the past few decades.

Hurricanes are defined as storms that originate in the tropics and have winds of at least 120 km/h. The winds of a hurricane revolve in an anticlockwise direction around a centre of lower barometric pressure. When wind speeds are under 65 km/h it's called a tropical depression and when winds are between 65 and 120 km/h it's a tropical storm. ■

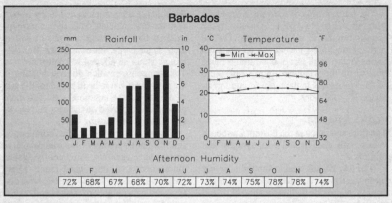

## Barbados

**Rainfall**

**Temperature**

**Afternoon Humidity**

| J | F | M | A | M | J | J | A | S | O | N | D |
|---|---|---|---|---|---|---|---|---|---|---|---|
| 72% | 68% | 67% | 68% | 70% | 72% | 73% | 74% | 75% | 78% | 78% | 74% |

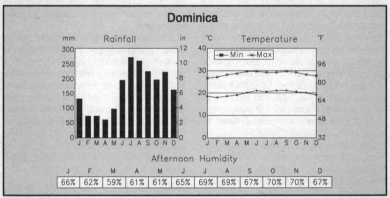

## Dominica

**Rainfall**

**Temperature**

**Afternoon Humidity**

| J | F | M | A | M | J | J | A | S | O | N | D |
|---|---|---|---|---|---|---|---|---|---|---|---|
| 66% | 62% | 59% | 61% | 61% | 65% | 69% | 69% | 67% | 70% | 70% | 67% |

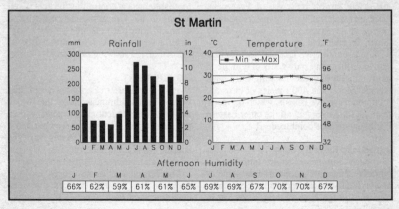

## St Martin

**Rainfall**

**Temperature**

**Afternoon Humidity**

| J | F | M | A | M | J | J | A | S | O | N | D |
|---|---|---|---|---|---|---|---|---|---|---|---|
| 66% | 62% | 59% | 61% | 61% | 65% | 69% | 69% | 67% | 70% | 70% | 67% |

The rainiest time of the year is generally May through November. On low-lying islands rainfall is relatively light. On the high, mountainous islands the precipitation varies greatly with location: rainfall is much heavier on the windward (north-east) sides of the islands and in the interiors and lighter on the leeward sides.

## FLORA & FAUNA

The flora and fauna in the Eastern Caribbean varies with each island's topography and rainfall.

The low islands tend to support a largely scrub vegetation and are pocketed with salt ponds that provide habitat for shorebirds and seabirds. The mountainous islands have far more diverse ecosystems that include lush interior rainforests of tall trees, ferns, climbing vines and a variety of colourful forest birds. Native parrots make their home in the mountainous rainforests of Dominica, St Lucia, St Vincent and Trinidad and Tobago. In many ways, location is as much a determining factor in the types and variation of native fauna as are rainfall and topography.

As a general rule the more isolated an island is from its nearest neighbour and the farther it is from a continental land mass, the more restrictive its native flora and fauna. On isolated Barbados, for instance, indigenous mammals are largely limited to a handful of bat species, while on Trinidad and Tobago, just a few km off the coast of Venezuela, there are a hundred types of mammals replicating those found on the nearby South American mainland.

Correspondingly, Trinidad and Tobago also have the greatest diversity of bird life to be found among the Eastern Caribbean islands. More than 400 species of birds are found on these two islands, which is greater than the total found on all the other Eastern Caribbean islands combined.

### Introduced Flora & Fauna

The early European settlers introduced a number of creatures to the islands, some as an inevitable consequence of their presence, others by design. Rats, nesting in crevices in the holds of their ships, sailed to the islands with the first colonists. Plantation managers, irritated by the damage the rats caused to their sugar crops, introduced the Burmese mongoose in an attempt to control the rats. The mongooses, which do their hunting in the day, turned out to be ill suited for the task of preying on the nocturnal rats. The mongoose instead preyed on the eggs and chicks of native ground-nesting birds.

Having evolved with limited competition and few native predators, the islands' native species have generally fared poorly against more aggressive, introduced fauna. Many species of birds, including parrots, have disappeared on a number of islands and others, including all of the surviving populations of parrots in the Eastern Caribbean, are now endangered.

The foraging animals introduced by colonists - particularly goats, which continue to roam freely on many islands - have had a similarly devastating effect on native flora. Their grazing has undermined fragile native ecosystems and spelled extinction for many island plants. Erosion, deforestation and thousands of introduced plants which compete with and choke out native vegetation have all taken their toll. In all, an estimated half of the native flora on the islands has already become extinct or is currently endangered.

New conservation efforts, ranging from recent attempts at controlling the goat populations in the Grenadines to concentrated efforts to bring the remaining Eastern Caribbean parrots back from the brink of extinction, are showing promise.

## GOVERNMENT

Most of those Eastern Caribbean islands that were formerly administered by the British are now independent democracies with a parliamentarian form of government and a Commonwealth affiliation. A couple of the islands, Montserrat and Anguilla, continue by their own request as British colonies.

The French islands have been incorporated in the French fold as overseas departments of France, with a status on par with that of the 96 departments that comprise mainland France.

Saba, St Eustatius and the Dutch side of St Martin are part of the Netherlands Antilles, a union that also includes the southern Caribbean islands of Curacao and Bonaire. The Netherlands Antilles is a parliamentary democracy linked to the Netherlands and administered by a governor who is appointed by the Queen.

## ECONOMY

The economies of many Eastern Caribbean islands are still heavily dependent upon the West, either for direct financial assistance or to provide favourable markets for island products.

On many islands agriculture remains the most important sector of the economy. Much of the arable land on some islands, such as Barbados and St Kitts, is still planted in sugar cane, while bananas are the major export crop on high, rainy islands like Dominica, St Vincent and St Lucia.

In part because of depressed world markets for the Caribbean's agricultural products, tourism has become an increasingly important industry for most of the islands. Trinidad, the most resource-rich island in the Eastern Caribbean, has oil, asphalt and other petroleum-based industries. Elsewhere in the region, with the exception of rum distilleries and a few small garment and electronics-assembly factories, there's very little industry.

Most trade is with the USA and Europe. In part due to their lengthy colonial history, the Eastern Caribbean islands do not trade extensively among themselves and customs barriers between islands have thus far frustrated the development of strong regional markets.

## POPULATION & PEOPLE

The population of the Eastern Caribbean is nearly three million, of which Trinidad accounts for more than a third.

Population densities vary greatly. One of the world's most densely populated countries is Barbados, which has 254,000 people and a population density of 591 people per sq km. Some of the smaller islands, including St Barts, Saba and St Eustatius, have fewer than 5000 people.

With some islands, like Grenada, there are more native islanders living abroad than at home. Most overseas West Indians live in the UK, USA or France.

With the Eastern Caribbean taken as a whole, the vast majority of islanders are of African ancestry. This varies between islands, however. There are also sizeable numbers of people of European and East Indian ancestry, as well as many of mixed ethnicities and smaller numbers from the Middle East, Asia and the Americas.

Although the native Caribs were almost completely wiped out by early colonists, about 3000 Caribs still live on the east side of Dominica and there are smaller native populations on St Vincent and Trinidad.

## EDUCATION

All the islands of the Eastern Caribbean have compulsory education for children, though the number of years varies. Most educational systems are modelled on either the French, British or Dutch systems.

The University of the West Indies, the largest university in the English Caribbean, has campuses in Trinidad and Barbados. On the French islands, the Université des Antilles-Guyane has campuses in Guadeloupe and Martinique.

Barbados has a literacy rate of 99%, the same as Australia and the USA. Literacy rates on other islands (figures vary according to source) range from about 78% in St Lucia to 96% in Trinidad and Tobago.

## ARTS

Notable figures in literature include novelists V S Naipaul of Trinidad, George Lamming of Barbados, Jamaica Kincaid of Antigua, Maryse Condé of Guadeloupe, Jean Rhys of Dominica and playwright/poet Derek Walcott, a native of St Lucia, who won the 1992 Nobel Prize in Literature.

On the French islands, the most renowned poet was Saint-John Perse of Guadeloupe, who won the Nobel Prize for Literature in 1960 for the evocative imagery of his poetry. Martinique has also produced two notable contemporary poets, Aimé Césaire and Édouard Glissant, both of whom write about the struggles of Blacks seeking their cultural identity under the burden of colonial influences. The most celebrated artist to have worked in the Eastern Caribbean was Paul Gauguin, who lived on Martinique for five months in 1887.

West Indian architecture is a blending of European tradition and tropical design. When European settlers moved to the islands they tended to build cities in grid patterns, with houses in orderly rows. Many in-town buildings are substantial two-storey structures of stone and wood. Houses are often painted in bright colours such as turquoise, lime, pink and yellow. Peaked corrugated iron roofs that turn a rusty red add a distinctive element, as does frilly architecture such as gingerbread trim, verandah latticework and wooden shutters.

## Music

The Caribbean has a rich musical heritage. Most of the music has its roots in African folk music and drumming, with some Spanish, French and English/Irish influences.

In the Eastern Caribbean, reggae and calypso are the two types of music heard most often, their catchy, singable tunes blasted in minibuses and emanating from restaurants and beachside bars. Those visiting Trinidad in the months leading up to Carnival should be sure to visit Port of Spain's panyards and calypso tents where steel pan bands practise their music in preparation for the Caribbean's grandest festival.

**Calypso** Calypso originated in Trinidad in the 18th century as satirical songs sung in French patois by slaves working on the plantations. Many of the songs mirrored their discontent and mocked their colonial masters, while in others the singers would try to top each other in a battle of verbal insults. The lyrics of early calypso songs were usually ad-libbed on the spot.

Contemporary calypso is nearly always sung in English and composed, choreographed and rehearsed in advance. Most popular are songs of biting social commentary, political satire or sexual innuendoes, usually laden with double entendres and local nuances. In most cases the melodies and rhythms of calypso are well established and it is mainly the lyrics that change from song to song.

Calypso and Carnival were linked almost from the beginning. Calypso competitions continue to be a major part of the Carnival festivities, with each singer trying to best the others for a prize and the title of king.

Trinidad's long-standing king of calypso is the Mighty Sparrow. Other major Trinidadian calypso artists include Cro Cro, Shadow, Pretender, Lord Kitchener, David Rudder, Sugar Aloes, Black Stalin, Denyse Plummer and Singing Sandra.

Relatively new crossover sounds include rapso, a combination of rap and calypso, and chutney, a blend of calypso and East Indian music.

**Soca** Blend soul with calypso and you've got soca, a dance music with bold rhythms, heavy on the bass sounds. Soca was created in the mid-1970s by Ras Shorty I of Trinidad. Other top soca stars include Arrow from Montserrat and Trinidad's SuperBlue.

**Steel Pan** The steel drum, also called pan, is a uniquely Trinidadian invention. It has its origins in the 1940s when aspiring musicians took discarded oil drums and hammered out the steel bottoms, tuning different sections to specific pitches. Steel pan drummers play together in bands, practicing in outdoor panyards and performing at Carnival during pan competitions. The distinctive, melodious sounds of the steel pan are found throughout the Caribbean, but are synonymous with Trinidad. Pan jazz, a fusion of jazz and steel pan music, has become increasingly popular.

**Ska** The predecessor to reggae, ska evolved in Jamaica in the 1950s as a blend of calypso,

Flora of the Eastern Caribbean
A (GB), B (TW), C (TW), D (NF), E (NF), F (NF), G (TW), H (NF), I (NF)

| A | | C |
|---|---|---|
| B | | |
| D | E | F |
| | | G |

Architecture of the Eastern Caribbean
A (TW), B (NF), C (NF), D (NF), E (TW), F (TW), G (TW)

rhythm and blues and African-Jamaican folk music. It has pop-style lyrics, jazzy horn riffs and a shuffling tempo.

**Reggae** Born in Jamaica and derived from a blend of ska, blues, calypso and rock, reggae is characterised by lyrics of social protest and a danceable syncopated rhythm. Popularised by the late Bob Marley, reggae's cheerful infectious beat is heard throughout the Eastern Caribbean.

**Zouk** Created in the French West Indies, zouk draws on the *biguine*, an Afro-French dance music with a bolero rhythm; the swing music of Haitian *compas*; bebop-like *cadence* and other French Caribbean folk forms. It has a Carnival-like rhythm with a hot dance beat. In recent years it has taken Paris by storm and is now as popular in Europe as it is in the Caribbean. The popular Martinique zouk band Kassav has moved to Paris and has made a number of top-selling recordings including the English-language album *Shades of Black*.

## CULTURE
Because the region is so diverse, there are many variations in local customs and lifestyles. The French West Indies are essentially provincial outposts of France, with French language, customs and food predominating. Some regions, like St Barts and Terre-de-Haut (off Guadeloupe), retain a character that approximates that of rural France, while others, such as Guadeloupe and Martinique, have a more strongly French Creole culture that incorporates African and West Indian influences.

On the islands with a British past, cultural influences largely represent a mix of African and British heritage. The latter predominates in institutional ways, including the form of government, education and the legal framework. African influences remain strong in music, dance and family life.

Throughout the Caribbean, there tend to be strong divisions of labour along gender lines: most of the hundreds of vendors in the marketplace are women, most of the taxi and minibus drivers are men.

Cricket is the region's most popular sport and a number of world-class cricket players have hailed from the Eastern Caribbean. Soccer is also very popular, especially on the French islands.

Most islanders dress neatly. Women's clothing is conservative and rather old-fashioned on some islands, smartly chic on others. Many women vendors in the marketplaces wear matronly dresses and tie up their hair in kerchiefs, while women who work in offices are apt to wear high heels, frosted lipsticks and the latest fashions. Generally the smaller and more rural the island, the more casual the dress.

As for visitors, neatness in dress and politeness in attitude goes a long way. As a rule, bathing suits, very short shorts and other skimpy clothing should not be worn in town or other non-beach areas – this holds true even on the French islands where topless bathing is *de rigueur* on the beach. Always start with 'Good Day' or 'Bonjour' before launching into a conversation or abruptly asking questions. Many people, including those in the marketplaces, do not like to be photographed; ask first, and respect the wishes of those who refuse.

## RELIGION
Roman Catholicism is the dominant religion

---

**Liming**
The tropical climate slows things down and most islanders in the Eastern Caribbean take life at an easy-going pace. Liming – to laze about, hang with friends and pass the time with small talk – is a popular pastime on every island. 'No problem' is the most common response to any request. ■

in the French islands, Protestantism on most of the English and Dutch islands.

There are also African-Christian traditions. Rastafarianism, a Jamaica-based cult dating from the late 1920s, has followers throughout the Eastern Caribbean. It looks to Africa as the promised land to which all believers will some day return, and to Haile Selassie, the late emperor of Ethiopia, as the Messiah. The name is derived from the emperor's pre-coronation name, Prince (Ras) Tafari.

Rastafarians are drawn to Ethiopia because of its biblical significance and believe that they are the reincarnations of the Old Testament prophets, exiled from their homelands because of the transgressions of their descendants. They embrace many Black Pride issues, let their hair grow in long rope-like dreadlocks and believe that the smoking of ganja (marijuana) holds sacramental value.

Rastafarianism has played an important role in the development of Jamaican ska and reggae music, whose rhythm is influenced by the Rastafarian akete drum. In addition to cutting social commentary, many popular reggae songs have lyrics of praise to Ras Tafari.

Some islanders believe in *obeah*, which is not a religion per se but embodies a type of black magic used to cast spells on one's enemy. Similar to Haitian voodoo practices, obeah uses conjurations, sorcery and magical rituals to align supernatural forces. Despite centuries of repression by Christian forces the practice of obeah continues to some extent on most Eastern Caribbean islands, although often in secret.

Hinduism or Islam is the faith of about 30% of the population of Trinidad; these Eastern religions also have followings on other islands (such as Guadeloupe) where there are sizeable minorities of East Indians.

## LANGUAGE

English is the main language spoken on all the islands in the Eastern Caribbean except for the French West Indies (Guadeloupe, St Barts, the French side of St Martin, and Martinique), where French is the primary language.

English speakers can travel throughout the Eastern Caribbean without major problems. The difficulty of getting around the French West Indies by those who do not speak French is generally exaggerated. Although many people outside the hotel and tourism industry don't speak English, as long as you have an English-French dictionary and phrasebook, a measure of patience and a sense of humour you should be able to get by.

Dutch is spoken on Saba, St Eustatius and St Martin, but it is a secondary language after English, though still the official language of government.

French creole and patois are also common on many Eastern Caribbean islands and often the first language spoken at home. Hindi is also spoken among family members on islands with large East Indian populations, most notably Trinidad.

---

**Some popular colloquialisms heard in the Eastern Caribbean are:**

**boy, girl** – commonly used by islanders when casually addressing adults as well as children
**fire a grog, fire one** – drink rum
**go so, swing so** – used in giving directions (be sure to watch the hand movements at the same time!)
**limin' (also lime, lime about)** – hanging out, relaxing
**no problem** – all-purpose answer to any request
**one time** – immediately, right away
**study** – take time to consider, think about
**wine** – sensuous dance movement winding the hips, essential to Carnival dancing
**workin' up** – dancing in general ■

# Facts for the Visitor

## PASSPORT & VISAS

Details on passports and visas vary from island to island and specific information is given under individual island chapters.

Note that upon arrival at many islands, the immigration officer will ask how long you're staying and stamp that exact number of days in your passport or on your entry card. Give yourself plenty of leeway, so if you stay longer than originally planned you won't need to make a trip to immigration or the police station for an extension. Another question commonly asked by the immigration officer is where you will be staying, so it's a good idea to have a hotel in mind, although it doesn't seem to matter where you actually end up staying.

One more thing to keep in mind as you travel throughout the region is that some islands require visitors to be in possession of either an onward or return ticket. As part of this policy, LIAT and other regional airlines often won't allow you to board a flight to an island unless you're in possession of an onward ticket out of that island (see Tickets Out in the Air Travel Glossary).

## DOCUMENTS

Bring your passport or other identifying documents required to enter all the islands you intend to visit (see Passport & Visas in the individual island sections). You'll need your home driving licence or an International Driving Permit (IDP) in order to rent a car. If you're going to St Lucia, an IDP will save you the price of a local licence there, but on the other islands there's no benefit in having an IDP in addition to your home licence.

An International Health Certificate is required only if you're coming from a country where yellow fever is a problem.

Divers should bring their certification cards.

## CUSTOMS

All islands in the Eastern Caribbean allow tourists to bring in a reasonable amount of personal items duty free, as well as an allowance of liquor and tobacco. For more details, see the individual island chapters.

Spear guns are prohibited in the waters around many islands; divers interested in spear-fishing should make advance enquiries. Most non-French islands prohibit firearms; yachters who have guns on board should declare them on entry. Some islands are free of rabies and have strict rules on the importation of animals; this is mainly of interest to sailors who might not be allowed to bring their pets onto land.

## MONEY

There are five official island currencies in the Eastern Caribbean, which can make things a bit confusing if you're jumping back and forth between islands. Fortunately the US dollar (US$) can also be used outright on virtually all the islands. Indeed, many Eastern Caribbean islands quote hotel prices and car rentals in US dollars. However, for most transactions you'll be better off exchanging your money into the local currency. British sterling (UK£) and Canadian dollars (C$) can also be readily exchanged at banks but are not commonly accepted by businesses.

### Currencies & Exchange Rates

**Eastern Caribbean Dollar** The Eastern Caribbean dollar (EC$) is the official currency of Anguilla, Antigua & Barbuda, Dominica, Grenada, Montserrat, St Kitts & Nevis, St Lucia and St Vincent & the Grenadines. One dollar is worth 100 cents. Coins are in 1, 2, 5, 10 and 25 cents and EC$1 denominations. Banknotes are in 5, 10, 20 and 100 dollar denominations.

The EC$ is pegged to the US$ at a rate of US$1=EC$2.70. The exchange rate given by banks (on islands where the EC$ is the official currency) is US$1=EC$2.6882 for travellers' cheques and EC$2.67 for cash. If you have leftover EC dollars you can sell them back at the rate of EC$2.7169=US$1.

Other major currencies, including British sterling and Canadian dollars, fluctuate against the EC$ in accordance with their value against the US$ on world markets.

When exchanging UK£ or C$ against EC$ there's a notably greater variation between buying and selling rates than there is for the US$. The margin between buying and selling is a bit over 2% for sterling and 4% for Canadian dollars when using travellers' cheques. Sterling notes command a 2% less favourable rate of exchange than sterling travellers' cheques.

**French Franc** The French franc (F) is the official currency of Martinique, Guadeloupe, St Barts and the French side of St Martin. One franc is worth 100 centimes. French coins come in denominations of 5, 10 and 20 centimes and ½, 1, 5 and 10 francs. Banknotes are issued in denominations of 20, 50, 100, 200 and 500 francs; the higher the denomination, the larger the size of the bill.

The French franc fluctuates daily with other currencies according to world markets. As we go to print, the current rate of exchange is:

| | | |
|---|---|---|
| A$1 | = | 4.16F |
| C$1 | = | 4.23F |
| DM1 | = | 3.43F |
| NZ$1 | = | 3.32F |
| UK£1 | = | 8.64F |
| US$1 | = | 5.83F |
| Japanese Y100 | = | 5.65F |

**Netherlands Antilles Guilder** The Netherlands Antilles guilder or florin (commonly written Naf at banks and Fls in stores) is the official currency of Saba, St Eustatius and Dutch St Martin.

The Netherlands Antilles guilder, which differs from the guilder used in the Netherlands, has coins in denominations of 1, 5, 10, 25 cents and Naf 1; banknotes in 5, 10, 25, 50, 100 and 250 guilders. Naf 10.50 is spoken '10 guilders 50'.

Islanders on the Dutch islands commonly carry both guilders and US dollars; businesses accept and give change in either. As there's no advantage in paying in guilders (and there's a small loss when exchanging money), most visitors simply use US dollars.

The Naf is pegged to the US dollar at US$1=Naf 1.77. Other major currencies fluctuate in accordance to their value with the US dollar in world markets.

**Barbados Dollar** The Barbados dollar (B$) is the official currency of Barbados. Details are in the Barbados chapter.

**Trinidad & Tobago Dollar** The Trinidad & Tobago dollar (TT$) is the official currency of that two-island nation. Details are in the Trinidad & Tobago chapter.

### Costs

Overall the Eastern Caribbean is a fairly expensive region and you'll need a tidy sum to explore it thoroughly. Still, costs can vary greatly depending upon which islands you visit, the type of accommodation you choose and how you travel.

Accommodation will generally be the heftiest part of a traveller's budget in the Eastern Caribbean. On islands such as Barbados, which has a good range of low and mid-priced accommodation, expenses for a conventional hotel room or apartment can be quite reasonable, whereas on pricier islands like Antigua it could easily cost twice as much for a comparable room. Of course the type of accommodation will also dictate cost – daily expenses can vary from US$25 at a cheap guesthouse to US$1000 at an exclusive resort.

Food is relatively expensive, in part because much of it is imported – prices are generally a good 50% higher than in the USA or Canada.

Transport costs vary greatly. Car rentals generally cost between US$30 and US$70 a day depending upon the island. There are public buses on the more developed islands, which provide a very cheap alternative for getting around.

For inter-island travel, there are some reasonably priced ferries, mostly in the Grenadines and around the French islands. Air travel between islands can be expensive, but there are numerous good deals floating around, including air passes with LIAT (the main regional airline) that can take you from one end of the Caribbean to the other for as little as US$200. See the Getting Around chapter for details.

There are also some little nagging costs that can add up quickly, particularly if you're island-hopping. Most of the English- speaking islands require car renters to buy a temporary local driving licence, which ranges from US$7 to US$15; most islands have airport departure taxes, commonly from US$10 to US$15; and many add tax and service charges (up to 25%) on top of quoted hotel rates and sometimes onto restaurant bills as well.

If you're buying air tickets in the Caribbean, try to buy them on a tax-free island, such as St Martin, as many Eastern Caribbean islands add 5% to 20% sales or VAT taxes to ticket sales.

### Credit Cards & Tipping

Major credit cards are widely, although not universally, accepted throughout the Eastern Caribbean. The most commonly accepted cards are Visa and MasterCard, followed by the American Express charge card. Automatic teller machines (ATMs) that will give advances on credit cards can be found on Barbados and the larger French islands.

The tipping situation varies. On some islands it's automatically added to your restaurant bill as a service charge, while on other islands you're expected to add a tip to the bill.

For specific details, see the Money section in the individual island chapters.

### WHEN TO GO

The main travel season in the Caribbean is from 15 December to 15 April, usually called 'winter'. Although this period does have drier and slightly cooler weather, the main variable in making it the high season is the weather *elsewhere*, as the bulk of Caribbean tourists are 'snow birds' escaping colder weather in North America and Europe.

You can enjoy steeply discounted 'summer' hotel prices by visiting in the low season, from mid-April to mid-December. In addition, most airfares to the Caribbean are cheaper during this period, the beaches are less crowded, tourist areas have a more relaxed pace and last-minute bookings for cars, flights and hotels are seldom a problem.

On the minus side, the tradewinds aren't as prevalent in summer, so the chance of encountering oppressively muggy weather is higher. Summer is also the hurricane season, albeit the odds of encountering a hurricane on any particular island aren't much higher than along the US east coast.

November and early December can be a pleasant time to visit. Many hotels have taken a late-summer break to spruce up, so their rooms are at their pre-season finest, the crowds are just beginning to show and the prices are still low.

### WHAT TO BRING

Travelling light, a good policy anywhere, is easy in the tropics as heavy jackets and bulky clothing are totally unnecessary.

Ideal clothes are those made of cotton, which breathes best in hot humid weather, are loose fitting and don't need to be tucked in, and can be hand washed in a sink and hung up to dry without wrinkling.

Dress in the Eastern Caribbean is casual. Sportswear, including shorts and neat T-shirts, is fine during the day in most places. For dinner at nice restaurants, a cotton dress for women and lightweight slacks for men are usually sufficient. Only a very few top-end restaurants on a few islands expect men to have a tie and jacket. One long-sleeved shirt, lightweight cotton jacket or windbreaker might be useful against indoor air-con and outside insects. You'll probably spend most of your time in sandals, but bring footwear with good traction for hiking off the beaten path.

A flashlight is good to have on hand for the occasional power blackout and to walk in some areas at night. Bird watchers might want binoculars. A Swiss Army knife is always worth its weight in gold. If you plan to do a lot of snorkelling, you'll save money by bringing your own snorkelling gear. You might want to consider a passport pouch or money belt to wear around your neck or waist.

Zip-lock plastic sandwich bags in a couple of sizes are indispensable for keeping things dry. You can use them to protect your film and camera equipment, to seal up airline tickets and passports, and to keep wet bathing suits away from the rest of your luggage.

A one-cup immersion heater, usually available for a few dollars from hardware or department stores, and a durable lightweight cup can come in handy. Not only can you boil water and make coffee and tea in your room but you can use it to make up a quick meal if you carry a few packets of instant oatmeal, soup, noodles or the like.

Medical supplies and toiletries are available in most places, though on the smaller islands the selection may be limited. See the Health section for suggestions on medical-related items.

Those who don't speak French and are planning to visit Martinique, Guadeloupe or St Barts should take along an English-French dictionary and phrasebook.

## TOURIST OFFICES

Most tourist offices will mail general tourist information about their islands upon request. The addresses and phone numbers are listed under Tourist Offices in the Facts for the Visitor section of each island chapter. The overseas tourist offices of the French West Indies are in the Martinique section.

## BUSINESS HOURS

On most islands, business offices are open from 8 or 9 am to 4 or 5 pm Monday to Friday. Shops and stores are typically open from around 9 am to 5 or 6 pm on weekdays and until noon on Saturday. However, there is variation between islands.

For specifics on business hours, as well as a listing of public holidays and cultural events, see Facts for the Visitor in each island chapter. Keep in mind that banks on many islands are only open to noon on the day preceding a public holiday.

---

**Never on Sunday**
On our first trip to the Caribbean, we asked a shopkeeper in Grenada about her hours of business: 'We're open daily,' she told us. 'Every day?' we asked. '*Every* day of the week', she emphasised. 'Even on Sundays?' we asked. 'Oh no, not on *Sundays*!' she answered.

And so we came to realise that in most of the Eastern Caribbean the word 'daily' – whether spoken, written in ads or posted on storefront signs – quite often means 'every day but Sunday'. ∎

---

## HOLIDAYS & CULTURAL EVENTS
Carnival is the major festival throughout the Eastern Caribbean. As elsewhere, it's traditionally been a pre-Lenten celebration – a period of merriment before the abstinence and fasting that many Christians, particularly Catholics, observe during Lent.

On Trinidad and on all of the French-influenced islands, Carnival remains strictly a pre-Lenten celebration, while on many of the British-influenced islands, Carnival celebrations are held at other times during the year.

The changing of Carnival dates has been largely the result of practical considerations – smaller islands simply couldn't compete with larger islands, particularly Trinidad, which attract the finest performers and the lion's share of visitors. As a result, visitors to the Eastern Caribbean can now find Carnival celebrations on one island or another throughout the year.

Carnival festivities usually include contests and performances by calypso singers and steel bands; the election of a Carnival 'king' and 'queen'; street dancing, called jump-ups; costume and dance competitions; and a parade with floats, music and masquerading revellers.

The following is a list major festivals and events held in the Eastern Caribbean. There are also numerous smaller festivities and events – see the individual island chapters for more details.

## January

The *Barbados Windsurfing World Cup* is held in Barbados.

The two-week *St Barts Music Festival*, which features jazz, chamber music and dance performances, is held in St Barts.

The *St Barth's Cup*, a three-day yachting race, is held in St Barts in late January.

## February

*Carnival* is celebrated in the days preceding Ash Wednesday (which falls in February or March) in Trinidad, Dominica, St Lucia, Martinique, Guadeloupe, St Barts and the French side of St Martin.

St Barts hosts the *St Barth Regatta* for four days in mid-February.

The week-long *Holetown Festival* in Barbados celebrates the arrival of the first English settlers to the island in 17 February 1627. A small four-day *Carnival* is held in Carriacou.

## March

Montserrat celebrates *St Patrick's Day* (17 March).

The *Bequia Regatta* is held on Easter weekend (March or April) in Bequia.

The *Oistins Fish Festival* is held on Easter weekend on Barbados.

## April

*Antigua Sailing Week*, which features yacht races, begins on the last Sunday in April and lasts one week.

*Carnival* is celebrated in Dutch St Martin for two weeks and usually begins the second week after Easter.

## May

The town of Saint-Pierre, Martinique, commemorates the eruption of Mont Pelée on 8 May 1902 with a jazz concert and a candlelight procession.

The *International Regatta of St Barthélemy* takes place in St Barts for over three days in mid-May.

The *St Lucian Jazz Festival* takes place in St Lucia in late May.

## June

*Fête La St Pierre*, held in Dominica on or near 29 June, includes a festive blessing of the fleet.

## July

*Crop-Over Festival* is a three-week, Carnival-like celebration in Barbados beginning in mid-July and ending on the first Monday in August.

*Bastille Day* is celebrated on 14 July in Martinique, Guadeloupe, St Barts and the French St Martin.

The *Tour de la Martinique*, a week-long cycling race, is held in Martinique in mid-July.

*Vincy Mas*, as Carnival is called in St Vincent, is usually held in the first two weeks of July.

Saba's Carnival, the week-long *Saba Summer Festival*, is held in late July.

*Carnival* is held in Antigua from the end of July, ending with a parade on the first Tuesday in August.

The *Carriacou Regatta*, held in late July or early August, features yacht races and other sporting events.

*Carnival* is held on St Eustatius in late July.

A *Heritage Festival* of traditional-style festivities is held in Tobago for two weeks in late July.

## August

*Carnival* is celebrated for a week in Anguilla, beginning on the weekend preceding the first Monday in August.

The *Tour des Yoles Rondes*, a week-long race of traditional sailboats, is held in Martinique in early August.

The *Fête des Cuisinières*, held in Guadeloupe in early August, honors women cooks.

The *Tour de la Guadeloupe*, a 10-day cycling race, is held in Guadeloupe in early August.

*Carnival* is celebrated in Grenada on the second weekend of August, ending on the following Tuesday.

The *Festival of St Barthélemy* (24 August) is the feast day for the island's patron saint.

Barbados holds the *Banks Field Hockey Festival* in late August.

## November

*Creole Day*, held in Dominica on the Friday preceding 3 November, features dancing, folkloric festivities and music.

The *Barbados International Surfing Championship* is held in early November in Barbados.

Trinidad holds a *Pan Jazz Festival*, featuring pan drummers and jazz musicians, for three days in November.

The *National Independence Festival of Creative Arts* takes place on Barbados throughout November, with dance, drama and music performances.

## December

The *Atlantic Rally for Cruisers*, a transatlantic yacht race, ends in St Lucia in December.

*Saba Days* are festivities held in Saba in early December.

*Run Barbados* is a marathon held on Barbados in early December.

*La Route du Rosé*, a transatlantic regatta of tall ships, ends in St Barts in mid-December.

The *Martinique Jazz Festival* is held in Martinique during December on odd-numbered years, and the *Martinique Guitar Festival* on even-numbered years; each lasts one week.

*Carnival* festivities take place on Montserrat from mid-December to New Year's Day, with the biggest events on 31 December.

*Carnival* is held on St Kitts from 26 December to 2 January.

## POST

Delivery time for airmail sent from the Eastern Caribbean varies greatly. From the French islands it generally takes about a week to European destinations and 10 days to the USA, while from some of the smaller independent nations, like St Vincent & the Grenadines, overseas mail can easily take two to three weeks from the postmark date.

Hotels and other businesses on the smaller islands often have no street address or post office box; when no address is given in this book, you can address correspondence by simply following the hotel name with the town, country and 'West Indies'.

You can receive mail by having it sent care of poste restante or general delivery to the general post office (GPO) on each island you're visiting. Specific information on island post offices, including hours and postage rates, is given in the individual island chapters.

## TELECOMMUNICATIONS

Most Eastern Caribbean islands have both coin phones and card phones, and local and

international phone calls can be made from either. You can also make phone calls, and send telexes and faxes, from the telephone company offices listed in the individual island chapters.

## Phonecards

Public card phones are very popular in the Eastern Caribbean. They operate on plastic phonecards the size of a credit card, which are inserted into the phone. Each phonecard has an original value and the cost of each call is deducted automatically as you talk. You can use your phonecard for subsequent calls until the initial value of the card completely runs out.

The card phones are convenient if you make long-distance calls or a lot of local calls, as you don't have to keep pumping in coins. On those few islands where coin phones have been virtually eliminated, however, the card phone concept can be a real pain when you want to make one quick call but are forced to find a phonecard vendor and pay for a card you don't want!

There's little advantage in buying phonecards in the larger denominations, as the per-unit cost is virtually the same on all cards. In addition, two of the dozen Caribbean Phone Cards we've purchased have failed before their value expired.

## Phone Systems

There are three main telephone systems in the Eastern Caribbean.

**French Islands** When calling from the French West Indies, to any other island in the French West Indies dial just the six-digit local number; to the Paris area, dial 16 + 1 + eight digits; to all other areas in mainland France, dial 16 + eight digits; to the USA or Canada, dial 19 + 1 + area code + seven digits; to other countries dial 19 + country code + area code + local number.

When calling to the French West Indies from other countries, dial the access code from the country you're calling from + 596 for Martinique or 590 for the other French West Indies + the six-digit local number.

The cheapest time to make calls within the French West Indies or to mainland France is from 9.30 pm to 5 am daily, the most expensive time is from 7 am to 1 pm and 2 to 5 pm Monday to Friday and 7 to 11.30 am on Saturday, with other times having a mid-range rate. The discounted hours are 30% to 65% cheaper than business hours.

The French phonecards, called *télécartes*, are sold in 50-unit and 120-unit measures, which cost 36F and 87F respectively. One unit is valid for a few minutes on a local call; 7.0 seconds to nearby Caribbean islands; 3.6 seconds to distant Caribbean islands, the USA or Canada; 3.0 seconds to most European countries; and 2.0 seconds to Australia. Calls between any two French West Indies islands are substantially cheaper than calls to non-French Caribbean islands.

**Dutch Islands** The Netherlands Antilles islands of Saba, St Eustatius and the Dutch side of St Martin have a country code of 599. To call these islands from overseas, dial the access code of the country you're calling from + 599 + 3 for St Eustatius, 4 for Saba or 5 for Dutch St Martin + the five-digit local number.

Landsradio, the Dutch telephone company, sells Netherlands Antilles phonecards for US$9.85 (17.35 Fls) for 60 units and US$16.75 (Fls 29.60) for 120 units. Their per-unit value is comparable to those used on the French islands.

**English Islands** The English-speaking islands of Anguilla, Antigua & Barbuda, St Kitts & Nevis, Montserrat, Dominica, St Lucia, St Vincent & the Grenadines, Grenada, Barbados and Trinidad & Tobago all have an area code of 809. They also have a similar telephone system, which on most islands is under the umbrella of the Cable & Wireless Company.

When direct dialling to these islands from North America, dial 1 + 809 + the seven-digit local number. When calling these islands from outside North America, dial the access code from the country you're calling from, followed by 809 and seven digits.

Rates for long-distance calls from these islands are similar but not identical. The typical cost for one minute's phone time varies from EC$1.50 to EC$2 to nearby islands and from EC$2.75 to EC$3.75 to more far-flung Caribbean islands, while calls to the Americas average EC$5.50 a minute, to Europe EC$8, to the rest of the world EC$9 or EC$10. These rates are during the high daytime period. In general, rates average about 20% cheaper in the evening from either 6 or 7 pm until either 6 or 7 am and all day on Sunday and public holidays.

Caribbean Phone Cards, which can be used on all these islands (as well as the British Virgin Islands, Cayman Islands and Turks & Caicos Islands) are sold in amounts of EC$10, EC$20, EC$40 and EC$60. You can use multiple phonecards on the same phone call. Shortly before a phonecard's time runs out, a buzzer goes off; if you then push the star button, on the bottom left side, the old card comes out and you can insert a second card without losing your connection.

## USA Direct

AT&T has a direct telephone service to the USA that can be accessed via public and hotel phones on most non-French islands.

To access USA Direct from Anguilla, Dominica, Grenada, Montserrat, St Kitts or Nevis dial 1-800-872-2881; from Saba or St Eustatius dial 001-800-872-2881; from Antigua, push the pound (#) symbol, followed by 1.

In addition, there are specific USA Direct phones at many airports, marinas and cruise ship docks and a few large resort hotels on the above islands as well as in St Martin, St Lucia, Barbados, Trinidad and Tobago.

USA Direct charges an initial fee of US$5.75 if you're calling collect or US$2.50 if you're using a calling card from either AT&T or your regional phone company at home. The charges then range from US$1.55 to US$2 for the first minute, and US$1.15 to US$1.31 for each additional minute, depending on which island you're calling from. Rates are the same regardless of the hour or day.

## TIME

All islands in the Eastern Caribbean are on Atlantic Time, four hours behind Greenwich Mean Time. Daylight-saving time is not observed.

Thus, when it is noon in the Eastern Caribbean (and not daylight-saving time elsewhere) the time in other parts of the world is: 11 am in Jamaica, New York, and Montreal, 8 am in Los Angeles and Vancouver, 4 pm in London, 5 pm in Paris, 2 am in Sydney and Melbourne, and 4 am in Auckland.

In summer, when North America and Europe go on daylight-saving time, it is the same time in New York and Montreal as it is in the Eastern Caribbean; Britain is five hours ahead, rather than four; France is six hours ahead, rather than five.

## ELECTRICITY

The electric current varies in the Eastern Caribbean.

In the French islands the current is 220 volts, 50/60 cycles, and a rounded two-pronged plug is used, the same type as in mainland France.

In the Dutch islands the current is 110 volts, 60 cycles, and a flat two-pronged plug is used, the same type as in the USA.

The former British West Indies are a mixed lot – a few use 110 volts, but most use 220 volts.

Whatever the current, you can still bring along small appliances. Most hotel bathrooms have a dual voltage outlet intended for electrical shavers and some hotels can provide adaptors for other items.

## LAUNDRY

Some of the islands have coin laundries, others have drop-off services for nearly the same price, and in others the only option is to send out laundry at a hotel. For convenience and to control your budget, it's a good idea to bring a little laundry soap and plan on doing some hand washing.

## WEIGHTS & MEASURES

Some islands use the metric system, others

use the imperial system and a few are in a transitional stage of moving from imperial to metric.

Throughout this book, we use the metric system (metres and km) to describe elevations, land area and other general use. But when it comes to road and walking distances, this book uses each island's measurement system. As roads and sights are often poorly (or not at all) marked, this was done to make it possible for people exploring by rental car to find places using their car odometer, which will almost always read in miles on islands with imperial systems and in km on islands with metric systems. On those islands where the imperial system is used, we have followed the imperial measurement with a metric conversion in parentheses.

Thus on an island such as Antigua, which uses the imperial system, directions might read 'turn left 1.25 miles (two km) after passing the abandoned windmill and then turn right on the unmarked road 2.75 miles (4.4 km) farther'. On St Martin, which uses the metric system, directions taking you through a maze of dirt roads to secluded Plum Bay are given in km.

## BOOKS

Information on maps, bookshops and books specific to individual islands are found in those island chapters. The following are books about the Eastern Caribbean in general.

### History & Culture

*From Columbus to Castro* by Eric Williams (Vintage Books, 1970) is an authoritative history book of the West Indies, written by the late prime minister of Trinidad & Tobago. It covers the period from the first European contact to the late 1960s and gives a good grasp of the dynamics of colonialism that shaped this region.

*A Short History of the West Indies* by J H Parry & Philip Sherlock (Macmillan Caribbean, 1988), now in its fourth edition, provides a historical overview of the West Indies, from colonial times through the post-

independent struggles experienced by the islands in the mid-1980s.

*Seeds of Change* (Smithsonian Institution Press, 1991), edited by Herman J Viola & Carolyn Margolis, is one of many books that appeared around the time of the Columbus Quincentennial. Like most of the others, it chronicles Columbus' four journeys and their impact on Caribbean history.

*Wild Majesty: Encounters with Caribs from Columbus to the Present Day* (Oxford, 1992), edited by Peter Hulme & Neil L Whitehead, is an anthology of writings about the Carib people, from the time of the first European contact, through the colonial period when the Caribs were annihilated on many islands and up to the present day.

### General

*Caribbean Companion: The A to Z Reference* by Brian Dyde (Macmillan Caribbean, 1992) is an inexpensive 192-page book written by a British expatriate living in Montserrat. It's a fun book to browse through, with general tidbits on a range of topics including sports, music, politics, people and culture. *Caribbean Camera: A Journey Through the Islands* by Oliver Benn (Macmillan Caribbean, 1992) is a 152-page coffee table book with photos of the islands that convey a sense of the Caribbean's cultural and environmental diversity.

### Literature

*Green Cane and Juicy Flotsam: Short Stories by Caribbean Women* (Rutgers University Press, 1991), edited by Carmen Esteves & Lizabeth Paravisini-Gebert, pulls together short works by Caribbean women writers, including stories by Maryse Condé and Jeanne Hyvrad about the French Caribbean and by Jean Rhys and Jamaica Kincaid about the English Caribbean.

*The Heinemann Book of Caribbean Poetry* (Heinemann, 1992), edited by Ian McDonald & Stewart Brown, is a collection of works by English-speaking Caribbean poets, including Olive Senior, Edward Brathwaite, Derek Walcott and numerous lesser known writers.

*The Traveller's Tree* by Patrick Leigh Fermor (Penguin Books, 1984), originally published in 1950, is a classic among Caribbean travel journals. It's an interesting account of Fermor's jaunt through the Lesser Antilles and on to Haiti, Jamaica and Cuba. The book gives vivid descriptions of the people and places visited, though many islands have certainly changed.

### Natural History

*The Nature of the Islands* by Virginia Barlow (Cruising Guide Publications, 1993) is the best overall guide to the flora and fauna of the Eastern Caribbean. This well-written book is easy to use, with descriptions of plants and animals accompanied by 40 colour photos and 140 drawings.

*Peterson's Field Guide to Birds of the West Indies* by James Bond (Houghton Mifflin, 1993) is a revision of *Birds of the West Indies*, the classic guide to the region's birdlife. This comprehensive book has detailed descriptions of each bird, including information on habitat, voice and range, all accompanied by illustrations.

*Birds of The Eastern Caribbean* by Peter Evans (Macmillan Caribbean, 1992) is a 168-page book covering birds found in the Eastern Caribbean islands. It has general introductory sections, species-by-species accounts and checklists. There are colour photos of some birds, illustrations of others.

*Diving Guide to the Eastern Caribbean* by Martha Gilkes (Macmillan Caribbean, 1994) provides information on the reefs, wrecks and popular diving sites of the region, with a chapter on Caribbean marine life.

### Cruising Guides

There are a number of cruising guides to the Eastern Caribbean. The most widely used are those published by Cruising Guide Publications: *Sailors Guide to the Windward Islands*, *Cruising Guide to the Leeward Islands* and *Cruising Guide to Trinidad and Tobago, Venezuela and Bonaire*, all three written by Chris Doyle. Updated every couple of years, these books are thoroughly researched and packed with information

from navigational approaches and entry regulations to where to pick up provisions and marine supplies.

Another well-regarded guide is *Street's Cruising Guide to the Eastern Caribbean* by Donald M Street Jr (W W Norton & Co, 1992).

Those new to sailing might want to read *Deck with a View: Vacation Sailing in the Caribbean* by Dale Ware & Dustine Davidson (Link International, 1992). It covers basic topics such as determining whether you have the personality to sail with a group, suggests sailing itineraries, details various yachting options and lists charter rental companies.

### Magazines

*Caribbean Travel & Life* (PO Box 2054, Marion, OH 43306 USA) is a four-colour monthly magazine covering travel in the Caribbean region. It has feature articles on specific destinations and regular columns on new resorts, food, shopping etc.

*Caribbean Sports & Travel* (1995 NE 150th St, Suite 107, North Miami, FL 33181 USA) is a four-colour quarterly magazine with an emphasis on sports travel in the Caribbean, covering such fields as cruising, deep-sea fishing, diving, golfing and the like. It has a calendar of events, sports-related news briefs and some general travel planning information.

### Resources

Macmillan Caribbean, a division of The Macmillan Press, publishes a range of books about the Caribbean. To order books or obtain a catalogue contact Macmillan Caribbean (☎ (0256) 29 242; fax (0256) 20 109), Houndmills, Basingstoke, Hampshire RG21 2XS, England.

Cruising Guide Publications (☎ (813) 733-5322 or ☎ (800) 330-9542; fax (813) 734-8179), PO Box 1017, Dunedin, FL 34697 USA, sells its own cruising guides and numerous other books about the Caribbean, and will send out a catalogue on request.

West Indies Books Unlimited (☎ (813) 954-8601), PO Box 2315, Sarasota, FL

34230 USA, sells Caribbean-related fiction and nonfiction and specialises in hard-to-find and out-of-print books.

## MAPS

You can buy maps after you arrive on the islands or order them in advance.

Ordnance Survey maps, which are generally the best maps available for the English-speaking islands, can be purchased by mail directly from Ordnance Survey International (☎ (0703) 79 2000; fax (0703) 79 2404), Romsey Rd, Maybush, Southampton SO9 4DH, England.

In addition, all Ordnance Survey and Institut Géographique National (IGN) maps listed in this book can be obtained from:

France
  Espace IGN, 107 rue La Boétie, 75008 Paris (☎ 1-43 98 85 00)
UK
  Stanfords, 12-14 Long Acre, London WC2E 9LP (☎ (071) 836-1321; fax (071) 836-0189)
USA
  Map Link, 25 E Mason St, Santa Barbara, CA 93101 (☎ (805) 965-4402; fax (805) 962-0884).

For marine charts, see the Yachting section in the Getting Around chapter.

## MEDIA
### Newspapers

Most Eastern Caribbean islands have their own newspapers – some published daily, others weekly – and these are well worth reading to gain insights into the local politics and culture. Foreign newspapers are usually available as well; try bookshops or the gift shops at top-end hotels.

*Caribbean Week* (Caribbean Communications, Lefferts Place, River Rd, St Michael, Barbados) is the most substantial weekly newspaper in the English-speaking Caribbean. It covers island news, politics, business, sports and cultural activities for the entire Caribbean region. Written in Barbados and printed in Florida, it is as widely circulated to islanders living abroad as it is to islanders within the Caribbean. Subscriptions cost US$26 for one year.

### Radio & TV

Most islands have their own radio stations, which is a great way to tune in to the latest calypso, reggae, soca and steel band music. Local radio stations are also a good source of regional news and occasionally offer up interesting glimpses of island life – such as the sombre reading of obituaries accompanied by appropriately maudlin music.

There's some kind of TV on almost every island, often relayed by satellite or cable. Not all hotels (not even all top-end hotels) offer TVs in the rooms.

## FILM & PHOTOGRAPHY

Print film is available on the main islands, but it's often harder to find slide film. There are same-day photo processing centres on the French islands and in heavily touristed areas on other large islands.

The high temperatures in the tropics, coupled with high humidity, greatly accelerate the deterioration of film, so the sooner you have exposed film developed, the better the results. If you're just in the Caribbean for a week or two it's no problem to wait until you get home, but if you're travelling for a long time consider making other arrangements. One way to avoid carting film around is to bring pre-paid mail bags with you and send it off along the way. We did this with our slide film and never lost anything in the mail, although we posted it from the larger islands in the expectations that the mail would be speedier.

Don't leave your camera in direct sunshine any longer than necessary. A locked car can heat up like an oven in just a few minutes.

Sand and water are intense reflectors and in bright light they'll often leave foreground subjects shadowy. You can try compensating by adjusting your f-stop or attaching a polarising filter, or both, but the most effective technique is to take photos in the gentler light of early morning and late afternoon.

## HEALTH

In general, the Eastern Caribbean is a fairly healthy place to visit. Still, infections, sunburn, diarrhoea and intestinal parasites all warrant precautions.

If you're coming from a cold, dry climate to the heat and humidity of the Caribbean you may find yourself easily fatigued and more susceptible to minor ailments. Acclimatise yourself by slowing down your pace for the first few days.

## Travel Health Guides
Two useful guides dealing with travellers' health issues are:

Travellers' Health, Dr Richard Dawood, Oxford University Press and Random House. This book discusses worldwide health issues; it's comprehensive, easy to read and authoritative, although it's rather large to lug around.
Travel with Children, Maureen Wheeler, Lonely Planet Publications. Includes basic advice on travel health for younger children.

## Predeparture Preparations
**Health Insurance** A travel insurance policy to cover theft, loss and medical problems is a wise idea. There are a wide variety of policies and your travel agent will have recommendations. Check the small print.

- Some policies specifically exclude 'dangerous activities' which can include scuba diving, motorcycling or trekking. If such activities are on your agenda, you don't want that sort of policy.
- You may prefer a policy which pays doctors or hospitals direct rather than you having to pay on the spot and claim later. If you have to claim later make sure you keep all documentation. Some policies ask you to call back (reverse charges) to a centre in your home country where an immediate assessment of your problem is made.
- Give serious consideration to a policy that covers emergency flights. Many islands in the Eastern Caribbean are not prepared to handle complicated medical problems, so for something serious a flight home may be the best option. In addition, some of the smaller islands have very limited or no medical facilities and medivac (medical evacuation) to a larger island (or Miami) is commonplace.

**Medical Kit** A small, straightforward medical kit is a wise thing to carry. A possible kit list includes:

- Aspirin, acetaminophen, ibuprofen or panadol – for pain or fever.
- Antihistamine (such as Benadryl) – useful as a decongestant for colds, allergies, to ease the itch from insect bites or to help prevent motion sickness.
- Kaolin preparation (Pepto-Bismol), Imodium or Lomotil – for stomach upsets or diarrhoea.
- Rehydration mixture – for treatment of severe diarrhoea; this is particularly important if travelling with children.
- Antiseptic and antibiotic ointment or powder – for cuts and grazes.
- Calamine lotion – to ease irritation from bites or stings.
- Bandages and Band-aids – for minor injuries.
- Scissors, tweezers and a digital thermometer (mercury thermometers are prohibited by airlines).
- Insect repellent, sunscreen lotion and water purification tablets.

**Health Preparations** Make sure you're healthy before you start travelling. Before embarking on a long trip it's wise to attend to any dental work that might be needed, as dental care varies greatly between islands. If you wear glasses, it's a good idea to take a spare pair and your prescription.

If you require a particular medication take an adequate supply, as it may not be available locally. But take the prescription with you just in case (with the generic rather than the brand name, which may not be available locally), as it will make getting replacements easier. It will also show that you legally use the medication – it's surprising how often over-the-counter drugs from one place are illegal without a prescription or even banned in another. Keep the medication in its original container.

A Medic Alert tag is a good idea if you have a medical condition that is not easily recognisable (heart trouble, diabetes, asthma, allergic reactions to antibiotics etc).

If you are sexually active, bring an adequate supply of your usual contraceptive devices.

**Immunisations** No immunisations are required to enter any of the islands in the Eastern Caribbean. However, travellers who have been in any country in the past six months where yellow fever is endemic are required to have a vaccination certificate showing immunisation against yellow fever. The disease in endemic in many South American and African countries between 15° north and 15° south of the equator. Countries commonly regarded at infected include Bolivia, Brazil, Colombia, Ecuador, French Guiana, Guyana, Panama, Peru, Surinam, Venezuela and numerous countries in central Africa.

All vaccinations should be recorded on an International Health Certificate, which is available from your physician or government health department.

### Basic Rules

Care in what you eat and drink is the most important health rule; stomach upsets are the most likely travel health problem, but the majority of these upsets will be relatively minor. Don't become paranoid, as trying the local food is part of the experience of travel after all.

**Water** Water quality varies from island to island. It's safe to drink from the tap in most places but if you don't know that for certain, always assume the worst.

In general the higher islands, which have abundant supplies of fresh water from the interior rainforests, have excellent drinking water. Some of the more developed low islands, such as St Martin, have desalination plants that provide potable but not necessarily tasty drinking water. The less developed low islands almost invariably get their water from rain catchment and as a rule their waters should be treated before drinking as the water can vary greatly in bacteria counts and purity.

Bottled water is available just about everywhere; coconut water, soft drinks and beer are other alternatives. Tea or coffee should also be OK, since the water should have been boiled.

**Water Purification** The simplest way of purifying water is to boil it thoroughly. Technically this means boiling for 10 minutes, something which happens very rarely!

Simple filtering will not remove all dangerous organisms, so if you cannot boil water it should be treated chemically. Chlorine tablets (Puritabs, Steritabs or other brand names) will kill many but not all pathogens. Iodine is very effective in purifying water and is available in tablet form (such as Potable Aqua), but follow the directions carefully and remember that too much iodine can be harmful.

If you can't find tablets, tincture of iodine (2%) or iodine crystals can be used. Two drops of tincture of iodine per litre or quart of clear water is the recommended dosage; the treated water should be left to stand for 30 minutes before drinking. Iodine crystals can also be used to purify water but this is a more complicated process, as you have to first prepare a saturated iodine solution. Iodine loses its effectiveness if exposed to air or damp so keep it in a tightly sealed container. Flavoured powder will disguise the taste of treated water and is a good idea if you are travelling with children.

**Food** Food in the Eastern Caribbean is usually sanitarily prepared. Thoroughly cooked food is safest but not if it has been left to cool or if it has been reheated. Take great care with fish or shellfish (including that in fancy buffets) and avoid undercooked meat. If a place looks clean and well run and if the vendor also looks clean and healthy, then the food is probably safe. In general, places that are packed with travellers or locals will be fine, while empty restaurants are questionable.

**Nutrition** Make sure your diet is well balanced and you get enough protein. Eat plenty of fruit; there's always some fruit that's plentiful and cheap – bananas, papayas and coconuts are good common sources of vitamins.

Because the Caribbean has a hot climate, make sure you drink enough – don't rely on feeling thirsty to indicate when you should drink. Not needing to urinate or very dark yellow urine is a danger sign. Always carry a water bottle with you on long trips, or if you're doing any hiking. Excessive sweating can lead to loss of salt and therefore muscle cramping. Salt tablets are not a good idea as a preventative, but in places where salt is not used much adding salt to food can help.

**Everyday Health** A normal body temperature is 98.6°F or 37°C; more than 2°C higher is a 'high' fever. A normal adult pulse rate is 60 to 80 per minute (children 80 to 100, babies 100 to 140). You should know how to take a temperature and a pulse rate. As a general rule the pulse increases about 20 beats per minute for each °C rise in fever.

Respiration (breathing) rate is also an indicator of illness. Count the number of breaths per minute: between 12 and 20 is normal for adults and older children (up to 30 for younger children, 40 for babies). People with a high fever or serious respiratory illness (like pneumonia) breathe more quickly than normal. More than 40 shallow breaths a minute usually means pneumonia.

Many health problems can be avoided by taking care of yourself. Wash your hands frequently – it's quite easy to contaminate your own food. When the water is suspect, clean your teeth with purified water rather than straight from the tap. Avoid climatic extremes: keep out of the sun when it's hot and avoid freezing blasts from air-con vents.

Dress sensibly: you can get dangerous cuts by walking barefoot over coral. Avoid insect bites by covering bare skin when insects are around, by screening windows or beds or by using insect repellents. Seek local advice: if you're told the water is unsafe because of jellyfish or bilharzia, don't go in. In situations where there is no information, discretion is the better part of valour.

**Medical Treatment**
Hospital locations and emergency numbers are given in each island chapter and certainly if you have a major ailment you shouldn't hesitate to use them. For less serious ailments, the front desk of your hotel or guesthouse can usually recommend a doctor, as can many tourist offices.

**Climatic & Geographical Considerations**
**Sunburn** Sunburn is a definite possibility in the Eastern Caribbean because the islands are in the tropics where fewer of the sun's rays are blocked by the atmosphere. Don't be fooled by what appears to be a hazy overcast day, as the rays still get through. The most severe sun is between 10 am and 2 pm. Fair-skinned people can get first and second-degree burns in the hot Caribbean sun, so particularly in the first few days meter out your time in the sun carefully.

Sunscreen with a SPF (sun protection factor) of 10 to 15 is recommended if you're not already tanned; if you're going into the water use one that's water resistant. Take extra care to cover areas which don't normally see sun – eg, your feet and thighs. A hat is a good idea for added protection, and if you have a fair complexion you might want to use zinc cream or some other barrier cream for your nose and lips. You'll not only be protecting against sunburn but also against potential skin cancer and premature ageing of the skin. Calamine lotion is good for mild sunburn.

Too much sunlight can also damage your eyes, whether it's direct or reflected (glare). Good sunglasses will help protect your eyes. Makes sure they're treated to absorb ultraviolet radiation – if not, they'll actually do more harm than good by dilating your pupils and making it easier for ultraviolet light to damage the retina.

**Prickly Heat** Prickly heat is an itchy rash caused by excessive perspiration trapped under the skin. It usually strikes people who have just arrived in a hot climate and whose pores have not yet opened sufficiently to cope with greater sweating. Keeping cool by bathing often, using a mild talcum powder or even resorting to air-conditioning may help until you acclimatise.

**Heat Exhaustion** Dehydration or salt deficiency can cause heat exhaustion. Take time to acclimatise to high temperatures and make sure you get sufficient liquids. Salt deficiency is characterised by fatigue, lethargy, headaches, giddiness and muscle cramps and in this case salt tablets may help. Vomiting or diarrhoea can deplete your liquid and salt levels.

Anhydrotic heat exhaustion, caused by an inability to sweat, is quite rare. Unlike the other forms of heat exhaustion it is likely to strike people who have been in a hot climate for some time, rather than newcomers.

**Heat Stroke** This serious, sometimes fatal, condition can occur if the body's heat-regulating mechanism breaks down and the body temperature rises to dangerous levels. Long, continuous periods of exposure to high temperatures can leave you vulnerable to heat stroke. You should avoid excessive alcohol or strenuous activity when you first arrive in a hot climate.

The symptoms are feeling unwell, not sweating very much or at all and a high body temperature (39°C to 41°C). Where sweating has ceased the skin becomes flushed and red. Severe, throbbing headaches and lack of coordination will also occur, and the sufferer may be confused or aggressive. Eventually the victim will become delirious or convulse. Hospitalisation is essential, but meanwhile get patients out of the sun, remove their clothing, cover them with a wet sheet or towel and then fan continually.

**Fungal Infections** The same climate that produce lush tropical rainforests also promotes a prolific growth of skin fungi and bacteria. Hot weather fungal infections are most likely to occur on the scalp, between the toes or fingers (athlete's foot), in the groin (jock itch) and on the body (ringworm). You get ringworm (which is a fungal infection, not a worm) from infected animals or by walking on damp areas, like shower floors.

To prevent fungal infections wear loose, comfortable clothes, avoid artificial fibres, wash frequently and dry carefully. If you do get an infection, wash the infected area daily with a disinfectant or medicated soap and water, and rinse and dry well. Apply an antifungal powder like the widely available Tinaderm. Try to expose the infected area to air or sunlight as much as possible and wash all towels and underwear in hot water as well as changing them often.

**Motion Sickness** Eating lightly before and during a trip will reduce the chances of motion sickness. If you are prone to motion sickness try to find a place that minimises disturbance – near the wing on aircraft, close to midships on boats, near the centre on buses. Fresh air usually helps; reading or cigarette smoke doesn't. Commercial anti-motion-sickness preparations, which can cause drowsiness, have to be taken before the trip commences; when you're feeling sick it's too late. Ginger is a natural preventative and is available in capsule form.

### Diseases of Insanitation

**Diarrhoea** A change of water, food or climate can all cause the runs; diarrhoea caused by contaminated food or water is more serious. Despite all your precautions you may still have a bout of mild travellers' diarrhoea but a few rushed toilet trips with no other symptoms is not indicative of a serious problem.

Moderate diarrhoea, involving half-a-dozen loose movements in a day, is more of a nuisance. Dehydration is the main danger with any diarrhoea, particularly for children, so fluid replenishment is the number one treatment. Weak black tea with a little sugar, soda water, or soft drinks allowed to go flat and diluted 50% with bottled water are all good. Coconuts, which are readily available on many islands, are not only a good source of uncontaminated water but they're also an excellent rehydration drink, full of vitamins and minerals.

With severe diarrhoea a rehydrating solution is necessary to replace minerals and salts. You should stick to a bland diet as you recover.

Lomotil or Imodium can be used to bring relief from the symptoms, although they do not cure the problem. Only use these drugs if absolutely necessary – eg, if you *must* travel. For children Imodium is preferable, but do not use these drugs if the patient has a high fever or is severely dehydrated.

Antibiotics can be very useful in treating severe diarrhoea especially if it is accompanied by nausea, vomiting, stomach cramps or mild fever. Ampicillin, a broad spectrum penicillin, is usually recommended. Two capsules of 250 mg each taken four times a day is the recommended dose for an adult. Children aged between eight and 12 years should have half the adult dose; younger children should have half a capsule four times a day. Note that if the patient is allergic to penicillin ampicillin should not be administered.

Three days of treatment should be sufficient and an improvement should occur within 24 hours. Ampicillin is a prescription drug and should only be taken on a doctor's advice.

**Dysentery** This serious illness is caused by contaminated food or water and is characterised by severe diarrhoea, often with blood or mucus in the stool. There are two kinds of dysentery. Bacillary dysentery is characterised by a high fever and rapid development; headache, vomiting and stomach pains are also symptoms. It generally does not last longer than a week, but it is highly contagious.

Amoebic dysentery is more gradual in developing, has no fever or vomiting but is a more serious illness. It is not a self-limiting disease: it will persist until treated and can recur and cause long-term damage.

A stool test is necessary to diagnose which kind of dysentery you have, so you should seek medical help urgently. In case of an emergency, note that tetracycline is the prescribed treatment for bacillary dysentery, metronidazole for amoebic dysentery.

**Cholera** There is currently no cholera in the Eastern Caribbean, but as it has been spreading throughout South America some health officials expect cholera to soon make an appearance in the Caribbean as well.

Cholera vaccination is not very effective. However, outbreaks of cholera are generally widely reported, so you can avoid such problem areas. The disease is characterised by a sudden onset of acute diarrhoea with 'rice water' stools, vomiting, muscular cramps, and extreme weakness. You need medical help and treatment for dehydration, which can be extreme.

**Hepatitis** Hepatitis A is the more common form of this disease and is spread by contaminated food or water. Protection is through the new vaccine Havrix or the antibody gammaglobulin. The antibody is short-lasting.

The first symptoms are fever, chills, headache, fatigue, feelings of weakness and aches and pains. This is followed by loss of appetite, nausea, vomiting, abdominal pain, dark urine, light-coloured faeces and jaundiced skin; the whites of the eyes may also turn yellow. In some cases there may just be a feeling of being unwell or tired, accompanied by loss of appetite, aches and pains and the jaundiced effect. You should seek medical advice, but in general there is not much you can do apart from resting, drinking lots of fluids, eating lightly and avoiding fatty foods. People who have had hepatitis must forego alcohol for six months after the illness, as hepatitis attacks the liver and it needs that amount of time to recover.

Hepatitis B, which used to be called serum hepatitis, is spread through sexual contact or through skin penetration – it can be transmitted via dirty needles or blood transfusions, for instance. Avoid having your ears pierced, tattoos done or injections where you have doubts about the sanitary conditions.

The symptoms of type B are much the same as type A except that they are more severe and may lead to irreparable liver damage or even liver cancer. Although there is no treatment for hepatitis B, an effective prophylactic vaccine is readily available in most countries. The immunisation schedule requires two injections at least a month apart followed by a third dose five months after the second. Persons who should receive a hepatitis B vaccination include anyone who anticipates contact with blood or other bodily secretions, either as a health care worker or through sexual contact with the local population, particularly those who intend to stay in the country for a long period of time.

Hepatitis Non-A Non-B is a blanket term formerly used for several different strains of hepatitis, which have now been separately identified. Hepatitis C is similar to B but is less common. Hepatitis D (the 'delta particle') is also similar to B and always occurs in concert with it; its occurrence is currently limited to IV drug users. Hepatitis E, however, is similar to A and is spread in the same manner, by water or food contamination.

Tests are available for these strands, but are very expensive. Travellers shouldn't be too paranoid about this apparent proliferation of hepatitis strains; they are fairly rare (so far) and following the same precautions as for A and B should be all that's necessary to avoid them.

### Diseases Spread by People & Animals

**Rabies** All islands north of (and including) St Vincent & the Grenadines are reportedly rabies-free. Rabies can be caused by a bite or scratch by an infected animal. Mongoose and dogs are noted carriers. Any bite, scratch or even lick from a mammal should be cleaned immediately and thoroughly. Scrub with soap and running water, and then clean with an alcohol solution. If there is any possibility that the animal is infected medical help should be sought immediately. Even if the animal is not rabid, all bites should be treated seriously as they can become infected or can result in tetanus.

**Bilharzia** Bilharzia, also called schistosomiasis, is endemic in Guadeloupe, Martinique and St Lucia and may occur sporadically on other islands, including Antigua and Montserrat.

Bilharzia is carried in water by minute worms. The larvae infect certain varieties of freshwater snails found in rivers, streams, lakes and particularly behind dams. The worms multiply and are eventually discharged into the water surrounding the snails.

The worms attach themselves to your intestines or bladder, where they produce large numbers of eggs. The worm enters through the skin, and the first symptom may be a tingling and sometimes a light rash around the area where it entered. Weeks later, when the worm is busy producing eggs, a high fever may develop. A general feeling of being unwell may be the first symptom; once the disease is established abdominal pain and blood in the urine are other signs.

Avoiding swimming or bathing in freshwater where bilharzia is present is the main method of preventing the disease. If you do get wet in a questionable area, dry off quickly and dry your clothes as well. Seek medical attention if you have been exposed to the disease and tell the doctor of your suspicions, as bilharzia in the early stages can be confused with malaria or typhoid.

**Leptospirosis** Visitors should be aware of leptospirosis, a bacterial disease found in some freshwater streams and ponds. The disease is transmitted from animals such as rats and mongoose.

Humans most often pick up the disease by swimming or wading in freshwater contaminated by animal urine. Leptospirosis enters the body through the nose, eyes, mouth or cuts in the skin. Symptoms, which resemble the flu, can occur within two to 20 days after exposure and may include fever, chills, sweating, headaches, muscle pains, vomiting and diarrhoea. More severe symptoms include blood in the urine and jaundice. Symptoms may last from a few days to several weeks and in rare cases can result in death.

As a precaution avoid swimming and wading in freshwater, especially if you have open cuts.

**Sexually Transmitted Diseases** Sexual contact with an infected sexual partner spreads these diseases. While abstinence is the only 100% preventative, using condoms is also effective. Gonorrhoea and syphilis are the most common of these diseases; sores, blisters or rashes around the genitals, discharges or pain when urinating are common symptoms. Symptoms may be less marked or not observed at all in women. Syphilis symptoms eventually disappear completely but the disease continues and can cause severe problems in later years. The treatment of gonorrhoea and syphilis is by antibiotics.

There are numerous other sexually transmitted diseases, most of which have effective treatments. However, there is no cure for herpes or HIV/AIDS. Using condoms decreases but does not eliminate your chances of contracting these diseases.

AIDS can also be spread through infected blood transfusions or dirty needles – vaccinations, acupuncture, tattooing and ear or nose piercing can potentially be as dangerous as intravenous drug use if the equipment is not clean. If you do need an injection, it may be a good idea to buy a new syringe from a pharmacy and ask the doctor to use it. You may also want to take a couple of syringes with you, in case of emergency.

### Insect-Borne Diseases

There is no malaria in the Eastern Caribbean, although dengue fever is endemic to most of the region.

**Dengue Fever** There is no prophylactic available for this mosquito-spread disease; the main preventative measure is to avoid mosquito bites. Use mosquito repellents containing the compound DEET on exposed areas and a mosquito net – it may be worth taking your own.

A sudden onset of fever, headaches and severe joint and muscle pains are the first signs before a rash starts on the trunk of the body and spreads to the limbs and face. After a further few days, the fever will subside and recovery will begin. Serious complications are not common.

### Cuts, Bites & Stings

**Cuts & Scratches** Skin punctures can easily become infected in hot climates and may be difficult to heal. Treat any cut with an anti-

septic solution. Where possible avoid bandages and Band-aids, which can keep wounds wet. Coral cuts are notoriously slow to heal, as the coral injects a weak venom into the wound. Avoid coral cuts by wearing shoes when walking on reefs, and clean any cut thoroughly.

**Snakes** The poisonous fer-de-lance snake is present in Martinique, St Lucia and Trinidad. It's a very deadly snake as it has an anti-coagulating agent in its venom. However, bites are not that common.

To minimise your chances of being bitten always wear boots, socks and long trousers when walking through undergrowth where snakes may be present and don't put your hands into holes and crevices.

Snake bites do not cause instantaneous death and antivenenes are usually available. Keep the victim calm and still, wrap the bitten limb tightly, as you would for a sprained ankle, and then attach a splint to immobilise it. Then seek medical help, if possible with the dead snake for identification. Don't attempt to catch the snake if there is even a remote possibility of being bitten again. Tourniquets and sucking out the poison are now comprehensively discredited.

**Jellyfish** Jellyfish make only periodic appearances in most places that they're found and local advice is the best way of avoiding contact with these sea creatures and their stinging tentacles. Stings from most jellyfish are painful. Dousing in vinegar will de-activate any stingers which have not 'fired'. Calamine lotion, antihistamines and analgesics may reduce the reaction and relieve the pain.

### Women's Health

**Gynaecological Problems** Poor diet, lowered resistance through the use of antibiotics for stomach upsets and even contraceptive pills can lead to vaginal infections when travelling in hot climates. Keeping the genital area clean and wearing skirts or loose-fitting trousers and cotton underwear will help to prevent infections.

Yeast infections, characterised by a rash, itch and discharge, can be treated with a water-diluted vinegar or even lemon-juice douche or with yoghurt. Nystatin suppositories are the usual medical prescription.

Trichomonas is a more serious infection; symptoms are a discharge and a burning sensation when urinating. Male sexual partners must also be treated. If a vinegar-water douche is not effective medical attention should be sought. Metronidazole (Flagyl) is the prescribed drug.

**Pregnancy** Most miscarriages occur during the first three months of pregnancy, so this is the most risky time to travel. The last three months should also be spent within reasonable distance of good medical care, as quite serious problems can develop at this time. Pregnant women should avoid all unnecessary medication. Additional care should be taken to prevent illness and particular attention should be paid to diet and nutrition.

Women travellers often find that their periods become irregular or even cease while they're on the road. Remember that a missed period in these circumstances doesn't necessarily indicate pregnancy. There are health posts or Family Planning clinics in many small and large urban centres in developing countries, where you can seek advice and have a urine test to determine whether you are pregnant or not.

## WOMEN TRAVELLERS

Although most islands in the Eastern Caribbean shouldn't prove a hassle, women travelling alone may occasionally encounter unwanted attention, catcalls, come-ons and the like.

In terms of physical danger, heading off into the wilderness alone, walking in dark places on most islands, hitching or picking up male hitchhikers are all potentially dangerous.

## DANGERS & ANNOYANCES

In terms of individual safety and crime, the situation is quite varied in the Eastern Caribbean. For instance, it's hard to imagine a more tranquil area than Saba, where most people don't even have locks on their doors, while walking the streets of Port of Spain, Trinidad, after dark can certainly be a risky venture. Consequently the precautions you should take depend on which island you're visiting. For a better grasp of the situation, see the individual island chapters.

As for nasty insects, you can expect to find mosquitoes and sand flies throughout the region, both of which can be quite voracious, so consider bringing insect repellent. In addition, a few of the islands have chiggers, poisonous snakes (see the Health section) and centipedes.

All visitors should learn to identify manchineel trees, which grow on beaches throughout the Eastern Caribbean. The fruit of the manchineel, which looks like small green apples, is very poisonous, and the milky sap given off by the fruit and leaves can cause severe skin blisters, similar to the reaction caused by poison oak. If the sap is rubbed in your eyes, it can cause temporary blindness. Never take shelter under the trees during a rainstorm, as the sap can be washed off the tree and onto anyone sitting below.

Manchineel trees can be quite sizeable, growing as high as 12 metres, with widely spreading branches. The leaves are green, shiny and elliptic in shape. On many of the more visited beaches, some of the trees will be marked with red paint or warning signs. Manchineel is called *mancenilla* on the French islands and *anjenelle* in Trinidad and Tobago.

## WORK

The Eastern Caribbean has high unemployment and low wages, as well as strict immigration policies aimed at preventing foreign visitors from taking up work.

Generally the best bet for working is to crew up with a boat. As boathands aren't usually working on any one island in particular, the work situation is more flexible and it's easier to avoid hassles with immigration. Marinas are a good place to look for jobs on yachts; check the bulletin board notices, strike up conversations with skippers or ask around at the nearest bar – most marinas have a watering hole where sailors hang out.

## ACTIVITIES
There are a slew of activities available throughout the Eastern Caribbean, including diving, windsurfing, hiking, horse riding, golf, tennis and endless catamaran cruises and sunset sails. Details on all activities are given in the individual island chapters.

Most islands in the Eastern Caribbean have good diving locales. Generally no two divers agree on the best sites for diving but among the places in vogue these days are Dominica, Saba, Tobago, St Kitts and St Vincent and the Grenadines.

In terms of windsurfing, Guadeloupe, St Barts and Barbados are special places that have competitions and hotels dedicated to windsurfers. For regular surfing, Barbados, the farthest out in the Atlantic, has the finest conditions.

Hiking enthusiasts will find excellent tracks through the rainforest and mountains on Dominica, Guadeloupe and Martinique while visitors seeking a birdwatching holiday will discover the greatest abundance and variety of birds on the islands of Trinidad and Tobago.

## ACCOMMODATION
There's a wide range of accommodation available in the Eastern Caribbean, from inexpensive guesthouses and good-value self-catering apartments to luxury villa resorts. However, not all islands have rooms in all price categories – and a few have no low-end accommodation at all. Accommodation options are detailed in each island chapter.

In this book the phrase 'in summer' refers to the low season and 'in winter' refers to the high season. At nearly all hotels, summer rates are in effect from 15 April to 14 December, winter rates from 15 December to 14 April. Perhaps 10% of the hotels in the Eastern Caribbean make some minor deviations from these dates, usually with the addition of a mid-range rate in the spring and autumn and/or with higher rates for a few weeks at the end of December and the beginning of January.

Many hotels close for a month or so in late summer, usually around September. If business doesn't look promising, some of the smaller hotels and guesthouses might even close down for the entire summer.

'Private bath' means that the room has its own toilet and shower – it does not necessarily mean that it has a bathtub, and in most cases it will not.

When you're looking for a hotel keep in mind that new hotels, especially first-class hotels, often have enticing rates for the first couple of years until they build up a clientele. Conversely, some of the busier older hotels are not good value but have simply built up name recognition over the years.

Camping is very limited in the Eastern Caribbean – the only established camping is at a handful of small, private camping grounds on Guadeloupe and Martinique.

At the national park in Grenada, camping is officially allowed but there are no facilities; other than that, there are no established camp sites in the English-speaking Eastern Caribbean and freelance camping is either illegal or discouraged.

### Reservation Systems
Reservations at some hotels and guesthouses can be made through overseas booking agencies. Those that operate on a single island are listed under that island. The following reservation services book many places on multiple islands – as it may be easier and cheaper to enquire about many hotels in a single call, you might want to try them first.

International Travel & Resorts
ITR, the largest single reservation system operating throughout the Caribbean, books numerous hotels in the moderate and upper ranges. ITR will send out individual hotel brochures on request, as well as an annual directory.
The reservation number for the USA, Canada, Puerto Rico and the US Virgin Islands is ☎ (800) 223-9815 or ☎ (212) 545-8469; in Germany it's ☎ (89) 55 5339.

Resinter

Resinter books all PLM Azur, Marine, Novotel, Pullman and Sofitel hotel chains, which together account for nearly a third of the hotel rooms on Martinique and Guadeloupe, as well as a few places on St Martin, St Barts and St Lucia.

Resinter's reservation numbers are ☎ (800) 221-4542 in the USA and Canada; ☎ (1) 60 77 27 27 in France; ☎ (071) 724-1000 in the UK; ☎ (6196) 48 3800 in Germany; ☎ (02) 29 51 71 01 in Italy; ☎ (01) 302-09-48 in Switzerland; ☎ 800 185 95 in Denmark; and ☎ (020) 793 153 in Sweden.

WIMCO

The West Indies Management Company (WIMCO), PO Box 1461, Newport, RI 02840 USA, specialises in renting out exclusive villa properties. Its extensive listings include villas on Mustique, St Martin, St Barts, Montserrat, Anguilla, Nevis and Barbados.

Reservation numbers are ☎ (800) 932-3222 or ☎ (401) 849-8012 in the USA; ☎ (0-800) 89 8318 in the UK; ☎ 05 90 16 20 in France; and ☎ (01) 30 81 57 30 in Germany.

## FOOD

Foods in the Eastern Caribbean reflect the mix of cultures. Throughout the region you'll find West Indian food – predominantly local root crops, vegetables, fresh seafood and goat – prepared with African and Western influences. Also prevalent on most islands is Creole food, a spicy mix of French and West Indian flavours. On the French islands, pâtisseries, crêpe shops and sidewalk cafés are nearly as prevalent as they would be in a Paris suburb.

East Indian, British, North American and continental foods can also be found in varying degrees throughout the region. Barbados has plenty of places selling English-style fish & chips, on St Eustatius you can enjoy a Dutch smorgasbord breakfast of deli meats and cheeses, while moderately priced pizza and Italian food can be found on most islands.

A few chain restaurants like Kentucky Fried Chicken are common on the bigger islands but the quintessential fast food in the region remains a West Indian creation – the roti. It's comprised of a curried filling, most commonly potatoes and chicken, that's placed inside a tortilla-like wrapping and

eaten much like a burrito. It's cheap and as filling as a good-sized sandwich.

Public markets are the place to go for fresh local fruit and produce – that's where it's at its freshest and you're contributing 100% of your money to the local economy by buying it direct from the farmer. On larger islands, the capital city has a produce market that's open everyday but Sunday. On other islands they're commonly held only a couple of days a week. Saturday is invariably the biggest and liveliest market day everywhere. Fishers often sell fresh fish directly from the beach and announce their presence by blowing a conch shell.

## DRINKS

With their histories tied to sugar cane, it's only natural that rum remains the most

## Common Dishes of the Eastern Caribbean

**accras**: Creole-style cod or vegetable fritters

**bake**: a sandwich made with fried bread and usually filled with shark or other fish

**blaff**: a seafood preparation poached in a spicy broth

**callaloo soup**: the quintessential Eastern Caribbean soup, made with dasheen leaves and often with coconut milk; it resembles a creamy spinach soup

**christophene**: also known as chayote, a common Caribbean vegetable shaped like a large pear; it can be eaten raw in salads, used in soup or cooked like a squash

**colombo**: a spicy, East Indian-influenced dish that resembles curry

**conch**: also called *lambi*, the chewy meat of a large gastropod, it's common throughout the Caribbean and is often prepared in a spicy Creole sauce

**conkies**: a mixture of cornflour, coconut, pumpkin, sweet potatoes, raisins and spice, steamed in a plantain leaf

**cou-cou**: a creamy cornflour and okra mash, commonly served with salt fish

**crabes farcis**: spicy stuffed land crabs

**cutter**: a salt-bread roll used to make meat and fish sandwiches, or the name of such a sandwich

**dasheen**: a type of taro; the leaves are known as callaloo and cooked much like spinach or turnip leaves, and the starchy tuberous root is boiled and eaten like a potato

**dolphin**: a common type of white-meat fish, also called mahimahi; no relation to the marine mammal

**flying fish**: a grey-meat fish named for its ability to skim above the water; particularly plentiful in Barbados

**goat water**: a spicy goat meat stew often flavoured with cloves and rum

**jambayala**: a Creole dish usually consisting of rice cooked with ham, chicken or shellfish, spices, tomatoes, onions and peppers

**johnnycake**: a cornflour griddle cake

**jug-jug**: a mixture of Guinea cornflour, green peas and salted meat

**mahimahi**: see dolphin

**mauby**: a bittersweet drink made from the bark of the mauby tree, sweetened with sugar and spices

**mountain chicken**: the legs of the *crapaud*, a type of frog

**oil down**: a mix of breadfruit, pork, callaloo and coconut milk

**pepperpot**: a spicy stew made with various meats and accompanied by peppers and cassareep

**pigeon peas**: the brown, pea-like seeds of a tropical shrub which are cooked like peas and served mixed with rice

**raw bar**: a place that serves raw seafood, particularly clams and oysters on the half shell

**roti**: a curry filling, commonly potatoes and chicken, rolled inside a tortilla-like flat bread

**souse**: a dish made out of a pickled pig's head and belly, spices and a few vegetables, commonly served with a pig-blood sausage called pudding ■

common alcoholic beverage throughout the Eastern Caribbean. Most larger islands produce their own rum. Some like Martinique and Guadeloupe use freshly harvested sugar cane, while others like Grenada import molasses to produce their rum. There are scores of labels, from internationally recognised favourites like the Barbadian-produced Mount Gay to small obscure distilleries producing solely for local consumption. Rum is invariably cheap throughout the islands.

Certainly the most popular beer in the Eastern Caribbean is Carib, first brewed in Trinidad in 1951, and now also brewed in St Kitts and Grenada. You'll see advertisements all around the region proclaiming 'In This Country a Beer is a Carib'. In and around the Dutch islands, Heineken is the beer of choice.

Inexpensive drinking coconuts make a nice option to a sugar-laden soft drink and can be purchased from street vendors in many places. Another nice drink found in many places is sorrel, a lightly tart, bright-red drink rich in Vitamin C that's made from the flowers of the sorrel plant.

Bottled water is available at stores on all

**Tropical Fruits**

Many Eastern Caribbean islands have a variety of tropical fruits that can be found in the marketplace. Some of the more widespread ones are as follows:

**breadfruit**: a large, round, green fruit; this Caribbean staple is comparable to potatoes in its carbohydrate content and is prepared in much the same way

**guava**: a round, yellow fruit about six cm in diameter, it has a moist, pink, seedy flesh, all of which is edible. Guavas can be a little tart but tend to sweeten as they ripen. They're a good source of vitamin C and niacin

**mango**: big old mango trees are abundant in the Caribbean, with juicy oblong fruits that are about eight cm in diameter and 12 cm long. The fruits start out green but take on deeper colours as they ripen, usually reddening to an apricot colour. Mangoe is sweet and a good source of vitamins A and C; it's mainly a summer fruit

**papaya**: usually called paw paw in the Eastern Caribbean, this sweet orange fruit, which is harvested year-round, is a good source of calcium and vitamins A and C

**passionfruit**: a vine with beautiful flowers which grow into small, round fruits; the thick skin of the fruit is generally purple or yellow and wrinkles as it ripens. The pulp inside is juicy, seedy and slightly tart

**pineapple**: there are a variety of pineapples found throughout the Caribbean; the small ones known as black pineapples are among the sweetest

**plantain**: a starchy fruit of the banana family, usually fried or grilled like a vegetable

**soursop**: a large green fruit with a pulpy texture that's slightly acidic and is often made into a vitamin-rich drink

**starfruit**: also called carambola, this translucent yellow-green fruit has five ribs like the points of a star; it has a crisp, juicy pulp and can be eaten without being peeled

**tamarind**: the pod of a large tropical tree of the legume family; the juicy, acidic pulp of the seeds is used in beverages ■

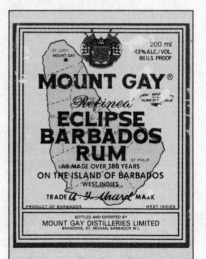

Mount Gay rum label

islands. Water is safe to drink from the tap on many but not all islands. See the individual island chapters for details.

**ENTERTAINMENT**

Whether you'd prefer to listen to Anguillian folk songs or check out the best bars on Barbados, the Eastern Caribbean's rich musical and cultural heritage ensures that you won't be at a loss for things to do after the sun goes down. More information is given in individual island chapters.

**THINGS TO BUY**

St Martin is the most popular island for duty-free shopping, but virtually any island that has large cruise ship facilities will have at least a few generic duty-free shops selling liquor, perfumes, jewellery and some designer clothing.

There are a lot of wood carvings from Bali, colourfully painted ceramic buses and

## Things Not to Buy

Sea turtle shells make beautiful jewellery – too beautiful, in fact, for the welfare of the turtles, which are endangered worldwide. Buying any turtle products increases the demand for hunting the turtles. Turtle shell jewellery is prohibited entry into the USA, Canada, Australia and most other countries.

The importation of black coral is likewise banned in more than 100 countries. The purchase of other corals, which are often taken live from their fragile reef ecosystems and sold in chunks or made into jewellery, should also give pause to the environmentally conscious. ■

market scenes made in Colombia and folk paintings from Haiti – some quite nice, but not made in the Eastern Caribbean.

Quality crafts that are made in the Eastern Caribbean include dolls in native Creole costumes, basketwork and stylish cotton clothing. Caribelle Batik makes nice batik clothing, as well as wall hangings with Caribbean scenes, which are for sale on several islands. Locally grown spices make nice lightweight souvenirs. And of course there's rum.

# Getting There & Away

## AIR

This section is an overview of international flights to the Eastern Caribbean. More specific details, including fare information, is in the Getting There & Away section of each island chapter.

Information on LIAT and other regional airlines flying within the Eastern Caribbean is in the Getting Around chapter.

The phone numbers listed in this section are the airline reservation numbers from the countries indicated.

### Scheduled Flights

**To/From the USA** There are more flights from the USA to the Eastern Caribbean than from any other part of the world.

American Airlines (☎ (800) 433-7300) is the main US carrier into the region. American has direct flights from the USA to a few of the larger islands, although to most destinations travellers must transit in San Juan, Puerto Rico, and then continue on American's inter-island carrier American Eagle. Overall, American's inter-island schedule coordinates quite closely with its flights between the US mainland and San Juan, making for convenient connections.

Continental Airlines (☎ (800) 525-0280) is the only other US carrier flying to the Eastern Caribbean and has a daily New York-St Martin flight.

The Trinidad-based airline BWIA (☎ (800) 327-7401) has a fairly extensive schedule between Miami and New York and the larger non-French islands of the Eastern Caribbean.

Air France (☎ (800) 327-2747) has a weekly flight from Miami to Guadeloupe and Martinique.

**To/From Canada** Air Canada (☎ (800) 268-7240) has direct flights from Toronto to Barbados, St Lucia and Trinidad.

BWIA (☎ (800) 327-7401) flies from Toronto to Barbados, Antigua and Trinidad.

**To/From the UK** BWIA (☎ (071) 839-9333) and British Airways (☎ (081) 897-4000) both have flights from London to Antigua, St Lucia, Barbados, Grenada and Trinidad.

**To/From Europe** Paris is the main European gateway to the Eastern Caribbean. Air France (☎ 44 08 22 22) flies from Paris to Martinique, Guadeloupe and St Martin. Air Outre Mer, or AOM (☎ 49 79 12 34), flies from Paris to Martinique and Guadeloupe. Air Corsair and Air Martinique (☎ 42 56 21 00) fly between Paris and Martinique.

BWIA (☎ (069) 628 025) and Lufthansa (☎ (069) 255 255) have direct flights from Frankfurt to Antigua and KLM has flights from Amsterdam to St Martin.

**To/From South America** There are connections between South America and the Eastern Caribbean with LIAT, Aeropostal, Aerotuy, Air France and United Airlines.

**To/From Australia & New Zealand** The main routing and cheapest fares to the Eastern Caribbean are via the USA. At the time of writing, the minimum return fare from Melbourne or Sydney to Los Angeles was A$1360 (low season) and A$1675 (high season). Excursion fares from Los Angeles to, for example, Barbados, start at A$776 return, and to Martinique, A$864 return. Cheaper fares may be available on application; check with your local travel agency.

### Charters

Charters from the USA, Canada, the UK and Europe offer another option for getting to the islands. Fares are often cheaper than on regularly scheduled commercial airlines, but you usually have to go and come back on a specific flight, commonly with a week-long stay, and you'll probably have no flexibility in extending your stay.

In the high season, charters often operate with such frequency that they carry more passengers to some islands than do the scheduled airlines.

Although charter companies do most of their business booking package tours that include both hotel and air, they commonly find themselves with a few empty seats on planes that they've chartered. Some companies will then sell these empty seats for bargain prices a week or two prior to departure.

In the USA you can sometimes find these seats advertised in the travel pages of larger Sunday news *New York Times* and the *Boston Globe*. Travel agents that specialise in discount travel can also be quite helpful.

## SEA
This section covers getting to the Eastern Caribbean from outside the region. Details on yacht chartering and information on ferries that connect one Eastern Caribbean island to another are in the Boat section of the Getting Around chapter.

### Banana Boat
There are two cargo lines that carry passengers on regularly scheduled voyages across the Atlantic to the Eastern Caribbean. Note that as cabin space is very limited, both commonly book up far in advance.

**To/From the UK** The Geest Line sails from Southampton, England every other Thursday. The boats carry cargo on the outbound journey and return with their refrigerated holds full of bananas. They are also equipped with five double and two single passenger cabins.

The ships call on Barbados, Antigua, St Kitts, Dominica, St Lucia, Grenada, St Vincent and Trinidad. Return journeys are typically 26 days. The return fare per person, in either a single or double cabin, is £2478 in July and August and £2915 the rest of the year. One-way fares to most islands are £1601 in July and August and £1884 the rest of the year. Prices include three meals a day and afternoon tea. There's a small bar, a lounge and a 'dip' pool. The cabins are straightforward but have air-con and private bathrooms.

Eastern Caribbean Boat Service

Bookings can be made through the Geest Line (☎ (0703) 33 3388; fax (0703) 71 4059), PO Box 154, Windward Terminal, Herbert Walker Ave, Southampton SO1 0XP. In the Caribbean information can be obtained by calling:

| | |
|---|---|
| Antigua: | ☎ 462-0854 |
| Barbados: | ☎ 429-9688 |
| Dominica: | ☎ 448-2320 |
| Grenada: | ☎ 440-2473 |
| St Kitts: | ☎ 465-4086 |
| St Lucia: | ☎ 452-2561 |
| St Vincent: | ☎ 456-1855 |
| Trinidad: | ☎ 625-6970 |

**To/From France** The Compagnie Générale Maritime (CGM) sails weekly between the French West Indies and mainland France. The vessels, which are modern cargo ships that carry bananas and limes to France, have a dozen comfortable passenger cabins, a TV room and a swimming pool. French meals with wine are included in the tariff, which is approximately US$1250 (one way) for the nine-day voyage. A ship leaves Guadeloupe every Thursday evening, overnights in Martinique where it takes on more cargo and then leaves Fort-de-France on Friday evening.

Passage can be booked through Transat Antilles Voyages (☎ 83 04 43), Quai Lefevre, Pointe-à-Pitre, Guadeloupe, or through the CGM office in Martinique (☎ 55 32 00) or Paris (☎ 46 25 70 00).

## Cruise Ship

Some two million cruise ship passengers sail the Caribbean annually, making the Caribbean the world's largest cruise ship destination. The ships average four to five ports of call each, adding up to a whopping nine million 'passenger visits' throughout the region.

The most visited ports in the Eastern Caribbean are St Martin, with 500,000 passenger arrivals, Barbados and Martinique, each with 400,000 passenger arrivals, followed in order by Antigua, Guadeloupe, Grenada, St Lucia, Dominica, St Kitts, St Vincent & the Grenadines and Trinidad & Tobago.

The typical cruise ship holiday is the ultimate package tour. Other than the effort involved in selecting a cruise, it requires minimal planning – just pay and show up – and for many people this is a large part of the appeal.

Some cruise lines put more emphasis on the thrill of cruising around the seas on a floating resort than they do on visiting any actual destination. If 'being there' is more important than 'getting there', travellers will need to choose a cruise accordingly.

For the most part, the smaller 'unconventional' ships put greater emphasis on the local aspects of their cruises, both in terms of the time spent on land and the degree of interaction with islanders and their environment. While the majority of mainstream cruises take in fine scenery along the way, the time spent on the islands is generally quite limited and the opportunities to experience a sense of island life is more restricted.

Still, the fact that most cruise ships call on many islands in a short time can be useful as an overview for those who plan to come back to the region later but haven't decided which islands to visit.

Because travel in the Eastern Caribbean can be expensive and because cruises cover rooms, meals, entertainment and transportation in one all-inclusive price, cruises can also be comparatively economical. All cruises will cost more than budget-end independent travel, but the least expensive cruises will not necessarily cost more than a conventional air/hotel package tour or a privately booked holiday at a resort hotel.

**Cost** Cruise lines do not divide passengers into class categories, but rather provide the same meals and amenities for all passengers on each ship.

Virtually all cruises are offered at a range of rates, however, depending mainly on the size, type and location of the cabin. Bottom-end cabins might well be uncomfortably cramped and poorly located, while top-end cabins are often spacious, luxurious suites. Price also depends on the season and dates of the cruise, the number of people in each cabin, transportation options between your home and the departure point and, of course, which cruise line you choose. In addition, discounts off the brochure rates are commonplace.

Standard rates are quoted per person, based on double occupancy. A third and fourth person (child or adult) in the same cabin is often given a heavily discounted rate.

Provisions vary widely for single travellers who occupy a double cabin; a few cruise lines allow this at no extra charge, while most charge from 110% to 200% of the standard rate. Some cruise lines offer single cabins and some have a singles share programme in which they attempt to match up compatible (same-sex) cabin mates to share the double cabins.

Some cruise lines provide a free or discounted airfare to and from the port of embarkation in their quoted rates (and will provide a rebate if you make your own transportation arrangements), while others do not.

Most cruises to the Eastern Caribbean end up costing around US$125 to US$350 per person per day, including airfare from a major US gateway city.

Meals, which are typically frequent and elaborate, are included in the cruise price. Alcoholic drinks are usually not included and are comparable in price to those in bars back home. Some cruise lines also charge for soft drinks.

Guided land tours are almost always offered at each port of call, generally for about US$25 to US$100 each. If you opt to see the sights yourself, you'll need to budget for taxis, admission fees etc.

Entertainment shows and most on-board activities are included in the cruise price but personal services such as hairstyling and laundry usually cost extra as do most shore-side activities, such as diving or windsurfing.

Some cruise lines include tipping in the quoted price. Most do not, however, and usually suggest that each passenger tip, per day, US$3 to the cabin steward, US$3 to the dining room waiter and US$1.50 to the table attendant, given in a lump sum on the last night of the cruise. For cocktail waiters, a 15% tip is sometimes included in the drink price and if not is generally given on the spot.

Port charges, which generally range from US$2 to US$6 per port, are sometimes extra. Be sure to check the fine print about deposits, cancellation and refund policies and travel insurance.

**Discounts** When all is said and done, very few cruises are sold at the brochure rates.

Many cruise lines offer discounts for early reservations and also give last-minute discounts. Just a few years ago the cheapest rates were those obtained at the last minute – essentially stand-by rates for whatever cabins had not been booked – but a concerted effort by the cruise lines to reverse this trend has been largely successful. These days, the general rule is the earlier the booking the greater the discount (and, of course, the better the cabin selection).

As an example, Holland America Line starts out with early-booking discounts of as much as 43% off the brochure rates, lowering the discount rate as the sailing date gets closer.

Still, cruise lines want to sail full, so if there are leftover seats at the end, there will be discounts available.

And then there are promotions: some cruise lines offer a 50% discount for the second person on designated sailings, offer free cabin upgrades if certain qualifications are met, run two-for-one specials in selected markets, offer discounts to senior citizens etc.

**Booking a Cruise** A good travel agent should be able to work through the maze, providing comparisons on cruise lines, itineraries, facilities, rates and discounts. Be aware that the industry has also attracted the occasional fly-by-night company that advertises heavily, then takes the money and runs, so be sure you're dealing with a reputable agent.

Those travel agents most knowledgeable about cruises are apt to belong to Cruise Lines International Association (CLIA), an organisation of 32 cruise lines that works in affiliation with about 20,000 North American travel agencies. You might also want to find a travel agent who subscribes to the *Official Cruise Guide*, which is a good source of information on cruise lines, listing schedules and facilities for virtually all ships.

Your local travel agent may be able to provide all the help you need. If not, there are numerous travel agents that specialise only in cruises and are therefore generally up to speed on the latest promotional deals and other discounts. In the USA, a few of those that book widely in the Eastern Caribbean are:

Cruise Time, 301 Maple Ave W, Suite H, Poplar Bldg, Vienna, VA 22180 (☎ (800) 627-6131)
Cruises Inc, 5000 Campuswood Drive, East Syracuse, NY 13057 (☎ (800) 854-0500, (315) 463-9695)
NABA Cruise Consultants, 2297 Whitney Ave, Hamden, CT 06518 (☎ (800) 775-1884, (203) 288-1884)
White Travel Service, 127 Park Rd, West Hartford, CT 06119 (☎ (800) 547-4790, (203) 233-2648)
World Wide Cruises, 8059 W McNab Rd, Ft Lauderdale, FL 33321 (☎ (800) 882-9000, (305) 720-9000)

For travellers with disabilities, Flying Wheels Travel (☎ (507) 451-5005, (800) 535-6790), PO Box 382, Owatonna, MN 55060, USA, specialises in booking handicapped-accessible Caribbean cruises.

**Choosing a Cruise** In addition to finding a cruise that fits your budget, here are some other things to consider:

**Schedule** Most cruises last between one and two weeks, though there are a few that are shorter or longer.

Caribbean cruises are most popular and thus most expensive during the northern hemisphere's midwinter (with the peak time being the Christmas/New Year holidays) and least crowded in autumn, with spring and summer in between.

**Departure Point** Most cruises that take in the Eastern Caribbean depart from Miami or Fort Lauderdale, Florida; San Juan, Puerto Rico; St Thomas, US Virgin Islands; or from within the Eastern Caribbean itself.

The cost and ease of getting to the departure point should be considered when choosing a cruise. Also important is your interest in the port and nearby islands if you plan to extend your holiday either before or after the cruise.

**Itinerary** Consider which islands you want to visit. The largest cruise ships generally stop only at islands with substantial port facilities, such as St Martin, Antigua, Guadeloupe, Martinique, Dominica, St Lucia and Grenada, while some of the smaller 'unconventional' ships are able to take in less visited islands like Saba, Montserrat and the Grenadines.

**Ship Type & Facilities** The conventional cruise ship is indeed a floating resort, some holding a good 2500 passengers, with multiple swimming pools, Las Vegas-type entertainment, casinos and discos.

Smaller ships, which might have between 50 and 250 passengers, will have less lavish entertainment but are more personal and can pull into smaller ports, marinas and snorkelling coves.

There is a huge variety in style. Some cruise lines appeal to active vacationers who enjoy water sports, hiking and exploration. Some are luxury boats, with a sophisticated ambience and prices to match. Some don't accept young children. Others are more middle-class, welcoming young families, retired seniors, singles and couples alike, with activities for all ages and interests. Likewise, dress codes, meal quality and types of shore excursions vary.

Some ships can accommodate special diets with advance notice. Many ships are handicapped-accessible, although details such as the measurement of bathroom clearance for wheelchairs should be checked carefully, as problems with cabins for the disabled are not uncommon. In general, the newer ships are more accessible, with fewer barriers, larger cabins situated near elevators and wider doorways and halls.

Again, a good travel agent can help match cruises to each customer's interests.

**Cabin** Outside cabins are best and least claustrophobic, as you get a view. The higher decks are preferable, as are of course the largest and fanciest cabins, and prices will correspond accordingly. Although modern cruise ships have stabilisers to prevent roll, if you're prone to motion sickness you might want to get a cabin in the centre of the ship which is more stable and rocks less in bad weather.

The inside cabins (with no portholes) on the lowest decks are the least desirable, but also the cheapest. Bottom-end cabins sometimes have bunk-style beds and minuscule bathrooms and can be uncomfortably cramped. Avoid the cabins nearest the engine room, as they may be noisy.

**Sanitation** All cruise ships that arrive in US ports – which includes the majority that sail the Caribbean – are subject to unannounced US sanitation inspections. The inspectors rate ships in four categories: potable water supply; food preparation and holding; potential contamination of food; and general cleanliness, storage and repair.

A summary sheet that lists ships, the latest date of inspection and their ratings is published weekly and may be obtained free by writing to: Chief, Vessel Sanitation Program, National Center for Environmental Health, 1015 North American Way, Room 107, Miami, FL 33132, USA.

**Environmental Sensitivity** Not all cruise ships have equally clean environmental records and this should be taken into account when choosing a cruise vacation. When you book a cruise ship, be sure to ask the travel agent about the cruise line's policy for dumping wastes and whether the company has been cited for violating marine pollution laws.

While on your cruise, be inquisitive about the ship's recycling programme and how waste is being handled and disposed – it will help raise the level of environmental consciousness. If you do sight any violations, report them to the Center for Marine Conservation (see the following section) and to your travel agent back home, so the information can be used by travellers who come after you.

**Environmental Considerations** The US government's National Oceanic and Atmospheric Administration (NOAA) is responsible for tracking down ships that illegally dump wastes at sea within the USA's 200-mile territorial limit. Efforts are concentrated on cruise ships, which tend to carry more garbage than other vessels.

NOAA's main educational and tracking arm is the Center for Marine Conservation (CMC), a nonprofit organisation dedicated to the conservation of marine wildlife. CMC is responsible for compiling information on violators but as it doesn't have the capacity to have staff on board cruise ships, it relies almost solely upon cruise passengers to report pollution violations.

The centre will send anyone planning to

---

**MARPOL Annex V**

Marine pollution is a serious issue in the Caribbean and cruise ships dumping rubbish overboard have traditionally been a major part of the problem. Annex V of MARPOL 73/78, an international treaty resulting from the 1973 International Convention for the Prevention of Pollution from Ships, makes it illegal to dump plastics anywhere at sea and also places near-shore restrictions on the disposal of other solid waste. Some garbage can still be dumped, as long as it's disposed of at least three miles (4.8 km) offshore; bottles and cans cannot be dumped within 12 miles (19.3 km) of land.

Despite the limits of the treaty, which went into effect in 1988, most countries have paid little heed to enforcing the regulations and many cruise ships have continued to dump garbage at random.

The USA, from whose waters most Caribbean cruise ships depart, has recently begun to crack down on violators within its 200-mile (322 km) territorial limit.

In 1993 the cruise ship industry got a wake-up call when the *Regal Princess* of Princess Cruises received the maximum fine of US$500,000 for dumping 20 plastic bags full of garbage off the Florida Keys. The successful prosecution was the consequence of a cruise passenger's video-taping of the dumping. ■

go on a cruise (or who is otherwise interested) a free packet that includes information about the problem, a list of cruise lines that have been implicated in illegal dumping since 1988 and a form for reporting unlawful dumpings.

The government also provides a monetary incentive for passengers to assist with enforcement. If a citizen provides information leading to fines, the court may award that person up to one-half of the fine, which can be as much as US$250,000!

The information packets are available by writing to the Center for Marine Conservation (☎ (202) 429-5609), 1725 DeSales St NW, Washington DC 20036.

**Other Considerations** Cruise ship passengers that show interest in the local culture and put money directly into the hands of small merchants are more appreciated by islanders than those that stay wrapped in the cocoon of organised land tours or see nothing beyond the duty-free shops.

While the cruise line's optional land tours are generally conveniently packaged to take in many of the island's sightseeing highlights, they also move quickly and tend to shield visitors from interaction with the local people. In addition, a fair percentage of the money paid for these tours stays with the cruise line organisers rather than going into the local economy.

On some islands you might want to take a closer look at a smaller area rather than trying to breeze around the whole island on a tour. It can be a fun alternative to wander the streets of the main town, poke into little shops, eat at local restaurants and buy souvenirs from street vendors and small businesses where you can chat with the owners. Buy local rums in small shops instead of on board ship – you might even save money in the process.

**Cruise Ship Lines** Most travel agents have stacks of cruise ship brochures available for the taking. Brochures can also be obtained by contacting the cruise lines directly.

The following cruise lines sail to one or more of the islands of the Eastern Caribbean. In some cases, not all ports of call listed are visited on a single cruise. While only Eastern Caribbean ports of call are listed, other parts of the Caribbean might also be visited during the same cruise.

The 800 phone numbers are toll-free from the USA and sometimes from Canada.

**Conventional Cruises** Contact details and ports of call of conventional cruise lines are as follows:

American Canadian Caribbean Line, PO Box 368, Warren, RI 02885 (☎ (800) 556-7450, ☎ (401) 247-0955).
Ships from Antigua. Ports of call include Guadeloupe, Dominica, Martinique, St Lucia, St Vincent, Bequia, Canouan, Mayreau, Carriacou and Grenada.

Carnival Cruise Lines, Carnival Place, 3655 NW 87 Ave, Miami, FL 33178 (☎ (800) 327-2058, ☎ (305) 599-2200).
Ships depart from Miami, Ocho Rios and San Juan. Ports of call include Dominica, Grenada, Guadeloupe, Martinique, Mayreau and St Lucia.

Costa Cruise Line, World Trade Center, 80 SW 8th St, 27th Floor, Miami, FL 33130 (☎ (800) 462-6782, ☎ (305) 358-7325).
Billed as 'Italian-style cruising', ships depart from San Juan. Ports of call include Barbados, Martinique and St Martin.

Crystal Cruises, 2121 Ave of the Stars, Los Angeles, CA 90067 (☎ (800) 446-6645).
Ships depart from San Juan, New York and Fort Lauderdale as well as Acapulco and Los Angeles via the Panama Canal. Ports of call include St Martin, Antigua, St Barts, Martinique, Barbados and Grenada.

Cunard Line, 555 Fifth Ave, New York, NY 10017 (☎ (800) 528-6273, ☎ (212) 880-7500).
Ships depart from Barbados, Fort Lauderdale, New York, San Juan and St Thomas. Ports of call include Grenada, Martinique, St Martin and Trinidad.

Dolphin Cruise Line, 901 S America Way, Miami, FL 33132 (☎ (800) 222-1003, ☎ (305) 358-5122).
Ships depart from Aruba. Ports of call include Martinique, Barbados and Dominica.

Holland America Line, 300 Elliott Ave West, Seattle, WA 98119 (☎ (800) 426-0327, ☎ (206) 281-3535).
Ships depart from Fort Lauderdale, Tampa, New York and Newport News, Virginia. Ports of call include Barbados, Dominica, Grenada, Martinique, St Kitts, St Lucia and St Martin.

Norwegian Cruise Line, 95 Merrick Way, Coral Gables, FL 33134 (☎ (800) 327-7030, ☎ (305) 445-0866).

Ships depart from Miami and San Juan. Ports of call include Antigua, Barbados, Martinique, St Lucia and St Martin.

Princess Cruises, 10100 Santa Monica Blvd, Los Angeles, CA 90067 (☎ (800) 568-3262, ☎ (310) 553-1770).

Ships depart from Fort Lauderdale and San Juan. Ports of call include Barbados, Martinique, Mayreau and St Martin.

Regency Cruises, 260 Madison Ave, New York, NY 10016 (☎ (800) 388-5500, ☎ (212) 972-4499).

Ships depart from San Juan and New York. Ports of call include St Martin, Antigua, St Barts, St Kitts, Martinique, St Lucia, Grenada, Barbados and Trinidad.

Renaissance Cruises, PO Box 350307, Fort Lauderdale, FL 33335 (☎ (800) 525-5350, ☎ (305) 463-0982).

Ships depart from Antigua. Ports of call include St Martin, Guadeloupe, St Barts, Dominica, Grenada, Union Island, Bequia, Martinique and Montserrat.

Royal Caribbean Cruise Line, 1050 Caribbean Way, Miami, FL 33132 (☎ (800) 327-6700, ☎ (305) 539-6000).

Ships depart from San Juan. Ports of call include Antigua, Barbados, Guadeloupe, Martinique, St Barts and St Martin.

Royal Viking Line, 95 Merrick Way, Coral Gables, FL 33134 (☎ (800) 634-8000, ☎ (305) 447-9660).

Ships depart from Fort Lauderdale. Ports of call include Barbados, Grenada, St Lucia and Tobago.

Seabourn Cruise Line, 55 Francisco St, San Francisco, CA 94133 (☎ (800) 929-9595, ☎ (415) 391-7444).

Ships depart from Fort Lauderdale and St Thomas. Ports of call include St Martin, Antigua, St Barts and Mayreau.

Seawind Cruise Line, 1750 Coral Way, Miami, FL 33145 (☎ (800) 854-9876, ☎ (305) 285-9494).

Ships depart from Aruba. Ports of call include Grenada, Barbados and St Lucia.

Silversea, 110 East Broward Blvd, Fort Lauderdale, FL 33301 (☎ (800) 722-6655, ☎ (305) 522-4477).

Ships depart from Nassau and from San Francisco via the Panama Canal. Ports of call include Antigua, Martinique, Barbados, Grenada and Bequia.

Sun Line Cruises, 1 Rockefeller Plaza, New York, NY 10020 (☎ (212) 397-6400; in the USA: ☎ (800) 872-6400, in Canada: ☎ (800) 368-3888).

Ships depart from Fort Lauderdale. Ports of call include Antigua, Barbados, Bequia, Guadeloupe, Martinique, St Martin, St Vincent, Tobago and Trinidad, in conjunction with an Amazon River cruise.

**Unconventional Cruises** In addition to the cruises listed here, see the Yacht section for information on cruising the Caribbean by yacht and Diving in the Tours section for information on live-aboard dive boats.

Clipper Cruise Line, 7711 Bonhomme Ave, St Louis, MO 63105 (☎ (800) 325-0010, ☎ (314) 727-2929).

While it's a conventional cruise ship, the *Yorktown Clipper* carries only 138 passengers and has a shallow draft, enabling it to navigate secluded waterways. One tour departs from Grenada and visits Anguilla, Antigua, Bequia, Dominica, Îles des Saintes, Saba, St Eustatius, St Kitts, St Lucia and Union Island. Another departs from Curacao and includes Tobago and Trinidad en route to a tour of Venezuela's Orinoco River.

Club Med, 40 West 57th St, New York, NY 10019 (☎ (800) 453-7447).

The 188-metre *Club Med I* has computerised sails and a high-tech design, holds 386 passengers and operates much like any other all-inclusive Club Med resort, except that it's at sea. Departs from Martinique. Ports of call include Marie-Galante, St Kitts, Nevis, St Martin, Tintamarre, Dominica, Les Saintes, St Barts and Antigua.

*Le Ponant* is booked through Elite Travel International, 208 East 58th St, New York, NY 10022 (☎ (212) 752-5440; fax (212) 752-5507).

This 88-metre, 64-passenger French sailing ship departs from Guadeloupe. Ports of call include Anguilla, Antigua, Dominica, Îles des Saintes, Martinique, St Barts, St Lucia, St Martin, Bequia, Mayreau and the Tobago Cays.

*Sea Cloud* is booked through Cruise Company of Greenwich, 31 Brookside Drive, Greenwich, CT 06830 (☎ (800) 825-0826, ☎ (203) 622-0203).

This four-masted 110-metre tall ship has luxury accommodation and departs from Antigua. Ports of call include Bequia, Palm Island, Grenada, Carriacou, St Kitts, Nevis, St Lucia, Martinique, Dominica, Barbuda, St Barts, Anguilla and St Martin.

Star Clippers, 4101 Salzedo Ave, Coral Gables, FL 33146 (☎ (800) 442-0551).

These modern four-masted clipper ships have tall ship designs and carry 180 passengers. They depart from Antigua and St Martin. Ports of call include Anguilla, Dominica, Îles des Saintes, Martinique, Saba, St Barts, St Eustatius, St Kitts and Nevis, St Lucia, St Vincent, Mayreau, Union and the Tobago Cays.

Tall Ship Adventures, 1010 South Joliet St, Suite 200, Aurora, CO 80012 (☎ (800) 662-0090, ☎ (303) 341-0345).

The *Sir Francis Drake*, a 50-metre three-masted schooner, is an original tall ship built in 1917. Cruises are mostly around the Virgin Islands, but in the summer there's a one-week cruise that departs from St Martin and takes in Tintamarre, St Barts and Anguilla. The boat holds 34 passengers.

Windjammer Barefoot Cruises, PO Box 120, Miami Beach, FL 33119 (☎ (800) 327-2601, ☎ (305) 672-6453).

The fleet consists of a restored 86-metre four-masted stay-sail rigged schooner and other tall sailing ships, carrying from 65 to 126 passengers. They tend to attract a younger, more active and budget-minded crowd. Departs from Freeport, Antigua, Grenada and St Martin. Ports of call include Anguilla, Dominica, Guadeloupe, the Iles des Saintes, Martinique, Montserrat, Saba, St Barts, St Eustatius, St Kitts, Nevis, St Lucia, St Vincent, Bequia, Canouan, Mayreau, Union Island, Palm Island, the Tobago Cays and Carriacou.

Windstar Cruises, 300 Elliott Ave West, Seattle, WA 98119 (☎ (800) 258-7245, ☎ (206) 281-3535).

The luxury four-masted 134-metre boats have high-tech, computer-operated sails and take 148 passengers. They depart from Barbados. Ports of call include Grenada, Carriacou, Bequia, the Tobago Cays, the Îles des Saintes, Martinique, St Kitts, St Barts, St Lucia and St Martin.

## TOURS

There are scores of conventional package tours to the Eastern Caribbean available from the USA, Canada and Europe. Most are a week in duration, though they sometimes can be extended. If you are going to the Caribbean for just a short holiday, package tours can be quite economical. If you were to book the same hotel and flight separately, it would cost substantially more. In the USA in particular package tours are highly competitive, with week-long tours that include hotel and airfare from the US east coast for as little as US$500. The ads found in the travel sections of big-city Sunday newspapers are a good source of information. Package tours represent a substantial part of the bookings for most travel agents, and they can usually pile you high with tour brochures.

Bargain hunters can sometimes find some good last-minute deals as consolidators that book out a block of hotel rooms and aeroplane seats often have to pay for them whether they're full or not – it's to their advantage to let them go cheaply (even below cost) a week or two prior to the flight. If you're flexible enough to book a discounted package on relatively short notice, let your travel agent know so he or she can keep you posted.

### Birding & Natural History Tours

The National Audubon Society (☎ (212) 979-3000; fax (212) 979-3188), 700 Broadway, New York, NY 10003 USA, offers tours with natural history oriented itineraries and led by Audubon staff members. Most of the society's Caribbean tours are aboard regularly scheduled cruises, such as the 10-day sail through the Leeward and Windward islands aboard Clipper Cruise Line's 138-passenger *Yorktown Clipper* (from US$2400) and an eight-day birdwatcher's trip to Trinidad and Venezuela aboard the 80-passenger *Polaris* (from US$2890). Prices do not include airfares.

The Massachusetts Audubon Society (☎ (617) 259-9500, ☎ (800) 289-9504) Lincoln, MA 01773 USA, offers a couple of ornithologist-led, 10-day birdwatching tours to Trinidad and Tobago each winter. Accommodation is at the *Asa Wright Nature Center* in Trinidad and the *Blue Waters Inn* on Tobago. The cost is around US$2300, including airfare to and from Miami.

Caligo Ventures (☎ (914) 273-6333, ☎ (800) 426-7781), 156 Bedford Rd, Armonk, NY 10504 USA, also runs birding tours to Trinidad and Tobago, with stays at the *Asa Wright Nature Centre* and the *Blue Waters Inn*. Low-season tours cost around US$1000 for a one-week tour to Trinidad and US$1345 for a 10-day tour to both Trinidad and Tobago, including the airfare from either New York or Miami.

The Smithsonian Institution (☎ (202) 357-4700), 1100 Jefferson Drive SW, Washington DC 20560 USA, leads natural history tours and cruises to the Eastern Caribbean, including to Dominica, Trinidad and Tobago.

## Volunteer Programmes

The Foundation for Field Research (☎ (619) 687-3584), PO Box 910078, San Diego, CA 92191, USA, has work-study tours in Grenada that include primate research and the underwater mapping of the original French settlement that's now submerged in St George's Harbour. Stays of up to two weeks cost from US$105 to US$130 per day, depending on the project; the fee includes accommodation and meals but not the airfare to Grenada.

Caribbean Volunteer Expeditions (☎ (607) 962-7846), PO Box 388, Corning, NY 14830, USA, sends volunteers to work at historic sites with local national trusts or national park departments. Fees typically range from US$300 to US$800 per week, including accommodation, food and land transportation, but not airfare.

## Dive Tours

PADI International has dive package tours to St Vincent, Bequia and Anse Chastanet in St Lucia. Rates per person based on double occupancy for a week-long hotel/dive package start in the low season at US$724 in Bequia, US$747 in St Vincent and US$1073 in St Lucia. The airfare to the island costs extra. Arrangements can be made at any PADI dive centre worldwide, or in the USA by calling ☎ (800) 729-7234.

Explorer Ventures (☎ (203) 259-9321; fax (203) 259-9896; in the USA and Canada: ☎ (800) 322-3577), 10 Fencerow Dr, Fairfield CT 06430 USA, books the M/V *Caribbean Explorer*, an 18-passenger live-aboard dive boat. One-week tours depart from St Martin on Saturday, take in two days of diving on St Kitts and four days of diving on Saba, before returning to St Martin. The cost of US$1395 per person, based on double occupancy, includes on-board accommoda-

tion, meals, five dives daily and the use of tanks, weights and belts. The airfare is not included. There is usually a US$300 discount for early bookings.

Caribbean Adventures (☎ (205) 757-4222, ☎ (800) 934-3483; fax (205) 764-6388), 328 Cox Creek Parkway, Florence, AL 35630, has dive tours to Dominica for US$800 which includes seven nights accommodation, 10 dives, breakfast and dinners. This company also arranges tours to Saba, St Eustatius, St Vincent & the Grenadines and can book the aforementioned M/V *Caribbean Explorer*.

In addition, most dive shops listed in this book can arrange package tours that include accommodation and diving fees, so if you're interested in a specific island consider contacting the dive shops directly.

## Surfing Tours

Surfing package tours to Barbados are offered by Morris Overseas Tours (☎ (407) 725-4809, ☎ (800) 777-6853; fax (407) 725-7956), 400 Ave B, Melbourne Beach, FL 32951 USA. Tours start at US$499 (low season, midweek departure) per person, based on triple occupancy, including airfare from Miami (free surfboard transportation) and six nights at the *Edgewater Inn* on Barbados' east coast.

## Clothing-Optional Tours

At least three US tour companies cater to those looking for a holiday *au naturel*. The most common destinations are Orient Beach on St Martin and Hawksbill Beach Resort on Antigua. There are also clothing-optional cruises on the *Star Clipper*.

Bare Necessities, 1502-A West Ave, Austin, TX 78701 (☎ (512) 499-0405, ☎ (800) 743-0405)

Travel Au Naturel, 35246 US 19 N, Suite 112, Palm Harbor, FL 34684 (☎ (800) 728-0185)

Travel Naturally, PO Box 2089, Mango, FL 33550 (☎ (813) 648-9990, ☎ (800) 462-6833)

# Getting Around

## AIR

LIAT is the Caribbean's main inter-island carrier, connecting a total of 25 destinations from Puerto Rico to Caracas, most of which fall within the Eastern Caribbean. The airline has nearly 150 flights each day, which accounts for roughly half of all inter-island flights in the region.

BWIA, the Trinidad-based airline, flies between some of the larger islands of the Eastern Caribbean but is predominantly an international carrier and has a far more limited inter-island schedule than LIAT.

Other airlines cover only a segment of the Eastern Caribbean. Winair services the islands around St Martin, from Anguilla to St Kitts. Airlines of Carriacou is a puddle jumper connecting the Grenadine islands between St Vincent and Grenada. In the French West Indies, Air Guadeloupe and Air Martinique are the main carriers, followed by tiny Air Saint-Barthelemy.

There are also smaller airlines that fly between a couple of islands on scheduled flights, but do most of their business as charters.

Specific airfare and schedule information on air travel is in each individual island chapter. Like everything else, they are subject to change and it's certainly a wise idea to pick up the latest LIAT schedule from an airline counter as soon as you arrive in the islands. Details on LIAT's inter-island network follows.

## LIAT

LIAT, formerly Leeward Islands Air Transport, is owned by the governments of a dozen Caribbean islands and is home-based in Antigua.

In addition to straightforward one-way and excursion tickets, LIAT offers a varied but confusing array of discounted fares and passes. As any extensive travel in the Caribbean is almost certain to involve flights on

LIAT, you can save yourself a great deal of money by figuring out the various options in advance and deciding which one best suits your itinerary.

LIAT offers a range of excursion fares, including the standard type valid for either 21 or 30 days that usually allows for two en-route stopovers and costs an average of 50% more than a one-way ticket. These excursion tickets are available on most, but not all, LIAT routes and can be purchased either before or after you arrive in the Caribbean – they have no advance purchase requirements and are fully refundable.

In addition, LIAT offers some deeply discounted one-day and seven-day excursion tickets on selected routes; these tickets are often cheaper than the price of a one-way ticket. Some one-day and seven-day tickets can only be purchased on the island where they originate and getting information on these tickets outside the islands is difficult. Essentially, short-stay tickets are marketed to local residents as an affordable opportunity to go to a neighbouring island for a shopping spree or short holiday. However, you don't need to be a Caribbean resident to buy them.

LIAT also has senior citizen fares and youth fares that normally cut as much as 50% off the regular fares; airpasses are not discounted.

LIAT's reservation number in the USA is ☎ (800) 253-5011 or ☎ (212) 251-1717. In the UK, TransAtlantic Wings (☎ (01) 602-4021) handles LIAT bookings and is quite knowledgeable about its various tickets. In France LIAT can be booked through Air France and in Germany through Lufthansa.

**Long-Distance Fares** Long distance (YD) fares are both LIAT's best kept secret and top bargain. The fares are available on selected long-distance routes such as Barbados to St Martin. If you're travelling to and from the

**Conflicting Info**

LIAT's various fares can be confusing. Indeed, even some LIAT agents don't seem to understand them and you are apt to get conflicting information on different islands.

Prior to one of our visits to the Caribbean, after booking an open-jaw ticket into Trinidad and out of St Kitts with an international carrier, we called LIAT's USA office to book a long-distance (YD) fare ticket that would allow us to stop at all the islands in between. That office told us YD tickets no longer existed. We then called LIAT's Trinidad office direct; they said 'no problem' and booked us YD tickets with stops at every LIAT destination between Trinidad and St Kitts: Tobago, Grenada, Carriacou, Union Island, Bequia, St Vincent, St Lucia, Martinique, Dominica, Guadeloupe and Antigua. The price of this ticket was less than half the cost of the Super Explorer Pass that the USA office thought was our best option.

We had an en-route stopover in Barbados on our international flight to Trinidad. At the Barbados airport, LIAT had no problem selling us the YD ticket we had booked, but they insisted that the three Grenadine islands between Grenada and St Vincent couldn't be included. After we arrived in Trinidad, however, the LIAT agent there readily changed our tickets to include the three Grenadine islands at no additional cost! ■

Caribbean on an open-jaw ticket (for instance, flying into Trinidad and out of St Martin), YD fares allow you to visit a broad sweep of islands at a low fare. Quite remarkably, YD fares are cheaper (by roughly a third) than regular one-way fares but allow unlimited en-route stopovers and have virtually no restrictions. They are valid for a year and you can change your flight dates or have the ticket rewritten to delete or add islands without additional fees. The hard part is getting information on YD fares, as even some LIAT offices don't seem to know they exist. If you can't get information from your local travel agent, consider calling either the Barbados (☎ (809) 623-1837) or Trinidad (☎ (809) 436-6224) LIAT offices directly to make reservations.

**Airpasses** The following LIAT airpasses can be an excellent deal for anyone interested in doing some serious island hopping.

*LIAT Super Explorer* The king of the passes is the LIAT Super Explorer, which costs US$367 and is valid for 30 days of travel to any or all of the 25 destinations served by LIAT. You can only visit each destination once, although you can go through an airport any number of times as required for onward connections.

There's no advance purchase requirement. Passes can be purchased at home (but not in

Venezuela) before your trip or after you arrive in the Caribbean. You must decide your itinerary at the time of purchase and any subsequent changes are subject to a US$25 surcharge.

Although LIAT's US office and at least a few Caribbean LIAT offices insist that you schedule each flight at the time of purchase, some passengers are able to buy and use the tickets on an open basis, making reservations for each segment just a few days in advance. Once you start to use the pass, the remainder of the pass coupons cannot be refunded or used as payment toward another ticket.

*LIAT Explorer* The LIAT Explorer is a good pass if you just want to visit a few islands, especially if they're far flung. The pass allows you to visit any three islands in LIAT's network, costs US$199 and is valid for 21 days. The ticket must be purchased before you arrive in the Caribbean and must begin and end on the same island. Once ticketed, no changes are allowed.

*LIAT Eastern Caribbean Airpass* LIAT's Eastern Caribbean Airpass is sold only in Europe and the UK in conjunction with a transatlantic ticket. A minimum of three tickets and a maximum of six tickets can be purchased for travel throughout LIAT's entire Caribbean network. Coupons cost US$60 each for weekday travel, US$70 for weekend flights. Once ticketed, no changes are allowed.

## BWIA

BWIA has a 'butterfly' fare for US$356 that's valid for 30 days and allows travellers to visit all of its Caribbean destinations. All travel is on wide-bodied aircraft, as each inter-Caribbean flight is a leg of an international flight. However, BWIA has just completed some major downsizing and at least temporarily has dropped a number of its Caribbean destinations. Currently BWIA serves Barbados, Antigua, Grenada, St Lucia, Trinidad, Tobago, Jamaica, Georgetown and Guyana only. On this 30-day pass, the itinerary must be set in advance and there's a US$20 charge to make changes. Each destination can be visited only once, other than for connecting flights.

BWIA's reservation numbers are ☎ (800) 327-7401 in the USA and Canada; ☎ (071) 839-9333 in the UK; and ☎ 62 8025 in Germany.

## BUS

There's inexpensive bus service on most islands, although the word 'bus' has different meanings in different places. Some islands have full-sized buses, while on others a bus is simply a pick-up truck with wooden benches in the back.

Perhaps the most common type of bus is the Toyota minivan, the sort that accommodates a family of six elsewhere. However, in the Eastern Caribbean these minivans have four or five rows of seats, as well as jump seats in the aisle that fold down as the rows

fill. As more and more people get on, the bus becomes an uninterrupted mass of humanity – children move onto their parents' laps, schoolkids share seats, people squeeze together and everyone generally accepts the crowding with good nature. Whenever someone gets off the back of a crowded minivan, it takes on the element of a human Rubik's Cube, with the jump seats folding up and down and everyone shuffling places; on some buses there's actually a 'conductor' to direct the seating.

Buses are often the primary means of commuting to work or school and thus are most frequent in the mornings and from mid to late afternoon. There's generally good bus service on Saturday as well, as it's the big market day. On Sunday, bus service on many islands virtually grinds to a halt.

## TAXI

Taxis are available on virtually all of the populated islands, with the exception of a few that don't have roads! Details are in the individual island chapters.

## CAR & MOTORBIKE
### Road Rules

On islands that were formerly British, driving is on the left-hand side of the road and on the French and Dutch islands it is on the right-hand side.

On the French islands, note that there's a rather confusing *priorité à droite* rule in which any car approaching an intersection from a road to your right has the right-of-way; you must slow down or stop to let them pass.

---

**Whenever It Arrives**

Those acronym-named airlines that fly around the Caribbean bear the brunt of a lot of jokes from islanders.

BWIA is mocked as 'But Will It Arrive?' LIAT is said to stand for 'Luggage In Another Terminal' or 'Leave Island Any Time' and WIA (Winair) becomes 'Whenever It Arrives'.

Despite this good-natured ribbing, during scores of flights we have never lost luggage and all the airlines have gotten us where we wanted to go. Well, there is one oddity – flights often leave a good 20 minutes *early* with no advance warning! ∎

## Rental

Car rentals are available on all islands, with the exception of a few very small ones. On most islands there are affiliates of one or more of the international chains like Hertz, Avis, Budget and National/Europcar.

You can often get a better deal by booking a car in advance before you go. On St Lucia, for example, National's cheapest walk-in rate is US$46 plus a mileage charge, but with an advance booking made from abroad you can reserve the same car with unlimited mileage for US$30.

Even on islands like Martinique and Guadeloupe, where the advance booking price is often the same as the walk-in price, reservations are a good idea. Without one, you may arrive at the airport and find the cheaper cars all sold out – a situation that's not uncommon in winter.

Island car rental agents frequently affiliate and disaffiliate with international chains, particularly on the smaller islands, so even if there's not an affiliate listed in the island's car rental section it's worth checking the latest status with the international firms mentioned above.

On many islands you need to be 25 years old to rent a car, and some car rental companies will not rent to drivers over 70.

## BICYCLE

Some of the islands have bicycles for rent and this is noted in those island chapters.

Cyclists should ride on the same side of the road as car traffic.

## HITCHING

Hitching is common amongst islanders on several islands, though the practice among foreign visitors, particularly outside the French islands, is not very common.

Hitching is never entirely safe in any country in the world, and we don't recommend it. Travellers who decide to hitch should understand that they are taking a small but potentially serious risk. People who do choose to hitch will be safer if they travel in pairs and let someone know where they are planning to go.

## BOAT
### Ferry

There are daily, or near-daily, ferry services between St Martin and Anguilla, St Kitts and Nevis, St Vincent and Bequia, Grenada and Carriacou, and Trinidad and Tobago, as well as from the main part of Guadeloupe to the outlying islands of Terre-de-Haut, Marie-Galante and La Désirade. In the Grenadines, a thrice-weekly ferry connects St Vincent and Bequia with Mayreau, Canouan and Union Island. Catamarans sail between St Martin and St Barts for day trips and will take one-way passengers, in effect acting as a ferry service.

Two fast-speed catamaran ferries, the *Caribbean Express* and the *Madikera*, connect the islands of Guadeloupe, Dominica and Martinique several days a week.

Details on all these boats are in individual island chapter.

### Windward Lines

Windward Lines Limited operates the 55-metre passenger/cargo boat M/V *Windward* between St Lucia (Castries), Barbados (Bridgetown), St Vincent (Kingstown), Trinidad (Port of Spain) and Venezuela (Guiria). As it's primarily a cargo boat it lays over at each port for several hours which, while not the most expedient way to travel, gives passengers time to do some exploring.

On the southbound schedule, arrival and departure times are as follows:

| | |
|---|---|
| Departs St Lucia | 7 am (Sun) |
| Arrives Barbados | 7 pm (Sun) |
| Departs Barbados | 10 pm (Sun) |
| Arrives St Vincent | 7 am (Mon) |
| Departs St Vincent | 5 pm (Mon) |
| Arrives Trinidad | 8 am (Tue) |
| Departs Trinidad | 8 pm (Tue) |
| Arrives Venezuela | 7 am (Wed) |

On the northbound schedule, sailing times are as follows:

| | |
|---|---|
| Departs Venezuela | 11 pm (Wed) |
| Arrives Trinidad | 7 am (Thur) |
| Departs Trinidad | 4 pm (Thur) |
| Arrives St Vincent | 7 am (Fri) |
| Departs St Vincent | 10 am (Fri) |
| Arrives Barbados | 7 pm (Fri) |
| Departs Barbados | 11 pm (Fri) |
| Arrives St Lucia | 7 am (Sat) |

Return fares from St Vincent are US$60 to St Lucia, US$71 to Barbados, US$90 to Trinidad and US$138 to Venezuela. Other return fares are US$60 between St Lucia and Barbados, US$60 between Trinidad and Venezuela, US$90 between Trinidad and Barbados, US$95 between Trinidad and St Lucia, US$148 between Venezuela and Barbados, and US$158 between Venezuela and St Lucia.

One-way fares are 65% of the return fares. Children under two years of age travel free of charge, while those aged two to 12 travel at half price. Seniors aged 70 and over get a 25% discount. There are cabins to accommodate 70 people; the cabin cost is an additional US$10 per berth per night, based on double occupancy.

There's a restaurant and a duty-free shop on board. Check-in is one hour before the scheduled departure time.

Booking agents for Windward Lines are:

**Barbados**
Windward Agencies, 7 James Fort, Hincks St, Bridgetown (☎ (809) 431-0449; fax (809) 431-0452)

**St Vincent**
Perry's Customs & Shipping Agency, Sharpe St, PO Box 247, Kingstown (☎ (809) 457-2920; fax (809) 456-2619)
**Trinidad**
Global Steamship Agencies, Mariners Club, Wrightson Rd, Port of Spain (☎ (809) 624-2279; fax (809) 627-5091)
**Venezuela**
Acosta Asociados, Calle Bolivar 31, Guiria (☎ (58) 948-1679; fax (58) 948-1112)

### Yacht

The Caribbean is one of the world's prime yachting locales, offering diversity, warm weather and fine scenery. The many small islands grouped closely together are not only fun to explore but also form a barrier against the raging Atlantic, providing relatively calm sailing waters in the Caribbean Sea.

In the Eastern Caribbean, the major yachting bases are in St Martin, Antigua, Guadeloupe, Martinique, St Lucia, St Vincent and Grenada.

It's easiest to sail down-island, from north to south, as on the reverse boats must beat back into the wind. Because of this, several yacht charter companies allow sailors to take the boats in just one direction, later arranging for its own crew to bring the boats back to home base.

Information on ports, marinas and immigration clearances are listed in the individual island chapters.

**Yacht Chartering** There are two basic types of yacht charters: bareboat and crewed. In addition, some yacht charter companies offer live-aboard sailing courses, land/sail tours, flotilla sails (a group of bareboats accompanied by a lead boat with an experienced crew) and other variations.

***Bareboat Charter*** With a bareboat charter you rent just the boat. You are the captain and you sail where you want, when you want, on your own (more or less, anyway – you must stay within designated geographical areas and night sailing may be prohibited).

You must be an experienced sailor to charter the boat. Although in most cases you won't need proof of having completed a sailing course, any certification or the like, you will need to fill out a written sailing resume which satisfies the charter company that you can handle the boat. You should have experience in sailing a similar-sized boat, in anchoring and in reading charts. Some companies will give you a trial check-out at the dock before allowing you to sail away.

Bareboat yachts generally come stocked with linen, kitchen supplies, fuel, water, dinghy, outboard, charts, cruising guides, cellular phone and other gear. Provisioning (stocking the boat with food) is not provided, except at an additional fee.

The charter company can provide a licensed skipper (generally from US$100 to US$140 a day) or a cook (about US$85 to US$100 a day) if you don't want to do all the work (this is sometimes called a semi-bareboat charter), but you still maintain responsibility for the boat.

You'll have to pay a security deposit and should check the fine print in regards to refunds, insurance and cancellation penalties.

***Crewed Charter*** With a crewed charter, the yacht comes with a captain, crew, cook and provisions. You don't have to know how to sail, or anything else about boats. You can either make your own detailed itinerary or provide a vague idea of the kind of places you'd like to visit and let the captain decide where to anchor.

**Cost** Rates vary greatly. The better established companies generally charge more than small, little-known operators and large ritzy yachts of course cost more than smaller, less luxurious boats. These days, many yachts have amenities such as TV, video, CD player, ice-maker, snorkelling equipment etc on board – more toys add to the cost.

Although a whole book could be written just comparing prices, the following gives a sense of mid-range prices. ATM, which is one of the larger companies and has some 200 boats at four islands, rents a 9.8-metre

*Prestige* at a weekly bareboat charter rate of US$1346 from May to October, US$1888 from January to May. The boat holds four passengers comfortably, or six in a squeeze. A 15.8-metre yacht that holds eight to 12 costs US$3911/5444 respectively. There's a shoulder season rate from November to mid-December, while prices jump up steeply around the Christmas and New Year holidays. ATM does not charge a drop-off fee for boats taken one way between any of its ports.

For fully crewed charters, including a skipper, a hostess/cook and 'gourmet' meals, ATM's *daily* rate for five to eight people aboard a 14.6-metre catamaran is US$1160 from May to mid-December, US$1360 from January to April.

At the lower end, there are other small crewed yachts in the Caribbean priced from around US$2500 a week.

**Yacht Charter Companies** The following charter companies offer both bareboat and crewed yacht charters in the Eastern Caribbean. Listings begin with the yacht charter company's US or European office(s), followed by the island addresses where the charter boats are based.

ATM/Stardust, 2280 University Dr, Suite 102, Newport Beach, CA 92660 (☎ (714) 650-0889, ☎ (800) 634-8822; fax (714) 642-1318)
    BP 615, 97150 Anse Marcel, St Martin (☎ (590) 74 98 17; fax (590) 74 88 12)
    Blue Lagoon, 97190 Gosier, Guadeloupe (☎ (590) 90 92 02; fax (590) 90 97 99)
    Le Marin, 97290 Marin, Martinique (☎ (596) 74 98 17; fax (596) 74 88 12)
    Clifton, Union Island, St Vincent & the Grenadines (☎ & fax (809) 458-8581)
Barefoot Yacht Charters, 2550 Stag Run Blvd, No 519, Clearwater, FL 34625 (☎ (813) 799-1858, ☎ (800) 677-3195; fax (813) 797-3195)
    PO Box 39, Blue Lagoon, St Vincent & the Grenadines (☎ (809) 456-9334; fax (809) 456-9238)
First Class Yachting (FCY), PO Box 2012, Gros Islet, Rodney Bay Marina, St Lucia (☎ (809) 452-0367)
The Moorings, 19345 US Hwy 19 N, 4th Floor, Clearwater, FL 34624 (☎ (813) 535-1446, ☎ (800) 535-7289; fax (813) 530-9747)

Port de Plaisance du Marin, Martinique (☎ (596) 74 75 39; fax (596) 74 76 44)

Marigot Bay, St Lucia (☎ (809) 453-4357)

Secret Harbour, St George's, Grenada (☎ (590) 444-4924)

Bas du Fort Marina, Point-à-Pitre, Guadeloupe (☎ (590) 90 81 81)

Captain Oliver's Marina, Oyster Pond, St Martin (☎ (590) 87 32 55)

Nautor's Swan Charters, 55 America's Cup Ave, Newport RI 02840 (☎ (401) 846-8404, ☎ (800) 356-7926; fax (401) 846-7349)

11 Ave des Trois Fontaines, 74600 Seynod, Annecy, France (☎ 50 46 8471; fax 50 46 85 08)

Port Lonvilliers, Anse Marcel – BP 335, Marigot 97150, St Martin (☎ (590) 97 35 48; fax (590) 87 35 50)

Privilege Charters, 1650 SE 17th St, Suite 204, Fort Lauderdale, FL 33316 (☎ (305) 462-6706, ☎ (800) 262-0308; fax (305) 462-6104)

Marigot, St Martin (☎ (590) 87 02 82; fax (590) 87 01 55)

Marina Bas du Fort, Guadeloupe (☎ (590) 90 71 89; fax (590) 90 72 93)

Star Voyage, 5 rue Lincoln, 75008 Paris, France (☎ 42 56 15 62)

Pointe du Bout Marina, Trois-Ilets, Martinique (☎ (596) 66 00 72; fax (596) 66 02 11)

Marina du Marin, Martinique (☎ (596) 74 70 92)

Sun Yacht Charters, PO Box 737, Camden, ME 04838 (☎ 207) 236-9611, ☎ (800) 772-3500; fax (207) 236-3972)

Captain Oliver's Marina, Oyster Pond, St Martin (☎ (590) 87 30 49)

English Harbour, Antigua (☎ (809) 460-2615)

Sunsail, 3347 NW 55th St, Fort Lauderdale, FL 33309 (☎ (800) 327-2276; fax (305) 485-5072)

Marina Bas du Fort, Guadeloupe (☎ (590) 90 82 80)

Marigot, St Martin (☎ (590) 87 83 41)

Rodney Bay Marina, St Lucia (☎ (809) 452-8648)

Marina du Marin, Martinique (☎ (596) 74 77 61)

Trade Wind, PO Box 1186, Court Circle, Gloucester, VA 23061 (☎ (804) 694-0881, ☎ (800) 825-7245; fax (804) 693-7245)

Marina Bas du Fort, Guadeloupe (☎ (590) 90 76 77)

Box 2158, Rodney Bay Marina, St Lucia (☎ (809) 452-8424; fax (809) 452-8442)

Blue Lagoon, St Vincent (☎ (809) 456-9736; fax (809) 456-9737)

**Charter Brokers** For those who don't want to be bothered shopping around, charter yacht brokers can help. Brokers work on commission, like travel agents, with no charge to the customer – you tell them your budget and requirements and they help make a match.

A few of the better known charter yacht brokers in the USA are:

Ed Hamilton & Co, PO Box 430, N Whitehead, ME 04353 (☎ (207) 549-7855, ☎ (800) 621-7855; fax (207) 549-7822)

Lynn Jachney Charters, PO Box 302, Marblehead MA 01945 (☎ (800) 223-2050; fax (617) 639-0216)

Nicholson Yacht Charters, 432 Columbia St, Cambridge, MA 02141 (☎ (617) 225-0555, ☎ (800) 662-6066; fax (617) 225-0190)

Russell Yacht Charters, 404 Hulls Hwy, Suite 102, Southport, CT 06490 (☎ (800) 635-8895; fax (203) 255-3426)

**Other Sailing Options** Another option is to book a tour package aboard a yacht, much the same as you would book a traditional cruise. The schedule, itinerary and price will already be fixed and you will sail with a few other passengers who have booked the same yacht. Many yacht charter companies, including The Moorings, provide this service.

If you just want to work in a couple of days of sailing after you arrive in the Caribbean, you may be able to find something on the spot. On many islands, small one-boat operators advertise trips to neighbouring islands; look for flyers, ask at local tour companies or check with the tourist offices.

For sails on tall ships, windjammers and the like, see Unconventional Cruises in the Cruise Ship section of the Getting There & Away chapter.

**Hitching a Ride on a Yacht** Marinas have general notice boards, and these sometimes have a posting or two by yachters looking for crew or passengers. If you don't find anything promising on the boards, you can add a notice of your own. It should include where you want to go; what you're willing to do in exchange for passage, such as cooking and cleaning; the date; and where you can be contacted.

In addition to the notice boards, there's always a bar or restaurant, usually at or near the marinas, that serves as a favourite haunt for sailors and serves as a ready place to make contacts.

**Resources** Cruising guides to the Eastern Caribbean are listed under Books in the Facts for the Visitor section.

**Maps & Charts** To navigate through the islands of the Eastern Caribbean, yachters will need either Imray yachting charts, US Defence Mapping Agency charts or British Admiralty charts.

Charts are available throughout the islands, especially at boating supply shops at marinas and in some bookstores. They can also be ordered in advance from Bluewater Books & Charts (☎ (305) 763-6533, ☎ (800)

942-2583), 1481 SE 17th St Causeway, Fort Lauderdale FL 33316, USA.

**Magazines** There are various sailing magazines published worldwide. The following have articles and tips for sailors, ads for yacht charter companies and charter brokers and sometimes a few classified ads for crew positions:

*Cruising World*, PO Box 3400, Newport RI 02840, USA (☎ (401) 847-1588, ☎ (800) 727-8473)
*Sail*, 275 Washington St, Newton, MA 02158, USA (☎ (617) 964-3030, ☎ (800) 745-7245; fax (617) 964-8948)
*Yachting*, 2 Park Ave, New York NY 10016, USA (☎ (212) 779-5300, ☎ (800) 999-0869; fax (212) 725-1035)

# Anguilla

The interior of Anguilla is flat, dry and scrubby, pockmarked with salt ponds and devoid of dramatic scenery. Anguilla's main attraction certainly lies in its fringing beaches, but there are also some offshore coral-encrusted islets that offer good opportunities for bathing, snorkelling and diving.

Inexpensive ferries shuttle between Anguilla and St Martin twice an hour, making Anguilla easy to visit as a day trip.

## ORIENTATION

The airport is in The Valley, the capital, which is right in the centre of the island. The ferry terminal is four miles (6.4 km) west of The Valley in the small village of Blowing Point.

From The Valley a single road leads to the west end of the island and two main roads head to the east end. All other island roads, including the spur roads to the beaches, branch off from these central arteries.

Anguilla's main appeal to visitors is its beautiful beaches – long, uncrowded stretches of powdery white coral sands and clear aquamarine waters.

Although it's just a few km across the channel from bustling St Martin, Anguilla retains the laid-back character of a sleepy backwater. The island is small and lightly populated, the islanders friendly and easy going.

Anguilla, which had almost no visitor facilities just a decade ago, made a decision in the 1980s to develop tourism with a slant towards luxury hotels and villas. It has since become one of the trendier top-end destinations in the Eastern Caribbean.

Although attention goes to the new exclusive resorts that are scattered along some of the island's finest beaches, there are also a number of small, locally owned guesthouses and apartments that make Anguilla accessible to holiday-makers on a more moderate budget.

# Facts about the Island

## HISTORY

The first Amerindians settled on Anguilla about 3500 years ago. Archaeological finds indicate that the island was a major regional centre for the Arawak Indians, who had sizeable villages at Sandy Ground, Meads Bay, Rendezvous Bay and Island Harbour.

The Carib Indians, who eventually overpowered the Arawaks, called the island Malliouhana. Early Spanish explorers named the island Anguilla, which means 'eel', apparently because of its elongated shape.

The British established the first permanent European colony on Anguilla in 1650 and despite a few invasion attempts by the French it has remained a Crown Colony since. While arid conditions thwarted attempts to develop large plantations, the

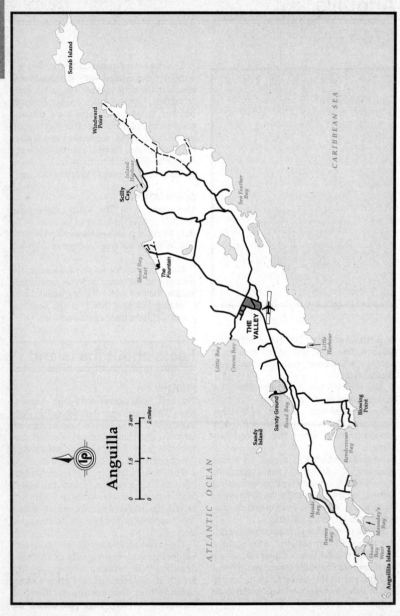

island did become an exporter of tobacco, cotton and salt. In the early 1800s Anguilla's population began to taper off from a peak of 10,500 and the island slid into a slow decline, largely forgotten by the rest of the world.

In 1967 Britain, in an attempt to loosen its colonial ties, lumped Anguilla into an alignment with the islands of St Kitts & Nevis, the nearest British dependencies. The intent was for the three islands to form a new Caribbean nation, the Associated State of St Kitts-Nevis-Anguilla, with Britain continuing to hold the reins on foreign affairs and defence.

Anguillians wanted no part of the new state, which they viewed as subjugation to a more powerful St Kitts. Within a few months, the Anguillians had armed themselves and revolted, forcing the St Kitts police off the island and blocking the runway to prevent a 'reinvasion' by Kittitian forces.

The British, concerned with the potential for bloodshed should St Kitts attempt to force its will upon the Anguillians, stationed Royal Marines in the waters off Anguilla. After two years of failed attempts to negotiate a solution, British forces invaded Anguilla in 1969. Rather than resisting, the islanders, content that some resolution was in the making, welcomed the first wave of British paratroopers, giving the event the bizarre aura of an Independence Day celebration.

The Anguillians eventually got their way: Britain agreed to drop the idea of Anguillian union with St Kitts and to continue British administration of the island under a modified colonial status that granted Anguilla a heightened degree of home rule.

Incidentally, throughout the entire two-year rebellion, including the early days of the revolt when shots were fired at the St Kitts police, there were no fatalities.

## GEOGRAPHY
Anguilla, which lies eight km north of St Martin, is the most northerly of the Leeward Islands. The island is about 26 km long and five km wide and has an indented shoreline punctuated generously with white-sand beaches. The terrain is relatively flat; the highest of the island's rolling hills, Crocus Hill, reaches a mere 65 metres above sea level.

A number of unpopulated offshore islands – including Scrub Island, Dog Island, Prickly Pear Cays and distant Sombrero Island – are also part of Anguilla and bring the total land area of the territory to 155 sq km.

## CLIMATE
The average annual temperature is 27°C (81°F), with the hottest weather occurring during the hurricane season from June to October. The average annual rainfall is 89 cm (35 inches), though it varies greatly from year to year. The lightest rainfall is generally from February to April, and the heaviest from August to November.

## FLORA & FAUNA
Anguilla's vegetation is a dryland type that's been degraded by overgrazing, particularly from free-ranging goats. Seagrape and coconut palms grow in beach areas, as do poisonous manchineel trees. The island's numerous salt ponds attract lots of migratory waterbirds, including egrets, herons and stilts.

## GOVERNMENT
As a result of its revolt from St Kitts, Anguilla remains a British dependency. Under the new Anguilla constitution, which came into effect in 1982, Britain is represented by a governor appointed by the Queen. The governor presides over an appointed Executive Council and an elected House of Assembly.

## ECONOMY
Many Anguillians still make a living from catching lobsters and fish, though since the 1980s there has been a dramatic shift in the economy towards the tourism industry. Anguilla gets about 90,000 tourists annually, of which 60,000 are day visitors.

## POPULATION & PEOPLE
The population is around 8000. The majority of islanders are of African descent, though

there's a bit of an admixture of Irish blood, particularly among people on the eastern end of the island.

## CULTURE

Anguilla has a typical West Indian culture with a blend of British and African influences. Because of the dry and barren nature of the island, the small population on Anguilla has traditionally struggled to make ends meet and has looked towards the sea, in the form of fishing and boatbuilding, for its livelihood. One consequence of this seafaring heritage is a penchant for boat racing.

### Dress Conventions

Dress is casual and simple cotton clothing is suitable attire for any occasion. In the more upmarket restaurants, men will want to wear long pants, but ties and jackets are not necessary. To avoid offence, swimwear should be restricted to the beach.

### RELIGION

There are Anglican, Methodist, Roman Catholic, Seventh Day Adventist, Baptist and Church of God churches on Anguilla.

### LANGUAGE

English is the official language, spoken with a distinctive lilt.

# Facts for the Visitor

## PASSPORT & VISAS

US and Canadian citizens can enter Anguilla with proof of citizenship in the form of a birth certificate with a raised seal or a voter's registration card accompanied by an official photo ID such as a driving licence. Citizens of most other nations require passports.

## CUSTOMS

A carton of cigarettes, a bottle of liquor and four ounces of perfume may be brought in duty free.

## MONEY

The Eastern Caribbean dollar (EC$) is the official currency. Generally hotels, car rental agents and restaurants list prices in US dollars, while grocers and local shops mark prices in EC dollars, but you can readily use either currency and most places give a fair rate of exchange.

Barclays Bank, Scotiabank and a few local banks are located in The Valley. Barclays is open from 8 am to 1 pm on weekdays, plus 3 to 5 pm on Friday, while most other banks are open longer hours.

Visa, MasterCard and American Express cards are accepted at many (but not all) hotels and moderate to high-end restaurants.

A 15% service charge is added to most restaurant bills and no further tipping is necessary. An 8% government tax and a 10% service charge is added onto hotel bills. In addition, a few hotels and restaurants, particularly in the Shoal Bay East area, needle you with a 4% to 5% surcharge if you pay by credit card.

## TOURIST OFFICES

The tourism department's central office is in the government offices complex in The Valley.

When requesting information by mail, write to: The Anguilla Department of Tourism (☎ 2759; fax 3389), The Valley, Anguilla, British West Indies.

There are tourist information booths in the airport and at the Blowing Point ferry terminal. Essentially they're just places to get brochures and tourist handouts – be sure to pick up *What We Do In Anguilla* and *Anguilla Life*.

### Overseas Reps

Tourist information can be obtained from the following overseas agencies:

UK
    Anguilla Tourist Office, Windotel, 3 Epirus Rd, London 3W67UJ (☎ (01) 937-7725; fax (01) 938-4793)

Top Left: Island Harbour, Anguilla (TW)
Top Middle: St John's street scene, Antigua (TW)
Top Right: Steel Band at Shirley Heights, Antigua (NF)
Middle: English Harbour, Antigua (TW)
Bottom: Hammock and beach cottage at Sandy Ground, Anguilla (NF)

Top Left: Green Monkey at Barbados Wildlife Reserve (NF)
Top Right: Folkestone Beach, Barbados (GB)
Bottom Left: A path through flower forest, Barbados (GB)
Bottom Right: Morgan Lewis mill, Barbados (TW)

USA
Anguilla Tourist Information & Reservations Office, c/o Medhurst & Associates Inc, 775 Park Ave, Huntington, NY 11723 (☎ (800) 553-4939; fax (516) 425-0903)

## BUSINESS HOURS
Business hours are generally 8 am to noon and 1 to 4 pm weekdays.

## HOLIDAYS
Public holidays observed in Anguilla are:

| | |
|---|---|
| *New Year's Day* | – 1 January |
| *Good Friday* | – late March/early April |
| *Easter Monday* | – late March/early April |
| *Labour Day* | – 1 May |
| *Whit Monday* | – eighth Monday after Easter |
| *Anguilla Day* | – 30 May |
| *Queen's Birthday* | – 11 June |
| *August Monday (EmancipationDay)* | – first Monday in August |
| *August Thursday* | – first Thursday in August |
| *Constitution Day* | – 6 August |
| *Separation Day* | – 19 December |
| *Christmas Day* | – 25 December |
| *Boxing Day* | – 26 December |

Note that holidays that fall on the weekend are often taken on the following Monday.

## CULTURAL EVENTS
Anguilla's main festival is its week-long Carnival, which starts on the weekend preceding August Monday and includes boat races, costumed parades, contests, music and dancing.

## POST
Anguilla's post office is in The Valley and is open from 8 am to noon and 1 to 3.30 pm Monday to Friday.

If you want to send mail to Anguilla, simply follow the business name with the post office box or the village/beach and 'Anguilla, British West Indies'.

## TELECOMMUNICATIONS
Both coin and card phones are common around the island. You can also make calls, as well as send faxes and telegrams, at the Cable & Wireless office in The Valley, which is open from 8 am to 6 pm weekdays, 9 am to 1 pm on Saturday and 10 am to 2 pm on Sunday.

Phonecards are sold at the Cable & Wireless office, the airport, ferry terminal and several shops. When making a local call, dial just the last four digits. When calling Anguilla from overseas, dial the area code 809 and then the prefix 497 before the four-digit number.

## ELECTRICITY
Electricity is 110 volts, 60 cycles, and a plug with two flat prongs is used, the same as in the USA.

## WEIGHTS & MEASURES
Anguilla uses the imperial system. Speed limit signs are in miles as are most car odometers.

## MEDIA
The island's monthly newspaper, *What We Do In Anguilla*, has tourist information, restaurant listings, a bit of community news and lots of ads. *Anguilla Life* magazine, published three times a year, features articles on everything from archaeology to cultural events and island happenings. Both are free and can be picked up at the airport, ferry terminal and some hotels.

The local government-run radio station is Radio Anguilla at 1505 AM.

## HEALTH
The island's 36-bed hospital (☎ 2551) is in The Valley. See the introductory Facts for the Visitor chapter for information on travel health.

## DANGERS & ANNOYANCES
Anguilla has very little crime and no unusual safety precautions are necessary.

## EMERGENCIES
For police, fire or ambulance emergencies call 911.

## ACTIVITIES
### Beaches & Swimming
Anguilla has lots of lovely white-sand

beaches and you never have to go far to find one. Sandy Ground has calm turquoise waters, as do the glorious sweeps at Shoal Bay East and Rendezvous Bay. Other top beaches worth a visit include Meads Bay and Shoal Bay West.

### Diving & Snorkelling

Anguilla has clear water and good reef formations. In addition, since 1985 nine ships have been deliberately sunk to create dive sites; they lie on sandy bottoms in depths of 12 to 25 metres and attract numerous fish.

Offshore islands popular for diving include Prickly Pear Cays, which has ledges, caverns, barracudas and nurse sharks; Dog Island, a drift dive along a rockface with good marine life; and Sandy Island, which has soft corals and sea fans.

The conservation-minded Tamariain Dive Shop (☎ 2020; fax 5125), PO Box 147, is a five-star PADI facility at Sandy Ground. One-tank boat dives cost US$35, two-tank dives US$60 and night dives US$45, with a minimum of two people. Resort courses are offered for US$80, open-water certification courses for US$375 and open-water referral courses for US$200. Snorkel sets rent for US$6 a day. It's open from 8 am to 4.30 pm daily.

Shoal Bay East, Sandy Island and Little Bay are popular snorkelling spots.

### HIGHLIGHTS

Beaches, beaches, beaches – Anguilla has some of the region's finest. If you don't dive, at least consider taking a snorkelling tour and a visit to one of the offshore islets.

### ACCOMMODATION

Anguilla has a reputation of being an expensive destination and for the most part accommodation is pricey.

At the low end there are a few *very* basic rooms as cheap as US$30, but they're at local boarding houses located in The Valley and are quite rudimentary. The middle range varies widely, beginning with US$75 apartments and moving up to small beachside hotels with US$250 rooms. At the top end

there are some fine luxury hotels, with prices generally beginning around US$500.

In the summer many top-end and mid-range hotels drop prices substantially, while some low-end and mid-range places close down entirely if bookings are slack.

Despite their high prices, even many mid-range hotels lack TV and air-con. The latter is especially noteworthy for summer travellers, as many spots on the island (Sandy Ground is one place in particular) have periods of dead air when nights can be unbearably muggy.

### FOOD

Lobster (common spiny lobster) and crayfish (spotted spiny lobster) are two locally caught Anguillian specialities. The crayfish, while smaller than the lobster, are reasonably sized creatures with sweet moist meat that are commonly served three to an order.

Although a few traditional staples, such as corn and pigeon peas, are still grown on Anguilla, most food is imported and prices are higher than on neighbouring islands.

### DRINKS

Tap water comes from rainwater catchment systems and thus should be boiled before drinking. Bottled water is readily available in grocery stores.

### ENTERTAINMENT

Uncle Ernie's at Shoal Bay East, Johnno's Beach Bar at Sandy Ground, Smitty's at Island Harbour and Scilly Cay, just off Island Harbour, have live bands on Sunday afternoons.

Johnno's Beach Bar has live music and dancing from 8 pm on Saturday. Red Dragon Disco in South Hill has a DJ or band on Saturday (and some Fridays), starting around 11 pm. La Sirena hotel at Meads Bay has a dinner show featuring Anguillian folk songs and dance at 8 pm Thursday.

Several of the larger hotels and restaurants have steel drum bands, guitarists or other live music a few nights a week. See *What We Do In Anguilla* for the current entertainment schedule.

## THINGS TO BUY

There are a couple of quality galleries in The Valley. The New World Gallery, operated by artist Penny Slinger, who painted the traditional-theme murals at the airport, features local art work and changing exhibits of international calibre.

Adjacent to the New World Gallery is the Devonish Cotton Gin Gallery, the showroom of Barbadian artist Courtney Devonish who creates some nice pottery and wood sculptures that sell for moderate prices.

The Anguilla Arts & Crafts Centre near the museum sells locally made silk-screened clothing, T-shirts, pottery, prints, leatherwork, baskets and other items.

# Getting There & Away

## AIR

There are no direct trans-Atlantic flights to Anguilla. However, it's possible to make same-day international connections via San Juan or St Martin.

American Eagle (☎ 3131) has two flights a day to Anguilla from San Juan. The cheapest fare, which allows a stay of up to 30 days, is US$120 return with a seven-day advance purchase. The one-way fare is US$110.

American Airlines' New York-Anguilla (via San Juan) 30-day excursion ticket is about US$500, with a 14-day advance purchase condition, although sometimes promotional fares between the US mainland and San Juan make it cheaper to buy separate New York-San Juan and San Juan-Anguilla tickets. Winair (☎ 2748) has a few flights daily between St Martin and Anguilla. The fare is US$25 each way.

LIAT (☎ 2238) has direct daily flights to Anguilla from St Martin, St Thomas, St Kitts and Antigua. The St Martin-Anguilla fare is US$26 one way, US$50 return; the St Thomas-Anguilla fare is US$76 one way, US$121 return; the St Kitts-Anguilla fare is US$56 one way, US$105 return; and the Antigua-Anguilla fare is US$79 one way, US$149 return.

Tyden Air (☎ 2719, in the USA (800) 842-0261) flies to Anguilla from St Martin in the afternoon, connecting with flights on American and Continental airlines. The cost is US$25 one way. Tyden has a day trip to St Barts on Monday, Wednesday and Friday, leaving Anguilla at 9 am and departing St Barts at 4.30 pm. The cost is US$75 one way, US$100 return.

Air Anguilla (☎ 2643) offers charter services.

### Airport Information

Anguilla's Wallblake Airport is small and modern. There are counters for LIAT, Winair, American Eagle, Air Anguilla and Tyden Air; a tourist information booth open from 7.30 am to 5 pm daily; and pay phones near the arrivals exit.

There are no car rental booths. The nearest company, Island Car Rentals, is a five-minute walk north of the airport.

**To/From the Airport** See Taxi in the Getting Around section of this chapter for information on travel from the airport to various points around Anguilla.

### SEA
### Ferry

Ferries make the 20-minute run from Marigot Bay in St Martin to Blowing Point in Anguilla every 30 minutes from 8 am to 5.30 pm (7.30 am to 5 pm from Anguilla to St Martin).

In addition, night ferries depart Marigot Bay at 7 and 10.45 pm and depart Blowing Point at 6.15 and 10 pm.

The one-way fare is US$9 in the day, US$11 at night. Sign the passenger registration list and pay the US$2 departure tax as soon as you arrive at the dock (for departures in either direction). The fare for the passage is paid on board the boat.

### Yacht

The main port of entry is at Sandy Ground in Road Bay. The immigration and customs office is open daily from 8.30 am to noon and 1 to 4 pm (closed Saturday mornings).

## LEAVING ANGUILLA

There's an airport departure tax of US$6 and a ferry departure tax of US$2. There are no departure taxes for children aged 11 and under.

# Getting Around

There's no bus service on the island and it's difficult to get around without renting a vehicle. See under Rental below.

---

### Rerouting

Most roads on Anguilla are not marked with names or numbers, although hotel and restaurant signs point the way to many beaches. Beware of the occasional renegade restaurant sign that appears to point to someplace nearby but is actually an attempt to reroute you halfway across the island. ■

---

## TAXI

Taxis are readily available at the airport and the ferry terminal. The minimum charge is US$5. Rates from the airport are US$8 to Sandy Ground, US$10 to Shoal Bay East and US$14 to Meads Bay. From Blowing Point, it costs US$10 to Sandy Ground or The Valley, US$15 to Shoal Bay East. These rates are for one or two people; each additional person is charged US$3.

## CAR & MOTORBIKE
### Road Rules

In Anguilla, you drive on the left. Virtually all rental cars have left-hand drive, however – a situation that can be quite disorienting!

Visitors must buy a temporary Anguillian driving licence for US$7, which is issued on the spot by the car rental companies.

The roads are generally well maintained and relatively wide by Caribbean standards. Be cautious of stray goats that occasionally bolt onto the road.

There are petrol stations in The Valley, in Island Harbour and on the road to Blowing Point. The one in The Valley is open from 7 am to 9 pm Monday to Saturday and from 9 am to 1 pm on Sunday.

### Rental

Compact air-con cars rent for about US$35 a day with free unlimited mileage. Jeeps cost just a few dollars more.

Triple K Car Rental (☎ 2934; fax 2503), Anguilla's Hertz agent, is a friendly operation that provides free pick-up and drop-off at the ferry terminal or airport. Its office in The Valley is open daily from 8 am to 5 pm (from noon on Sunday), but will deliver cars at other times with advance reservations.

Other major rental agencies include Island Car Rentals (☎ 2723; 4330 after 5 pm) on Airport Rd and Budget (☎ 2217) on Stoney Ground Rd, both in The Valley, and Connor's Car Rental (☎ 6433) at the intersection of the north end of Blowing Point Rd.

Boo's Cycle Rental (☎ 2323), on the road between The Valley and Sandy Ground, rents mopeds for US$16 a day, scooters for US$20 and Yamaha 135RX motorbikes for US$22. They also have hourly and weekly rates.

### BICYCLE

Island Tours (☎ 5810), on the main road near the Island Harbour Rd traffic lights, rents mountain bikes.

### TOURS

Taxi drivers provide tours of the island for US$40 for one or two people, US$5 for each additional person.

Among the offshore islands, one of the most popular destinations is Prickly Pear Cays, which has excellent snorkelling conditions. Boats leave Sandy Ground for Prickly Pear at around 10 am, returning around 4 pm. The cost is about US$70 for adults, US$45 for children, including lunch, drinks and snorkelling gear.

Also popular and a bit cheaper are sails to secluded Little Bay, on Anguilla's east coast, which is a lovely cliff-backed cove with a little white-sand beach and fine snorkelling.

The following offer sails to both: Suntastic Yacht Cruises (☎ 3400), Princess Soya Cruises (☎ 2671) and Enchanted Island Cruises (☎ 3111). There may also be some upstart companies making the same runs at discounted prices – ask around.

For information on boats to Sandy Island see the Sandy Ground section.

# The Valley

The Valley, the island's only real town, is the geographic, commercial and political centre of Anguilla. It's not a very large town, but it's rather spread out and rambling. In part because the British moved the administration of the island to St Kitts back in 1825, there are no quaint colonial government buildings or even a central square. Most buildings are the functional type, taking on the appearance of small shopping centres.

There's a new **museum** in the centre of town, between Wallblake and Airport roads, which has displays covering everything from Amerindian artefacts and natural history to the 1967 revolution.

The Valley's most interesting building is the **Wallblake House**, which was built in 1787 and is one of the oldest structures on the island. The house can only be viewed from the exterior as it's the rectory for the Roman Catholic church. You can, however, view the interior of the adjacent church, which has a unique design incorporating a decorative stone front, open-air side walls and a ceiling shaped like the hull of a ship.

### Places to Stay

*Casa Nadine Guest House* (☎ 2358), PO Box 10, is a local boarding house with a friendly manager and 11 very basic rooms, each with a private shower and toilet. Singles/doubles cost US$20/30.

*Lloyd's Guest House* (☎ 2351), PO Box

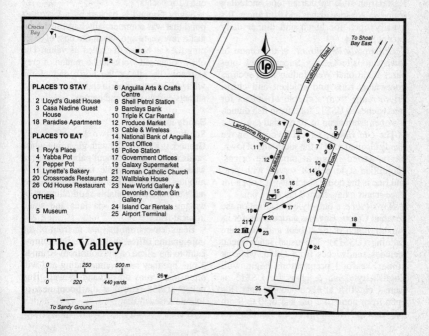

**PLACES TO STAY**

2 Lloyd's Guest House
3 Casa Nadine Guest House
18 Paradise Apartments

**PLACES TO EAT**

1 Roy's Place
4 Yabba Pot
7 Pepper Pot
11 Lynette's Bakery
20 Crossroads Restaurant
26 Old House Restaurant

**OTHER**

5 Museum

6 Anguilla Arts & Crafts Centre
8 Shell Petrol Station
9 Barclays Bank
10 Triple K Car Rental
12 Produce Market
13 Cable & Wireless
14 National Bank of Anguilla
15 Post Office
16 Police Station
17 Government Offices
19 Galaxy Supermarket
21 Roman Catholic Church
22 Wallblake House
23 New World Gallery & Devonish Cotton Gin Gallery
24 Island Car Rentals
25 Airport Terminal

**The Valley**

Crocus Bay

To Shoal Bay East

Landsome Road

Wallblake Road

Airport Road

0    250    500 m
0    220    440 yards

To Sandy Ground

52, is an old-fashioned guesthouse with a dozen rooms. All are very straightforward, but they do have private bathrooms and the year-round rate of US$50 includes breakfast. Lloyd's also has a few apartments with kitchenettes down at Crocus Bay that it sometimes lets out for the same price.

*Paradise Apartments* (☎ 2168; fax 5381) is opposite the Central Baptist Church in the Rey Hill area, not far from the airport. The two-storey building has four modern apartments, each with a large bedroom, bathroom, separate kitchen, ceiling fans and a view of The Valley. Rates are US$60/85 in summer/winter.

### Places to Eat

The *Pepper Pot*, west of Barclays Bank, has good chicken rotis for EC$8 as well as cheap burgers and sandwiches. It's open for breakfast and lunch from Monday to Saturday, closing around 5 pm.

*Yabba Pot* on Wallblake Rd serves Rastafarian-style vegetarian food, including soups, salads, rice dishes and fruit juices. It's usually open for lunch and dinner daily except Sunday.

*Crossroads Restaurant*, in the centre of town opposite Galaxy Supermarket, prepares traditional West Indian food such as goatwater, rotis and chicken and chips. Prices range from a couple of dollars for sandwiches to US$12 for a fresh fish dinner. It's open from noon to 10 pm daily.

The *Old House*, a local favourite on the Sandy Ground road at the south side of town, has a varied menu at moderate prices. Anguillian-style potfish served with peas and rice is the house speciality. It's open for three meals a day, from 7 am to 11 pm.

*Roy's Place*, a pub-style restaurant on the beach at Crocus Bay, has a reputation for its Sunday lunch of roast beef and Yorkshire pudding (US$15). The usual lunch menu includes sandwiches from US$5, while at dinner, seafood preparations begin with English-style fish & chips for US$15 or there's crayfish at about double that. It's open from noon to 2 pm and 6.30 to 9 pm daily except Monday. For the island's best

breakfast deal, try *Lynette's Bakery* on Landsome Rd where you can get a big slab of warm tasty bread pudding for a mere EC$1.25. It's closed on Sunday.

The Galaxy Supermarket on Wallblake Rd is a good-sized grocers open to 7.30 pm weekdays, to 9 pm on Saturday. Near the corner of Wallblake and Landsome there's a produce market, but be prepared for high prices.

# Central & West Anguilla

## SANDY GROUND/ROAD BAY

Sandy Ground, a small village fronting Road Bay, is the closest thing Anguilla has to a travellers' haunt. It has a nice white-sand beach lined with good beachside restaurants, a dive shop and a few low-key places to stay. The fishhook-shaped bay is one of the most protected on the island and the main port of entry for yachts.

Sandy Ground is backed by a large salt pond that was commercially harvested until just a few years ago, when the cost of shipping the salt began to exceed its value. The old wooden salt works and a mound of grey salt now lie idle at the north end of the village. The quieter north end of the salt pond attracts egrets, stilts and herons.

### Sandy Island

Sandy Island, lying two km off Sandy Ground, is a small islet with gleaming white sands and a dozen coconut palms – you can walk around the whole thing in just 10 minutes. The island is surrounded by shallow reefs that offer reasonable snorkelling, with waving finger corals, sea fans and small tropical fish.

Boats leave from the pier in front of the immigration office, making the five-minute jaunt to the island on the hour from 10 am to 3 pm, but they're accommodating and will often make runs on demand as well. Buy tickets (US$8 return) at the booth next to Johnno's Beach Bar.

There's a beach bar on the island that sells

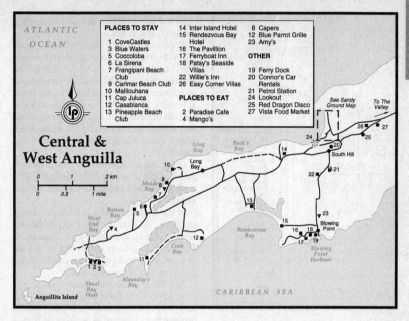

| PLACES TO STAY | 14 | Inter Island Hotel | 8 | Capers |
|---|---|---|---|---|
| | 15 | Rendezvous Bay | 12 | Blue Parrot Grille |
| 1 CoveCastles | | Hotel | 23 | Amy's |
| 3 Blue Waters | 16 | The Pavillion | | |
| 5 Coccoloba | 17 | Ferryboat Inn | **OTHER** | |
| 6 La Sirena | 18 | Patsy's Seaside | | |
| 7 Frangipani Beach | | Villas | 19 | Ferry Dock |
| Club | 22 | Willie's Inn | 20 | Connor's Car |
| 9 Carimar Beach Club | 26 | Easy Corner Villas | | Rentals |
| 10 Malliouhana | | | 21 | Petrol Station |
| 11 Cap Juluca | **PLACES TO EAT** | | 24 | Lookout |
| 12 Casablanca | | | 25 | Red Dragon Disco |
| 13 Pineapple Beach | 2 | Paradise Cafe | 27 | Vista Food Market |
| Club | 4 | Mango's | | |

**Central & West Anguilla**

ATLANTIC OCEAN

CARIBBEAN SEA

Anguillita Island

---

US$2 beers and plate lunches from US$10 (chicken) to US$25 (lobster).

### Places to Stay

*Syd-An's Apartments* (☎ 3180; fax 5381), on the beach road in the village centre, has six apartments that are a bit wear-worn but adequate, each with kitchen facilities and fans. Singles/doubles cost from US$45/60 in summer, US$60/75 in winter.

The *Sea View Guest House* (☎ 2427), on the beach road opposite the dive shop, is a tidy two-storey building with three fan-cooled apartments. Rates are US$48 for a one-bedroom apartment, US$90 for a three-bedroom apartment.

The *Pond Dipper Guest House* (☎ 2315), on the 2nd floor of a family home, has three bedrooms with a shared kitchen and sitting room. Two of the bedrooms – one with three twin beds and another with a double bed – share a bathroom. The third bedroom has a double bed and private bathroom. The rooms

are spartan, with standing fans being the main amenity; each rents for US$50/60 in summer/winter.

Sandy Ground's only hotel, *The Mariners* (☎ 2671; fax 2901; in the USA ☎ (800) 848-7938), is at the quieter south end of the beach. Most rooms are in a cluster of attractive West Indian-style cottages with brightly painted shutters and gingerbread trim. The interiors are simple but comfortable with screened louvred windows, ceiling fans and phones. There are hammocks tied to the palm trees along the beach and guests have free use of snorkel gear, Sunfish boats, windsurfing equipment and the tennis court. Singles/doubles begin at US$135/145 in summer, US$210/235 in winter. There are also air-con rooms with less atmosphere in a two-storey cliffside block for the same price.

### Places to Eat

*Johnno's Beach Bar* is a casual open-air restaurant on the beach with picnic tables and a

ANGUILLA

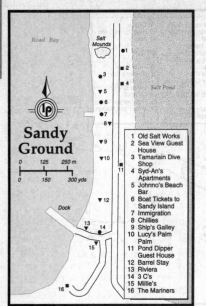

Road Bay

Salt Mounds

Salt Pond

Sandy Ground

| 0 | 125 | 250 m |
| 0 | 150 | 300 yds |

Dock

| | |
|---|---|
| 1 | Old Salt Works |
| 2 | Sea View Guest House |
| 3 | Tamariain Dive Shop |
| 4 | Syd-An's Apartments |
| 5 | Johnno's Beach Bar |
| 6 | Boat Tickets to Sandy Island |
| 7 | Immigration |
| 8 | Chillies |
| 9 | Ship's Galley |
| 10 | Lucy's Palm Palm |
| 11 | Pond Dipper Guest House |
| 12 | Barrel Stay |
| 13 | Riviera |
| 14 | 3 C's |
| 15 | Millie's |
| 16 | The Mariners |

simple menu. A burger and fries cost US$5.50, chicken or ribs US$8.50 and catch of the day US$12. It's open daily for lunch and dinner, and is especially lively on Saturday nights and Sunday when there's a live band.

*Chillies*, in the village centre, is a laid-back Mexican restaurant with reasonably good food and big servings. Two chicken tacos or enchiladas with rice and beans cost US$8.50. There are also burritos, tostadas, quesadillas and fajitas and most dishes can be served vegetarian. It's open daily for lunch and dinner.

The popular seaside *Barrel Stay* (☎ 2831), which takes its name from the old rum-barrel stays that comprise the restaurant rails, has Sandy Ground's most romantic setting. Fresh fish is prepared in a number of creative ways, including almondine and Vietnamese, and costs US$23, while conch Creole costs US$20 and grilled lobster is US$30; all prices are à la carte. Don't miss the fish soup,

regarded as Anguilla's best. It's open daily for lunch and dinner.

*Riviera* has a pleasant beachfront veran-dah and serves reasonably good French fare. The kitchen does a nice job with grilled crayfish which costs US$30; other main dishes such as chicken and red snapper begin at US$20. There are often a few good-value specials that essentially throw in an appetiser and dessert for the same price as the main course alone. It's open daily for lunch and dinner.

Other restaurants on the beach include *Lucy's Palm Palm* and the nearby *Ship's Galley*, both with moderately priced seafood dishes.

In the evenings *Millie's*, a simple corner eatery on the road to the dock, barbecues chicken legs on an outdoor grill. Opposite is 3 C's, a small grocery store open from 8 am to 4 pm and 5 to 8 pm Monday to Saturday and from 8 to 10 am on Sunday.

For more extensive grocery shopping, drive up to Vista Food Market, a mile (1.6 km) away at the roundabout. It's the island's best stocked supermarket and is open from 8 am to 6 pm Monday to Saturday.

## SOUTH HILL
South Hill, the village that rises above the south end of Road Bay, is essentially a resi-dential area although there are a couple of places to stay. There are no sights in South Hill, but you can take the one-way road that goes west to east above the cliffs for some fine views of Sandy Ground, Road Bay and Sandy Island.

### Places to Stay
*Easy Corner Villas* (☎ 6433; fax 6410), PO Box 65, on a hillside just west of Vista Food Market, has 12 modern self-catering apart-ments, with balconies overlooking Sandy Ground. Rates are US$160/195/240 for one/two/three-bedroom apartments in winter and are US$40 less in summer. Studio units cost US$90/110 in summer/winter. The office is at Connor's Car Rental, a mile (1.6 km) to the west on the same road.

*Inter Island Hotel* (☎ 6259; fax 5381), an

older two-storey hostelry at the side of the main road, has 14 rather plain units. Many rooms are on the small side, though some have balconies with distant ocean views. While the hotel is rather oddly located, several beaches are within a 10-minute drive. Rates are the big plus here: US$35/60 for singles/doubles in standard rooms, US$70 for one-bedroom apartments, and US$95 for two-bedroom apartments for up to four people.

## BLOWING POINT

Blowing Point, where the ferry from St Martin docks, is mainly a residential area and not a major tourist centre. There is a modest beach west of the immigration office as well as a few reasonably priced apartment-style places to stay, but most visitors arriving for a day visit will want to make their way to better beaches elsewhere around the island.

### Places to Stay

The first three places listed are within a 10-minute walk from the ferry, on the first road to the left after leaving the terminal.

The *Ferryboat Inn* (☎ 6613; fax 3309) has six apartments on the beach. Units are large and modern with rattan furnishings, sliding glass doors to a porch or balcony, ceiling fans and TV. Rates are US$75 in summer and from US$125 in winter.

*The Pavillion* (☎ 6395; fax 6234), directly opposite the Ferryboat Inn, is a modern three-storey building with eight one-bedroom apartments for US$60/80 in summer/winter and a two-bedroom apartment for US$90/120. Units have full kitchens, balconies, ceiling fans and TV.

Nearby *Patsy's Seaside Villas* (☎ 6297; fax 5381) also has a couple of beachside units with kitchens, ceiling fans and TV. Rates are US$70 in summer, US$100 in winter.

*Willie's Inn* (☎ 6225; fax 5381), a mile (1.6 km) up from the ferry dock, is a two-storey building with 16 good-value apartments. Units are fan-cooled and have kitchenettes with hot plates, refrigerators and

toasters. Singles/doubles cost US$40/50 in summer, US$50/75 in winter.

### Places to Eat

There's no food (or even water!) at the ferry terminal but there are a couple of local snack shops up the road from the dock. The nicest of these is *Amy's*, a small bakery with half a dozen café-style tables. In addition to inexpensive slices of banana bread and carrot cake, you can get pancakes for breakfast and sandwiches for lunch for US$5 to US$7. It's open from 7.30 am to 2.30 pm daily except Sunday.

On the right side of the road just outside the dock, there's sometimes a man with a smoke-grill who cooks some of the best grilled ribs and fish on the island.

*Ferryboat Inn* has a casual open-air beachfront restaurant a few minutes west of the dock. A burger and fries cost US$6.50, grilled chicken US$12 and fresh fish a couple of dollars more. It's open for lunch and dinner and takes credit cards.

## RENDEZVOUS BAY

Rendezvous Bay is a gorgeous arc of white sand that stretches for more than 1.2 miles (two km). There's a hotel at either end and one in the middle, but otherwise it's delightfully free of development. This sheltered bay has protected turquoise waters, a nice sandy bottom and a straight-on view of hilly St Martin to the south.

Rendezvous Bay is well known in local history as the site of a 1796 invasion by French forces who hastily plundered the island before British troops from St Kitts came to the rescue.

Public beach access is at the east side of the Pineapple Beach Club. After turning south off the main road towards the hotel, simply continue along the dirt road that skirts the salt pond until you reach the beach. Upwinds Water Sports, next to the hotel restaurant, rents windsurfing gear.

### Places to Stay

*Rendezvous Bay Hotel* (☎ 6549; fax 6026; in the USA ☎ (800) 274-4893), PO Box 31, is at the east end of Rendezvous Bay and reached via Blowing Point. There are 20 straightforward motel-like units with fans that cost US$75/100 in summer/winter and 24 spiffier villa units with air-con, fans, refrigerators and porches that cost from US$100/175. There are also studios with kitchens for US$125/200. The hotel has a restaurant, pool, tennis courts and a common room with TV.

*Pineapple Beach Club* (☎ 6061; fax 6019; in the USA ☎ (800) 345-0356) sits by itself on a quiet stretch of beach at the centre of Rendezvous Bay. It's a collection of cottages built in traditional West Indies design and tastefully furnished with colonial decor. This would be a nice place to get away from it all – the rooms are comfortable and the staff friendly. There's a restaurant, bar and pool. Rates, which include meals and water sports, start at US$220/340 singles/doubles in summer, US$320/400 in winter.

*Casablanca* (☎ 6999; fax 6899; in the USA and Canada ☎ (800) 231-1945) is the new 76-room Moroccan-style resort at the west end of Rendezvous Bay. With its pink exterior and exotic arches, it certainly looks quite apropos for the desert – if not necessarily an Anguillian one. The whole place exudes a fantasy element, from elaborate tile mosaics in the lobby to the Bogart-reminiscent Café American bar, and the spacious rooms have Moorish decor, Italian marble baths and satellite TV. There's a large pool, tennis courts and a fitness room. Daily rates begin at US$700 in summer, US$800 in winter, per couple all-inclusive.

### Places to Eat
Casablanca has a couple of restaurants. The *Blue Parrot Grille* is a pleasantly upscale poolside café featuring seafood dishes like red snapper (US$25) and lobster with crayfish (US$32). More formal and expensive is the *Casablanca* restaurant, which serves classic French and continental fare. Worth checking out is the US$25 Sunday brunch (half price for children), from 11.30 am to 3 pm, which includes various salads, couscous, poached salmon, roast beef, fresh fruit

and pastries; there's live brunch music and diners are free to use the pool.

### MEADS BAY
Meads Bay boasts a lovely mile-long sweep of white sand with calm turquoise waters. It's a good beach for swimming and a great one for strolling.

Although a couple of the island's trendiest hotels and a few small condominium complexes are scattered along the beach, Meads Bay is certainly not crowded – some of the hotels are a good five-minute walk from their nearest neighbour. The bay is backed by a salt pond for most of its length. There are annual boat races from the beach on the first Thursday in August.

### Places to Stay
*La Sirena* (☎ 6827; in North America ☎ (800) 332-9358, in London ☎ (071) 937-7725), PO Box 200, is at the west end of Meads Bay. There are 27 rooms in low-rise whitewashed buildings with red tile roofs, each room with ceiling fans, a phone and minibar. Even though it's the cheapest of the area's hotels, it's a pleasant enough place, with singles/doubles from US$95/120 in summer, US$140/190 in winter.

*Carimar Beach Club* (☎ 6881; fax 6071; in the USA ☎ (800) 235-8667), PO Box 327, is a pleasant, contemporary, two-storey beachfront condominium complex on the east side of Mead's Bay. The 23 units have full kitchens, a living/dining room and a balcony or patio. One-bedroom apartments begin at US$225/300 in summer/winter, two bedrooms from US$280/400. From April to 15 December there's a special rate for stays of five days or more that begins at US$120 per night.

*Coccoloba* (☎ 6871; fax 6332; in the USA ☎ (800) 982-7729) is on the promontory that separates Meads Bay from neighbouring Barnes Bay. This trendy upper-end hotel has standard hotel rooms from US$195 to US$360 depending on the season and pleasant gingerbread-trim villas that begin at US$295 in summer, US$350 in spring and autumn and US$460 in winter. *Malliouhana*

*Hotel* (☎ 6111; fax 6011; in the USA ☎ (800) 835-0796), PO Box 173, on a low cliff at the east end of Meads Bay, is one of the island's most fashionable luxury hotels. Its large open-air lobbies are decorated with Haitian and East Indian art. The rooms are air-conditioned and have tile floors, marble baths, rattan furnishings, original art work and large patios. Prices begin at US$240 in summer, US$320 in autumn and spring and US$480 in winter. Credit cards are not accepted.

The *Frangipani Beach Club* (☎ 6442; fax 6440; in the USA ☎ (800) 892-4564), on the quiet west side of Meads Bay, is a small condominium complex of Spanish design. Its large suites have air-con, ceiling fans, full kitchens, individual washer/dryers, marbled bathrooms, king-size beds and beachfront terraces. Rates for one-bedroom suites are US$250/450 in summer/winter; two-bedroom suites cost US$390/765. There are also some hotel-style rooms available from US$165/325.

### Places to Eat

*Capers* (☎ 6369) is a casual open-air restaurant on the beach between the Frangipani and Carimar condo complexes. The food is good and the menu varied. The house speciality, Vietnamese spring rolls (US$8), makes a good starter, while main courses include grilled mahimahi with pineapple salsa for US$21, lobster for US$28 and pasta of the day for US$18. It's open for dinner only, from 6 to 10 pm daily except Monday.

*Mango's* is a very pleasant and popular beachside restaurant at the west end of Barnes Bay, adjacent to Meads Bay. Main courses include a vegetarian couscous plate for US$13, chicken in a tasty mango sauce for US$17 and blackened lobster for US$30. Starters such as gazpacho soup or Caesar salad cost US$5, as do many of the home-made desserts. It's open for dinner with two seatings (☎ 6497 for reservations), closed on Tuesday. During the winter, Mango's is also open for lunch.

There are also expensive restaurants at the hotels. At the highly regarded *Malliouhana*, which has classic French cuisine and a lovely ocean view, dinner for two will run to a good US$100.

### SHOAL BAY WEST

Shoal Bay West is a curving half-moon bay fringed by a pretty white-sand beach. The waters are clear and sheltered. It's rather remote, with just two small resorts and a pink beach estate belonging to actor Chuck Norris. The salt pond that backs the beach was used to harvest salt until just a few decades ago.

There's another glistening white-sand beach, Maunday's Bay, to the east, but it's largely dominated by Cap Juluca, an exclusive resort of Moorish design.

### Places to Stay

*CoveCastles* (☎ 6801; fax 6051), PO Box 248, is a complex of 12 stark white villas with a futuristic sculptural design that's won kudos in architectural circles. The villas are handsomely decorated with all rooms facing the sea. They have cable TV, phones, hammocks on the terraces, full kitchens right down to the crystal and rates that start at US$320/590 in summer/winter.

*Blue Waters* (☎ 6292; fax 3309), PO Box 69, is just down the beach from CoveCastles. A bit more conventional in design, it's a modern two-storey building with nine apartments, each with a beachfront balcony or terrace, a kitchen, ceiling fans and TV. Summer/winter rates are US$100/165 for a one-bedroom unit, US$145/240 for a two-bedroom unit.

### Places to Eat

*Paradise Cafe* (☎ 6010), next to Blue Waters, is a pleasant seaside café open daily except Monday. At lunch (noon to 2.30 pm), pizza or a steak sandwich with fries cost around US$10. Dinner features a more exotic menu with main dishes such as Thai curry, Sichuan tenderloin, Indonesian crayfish or West Indian bouillabaisse in the US$17 to US$24 range.

# East Anguilla

## SHOAL BAY EAST

Shoal Bay, often referred to as Shoal Bay East to distinguish it from Shoal Bay West, is considered by many to be Anguilla's premier beach. Located at the north-east side of the island, Shoal Bay East is broad and long with radiant white sands and turquoise waters that are ideal for swimming, snorkelling and just plain lazing. There are a couple of hotels and restaurants on the beach, but virtually no other development in sight.

A trailer behind Uncle Ernie's beach bar rents snorkel gear (US$9 a day), lounge chairs and umbrellas.

### The Fountain

The island's top archaeological site is the Fountain, a huge underground cave located along a rocky pathway a few hundred metres south-east of the Fountain Beach Hotel.

The cave, which draws its name from its former importance as a freshwater spring, contains scores of Amerindian petroglyphs, including a rare stalagmite carving of Jocahu, the Arawak God of Creation. The Fountain is thought to have been a major regional worship site and a place of pilgrimage for Amerindians. A national park, with the Fountain at its centrepiece, has been proposed. In the meantime the Fountain remains the domain of archaeologists only and the ladder leading down into the cave has been fenced off to protect the site from damage.

### Places to Stay

*Fountain Beach Hotel* (☎ & fax 3491; in the USA ☎ (800) 633-7411), at the secluded west end of Shoal Bay, is a modern little hotel with half a dozen units and a lightly posh Italian decor. There's a poolside hotel room without kitchen that costs US$90/150 in summer/winter, a junior suite for US$155/225 and larger one and two-bedroom suites priced about 25% and 50% more. Suites have full kitchens, comfortable living rooms with sofabeds and beachfront porches. It's closed in September.

*Shoal Bay Resort Hotel* (☎ 2011; fax 3355), PO Box 51, has 26 condo-style apartments in two and three-storey buildings that are set back just a touch from the beach. They are modern and comfortable, each with one bedroom, a kitchen, a living room with queen-sized sofabed, a patio or balcony, a phone and ceiling fans. Rates are US$130/195 for two people in summer/ winter, plus US$40 for each additional person. Despite the 'resort hotel' label, there's no restaurant, pool or other common facilities.

The beachfront *Shoal Bay Villas* (☎ 2051; fax 3631; in the USA ☎ (800) 722-7045), PO Box 81, has 13 comfortable units with tropical decor. For two people in summer/ winter, studios cost US$125/210, and one-bedroom apartments are US$150/230. Two-bedroom apartments cost US$240/360 for up to four people. All have ceiling fans, a kitchen and a patio or balcony. There's a nice pool. In winter there's a seven-night minimum stay.

There are two apartment-style places at the east side of Shoal Bay within walking distance of the beach. *Milly's Inn* (☎ 2465; fax 5591; in the USA ☎ (800) 626-6161), about five minutes from the beach, is a modern two-storey building with just four units, each with a full kitchen, ceiling fans, white tile floors and a large ocean-view balcony. The rate is US$100 in summer, US$150 in winter.

*The Allamanda* (☎ 5217), about a 10-minute walk from the beach, has 16 one-bedroom apartments in a single three-storey building. The apartments, which are quite straightforward, have a small separate kitchen, living room, TV and ceiling fans, and cost US$80 or US$100 depending on whether there's one or two beds.

### Places to Eat

At *Uncle Ernie's*, a popular local beach bar immediately west of Shoal Bay Villas, you can get barbecued chicken, ribs or a cheeseburger for US$6 and wash it down with a US$1 Heineken. It's open from 10 am to 8 pm daily. The neighbouring beachfront bar

*Trader's Vic* has the same sort of barbecue setup.

*Ristorante La Fontana* (☎ 3492) at Fountain Beach Hotel serves authentic Italian food in a romantic setting right on the beach. Light, delicious pastas or fish and meat main dishes cost US$13 to US$20. There's a good Italian wine selection and homemade sorbet and ice cream. It's open for breakfast, lunch and dinner, though it's closed during most of the low season and on Wednesday all year round.

*Reefside Restaurant* at Shoal Bay Villas has open-air beachfront dining for three meals a day. At lunch, served until 3.30 pm, you can get chicken rotis and burgers at moderate prices. At dinner, fresh seafood and meat dishes range from US$16 to US$26. There's a happy hour from 6.30 to 7.30 pm.

## ISLAND HARBOUR

Island Harbour is a working fishing village, not a resort area, and its beach is lined with brightly coloured fishing boats rather than chaise lounges. Still it does have a few places to stay and eat and some travellers make their base here.

The area's historic site, albeit sadly neglected, is **Big Spring**, a partially collapsed cave 10 metres west of the Island Pub supermarket. The cave contains Amerindian petroglyphs and an underwater spring that once served as the village water source. However, the site is caught up in a land dispute between the government and the store owner and the cave cannot be entered.

Just off Island Harbour, in the centre of the bay, is the tiny private island of **Scilly Cay**, which has a restaurant and bar and is fringed with a beach of bone-white sands.

### Scrub Island

Scrub Island is the four-km-long island that lies just off Anguilla's north-eastern tip. Befitting its name the island has scrubby vegetation and is inhabited only by goats. It has a beach on its west side, a blocked-off airstrip that's rumoured to have once been used by cocaine runners and some good snorkelling spots. If you don't have your own boat, Smitty's beachside bar (☎ 4300) can arrange one to take you to the island for US$40. There are no facilities; bring your own picnic.

### Places to Stay

*Ocean View Inn* (☎ 4477; fax 3180), opposite the dock to Scilly Cay, has two modern 2nd-floor apartments, one with two bedrooms and the other with three. Each has a large dining/living room area, a full kitchen, screened louvred windows and ceiling fans. Rates begin at US$100.

*Harbour Villas* (☎ 4433; fax 2149), on a hillside half a mile (800 metres) north of Ocean View Inn, has 16 spacious condos in two-storey buildings. The apartments have full kitchens, bedroom ceiling fans and balconies with views of Scilly Cay. Summer/winter rates are US$65/110 for one-bedroom units, US$95/125 for two bedrooms, though when things are slow you can sometimes negotiate a bit of a discount.

The new *Arawak Beach Resort* (☎ 4888; fax 4898), PO Box 98, on the west side of the harbour, has 14 villas in two-storey buildings that supposedly take influences from the ancient Arawaks who once occupied the site. Rates start at US$180 in summer, US$250 in winter.

### Places to Eat

*Smitty's* is a beachside bar and restaurant with simple barbecue fare: hamburgers cost US$5, ribs, chicken or fish with fries US$10 and lobster about US$20. There's a live band from 7.30 pm on Thursday and all day on Sunday.

*Hibernia* (☎ 4290), half a mile (800 metres) east of Island Harbour in the Harbour View residential area, is one of the island's top restaurants and features Caribbean nouvelle cuisine with Asian hints. There's verandah dining and a hillside setting with a spectacular sea view. Starters cost US$6 to US$9. Main courses range from a US$17 chicken dish to creative seafood dishes such as Thai-style bouillabaisse or grilled crayfish in a vanilla-ginger sauce for US$28. It's open for dinner from Tuesday to Sunday. During the winter, it's also open for lunch.

*Scilly Cay* (☎ 5123) has a casual lunchtime restaurant with chicken for US$20, lobster for US$35, and a bar that's open from 11 am to 6 pm. Guests can pick up a free boat shuttle by going to the Island Harbour pier and waving towards the island. A string band plays on Sunday, a guitarist on Wednesday. It's closed on Monday.

# Antigua & Barbuda

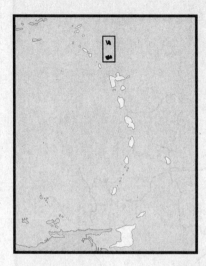

Antigua's chief drawing cards are its fine beaches and abundance of colonial-era historic sites. Old stone windmills from long-abandoned sugar plantations are so plentiful that they are the island's chief landmarks. The renovated colonial-era naval base of Nelson's Dockyard now attracts yachters from around the world and the scattered ruins of an extensive hilltop fortress are found at neighbouring Shirley Heights.

Antigua's hotels are spread out along its sandy beaches; Dickenson Bay and neighbouring Runaway Bay have the most places to stay but there are remote resorts scattered around the island.

While the seaward view from the beach is generally quite lovely, the interior of Antigua is not as pristine in appearance – many places are scruffy and quite heavily littered.

Barbuda, 40 km to the north, is the other half of the dual-island nation of Antigua & Barbuda. This quiet, single-village island has less than 2% of the nation's population.

Barbuda gets very few visitors, mainly bird watchers who come to see its frigatebird colony and a few yachters who enjoy its clear waters and remote beaches. Information on visiting Barbuda is at the end of this chapter.

## ORIENTATION
The airport is at the north-east side of the island, about a 15-minute drive from either St John's or Dickenson Bay.

# Facts about the Islands

## HISTORY
The first permanent residents are thought to have been migrating Arawaks who established agricultural communities on both Antigua and Barbuda about 2000 years ago. Around 1200 AD the Arawaks were forced out by invading Caribs, who used the islands as bases for their forays in the region but apparently didn't settle them.

Columbus sighted Antigua in 1493 and named it after a church in Seville, Spain. In 1632 the British colonised Antigua, establishing a settlement at Parham on the east side of the island. The settlers started planting indigo and tobacco but a glut in the market for those crops soon undermined prices.

In 1674, Sir Christopher Codrington arrived on Antigua and established the first sugar plantation, Betty's Hope. By the end of the century, a plantation economy had developed, slaves were imported and the central valleys were deforested and planted in cane. To feed the slaves, Codrington leased the island of Barbuda from the British Crown and planted it with food crops.

As Antigua prospered the British built numerous fortifications around the island, turning it into one of their most secure bases in the Caribbean. The military couldn't secure the economy, however, and in the

ANTIGUA

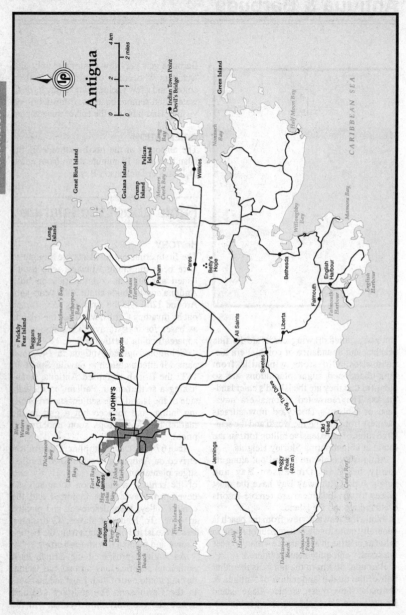

early 1800s the sugar market began to bottom out. With the abolition of slavery in 1834 the plantations went into a steady decline. Unlike on some other Caribbean islands, as the plantations went under the land was not turned over to former slaves but was consolidated under the ownership of a few landowners. Consequently the lot of most people only worsened. Many former slaves moved off the plantation and into shanty towns, while others crowded onto properties held by the church.

A military-related construction boom during WW II and the development of a tourist industry during the post-war period helped spur economic growth, although the shanty towns that remain along the outskirts of St John's are ample evidence that not everyone has benefited.

After more than 300 years of colonial rule, in 1967 Antigua achieved a measure of self-government as an Associated State of the United Kingdom and on 1 November 1981 the country achieved full independence.

### GEOGRAPHY

The island of Antigua has a land area of 280 sq km. It is vaguely rounded in shape, averaging about 18 km across. Antigua's deeply indented coastline is cut by numerous coves and bays, many lined with white-sand beaches. The south-west corner is volcanic in origin and quite hilly, rising to 402 metres at Boggy Peak, the island's highest point. The rest of the island, which is predominantly of limestone and coral formation, is given to a more gently undulating terrain of open plains and scrubland.

The island of Barbuda, 40 km north of Antigua, has a land area of 161 sq km. A low-lying coral island, Barbuda's highest point is a mere 44 metres. The west side of Barbuda encompasses the expansive Codrington Lagoon, which is bound by a long undeveloped barrier beach.

The country's boundaries also include Redonda, an uninhabited rocky islet about one sq km in size which lies 40 km south-west of Antigua.

### CLIMATE

In January and February, the coolest months, the daily high temperature averages 27°C (81°F), while the nightly low temperature averages 22°C (72°F). In July and August, the hottest months, the high averages 30°C (86°F), the low 25°C (77°F).

Antigua is relatively dry, averaging about 115 cm of rain annually. The rainiest months are September to November when measurable precipitation occurs on average eight days each month. February to April is the driest period with an average of three rainy days each month.

### FLORA & FAUNA

As a consequence of colonial-era deforestation most of Antigua's vegetation is dryland scrub. The island's marshes and salt ponds attract a fair number of stilts, egrets, ducks and pelicans, while hummingbirds are found in garden settings.

Barbuda's Codrington Lagoon has the largest frigatebird colony in the Lesser Antilles.

### GOVERNMENT

The nation of Antigua & Barbuda, part of the Commonwealth, has a parliamentary system of government which is led by a prime minister and modelled after the British system. There's an elected 17-member House of Representatives and an appointed 17-member Senate. Elections are held at least once every five years.

The British monarchy is represented by a Governor-General who has a role in appointing members of the senate but is otherwise largely an advisory figure.

Despite leading a government marred by political scandals, Prime Minister Vere Cornwall Bird has held the nation's highest position since independence. Now in his eighties, it's expected that one of his two rival sons will vie to replace him when his current term ends in 1994.

The oldest son, Vere Bird Jr, received international attention in 1991 as the subject of a judicial enquiry into his involvement in smuggling Israeli weapons to the Medellin

ANTIGUA

ANTIGUA

drug cartel. His signature on documents, which were required by Israeli authorities to prove the weapons were bound for a legitimate buyer, allowed the cargo to be shipped to a nonexistent officer of the Antigua Defence Force. After eight hours in port the weapons were transferred to a Columbian boat and shipped to the cartel without interference by customs. As a consequence of the enquiry Vere Bird Jr was pressured into resigning his cabinet post but he remains a member of parliament.

## ECONOMY

Tourism is the island's main industry, accounting for about half of the workforce. Agriculture and fishing employ about 10% of the workforce. There's a bit of small-scale manufacturing, primarily in garment and electronic assembly.

## POPULATION & PEOPLE

About 65,000 people live on Antigua. Approximately 90% are of African descent. There are also small minority populations of British, Portuguese and Lebanese ancestry. The population of Barbuda is approximately 1100.

## ARTS & CULTURE

Away from the resorts Antigua retains a traditional West Indian character. It's manifested in the gingerbread architecture found around the capital, the popularity of steel band, calypso and reggae music and in festivities such as Carnival. English traditions also play an important role, as is evident in the national sport of cricket. Antigua has also produced the renowned novelist Jamaica Kincaid (see Books for more details).

### Dress Conventions

Dress is casual and simple cotton clothing is suitable attire for most occasions. In a few of the most upmarket resort restaurants, jackets and ties are required of men. To avoid offence, swimwear should be restricted to the beach.

## RELIGION

Nearly half of all Antiguans are members of the Anglican Church. Other denominations include Roman Catholic, Moravian, Methodist, Seventh Day Adventist and Rastafarian.

## LANGUAGE

English is the official language, most often spoken with a distinctive Antiguan lilt.

# Facts for the Visitor

## PASSPORT & VISAS

Visitors from the USA, Canada, the UK and British Territories may enter for stays of less than six months with either a valid passport or a birth certificate with a raised seal and a photo ID.

Australian, New Zealand, Japanese and all West European citizens must have passports but do not need visas.

Officially all visitors need a return or onward ticket.

## CUSTOMS

Arriving passengers may bring in a carton of cigarettes, one quart of liquor and six ounces of perfume duty free.

## MONEY

The currency of Antigua & Barbuda is the Eastern Caribbean dollar (EC$) and the official exchange rate is US$1=EC$2.70.

US dollars are widely accepted. However, unless a bill is posted in US dollars, as is the norm with accommodation, it usually works out better to pay in EC dollars.

MasterCard, Visa and American Express are widely accepted. Credit card charges are made in US dollars, so businesses that quote prices in EC dollars must convert the bill to a US dollar total. Whenever you intend to pay by credit card it's a good idea to ask the exchange rate first, as some places use EC$2.60 or EC$2.65 to US$1, but others use EC$2.50, a hefty 8% overcharge.

A 10% service charge is added to most

restaurant bills, in which case no further tipping is necessary.

## TOURIST OFFICES

The main tourist office is on Thames St in St John's. When requesting information by mail, write to: Antigua Department of Tourism (☎ 462-0480), PO Box 363, St John's, Antigua, West Indies. There's also a tourist information booth at the airport.

### Overseas Reps

Tourist offices abroad include:

**Canada**
Antigua & Barbuda Department of Tourism, 60 St Clair Ave E, Suite 205, Toronto, Ontario M4T 1N5 (☎ (416) 961-3085; fax (416) 961-7218)
**Germany**
Antigua & Barbuda German Office, Postfach 1331, Minnholzweg 2, 6242 Kronberg 1 (☎ (061) 73-5011; fax (061) 73-7299)
**Hong Kong**
Consulate of Antigua & Barbuda; 905 Star House, 3 Salisbury Rd, Tsimshatsui, Kowloon (☎ (852) 736-8033)
**UK**
Antigua & Barbuda Department of Tourism & Trade, Antigua House, 15 Thayer St, London W1M 5DL, England (☎ (071) 486-7073; fax (071) 486-9970)
**USA**
Antigua Department of Tourism, 610 Fifth Ave, Suite 311, New York, NY 10020 (☎ (212) 541-4117; fax (212) 757-1607)

## BUSINESS HOURS

Typical business hours are 8 am to noon and 1 to 4 pm Monday to Friday.

## HOLIDAYS

Public holidays in Antigua & Barbuda are:

| | |
|---|---|
| *New Year's Day* | – 1 January |
| *Good Friday* | – late March/early April |
| *Easter Monday* | – late March/early April |
| *Labour Day* | – first Monday in May |
| *Whit Monday* | – eighth Monday after Easter |
| *Queen's Birthday* | – second Saturday in June |
| *Carnival Monday* | – first Monday in August |
| Carnival Tuesday | – first Tuesday in August |
| *Merchants Day* | |
| (only shops closed) | – first Monday in October |
| *Antigua & Barbuda* | |
| *Independence Day* | – 1 November |
| *Christmas Day* | – 25 December |
| *Boxing Day* | – 26 December |

## CULTURAL EVENTS

Carnival, Antigua's big annual festival, is held from the end of July and culminates in a parade on the first Tuesday in August. Calypso music, steel bands, masqueraders, floats and street jump-ups (dancing and general merry-making) are all part of the celebrations.

Antigua Sailing Week is a major week-long yachting event that begins on the last Sunday in April. It generally attracts about 150 boats from a few dozen countries and consists of five races, mostly on the south and west sides of the island.

## POST

The main post office is in St John's and there are branch post offices at English Harbour (at the entrance to Nelson's Dockyard) and the airport. The rate to send a postcard to North America or the UK is EC$.30; to Australia or Europe EC$.40; a half-ounce letter costs EC$.60 and EC$1 respectively.

Mail sent to Antigua should have the post office box followed by 'St John's, Antigua, West Indies'.

## TELECOMMUNICATIONS

Almost all pay phones have been converted to the Caribbean Phone Card system. Phonecards can be bought from vendors in areas near the phones and from the Cable & Wireless offices in St John's or English Harbour. They're priced from EC$10 to EC$60, depending on the number of time units they have.

Avoid the credit card phones found at the airport and in some hotel lobbies as they charge a steep US$2 per minute locally, US$4 to other Caribbean islands or the USA and as much as US$8 elsewhere.

When calling Antigua from overseas dial the 809 area code, followed by the seven-digit local phone number.

More information on phonecards and

ANTIGUA

making long-distance calls is under Tele-communications in the Facts for the Visitor chapter in the front of the book.

## ELECTRICITY

Most hotels operate on 110 volts AC, 60 cycles; however, some places use 220 volts. Check before plugging anything in.

## WEIGHTS & MEASURES

Antigua uses the imperial system of measurement. Car odometers register in miles, speed limits are posted in miles per hour and petrol is sold by the gallon.

## BOOKS & MAPS

Antigua's best known writer is Jamaica Kincaid who has authored a number of novels and essays including *A Small Place* (1988) which gives a scathing account of the effects of tourism on Antigua. Kincaid's collection of stories *At the Bottom of the River* and the novel *Annie John* are two of her more internationally recognised works.

Desmond Nicholson, director of the island museum at Nelson's Dockyard, has published several works on local history, including *Antigua, Barbuda & Redonda: A Historical Sketch*, which is sold for US$10 at the museum.

The best road map of Antigua is the 1:50,000 scale British Ordnance Survey map, *Tourist Map of Antigua*, reprinted in 1992. It can be bought at the Map Shop in St John's (EC$20) and a few other places around the island.

## MEDIA

The island has no daily newspaper, but there are a couple of weeklies. The best source of tourist information is the glossy 100-page *Antigua & Barbuda Adventure*, a free magazine published in spring and autumn, which has facts about the island, a couple of feature stories and listings and prices for most of Antigua's accommodation. Less comprehensive, but similar in style, is the pocket-sized *The Antiguan*. Both can be picked up at the tourist office and at some hotels.

## HEALTH

Antigua's 225-bed Holberton Hospital (☎ 462-0251) is on the eastern outskirts of St John's, just off the Queen Elizabeth Highway. See the introductory Facts for the Visitor chapter for information on travel health.

## DANGERS & ANNOYANCES

Visitors should be careful not to leave valuables unattended and should be cautious walking in secluded places after dark.

## EMERGENCIES

The police headquarters (☎ 462-0125) is on American Rd on the eastern outskirts of St John's. There are substations near Nelson's Dockyard at English Harbour and in central St John's on Newgate St.

## ACTIVITIES

Major resort areas, including Dickenson Bay, have water-sports beach huts that rent small sailing boats and windsurfing gear for around US$20 an hour and snorkelling equipment for US$20 for two hours.

### Beaches & Swimming

Antigua's tourist office boasts that the island has 365 beaches, 'one for each day of the year'. While the count may be suspect, the island certainly doesn't lack in lovely strands. Most of Antigua's beaches have white or light golden sands, many are protected by coral reefs and all are officially public. You can find nice sandy stretches all around the island and, generally, wherever there's a resort there's a nice beach. Prime beaches on the east coast include: the adjacent Dickenson and Runaway beaches, Deep Bay and Hawksbill Beach to the west of St John's and Darkwood Beach to the south. On the east coast Half Moon Bay is a top contender. Those based in the English Harbour area can make their way to Galleon Beach and the secluded Pigeon Beach.

The far ends of some public beaches, including the north side of Dickenson, are favoured by topless bathers, and nude bathing is practised along a section of Hawksbill Beach.

## Diving

Antigua has some excellent diving with coral canyons, wall drops and sea caves hosting a range of marine creatures including turtles, sharks, barracuda and colourful reef fish. Popular diving sites include the three-km-long Cades Reef whose clear calm waters have an abundance of fish and numerous soft and hard corals, and Ariadne Shoal which offers reefs teaming with large fish, lobsters and nurse sharks. A fun spot for both divers and snorkellers is *Jettias*, a 310-foot steamer that sank in 1917 and now provides a habitat for reef fish and coral. The deepest end of the wreck is in about 10 metres of water while the shallowest part comes up almost to the surface.

**Dive Shops** Dive shops on Antigua include the following:

Dive Runaway, PO Box 1603 (☎ 462-2626; fax 462-3484); at the Runaway Beach Club on Runaway Beach.

Dive Antigua, PO Box 251 (☎ 462-3483; fax 462-7787); at Halcyon Cove Beach Resort on Dickenson Beach.

Dockyard Divers, PO Box 184 (☎ 460-1178; fax 460-1179); at Nelson's Dockyard.

Jolly Dive, PO Box 744 (☎ & fax 462-8305); at Jolly Harbour.

The going rate is about US$40 for a one-tank dive, US$60 for a two-tank dive and US$50 for a night dive. All four dive shops provide certification courses for about US$375. They also offer a one-day resort course that includes a reef dive – the cost is US$65 at Dive Runaway, US$99 at Dockyard Divers and US$75 at the other two shops.

## Snorkelling

Dive Runaway takes snorkellers out with divers for just US$10, plus US$10 to rent the snorkel equipment if you don't have your own. It's best to pick a day when they are going to the *Jettias* wreck, but that shouldn't be too hard to do as it's one of their more popular dives. Dockyard Divers takes snorkellers out for US$16 which includes gear, while Dive Antigua charges US$20. For snorkelling from the shore, the wreck of the *Andes* near the Royal Antiguan Hotel and the reef fronting nearby Hawksbill Beach are popular spots. For information on snorkelling with glass bottom boat tours, see Tours in the Getting Around section of this chapter.

## Windsurfing

The sheltered west coast is best for beginners, while the open east coast has conditions more suitable for advanced windsurfers.

At Dickenson Bay, Patrick's Windsurfing School (☎ 462-0256, extension 217) in front of Halcyon Cove Beach Resort gives two-hour lessons for US$40.

The Lord Nelson Beach Hotel (☎ 462-3094) on Dutchman's Bay at the north-east side of Antigua has a windsurfing school for more advanced windsurfers.

### Fishing

Shorty's Water Activities (☎ 462-3626) at Dickenson Bay offers a deep-sea fishing trip from 8 am to noon for US$180. The tourist office can provide a list of other deep-sea fishing boats, most of which charge US$450 for a half day.

### Tennis

There are tennis courts at many larger resort hotels and occasional competitions at Half Moon Bay, St James Club and Curtain Bluff hotels. Temo Sports complex, on the south side of Falmouth Harbour, has two lit tennis courts as well as squash courts.

### Golf

The Cedar Valley Golf Club (☎ 462-0161), a 10-minute drive north of St John's, has an 18-hole, par 70 course, and Half Moon Bay Hotel (☎ 460-4300) has a nine-hole course. Both rent carts and other equipment.

### HIGHLIGHTS

There are a couple of places in Antigua that are heavily laden with colonial atmosphere – Nelson's Dockyard is a special place that shouldn't be missed. The Sunday barbecue at Shirley Heights is lots of fun and the setting and view are superb. And then of course there are the beautiful beaches and good snorkelling and diving.

### ACCOMMODATION

There's not a great deal of inexpensive accommodation on Antigua; rather dreary guesthouses in St John's comprise most of the bottom-end places. There are a few good-value, moderate-range places around the island, with prices beginning at about US$60 a double in summer, closer to US$100 in winter. Still, most of what Antigua has to offer is easily priced at double that.

Top-end resorts average about US$300 in winter for 'standard' rooms – and many of these rooms really are quite standard despite the price. For better amenities, more space or

an ocean view, guests often have to step up to a more expensive room category.

If you plan on travelling in late summer keep in mind that many of Antigua's hotels close for the month of September and some extend that a few weeks in either direction.

On top of the rates given throughout this chapter, a 7% government tax and 10% service charge is added to accommodation bills.

### FOOD

There's a fairly good range of West Indian, French, Italian, English and North American food around the island. Most restaurants feature fresh seafood, with the catch of the day commonly being one of the better value options.

For a good cheap local snack, order a roti, the West Indian version of a burrito that's filled with curried potatoes, chicken or beef.

Try one of the locally grown black pineapples, which are quite sweet, rather small and, despite the name, not at all black.

### DRINKS

When it's working, the island's desalination plant provides most of Antigua's water supply. If the water source where you're staying comes from catchment it should be treated before drinking.

Cavalier and English Harbour rums are made locally.

### ENTERTAINMENT

Two of the nicest music scenes are at Miller's by the Sea on Dickenson Bay, where you can catch live jazz and reggae performances, and at Shirley Heights Lookout, above English Harbour, which has steel band music and reggae. Many restaurants and hotels schedule live music a few days a week; ask at the tourist office for the latest *Antiguan Nights*, a weekly entertainment calendar.

There are three casinos on Antigua: at Heritage Quay in St John's, at the Royal Antiguan hotel west of St John's and at the St James Club on the south-east side of the island.

## THINGS TO BUY

There's a small handicraft centre in St John's next to the tourist office. Caribelle Batiks in St John's sells quality Caribbean-made wall hangings and clothing.

The Art Centre, near Limey's at Nelson's Dockyard, sells local art and inexpensive prints. T-shirts, jewellery and other souvenirs are sold by vendors at Dickenson Bay, at the entrance to Nelson's Dockyard and in St John's along the road between the two quays.

You can buy 'duty-free' liquor at Heritage Quay or the airport departure lounge, with Johnny Walker Red selling for US$13 and Antiguan rum for US$5. Rum can also be bought in local shops around the island for the same price.

# Getting There & Away

### AIR
### To/From the USA
American Airlines (☎ 462-0952) has three daily flights between Antigua and San Juan that connect with direct flights to Boston, New York and Miami. Fares depend on the season, but from the US east coast they generally begin at around US$450 return for a ticket allowing stays of up to 30 days.

BWIA (☎ 462-0262) has daily nonstop flights to Antigua from New York and Miami and offers fares competitive with those of American Airlines.

### To/From Canada
BWIA flies three times a week between Toronto and Antigua, charging C$579. Tickets must be purchased 14 days in advance and allow a 21-day maximum stay. On days they don't fly direct to Antigua, you can fly BWIA to Barbados and connect with LIAT on to Antigua at the same fare for weekday travel, slightly higher on weekends.

### To/From the UK
British Airways (☎ 462-0876) has direct flights from London on Wednesday, Thursday, Saturday and Sunday. Fares vary a bit with the season but are around US$1100 (£685) for a 21-day advance purchase ticket allowing stays of up to six months.

### To/From Europe
Lufthansa (☎ 462-0983) has Tuesday and Friday flights from Frankfurt with a regular one-way fare of US$1382, a 90-day return fare of US$1922.

### Within the Caribbean
As LIAT is home-based in Antigua, there are either direct or connecting flights from Antigua to all destinations in LIAT's network.

LIAT flights from Antigua to Montserrat cost US$66 return; to St Kitts US$53 one way, US$97 return; to St Martin US$80 one way, US$94 for same-day return and US$144 for 21-day return; to Martinique (stops allowed in Dominica and Guadeloupe) US$204 for a 30-day return ticket. For same-day excursions to other islands see the Tours section of this chapter.

The LIAT ticketing and reservation office (☎ 462-0700) is at the airport, tucked behind the American Airlines check-in counter. It's open from 6.15 am to 6 pm daily.

### Airport Information
Travellers island hopping through the Eastern Caribbean can expect to do some transiting through Antigua's V C Bird International Airport, a rather poorly designed facility.

Despite there being a transit door directly from the tarmac to the departure lounge, transit passengers are forced to walk past it, recheck in at a transit booth and then clear security (and the baggage X-ray machine) before entering the departure lounge.

The departure lounge has a couple of souvenir and duty-free liquor shops and coin and card phones. The bar sells drinks but not food, and security will generally not allow transit passengers to visit the restaurant on the 2nd floor – noteworthy because there are sometimes long layovers on LIAT connections.

Those not in transit will find a tourist information booth between immigration and customs. The staff distributes maps and brochures and can help with booking rooms. Outside the arrivals exit, there are agents for a dozen car rental companies. Nearby is a post office and an exchange bank that's open from 9 am to 3 pm Monday to Friday and from 1.30 to 7.30 pm on Saturday. One of the three phones marked 'card' at the right of the airline ticket counters is a coin phone.

**To/From the Airport** There are taxis and car rentals at the airport (see the Getting Around section below), but there's no airport bus service.

### SEA
### Yacht
Yachts can clear customs at Nelson's Dockyard in English Harbour (VHF channel 16; for more information see under English Harbour later in this chapter); at the Deep Water Harbour at the north side of St John's; and at Crabbs Marina in Parham Sound. In the future Jolly Harbour expects to be added to the list. If you're going on to Barbuda ask for a cruising permit, which will allow you to visit that island without further formalities.

Antigua has many protected harbours and bays and fine anchorages are found all around the island. Full-service marinas are located at English Harbour, Falmouth Harbour, Jolly Harbour and Parham Sound.

Boaters can make reservations at many restaurants around Falmouth Harbour and English Harbour via VHF channel 68.

Yacht charters can be arranged through Sun Yacht Charters (☎ 460-2615) at English Harbour.

### Cruise Ship
Antigua is a port of call for numerous cruise ships. The island's new cruise ship terminal, at Heritage Quay in St John's Harbour, has a duty-free shopping centre and a casino. Heritage Quay is within easy walking distance of

St John's main sites: the museum, cathedral and historic Redcliffe Quay.

### LEAVING ANTIGUA & BARBUDA
There's an EC$25 departure tax.

# Getting Around

Finding your way around is difficult on Antigua. Virtually none of the roads are posted other than by private signs pointing the way to restaurants, hotels and a few other tourist spots. Beyond that the best landmarks are windmills, which are shown on the Ordnance Survey map of Antigua – a very handy item to have if you intend to do any exploring.

### BUS
Antigua's buses are privately owned and are predominantly minivans, although there are a few mid-sized buses as well. Buses from St John's to Falmouth and English Harbour are plentiful, cost EC$2 and take about 30 minutes. They start early and generally run until about 7 pm. Rush hour is particularly bustling, with lots of buses between 4 and 5 pm. There are very few buses on Sunday.

The main bus station in St John's is opposite the public market. Buses line up two or three across, all competing by revving up their engines and pretending to be on the verge of leaving so passengers will pile in – however, most buses don't actually leave until they're full.

Buses to Old Road also leave from St John's market.

Buses to the east side of the island leave from the East Bus Station, near the corner of Independence Ave and High St, and go to Piggots and Willikies.

There's no bus service to the airport, Dickenson Bay or other resort areas on the northern part of the island.

### TAXI
Taxi fares are regulated by the government, but confirm the fare with the driver before

riding away. Fares from the airport are: US$7 to St John's, US$11 to Runaway Bay or Dickenson Bay, US$16 to Jolly Harbour and US$21 to English Harbour.

From Nelson's Dockyard at English Harbour, taxi fares are US$20 to St John's, US$25 to Runaway Bay.

In St John's there's a taxi stand opposite the public market and taxi drivers also hang around Heritage Quay. Most hotels have taxis assigned to them; if you don't find one, ask at reception.

## CAR & MOTORBIKE
### Road Rules
To drive on Antigua you need to buy a temporary 90-day licence, which is usually obtainable from car rental agents but can also be picked up at the Inland Revenue Department on Newgate St in St John's. Simply show your home licence and dish out EC$30.

Driving is on the left. Many rental cars have steering wheels on the left, which can be disorienting.

Antigua has some of the most potholed roads in the Eastern Caribbean. Even the newer roads aren't maintained and can surprise you with unexpected craters.

Be aware of goats darting across the road and of narrow roads in built-up areas which can be crowded with children after school gets out.

The speed limit is generally 20 mph in villages and 40 mph in rural areas. There are numerous petrol stations scattered around the island, including one just outside the airport terminal. Petrol sells for EC$5.70 per gallon.

### Rental
There are more than a dozen car rental agencies on Antigua, most with representatives at the airport. Avis and Budget have cars from about US$40 a day, Hertz and Dollar from about US$50, and the local agencies have similar rates.

In part due to the poor condition of roads, all but the newest cars are generally quite beat. Your best bet (though not a sure bet) on getting a roadworthy car is to book with one of the international agencies. Most car rental firms will deliver cars to your hotel free of charge.

Local numbers include:

| | |
|---|---|
| Avis | – ☎ 462-2840 |
| Budget | – ☎ 462-3009 |
| Capital Rentals | – ☎ 462-0863 |
| Dollar | – ☎ 462-0362; |
| at Jolly Harbour | – ☎ 462-1048 or VHF 14 |
| Hertz | – ☎ 462-4114 |
| Jacobs Rent-A-Car | – ☎ 461-0399 |
| National Car Rental | – ☎ 462-2113 |
| United Rent-A-Car | – ☎ 462-3021 |

### BICYCLE
Sun Cycles (☎ 461-0324), Nelson Drive, Hodges Bay, rents mountain bikes for US$15 the first day and US$10 for each additional day and will deliver and pick up at no extra charge.

The marina office at Jolly Harbour also rents bicycles.

### TOURS
#### Air Tours
LIAT (☎ 462-0818) offers day-tour packages from Antigua to Montserrat or Nevis for US$125, to St Kitts for US$130, to Dominica for US$165 and to Guadeloupe for US$175, each including airfare, a guided sightseeing tour and lunch.

#### Land Tours
Touring the island by taxi costs about US$75 per car for a half-day tour that takes in Nelson's Dockyard and Shirley Heights or US$140 for a full-day tour.

#### Boat Tours
Tony's Glass Bottom Boat (☎ 461-5705 or 462-0256 extension 217), on the beach fronting Halcyon Cove Beach Resort at Dickenson Bay, has a two-hour snorkelling trip to the shallow waters of Paradise Reef at 10 am, noon and 2 pm. It costs US$20 including equipment and drinks.

Shorty's Water Activities (☎ 462-3626), near Millers by the Sea at Dickenson Bay, has a similar glass bottom boat trip with

ANTIGUA

similar prices and tour times. Shorty's also makes a day trip to Bird Island, a small volcanic island a few km off the north-east coast of Antigua, at 10 am on Tuesday and Friday for US$55.

Wadadli Watersports (☎ 462-2980) offers a number of catamaran trips, including one that has snorkelling time at Cades Reef and another at Bird Island. Both trips include lunch, cost US$60 and pick up guests at Dickenson Bay, the Royal Antiguan hotel and Jolly Beach.

The Jolly Roger 'pirate ship' (☎ 462-2064) is a party boat that leaves from Buccaneer Cove at Dickenson Bay and offers a day trip of snorkelling, plank-walking and rope swinging for US$45.

There are numerous other small companies that offer various day sails for around US$50 to US$75 and advertise with flyers and in the tourist magazines.

# St John's

St John's, Antigua's capital and commercial centre, has a population of about 30,000,

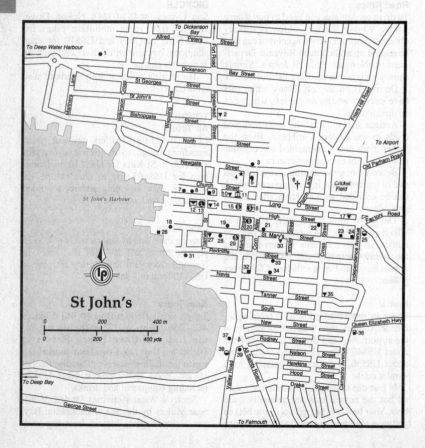

making it home to more than a third of the island's residents.

Most of the town's tourist activity is centred around two harbourfront complexes, Heritage Quay and Redcliffe Quay, which are a few minutes' walk apart along a street lined with sidewalk vendors.

Heritage Quay, where cruise ship passengers disembark, is a modern complex with a

casino, a hotel, a couple of restaurants and a few dozen duty-free shops selling designer clothing, perfumes, cameras and liquor.

Much more engaging is Redcliffe Quay, where a cluster of period stone buildings and wooden huts have been restored to house gift shops, art galleries and restaurants. Redcliffe Quay appeals to both islanders and tourists and is a popular spot for lunch.

Most of the rest of St John's is largely unaffected by tourism and remains solidly West Indian in flavour. The town centre is a rather bustling scene, with shoppers making the rounds, taxis crowding narrow roads and businesspeople rushing to and from work. St John's also has depressed corners with deep poverty.

### Information

**Tourist Office** The tourist office, on Thames St, is open from 8 am to 4.30 pm Monday to Thursday, until 3 pm on Friday.

**Money** The Bureau de Change at Heritage Quay exchanges US dollars and travellers' cheques at the same rate as the banks, but without any fees. It's open from 9 am to 4 pm Monday to Friday, until 2 pm on Saturday.

The Royal Bank of Canada on Market St doesn't charge a commission on US dollar travellers' cheques if the amount being exchanged is over EC$1000, but charges EC$5 for amounts under that. It's open from 8 am to 3 pm Monday to Thursday, until 5 pm on Friday.

**Post** The post office, at the west end of Long St, is open weekdays from 8.15 am to noon and 1 to 4 pm, except on Friday when it closes at 5 pm.

**Telecommunications** Cable & Wireless on St Mary's St sells phonecards and is open from 8 am to 6 pm Monday to Friday, until noon on Saturday.

**Bookshops** The Map Shop on St Mary's St sells Caribbean charts, survey maps of

Antigua & Barbuda and other Caribbean islands as well as books on Caribbean history, culture, birds, flowers etc. It's open from 9 am to 5 pm weekdays, until 2 pm on Saturday.

### Museum of Antigua & Barbuda

The Museum of Antigua & Barbuda, on the corner of Market and Long Sts, occupies the old courthouse, a stone building that dates from 1750. The museum has a rather eclectic collection of displays on island history. There's a touchable section with stone pestles and conch shell tools, a reconstructed Arawak house and modest displays on natural history, the colonial era and the struggle for emancipation. It's open from 8.30 am to 4 pm Monday to Thursday, until 3 pm on Friday, and from 10 am to 2 pm on Saturday. Admission is free but an EC$5 donation is encouraged.

### St John's Anglican Cathedral

The twin-spired St John's Anglican Cathedral is the town's most dominant landmark. The original church dated to 1682 but the current stone structure was erected in 1843, following a devastating earthquake. The interior of the cathedral can be viewed when the caretaker is around, which is usually until 5 pm. At the south side of the cathedral are interesting old moss-covered tombstones, many dating from the 1700s.

### Fort James

Fort James, a small fort at the north side of St John's Harbour, was first built in 1675, but most of the present structure dates from 1739. It still has a few of its original 36 cannons, a powder magazine and a fair portion of its walls intact. A couple of islanders are in the process of turning a section at the north end of the fort into an informal restaurant and bar.

Fort Bay, which stretches north from the fort, is the closest beach to St John's and is thus popular with islanders.

### Places to Stay

The *Palm View Guest House* (☎ 462-1299),

57 St Mary's St, has three very simple, clean rooms upstairs in an elderly couple's home. Rooms are large with private baths and mosquito nets and guests share a sitting room and kitchen. It's a good value at US$15 per person and a nice opportunity to put your money directly into the local economy.

Another guesthouse is the four-room *Roslyn's Guest House* (☎ 462-0762), about a 15-minute walk north of town on Fort Rd, which has singles/doubles for US$35/45.

*Joe Mike's Hotel Plaza* (☎ 462-1142; fax 462-1187), PO Box 136, on the corner of Corn Alley & Nevis St, is an older in-town hotel. Rooms are rather basic, but are clean and have air-con, phone and either a double bed or two twin beds. Singles/doubles cost US$45/50 year-round.

Another option might be the *Spanish Main Inn* (☎ 462-0660), an older two-storey wooden building on the heavily trafficked Independence Ave. It's been undergoing renovations but should reopen soon with moderate prices.

The best rooms in town are at the *Heritage Hotel* (☎ 462-1247; fax 462-2262) at Heritage Quay. There are 22 huge, modern flats, each with a full kitchen, cable TV, phone, thermostatic air-con, bathtub, bedroom with two double beds and a living room with two couches, one of them a sofabed. Some units have scenic harbourside verandahs, however, the harbour has a pollution problem and the waters can get a bit odoriferous. While geared for businesspeople, this hotel could also be convenient for a family. Singles/doubles cost US$90/120 throughout the year.

### Places to Eat

**Redcliffe Quay** The *Curry House*, in one of the huts at the west side of Redcliffe Quay, makes very nice vegetarian, chicken or beef rotis for EC$9, conch or shrimp rotis for a dollar more. It's open from 10 am to 6 pm Monday to Saturday. Also in a little hut is *The Quencher*, which has burgers and local dishes such as saltfish and bread for EC$6 and a daily lunch special for EC$10.

*Redcliffe Tavern*, in a nicely restored brick building, is quite a trendy lunch spot. The varied menu includes quiche and salad or a barbecue chicken platter for EC$22 and a smoked salmon salad for EC$38. There's also a deli-style takeaway window at the back. It's open from 8 am to 11.30 pm Monday to Saturday.

*Pizzas on the Quay* is a locally popular restaurant serving rather ordinary pizzas from EC$34 to EC$56 as well as salads and sandwiches. It's open to 11 pm Monday to Saturday.

**Around Town** The *Pizza House* on the waterfront at Heritage Quay has chicken curry and grilled fish dishes for around EC$20, sandwiches for about half that price and pizza by the slice.

*China Restaurant* on St Mary's St has vegetarian dishes for EC$15 and an array of standard Chinese meat dishes for around EC$25. It's open from 11.30 am to 2.30 pm Monday to Saturday and from 6 to 11 pm nightly.

*Hemingway's*, at the west end of St Mary's St, has verandah dining on the 2nd floor of an attractive 19th-century West Indian building. At lunch, sandwiches average EC$17 while catch of the day is about double that. Dinner offerings range from vegetarian pasta for EC$24 to coconut shrimp or lobster for EC$60. It's open from 8 am to 5 pm on Monday, 8 am to 11 pm Tuesday to Saturday.

The *Lemon Tree*, on Long St just west of the museum, is a rather elegant restaurant that's quite popular if not always consistent. The varied menu includes burritos or vegetarian crêpes for EC$18 at lunch or dinner, while other dinner dishes range from flying fish for EC$25 to broiled lobster for EC$66. There's live jazz some nights. Across the street, *Brother B's* sells soul food and juices.

*Chez Pascal* (☎ 462-3232), on the corner of Cross and Tanner Sts, is a pleasant French restaurant operated by a family from Lyon. The à la carte menu features an array of seafood dishes averaging EC$65, as well as either rack of lamb or chateaubriand for two for EC$180. Traditional French appetisers,

soups and salads are priced from EC$20. It's open from 6 to 11 pm Tuesday to Saturday in summer, for lunch and dinner in winter.

*Kentucky Fried Chicken* is opposite the tourist office and open from 10.30 am to 11 pm, to midnight on weekends.

The *Golden Crust Bakery* on Long St has bakery products made without animal fats, chemicals or preservatives. *Galstron's Bakery* on Popeshead St has simple breads and pastries and is open from 6 am to 10 pm.

There are two adjacent supermarkets north of the post office: Brysons is better stocked while Dew's is open longer hours (8 am to 6 pm Monday to Thursday, until 10 pm on Friday and Saturday). Antigua's largest and most modern supermarket is Food City, on Dickenson Bay St about halfway to the Deep Water Harbour. Open daily from 7 am to 11 pm, it has a full deli and a bakery with tasty cinnamon rolls.

The public produce market at the south end of Market St is open from 6 am to 6 pm Monday to Saturday.

# Around Antigua

## RUNAWAY BAY

Runaway Bay is a quiet area with an attractive white-sand beach, calm waters, a dive shop and a handful of small hotels and restaurants. Those staying here who want more action often wander over to the adjacent Dickenson Bay. A channel dug a few years back for a marina project (which was halted after hitting rock) cuts off shoreline access between Runaway and Dickenson bays but it's just a short walk along the road between the two areas.

Pelicans dive for food in the inlet created by the new channel and also along Corbinson Point, the rocky outcrop at the north end of the bay. The point is the site of an old fort, but there's little left to see. A large salt pond stretches along the inland side of Runaway Bay and in the evening egrets come to roost at the pond's southern end.

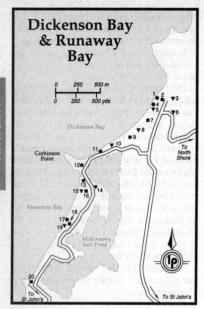

## Dickenson Bay & Runaway Bay

0   250   500 m
0   250   500 yds

*Dickenson Bay*

Corbinson Point

*Runaway Bay*

McKinnons Salt Pond

To North Shore

To St John's

**PLACES TO STAY**

2   Halcyon Cove Beach Resort
7   Sandals Antigua
9   Antigua Village
12  Marina Bay Beach Resort
13  Sunset Cove Resort
16  Barrymore Beach Club
18  Runaway Beach Club
20  Sand Haven Beach Hotel

**PLACES TO EAT**

2   Warri Pier & Arawak Terrace
3   Clouds
5   Millers by the Sea
6   Pari's Pizza
8   Spinnaker's
10  Coconut Grove
14  French Quarter
15  Frank's Strand Cafe
19  Lobster Pot

**OTHER**

1   Water Sports Booths
4   Shorty's Water Activities
11  Buccaneer Cove
17  Dive Runaway

## Places to Stay

*Sunset Cove Resort* (☎ 462-3762; fax 462-2684), PO Box 1262, is the best deal on the beach. This low-profile development has 33 modern units in two and three-storey buildings. Standard hotel rooms, which cost US$65/90 in summer/winter, have ceramic tile floors, rattan furnishings, tiny kitchenettes, nice balconies, TVs, air-con and ceiling fans. Ask for one of the top-floor units, which have high ceilings. Studio units, which cost US$85/110 in summer/winter for up to four people, have full kitchens and a living room that doubles as the bedroom, with a pull-down double bed and a queen-sized sofabed. One and two-bedroom units are also available. There's a pool.

The *Barrymore Beach Club* (☎ 462-4101; fax 462-4101; in the USA fax (800) 542-2779), PO Box 1774, is a smaller 36-room complex which is on a fine section of the beach. Cheapest are the hotel-style rooms, which are nice enough but still a bit expen-

sive, costing US$70/115 in summer/winter. One-bedroom apartments with kitchens cost from US$105/175, two-bedroom apartments from US$150/295. Units have screened louvred windows and ceiling fans but no air-con, TV or phone. The 2nd-floor units, which have raised wooden ceilings, are the best.

The largest hotel on Runaway Bay is *Runaway Beach Club* (☎ 462-1318; fax 462-4172; in the USA ☎ (800) 742-4276), PO Box 874, with 52 units. Standard rooms are good-sized but straightforward with twin or double beds, ceiling fans, showers and screened louvred windows; they cost from US$60/80 in summer/winter. Studio units, which have kitchenettes and balconies, cost from US$95/170, while two-bedroom units cost US$150/350.

*Sand Haven Beach Hotel* (☎ 463-4491), PO Box 405, is a small 14-unit hotel isolated at the south end of Runaway Bay. Because it's a bit out of the way, it's not a great choice if you don't have a car although there is a small restaurant on site. Prices are US$60 for standard rooms with two twin beds and US$80 to US$100 for a couple of larger family rooms. All have a terrace or balcony, ceiling fans and coffeemakers.

**Places to Eat**

The *French Quarter* is a somewhat upscale Creole restaurant with an interior resembling the ballroom of a 1920s hotel. The best value is the twilight dinner, offered from 5.30 to 7 pm, which comes with a starter, main course and dessert. The price depends on the main dish, ranging from pasta jambalaya (a nicely spiced dish of mixed vegetables, seafood and pasta) for EC$26 to leg of lamb for EC$50. It's open for dinner only, to 1 am nightly, with live jazz every night but Tuesday.

*Lobster Pot* (☎ 462-2855) at Runaway Beach Club has an appealing beachside setting and nice food although the service can be quite slow. The fresh salads (EC$18) are very good and the coconut curried chicken and shrimp (EC$55) is a tasty main dish. Fresh fish dishes cost from EC$45 (EC$30 at lunch) and come with a choice of preparations; skip the salsa topping, a bland mix of canned corn and diced tomatoes. Lobster Pot also serves a rather pricey breakfast and a varied, moderately priced lunch menu. At dinner, call ahead to reserve one of the waterfront tables.

The open-air *Frank's Strand Cafe* at the Barrymore Beach Club serves standard breakfast and lunch fare at moderate prices and has relatively inexpensive dinners ranging from spareribs for EC$23 to lobster for EC$62. Both curried chicken and wiener schnitzel are nicely prepared mid-range dishes. Wednesday dinners come with a complimentary salad bar, happy hour is from 4.30 to 6.30 pm daily and on some nights there's live entertainment.

**DICKENSON BAY**

Dickenson Bay is Antigua's main moderate-range resort area. Like neighbouring Runaway Bay, Dickenson Bay is fronted by a long sandy beach with turquoise waters and good swimming conditions.

All of Dickenson Bay's action is centred on the beach, where there are water sports booths, open-air restaurants and half a dozen hotels and condominiums. While it's much more touristy than Runaway Bay, it's not over touristed and can be a fun scene with live reggae music, vendors selling T-shirts and jewellery, and women braiding hair.

**Places to Stay**

*Marina Bay Beach Resort* (☎ 462-3254; fax 462-2151; in the USA ☎ (800) 223-6510) is a two and three-storey condo complex on the point separating the two bays. The 27 spacious one-bedroom units are sleek and contemporary with kitchens, air-con, cable TV, phone and balconies or patios. Singles/doubles cost US$75/125 in summer, US$120/175 in winter, and up to two children under 12 may stay for free.

*Antigua Village* (☎ 462-2930; fax 462-0375; in the USA and Canada ☎ (800) 742-4276), PO Box 649, is a large condominium complex, with 100 units spread around nicely landscaped grounds. Each is quite pleasant with cooking facilities, air-con, ceiling fans, and patios or balconies. It's a good value in summer, when studios cost US$95, one-bedroom apartments US$115 and two-bedroom apartments US$210. In winter it's a more pricey US$170/210/380 respectively. Add another 20% for a beach-front unit. There's a pool.

The 209-room *Halcyon Cove Beach Resort* (☎ 462-0256; fax 462-0271), PO Box 251, is a welcoming low-key beachfront resort hotel at the north end of Dickenson Bay. Five categories include fan-cooled standard rooms at US$84/168 in summer/winter and air-con oceanfront rooms at US$198/282. There are mid-range rates in November and January and steeply increased rates during the Christmas holidays. Rooms vary a bit even within a category, but all are spotlessly clean and most are quite pleasant. There's a pool and tennis courts and guests have free use of snorkelling gear, windsurfing equipment and pedal boats.

ANTIGUA

*Sandals Antigua* (☎ 462-0267) is a busy couples-only resort and a rather hyped scene in comparison to nearby Halcyon Cove. There are 149 rooms, four pools, a sauna and gym, three restaurants, tennis courts and various water sports. All-inclusive rates per couple start at US$1485/1760 in summer/winter for three nights. For EC$450 per couple, non-guests can use Sandals' facilities (including open bar and restaurants) from 10 am to 6 pm or for EC$250 from 6 pm to 2 am.

## Places to Eat

Halcyon Cove Beach Resort has two ocean-view restaurants that make fine spots for a sunset drink or dinner. The *Warri Pier* has a pleasant locale, set at the end of a private pier that juts out from the beach fronting the hotel. From noon to 10 pm daily, you can get a bowl of callaloo soup or a sandwich for EC$12 or warri (marlin), West Indian curry or catch of the day for EC$26. Prices include service and tax.

*Clouds*, on a steep hill above the hotel, opens for cocktails at 5.30 pm, dinner at 7.30 pm. This upscale restaurant has consistently good food. There's a shuttle service from the hotel lobby, where the daily set menu (around US$32) is posted.

Halcyon Cove's third restaurant, *Arawak Terrace*, has a daily breakfast buffet (7 to 11 am) where you can fill up on continental fare for EC$22 or choose from the full table which includes hot dishes for EC$30.

*Millers by the Sea* (☎ 462-2393) is a local beachside restaurant with good food, friendly service and live music (often reggae or jazz) at noon and dinnertime daily. Western-style breakfasts average EC$15. The Creole fish is a nice dish at lunch for EC$18, at dinner for EC$25. Other offerings include burgers, curried conch, shrimp scampi and grilled lobster. Every Thursday there's a buffet barbecue with grilled steaks, ribs and lobster for EC$65. Happy hour, from 5 to 7 pm weekdays, features two-for-one drinks.

*Pari's Pizza* (☎ 462-1501), about 200 metres east of Halcyon Cove on the inland road, is locally popular for takeaway pizza. Cheese pizzas cost from EC$22 (small) to EC$36 (extra large), plus a few dollars more for each topping. You can also eat in or have your pizza delivered. Pari's is open from 5.30 to 11.30 pm daily except Monday.

*Spinnaker's*, near Sandals, is a very pleasant restaurant on the beach. Breakfast, served until 10.30 am, features the usual fare at reasonable prices and a bottomless cup of coffee for EC$3. At lunch, from 11 am to 5.30 pm, you can get salads, sandwiches and omelettes for around EC$20 or a few hot seafood dishes for EC$35. At dinner (6.30 to 10.30 pm) there are three vegetarian options for EC$30, while steak, red snapper or jumbo shrimp, all served with a side salad, are double that price.

*Coconut Grove* is another casual beach-front restaurant with moderately priced breakfasts and lunchtime sandwiches. At dinner, seafood dishes range from catch of the day for EC$50 to lobster for EC$70. There's a piano player or other entertainment a few nights a week.

There's a very small grocery store at Antigua Village that's open from 8.30 am to 7 pm daily.

## NORTH SHORE

The northern part of the island between Dickenson Bay and the airport has the island's most well-to-do residential areas, a golf course, some exclusive villa developments and two small resorts.

## Places to Stay

The secluded, British-run *Blue Waters Beach Hotel* (☎ 462-0290; fax 462-0293; in the USA ☎ (800) 372-1323, in the UK (081) 367-5175), PO Box 256, is on a nice little sandy beach at Blue Waters Bay. There are 46 air-con rooms and eight villas in condo-like two-storey buildings, with private balconies, minibars, phones and room safes. Single/double rates for standard rooms are US$120/140 in summer, US$200/235 in winter, while roomy one-bedroom villas rent for US$270 in summer, US$430 in winter.

Rates include use of windsurfing equipment, snorkelling gear, sailboats and tennis.

The *Hodges Bay Club* (☎ 462-2300; fax 462-1962; in the USA ☎ (800) 432-4229), PO Box 1327, is a new upscale villa-style resort on a sandy beach near Beggars Point. Units are modern with full kitchens, cathedral ceilings, air-con, cable TV, phones and terraces or balconies. Rates for ocean-view one-bedroom units are US$170/300 in summer/winter, two-bedroom units start at US$225/400. Due to low occupancy, the resort sometimes offers a US$50 reduction on nightly rates in summer to guests staying three nights or more. There's a pool, tennis courts and complimentary sailing, windsurfing and snorkelling gear.

### Places to Eat

*Le Bistro* (☎ 462-3881) is a well-regarded restaurant serving traditional French food. Snapper, grilled lobster and a number of meat dishes are priced around EC$65, while hors d'oeuvres are about half that. It's open for dinner only, closed on Monday (and in June and July) and reservations are required. Le Bistro is about a third of a mile (500 metres) south of Beggars Point and just a bit inland from the main road; a sign marks the turn-off.

The Blue Waters Beach Hotel's *Garden Restaurant* has a nice ocean view and serves continental breakfast for EC$16 or a reasonably good breakfast buffet with the likes of bacon, eggs, fruit, yoghurt, croissants and juice for EC$32. At dinner there's a barbecue on Tuesday, a West Indian buffet on Friday and a fixed-price (EC$95) table d'hôte dinner on other nights.

The *Pelican Club* has an upmarket setting right on the waterfront at the Hodges Bay Club. Full breakfasts and lunchtime salads, sandwiches and burgers average about EC$30. At dinner, pasta, fish and chicken dishes start at EC$40, while surf and turf costs EC$74.

### AROUND THE AIRPORT

There are no real sights around the airport and it's certainly not a prime tourist destination, but there are four relatively inexpensive places to stay, two just outside the airport and two others on small beaches a mile (1.6 km) north of the runway.

### Places to Stay

The *Airport Hotel* (☎ 462-1192; fax 462-0926), PO Box 700, is a concrete motel-style place next to the West Indies petrol station, about a 10-minute walk from the airport terminal. The rooms are quite simple but have TV and the hotel provides free transport to and from the airport. Singles/doubles cost US$45/65 year-round.

Also motel style but spiffier is the *Antigua Sugar Mill Hotel* (☎ 462-3044; fax 462-1500), PO Box 319, half a mile (800 metres) from the airport terminal, north along the main road. There are 22 rooms with air-con, cable TV and phone and the grounds have a pool and the remains of a sugar mill. Single/double standard rooms cost US$50/60 in summer, US$70/80 in winter.

The *Lord Nelson Beach Hotel* (☎ 462-3094; fax 462-0751), PO Box 155, is an unpretentious family-run operation with 16 simple ocean-fronting rooms right on the beach at Dutchman's Bay. There's a windsurfing school here and scuba diving can also be arranged. Singles/doubles cost US$55/65 in summer, US$72/95 in winter.

The *Antigua Beachcomber Hotel* (☎ 462-3100), PO Box 10, on Winthorpes Bay, is 500 metres south of Lord Nelson Beach Hotel, although a small headland topped with an oil depot separates the two. Rooms are in two-storey motel-style row buildings and are on par with those of a mid-range motel. Singles/doubles cost US$60/80 in summer, US$80/100 in winter. Although it's not the most pristine of locations there is a little sandy beach.

### Places to Eat

Dining in this area is largely limited to the restaurants in the four hotels, with the most extensive menu at the *Antigua Beachcomber*. You can also get moderately priced sandwiches, omelettes and other simple eats from 7 am to 10 pm daily at the *Lord Nelson*

*Restaurant* on the 2nd floor of the airport terminal.

## DEEP BAY

Deep Bay, west of St John's, is a pleasant little bay with a sandy beach and protected waters. The Royal Antiguan hotel sits above the beach and there's a fair amount of resort activity, but it's a good-sized strand and a nice swimming spot.

The coral-encrusted wreck of the *Andes* lies in the middle of the bay, its mast reaching almost a metre above water. Nearly 100 years have passed since this barque caught fire and went down, complete with a load of pitch from Trinidad. It's shallow enough to be snorkelled but divers tend to bypass it as ooze still kicks up pretty easily from the bottom.

The remains of **Fort Barrington**, which once protected the southern entrance of St John's Harbour, is atop the promontory that juts out at the northern end of the bay. Originally constructed in the mid-17th century, most of the present fortifications date to 1779. To hike up to the fort, simply begin walking north along the beach at Deep Bay; the trail takes about 10 minutes.

A salt pond separates Deep Bay from the smaller Hog John Bay, where there's another sandy beach and a couple of hotels.

### Places to Stay

*Pillar Rock* (☎ 462-2326; fax 462-2327; in the USA and Canada ☎ (800) 223-9815), PO Box 1226, on Hog John Bay, is a 30-unit complex with a bit of Mediterranean flavour. There are one-bedroom villas with kitchens, living rooms and separate bedrooms that rent for US$200/250 in summer/winter, or you can rent just a room for US$100/130. All units have ceiling fans and air-con.

*Yepton Beach Resort* (☎ 462-2520; in the USA ☎ (800) 361-4621), PO Box 1427, on Hog John Bay, has 38 modern air-con units with ocean-fronting balconies or patios. Studios are spacious with full kitchens and living rooms and cost US$150/220 in summer/winter. Hotel-style rooms cost US$110/170 and one and two-bedroom

apartments are also available. This pleasant little resort has complimentary windsurfing, sailing, snorkelling and tennis.

With nine stories and 282 rooms, the *Royal Antiguan*, a member of the Ramada Renaissance chain (☎ 462-3733; fax 462-3732), PO Box 1322, on Deep Bay, is the island's only high-rise resort. It has a casino, a free-form pool, eight tennis courts and a pro shop, a dive shop and complimentary use of windsurfing equipment, kayaks and snorkelling gear. Rooms are comfortable and well appointed, each with a TV, VCR, phone, minibar, bathtub and central air-con. Rates for standard rooms are US$110/175 in summer/winter, while ocean-view rooms with balconies cost US$160/250. There's a daily shuttle (US$6 return) to St John's. Reservations can be made worldwide through Ramada (in the USA ☎ (800) 228-9898).

Less than two miles (3.2 km) south of the Royal Antiguan is the *Hawksbill Beach Resort* (☎ 462-0301; fax 462-1515; in the USA ☎ (800) 223-6510), PO Box 108, a rather exclusive place that encompasses a couple of nice secluded beaches. A noteworthy geological feature is the offshore rock shaped like a hawk's head, for which the beach and resort are named. There are 88 rooms, ranging from pleasant cottages to more traditional two-storey buildings. Rates for singles/doubles begin at US$131/168 in summer, US$247/299 in winter, with breakfast included. The resort has an expensive restaurant, a pool, a tennis court and the usual water sports.

### Places to Eat

*The Pavilion* (☎ 462-2325) at Pillar Rock is one of the better value places in the area, with a variety of pastas and pizzas from US$10 to US$13.

Yepton Beach Resort's *Patio Caribe* has burgers, salads and fish & chips from US$7 to US$10 from noon to 2 pm.

The Royal Antiguan has a few dining options: the beachside *Andes* is primarily a lunch spot with US$10 burgers and similar fare; the *Lagoon Cafe* has a typical hotel menu with US$7 sandwiches and hot meals for about double that and there's a fancier dinner restaurant.

## JOLLY HARBOUR

Jolly Harbour is a new marina and dockside condominium village on Antigua's west coast. Marina facilities include a pharmacy, supermarket, liquor store, small camera shop, La Marine boat rentals and charters, restaurants and handicraft, beachwear and gift shops. The Swiss American Bank sells phonecards, changes travellers' cheques free of charge, and is open from 9 am to 12.30 pm and 1.30 to 3 pm weekdays. The Flower Basket carries international newspapers and magazines and rents videos. There are free-use showers in the main complex.

Boaters will find 150 slips (some which can accommodate boats up to 60-metres long), fuel facilities, 30/50/100 amps 110/220 volt power and a boat yard with a 70-tonne lift and repair facilities.

There's a nice white-sand beach south of the marina at Club Antigua.

### Places to Stay

*Jolly Harbour Beach Resort* (☎ 462-6166; fax 462-6167), PO Box 1793, is a large complex with rows of condos built on artificial breakwaters. Each unit is townhouse-style, the downstairs with a full kitchen, living/dining room and a terrace that looks out onto a private boat mooring. Upstairs are two bedrooms (one with a double bed, the other with two twins), two bathrooms and a balcony. Plans call for more than 1000 units to be built, which will be sold to individuals who can opt to put them in a rental pool. In part because it's new and a bit disrupted by continuing construction, the rates are a bargain at US$60 for up to two people, US$15 for each additional person. Monthly rates of US$700 are available. Facilities include a swimming pool, tennis courts and a planned 18-hole golf course.

*Club Antigua* (☎ 462-0061; fax 462-1827; in the USA and Canada ☎ (800) 777-1250), PO Box 744, is a bustling all-inclusive 427-room beachfront resort. Singles/doubles cost US$105/210 in summer, US$209/286 in winter, including all food, drinks, water sports, tennis and entertainment (other than the slot machines). For US$70 non-guests can use the resort facilities, including food and drinks, from 10 am until the disco closes, or pay US$40 for a half day.

### Places to Eat

The most popular restaurant at the marina is *Al Porto*, a busy place with good pizza and pasta dishes in the EC$20 to EC$30 range and pricier meat dishes. Lunch is served daily from noon to 3 pm, dinner from 7 to 10 pm and there's a happy hour from 6 to 7 pm. The *Harbour Cafe* has a varied menu that includes French, Spanish and Brazilian dishes from EC$35 to EC$65, plus moderately priced lunchtime sandwiches. Both restaurants have open-air harbourfront dining as well as indoor seating.

The marina's PJ's Supermarket & Deli sells sandwiches or half a barbecued chicken for EC$10. It's open from 9 am to 6 pm Monday to Saturday, noon to 4 pm on Sunday.

## DARKWOOD BEACH

Darkwood, an undeveloped roadside beach two miles (3.2 km) south of Jolly Harbour, is a pleasant strand with mounds of light sand chock-full of bits of shells and coral. The only development here is a bar with beachside picnic tables that serves reasonably priced breakfasts, burgers and a few hot dishes.

## JOHNSON'S POINT BEACH

Johnson's Point Beach, at the south-west corner of the island, is a fine stretch of white sand with a couple of good-value places to stay. Midway between St John's and English Harbour, it might suit some people who want to avoid the more touristed parts of the island without being totally secluded. It's not quite as out of the way as it seems, as buses (EC$1.50) go by about every half-hour (except on Sunday) on the way to St John's.

## Places to Stay

The *Blue Heron Hotel* (☎ 462-8564; fax 462-8005), PO Box 1715, is a quiet 40-room hotel right on the beach. Most of the units face the water; those on the upper floor have balconies, those on the ground level have patios. Rooms are suitably straightforward with queen-size beds and TV. The 10 standard rooms cost US$57/77 in summer/winter, while air-con superior rooms cost US$77/102, although all rates nearly double for a few weeks around the Christmas holidays. Guests can use sailing boats, windsurfing equipment and snorkel gear free of charge.

The *Golden Rock Beach Apartments* (☎ 462-1442) is a friendly, family-run operation in a simple two-storey building opposite the beach. There are six unpretentious rooms. The smallest rents for US$35/45 for singles/doubles in summer, US$45/60 in winter. The largest is a good-sized studio which in summer costs US$55 if you don't use the kitchen, US$75 if you do, and in winter costs US$90 regardless.

## Places to Eat

*Vienna Beach Bar* at Golden Rock Beach Apartments is a tiny restaurant open for three meals a day. At breakfast bacon & eggs cost EC$8. Hot meals include catch of the day (EC$27), lobster (EC$54) and a couple of Austrian and Greek specialities.

The restaurant at the *Blue Heron Hotel* serves a continental (EC$22) and full (EC$32) breakfast, while at lunch there are burgers, salads and sandwiches from about EC$15. Dinner features seafood main dishes beginning at EC$50.

## FIG TREE DRIVE

After Johnson's Point Beach, the road passes pineapple patches, tall century plants and pastures with grazing cattle and donkeys. There are high hills on the inland side of the road, topped by the 402-metre Boggy Peak, the island's highest point.

Old Road, a village with both a fair amount of poverty and the luxury Curtain Bluff hotel, marks the start of Fig Tree Drive. From here the terrain gets lusher as the road winds up through the hills. The narrow road is lined with bananas (called 'fig' in Antigua), coconut palms and big old mango trees. It's not jungle or rainforest, but it is refreshingly green and makes a pleasant rural drive. There are a couple of snack bars that sell fresh fruit and juices along the way.

Fig Tree Drive ends in the village of Swetes. On the way to Falmouth Harbour you'll pass through the village of Liberta and by the St Barnabus Anglican Chapel, an attractive green stone and brick church built in 1842.

## FALMOUTH HARBOUR

Falmouth Harbour is a large, protected, horseshoe-shaped bay. There are two main centres of activity: the north side of the harbour, where the small village of Falmouth is located, and the more visitor-oriented east side of the harbour, which has most of the restaurants. The east side of the harbour is about a 15-minute walk from Nelson's Dockyard.

## St Paul's Church

St Paul's Anglican Church, on the main road in Falmouth's centre, was Antigua's first church, established in 1676. In its early days the church doubled as the island's courthouse. If you poke around the overgrown churchyard you can find some interesting and quite readable gravestones. Charles Pitt, the brother of the English prime minister, was buried here in 1780, and beside his site is the excessively loquacious memorial to Brigadier General Andrew Dunlop, who died of yellow fever.

## Places to Stay

*Falmouth Harbour Beach Apartments* (☎ 460-1027; fax 460-1534), on the east side of Falmouth Harbour, has 28 studios in half a dozen two-storey buildings. The studios have verandahs or patios, full kitchens, two twin beds and ceiling fans, but no air-con or TV. Though the beach fronting the hotel isn't special, there's a nice beach about 10

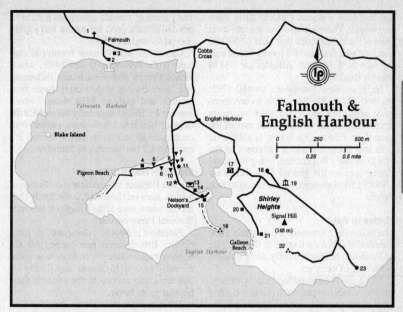

## Falmouth & English Harbour

0    250    500 m

0    0.25    0.5 mile

**ANTIGUA**

### PLACES TO STAY

2  Catamaran Hotel & Marina
3  Harbour View Apartments
4  Falmouth Harbour Beach Apartments
14  Admiral's Inn
15  Copper & Lumber Store Hotel
20  Inn at English Harbour
21  Galleon Beach Club

### PLACES TO EAT

5  G & T Pizza
6  Temo Sports Complex
7  Kwik Stop
8  La Perruche
9  Maracuja

10  Le Cape Horn
11  Carib Marine GroceryStore
22  Shirley Heights Lookout

### OTHER

1  St Paul's Anglican Church
5  Antigua Yacht Club
12  Police Station
13  Post Office & Entrance to Nelson'
    Dockyard
16  Fort Berkley
17  Clarence House
18  Dow's Hill Interpretation Centre
19  Shirley Heights Museum
22  Fort Shirley
23  Blockhouse Hill

minutes' walk to the east. Most singles/ doubles cost US$60/78 in summer, US$92/ 114 in winter. Beachfront rooms cost US$6 to US$12 more. The complex has the same management as the Admiral's Inn.

The *Catamaran Hotel & Marina* (☎ 460-

1036; fax 460-1506), PO Box 958, is on a little beach at the north side of Falmouth Harbour and has its own 30-berth marina. This pleasant 16-room hotel is one of the area's better value places. The deluxe rooms on the 2nd floor have four-poster queen beds and bathtubs and cost US$85/120 in summer/winter. There are also four ground-level units with kitchenettes that cost US$70/80 and four simpler standard rooms with standing fans for US$55/65. All rates are US$10 less for singles.

*Harbour View Apartments* (☎ 460-1762; fax 460-1871), PO Box 20, is a contemporary complex with six two-bedroom apartments on the beach a little east of the catamaran marina. Each unit is split level with two bedrooms and a bathroom on the 2nd floor and a full kitchen, living room and dining area on the ground floor. Rates are US$85/150 in summer/winter for up to four people.

### Places to Eat

The following restaurants are all within a few minutes' walk of each other at the east side of Falmouth Harbour, mostly along the road to Nelson's Dockyard.

*Maracuja* is a natural food café with inexpensive salads, crêpes, fresh juices and a few chalkboard specials such as eggplant parmesan for around EC$20. It's open from 8.30 am to 2.30 pm and 5.30 to 9 pm daily except Monday. *Kwik Stop*, next door, serves simple fare for breakfast, lunch and dinner with sandwiches, burgers and rotis costing about EC$10.

The restaurant at *Temo Sports* complex has a country club setting, cheap sandwiches and lunch specials like conch salad or barbecued ribs for EC$25.

The popular *G & T Pizza*, downstairs at the Antigua Yacht Club, has good pizzas costing from EC$31 to EC$52, simple salads and a pleasant casual setting with picnic tables on the waterfront. Food is served from noon to 10.30 pm, drinks until midnight, and there's a happy hour from 5 to 6 pm. It's closed on Tuesday.

*Le Cap Horn* (☎ 460-3336) has two sides: a pizzeria and a French restaurant. The pizzeria makes brick-oven pizza ranging from EC$26 for tomato and cheese to EC$34 for seafood, as well as pasta dishes and a meal of the day in the same price range. From 6 to 7 pm Monday to Friday, pizza is half price.

The French restaurant, open from 6.30 to 11 pm daily, has a good reputation and a daily special for about EC$50.

One of the island's more creative restaurants is *La Perruche* (☎ 460-3040), which blends French and West Indian influences and specialises in dishes using fresh local produce and seafood. Main dishes, which average EC$60, change daily but include the likes of blackened tuna with passion fruit chutney or lobster on spinach fettucine. It's open from 7 pm Monday to Saturday.

### ENGLISH HARBOUR

English Harbour has the richest collection of historic sites on the island; collectively they are the centrepiece of the Antigua & Barbuda National Parks system.

Foremost is Nelson's Dockyard, an 18th-century British naval base named for the English captain Horatio Nelson, who spent the early years of his career here. Today it's still attracting sailors as the island's most popular yacht haven.

There are also two hilltop forts flanking the entrance to the harbour, a couple of museums and an interpretation centre. You could easily spend the better part of a day roaming around the sites. Buses from St John's end right at Nelson's Dockyard, but you'd need a car to explore the Shirley Heights area on the opposite side of the harbour.

English Harbour is separated from Falmouth Harbour by a neck of land that at its narrowest is just a few hundred metres wide.

### Information

**Money** The Swiss American Bank opposite the Admiral's Inn exchanges US dollar travellers' cheques to EC currency free of charge. It's open weekdays from 9.15 am to 1 pm and 2 to 4 pm (to 5 pm on Friday) and on Saturday from 9.15 am to 1 pm.

**Post & Telecommunications** The post office at the entrance of Nelson's Dockyard is open from 8.15 am to noon and 1 to 3.45 pm Monday to Friday. You can buy phonecards next door at Cable & Wireless; there are card phones and one coin phone outside the office.

**For Boaters** The following facilities are all inside Nelson's Dockyard. The customs office, on the ground level of the old Officer's Quarters building at the south-east side of the marina, opens from 8.30 am to 3.30 pm daily but closes at noon for lunch. Lockers, south of the customs office, sells nautical charts. There are notices for crew wanted/available at Limey's and several other places around the dockyard. Showers (US$1) and laundry facilities (US$8 a load) are open from 6 am to 6 pm daily.

### Nelson's Dockyard

This historic dockyard is Antigua's most popular tourist sight as well as the island's main port of entry for yachts. The dockyard, which dates to 1743, was abandoned in 1899 following a decline in Antigua's economic and strategic importance to the British Crown.

Restoration work began in the 1950s and the former royal naval base now has a new life closely paralleling its old one – that of an active dockyard.

The handsome old brick and stone buildings have been converted into yachting and tourist-related facilities. Many duplicate the original use of the buildings. The bakery, for instance, was originally the officers' kitchen and still has the old stone hearth, while some of the hotel rooms that now house travellers were once used as quarters for sailors whose ships were being careened.

The dockyard is English Harbour's main centre of activity, with a small market selling T-shirts and souvenirs, a handful of restaurants, two inns, a couple of banks, a dive shop, a travel agency, a pharmacy and numerous boating facilities – all occupying old naval buildings. Take time to stop at the numerous interpretive plaques that explain the history of the various buildings.

Upon entering, pick up the free map that shows the dockyard sights and businesses. Admission costs EC$4 for adults, free for children under 12.

**Museum** The dockyard's small museum occupies a former officers' house and features an assorted collection of nautical memorabilia, including uniform buttons, clay pipes, rusty swords, muskets and cannonballs. Models of a mid-19th-century schooner and naval brig round off the display. The museum's small gift shop sells books and maps. Admission is free.

### Fort Berkley

A pleasant 10-minute stroll starting behind the Copper & Lumber Store Hotel leads to the site of this small fort, which overlooks the western entrance of English Harbour. The fort, dating to 1704, served as the harbour's first line of defence. You'll find intact walls, a powder magazine, a small guard house and a solitary cannon, the last of 25 cannons that once lined the fortress walls. There's also a fine harbour view at the top. The dirt path up is well maintained and passes lots of yucca and succulents, including tall dildo cactus and the stubby Turk's-head cactus, easily identified by its round red head.

### Clarence House

Clarence House, on the road to Shirley Heights, was built in 1786 for the Duke of Clarence, who later became King William IV. The ageing Georgian-style residence has period furnishings and is now used as the country residence of the governor. When the governor is not present, the caretaker gives tours, usually from 9 am to 3.30 pm weekdays and on Saturday mornings. There's no entry fee but a tip after the tour is appropriate.

### Shirley Heights

Shirley Heights is a fun place to explore with its scattered 18th-century fort ruins and wonderful hilltop views. A bit over a mile (1.6 km) up Shirley Heights Rd you'll find a modest museum in the old Royal Artillery Quarters and an interpretive centre featuring an audio-visual presentation (US$4).

For the best views and main concentration of ruins continue past the museum; the road will fork after about half a mile (800 metres).

The left fork leads shortly to Blockhouse Hill, where you'll find remains of the Officers' Quarters dating to 1787 and a clear-on view of sheltered Mamora Bay to the east. The right fork leads to Fort Shirley, which has more ruins, including one that's been turned into a casual restaurant and bar. There's a sweeping view of English Harbour from the rear of the restaurant while from the top of Signal Hill (148 metres), just a minute's walk from the parking lot, you can see Montserrat 45 km to the south-west and Guadeloupe 64 km to the south.

## Places to Stay

The *Admiral's Inn* (☎ 460-1027; fax 460-1534), PO Box 713, built as a warehouse in 1788, has 10 rooms above the restaurant in the original brick building and four rooms in a separate annexe. Rooms vary in size and decor and some are quite small. Room No 5 is larger and a good choice in the moderate category, while No 3, a quiet corner room with a ceiling fan and a fine harbour view, is recommended in the superior category; both have air-con and ceilings with hand-hewn open beams. In summer, singles/doubles cost US$62/76 for moderate rooms, US$66/84 for superior rooms. In winter, moderate rooms cost US$88/112, superior rooms US$94/124. Rates include the use of Sunfish sailing boats and snorkelling gear, and transport to nearby beaches. For reservations call: in the USA ☎ (800) 223-5695, in Canada (800) 387-8031, in the UK (081) 940-3399.

The *Copper & Lumber Store Hotel* (☎ 460-1058; fax 460-1529; in the USA ☎ (800) 633-7411, in the UK ☎ (0453) 835801) was built in the 1780s to store the copper and lumber needed for ship repairs. It now has 13 studios and suites, all with kitchens and ceiling fans. Rates range from US$160 to US$280 in winter, US$80 to US$140 in summer, the higher rates for those with antique furnishings.

The *Galleon Beach Club* (☎ 460-1024; fax 463-1450), PO Box 1003, is a quiet resort on Galleon Beach at the south-east side of English Harbour. Accommodation is in cottages spread along the beach. All 36 units have a kitchen, a deck and a living room with a sofabed. One-bedroom cottages cost US$135/230 in summer/winter and two-bedroom cottages cost US$170/290. Each bedroom sleeps two people and two more can sleep on the sofabed at no extra cost. There's an Italian restaurant on site, a couple of tennis courts and some water sports activities.

The *Inn at English Harbour* (☎ 460-1014; fax 460-1603; in the USA (☎ (800) 223-6510, in the UK (071) 730-7144), PO Box 187, is another small beach resort on the south-east side of English Harbour. Rooms are in two-storey buildings and are a bit on the small side but most have beachfront balconies. Rates include breakfast, dinner and water sports and begin at US$150/200 for singles/doubles in summer, US$270/340 in winter.

## Places to Eat

The *Dockyard Bakery*, behind the museum at Nelson's Dockyard, has good breads, guava danish, carrot cake and other pastries at reasonable prices. You can also get takeaway coffee (EC$1.50) and sip it under the 300-year-old sandbox tree that fronts the bakery. It's open from 7.30 am to 4 pm weekdays, until 3 pm on Friday.

*Limey's* is Nelson's Dockyard's cheapest meal spot, serving inexpensive diner-quality food. There's an indoor dining room but it's better to grab one of the picnic tables out on the balcony and enjoy the harbour view. Sandwiches cost EC$8, chicken & fries EC$12 and fresh fish is priced from EC$25. It's open until 6 pm in summer, until 10 pm in winter.

*Carib Marine* is a good little grocery store, a five-minute walk from the entrance to Nelson's Dockyard. It sells rounds of crispy brick-oven bread that's baked daily – with a slab of cheese it makes a good inexpensive lunch and there are picnic tables outside where you can eat. The store's small deli also makes sandwiches for EC$5. It's open from 8.30 am to 5 pm Monday to Saturday. The store sells liquor and ice and has its own dinghy dock.

The *Admiral's Inn* is open for three meals daily. The changing chalkboard menu usually has such things as salads, cheeseburgers and curried conch and rice for around EC$30 at lunch, while at dinner there are more elaborate dishes. There's both indoor dining and outdoor harbourfront tables.

The *Copper & Lumber Store Hotel* has a pub serving the likes of shepherds pie, chicken salad and barbecued spareribs & chips for EC$25. There's a happy hour from 6 to 8 pm with two-for-one drinks. The hotel also has a more formal restaurant, *The Wardroom*, which has an English breakfast for EC$28 and dinner at upmarket prices.

*Shirley Heights Lookout* (☎ 460-1785), in a vintage 1791 guard house at Fort Shirley, has a fantastic view of English Harbour and serves three meals a day at moderate prices. It's best known for its Sunday barbecues which are accompanied with steel band music from 3 to 6 pm and reggae from 6 to 9 pm, with lots of dancing towards the end of the evening. There's no admission fee, drinks are reasonably priced and a simple hamburger or chicken plate with salad costs EC$20, a rib plate EC$38. The barbecue and steel band music has also started up on a trial basis on Thursday from 3.30 to 8 pm. All in all it's one of the island's nicest scenes.

## HALF MOON BAY

Half Moon Bay, on the south-eastern side of the island, is a C-shaped bay with a beautiful white-sand beach and turquoise waters. It's largely undeveloped, though there's a hotel at the south side of the bay and a snack bar by the beach.

### Places to Stay

The *Half Moon Bay Hotel* (☎ 460-4300; fax 460-4306; in the USA ☎ (800) 223-6510), PO Box 144, is a 100-room resort on a rise overlooking the beach. Amenities include a pool, tennis courts and a nine-hole golf course. Rates include all meals, with singles beginning at US$130/260 in summer/winter, doubles from US$210/340. Partly because it's so secluded the resort has had serious

occupancy problems and its future is a bit iffy.

## LONG BAY

Long Bay, on the east side of Antigua, has clear blue waters and a quite appealing white-sand beach that's reef protected and good for snorkelling. There are two exclusive resorts at either end of the beach and a moderately priced condominium hotel within walking distance. Other than a few private homes there's little else in the neighbourhood and unless you're looking for total seclusion or don't mind paying some hefty taxi fares you'll need a car if you make a base in this area.

### Devil's Bridge

Devil's Bridge is a modest little coastal sea arch at Indian Town Point, an area thought to have been the site of an early Arawak settlement. To get there, turn east onto the paved road a third of a mile (500 metres) before the Long Bay Hotel turn-off. The road ends after a mile (1.6 km) at a turn-around; from there the arch is less than a minute's walk to the east. Be careful walking near the arch as the Atlantic breakers that have cut the arch out of these limestone cliffs occasionally sweep over the top.

### Places to Stay & Eat

*Banana Cove at Dian Bay* (☎ 463-2003; fax 463-2425), PO Box 321, is a nice 30-unit condominium on a quiet peninsula about 500 metres east of Long Bay beach. One-bedroom suites have a big kitchen, living/dining room, separate bedroom, bathroom with a tub and big balconies. Most of the upper-floor poolside units have a view of the ocean across the pool and are one of the island's better value choices at US$60 in summer, US$90 in winter. Ocean-view units are US$20 more, while two-bedroom suites cost US$120/175 in summer/winter. There's a small restaurant serving standard breakfast fare, sandwiches and salads at moderate prices. Guests can also buy a US$40 voucher for a full course dinner with wine at the Pineapple Beach Club. Use of snorkelling and windsurfing equipment is complimentary.

The *Long Bay Hotel* (☎ 463-2005; fax 463-2439), PO Box 442, on the east end of Long Bay, is an upscale family-run hotel that caters to a fair number of returning visitors. The 20 rooms start at US$150/250 for singles/doubles in summer and US$270/350 in winter, including breakfast and dinner, while the six cottages start at US$165 in summer and US$220 in winter, with kitchen facilities but no meals. Tennis and water sports are complimentary. The hotel restaurant has candlelight dining with an ocean view; there's a three-course dinner of the day for EC$90 or a range of main dishes from EC$40 to EC$70.

The *Pineapple Beach Club* (☎ 463-2006; fax 463-2452; in the USA ☎ (800) 345-0356), PO Box 54, is a 116-room all-inclusive resort on the west end of Long Bay. It has a California owner and a relaxed atmosphere. Single/double rates, which begin at US$220/300 in summer and US$270/370 in winter, include meals, drinks, water sports activities, entertainment and tipping and taxes.

**BETTY'S HOPE**

Betty's Hope, just east of the village of Pares, was the island's first sugar plantation, built by Christopher Codrington in 1674 and named in honour of his daughter Betty. Ruins of two old stone windmills, a still house and a few other stone structures remain on the site, which is now under the jurisdiction of the Museum of Antigua & Barbuda. Ambitious plans call for an extensive restoration of the plantation and development of a 'living history' museum. The rough dirt road into Betty's Hope is signposted. It's open from 9 am to 5 pm Tuesday to Saturday.

# Barbuda

Barbuda, 40 km north of Antigua, remains one of the Eastern Caribbean's least visited places. Other than its frigatebird colony and its beautiful beaches, most of which are best accessed by private boat, there's not much to attract tourists to this low scrubby island.

The only village, Codrington, is home to most residents and is the site of the island's airport. Barbuda has two small exclusive resorts at its southern tip, although these club-like places are so removed from the rest of the island that they have their own landing strip and haven't done much to upset Barbuda's isolation.

Most of the 1100 islanders share half a dozen surnames and can trace their lineage to a small group of slaves brought to Barbuda by Sir Codrington, who leased the island in 1685 from the Crown. The slaves raised livestock and grew food crops, turning Barbuda into a breadbasket to feed labourers working the sugar plantations on Antigua.

The Codrington family managed to keep the lease, which was negotiated at an annual rental payment of 'one fattened sheep', for nearly two centuries. Their legacy remains well beyond the town's name – from the communal land-use policies that still govern on Barbuda to the introduced goats, sheep and feral donkeys that range freely, much to the detriment of the island flora.

Besides having the Caribbean's largest colony of frigatebirds, Barbuda hosts tropical mockingbirds, warblers, pelicans, ibis, oystercatchers, herons and numerous ducks. The island also has wild boar and white-tailed deer, both of which are legally hunted.

**CODRINGTON**

Codrington is a modest, low-key place. The town begins at the airport – simply walk to the north and you're in the centre of it. Codrington has Barbuda's post office, bank and police station as well as a government house that dates to 1743.

This is not a town set up for visitors – only one of the places that rents rooms bothers to put up a sign and there are no restaurants with regular hours. You can get sandwiches at two snack shops, one adjacent to the bakery and the other a bit farther down the same road.

The town is on the inland side of

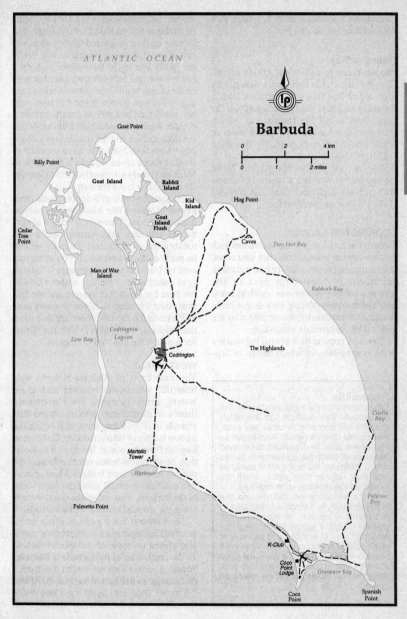

ATLANTIC OCEAN

Goat Point

Billy Point

**Goat Island**

**Rabbit Island**

**Kid Island**

Hog Point

Cedar Tree Point

**Goat Island Flush**

Caves

Two Feet Bay

Man of War Island

Rubbish Bay

Codrington Lagoon

Low Bay

Codrington

The Highlands

Castle Bay

Martello Tower

Harbour

Pelican Bay

Palmetto Point

K-Club

Coco Point Lodge

Gravenor Bay

Spanish Point

Coco Point

**Barbuda**

0        2        4 km

0    1    2 miles

Codrington Lagoon, a hefty 3.5 miles (5.6 km) north of the nearest beach.

## Places to Stay

*Thomas Guest House* (☎ 460-0004), a block from the airport, has four rooms with private bath and ceiling fans which rent for US$25 for either single or double occupancy. If the guesthouse is full Mr Thomas can usually refer you to someone else with a room or small house for rent, generally for about US$30 to US$70.

Another option is MacArthur Nedd (☎ 460-0059), who has a handful of rooms with private bath and fans that rent for US$35/60 for singles/doubles.

## CODRINGTON LAGOON

Codrington Lagoon, the expansive brackish estuary that runs along Barbuda's west coast, is an intriguing destination for bird watchers. Thousands of frigatebirds nest in the lagoon's scrubby mangroves – with as many as a dozen birds roosting on a single bush. Because of the density, the nesting sites are abuzz with contentious squawking.

The most popular time to visit the rookery is the mating season, which begins in Sep-

tember and continues until January. Male frigatebirds put on a colourful display, ballooning up their bright red throat pouches as part of the elaborate courtship rituals. While the males line up in the bushes, arch their heads back and puff out their pouches with an air of machismo, the females take to the sky. When one spots a suitor that impresses her, she'll land and initiate a mating ritual.

After mating, a nest is built from twigs that the male gathers and the female lays a single egg which both birds take turns incubating. It takes about seven weeks for the chick to hatch and nearly six months for it to learn to fly and finally leave the nest.

The nesting site is in the upper lagoon area known as Man of War Island and can only be reached by boat. There are a couple of outboards that can take visitors out to the rookery, but arrangements generally need to be made a day in advance. If you're staying over on Barbuda you can arrange it through your guesthouse – the cost is about US$40 per boat for up to four people and the trip lasts about 75 minutes. If you're going over to Barbuda for the day, there are day tours that include the rookery (see the Tours section near the end of this chapter).

## WEST COAST

The west coast of Barbuda is lined with beautiful white-sand beaches and azure waters. From Palmetto Point northward there's a magnificent pinkish strand that extends nearly 18 km, most of it lining the narrow barrier of land separating Codrington Lagoon from the ocean. Because of its isolation, however, the beach remains largely the domain of a few lone boaters. More accessible beaches are found along the coast south of the harbour, with one of the finest sweeps along the stretch between the two resorts.

The **harbour** has a customs office and a sandloading operation – Barbuda's sands also glisten on some of Antigua's beaches! To the north-west of the harbour is **Martello Tower**, a former lookout station that from a distance looks like an old sugar mill. About 0.6 miles (one km) north of Coco Point there's a nice white-sand strand with

---

**Frigatebirds**

Frigatebirds skim the water's surface for fish but because their feathers lack the water-resistant oils common to other sea birds, they cannot dive into water. Also known as man-of-war birds, the frigatebird has evolved into an aerial pirate that supplements its own fishing efforts by harassing other sea birds until they release their catch, which the frigatebird then swoops up in mid-flight.

While awkward on the ground the frigatebird, with its distinctive forked tail and two-metre wingspan, is mesmerisingly graceful in flight. It has the lightest weight-to-wingspan ratio of any bird and can soar at great heights for hours on end – making it possible for the bird to feed along the coast of distant islands and return home to roost at sunset without landing anywhere other than its nesting site. ∎

nearshore coral formations that provide good snorkelling.

The pristine waters of **Gravenor Bay**, between Coco Point and Spanish Point, is a favoured yacht anchorage with reef formations and excellent snorkelling. Near the centre of the bay there's an old deteriorating pier, while the ruins of a small **tower** lie about 0.6 miles (one km) away to the east.

Archaeologists believe the uninhabited peninsula leading to **Spanish Point** was once the site of a major Arawak settlement. A dirt track connects both ends of the bay and another leads northward from the east side of the salt pond.

### Places to Stay

The *K-Club* (☎ 460-0301; fax 460-0305) is the handiwork of Italian fashion designer Mariuccia 'Krizia' Mandelli. This new beachfront resort has 33 upmarket, contemporary cottages and its own nine-hole golf course. While the K in the name also stands for Krizia, the daily rates just happen to hover at a cool K, US$1000 inclusive. For about US$100, non-guests can have lunch or dinner at the resort.

*Coco Point Lodge* (☎ 462-3816), located about a mile (1.6 km) south of K-Club, is a US-owned, members-only club on a lovely beach. The cheapest of the 36 rooms and suites begin at around US$500, plus membership fees. It's open from November to April and doesn't welcome non-guests.

### CAVES

If you feel like taking a look down under, there are some caves about five miles (eight km) north-east of Codrington, though if it's been raining recently mud holes may well make it impossible to visit them. Dark Cave is an expansive underground cavern with pools of deep water while another cave near Two Feet Bay is said to contain the faded drawings of Arawak Indians.

### GETTING THERE & AWAY
### Air

The only scheduled air service is into Codrington airport. LIAT has two daily flights making the 20-minute skip between Antigua and Barbuda. Flights leave Antigua at 8.35 am and 3.30 pm and depart Barbuda for Antigua 30 minutes later. The fare is US$27 one way, US$38 for an excursion ticket.

Carib Aviation (☎ 462-3147) deals mainly in charters but will also take passengers on the return sector of the twice weekly flights that it runs for the island bank. On Thursday afternoons you can take the flight to Barbuda, while on Wednesday mornings you can hop it to Antigua. The one-way cost is EC$55.

### Boat

Barbuda's reefs, which extend many km from shore, are thought to have claimed a good 200 ships since colonial times – a rather impressive number considering Barbuda has never been a major port. Some reefs still remain poorly charted and the challenge of navigating through them is one reason Barbuda remains well off the beaten path. If you're sailing to the island bring everything you'll need in advance as there are no yachting facilities on Barbuda.

There's no scheduled passenger boat service to Barbuda but if you want to try your luck hitching with a private yacht, check around at the marinas on Antigua.

### Tours

Barbuda has a reputation for tours that fail to materialise, a driver that doesn't show up at the airport or some other missing link. Confirm all reservations.

If you book a tour with LIAT be sure to get a contact number on Barbuda; consider calling that person in advance to reconfirm your tour directly with them.

LIAT charges US$125 for a day tour that includes airfare, a boat ride to the frigatebird rookery, a visit to the caves, some time on the beach and lunch. Some Antiguan travel agents including Caribrep (☎ 462-0818) and Wadadli Travel & Tours (☎ 462-2227) also offers the same package.

On Barbuda, the people who operated outings for the now-closed Sunset View

Hotel still offer a tour consisting of a guided walk through the village and a visit to the rookery and beach. It includes a lobster lunch but not the airfare to Barbuda and costs US$60 per person with a minimum of two people. Make reservations (☎ 460-0266) in advance.

## GETTING AROUND

Barbuda has no public transportation. Distances are too great and the dusty dirt roads too hot to make walking a practical means of exploring. There isn't an established taxi service, but you might be able to arrange to hire someone to drive you around – ask the LIAT agent or at your guesthouse.

Car rental is another option, although the individuals who rent vehicles change from time to time and tracking them down can be tricky. A good place to start is with Netta Williams (☎ 460-0047), who has a couple of small Suzuki 4WDs that rent for EC$120 for 24 hours, EC$100 if you're flying in and out the same day.

# Barbados

Barbados, the easternmost island in the Caribbean, is one of the most successful at luring visitors to its shores. It has fringing white-sand beaches, a good range of places to stay and eat and enough organised activities to make for a solid holiday destination.

The west and south coasts, where most visitor accommodation is centred, are quite built up with an intermingling of tourist and residential areas. The interior is predominantly rural with undulating hills of sugar cane, grazing sheep and scattered villages.

Perhaps no other Caribbean island has been as strongly influenced by the British as Barbados. It's visible in the national passion for cricket, the old stone Anglican churches found in every parish, the well-tended gardens fronting islanders' homes and the Saturday horse races.

But the 'Little England' analogy only goes so far. Bajans, as islanders call themselves, also draw heavily from West Indian influences. Some of the finest calypso musicians

in the Caribbean have hailed from Barbados. The countryside is dotted with rum shops, not pubs, and West Indian cuisine, not kidney pie, is the mainstay of Bajan diets.

For many visitors Barbados can make for a comfortable mix of the familiar peppered with just enough local flavour to feel exotic. The island handles tourism well, people are friendly and it makes a good choice for a tame destination.

## ORIENTATION

Barbados is divided into 11 parishes. The airport and the south coast resorts are in the parish of Christ Church, while most of the west coast resorts are in St James. Addresses commonly list both the village and parish name.

The island's major highways, numbered 1 to 7 from north to south, all begin in Bridgetown. The airport is on the south-east side of the island, 16 km from Bridgetown. Hwy 7 leads from the airport through the south-coast resort area, but if you're heading to Bridgetown or the west coast, the new bypass road, the ABC Highway, is much quicker than the coastal road. The ABC Highway is a combination of the Adams, Barrow and Cummings highways.

Most of the island's rural sights – plantation houses, gardens and parks – are scattered throughout the interior. With a car you could see the bulk of them in one frenetic day or all of them in a couple days of leisurely exploring.

# Facts about the Island

## HISTORY

The original inhabitants of Barbados were Arawak Indians, who were driven off the island around 1200 AD by invading Carib Indians from Venezuela. The Caribs themselves abandoned Barbados around the time

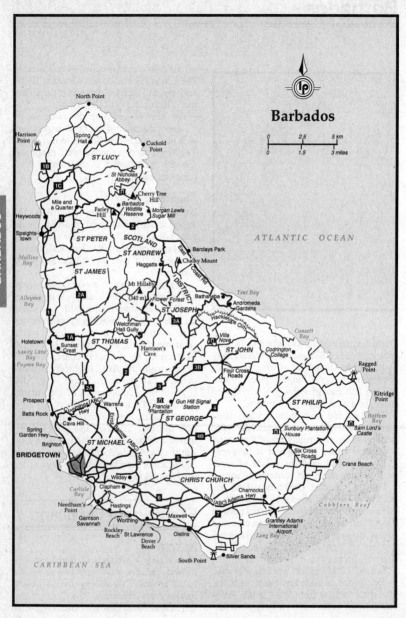

BARBADOS

the first Europeans sailed into the region. Although the conditions of their departure are unclear, some historians believe the Spanish might have landed on Barbados in the early 1500s and taken some of the Caribs as slaves, prompting the rest of the tribe to flee to the safety of more protected, mountainous islands such as St Lucia.

Portuguese explorer Pedro a Campos stopped on Barbados in 1536 en route to Brazil. Though he had no interest in settling the island it's thought that he introduced pigs to Barbados with the intention of having them as a food source on return voyages. It was Campos who named the island Los Barbados ('the bearded ones'), presumably after the island's fig trees, whose long hanging aerial roots have a beard-like resemblance.

In 1625 Captain John Powell landed on Barbados and claimed the uninhabited island for England. Two years later, his brother Captain Henry Powell landed with a party of 80 settlers as well as 10 slaves captured en route from a trading vessel. The group established the island's first European settlement, Jamestown, on the west coast at what is now Holetown. More settlers followed in their wake and by the end of 1628 the colony's population had grown to 2000.

Within a few years the colonists had cleared much of the native forest and planted tobacco and cotton. In the 1640s they replanted their fields in sugar. The new sugar plantations were labour intensive and the planters, who had previously relied upon indentured servants, began to import large numbers of African slaves. Their estates, the first large sugar plantations in the Caribbean, proved immensely profitable and by the mid-17th century the islanders – or at least the White planters and merchants – were thriving.

In 1639, island freeholders formed a Legislative Assembly, only the second such parliament established in a British colony (Bermuda was the first). Barbados was loyal to the Crown during Britain's civil wars, and following the beheading of King Charles I in 1649, Oliver Cromwell decided to send a force to establish his authority over Barbados. The invading fleet arrived in 1651 and by the following year Barbados had surrendered and signed the Articles of Capitulation, which formed the basis for the Charter of Barbados. The charter guaranteed government by a governor and a freely elected assembly as well as freedom from taxation without local consent. In 1660, when the British Crown was restored, this charter, with a certain ironic twist, provided Barbados with a greater measure of independence from the English monarchy than that of other British colonies.

The sugar industry continued to boom during the next century and even after abolition Barbadian planters continued to prosper. When slaves were emancipated in 1834, their difficult living conditions remained largely unchanged. Virtually all of the arable land continued to be owned by large estates and most Black islanders found few options other than staying on with the plantations. Those who did move off often ended up in shanty towns in abject poverty.

During the economic depression of the 1930s, unemployment shot upwards, living conditions deteriorated and street riots broke out. As a consequence the British Colonial Welfare and Development Office was established, providing sizeable sums of money for Barbados and other Caribbean colonies. To counter growing political unrest, the British reluctantly gave Black reformers a role in the political process. One of those reformers, Grantley Adams, would become the first premier of Barbados a decade later and eventually be knighted by the queen.

Barbados was far enough afield to avoid the hostile British-French rivalry that marked the history of the Windward and Leeward Islands. Instead it experienced an unbroken period of British rule that lasted almost 350 years.

Barbados gained internal self-government in 1961 and became an independent nation on 30 November 1966, with Errol Barrow as its first prime minister.

## GEOGRAPHY
Barbados lies 160 km east of the Windward

BARBADOS

Islands. It is somewhat pear shaped, measuring 34 km from north to south and 22 km at its widest, and has a total land area of 430 sq km.

The island is largely composed of coral accumulations built upon sedimentary rocks. Water permeates its soft coral cap, creating underground streams, springs and limestone caverns. The most notable of the caverns, Harrison's Cave, is one of the island's leading tourist attractions.

Most of the island's terrain is relatively flat, rising to low gentle hills in the interior. However, the north-eastern part of the island, known as the Scotland District, rises to a relatively lofty 340 metres at the island's highest point, Mt Hillaby.

The west coast has white-sand beaches and calm turquoise waters, while the east side of the island has turbulent Atlantic waters and a coastline punctuated by coastal cliffs. Coral reefs surround most of the island.

## CLIMATE

In January the average daily high temperature is 28°C (83°F) while the low averages 21°C (70°F). In July the average daily high is 30°C (86°F) while the low averages 23°C (74°F).

February to May are the driest months,

with a mean relative humidity around 68%. The rest of the year the humidity averages between 74% and 79%. In July, the wettest month, there's measurable rainfall for an average of 18 days, while April, the driest month, averages seven days. Annual rainfall averages 1275 mm (51 inches).

## FLORA & FAUNA

As most of Barbados' native forest was levelled by early settlers to clear tracts of farmland, the landscape is predominantly one of sugar-cane fields, pasture and scrubland. The small sections of native woodlands that still remain are mainly in gullies and clifflands too steep for cultivation.

One of the island's more notable trees is the bearded fig tree (*ficus citrofolia*), for which the island was named. Other trees common to Barbados are palms, casuarina, locust, white cedar, poinciana and mahogany. There are also a fair number of flowering plants on the island and some attractive cultivated gardens that are open to visitors.

There are a few introduced mammals found in the wild, including green monkeys, mongoose, European hares, mice and rats. Found only on Barbados is the non-poisonous and rarely seen grass snake *Liophis perfuscus*. The island also has a small harm-

---

**Green Monkeys**
The green monkeys that inhabit Barbados were introduced as pets from West Africa some 350 years ago. The monkeys quickly found their way into the wild where they fared well, free of any predators other than humans.

Today the island's monkey population is estimated at between 5000 to 10,000. They are shy of people and live mainly in forested gullies, travelling in groups of about a dozen. Like most other primates, they are active from dawn to dusk and sleep at night.

Green monkeys are not rare or endangered either in Barbados or worldwide. Indeed, because monkeys have many of the same food preferences as humans, they are considered a pest by Barbadian farmers who can lose as much as a third of their banana, mango and papaya crops to the monkeys.

Consequently, the government has long encouraged the hunting of monkeys. The first bounties were introduced in the late 1600s, with five shillings offered for each monkey head delivered to the parish church. In 1975 the Ministry of Agriculture introduced a new bounty of B$5 for each monkey tail received. After the Barbados Primate Research Center was founded in 1982, it began to offer a more enticing B$50 reward for each monkey captured alive and delivered unharmed to the centre. As a result many farmers now trap, rather than shoot, the monkeys. ■

Barbados coat of arms

Universal suffrage dates from 1951. The two main political parties are the Barbados Labour Party (BLP), formed in 1938 by Grantley Adams, and the Democratic Labour Party (DLP), which splintered from the BLP in 1955. Both parties have moderate socialist platforms.

## ECONOMY

Sugar, the mainstay of the Barbadian economy for 300 years, was nudged into second place by tourism in 1970. Since then tourism has continued to grow and now accounts for nearly 50% of the island's GNP.

Sugar, and its byproducts of rum and molasses, are still leading exports, but the amount of land devoted to sugar cane is gradually declining and a policy of agricultural diversification is underway. Other crops are yams, sweet potatoes, corn and sea-island cotton.

In total, agriculture accounts for about 10% of the labour force and the fishing industry accounts for another 5%. There's also a small light industry sector that includes the manufacturing of clothing, pharmaceuticals and computer components. Barbados meets nearly half of its energy needs from domestic oil and natural gas production; there's a refinery in Bridgetown.

less blind snake, whistling frogs, lizards, red-footed tortoises and eight species of bats.

Hawksbill turtles come ashore to lay their eggs on sandy beaches around Barbados on a regular basis, and the leatherback turtle is an occasional nester.

More than 180 species of birds have been sighted on Barbados. Most are migrating shorebirds and waders that breed in North America and stop over in Barbados en route to winter feeding grounds in South America. Only 28 species nest on Barbados; these include wood doves, blackbirds, banana-quits, guinea fowl, cattle egrets, herons, finches and three kinds of hummingbirds.

## GOVERNMENT

Barbados is an independent state within the Commonwealth. It has a bicameral parliament consisting of a House of Assembly with 28 elected members, who serve for a maximum five-year term, and a Senate with 21 appointed members. Executive power is vested in the Prime Minister, who is generally the leader of the majority party in the Assembly. A Governor-General representing the Queen is the official head of state, but the role is mainly ceremonial in nature.

### Early Tourists

In 1751 at age 19, some 38 years before he would become the first US president, George Washington visited Barbados as a companion to his half-brother Lawrence, who suffered from tuberculosis. It was hoped the tropical climate would prove therapeutic.

The two rented a house in the Garrison area south of Bridgetown (at a place where the Bush Hill House now stands) and stayed on the island for six weeks. Unfortunately, George contracted smallpox while on Barbados, which left his face permanently scarred, and Lawrence died the following year. The Barbados trip was the only overseas journey George Washington ever made. ■

BARBADOS

BARBADOS

## POPULATION & PEOPLE

The population of Barbados is approximately 254,000. Over 90% of Bajans are Black, of African descent. The remainder are mostly English and Scottish, along with a small minority of East Indians. Although there are many small villages throughout Barbados, the vast majority of people live along the leeward Caribbean side of the island, in an urban sweep running from Speightstown in the north-west to Oistins in the south.

## ARTS & CULTURE

The national sport, if not the national obsession, is cricket. Barbadians boast more world-class cricket players than any other nation, at least on a per capita basis. One of the world's top all-rounders, Bajan native Garfield Sobers, was knighted by Queen Elizabeth II during her 1975 visit to Barbados, while another cricket hero, Sir Frank Worrell, appears on the face of the five-dollar bill.

Island architectural styles have their roots in the colonial era when virtually all land belonged to large sugar estates. The island still has a number of grand plantation homes as well as numerous chattel houses, the latter a simple rectangular wooden home built upon cement or stone blocks which allowed it to be moved.

Despite the British influence, West Indian culture is also strong in terms of family life, food and music. Barbadian contributions to West Indian music are renowned in the region, having produced such greats as the calypso artist the Mighty Gabby, whose songs on cultural identity and political protest speak for emerging black pride throughout the Caribbean.

### Dress Conventions

Shorts are not appropriate in nightclubs or in most restaurants at dinner time. Topless sunbathing is illegal.

### RELIGION

The majority of the population is Anglican. Other religious denominations on Barbados include Methodist, Moravian, Roman Catholic, First Church of Christ Scientist, Jehovah's Witnesses, Mormons, Baha'i, Muslim and Jewish. For a current calendar of religious services see the 'Time For Worship' page in the free tourist publication *The Visitor*.

### LANGUAGE

The island's language is English, spoken with a distinctive Bajan accent.

# Facts for the Visitor

## VISAS & EMBASSIES

Citizens of the USA and Canada who are travelling directly from their home countries can enter Barbados without a passport for stays of less than three months, as long as they have an original birth certificate or naturalisation certificate along with a photo ID such as a driving licence. Citizens of all other countries must have a valid passport.

Visas are required for citizens from

Sir Frank Worrell

Eastern European countries, the former USSR, Cuba, China, Taiwan, India, Pakistan, South Africa, non-Commonwealth African countries and all South American countries except Argentina, Brazil, Colombia and Venezuela.

All visitors are officially required to be in possession of an onward or return ticket.

### Foreign Embassies in Barbados

Foreign embassies and consulates in Barbados are:

Belgium
    Consulate of Belgium, 609 Rockley Resort, Christ Church (☎ 435-7704)
Brazil
    Embassy of Brazil, 3rd Floor, Sunjet House, Fairchild St, Bridgetown (☎ 427-1735)
Canada
    Canadian High Commission, Bishop's Court Hill, Pine Rd, St Michael (☎ 429-3550)
China
    Embassy of the People's Republic of China, 17 Golf View Terrace, Rockley, Christ Church (☎ 435-6890)
Colombia
    Embassy of Colombia, Rosemary, Dayrells Rd, Rockley, Christ Church (☎ 429-6821)
Costa Rica
    Embassy of Costa Rica, Mahogany Ave, Sunset Ridge (☎ 432-0194)
France
    French Consular Agent, Shirley House, Hastings, Christ Church (☎ 435-6847)
Netherlands
    Netherlands Consulate, Chickmont Foods, Balls, Christ Church (☎ 428-0420)
Trinidad & Tobago
    Trinidad & Tobago High Commission, Cockspur House, Nile St, Bridgetown (☎ 429-9600)
UK
    British High Commission, Lower Collymore Rock, St Michael (☎ 436-6694)
USA
    US Embassy, Broad St, Bridgetown (☎ 436-4950)
Venezuela
    Venezuelan Embassy, Hastings, Christ Church (☎ 435-7619)

### CUSTOMS

Visitors may bring in one litre of spirits or wine, 200 cigarettes (or 100 cigars) and a reasonable amount of personal effects. Most items intended as gifts for people in Barbados are charged a 30% duty.

### MONEY

Banks exchange Barbados dollars at the rate of B$1.98 for US$1 in cash, B$1.99 for US$1 in travellers' cheques. To exchange Barbados dollars back to US dollars the rate is B$2.04 to US$1. Cash and travellers' cheques in British, Canadian and German currencies can also be readily exchanged at banks, with rates fluctuating daily according to international monetary markets.

Banks charge a stamp fee for each travellers' cheque cashed – 10 cents for up to the equivalent of B$50, 50 cents for larger cheques – and generally a commission of B$1 to B$3, depending on the amount of money exchanged. American Express in Bridgetown cashes American Express travellers' cheques without a commission charge.

You'll certainly want some Barbados dollars for incidentals but most larger payments can be made in US dollars or with a credit card. Hotels and guesthouses quote rates in US dollars, although you can use either US or Barbadian currency to settle the account; most give an exchange rate of B$2 to US$1 for travellers' cheques or cash. When using a credit card, charges are made in Barbados dollars and calculated by the bank at the rate of B$1.97 to US$1.

Most restaurants, hotels and shops accept Visa, MasterCard and American Express cards. A few also accept the Discover Card.

Banks are easy to find in larger towns and major tourist areas. Visa card holders can obtain cash advances from automatic teller machines (ATMs) at many Royal Bank of Canada and Barclays Bank branches. There's an ATM at the airport.

### Currency

Notes come in B$2 (blue), B$5 (green), B$10 (brown), B$20 (purple), B$50 (orange) and B$100 (grey) denominations.

There are 1 cent copper coins, 5 cent bronze coins and 10 cent, 25 cent and B$1 silver-coloured coins. All are round except the dollar coin which has seven sides.

## TOURIST OFFICES

The Barbados Board of Tourism has its main office (☎ 427-2623; fax 426-4080) on Harbour Rd in Bridgetown and a booth (☎ 428-0937) at the airport. When requesting information by mail, write to: Barbados Board of Tourism, PO Box 242, Bridgetown, Barbados, West Indies.

### Overseas Reps

Overseas offices of the Barbados Board of Tourism include:

Canada
    5160 Yonge St, 18th Floor, North York, Ontario M2N 6L9 (☎ (416) 512-6569, ☎ (800) 268-9122; fax (416) 512-6581)
    615 Dorchester Blvd West, Suite 960, Montreal, Quebec H3B 1P5 (☎ (514) 861-0085; fax (514) 861-7917)
France
    Caraibes 102, 102 Ave des Champs-Elysees, 75008 Paris (☎ 45 62 62 62; fax 40 74 07 01)
Germany
    Rathenauplatz 1a, 6000 Frankfurt am Main 1 (☎ (069) 28-09-82; fax (069) 29-47-82)
Sweden
    Target Marketing of Scandinavia, Kamma Kargafam 41, 5-111, 24, Stockholm (☎ (468) 115-282; fax (468) 206-317)
UK
    263 Tottenham Court Rd, London W1P 9AA (☎ (441) 636-9448; fax (441) 637-1496)
USA
    800 Second Ave, New York, NY 10017 (☎ (212) 986-6516, ☎ (800) 221-9831; fax (212) 573-9850)
    3440 Wilshire Blvd, Suite 1215, Los Angeles, CA 90010 (☎ (213) 380-2198; fax (213) 384-2763)

## BUSINESS HOURS

Most banks are open from 8 am to 3 pm Monday to Thursday, until 5 pm on Friday. A few branches are also open from 9 am to noon on Saturday.

Most stores are open from 8 am to 4 pm Monday to Friday and to noon on Saturday. Supermarkets are generally open until 6 pm.

Many restaurants and visitor attractions are closed on public holidays.

## HOLIDAYS

Public holidays are:

| | | |
|---|---|---|
| *New Year's Day* | – | 1 January |
| *Errol Barrow Day* | – | 21 January |
| *Good Friday* | – | late March/early April |
| *Easter Monday* | – | late March/early April |
| *May Day* | – | 1 May |
| *Whit Monday* | – | eighth Monday after Easter |
| *Kadooment Day* | – | first Monday in August |
| *United Nations Day* | – | first Monday in October |
| *Independence Day* | – | 30 November |
| *Christmas Day* | – | 25 December |
| *Boxing Day* | – | 26 December |

## CULTURAL EVENTS

The island's top event is the Crop-Over Festival, which originated in colonial times as a celebration to mark the end of the sugar cane harvest. Festivities stretch over a three-week period beginning in mid-July. There are spirited calypso competitions, fairs and other activities around the island. The festival culminates with a Carnival-like costume parade on Kadooment Day, a national holiday.

In February, the Holetown Festival celebrates the 17 February 1627 arrival of the first English settlers on Barbados. Holetown's week-long festivities include street fairs, a music festival at the historic parish church and a road race.

The Oistins Fish Festival, held over Easter weekend, commemorates the signing of the Charter of Barbados. It's a seaside festivity with events focusing on boat races, fishboning competitions, local foods, crafts and dancing.

The National Independence Festival of Creative Arts, held throughout November, features talent contests in dance, drama, singing and the like. Performances by the finalists are held on Independence Day, 30 November.

There are also a handful of international sporting events, including the Barbados Windsurfing World Cup, held at Silver Sands in January; the Barbados International Surfing Championship, held in early November at Bathsheba; Banks Field Hockey Festival, in late August; and Run Barbados, a marathon held in early December.

## POST

The general post office, in Cheapside, Bridgetown, is open from 8 am to 5 pm Monday to Friday. There's a district post office in every parish, open weekdays from 8 am to noon and 1 to 3.15 pm (3 pm on Monday).

Airmail postage rates for a postcard are 45 cents to other Caribbean countries, 65 cents to the USA and Canada and 70 cents to the UK and Europe. For a letter up to 10 grams it's 70 cents to other Caribbean countries, 90 cents to the USA and Canada and B$1.10 to Europe.

Mail service is quite efficient and mail is dispatched daily to both London and New York.

When addressing mail to Barbados from overseas, follow the town and/or parish name with 'Barbados, West Indies'.

## TELECOMMUNICATIONS

Local phone numbers have seven digits. When calling Barbados from overseas, add the area code 809.

Barbados has both coin and card phones. At coin phones, you'll get five minutes' calling time to anywhere on the island for each 25 cents; 5, 10 and 25 cent coins are accepted.

There are card phones at the airport, Bridgetown Harbour, major shopping centres and in other heavily trafficked public places although, to date, card phones are not as widespread as coin phones.

Barbados phonecards are available in B$10, B$20, B$40 and B$60 denominations and are sold at the airport, phone company (Bartel) offices, Cave Shepherd branches, '99' convenience stores and Super-Centre supermarkets, among other places.

More information on phonecards and making long distance phone calls is under Telecommunications in the Facts for the Visitor chapter at the front of the book.

## ELECTRICITY

Electricity in Barbados is 110 volts AC, 50 cycles, with a flat two-pronged plug; many hotels have 240 volt converter outlets in the bathrooms.

## WEIGHTS & MEASURES

Despite its British heritage, Barbados has gone metric. Road signs and car odometers are in km, weights are in grams and kg. However, the transition to metric is fairly recent and many islanders still give directions in feet and miles.

## BOOKS

There are numerous books on Barbadian history and sights.

*The Barbados Garrison and its Buildings* by Warren Alleyne & Jill Sheppard (1990, paperback) is a well-written little book describing the many historic buildings that comprise the Garrison area.

Other books include *Barbados: Portrait of an Island*, a smart hardcover coffee-table book by Dick Scoones; *Treasures of Barbados*, a hardcover 96-page book on the island's architecture by Henry Fraser, the president of the Barbados National Trust; and books on Barbadian political figures, including *Tom Adams: A Biography* and *Grantley Adams and the Social Revolution*, both by local historian F A Hoyos.

The acclaimed novel *The Castle of My Skin* by Barbadian author George Lamming gives a good sense of what it was like growing up Black in colonial Barbados.

### Bookshops

In Bridgetown, the Cloister Bookstore on Hincks St, near Immigration, is a comprehensive bookshop. The Cave Shepherd department store on Broad St also has a fairly good selection of books, as does Brydens Bookshop behind Cave Shepherd on the corner of Victoria St and Bolton Lane. Other Cave Shepherd stores around the island also have book sections.

### Libraries

The central public library is on Coleridge St in Bridgetown and there are seven branch libraries, including ones in Holetown, Oistins and Speightstown. Visitors may check

BARBADOS

out library books on payment of a B\$20 refundable deposit. The libraries are open Monday to Saturday, from 9 am to 5 pm in Bridgetown and from 10 am to 6 pm at the branches.

## MAPS

If you intend to explore the island on your own, a good map will certainly come in handy. The best overall map of the island is the Ordnance Survey 1:50,000 map of Barbados. It costs B\$26 and can be purchased at the Barbados Museum and larger bookshops.

Although they don't show topographical detail, there are a couple of reasonably good free maps as well, including a road map distributed by the tourist office.

## MEDIA

Barbados has two daily newspapers, the *Barbados Advocate* and the *Nation*. British and US newspapers are available at convenience stores in the main tourist areas. Worth picking up are the weekly *The Visitor*, the bi-monthly *Sunseeker* and the monthly *What's On*, all free tourist publications with lots of ads and general information.

In addition to the government-owned TV station, CBC, which broadcasts on Channel 8, a number of international TV networks, including CNN, ESPN and TNT, are picked up by satellite. There are seven radio stations on Barbados.

## HEALTH

There's a 600-bed government hospital in Bridgetown, the Queen Elizabeth Hospital (☎ 436-6450) on Martindales Rd, and several clinics around the island.

For divers who get the bends, the Barbados Defence Force (☎ 436-6185) maintains a decompression chamber in the Garrison area of Bridgetown.

Leptospirosis, which can be carried by mongooses, can be present in freshwater streams. For more information see Health in the Facts for the Visitor chapter.

## DANGERS & ANNOYANCES

Crime, including assaults on tourists, is certainly not unknown on Barbados. Still, the crime statistics are not alarming and the usual precautions should suffice.

Portuguese men-o-war (a type of poisonous jellyfish) are occasionally encountered in Barbadian waters and poisonous manchineel trees grow along some beaches.

## EMERGENCIES

Emergency medivac service is available 24 hours a day from Air Ambulance America (☎ (800) 222-3564) and Air Ambulance Network (☎ (800) 762-7022), or call collect to Miami ☎ (305) 447-0458.

Emergency telephone numbers in Barbardos are:

| | |
|---|---|
| Ambulance | ☎ 115 |
| Fire | ☎ 113 |
| Police | ☎ 112 (☎ 436-6600 for routine police matters) |

## ACTIVITIES

Barbados has a plethora of civic clubs and special interest groups, covering everything from flower arranging and Scottish dance to taekwondo and transcendental meditation. Many are open to short-term visitors; meeting times and contact numbers are listed in the *Sunseeker* and *The Visitor* tourist publications.

### Beaches & Swimming

Some of the island's prettiest beaches and calmest waters are along the west coast. Top spots include Paynes Bay, Sandy Bay and Mullins Bay – all lovely white-sand beaches that are easily accessible.

The south-west side of the island also has some fine beaches, including Sandy Beach in Worthing and Dover Beach. On the south-east side is Crane Beach, a scenic stretch of pink-tinged sand that's popular with body-surfers but rough for swimming.

The east coast has dangerous water conditions, including rocky nearshore shelves and strong currents, and only the most confident swimmers should take to the waters. The

Bathsheba area, in particular, has been the scene of a number of visitor drownings.

## Diving & Snorkelling

The west coast of Barbados has reef dives with soft corals, gorgonians and colourful sponges. There are also about a dozen shipwrecks. The largest, the 111-metre freighter *Stavronikita*, was scuttled by the government in 1978 to create an artificial reef. It sits upright off the central west coast in 42 metres of water, with the rigging reaching to within six metres of the surface. The coral-encrusted tug *Berwyn*, which sank in 1919 at Carlisle Bay, lays in only seven metres of water and makes for good snorkelling as well as diving.

One-tank dives with gear average US$40, two-tank dives US$70. For beginners who want to try the waters, the following companies offer a brief resort course and a shallow dive for US$45. They also offer full certification courses in either PADI or NAUI.

Dive Boat Safari at the Barbados Hilton, Aquatic Gap, St Michael (☎ 427-4350, fax 436-8946)

The Dive Shop, Aquatic Gap, St Michael (☎ 426-9947)

Exploresub Barbados, St Lawrence Gap, Christ Church (☎ 435-6542)

Underwater Barbados, Hastings, Christ Church (☎ 426-0655)

Willie's Watersports, Heywoods Resort, St Peters (☎ 422-4900, extension 2831)

Dive Boat Safari also offers a one-hour snorkelling tour that includes the *Berwyn* for US$15.

## Windsurfing

Barbados has good windsurfing conditions, with the best winds and waves from November to June. Maxwell is a popular area for intermediate-level windsurfers, while the Silver Sands area, at the southern tip of the island, has excellent conditions for advanced windsurfing.

**Rentals** Club Mistral rents windsurfing gear daily year-round at its Windsurfing Club (☎ 428-7277) in Maxwell and from November to May at the Silver Sands Resort (☎ 428-6001).

At Maxwell, a range of boards and wave and slalom sails rent for US$18/50/200 per hour/day/week. At Silver Sands, they rent only short boards (sinkers) and wave sails, for US$20/60/230.

Weather permitting, which is mainly in summer, Club Mistral gives lessons to beginners in Maxwell. Group lessons cost US$25 an hour, private lessons US$55, including gear.

Silver Rock Windsurfing at the Silver Rock Hotel (☎ 428-2866), Silver Sands, rents windsurfing gear for advanced sailors.

Other sites that rent windsurfing gear include Jolly Roger Watersports (☎ 432-1311), Sunset Crest, St James, and the Barbados Hilton (☎ 436-3549) in Bridgetown.

## Surfing

Barbados has some excellent surfing action. The biggest swells hit the east coast, with the prime surfing taking place at the Soup Bowl, off Bathsheba.

South Point and Rockley Beach on the south coast are sometimes good for surfing and the west coast can have surfable waves as well.

Though winter sees the highest swells, surfers will generally find reasonably good conditions on Barbados year-round. The water tends to be flattest in May and June.

## Hiking

Each Sunday at 6 am and 3 pm, the Barbados National Trust (☎ 426-2421) leads guided hikes in the countryside. Hikers are divided into three categories ranked by pace: fast, medium and stop-and-stare. Hike leaders share insights on local history, geology, flora and fauna. Locations vary, but all hikes end where they start, last around three hours and cover about eight km. There is no fee. Schedule information can be found in the free tourist publications or is available by calling the trust.

## Horse Riding

The Wilcox Riding Stable (☎ 428-3610) near the airport, the Brighton Riding Stables (☎ 425-9381) in the Black Rock area north of Bridgetown and Tony's Riding Stables (☎ 422-1549) near Mullins Bay all offer one-hour rides along the beach, for B$55 to B$60 including transportation.

Rides in the countryside are offered by Beau Geste Farm (☎ 429-0139) near Gun Hill and Caribbean International Riding Centre (☎ 433-1453), Auburn, St Joseph. Most stables are closed on Sunday.

## Tennis

There are tennis courts at several resort hotels, including the Casuarina Beach Club at Dover, Southern Palms Beach Club in St Lawrence, the Barbados Hilton in Bridgetown and Marriott's Sam Lord's Castle and the Crane Beach Hotel, both on the east coast. There are public tennis courts at Folkestone Park in Holetown and at the Garrison area south of Bridgetown centre.

## Golf

There's an 18-hole course at the Sandy Lane Hotel & Golf Club (☎ 432-1145) in St James. Green fees for non-guests are US$60/75 in summer/winter, plus US$50 for a cart; clubs, caddies, pull carts and lessons are available.

The Heywoods Golf Club (☎ 435-7880) just north of Speightstown and the Rockley Resort Golf Club (☎ 435-7880) on the south coast both have nine-hole courses. Green fees are about US$20; club and cart rentals are available.

The Belair Par 3 Golf Course (☎ 423-4653), on the east coast near Sam Lord's Castle, is open daily from 7 am to 4 pm. Green fees are US$12.50 for nine holes; club rentals cost US$2.50.

## HIGHLIGHTS

The island's highlights include the fine white-sand beaches that fringe the west and south coasts, the impressive subterranean sights at Harrison's Cave and the tours of 17th-century plantation houses. Also well worthwhile is a visit to the Barbados Museum and a stroll through the surrounding Garrison area. Another fun way to spend an

---

### Barbados National Trust Properties

The Barbados National Trust is a nonprofit organisation dedicated to the preservation of the island's historic sites and areas of environmental significance. Founded in 1961, the trust is the caretaker of a number of the island's leading visitor attractions. In some cases the trust owns the property outright but in other cases, as with the great houses, it mainly assists in managing visitor access to the property, which otherwise remains in private hands.

Properties under the Barbados National Trust umbrella include the Barbados Museum, Barbados Synagogue, Gun Hill Signal Station, Welchman Hall Gully, Francia Plantation House, Villa Nova, Sunbury Plantation House, St Nicholas Abbey, Morgan Lewis Sugar Mill, Andromeda Botanic Gardens and Codrington College.

The trust sells a Heritage Passport which provides admission to all 11 of its sites for B$50 and a mini-passport that allows admission to five sites for B$24. The passports can be purchased at any of the above sites. Each property can also be visited by paying a single admission fee and if you don't intend to take in a lot of sites, that's generally the most economical way to go. ■

afternoon is to join the crowd at a cricket match or a Saturday horse race.

## ACCOMMODATION

Barbados has a good variety of low and mid-range places to stay. Some could use a fresh coat of paint but most are comfortable and good value by Caribbean standards. There are also some fine top-end resorts.

Most of the upmarket resorts are along the west coast in the parish of St James, a relatively quiet and subdued area. The south coast, which generally attracts a younger crowd, has most of the low and mid-range accommodation. There's a light scattering of places to stay elsewhere on the island, including a few secluded options on the east and south-east coast.

For the past few years, low occupancy rates have forced many places to set aside the rack rates listed in their brochures and to discount by a third or more. Consequently, Barbados offers some excellent deals, even in the high season.

As most hotels don't include breakfast, many charge the same rate for single or double occupancy. Some places have three rate schedules: a low rate for summer, a marginally more expensive spring and autumn rate and a high rate for winter.

If you arrive without a reservation the tourist office at the airport can book you a room. There's no charge for the service and they can always come up with something in every price range. The tourist office also keeps a short list of families that rent out bedrooms in their homes, from about US$25 to US$50 a night. Most hotels add a 5% government tax and a 10% service charge.

Camping is generally not allowed on Barbados, except for organised outings by designated youth groups.

### Reservation Service

The Barbados Hotel Association (☎ (402) 398-3217 or ☎ (800) 462-2526 from the USA, ☎ (800) 822-2077 from Canada) has a booking service that handles about 75% of the island's hotels. They don't cover the very cheapest budget hotels or guesthouses, but otherwise book a full spectrum, from small hotels and apartments to luxury resorts. Member hotels change a bit from year to year but include most places listed in this chapter.

There are no fees to make a reservation (although a credit card guarantee is usually required) and bookings are made at established rates. The only thing to keep in mind is that island hotels sometimes offer discounted promotional rates that are available only by booking directly with the hotel.

### Villas

There are numerous individually owned villas available for rent. They are generally quite exclusive. All have maid service, most have a cook and some also have a butler. About half of the villas have private pools.

WIMCO books about 150 of these properties, with weekly prices ranging from about US$1200 for a simple one-bedroom villa to US$25,000 for an eight-bedroom great house. Summer prices are 30% to 60% cheaper. For reservations contact WIMCO (☎ (401) 849-8012), PO Box 1461, Newport, RI 02840. Toll free numbers are ☎ (800) 932-3222 in the USA, ☎ 05 90 16 20 from France and ☎ (0-800) 89-8318 from the UK.

## FOOD

Barbados has a range of Western fare from fast-food pizza and fried chicken to fine continental cuisine. In addition there's spicier Bajan and Caribbean food to choose from. Some of the more popular local foods, many of which borrow heavily from African and Indian influences, include conkies, cou-cou, cutter, flying fish, jug-jug and souse. For further information, see the food glossary on page 48 of the Facts for the Visitor chapter.

Other common local foods include pigeon peas and rice, pumpkin fritters, fried plantains and coconut pie.

## DRINKS

Tap water is safe to drink; it comes from underground reservoirs that are naturally filtered by the island's thick limestone cap.

Barbadian rum is considered some of the

finest in the Caribbean, with Mount Gay being the largest and best known label. A litre of rum costs about B$12. The island beer, Banks, is a pretty good brew.

## ENTERTAINMENT

The south coast of Barbados has a lively night scene. Most clubs open around 9.30 pm and continue into the wee hours of the morning, often until 3 am. Music is usually a mix of reggae, calypso and rock.

Harbour Lights, an open-air nightclub on Bay St (Hwy 7) at the south end of Bridgetown, has dancing and live bands nightly, except on Tuesday and Wednesday when there's a DJ. The cover charge is usually B$10 to B$15. On Wednesday, it's B$18 but includes all you can drink. Wednesday, Friday and Saturday are the liveliest nights.

The other Bridgetown club is the Warehouse, on Cavans Lane near the Careenage (a boat mooring area), popular with people aged 18 to 25, and as a late night spot for party-goers coming from other clubs.

Ship Inn is the most happening place in the St Lawrence area, with Tuesday the hottest night. The cover charge is B$9, with B$6 redeemable in drinks or food. The nearby After Dark is a popular mingling place for locals and tourists and is generally at its best on Friday and Saturday.

Waterfront Cafe, at the Careenage in Bridgetown, is the place to go for live jazz, with entertainment from 8 to 11.30 pm

Wednesday to Saturday. There's no cover charge. Saxophonist Arturo Tappin, one of the best jazz musicians in the Caribbean, performs on weekends.

'1627 and All That', a colourful dramatisation of the island's history through music and folk dance, is held Sunday and Thursday evenings at the Barbados Museum. It's all good fun and the price of B$85 for adults, B$40 for children, includes the show, a Bajan dinner buffet, drinks, a museum tour and transportation. For reservations call ☎ 435-6900.

The Plantation Restaurant (☎ 428-5048) on Hwy 7 in St Lawrence puts on a flamboyant costumed cabaret show with dancing, fire eating and steel band music on Monday, Wednesday and Friday. The show and drinks alone costs B$35; with a buffet dinner and transportation it's B$84.

Entertainment schedules can be found in the *Sunseeker* and *The Visitor* tourist publications.

## THINGS TO BUY

In Bridgetown, the government-sponsored Pelican Village, opposite the tourist office, has scores of kiosks selling local arts and crafts. The Women's Self Help Association on Broad St also has island crafts, including nice handmade dolls, while the Verandah Art Gallery directly above sells local paintings.

You can shop duty free (upon presentation of your passport) at a number of shops, including Cave Shepherd, the island's largest department store chain. It has a branch on Broad St, Bridgetown's main shopping street.

For an unusual souvenir you might want to pick up a packed box of frozen flying fish at the airport departure lounge.

# Getting There & Away

### AIR
#### Airlines
Most airlines have offices in Bridgetown: American Airlines is upstairs in the Cave

Steel-band player

Shepherd department store on Broad St; British Airways is on Fairchild St; BWIA is on the corner of Fairchild and Probyn Sts; and LIAT is on St Michael's Row opposite St Michael's Cathedral. All are open from 8 am to 4 pm weekdays.

You can also purchase tickets at the airport counters but it's best to avoid heavy flight times; in LIAT's case that's usually early morning and late afternoon.

Airline reservation numbers on Barbados are:

| | |
|---|---|
| Aeropostal | – ☎ 427-7781 |
| Air Canada | – ☎ 428-5077 |
| Air Martinique | – ☎ 436-1858 |
| American Airlines | – ☎ 428-4170/1684 |
| BWIA | – ☎ 426-2111, |
| airport | – ☎ 428-1650 |
| British Airways | – ☎ 436-6413, |
| airport | – ☎ 428-1660 |
| LIAT | – ☎ 436-6224, |
| airport | – ☎ 428-0986 |
| Mustique Airways | – ☎ 428-1638 |

## To/From the USA

Both American Airlines and BWIA fly to Barbados daily from New York and Miami. Although fares fluctuate, American Airlines often offers the best deals, with 30-day excursion fares from Miami beginning around US$280 in the low season, US$380 in winter. American's fares from New York begin around US$300 in the low season, US$450 in winter.

BWIA offers a 21-day excursion fare of US$400 from Miami, US$465 from New York.

## To/From Canada

Air Canada flies from Toronto to Barbados on Thursday, Friday, Saturday and Sunday and from Montreal to Barbados on Sunday only. The cheapest excursion fare, with a minimum stay of seven days and a maximum of 21 days, costs C$579. Tickets require a 14-day advance purchase.

BWIA flies from Toronto to Barbados on Sunday, Monday, Thursday, Friday and Saturday. Fares begin at C$593 for an excursion

ticket with the same conditions as the afore-mentioned Air Canada ticket.

## To/From the UK

British Airways flies to Barbados from London's Gatwick Airport on Tuesday, Wednesday, Friday and Saturday and from Heathrow Airport on Saturday and Sunday. The least expensive return fare is UK£685, with a seven-day minimum stay, a 180-day maximum stay and a 21-day advance purchase.

BWIA offers the same ticket and fare, flying from Heathrow to Barbados on Saturday and Monday.

## To/From Europe

BWIA flies to Barbados from Frankfurt on Friday, with an excursion fare of DM1945, and from Zurich on Saturday, with an excursion fare of US$1538. Both fares require a minimum stay of seven days and allow a maximum stay of six months.

## To/From South America

Aeropostal flies to Barbados from Porlamar on Venezuela's Margarita Island on Monday and Friday for US$100 each way. Aeropostal also has an excursion ticket from Caracas to Barbados, with a stopover on Margarita Island, for US$285 return; this has a minimum seven-day stay and a maximum 17-day stay.

BWIA flies daily to Barbados from Georgetown, Guyana, via Trinidad. The one-way fare costs US$172, while a 30-day excursion ticket is US$193. In addition, LIAT flies between Georgetown and Barbados four times a week.

## Within the Caribbean

LIAT has direct daily flights to Barbados from Antigua, St Lucia, Grenada and St Vincent. Frequencies range from twice daily from Grenada to almost a dozen flights from St Vincent. There are connecting LIAT flights to other islands throughout the Caribbean.

LIAT's fare between Barbados and St Lucia is US$78 one way, US$124 for a 30-

BARBADOS

day excursion. Other one-way/excursion fares to Barbados are US$116/152 from Grenada, US$110/145 from St Vincent & US$204/268 from Antigua.

LIAT also offers some good-value long-distance (YD) fares to and from points farther north; from St Martin to Barbados the cost is US$209 one way with unlimited en route stopovers. You'll have to insist on the YD fare as the regular one-way fare is about 15% more and allows only one stopover. There's also a 21-day excursion ticket from St Martin to Barbados (two stopovers allowed) for US$304.

Air Martinique has an excursion ticket from Martinique to Barbados, valid for stays of four to 21 days, that costs US$210.

Though it's mainly a charter airline, Mustique Airways has once-daily scheduled flights to St Vincent and the Grenadines. One-way fares from Barbados are US$80 to St Vincent, $85 to Mustique or Bequia and US$110 to Union; return fares are double.

BWIA has direct flights daily between Barbados and Antigua, Grenada and Trinidad; on Thursday from Tobago; and on Friday from St Lucia. BWIA's one-way/excursion fares to Barbados are US$78/124 from St Lucia, US$116/152 from Grenada, US$123/155 from Tobago or Trinidad and US$204/268 from Antigua. The excursion fares have no minimum stay requirements and allow a 30-day maximum stay.

Tickets purchased in Barbados for flights originating in Barbados have a whopping 20% tax added on. However, if you buy a ticket in Barbados for flights originating on another island the tax is not added.

### Airport Information

In season, a steel band and complimentary rum punch greets arriving passengers.

The tourist office booth, open from 8 am to midnight or until the last flight arrives, can help you book a room and is a good place to pick up tourist brochures. Opposite is Barbados National Bank's exchange booth, open daily from 8 am to midnight. Outside customs there are card and coin phones, a post office and a couple of places to grab something to eat.

The departure lounge has shops selling duty-free liquor, watches and jewellery as well as a money-exchange window.

**To/From the Airport** If you're travelling very light, it's possible to walk out to the road and wait for a passing bus. Otherwise, if you're not renting a car, you'll find a line of taxis outside the arrival lounge.

Taxi rates from the airport are about B$20 to St Lawrence, B$30 to central Bridgetown, B$38 to Holetown and B$48 to Speightstown.

### SEA

Because of Barbados' easterly position and challenging sailing conditions, it is well off the main track for most sailors and there is no yacht charter industry on the island.

There is a passenger/cargo boat, the M/V *Windward*, which links Barbados with St Lucia, St Vincent, Trinidad and Venezuela. Details are under Boat in the Getting Around chapter in the front of the book.

### Cruise Ship

About 450,000 cruise ship passengers arrive in Barbados each year. Ships dock at Bridgetown Harbour, about a km west of the city centre. The port has a new commercial centre, with about 20 shops selling duty-free goods.

### LEAVING BARBADOS

Barbados has a departure tax of B$25.

# Getting Around

## BUS

There are three kinds of buses: government-operated public buses, which are blue with a yellow stripe and have the most extensive routes; a privately operated minibus system, which uses intermediate-sized buses painted yellow with a blue stripe; and route taxis.

The latter are individually owned minivans that have 'ZR' on their licence plates and ply shorter, heavily travelled routes. Some islanders prefer the minibuses, which are generally better maintained than the government buses and don't pack passengers as sardine-like as the route taxis.

All three types of buses charge the same fare: B$1.50 to any place on the island.

Most buses transit through Bridgetown although a few north-south buses bypass the city. It's possible to get to virtually any place on the island by public bus. Buses to the south-east part of the island generally transit through Oistins, while those to Bathsheba on the east coast generally transit through Speightstown. Buses leave Speightstown for Bathsheba on odd-numbered hours (9 am etc) and return from Bathsheba on the even hour. For detailed route information call the Transport Board (☎ 436-6820).

Bus stops around the island are marked with red and white signs printed with the direction the bus is heading in ('To City' or 'Out of City'). Buses usually have their destinations posted on or above the front windscreen.

Buses along the main routes, such as Bridgetown to Oistins or Speightstown, are frequent, running from dawn to around midnight.

### Bridgetown Terminals

In Bridgetown, public buses going south and east leave from the Fairchild St Bus Terminal on the corner of Fairchild and Bridge Sts. Public buses going north up the west coast leave from the Jubilee (Lower Green) Terminal at the west end of Lower Broad St.

Minibuses use the River Bus Terminal, on the east side of the Fairchild St Public Market, for central and eastern routes. Minibuses going south leave from the corner of Probyn St and Jordan's Lane, while those going north up the west coast leave from near the general post office in Cheapside.

The route taxi terminal is on River Rd, at the east side of the Fairchild St Public Market.

### TAXI

Taxis have a 'Z' on the licence plate and usually a 'taxi' sign on the roof. They're easy to find and often wait at the side of the road in popular tourist areas.

Although fares are fixed by the government, taxis are not metered, so you should establish the fare before you start off. The rate per km is generally about B$1.50 and the flat hourly rate B$32.

---

**Have a Good Day**

In Bridgetown centre you can expect to have taxi drivers approach and ask if you need a tour or a ride, whether you look like you do or not. This is not a hassle scene, however, and if you politely decline they generally smile and respond with the likes of 'just stretching legs?' or 'you have a good day then'. ■

---

### CAR & MOTORBIKE
#### Road Rules

In Barbados, you drive on the left. Temporary driving permits are required; they cost B$10 and can be obtained through your car rental agency.

Highways are not very well marked, although key roundabouts and major intersections are usually signposted. The most consistent highway markings are often the low yellow cement posts at the side of the road; they show the highway number and below that the number of km from Bridgetown.

Finding major tourist sights, many of which are on country roads, is not too difficult as most have signs en route pointing the way. If you get lost don't hesitate to stop and ask for directions; this is common practice and Bajans are generally very helpful.

All primary and main secondary roads are sealed, although some are a bit narrow. There are lots of petrol stations around the island, including one outside the airport. Some stations in the Bridgetown area are open 24 hours a day.

**BARBADOS**

### Rental

Barbados doesn't have any car rental agents affiliated with major international rental chains. There are, instead, scores of small car rental companies, some so small that the number rings through to a private home. You simply call to book a car and someone will swing by your hotel to pick you up.

Despite the number of companies, prices don't seem to vary much. The going rate for a small car is about B$120 a day, B$300 for a three-day rental and B$500 a week, including unlimited mileage and insurance. Rental cars are marked with an 'H' on the licence plate.

While most car rental companies don't have booths at the airport there are a number of nearby agencies that will pick you up there. You can make a reservation on the spot using the courtesy car/hotel phone located between immigration and customs.

Courtesy Rent-A-Car (☎ 431-4160; fax 426-2276) is one of the island's larger companies and has an airport location.

Other car rental companies include:

A R Auto Rentals, Top Rock, Christ Church (☎ 428-9085; fax 420-6844)
Barbados Rent-A-Car, Tudor Bridge, St Michael (☎ 425-1388)
Direct Rentals, Enterprise, Christ Church (☎ 428-3133; fax 420-8190)
Hill's Car Rentals, Mason Hall St, St Michael (☎ 426-5280)
P & S Car Rentals, Cave Hill, St Michael (☎ 424-2052; fax 424-7591)
Rayside Car Rental, Charnocks, Christ Church (☎ 428-0264)
Sunny Isle Motors, Worthing, Christ Church (☎ 428-0264)
Sunset Crest Rent-A-Car, Sunset Crest, St James (☎ 432-1482; fax 432-1619)

### BICYCLE

M A Williams Rentals (☎ 427-3955) in Hastings rents 12-speed mountain bikes for B$25 for 24 hours or B$150 a week and requires a B$100 deposit or a major credit card. It's open from 9 am to 4 pm weekdays, to 3 pm on Saturday and Sunday. Club Mistral (☎ 428-7277) in Maxwell rents mountain bikes for B$30 a day.

### HITCHING

Hitchhiking is legal though not widespread, in part because buses are cheap and frequent. The usual safety precautions apply.

### TOURS

L E Williams Tour Co (☎ 427-1043) and Sunflower Tours (☎ 429-8941) both offer full-day sightseeing tours that concentrate on the perimeter of the island for B$100, lunch included, and have shorter tours of the interior, including one of Harrison's Cave and Flower Forest for B$70. Tour prices include entrance fees. There are also ads for a couple of other smaller tour companies in the free tourist magazines.

The going rate for custom tours by taxi drivers is B$32 an hour; however, you can usually negotiate with individual drivers to work out a better deal.

### Open Houses & Gardens

From January to April, the Barbados National Trust (☎ 436-9033) has an Open House programme offering visits to some of the island's grander private homes. A different house can be visited each Wednesday from 2.30 to 5.30 pm for an admission of B$12, which includes a drink. Should you be a member of the National Trust in the UK, Australia or New Zealand, the fee is only B$4. The Barbados Horticultural Society (☎ 428-5889) has an Open Garden programme that visits some of the more impressive private gardens. The gardens are open on Sunday from 2 to 6 pm and admission is B$5.

Schedules for both programmes are listed in the free tourist magazines.

### Distilleries & Breweries

'Where the Rum Come From' (☎ 435-6900) is a rather elaborate guided tour of the West India Rum Refinery, where Cockspur rum is made. Tours are on Wednesday and include a buffet lunch, steel band music and transportation to and from your hotel for B$55.

Mount Gay has a new visitors' centre (☎ 425-8757) built in a chattel-house style at its Bridgetown rum distillery. The centre, open from 9 am to 5 pm on weekdays and 10 am to 1 pm on Saturday, provides 30-minute tours and rum tasting for B$8.

The Mount Gay Visitor Centre is on the coastal road about a km north of Bridgetown Harbour, while the West India Rum Refinery is a km farther north.

Tours of the Banks beer brewery (☎ 429-2113) in Wildey, about three km east of Bridgetown centre, are conducted on Tuesday and Thursday (advance reservation required).

### Boat & Submarine Cruises

The *Jolly Roger* (☎ 436-6424), a party boat built to replicate a pirate ship, does a four-hour excursion which includes lunch, an open bar and snorkelling. It leaves from Bridgetown's Deep Water Harbour and anchors off Holetown at lunchtime. There's also a dinner cruise once or twice a week, which includes live calypso music. Both cruises cost B$105.

The same route is plied by the *Bajan Queen* (☎ 436-2149), a replica of a Mississippi riverboat, which does a sunset dinner cruise with an open bar and a live band on Wednesday and Saturday. The cost is B$105.

If you're looking for a mellower scene, there are also small sailboat cruises that include lunch, snorkelling and drinks for the same price as the party boats. These include the catamarans *Irish Mist* (☎ 436-9201), *Tiami* and *Windwarrior* (both ☎ 425-5800) and the sailboat *Secret Love* (☎ 437-7498). Most boats sail from Bridgetown at 10 am and return at 2.30 pm.

The *Atlantis* (☎ 436-8929), a 28-seater submarine lined on both sides with portholes, takes visitors on underwater tours of the coral reef off the island's west coast. Tours leave from Bridgetown numerous times daily and cost B$139 for adults, half price for children aged four to 12. Children under four are not taken. The office is at Horizon House, McGregor St, Bridgetown.

### Tours to Other Islands

The most popular day tour from Barbados is to the Grenadines. It generally starts with an early morning flight to Mustique and breakfast at the Cotton House, followed by a second flight to Union Island and a catamaran sail around the spectacular Tobago Cays, Palm Island and Mayreau. The tour includes a picnic lunch, complimentary drinks and a bit of beach and snorkelling time, returning to Barbados around 6.30 pm. The cost is US$285.

There are also day tours, utilising LIAT flights, to Grenada, St Lucia, Martinique and Dominica for around the same price.

The passenger-cargo ferry MV *Windward* can make for an interesting weekend budget trip from Barbados to St Lucia. The boat leaves Barbados at 11 pm on Friday and allows a full day of free time on St Lucia before departing from St Lucia at 7 am on Sunday. The crossing takes eight to 12 hours each way and costs from US$116 return, including a berth, breakfast and port charges. It can be booked through travel agents or tour companies.

Three of the largest tour companies are Caribbean Safari Tours (☎ 427-5100), Ship Inn Complex, St Lawrence Gap; Grenadine Tours (☎ 435-8451), 26 Hastings Plaza, Hastings, Christ Church; and Chantours (☎ 432-5591), Sunset Crest Plaza No 2, St James.

# Bridgetown

Bridgetown, the island capital, is a busy commercial city set on Carlisle Bay, the island's only natural harbour.

Architecturally, the city is a bit of a hodge-podge. Most of the main streets are quite modern and business-like in appearance, but there's also a handful of nicely restored colonial buildings as well as side streets that lead off into residential neighbourhoods sprinkled with rum shops and chattel houses.

The Careenage, a finger-like inlet lined with recreational boats, cuts into the heart of the city. At the south side of the Chamberlain Bridge, which crosses the Careenage to Trafalgar Square, is Independence Arch,

BARBADOS

BARBADOS

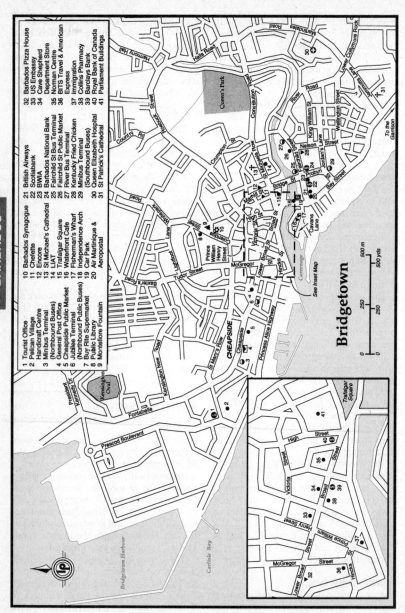

1 Tourist Office
2 Pelican Village Handicraft Centre
3 Minbus Terminal (Northbound Buses)
4 General Post Office
5 Cheapside Public Market
6 Jubilee Terminal (Northbound Public Buses)
7 Bur Rita Supermarket
8 Public Library
9 Montefiore Fountain
10 Barbados Synagogue
11 Chefette
12 Encore
13 St Michael's Cathedral
14 LIAT
15 Trafalgar Square
16 Waterfront Cafe
17 Fisherman's Wharf
18 Independence Arch
19 Car Park
20 Air Martinique & Aeropostal
21 British Airways
22 Scotiabank
23 BWIA
24 Barbados National Bank
25 Fairchild St Bus Terminal
26 Fairchild St Public Market
27 River Bus Terminal
28 Kentucky Fried Chicken
29 Minibus Terminal (Southbound Buses)
30 Queen Elizabeth Hospital
31 St Patrick's Cathedral
32 Barbados Pizza House
33 US Embassy
34 Cave Shepherd Department Store
35 Norman Centre
36 BITS Travel & American Express
37 Immigration
38 Collins Pharmacy
39 Barclays Bank
40 Royal Bank of Canada
41 Parliament Buildings

Bridgetown

which commemorates Bajan independence and has plaques honouring the island's first prime minister, Errol Barrow.

Bridgetown centre doesn't boast a lot of must-see sights but there's enough bustle to make an interesting half day of sauntering around. There are some good shopping opportunities, especially along Broad St and at the Pelican Village handicraft centre, and a couple of recommendable waterfront restaurants.

### Information
**Tourist Office** The tourist office is on Harbour Rd, opposite Pelican Village, at the west side of town. It's open from 8.30 am to 4.30 pm Monday to Friday.

**Money** There are numerous banks in the city including Barbados National Bank and Scotiabank near the bus terminals on Fairchild St and Royal Bank of Canada and Barclays Bank on Broad St near Trafalgar Square.

The American Express office, at BITS Travel (☎ 431-2423) on McGregor St, is open from 8 am to 4.30 pm Monday to Friday, to noon on Saturday.

**Post** The general post office is in Cheapside and is open from 8 am to 5 pm Monday to Friday.

**Pharmacy** Collins Pharmacy (☎ 426-4515) is on Broad St.

### Trafalgar Square
The triangular-shaped Trafalgar Square marks the bustling centre of the city. The square, which fronts the parliament buildings, has an obelisk monument honouring WW I dead and a water fountain commemorating the bringing of piped water to Bridgetown in 1861. At the west side of the square is a bronze statue of Lord Horatio Nelson, who sailed into Barbados in 1805, just months before dying at the Battle of Trafalgar. The statue was erected in 1813, three decades before its larger London counterpart.

### Parliament Buildings
On the north side of Trafalgar Square are two stone-block, Gothic-style government buildings constructed in 1871. The west-side building with the clock tower contains public offices. The building on the east side houses the Senate and House of Assembly and has stained glass windows of British monarchs and Oliver Cromwell. The parliament building is not generally open for public viewing, but it's sometimes possible to visit when parliament is in session; call ☎ 427-2019 during business hours.

> **Lord Nelson**
> Over the years the Lord Nelson statue, which stands in Trafalgar Square fronting Parliament, has been the centre of controversy among islanders, many of whom feel it too closely embraces the island's colonial past. In the 1970s, the Mighty Gabby, the island's leading calypso singer, had an immensely popular song called 'Take Down Nelson' which called for replacing the statue with one of a Bajan man. ■

### St Michael's Cathedral
St Michael's, the island's Anglican cathedral, is a five-minute walk east of Trafalgar Square. The original church, built in 1665 to accommodate 3000 worshippers, proved to be too much of a windscreen and came tumbling down in a hurricane a century later. The present structure dates to 1789 and seats 1600. At the time of construction it was said to have the widest arched ceiling of its type in the world.

Also interesting is the adjacent churchyard, where many island notables are buried. Under the big breadfruit tree you'll find the Adams family plot with the grave of Sir Grantley Adams, Barbados' first premier and the head of the West Indies Federation from 1958 to 1962. His son Tom, prime minister of Barbados from 1976 to 1985, is buried nearby.

### Barbados Synagogue

This small synagogue, built in 1833 and abandoned in 1929, has recently undergone a thorough restoration with the help of the local community and international Jewish organisations. The distinctive white building has a simple but handsome interior with brass chandeliers, a checkerboard marble floor and a columned ladies' balcony.

The first synagogue was built on this site in the 1600s, at which time Barbados had a Jewish population of more than 300. Many were refugees who had fled Portuguese and Dutch oppression in South America and became plantation owners in Barbados. Today the island's Jewish population is around 60.

The synagogue, once again a place of worship, is on Coleridge St, about a 10-minute walk from Trafalgar Square. Under the jurisdiction of the Barbados National Trust, the synagogue is open for viewing from 9 am to noon and 1 to 4 pm Monday to Friday. There's an old Jewish cemetery at the side.

Nearby, opposite the public library, is the **Montefiore Fountain**, a decorative little monument which was given to the city in 1864 by John Montefiore, a wealthy Jewish resident.

### Baxter's Rd

Baxter's Rd, at the north side of Bridgetown centre, has such a bustling night scene that it's been dubbed 'the street that never sleeps'. After the sun sets the pavement becomes thick with aproned women cooking fish in 'buck pots' over open fires; they also sell chicken, yams and roasted corn. The later it gets, the more enlivened it becomes, with rum shops and bars overflowing onto the street and calypso and reggae music wailing. Robust and colourful as it is, Baxter's Rd attracts a wide range of people, including a certain undesirable element. Use caution and common sense; it's best to go with a small group and stick to well-lit areas.

### Queen's Park

Queen's Park is a green space of grassy lawns and a popular place for island families to picnic and relax on Sunday afternoons.

On a knoll at the top of the park is a rather grand two-storey house which was once the residence of the commander of the British forces in the West Indies. Erected in 1786, it underwent a thorough restoration in 1973 and now houses a theatre and a gallery that exhibits local art. Nearby are a few cages with green monkeys and exotic birds and a lunchtime restaurant serving inexpensive Bajan fare.

One of the park's more unique features is the huge baobab tree, 18 metres in circumference, at the edge of the playground. A plaque at the site estimates the tree to be 1000 years old, the claim somewhat complicated by the fact that the tree is native to Africa, a continent which presumably had no contact with Barbados until the early 17th century.

There's no admission fee to the park or gallery; it's possible to drive in via the main Constitution Rd entrance.

### Observatory

The Harry Bayley Observatory (☎ 426-1317), east of central Bridgetown in the Clapham area, off Rendezvous Rd, is the headquarters of the Barbados Astronomical Society. The observatory is open to the public on Friday from 8.30 to 11.30 pm.

### The Garrison Area

About two km south of central Bridgetown is the Barbados Garrison. Spreading inland from the south side of Carlisle Bay, the garrison was the base of the British Windward and Leeward Islands Command in the 1800s.

A central focal point is the oval-shaped Savannah, which was once a large parade grounds and is now used for cricket games, jogging and Saturday horse races. Some of the Garrison's more ornate colonial buildings stand along the west side of the Savannah, most notably the salmon-coloured Main Guard with its four-sided clock tower. Fronting the Main Guard you'll find an impressive array of cannons. Barbados, incidentally, claims the world's largest collection of 17th-century iron cannons, including one of only two existing cannons bearing Cromwell's Republican Arms.

If you're interested in British military history, the entire Garrison area can be fascinating to explore. The first fortifications in the area went up as early as 1650, although many of the current buildings date to the mid-19th century, a consequence of the violent 1831 hurricane that destroyed virtually everything not made of stone or iron. In the grounds of the Hilton at Needham's Point you'll find the remains of the 17th-century Charles Fort and a nice coastal view.

### Barbados Museum

The Barbados Museum, on the north-east side of the Savannah, is housed in an early 19th-century military prison. It has engaging displays on all aspects of the island's history beginning with its early Amerindian inhabitants. Not surprisingly, the most extensive collections cover the colonial era, with exhibits on slavery and emancipation, military history and plantation house furniture, all accompanied by insightful narratives.

Among the museum's other offerings are a cell that looks as it would have to a prisoner in the 1800s, an African culture gallery, a children's gallery, natural history displays, changing exhibits of local contemporary art, a gift shop and a small café.

For a quick immersion into island history, you couldn't do better than to spend an hour or two here. The museum is open from 10 am to 6 pm Monday to Saturday. Admission is B$7 for adults, B$1 for children. The museum also sponsors a dinner show, detailed in the Entertainment section earlier in this chapter.

### Places to Stay

The *Barbados Hilton* (☎ 426-0200; fax 436-8946; in the USA ☎ (800) 445-8667), PO Box 510, Bridgetown, is at the tip of Needham's Point on the grounds of the former Charles Fort. It's a typical Hilton,

with a pool, health club, tennis courts, restaurants and 185 rooms, each with a phone, TV, minibar, air-con and balcony. The area is pleasant enough, and has a nice beach considering its proximity to the capital. Behind the hotel are some fort remains, complete with an embankment lined with replicas of the original cannons. Room rates are US$137/218 in summer/winter.

On the road into the Hilton, next to the Brown Sugar restaurant, is the *Island Inn Hotel* (☎ 436-6393), Aquatic Gap, St Michael. The hotel incorporates a restored 1804 garrison building that was originally a military rum store. There are 25 rooms, each with either a king or queen-sized bed, air-con and a phone. There's a bar, restaurant and pool. Singles/doubles cost US$125/175 in summer, US$165/225 in winter.

### Places to Eat

The best places to buy fruit and vegetables are at the Fairchild St and Cheapside public markets, which are open from 7 am to late afternoon Monday to Saturday. Produce vendors can also be found along the streets near Trafalgar Square. There are a couple of large supermarkets in town, including the Buy Rite Supermarket on Lower Broad St.

*Merle's Health Food*, upstairs in the Norman Centre on Broad St, has a B$10 vegetarian lunch from 11 am until mid-afternoon Monday to Saturday. Servings are generous and the food is good – typically brown rice, beans, local vegies and a salad. Merle's also makes peanut butter punch and a good mauby and sells herbal and ginseng drinks and a few packaged health food items. On the same floor is a stall with homemade ice cream and smoothies.

*Chefette*, on Marhill St, 100 metres north of Trafalgar St, is a busy fast-food spot with inexpensive rotis, burgers and fried chicken. *Encore*, a cafeteria-style restaurant opposite Chefette, has cheap Bajan fare and a pleasant dining area.

A popular lunch stop with shoppers and office workers is *Ideal Restaurant*, a cafeteria with inexpensive island food upstairs in

BARBADOS

the Cave Shepherd department store. A serving of flying fish or field peas and rice costs B$2.65 and there's a different full meal each day for B$10. It's open from 9 am to 3 pm on weekdays.

*Barbados Pizza House* (☎ 431-0500) on Broad St has good pizza priced from B$14 to B$27 depending on the size, plus a dollar or two for each topping. They also sell pizza by the slice for B$4 and English fish & chips for B$15.

Bridgetown's busiest lunch spot is *Fisherman's Wharf* (☎ 436-7778), opposite Independence Arch, which has a nice 2nd-floor waterfront setting overlooking the Careenage. At lunch there are a number of good-value dishes, including a nice spicy flying fish with fries and salad (B$15) and beef kebabs with a yoghurt chutney sauce (B$19); other offerings such as coconut shrimp are B$26. At dinner, served à la carte, most main courses are priced from B$30 to B$35. They make a generous rum punch and are open weekdays from 11.30 am to 3 pm and nightly from 6.30 to 10 pm.

The *Waterfront Cafe* (☎ 427-0093), on the ground floor of the same building, has both waterfront pavement dining and indoor seating. It has pepperpot for B$14 and dishes such as chicken satay or garlic shrimp for around B$25. The menu also includes gazpacho soup, good salads and a daily vegetarian special for B$20. There's a small dance floor and on some evenings there's live jazz. It's open Monday to Saturday from 10 am to midnight.

*Brown Sugar* (☎ 426-7684), at Aquatic Gap in the Garrison area, is a veritable greenhouse of hanging plants complete with a waterfall and whistling frogs. Its popular West Indian buffet, available from 11.30 am to 2.30 pm Monday to Friday, includes soup, salad, flying fish, pepperpot, salt fish, souse, peas and rice, pickled bananas and dessert for B$29. It's also open from 6 to 10 pm daily for dinner served ã la carte. Main dishes include the likes of seafood fettucine, jerk pork and coconut beer shrimp for B$25 to B$38, broiled lobster for B$60. Reservations are advised.

# South Coast

The south coast, from Hastings to Maxwell, has most of the island's low to mid-range accommodation. Virtually the entire strip is fringed with white-sand beaches and turquoise waters.

Hwy 7, a two-lane road, links the south-coast villages; buses and route taxis (No 11) run frequently along this route as they ply between Bridgetown and Oistins.

While the south coast is fairly well built up, some areas, such as the coastal roads in St Lawrence and Maxwell, are off the main strip and thus more lightly trafficked. As a rule the farther east you go from Bridgetown the less developed it is.

All the communities described in this section are in the parish of Christ Church, which ends at the airport. For the region east of the airport see the South-East section.

## HASTINGS & ROCKLEY

The Hastings-Rockley area is the first major tourist area east of Bridgetown. The centre of activity is Rockley Beach, a roadside white-sand beach with shade trees, snack wagons, clothing vendors and women braiding hair. It's a half-local, half-tourist scene and as Rockley Beach is a mere 10-minute bus ride from central Bridgetown, it attracts a crowd, especially on weekends.

### Places to Stay

*Abbeville Hotel* (☎ 435-7924; fax 435-8502), Rockley, Christ Church, is on the inland side of Hwy 7, a couple of minutes' walk from Rockley Beach. This older 18-room hotel has straightforward rooms with private baths. Singles/doubles cost US$45/50 for an air-con room, US$35/40 without air-con. All rates are US$5 cheaper in summer and major credit cards are accepted. The hotel's Bert's Bar is a popular local eating and drinking spot.

*Sichris Hotel* (☎ 435-7930; fax 435-8232), Worthing, Christ Church, on Hwy 7 opposite the Abbeville Hotel, has 24 air-con suites that are a bit less wearworn than most other moderately priced places in the area. All rooms have kitchenettes and phones but no TV. There's a pool. Studios cost US$75/85 in summer/winter. The one-bedroom apartments, which have balconies, cost US$85/100 in summer/winter.

The five-storey beachfront *Coconut Court Hotel* (☎ 427-1655; fax 429-8198), Hastings, Christ Church, is a good-value package resort hotel popular with Canadians. There are 30 ocean-view rooms with small refrigerators, coffeemakers and toaster-ovens that cost US$46/79 in summer/winter. There are also 60 spacious apartments with full kitchens that cost US$46/79 for a studio, US$50/89 for a one-bedroom apartment and US$86/159 for up to four people in a three-bedroom apartment. Rooms have ceiling fans and balconies; some have a double sofabed in the living room. There's no minimum stay. There's a nice beachside pool, a restaurant, a bar and water-sports rentals.

*Ocean View Hotel* (☎ 427-7821; fax 427-7826; in the USA ☎ (800) 225-2230), Hastings, Christ Church, is one of the island's oldest hotels. It has some classic touches, including a lobby filled with antiques and a nightclub featuring cabaret and '50s musicals. There are 31 rooms with varying decor; some have canopy beds and hardwood floors, others are quite basic, although all have phones and private baths. Ocean View is squeezed between the beach and road, so if you're sensitive to noise, avoid the roadside rooms. Singles/doubles cost US$40/50 for roadside rooms and US$55/65 for ocean-view rooms in summer, US$65/75 for roadside rooms and US$95/120 for ocean-view rooms in winter.

### Places to Eat

At the east end of Rockley Beach on Hwy 7 is a *Barbados Pizza House*, followed by *Shakey's Pizza*. Both are open from 11 am to 11 pm (later on weekends) and have the usual pizza and fast-food offerings as well as weekday lunch specials. On the same road 300 metres west of Shakey's is a *Kentucky*

*Fried Chicken*. The *Barbecue Barn*, opposite Rockley Beach, is a modern steakhouse restaurant with grilled chicken (B$15) and steak (B$17) served with a baked potato and garlic bread. There's a small but reasonable salad bar costing B$5 a serving with a meal, B$8 if purchased separately. In the same complex is a branch of the fast-food chain *Chefette* with burgers, rotis and fried chicken. Both places are open from 11 am to 11 pm daily.

*Sugar Reef Bar & Restaurant* (☎ 435-8074), on the west side of Rockley Beach, has a nice waterfront setting and good-value food. The menu ranges from inexpensive kebabs and barbecue spareribs to lobster. If you stick with the simpler offerings, you can get a solid meal for about B$25. It's open for lunch until 3 pm, dinner until 10 pm.

*Da Luciano* (☎ 427-5518), in a lovely old Barbadian house on Hwy 7 opposite Ocean View Hotel, offers fine dining and very good Italian food. A range of starters, including misto mare (mixed seafood) and antipasto, are priced from B$10 to B$20. The extensive main-course menu includes lots of pastas and a few dozen fish and meat dishes from B$30 to B$50. It's open from 6.30 to 10 pm nightly.

The *Ocean View Hotel* (☎ 427-7821) has a dining room overlooking the ocean and a kitchen that turns out traditional West Indian cuisine. At breakfast, French toast and coffee cost B$10 while lunch dishes such as lamb curry or an omelette with salad cost about twice that. From Thursday to Saturday, there's a Bajan dinner buffet with a cabaret show for B$75 and in the high season a Sunday lunch buffet, accompanied by a jazz band, for B$55.

### WORTHING

Worthing can make a nice base, particularly if you're on a tight budget but still want to be in the middle of things. It has inexpensive places to eat and a handful of cheap guesthouses that are either on the beach or a stone's throw from it.

Sandy Beach, which fronts Worthing, is a lovely broad beach of powdery white sand. The beach has just enough activity to be

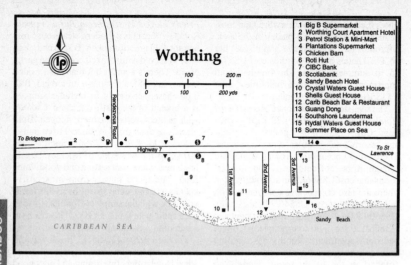

Worthing

| 0 | 100 | 200 m |
| 0 | 100 | 200 yds |

1 Big B Supermarket
2 Worthing Court Apartment Hotel
3 Petrol Station & Mini-Mart
4 Plantations Supermarket
5 Chicken Barn
6 Roti Hut
7 CIBC Bank
8 Scotiabank
9 Sandy Beach Hotel
10 Crystal Waters Guest House
11 Shells Guest House
12 Carib Beach Bar & Restaurant
13 Guang Dong
14 Southshore Laundermat
15 Hydal Waters Guest House
16 Summer Place on Sea

To Bridgetown
Rendezvous Road
Highway 7
1st Avenue
2nd Avenue
3rd Avenue
To St Lawrence
CARIBBEAN SEA
Sandy Beach

interesting but not so much that it feels crowded.

From Worthing it's just a five-minute stroll to St Lawrence, a walk that can be made along the beach at low tide.

### Information

There's a Scotiabank on Hwy 7 in front of Sandy Beach Hotel and a CIBC Bank opposite Scotiabank.

The Southshore Laundermat (435-7438), on Hwy 7 opposite the road to Summer Place by Sea, has a token-operated laundry costing B$4 to wash a load of clothes, B$4.25 to dry.

### Places to Stay

**Guesthouses** *Summer Place on Sea* (☎ 435-417, 435-7424), Worthing, Christ Church, is a pleasantly funky place with the feel of a beach cottage, set right on the sand. There are seven simple but clean rooms, each with a private bathroom, hot water and a fan. Two rooms also have kitchenettes. A TV and phone are available in the common room. Owner George de Mattos is a congenial host who hails from Trinidad but has been operating inns on Barbados for 25 years. Rates are US$35 for kitchenette units, US$20/30 a

single/double for the others. As lots of repeat visitors stay here, it can be challenging getting a room during the peak months of January to March and July and August – still it's worth a try anytime.

Nearby is *Rydal Waters Guest House* (☎ 435-7433), Worthing, Christ Church, in an older private home. The six rooms, which are all upstairs, have private baths, two twin beds and table fans. The guesthouse is not on the beach but it's barely a minute's walk away. Singles/doubles cost US$20/30 in winter, US$5 less in summer.

*Shells Guest House* (☎ 435-7253), 1st Ave, Worthing, Christ Church, has a Scandinavian manager and is popular with European budget travellers and gay visitors. There are eight simple rooms, all with ceiling fans, a small dresser and a lamp. The doubles have either a double bed with a private bathroom or two twin beds with a shared bathroom. The singles are small and have just a single bed and wash basin. Singles/doubles cost US$15/25 in summer, US$20/35 in winter, including continental breakfast. There a TV room and a bar.

*Crystal Waters Guest House* (☎ 435-7514), Worthing, Christ Church, is a small, older beachfront inn with a faded period character. The rooms are clean and have hardwood floors, twin beds with comfortable mattresses, dressers and private bathrooms. There's a spacious 2nd-floor sitting room with a TV and ocean view and a casual beachfront bar. Singles/doubles cost US$25/35 all year round.

**Hotels & Apartments** *Worthing Court Apartment Hotel* (☎ 435-7910; fax 435-7374), Worthing, Christ Church, on the inland side of Hwy 7, is a three-storey complex with 24 older but clean units. Rooms have rattan furnishings, kitchenettes, phones, air-con, radios and small balconies – most without views. Studios cost US$55/80 in summer/winter, one-bedroom apartments cost US$75/100. Singles cost US$5 to US$10 less; children under 10 are free. There's a pool.

*Sandy Beach Hotel* (☎ 435-8000; fax 435-8053), Worthing, Christ Church, is a modern and rather nondescript four-storey beachfront hotel, formerly a Best Western. All 89 units are suites with kitchenettes, dining areas, phones, air-con and a patio or balcony. The hotel has a pool and restaurant. Winter rates are pricey at US$185 for a one-bedroom unit, US$270 for a two-bedroom, two-bath unit, plus US$50 more for an ocean view. Rates drop a full 50% in summer.

**Places to Eat**

The popular *Carib Beach Bar & Restaurant*, right on Sandy Beach, has a lively bar at ground level and a casual restaurant upstairs. The menu is varied. The fish cutter sandwich is excellent value at B$6, fresh fish dishes cost B$14 to B$16 and servings are generous. There's live music from 3.30 to 7.30 pm on Sunday, as well as on Wednesday nights when there's a fish fry and Friday nights when there's a Bajan barbecue buffet; both start at 7.30 pm and cost B$25. The restaurant is open from 11.30 am to around 10 pm (to 7.30 pm on Sunday), but the bar stays open later. On weekdays there's a happy hour from 5 to 6 pm.

The *Roti Hut*, on Hwy 7 west of Sandy Beach Hotel, has good rotis ranging in price from B$3.20 for a potato version to B$8 for a shrimp roti. It's open from 11 am to 10 pm Monday to Thursday, until 11 pm on Friday and Saturday.

The *Chicken Barn*, on Hwy 7 opposite the Roti Hut, is a modern fried chicken restaurant with both eat-in and takeaway service. You can get simple salads, burgers for B$3 or fried chicken and chips for B$10.50. It's open from 10 am to 10.30 pm Monday to Saturday.

*Guang Dong* (☎ 435-7387), on the corner of Hwy 7 and 3rd Ave, has sweet and sour pork with chop suey and fried rice or a choice of three other combos for B$16 at lunchtime. Otherwise, there's a full range of standard Cantonese main dishes, most from B$16 to B$25. It's open daily from 11 am to 2 pm and 6 to 10 pm.

You can get a continental breakfast of juice, coffee, toast and bananas for B$5 until 10.30 am at *Shells Guest House*.

The Big B Supermarket, just 100 metres up Rendezvous Rd, has a wide range of imported foods, a deli with inexpensive local food (stew, souse etc) and a large liquor section. It's open from 8 am to 7 pm on Monday and Tuesday, until 8 pm Wednesday to Saturday. The nearby Plantations Supermarket, on the corner of Hwy 7 and Rendezvous Rd, is more like a large convenience store but it's open on Sunday. Some of the 24-hour petrol stations along Hwy 7 have mini-marts.

## ST LAWRENCE & DOVER

St Lawrence has the area's most active night scene as well as numerous good-value, midrange restaurants and places to stay, most of them fronting the ocean.

The western end of St Lawrence is at the junction of Little Bay and Hwy 7, but most of St Lawrence lies along the St Lawrence Coast Rd, in the area known as the Gap. While there's a lot happening in the Gap, the coastal road extends nearly two km and it's not a hectic scene.

Dover Beach, near the middle of the coastal road, is a nice broad white-sand

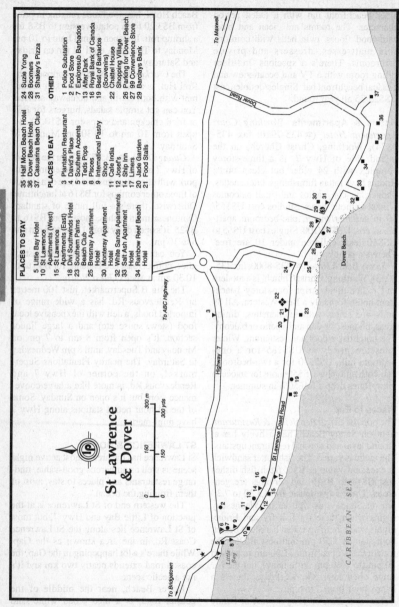

beach that attracts swimmers, bodysurfers, sailors and board surfers, depending on the water conditions. The beach also has a line of clothing stalls selling tropical print shirts and dresses.

## Information
On St Lawrence Coast Rd there's a Royal Bank of Canada beside Ship Inn and a Barclays Bank next to Shakey's Pizza. There's also a drugstore next to Shakey's.

You'll find a small store selling groceries and spirits on Hwy 7 about 100 metres east of Little Bay Hotel and a '99' convenience store opposite Boomers on St Lawrence Coast Rd, which is open from 8 am to 10 pm.

## Places to Stay – bottom end
A good value low-end place is *Salt Ash Apartment Hotel* (☎ 428-8753), St Lawrence Gap, Christ Church, a small family-run place that caters to both overseas and Caribbean travellers. The eight units are roomy and have air-con, private bathrooms with tubs, kitchenettes and balconies, some with fine ocean views. While certainly not fancy, it's quite adequate, right on the beach and costs just US$35/58 in summer/winter. There's a phone in the hall and a beachside snack bar.

Next door and also right on the beach is *White Sands Apartments* (☎ 428-7484), St Lawrence Gap, Christ Church, an older complex with 10 straightforward studio units, costing US$40/57 in summer/winter.

*Little Bay Hotel* (☎ 435-8574; fax 435-8586), St Lawrence Gap, Christ Church, is a pleasant little beachside hotel on Little Bay. All 10 rooms and apartments are comfortable, with balconies looking straight out onto the water, ceiling fans, refrigerators and private baths. The apartments have separate kitchens. The hotel, operated by a Canadian couple, costs US$45/55 in summer for rooms/apartments, US$70/90 in winter. If business is slow they generally discount the winter rates by about US$15, in which case they're a particularly good value.

The *St Lawrence Apartments* (☎ 435-6950), St Lawrence Gap, Christ Church, is

composed of two nearby apartment hotels with a total of 75 units. St Lawrence West has big studios with ceiling fans, air-con, phones, bathtubs, kitchens and large ocean-facing balconies that cost US$60/100 in summer/winter. St Lawrence East has essentially the same facilities, though its units are a bit smaller; studios, which rent for US$55/80, have kitchenettes (no ovens), and there are also one-bedroom apartments with full kitchens for US$60/90. Both complexes have swimming pools and are a good value, on par with many other places at far higher rates.

*Monteray Apartment Hotel* (☎ 428-9152; fax 428-7722), Dover, Christ Church, has roomy one-bedroom apartments, each with a full kitchen, a living room with a dining table, couch and chairs and a separate bedroom with two twin beds and a desk; rates are US$60/95 in summer/winter. There are also studio units that are similarly furnished but more compact and US$5 cheaper. The downstairs apartments have patios while the upper-level ones have small balconies. All 22 units have air-con and phones and there's a pool. The location behind Shakey's Pizza isn't inspirational but the place is tidy and a good value at these rates.

*Rainbow Reef Beach Hotel* (☎ 428-5110; fax 428-5395), Dover, Christ Church, is a modern 45-unit beachfront hotel. The standard rooms are small but comfortable, each with air-con, phone, TV and firm double beds and cost US$50/70 in summer/winter. There are also larger studios with kitchens and balconies for US$65/105 with garden views, US$75/130 with ocean views, and one-bedroom apartments at US$95/160, two-bedroom apartments at US$130/225. All rates are for up to two people. Additional adults cost US$25; there's no charge for children under 12. It has a pool, restaurant and nice strip of beach.

## Places to Stay – top end
*Bresmay Apartment Hotel* (☎ 428-6131; fax 428-7722), St Lawrence Gap, Christ Church, has two sections. The new section is on the beach and costs US$125/150 in summer/

winter for studios, US$165/190 for one-bedroom apartments. The older section, a small three-storey block building on the opposite side of the road, has studio units that are pleasant enough, but they face a pool and the hotel's Chinese restaurant rather than the beach. Rates in the older section are US$65/105, though they sometimes offer special walk-in rates discounted by about 20%. All units have kitchen facilities, phones, air-con and patios or balconies.

*Half Moon Beach Hotel* (☎ 428-7131; fax 428-6089), St Lawrence, Christ Church, has a nice beachside location and pleasant studios with air-con, ceiling fans, radios and phones. The living room, which is separated from the bedroom by a curtain, has rattan furnishings and a kitchenette. Most of the units also have ocean-fronting balconies. Rates are US$70/135 in summer/winter. There are also some cheaper hotel rooms, but they're generally rented on a long-term basis. There's a pool.

*Casuarina Beach Club* (☎ 428-3600; fax 428-1970), Dover, Christ Church, is popular with package-tour groups and families with children. The hotel is on a nice beach and is surrounded by coconut and casuarina trees. The 129 units have ceiling fans, air-con and phones. Rates for garden-view rooms are US$85/150 in summer/winter. Add US$10 more for a beachfront studio. One-bedroom apartments cost US$115/180, two-bedroom apartments cost US$160/280. Children under 12 are free and a third adult is US$10 more. There are tennis courts, a restaurant, bar and mini-mart.

Though it doesn't have as much of a following as the neighbouring Casuarina, the *Dover Beach Hotel* (☎ 428-8075; fax 428-2122), Dover, Christ Church, is a bit spiffier and cheaper. The 39 air-con studios and one-bedroom apartments have phones, radios, kitchens and private patios or balconies. It's on the beach and there's a pool, restaurant, bar and cocktail lounge. Rates range from US$78 to US$98 in summer, from US$100 to US$135 in winter. The lowest rates are for studios with garden views.

*Southern Palms Beach Club* (☎ 428-7171; fax 428-7175), St Lawrence, Christ Church, is a modern 100-room resort hotel with a fine beachfront location. The rooms have standard resort decor with tile floors, air-con and minibars but the lower priced ones, which begin at US$100/160 in summer/winter, are quite small. The more spacious suites that have kitchenettes cost US$135/250. The resort has two restaurants, a bar, two pools, tennis courts and complimentary Hobie Cat boats and windsurfing equipment.

Also in the area is the *Divi Southwinds Hotel*, a sprawling time-share resort.

### Places to Eat – cheap

*International Pastry Shop* is a wonderful little English-style bakery that makes whole-wheat raisin scones, coconut cakes, crispy French bread, cornish pastries and a range of other goodies. It opens at 8 am, has half a dozen café tables and makes a nice place for breakfast when there's always something warm coming out of the oven. The bakery is open daily until about 3 or 4 pm.

*Teds Pops* is a small ice-cream shop with a full range of ice cream and sherbet concoctions at reasonable prices. You can also get juices, beer, espresso and inexpensive sandwiches. It's open daily except Monday, from 11 am on weekdays and 2 pm on weekends, closing at midnight.

A collection of seven bubblegum-coloured chattel houses opposite Southern Palms has been turned into a little shopping centre. One houses *Friendly's*, a deli with pastries, meat pies and sandwiches, while another has an ice-cream shop. A couple of food stalls nearby sell tacos or burritos (B$8) and smoothies.

The Ship Inn, on St Lawrence Coast Rd, has a couple of dining spots: *The Courtyard* serves light fare for B$12 to B$25, while the *Captain's Carvery* has a rather average buffet dinner that includes a salad bar and slices from a prime roast for B$39.

*Limers* is one of the cheaper restaurants on the St Lawrence strip and features Bajan food and a simple island decor. Meals include barbecued chicken (B$15), fish fillet or beef pepperpot (B$18) and sirloin or fried shrimp (B$28). All dishes include rice or potatoes and a salad. It's open daily from 6 pm and there's a happy hour from 6 to 7 pm.

*Boomers*, on the roadside in the Dover Beach area, is a lively bar and restaurant that's very popular with expats and visitors. It has some reasonably priced breakfasts (from 8 to 11.30 am) including French toast or a cheese omelette, both with juice and coffee, for B$8.50. For around the same price you can get a flying fish sandwich or a hamburger at lunch (11.30 am to 3 pm) while dinner features a vegetarian plate for B$16, flying fish or Creole chicken for B$19 and shrimp or roast beef for B$28. All come with a vegetable and choice of baked potato or Bajan rice. The last order is taken around 9.45 pm but the bar usually stays open to about midnight.

*Shakey's Pizza*, near Boomers, has the usual pizza, pasta, submarine sandwich and burger menu. One of the more attractive deals is the business lunch, from 11 am to 3 pm, which features a dolphin (mahimahi) or flying fish sandwich with fries and a Coke for B$8.50.

*Jade Garden* (☎ 428-2759), across from the Southern Palms Beach Club, is an air-conditioned Chinese restaurant with a varied Cantonese and Sichuan menu. Most chicken, beef, fish and pork dishes, as well a handful of vegetarian offerings, cost B$16. A bowl of steamed rice is B$4 more. At lunch there's a special that includes soup, a choice of main dishes and rice or chow mein for B$17 or a simple takeaway box lunch for half that price. Lunch is from 11 am to 2.30 pm, dinner from 6 to 10.30 pm daily.

*Suzie Yong* (☎ 428-1865), a Chinese restaurant at Bresmay Apartment Hotel, has an open-air setting with prices similar to those at Jade Garden. Lunch specials cost from B$13 to B$18 and include a main dish and fried rice or chow mein. It's open from noon to 2.30 pm and 6 to 10 pm Tuesday to Sunday.

## Places to Eat – expensive

*Southern Accents* (☎ 435-8574) has al fresco patio dining with a romantic waterside setting on Little Bay. The staff are friendly, the food is fine if not necessarily inspired and prices are reasonable. Starters, including conch fritters and satays, are priced around B$12. Main courses include fried chicken, Bajan fish and Thai spicy noodles, all about B$25, and a few seafood dishes for B$30. At lunch there's a simple menu with cheese omelettes, burgers or flying fish cutters with salad or fries for around B$15.

*Pisces* (☎ 435-6564), at the west end of St Lawrence Coast Rd, is a sprawling and very popular waterfront restaurant with an interior chock-full of hanging philodendrons. Its varied menu includes Jamaican jerk chicken and blackened fish for around B$30 or a vegetarian platter and a daily pasta for a few dollars less. The menu tops off with lobster for B$60. A side salad or gazpacho soup costs another B$6. It's open daily for dinner only, from 6 pm.

*David's Place* (☎ 435-6550) is an upmarket dinner restaurant with a waterfront setting and good Bajan food. Main dishes, which include spicy fried chicken or pepperpot for B$35 and rabbit for B$48, come with peas and rice or chips and vegetables. Add another B$12 for a garden salad. It's open from 6 to 10 pm nightly and there's a loose dress code, which essentially means no shorts.

*Cafe India* (☎ 435-6531), the Gap's new Indian restaurant, has a slightly upmarket mood and an extensive menu of traditional Indian dishes. There are various curry, korma and biryani offerings, as well as a dozen vegetarian plates, averaging B$30. Other dishes include tandoori items such as chicken tikka and shish kebab, served with rice and salad, and a few European offerings like steak and fries from around B$35. At lunch, there's a fixed course special that includes a starter, main course and coffee or tea for B$19. Lunch is from noon to 2 pm on weekdays, dinner from 6 to 10.30 pm daily.

*Josef's* is a casually elegant restaurant with open-air dining and well-prepared seafood dishes. Starters, including escargot, smoked salmon and a savoury seafood crêpe, cost from B$14 to B$22. Main courses served with rice and vegetables include a Cajun-style blackened fish, kingfish in a curry and fruit sauce, and shrimp pernod – all priced around B$40. There are also half a dozen meat dishes, including rack of lamb and peppercorn steak. Lunch, from noon to 3 pm on weekdays, features lower priced specials ranging from chef's salad for B$18 to grilled sirloin for B$24. Dinner is daily from 6.30 to about 9.30 pm and dinner reservations are suggested.

## MAXWELL

Maxwell has two distinct but adjacent areas. Maxwell Rd (Hwy 7) is predominantly residential with a few small businesses and a couple of the area's older hotels. Maxwell Coast Rd, which curves south from the highway, is the more touristed area.

Maxwell is generally a quieter, cheaper area than St Lawrence, and some of its beaches are equally appealing. The dining options in Maxwell can quickly wear thin, however, and there's little nightlife. Depending on where you stay, St Lawrence is a 15 to 30-minute walk away, while the bus to Bridgetown takes roughly 20 minutes.

### Information

Winkles Washing Club, next to China Gardens, charges B$12 to wash, dry and fold a small load of laundry.

### Places to Stay

*Fairholme Hotel* (☎ 428-9425), Maxwell, Christ Church, set back 150 metres from Maxwell Rd, has simple, cheap accommodation. There are studios with cooking facilities, two single beds, private bathrooms and a faded decor; the 2nd-floor ones have balconies but their corrugated tin roofs can be noisy in the rain. The studios cost US$35/60 in summer/winter; optional air-con costs US$3 per eight hours. A better deal, especially in winter, are the 11 fan-cooled rooms in the main house. These are basic but clean, although only a plastic curtain, not a door, separates the toilet and shower from the sleeping area. Singles/doubles cost US$22/26 in summer, US$25/30 in winter. The hotel is quiet and the rear courtyard has a small but deep swimming pool. It's about five minutes on foot to the nearest beach or by bus to St Lawrence.

*Shangri-la Apartment Hotel* (☎ 428-9112; fax 428-3429), Maxwell Coast Rd,

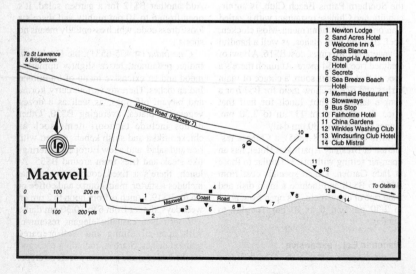

To St Lawrence & Bridgetown

Maxwell Road (Highway 7)

**Maxwell**

Maxwell Coast Road

To Oistins

0   100   200 m
0   100   200 yds

1  Newton Lodge
2  Sand Acres Hotel
3  Welcome Inn & Casa Blanca
4  Shangri-la Apartment Hotel
5  Secrets
6  Sea Breeze Beach Hotel
7  Mermaid Restaurant
8  Stowaways
9  Bus Stop
10  Fairholme Hotel
11  China Gardens
12  Winkles Washing Club
13  Windsurfing Club Hotel
14  Club Mistral

Christ Church, has pleasant, spacious studios and one and two-bedroom apartments. All have large bathrooms, fully equipped kitchens, ceiling fans, big balconies and either a queen or two twin beds. A few ground-level apartments also have air-con. The hotel books almost solely with tour groups and has withdrawn from reservation systems geared towards individuals, but it does offer walk-in rates comparable to those given to tour groups. If you arrive when it's not booked solid with a tour, this place can be a bargain with studios costing US$40/60 in summer/winter, one-bedroom units US$60/70 and two-bedroom units US$70/90. There's a pool, a poolside bar and restaurant and a car rental office on site.

The *Windsurfing Club Hotel* (☎ 428-9095), Maxwell, Christ Church, is an unpretentious and very casual seaside hotel catering to windsurfers. There are 14 straightforward rooms with private baths and fans; two rooms also have kitchenettes for the same price. It attracts an international crowd, has a cheap restaurant and is home to the Club Mistral operation. Rooms cost US$45/50 in summer, US$5 more in winter, but they often book solid with windsurfing tours.

*Sea Breeze Beach Hotel* (☎ 428-2825; fax 428-2872), Maxwell Coast Rd, Christ Church, is a rather pleasant beachfront resort. The 30 studios in the main three-storey building are smallish with kitchenettes, two single beds, ceiling fans, air-con, phones and bathrooms with tubs. The upper levels have pleasant little balconies, most fronting the sea. Rates are US$65/125 in summer/winter; add US$10 for an ocean-view room. There's also an older annexe with straightforward fan-cooled studios that rent for US$50/90 in summer/winter. There are no room TVs in either wing but there is a TV lounge and a pool.

*Sand Acres Hotel* (☎ 428-7141; fax 428-2524), Maxwell Coast Rd, Christ Church, has 37 spacious contemporary studios with kitchenettes, ocean-view balconies, air-con, TVs and phones. There's a restaurant, bar, tennis courts, a pool and a lovely stretch of beachfront. Studios cost US$70 in June, September and October; US$80 from 17 April to 28 May and in July and August; US$150 from mid-December to late March; and US$105 at other times. There are larger one-bedroom apartments for about 20% more. It's US$15 each for a third and fourth adult, but children under 15 are free.

*Newton Lodge*, opposite Sand Acres Hotel, is an intriguing old house with creaking hardwood floors, a formal dining room and a living room full of upholstered chairs and couches. There are five rooms, all full of character but no two alike. Choicest are No 3, a commodious room with a king bed, and No 2, which has an antique four-poster bed. Both have bathtubs. Guests may use the kitchen and the washing machine and dryer. All rooms cost a very reasonable US$35/50 in summer/winter. The rooms are booked through Sand Acres Hotel; it's best to make arrangements during the day. If the desk clerk doesn't seem familiar with the house, ask for Ms Yarde. As all the action and staff are across the street, the house might feel a bit too isolated for some people.

The *Welcome Inn* (☎ 428-9900; fax 428-8905), Maxwell Coast Rd, Christ Church, is the beach's biggest hotel, rising seven stories. This is a standard package-tour hotel with rooms that are average in both size and decor; all have kitchenettes, air-con, phones, simple rattan furnishings and balconies. Standard studios cost US$60/105 in summer/winter with a garden view, but it's worth the additional US$10 for an ocean view. Nicer still are the corner deluxe rooms which have queen beds and broad ocean views and cost US$85/125 in summer/winter. There's a TV lounge and a large swimming pool.

If you're staying in the area for awhile, there are a handful of apartment-for-rent signs along the north end of Maxwell Coast Rd that might be worth checking.

## Places to Eat

The dining room at the *Fairholme Hotel* offers a continental breakfast of toast, orange juice and coffee for B$5 or the same combo with the addition of a cheese omelette for

B$10. It also has a light lunch menu and dinner by reservation only. Breakfast is from 8 to 9.30 am, lunch from noon to 2 pm.

*China Gardens* (☎ 428-8179) on Maxwell Rd, just a few minutes' walk east of the Fairholme Hotel, has good-sized servings of average Chinese food at cheaper than average prices. Most dishes, including a good beef with vegetables plate, are priced from B$13 to B$19. It's open from 11 am to 2 pm and 6 to 10 pm and has both sit-down and takeaway service.

*Windsurfing Club Hotel* has a simple restaurant and bar with both indoor seating and seaside picnic tables. Burgers, sandwiches and salads cost from B$10 to B$12 and chalkboard specials like chicken or fish & chips are a few dollars more.

*Stowaways*, on the beach opposite the Fairholme Hotel, is a café that you might consider in a pinch. It has a simple menu, with sandwiches, fish cutters and burgers for B$7. There are also hot dishes from B$15 but it's best to stick to the sandwiches.

The *Mermaid Restaurant* (☎ 428-4116), on the east end of Maxwell Coast Rd, has the atmosphere of an upmarket beach house and a splendid waterfront view. There's a simple buffet breakfast of eggs, bacon, pancakes, juice and fruit for B$20, a somewhat more substantial Sunday brunch for B$25 and a Tuesday night Bajan barbecue buffet for B$30. The barbecue, which starts at 7 pm and is accompanied by a steel band, includes steak, fish, chicken, a few vegetable and salad dishes, dessert and coffee. On other nights there's an à la carte menu with main dishes from B$25.

*Casa Blanca*, at the Welcome Inn, has a rather touristy Bajan buffet complete with a dinner show of fire eaters, limbo dancers and calypso music. The food is quite simple but includes some fruit and salad. The buffet is on Tuesday nights from 7.30 pm and costs B$28.

Another possibility is *Secrets* (☎ 428-9525), a small restaurant on Maxwell Coast Rd. It has an à la carte menu and specialises in seafood, with dishes such as garlic shrimp with basil sauce over fettuccine for B$30.

Secrets is open from 6 to 10 pm nightly except on Sunday.

## OISTINS

Oistins, two km east of Maxwell, is a decidedly local town that's the centre of the island's fishing industry. There's a large and bustling fish market that's open daily from morning to night as long as the catch is coming in.

The Barbados Charter, the document that provided the island with its first constitutional protections, was signed in Oistins in 1652.

### Places to Eat

The most popular eatery in town is *Granny's*, a simple cafeteria-style place 200 metres east of the fish market. Fish cutters and rotis cost B$3, flying fish with rice and peas or coucou and salt fish cost B$8. As the food is served from steamer trays it's freshest at meal times; you can order takeaway or eat at the outdoor tables.

## SILVER SANDS

On the southernmost tip of the island, between Oistins and the airport, is the breezy Silver Sands area, a mecca for windsurfers. If you're not on the island for windsurfing, the location is a bit out of the way and the beaches to the west are better suited for tamer water activities.

### Places to Stay & Eat

*Round Rock Apartments* (☎ 428-7500), Silver Sands, Christ Church, a two-minute walk from the beach, has seven self-catering units that cost US$40/65 in summer/winter for a studio, US$50/90 for a two-bedroom apartment.

Not far from Silver Sands is the *Peach and Quiet Hotel* (☎ 428-5682), Inch Marlow, Christ Church, which has 22 airy rooms with private baths and little sitting areas that cost US$69 year-round. There's an oceanside pool and a buffet breakfast of juice, cereal, eggs and toast for an additional B$15.

*Silver Sands Resort* (☎ 428-6001; 428-3758), Silver Sands, Christ Church, is a

106-room resort on a sandy beach surrounded by casuarina trees. All rooms have air-con, phones and radios; some have kitchenettes. There are two pools, two tennis courts, two restaurants, a mini-mart and a Club Mistral shop. Rates begins at US$60 in summer, US$120 in winter.

The beachside *Silver Rock Hotel* (☎ 428-2866), Silver Sands, Christ Church, has 33 self-catering apartments that cost US$85 for a studio or US$115 for a one-bedroom unit in winter, both US$30 cheaper in summer. There's a pool and a reasonably priced restaurant featuring seafood and local dishes at lunch and dinner.

# South-East

St Philip, the diamond-shaped parish east of the airport, is relatively sparsely populated with a scattering of small villages but no large towns. Along the coast are a couple of resort hotels while inland, just north of Six Cross Roads, is one of the oldest plantation houses on the island.

## CRANE BEACH

Crane Beach, seven km north-east of the airport, is a broad white-sand beach backed by cliffs and fronted by aqua blue waters. Despite some storm erosion to the cliffs, this is still one of the loveliest beaches on the Atlantic coast. Public access to the beach can be found along the side roads north of the Crane Beach Hotel.

In terms of the view, the most spectacular angle is from the Crane Beach Hotel, which sits high on a cliff at the south end of the beach. So scenic is the setting that the hotel has managed to turn itself into a bit of a tourist attraction, charging B$10 to tour the grounds. In most cases no one is there to collect before 10 am and in any case the fee can be redeemed at the restaurant and bar.

### Places to Stay & Eat

*Crane Beach Hotel* (☎ 423-6220; fax 423-5343), St Philip, occupies an 18th-century

mansion and has 19 spacious rooms and suites with mahogany furnishings, hardwood floors and bathrooms with tubs. The suites have kitchens, queen-sized beds and either an ocean or pool view. Though each unit varies in size and decor, the rooms are some of the most atmospheric on the island. They cost US$100/160 in summer/winter, suites begin at US$140/250. The hotel also has a luxury four-bedroom mansion at the opposite end of the beach that rents in its entirety for US$850/1250.

The hotel's dining room has a fine view overlooking the beach. It offers a continental breakfast for B$14, a Bajan breakfast with flying fish and potatoes for B$20 and an American-style breakfast for B$23. Lunch and dinner, which are often accompanied by live music, feature a short but choice menu with the likes of lobster thermidor and veal a la Hamlet at moderately expensive prices.

## SAM LORD'S CASTLE

Sam Lord's Castle, the centrepiece of the Marriott hotel on Long Bay, is a limestone coral mansion with an interesting, albeit much embellished, history. The mansion was constructed in 1820 by Samuel Lord, who according to legend hung 'wrecker' lanterns off the point to lure ships onto nearby Cobbler's Reef. After the ships, which thought they were entering a safe harbour, crashed up on the reef, Lord purportedly went down to collect the cargo. Although there's little doubt that Lord was a scoundrel, most historians discount the lantern story as folklore.

Lord's former home, which looks more like a stately residence than a castle, contains the hotel reception and a museum-like collection of antique furnishings and paintings. It's interesting enough, but not a major sight worth going out of your way to see. The hotel charges non-guests a B$7 fee to enter the grounds.

### Places to Stay

*Marriott's Sam Lord's Castle* (☎ 423-7350; fax 423-5918), Long Bay, St Philip, has 248 rooms. A handful of these are on the 2nd floor of the 'castle' and have a colonial decor, but the rest of the accommodation is more typical Marriott fare, most in smaller buildings spread around the grounds. The hotel beach has a broad stretch of white sand backed by coconut palms; however, the waters can be dangerous. There are tennis courts and swimming pools. Summer rates begin at US$105, winter rates at US$195. In the off season, there are often week-long package tours from the US east coast that include airfare and a room for around US$600 per person.

### SUNBURY PLANTATION HOUSE

Sunbury Plantation House was built between 1660 and 1670 by an early Irish planter, Mathew Chapman. This handsome house changed hands once a century; the 1775 owners who hailed from Sunbury-on-Thames gave it its present name. In 1888 a Scottish planter purchased the property and after his two unmarried daughters died in 1981, the house was separated from the plantation and sold in auction. To the benefit of visitors, the present owners do not live here, making this the only Barbados plantation house that can be toured in its entirety. The tour is given by articulate guides who are well versed in local history and is the finest plantation house tour on the island.

The house has thick walls built of local coral blocks and ballast stones, the latter from the ships that set sail from England to pick up shipments of Barbadian sugar. The interior retains its plantation-era ambience and is furnished in antiques, many made from Barbadian mahogany. The cellar has a horse-drawn carriage, various riding paraphernalia and old cooking utensils.

The house can be toured daily, except on Christmas day, from 10 am to 4.30 pm. Admission costs B$8 for adults, B$4 for children under 12. Buses from Oistins can drop you at the gate.

### Places to Eat

The *Sunbury Plantation House* (☎ 423-6270) has a pleasant little outdoor café at the rear of the main building. Offerings include

English scones and a pot of tea for B$8 and quiche and salad or steak and kidney pie for B$12. An elaborate period-style dinner for up to 14 guests is held twice weekly in the plantation house; it includes a four-course meal, drinks and a house tour and costs US$60.

# West Coast

Barbados' west coast has lovely white-sand beaches and the majority of the island's luxury hotels. Most are in the parish of St James, which in colonial times was a popular holiday area for the upper crust of British society. Over the years their seaside estates have gradually been replaced by resorts, many of which still cater to the well-to-do.

Hwy 1, the two-lane road which runs north from Bridgetown to Speightstown, is bordered much of the way by a close mix of tourist facilities and residential areas.

### PAYNES BAY

Paynes Bay is a gently curving bay with a fine stretch of white sand and good swimming and snorkelling. There's beach parking and access near the Bamboo Beach Bar at the south end of the bay and opposite the Coach House Restaurant at the north end.

### Places to Stay

*Angler Apartments* (☎ & fax 432-0817), Clarke's Rd No 1, Derricks, St James, is inland on a side road about 200 metres southeast of the Coconut Creek Hotel. This locally owned, unpretentious operation has 13 older but clean apartments. The eight one-bedroom units each have a kitchen, a living room with a small bed and ceiling fan, a bedroom with either a double or two twin beds, a private bathroom and a radio. The five studios are similar but lack the living room. Cribs can be provided. Studios cost US$45/75 in summer/winter, one-bedroom units cost US$55/85. Guests can use the beach and pool at Coconut Creek Hotel.

*Coconut Creek Hotel* (☎ 432-0803; fax

422-1726), a km south of Paynes Bay (PO Box 429, Bridgetown), is a low-key, upmarket resort fronting a private shoreline with a couple of little sandy coves. There are 50 rooms in a collection of Mediterranean-style buildings with whitewashed walls and red tile roofs. Rooms are pleasant with rattan furnishings, ceiling fans, air-con and balconies. The resort has a pool, a restaurant and complimentary use of Hobie Cat boats and windsurfing gear. Singles/doubles begin at US$155/195 in summer, US$230/270 in winter, including breakfast and dinner.

*Treasure Beach Hotel* (☎ 432-1346; fax 432-1094) is a 25-room hotel right on the beach at Paynes Bay. Smaller and more personable than the area's larger resorts, it books heavily with repeat guests. Rooms have a ceiling fan, phone, refrigerator, air-con, rattan furnishings, two beds and a terrace. There's a pool. Rates, which include breakfast, begin at US$150/325 in summer/winter for double occupancy.

### Places to Eat
*Fathom's* (☎ 432-2568), on Hwy 1 near the south end of Paynes Bay, is a delightful open-air beachfront restaurant. It's top value both for its setting and its food. At lunch, starters range from a green salad for B$7 to octopus ceviche (raw octopus marinated in lime) for B$12, while flying fish cutters, chicken kebabs and spicy pork crêpes are B$12 to B$16. At dinner, starters are similarly priced while most main dishes, including jumbo shrimp, tuna steak and rack of lamb, cost B$32. It's open daily from 11 am to 3 pm and 6.30 to 9.30 pm. It's a good idea to make dinner reservations fairly early in the day.

*Treasure Beach Hotel* (☎ 432-1346) on Paynes Bay has one of the more highly regarded resort restaurants; head chef, Graham Newbould, was formerly personal chef to the Prince of Wales. The restaurant features a varied continental menu with lunch averaging about B$30 and dinner without wine about B$85. Lunch is served from noon to 2 pm, dinner from 7 to 9 pm and dress is semi-formal – essentially long

pants and a collared shirt for men. Dinner reservations are required.

## SANDY LANE BAY
Sandy Lane Bay has a wonderful white-sand beach backed by shade trees and fronted by lovely turquoise waters. It's popular for swimming and sunbathing. Much of the activity is centred near the Sandy Lane Hotel, where you'll often find a few jewellery vendors, hair braiders and someone offering horseback rides along the shore. When the surf is up there are usually a few surfers along the quieter south end of the beach.

There's public access to the beach on both sides of the Sandy Lane Hotel.

### Places to Stay & Eat
The 121-room *Sandy Lane Hotel* (☎ 432-1311; fax 432-2954; in the USA ☎ (800) 225-5843), St James, is the island's most exclusive resort, complete with marbled lobbies and grand facades. Founded by former British parliamentarian Ronald Tree in 1961, the hotel is now a member of the upmarket Forte hotel group. Rooms are posh with rates to match, beginning at US$720 (US$500 in summer) including breakfast and dinner for two. Guests have complimentary use of the fitness centre, tennis courts and the 18-hole golf course.

Sandy Lane's *SeaShell Restaurant* offers a lunch buffet for B$55. The main dinner dining room, the *Sandy Bay Restaurant*, is a more formal affair, with a table d'hôte menu for B$130.

## HOLETOWN
The first English settlers to Barbados landed at Holetown in 1627 aboard the *Olive Blossom*. An obelisk **monument and mural** along the main road in the town centre commemorates the event – albeit the date on the monument, which reads July 1605, is off by two decades.

Despite being the oldest town on the island, Holetown is more modern than traditional in appearance and is a rather busy town

BARBADOS

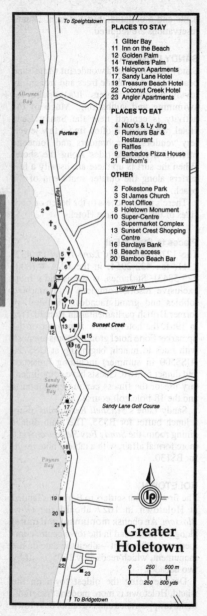

**PLACES TO STAY**

1  Glitter Bay
11  Inn on the Beach
12  Golden Palm
14  Travellers Palm
15  Halcyon Apartments
17  Sandy Lane Hotel
19  Treasure Beach Hotel
22  Coconut Creek Hotel
23  Angler Apartments

**PLACES TO EAT**

4  Nico's & Ly Jing
5  Rumours Bar & Restaurant
6  Raffles
9  Barbados Pizza House
21  Fathom's

**OTHER**

2  Folkestone Park
3  St James Church
7  Post Office
8  Holetown Monument
10  Super-Centre Supermarket Complex
13  Sunset Crest Shopping Centre
16  Barclays Bank
18  Beach access
20  Bamboo Beach Bar

**Greater Holetown**

0   250   500 m
0   250   500 yds

in the midst of St James' booming tourism industry.

**St James Church** on Hwy 1, just north of the town centre, is the site of the region's oldest church. The initial church, built in 1660, was replaced by a more substantial structure in the mid-19th century. However, a few vestiges of the original church remain, including a bell that was cast in the late 1600s and inscribed with the name of King William.

At the north side of Holetown is **Folkestone Park**, a public park with a rather narrow beach. It has reasonable surfing when the waves are up and snorkelling when it's calm. The underwater trail that once existed at this park is long gone but snorkellers can still find some coral and small tropicals, including angelfish and blue hunters, and a sunken barge at the south side of the beach can be explored. The park has a few picnic tables, a lifeguard and usually a couple of clothing vendors. A new interpretive centre with marine displays is scheduled to open in 1994. However, if you're just looking for a nice beach for sunbathing and swimming there are better ones in the area, including the strip that fronts Barbados Pizza House.

### Information

There's a Scotiabank next to Barbados Pizza House and opposite is the Super-Centre supermarket complex with a CBIC bank, travel agent and Texaco petrol station. The Sunset Crest Shopping Centre at the south side of town has a '99' convenience store, two banks, a laundry and a fruit stand.

### Places to Stay

The *Tropicana Beach Hotel* (☎ 422-2277), Lower Carlton, St James, three km north of Holetown, is an older triple-decker beachfront hotel. There are 20 studios and suites, each with a kitchen and all but one with either a patio or balcony overlooking the ocean. While not fancy, the units are quite sufficient and rate as one of the island's best value places at US$35 year-round. The prices, however, have only recently been dropped, so rates could change.

*Travellers Palm* (☎ 432-7722), 265 Palm Ave, Sunset Crest, St James, is a friendly apartment hotel at the south side of Holetown, about 500 metres inland from the coast. There are 16 pleasant apartments, each with a full kitchen, a separate bedroom with two twin beds and a dining room with seating for four. The bedroom air-conditioners are operated by tokens that cost US$5 for an eight-hour period. There's a pool and a small bar. While it's a 10-minute walk to the beach, the hotel is in a nice quiet neighbourhood and the price is a reasonable US$35/65 in summer/winter. Operated by a Manchester couple, Marilyn and Keith Rippingham, it books pretty solid with English tourists until December but is usually not full the rest of the winter. If business is slow the Rippinghams often let the units go for US$45 in winter.

Also in the same neighbourhood is *Halcyon Apartments* (☎ 432-6750; fax 432-7229), Palm Ave, Sunset Crest, St James. This is a rather sprawling complex with 73 apartments. Units have kitchenettes, living rooms, large bedrooms with twin beds, bathrooms with sunken tubs, phones, ceiling fans and token-operated air-con (B$8 for 10 hours). However, some rooms are a bit scruffy and overall it's rather average value at US$45/70 in summer/winter. There's a pool, tennis courts and a restaurant.

*Golden Palm* (☎ 432-6666, fax 432-1335; in the UK ☎ (0203) 42-2230, fax 46-6255), on the beach in Holetown, is a comfortable three-storey apartment hotel. The units are spacious, with a kitchen and dining area, separate bedroom, bathroom with tub and ocean-view balcony. Overall it's a good value for a mid-range beachfront hotel although the token-operated air-con (B$12) seems a bit miserly for this price range. Rates are US$65/115 in summer/winter for up to two people; children under 12 are free. There's a pool, a restaurant on site and a shopping centre just 300 metres away.

*Inn on the Beach* (☎ 432-0385; fax 432-2440), Holetown, St James, just south of Barbados Pizza House, is a very quiet place for being in the centre of Holetown. There are 20 pleasant air-con studios, all with kitchens, dining areas, oceanfront balconies, phones and tubs. There's a pool and it's on the beach. Singles/doubles cost US$60/75 in summer, US$125/140 in winter.

*Glitter Bay* (☎ 422-4111; fax 422-3940), Porters, St James, is a handsome 87-room complex a km north of Holetown. Accommodation is in three and four-storey Mediterranean-style buildings with red tile roofs and balconies draped with flowering plants. Rooms have ceiling fans, air-con, minibars and king-size beds. Room rates begin at US$175/345 in summer/winter, one-bedroom suites at US$195/445. There's a large free-form pool, complimentary water sports and an attractive beach. The site, incidentally, was once the home of British tycoon Sir Edward Cunard, a member of the family that founded the Cunard cruise line.

## Places to Eat

There's no shortage of places to eat in Holetown. In the parking lot of the Super-Centre supermarket complex you can usually find a few vendors selling fruit and drinking coconuts. Inside the complex is the *Brig* restaurant, which has simple fare like fish & chips or lasagne and salad for B$14; it's open from 8.30 am to 9.30 pm Monday to Saturday. At the side of the supermarket is *Cracker Barrel*, a cheap deli selling rotis for B$4, a quarter of a barbecued chicken for B$6 and other local food.

The open-air *Barbados Pizza House* (☎ 432-0227) has a great view overlooking the beach and good pizza by island standards. Prices begin at B$14 for a small cheese pizza, which makes a reasonable light lunch for two. Crust comes in either white or whole wheat; toppings cost B$1 each. There's a different Bajan lunch special each day except Sunday for B$8 and fish & chips and pastas are B$14. It's open from 10 am to 11 pm Sunday to Thursday, to midnight on Friday and Saturday.

There's a cluster of restaurants on 1st St and 2nd St, off Hwy 1 just south of the bridge. These include *Ly Jing*, which has a full range of Chinese dishes, most from B$15

to B$25; *Rumours Bar & Restaurant* with a
burger, steak and seafood menu; *Nico's* with
a more upmarket menu that includes fresh
seafood and French pâtés and wines; and
*Raffles*, a well-regarded dinner restaurant
featuring safari decor and a fixed five-course
menu of Caribbean food for B$110.

### MULLINS BEACH
Mullins is a popular roadside beach along
Hwy 1 between Holetown and Speightstown. The waters are usually very calm and
good for swimming and snorkelling.

### Places to Eat
The popular *Mullins Beach Bar & Restaurant* (☎ 422-1878), on Hwy 1 about a km
south of Speightstown, has good food and an
open verandah overlooking the sea and sand
at Mullins Beach. Lunch includes burgers
and fries (B$15), quiche and salad (B$20)
and a buffet (B$30) that's served from 11.30
am to 5.30 pm. At dinner there's a seafood
and steak menu, with starters priced between
B$10 and B$15 and main courses from B$22
to B$60. Dinner is served from 6.30 to 10.30
pm and drinks and dancing continue until
well after that. It's also open for breakfast
from 8.30 to 11.30 am.

### SPEIGHTSTOWN
Now a shadow of its former self, Speightstown was a thriving port in the days when
sugar was king. A main shipping line ran
from Speightstown to Bristol, England, and
trade was so extensive between the two areas
that Speightstown was once dubbed 'Little
Bristol'.

Today Speightstown is a decidedly Bajan
town, its side streets thick with older wooden
buildings with overhanging galleries. Unfortunately many of these historic buildings are
in a state of disrepair, some abandoned and
literally falling apart. If you have time to
spare, the waterfront is worth a stroll, not for
any particular sights but to soak up the
town's overall character.

### Places to Stay
If you're interested in staying in Speights-

town, apartment and house rentals can be
arranged at reasonable rates through
Clement (Junior) Armstrong, who manages
the Fisherman's Pub (☎ 422-2703).

There's also a modern mid-range resort,
*Heywoods* (☎ 422-4900), at the northern
outskirts of town, and the exclusive *Cob-
blers Cove* hotel (☎ 422-2291) to the south.

### Places to Eat
In the centre of town, opposite the post
office, is the Speightstown Mall which has a
fruit stand, *Kentucky Fried Chicken* and an
ice-cream shop (as well as Barclays Bank).
Vegetable and fruit vendors can be found
along the main street.

*Fisherman's Pub*, on Queen St down by
the waterfront, is a spirited, colourful place
with a solidly Bajan atmosphere and inexpensive local food. Essentially an oversized
beach shack, this is the town's most popular
eating and drinking spot.

A more upmarket in-town option is the
*Mango Cafe* (☎ 422-0704), open for dinner
only. Main dishes include chicken for B$26
and fisherman's platter for B$36, both served
with rice, vegetables and salad. Shrimp
cocktail or smoked salmon starters cost
B$14.

# Central & Eastern
# Barbados

From Bridgetown a series of highways fans
out into the interior. Any of these can make
a nice drive and there are scores of secondary
roads that add still more possibilities for
exploration.

The most popular touring route, which
takes in some of the finest scenery on Barbados as well as many of its leading attractions,
starts along Hwy 2, running north-east from
Bridgetown. The suburbs soon give way to
small villages, sugar cane fields and scrubby
pastureland with grazing black belly sheep.
About 10 km out of the city the road leads to
Welchman Hall Gully, Harrison's Cave and

the Flower Forest. Hwy 2 continues through the hilly Scotland District and then turns westward, leading to a scenic loop drive that takes in the Morgan Lewis Sugar Mill, the vista at Cherry Tree Hill, St Nicholas Abbey, Farley Hill and the Barbados Wildlife Reserve.

From there it's possible to head down the east coast to Bathsheba and return via Gun Hill Signal Station, with a detour via the Francia Plantation.

## WELCHMAN HALL GULLY
Welchman Hall Gully (☎ 438-6671), along Hwy 2 near the turn-off to Harrison's Cave, is a thickly wooded ravine with a walking track and nearly 200 species of tropical plants. Gullies like this were virtually the only places planters were unable to cultivate crops and thus represent an unspoiled slice of forest similar to the one that covered Barbados before the arrival of English settlers.

Geologically, this was once a part of the network of caverns that encompasses the nearby Harrison's Cave, but the caverns here collapsed eons ago, leaving an open gully. Admission is B$5 for adults, B$2.50 for children. It's open daily from 9 am to 5 pm. Parking for Welchman's Gully is a few hundred metres north of the entrance.

## HARRISON'S CAVE
Harrison's Cave, just off Hwy 2, is a fascinating network of limestone caverns, dripping stalactites and stalagmites, and subterranean streams and waterfalls. A battery-operated tram goes down into the cave, stopping en route to let passengers get out and closely examine some of the more impressive sites, including the Great Hall, a huge domed-shaped cavern, and Cascade Pool, an impressive body of crystal clear water 50 metres beneath the surface. The air temperature inside the cave is 26°C (78°F).

The underground tram tour lasts about 35 minutes, but it's usually preceded by a short video, so the whole thing takes about an hour. At certain times of the day it can get very busy with tour groups; to avoid a wait, call ☎ 438-6640 for reservations. The cost is

B$15 for adults, B$7.50 for children. There's a snack bar with drinks and sandwiches.

## FLOWER FOREST
Flower Forest, three km north of Harrison's Cave, at the western edge of the Scotland District, is a 50-acre botanical garden at the site of a former sugar estate. Paths meander through the grounds, which are now planted with virtually every plant found on Barbados, including lots of flowering species that bloom at a height ideal for photography. The gardens retain the estate's mature citrus and breadfruit trees, the latter having been introduced to Barbados from the South Pacific as an inexpensive food source for slaves.

Plaques display both the English and Latin names of flowers and trees, making this a particularly nice place to come if you want to identify flora you've seen around the island. The grounds also offer sweeping views of Chalky Mountain and the Atlantic Ocean to the east and of Mt Hillaby, the island's highest point, to the west. Some of the paths are wheelchair accessible.

It's open from 9 am to 5 pm daily. Admission is B$10 for adults, B$5 for children. There's a snack bar with moderately priced sandwiches and other simple fare.

## MORGAN LEWIS SUGAR MILL
Morgan Lewis Sugar Mill, at the side of the road two km south-east of Cherry Hill, claims to be both the largest and only completely intact sugar windmill surviving in the Caribbean. The interior of the mill has a simple display of historic photos, a few artefacts of the era and the original gears, shaft and grinding wheel. A stairway leads up around the works to the top where you can get a bit of a view of the surrounding area. The mill is open from 9 am to 5 pm Monday to Friday. Admission is B$2.

## CHERRY TREE HILL
Cherry Tree Hill, on the road that turns inland a km north of Morgan Lewis Sugar Mill, offers a fine vista of much of the east coast. The best views are just beneath the

summit at the roadside lookout next to the sugar cane fields. There's usually an elderly security guard there who is more than willing to spice up the view with a little local history.

A steep dirt track opposite the lookout leads to the top of the hill, but the view from there is largely blocked by trees. They are not cherry trees, incidentally; according to local lore, the cherry trees were chopped down long ago because passers-by kept taking the fruit.

## ST NICHOLAS ABBEY

St Nicholas Abbey, 750 metres west of Cherry Tree Hill, is one of the oldest plantation houses in the Caribbean. This unique Jacobean-style mansion with curly Dutch gables dates from the 1650s.

One of its early owners, Sir John Yeamans, led a 1663 expedition that colonised Carolina and became an early governor of that North American colony. For the last five generations it's been in the family of Colonel Stephen Cave, who resides in the house and manages the surrounding plantation.

Visitors can tour the ground floor of the mansion which has a fine collection of 19th-century Barbadian and English furnishings. One peculiar feature of the house is the inclusion of fireplaces, apparently the result of a strict adherence to a design drawn up in England that didn't give consideration to Barbados' tropical climate.

On the wall of the gift shop is a handwritten account of the plantation's property in 1822 that includes the names and prescribed value of each slave: 0 for the non-working elders and up to £150 for younger men.

Until the 20th century, each plantation on Barbados had its own windmill for crushing cane. The remains of this plantation's mill (and the tower from the former syrup factory) can be seen below the house. These days the sugar cane is hauled to the Portvale Sugar Factory near Holetown.

St Nicholas Abbey is open from 10 am to 3.30 pm Monday to Friday. If you time your visit accordingly you can also see a 15-minute film made in 1935 that shows some of the old sugar mills in action; it plays at

11.30 am and 2.30 pm. Admission is a bargain at B$5, with or without the movie.

## FARLEY HILL

Farley Hill National Park, off Hwy 2, is a pleasant hilltop park that would make a fine place to break out a picnic. The centrepiece of the park is the former mansion of Sir Graham Briggs, a wealthy 19th-century sugar baron whose guest list included the Duke of Edinburgh and King George V. In 1957, the stately Georgian-style mansion appeared in the movie *Island in the Sun*, starring Harry Belafonte. In 1965 a fire swept through the mansion, completely gutting the interior and burning away the roof. Today only the hollow coral block walls still stand – a rather haunting site that still retains a measure of grandeur.

Behind the mansion a hilltop gazebo and nearby benches offer a fine view clear out to East Point Lighthouse at the eastern tip of the island.

Farley Hill is open daily from 8.30 am to 6 pm. Admission is B$3 per car.

## BARBADOS WILDLIFE RESERVE

The Barbados Wildlife Reserve, opposite Farley Hill National Park, is a little free-range zoo with short paths that meander through mahogany woods of scurrying green monkeys, sluggish red-footed turtles and a

caiman pond. Other creatures that might be spotted include brocket deer, iguanas and agoutis. There's also a small aviary with macaws and cockatoos, as well as some caged parrots and uncaged peacocks and pelicans.

The free-roaming monkeys are the highlight. They are generally easy to spot but if you want to stack the odds in your favour come around 4 pm when feedings take place.

Green monkeys are predominantly brownish-grey, with highlights of white fur, but flecks of yellow and olive-green give them a greenish cast in some light, hence the name. On average, adult females weigh about three kg, males about five kg.

There are also caged monkeys on the grounds. The reserve is a project of the non-profit Barbados Primate Research Center, which was established in 1985 with assistance from the Canadian International Development Agency. The centre supports itself by supplying monkeys to laboratories in the USA and other countries for the production and testing of vaccines.

The reserve is open from 10 am to 5 pm daily. Admission is B$10 for adults, B$5 for children under 12. There's a snack bar.

## GUN HILL SIGNAL STATION

The 215-metre Gun Hill, off Hwy X in the centre of the island, boasts a small hilltop signal tower and a clear view of the surrounding valleys and the south-west coast.

The island was once connected by six such signal towers which used flags and lanterns to relay messages. The official function of the towers was to keep watch for approaching enemy ships but they also served colonial authorities as a mechanism for signalling an alarm in the event of a slave revolt.

The Gun Hill tower, which was built in 1818, now houses a couple of small displays of military artefacts and a pair of old cannons. The grounds are open from 9 am to 5 pm Monday to Saturday. Admission is B$5 for adults, B$2.50 for children.

Down the slope from the signal station is the British Regiment lion, carved from rock and painted white.

## FRANCIA PLANTATION

Francia Plantation, on the side road just south of Gun Hill, is an elegant plantation house with an interior of rich woods, period furnishings and an interesting collection of antique maps and prints. There are pleasant formal gardens out the back and some surrounding fields of vegetable crops.

The plantation was built at the turn of the century and is still occupied by descendants of the original French owner. The narrow km-long road into the plantation is nicely lined with mahogany trees. Francia Plantation can be visited from 10 am to 4 pm Monday to Friday. Admission is B$6.

## EAST COAST

The east coast has a predominantly rugged shoreline, turbulent seas and an unspoiled rural character. The East Coast Rd, which connects Hwy 2 with Bathsheba, is the only coastal road of any length on this side of the island.

Near the upper end of the East Coast Rd is **Barclays Park**, a public beach and picnic area donated to the government as an independence gift from Barclays Bank. Because of dangerous currents, the beach is best for picnicking and strolling.

**Bathsheba**, at the south end of the road, is the island's top surfing locale and has a picturesque coastline of high sea cliffs, untamed beaches and roaring Atlantic waters.

**Chalky Mount**, the white clay hills that rise inland of the East Coast Rd, are home to a couple of pottery shops. Visitors can view the operations and purchase items direct from the potters at reasonable prices. Access to Chalky Mount is from Hwy 2 near Haggatts.

### Places to Stay & Eat

There's a beachside snack bar at Barclays Park that serves simple fare including burgers, flying fish sandwiches and a few hot dishes. It's open daily for lunch only.

*Kingsley Inn* (☎ 433-9422; fax 433-9226), Cattlewash, St Joseph, on the East Coast Rd two km south of Barclays Park, is a pleasant little inn and restaurant that dates back to the early part of this century. It has a relaxed open-air setting and good Bajan food, including flying fish cutters, omelettes and salads for B$14 to B$28. There's a more elaborate fixed price meal that pairs chicken or a generous dolphin meunière with various local vegetables and a salad for B$34, or with the addition of soup and dessert for B$50.

Kingsley Inn also has seven rustic white-washed rooms with private baths, double beds, ceiling fans and pinewood floors that cost US$79/84 for singles/doubles in summer, US$92/101 in winter.

*Edgewater Inn* (☎ 433-9900), Bathsheba, St Joseph, has a fine cliffside setting above the beach at the north side of Bathsheba. There's a restaurant with sandwiches priced from B$8, hot dishes around B$20 and a Sunday buffet (12.30 to 3 pm) of chicken, flying fish, stew, salads and pie for B$25.

Edgewater Inn has 20 modern and comfortable ocean-facing rooms, each with a sitting area, mahogany furnishings, a tub, ceiling fan, air-con and a phone. There's a pool perched above the ocean and satellite TV in the lobby. Rates are a reasonable US$50/75 in summer/winter.

## ANDROMEDA BOTANIC GARDENS

Andromeda Botanic Gardens, off Hwy 3 a couple of km south of Bathsheba, was the private garden of the late Iris Bannochie, one of Barbados' foremost horticulturists. The gardens cover six acres and have a wide collection of introduced tropical plants, including orchids, ferns, water lilies, bougainvillea, cacti and palms. The property is managed by the Barbados National Trust and is open from 9 am to 5 pm daily. Admission is B$10 for adults, B$5 for children.

## VILLA NOVA

Villa Nova, in the western corner of St John parish, is an early 19th-century plantation house with a choice hilltop setting. The house, which is built of coral blocks, was once the centrepiece of a 400-hectare sugar estate. In 1907 it was separated from its adjacent cane fields and sold to the government, which used the house as a residence and clinic for the parish physician. In 1965 former British prime minister Sir Anthony Eden purchased the property as a winter home, added the pool and entertained a host of guests that included Queen Elizabeth II and Prince Philip. The present owners, who purchased the property in 1987, have opened it to visitors as a way to help with the upkeep.

The house has period furnishings but as it's a private home visitors are not allowed to tour the interior; viewing is rather disappointingly limited to peering in through the French doors and windows. It's 'open' from 10 am to 4 pm weekdays only and admission is B$8. Villa Nova is between Hwy 3 and 3B and the route is signposted.

# Dominica

Whether you approach Dominica by air or sea, the island looms above the horizon like no other in the Eastern Caribbean. Dominica's interior is solidly mountainous. Sharp steep ridges rise up from the coast and deep jungly river valleys run back down.

The island is strikingly rural and unspoiled. Most of the larger towns are set on the coast, but there are also tiny hamlets that snake along the mountain ridges. Even the capital of Roseau, whose sidewalks are lined with period wood and stone buildings, has the appearance of a forgotten frontier town.

Dominica has not only a rich West Indian tradition, the island is also home to the Eastern Caribbean's largest Carib Indian community.

Dominica, which fittingly dubs itself the 'Nature Island', shies away from packaged tourism and promotes itself instead as a 'non-tourist destination' for divers, hikers and naturalists. Indeed, it offers some of the Caribbean's most spectacular scenery, both

above and below the water. Many of the diving spots are still virgin and there's scarcely a soul on most of the trails. Hikes range from short walks to all-day treks and take in rainforests, waterfalls, rivers, lakes, bird sanctuaries, hot springs and other volcanic sites.

Dominica has beaches, but they are not exceptional and they're mostly of black sand. Because of this and because overseas visitors have to touch down on a neighbouring Caribbean island first (Dominica has no international jet traffic), the most popular way to see Dominica is as part of an island-hopping itinerary that also combines more traditional beach destinations.

## ORIENTATION

Most of Dominica's attractions and places to stay are along the west coast or in the mountains just inland from Roseau.

Dominica has two airports: Canefield, a 10-minute drive from Roseau, and Melville Hall, on the secluded north-east side of the island. If you're planning to base yourself in Roseau, avoid Melville Hall as it's a good 75-minute haul to the capital.

This is a large island, but the primary roads are well paved and getting around is easy. With a reasonably early start, it's possible to drive up the west coast from Roseau to Portsmouth, explore the Cabrits National Park, travel down the east coast through the Carib Territory and stop at the Emerald Pool on your way back across the island, all in a full-day outing.

# Facts about the Island

## HISTORY

The Caribs, who settled here in the 14th century, called the island Waitikubuli which means 'tall is her body'. Christopher Columbus, with less poetic flair, named the island

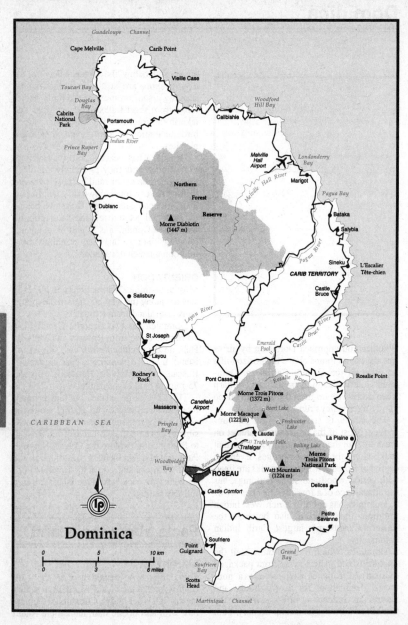

Dominica

after the day of the week that he spotted it – a Sunday – on 3 November 1493.

Daunted by fierce resistance from the Caribs and discouraged by the absence of gold, the Spanish took little interest in Dominica. France laid claim to the island in 1635 and a few years later sent a contingent of missionaries who were driven off by the unwelcoming Caribs. In 1660 the French and English signed a neutrality treaty in which they agreed to allow the island to remain a possession of the Caribs. Nevertheless, by the end of the century, French settlers from the neighbouring French West Indies began to establish plantations on Dominica. In the 1720s France sent a governor and took formal possession of the island.

For the remainder of the 18th century, Dominica was caught up in the French and British skirmishes that marked the era, with the island changing hands between the two powers several times. In 1763, under the Treaty of Paris, the French reluctantly ceded the island to the British. The French made attempts to recapture Dominica in 1795 and again in 1805 when they burned much of Roseau to the ground.

After 1805 the island remained firmly in the possession of the British who established sugar plantations on Dominica's more accessible slopes. The British administered the island as part of the Leeward Islands Federation until 1939 when it was transferred to the Windward Islands Federation. In 1967 Dominica gained autonomy in internal affairs as a West Indies Associated State and on 3 November 1978, the 485th anniversary of Columbus' 'discovery', Dominica became an independent republic within the Commonwealth.

The initial year of independence was a turbulent one. In June 1979 the island's first prime minister, Patrick John, was forced to resign after a series of corrupt schemes surfaced, including one clandestine land deal that attempted to transfer 15% of the island to US developers. In August 1979 hurricane David, packing winds of 240 km an hour, struck the island with devastating force, denuding vast tracts of forest, destroying the banana crops and wrecking havoc on much of Roseau. Overall 42 people were killed and 75% of the islanders' homes were destroyed or severely damaged.

In July 1980 Mary Eugenia Charles was elected Prime Minister, the first woman in the Caribbean to hold the office. Within a year of her inauguration she survived two unsuccessful coups, including a bizarre attempt orchestrated by Patrick John that involved mercenaries recruited from the Ku Klux Klan.

In October 1983, as chairperson of the Organization of East Caribbean States, Prime Minister Charles endorsed the US invasion of Grenada and sent a symbolic force of Dominican troops to participate. An appreciative USA responded by increasing foreign aid to Dominica, one consequence of which is the island's fine paved roads.

## GEOGRAPHY

Dominica is 46 km long and 25 km wide and has a total land mass of 750 sq km. It has the highest mountains in the Eastern Caribbean; the loftiest peak, Morne Diablotin, is 1447 metres high. The mountains, which act as a magnet for rain, serve as a water source for the more than 200 rivers that run down the mountain valleys. En route to the coast many of the rivers cascade over steep cliff faces, giving the island an abundance of waterfalls.

## CLIMATE

In January the average high temperature is 29°C (85°F) while the low averages 20°C (68°F). In July the average high is 32°C (90°F) while the low averages 22°C (72°F).

### Peaks & Valleys
It's said that when Christopher Columbus returned to Spain after his second voyage to the New World, King Ferdinand and Queen Isabella asked him to describe the island of Dominica. Columbus responded by crumpling up a piece of paper and tossing it, with all its sharp edges and folds, onto the table. That, he said, was Dominica. ∎

**DOMINICA**

The driest months are February to June, with a mean relative humidity of around 65%. During the rest of the year the humidity is in the low 70s. In August, the wettest month, there's measurable rainfall for an average of 22 days, while April, the driest month, averages 10 days. All these statistics are for Roseau – the mountains are cooler and wetter.

## FLORA & FAUNA

There have been 162 bird species sighted on Dominica, giving it some of the most diverse birdlife in the Eastern Caribbean. Of these, 59 species nest on the island, including two endemic and endangered parrot species.

Dominica's national bird, the Sisserou (*Amazona imperialis*), also called the imperial parrot, is about 50 cm long when full grown, the largest of all Amazon parrots. It has a dark purple breast and belly and a green back.

The Jaco (*Amazona arausiaca*) parrot is somewhat smaller, more green overall with bright splashes of varied colours. It is also called the red-necked parrot for the fluff of red feathers commonly found at the throat.

The island has large crapaud frogs, small tree frogs, many lizards, 13 bat species, 55 butterfly species, boa constrictors that grow nearly three metres in length and four other types of snakes (none poisonous).

Dominica is well known for its vast rainforests, but the island also has montane thickets, dry scrub woodlands, evergreen forests, fumarole vegetation, cloud forests and elfin woodlands. The most abundant tree on the island is the gommier, a huge tree that's traditionally been used to make dugout canoes.

## GOVERNMENT

Dominica, an independent republic within the British Commonwealth, has a unicameral Assembly comprising 21 elected members and nine appointed senators. Members of the Assembly normally sit for five-year terms. The executive branch is headed by a prime minister who represents the majority party in the Assembly. The current Prime Minister, Mary Eugenia Charles, has held the position since 1980.

In addition there's a well-developed system of local government that includes town councils in Roseau and Portsmouth and 25 village councils around the island.

## ECONOMY

Dominica's principal economic earnings are from agriculture. Bananas enjoyed a protected market in England until 1993, when the dismantling of trade restrictions between Western European nations opened the English market to substantially cheaper Central American bananas. The result has been a steep drop in the export value of the Dominican crop. The government is encouraging farmers to diversify in hopes of reducing economic dependency upon bananas, which account for 75% of Dominica's agricultural production.

Coconuts are the other major agricultural commodity. The largest island employer, Dominica Coconut Products, uses most of the coconut crop to produce body soaps and oils. Spices, coffee and citrus fruits are also grown for export.

Tourism is still small scale, with only

about 55,000 visitors coming to the island each year.

## POPULATION & PEOPLE
Dominica's population is approximately 73,000; about a third live in Roseau.

While most islanders are of African descent, about 3000 native Caribs also reside on Dominica, most of whom live on a 3700-acre reservation on the eastern side of the island.

## ARTS & CULTURE
Dominica draws upon a mix of cultures: there are as many French place names as English; African language, foods and customs mingle with European traditions as part of the island's Creole culture; and the Caribs still carve dugout canoes, build houses on stilts and weave distinctive basketwork. Rastafarian and Black pride influences, including dreadlocks and clothing in the African colours of red, green and yellow, are common on the island as well.

Dominica's most celebrated author, Jean Rhys, was born in Roseau in 1890. Although she moved to England at age 16 and only made one brief return visit to Dominica, much of her work draws upon her childhood experiences in the West Indies. Her most famous work, *Wide Sargasso Sea*, a novel set in Jamaica, was made into a film in 1993.

Cricket and soccer are the most popular sports on Dominica.

## RELIGION
In terms of religion, the French have had a more lasting influence on Dominica than the British and nearly 70% of the population is Roman Catholic. Other denominations include Anglican, Methodist, Pentecostal, Baptist, Seventh Day Adventist, Baha'i, Muslim and Rastafarian.

## LANGUAGE
English is the national language, but a French-based patois is also widely spoken.

# Facts for the Visitor

## PASSPORT & VISAS
Most visitors to Dominica must have a valid passport, however, US and Canadian citizens can enter with just proof of citizenship, such as a photo ID and an official birth certificate. French nationals may visit for up to two weeks with a Carte d'Indentité. Citizens of former Eastern Bloc countries require visas. A return or onward ticket is officially required of all visitors.

## CUSTOMS
Visitors may bring in 40 ounces (one litre) of wine or spirits and 200 cigarettes. Customs is often quite thorough in checking baggage.

## MONEY
Dominica uses the Eastern Caribbean dollar (EC$). The bank exchange rate for US$1 is EC$2.68 for travellers' cheques, EC$2.67 for cash. Barclays Bank, which has branches in Roseau and Portsmouth, charges an EC$2 commission plus 10 cents per cheque to cash travellers' cheques. The Royal Bank of Canada in Roseau charges an EC$5 commission to cash travellers' cheques.

US dollars are widely accepted by shops, restaurants and taxi drivers, although you'll often get an exchange rate of about EC$2.60.

Most hotels, car rental agencies, dive shops, tour operators and top-end restaurants accept MasterCard, Visa and American Express cards. Barclays gives cash advances on MasterCard, Visa and Discover cards.

## TOURIST OFFICES
The main tourist office is at the Old Market in Roseau and there are tourist information booths at each airport. When requesting information from overseas, address mail to: Division of Tourism (☎ 82351; fax 85840), National Development Corp, PO Box 73, Roseau, Commonwealth of Dominica, West Indies.

For visitors transiting through Antigua's international airport, there's a Dominica

DOMINICA

tourist information desk at the side of LIAT's transit counter.

## Overseas Reps

Dominica does not have its own overseas tourist offices, but information on Dominica can be obtained from:

Belgium
OECS Embassy, Rue des Aduatiques, 100, 1040 Brussels (☎ (322) 733-4328; fax (322) 735-7237)
Canada
OECS Mission in Canada, Suite 1050, 112 Kent St, Ottawa, Ontario KIP 5P2 (☎ (613) 236-8952; fax (613) 236-3042)
UK
Caribbean Tourism Organisation, Suite 3.15, Vigilant House, 120 Wilton Rd, Victoria, London SW1V 1JZ (☎ (071) 233-8382; fax (071) 873-8551)
USA
Caribbean Tourism Organisation, 20 East 46th St, New York, NY 10017 (☎ (212) 682-0435; fax (212) 697-4258)

## BUSINESS HOURS

Though they vary a bit, typical business hours are from 8 am to 1 pm and 2 to 4 pm Monday to Friday.

## HOLIDAYS

Public holidays on Dominica are:

| | | |
|---|---|---|
| New Year's Day | – | 1 January |
| Carnival | – | Monday & Tuesday preceding Ash Wednesday |
| Good Friday | – | late March/early April |
| Easter Monday | – | late March/early April |
| May Day | – | 1 May |
| Whit Monday | – | eighth Monday after Easter |
| August Monday | – | first Monday in August |
| Independence Day | – | 3 November |
| Community Service Day | – | 4 November |
| Christmas Day | – | 25 December |
| Boxing Day | – | 26 December |

## CULTURAL EVENTS

Dominica's Carnival celebrations are held during the traditional Mardi Gras period. In the two weeks prior to Lent, there are calypso competitions, a Carnival Queen contest, jump-ups and a costume parade.

Creole Day, usually held on the Friday before Independence Day, is a celebration of the island's Creole language and culture and includes traditional dancing, folklore and music.

Fête La St Pierre, the annual blessing of the fleet, takes place in fishing villages around the island on or near 29 June, the feast day of St Peter. Some villages make it an all-day event with parades, music and dancing.

## POST

The main post office is in Roseau; there are sub-post offices in larger villages. All post office boxes listed in this chapter are in Roseau, therefore box numbers should be followed by 'Roseau, Commonwealth of Dominica, West Indies'. When there's no post office box, the address should include the recipient's town. The use of 'Commonwealth' is to help prevent mail from being sent to the Dominican Republic by mistake.

Mail sent from Dominica to addresses in the Caribbean costs EC\$.65 for a letter and EC\$.35 for a postcard. Mail to any country outside the Caribbean costs EC\$0.95/0.55 for a letter/postcard.

## TELECOMMUNICATIONS

When making a local call on Dominica dial only the last five numbers. When calling from overseas dial 809-44 plus the local five-digit number.

Dominica has both coin and card phones, commonly side by side. You can buy phone cards at Cable & Wireless offices and at the Canefield Airport gift shop.

## ELECTRICITY

Electricity is 220/240 volts AC, 50 cycles. Incidentally, 70% of the island's electricity is hydro-generated.

## WEIGHTS & MEASURES

Dominica follows the imperial system of measurements. Car odometers and speed limits are given in miles.

Top Right: Hats for sale, Dominica (NF)
Top Middle: Annandale Falls, Grenada (NF)
Top Left: Grenadian man (NF)
Middle: Sisserou Express Bus, Botanical Gardens, Roseau, Dominica (GB)
Bottom: Prince Rupert Bay from Fort Shirley, Dominica (NF)

Top Left: Cascade aux Ecrevisses, Guadeloupe (NF)
Top Right: Produce seller, Pointe-à-Pitre market, Guadeloupe (NF)
Bottom: Ilet du Gosier, Guadeloupe (NF)

## BOOKS & MAPS

Jean Rhys touches lightly upon her life in Dominica in her books, *Voyage in the Dark* (1934) and her autobiography *Smile Please* (1979).

For a souvenir picture book of the island, take a look at *Dominica – Nature Island of the Caribbean*, available at island bookshops and a couple of the larger hotels.

The best map of the island is the detailed 1:50,000 British Ordnance Survey map, last published in 1991. It can be bought at the tourist office in Roseau for EC$22.

## MEDIA

There are three local radio stations, the government-owned DBS (88.1 FM; 595 AM) and two devoted to religious programming. You can also pick up stations from other islands, including a St Lucian station (98.1 FM) that plays reggae music.

Cable TV has nine channels with a mix of US network fare and local programming, including regional cricket matches. Channel 7 provides general information, exchange rates, a calendar of events and videos on island sightseeing and culture.

The island newspaper, *The New Chronicle*, is a weekly that's published on Friday.

## HEALTH

The Princess Margaret Hospital (☎ 82231) is in the Goodwill area at the north side of Roseau, off Federation Drive.

See the general introductory Facts for the Visitor chapter for information on travel health.

## DANGERS & ANNOYANCES

While Dominica is generally a safe place, thefts are not unknown and you shouldn't leave valuables unattended.

Roads on Dominica are narrow and you'll need to be quite cautious when walking in trafficked areas. That holds doubly true for Roseau where cars zip around at a fairly fast pace with drivers expecting pedestrians to grant them the right of way.

## EMERGENCY

For police, fire or ambulance attendance, call ☎ 999.

## ACTIVITIES
### Beaches & Swimming

While Dominica doesn't have the sort of gorgeous strands that make it onto brochure covers, it's not without beaches. On the calmer and more popular west coast they're predominantly black-sand beaches, with the best of the lot in the Portsmouth area.

The east coast is largely open seas with high surf and turbulent water conditions. There are a few pockets of golden sands just south of Calibishie that are sometimes calm enough for swimming and snorkelling and a couple of roadside brown-sand beaches a bit farther south.

### Diving

Dominica has superb diving. The island's rugged scenery continues underwater where it forms sheer drop-offs, volcanic arches, pinnacles and caves.

Many of Dominica's top dive sites are in the Soufriere Bay area. Scott's Head Drop is a shallow coral ledge that drops off abruptly to over 50 metres revealing a wall of huge tube sponges and soft corals. Just west of Scotts Head is The Pinnacle, which starts a few metres below the surface and drops down to a series of walls, arches and caves that are rife with stingrays, snappers, barracudas and parrotfish.

Calmer waters more suitable for snorkellers and amateur divers can be found at another undersea mound, the Soufriere Pinnacle, which rises 50 metres from the floor of the bay to within two metres of the surface and offers a wide range of corals and fish. Also popular for snorkellers and beginners is Champagne, a sub-aquatic hot spring off Pointe Guignard, where crystal bubbles rise from underwater vents.

The north side of the island still has lots of unexplored territory. Popular sites north of Roseau include the wrecks of a barge and tug off Canefield, Castaways Reef, Grande Savane, Rodney's Rock and Toucari Bay.

DOMINICA

**Dive Shops** Dive shops on Dominica include:

Anchorage Dive Centers, PO Box 34 (☎ 82638; fax 85680); this operation is based at the Anchorage Hotel in Castle Comfort and the Portsmouth Beach Hotel south of Portsmouth centre. Divemaster Fitzroy Armour is an accomplished underwater photographer and an active conservationist.

Castaways Dive Center, PO Box 5 (☎ 96244; fax 96246; in the USA and Canada ☎ (800) 525-3833); based at the Castaways Beach Hotel, midway along the west coast.

Dive Dominica, PO Box 63 (☎ 82188; fax 86088; in the USA ☎ (800) 544-7631); based at the Castle Comfort Lodge, just south of Roseau, this is the island's oldest dive shop.

East Carib Dive, PO Box 375 (☎ 96575; fax 96603; in the USA ☎ (908) 580-1375); this outfit, on a black sand beach 1.5 miles (2.4 km) north of Castaways Beach Hotel, is run by Gunther Glatz, a friendly divemaster from Germany.

The going rate is about US$40 for a one-tank dive and US$50 for a night dive. Anchorage has the best rates (US$60) for a two-tank dive. Dive Dominica (US$80) and Anchorage (US$90) offer one-day resort courses with an ocean dive. All four dive shops offer certification courses for around US$300 as well as hotel/dive packages.

**Snorkelling**
There's good snorkelling in the Soufriere Bay area and at Cabrits National Park.

All four dive shops listed in the previous diving section offer snorkelling tours or will take snorkellers out with divers. If you're chumming along with divers, make sure they're doing a shallow dive – staring down at a wreck 15 metres underwater isn't terribly interesting from the surface.

Castaways has a Saturday morning snorkelling tour, usually to Rodney's Rock. They require a minimum of four passengers and charge US$25 per person with gear, US$15 without. The shop also rents snorkelling gear for EC$20; there's fair snorkelling off the hotel beach. East Carib Dive charges US$20 for a snorkelling trip and also rents snorkelling gear for US$15 a day or US$10 a half day. Dive Dominica allows snorkellers to go out with divers for US$25, equipment included. Anchorage rents snorkelling gear for US$10 a day.

**Windsurfing & Sailing**
East Carib Dive (☎ 96575), near Salisbury, teaches five-hour windsurfing courses for beginners for US$110 and rents boards for US$8 an hour or US$110 a week.

Castaways Beach Hotel, also in the central coast area, rents sailing boats for EC$40 an hour.

**Whale Watching**
Whales and dolphins roam the deep waters off Dominica's coast. Resident toothed whales include the sperm whale, orca, pygmy sperm whale, pygmy killer whale, false killer whale and pilot whale. In winter,

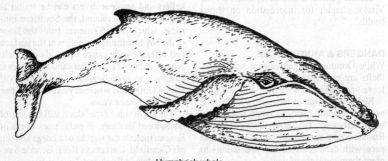

Humpback whale

migrating humpback whales are sometimes spotted as well.

Fitzroy Armour of Anchorage Dive Centers (☎ 82638) runs the island's only whale-watching boat tours. Tours leave mid-afternoon, last about four hours and cost US$50.

### Hiking
Dominica has some excellent hiking. Short walks lead to Emerald Pool and Trafalgar Falls, two of the island's most visited sights. Cabrits National Park has a couple of short hikes. The Morne Trois Pitons National Park offers serious treks into the wilderness, ranging from jaunts through verdant jungles to an all-day trek across a steaming volcanic valley that ends at a boiling lake.

Shorter hikes to more popular destinations can generally be done on your own but most wilderness treks require a guide who's familiar with the route. For further information, hikes are described in their relevant sections.

### HIGHLIGHTS
Diving and hiking are highlights on Dominica. Give yourself a few hours to stroll around Roseau and visit the town's botanical garden with its parrot aviary. The drive south to Scotts Head, and the walk out to the end of the peninsula, makes an enjoyable little outing. Other attractions that shouldn't be missed are Fort Shirley at Cabrits National Park and the short walks to Trafalgar Falls and Emerald Pool.

### ACCOMMODATION
Dominica has only about 600 rooms available for visitors, mainly in small, locally run hotels and guesthouses along the west side of the island. There are also three mountain lodges (Papillote, Roxy's and Springfield) just west of Morne Trois Pitons National Park that can make delightful places to stay for those who want to be on the edge of the jungle.

With a few exceptions, bottom-end accommodation is largely comprised of lacklustre guesthouses in the US$25 to US$45 range. The mid range, about US$50 to US$75, includes some of Dominica's best

values, even top-end hotels are quite reasonably priced, averaging US$100 to US$125.

Dominica has a 5% room tax and hotels add on a 10% service charge.

### FOOD
Dominica's national dish is the mountain chicken, which is not a chicken at all but the legs of a giant frog called the crapaud. Found at higher elevations, it's a protected species and can only be caught between autumn and February. Crapaud meat is white and tastes similar to chicken.

Creole food is quite prevalent on restaurant menus. Be sure to try callaloo soup; although no two recipes are identical, on Dominica it's almost invariably a flavourful, creamy concoction.

The island produces numerous fresh fruits, including bananas, coconuts, papayas, guavas, pineapples and mangoes, the latter so plentiful they commonly drop along the roadside.

### DRINKS
Rivers flowing down from the mountains provide Dominica with an abundant supply of pure, fresh drinking water. Water is generally safe to drink from the tap. Fresh fruit juices are inexpensive and readily available at most restaurants. You can also find good punch drinks made from fresh fruit and local rum.

### ENTERTAINMENT
A popular local meeting spot is the Pina Colada Bar, 30 Bath Rd, Roseau, which is open until about 11 pm and sometimes has live jazz. The Warehouse, a disco in the Canefield area, attracts a crowd on Saturday night. The village of Soufriere can be a fun place on Friday night with fish barbecues, local music and plenty of rum. Other entertainment is largely limited to a sunset drink at one of the hotel bars.

### THINGS TO BUY
Dominica has high-quality baskets of traditional Carib design. The prices are surprisingly moderate and the baskets can be

purchased at roadside stands in the Carib Territory or at handicraft shops in Roseau. The handicraft shops also sell woven placemats, hats, pocketbooks, Creole dolls, hot pepper sauce, Dominican coffee and coconut oil beauty products.

At Tropicrafts, at the east end of Queen Mary St in Roseau, you can watch women weaving huge floor mats of verti-vert, a native straw-like grass. Tropicrafts sells a wide range of souvenir items, although you can find cheaper prices at two smaller gift shops in the centre of Roseau, Dominica Handicrafts opposite Cable & Wireless and Caribana Handcrafts on Cork St.

# Getting There & Away

## AIR

There are no international flights into Dominica, so overseas visitors must first get to a gateway island. There are direct daily flights to Dominica from Antigua, Guadeloupe, Martinique, St Lucia and St Martin.

If you're island hopping, LIAT has numerous through fares that allow free stopovers on Dominica. Otherwise, a regular ticket from Antigua to Dominica costs US$83/158 one way/return, and a ticket from Martinique to Dominica costs US$96/181 one way/return. The fare from Guadeloupe to Dominica is US$81/136 one-way/return, and from St Lucia to Dominica it's US$83/ 150. Return fares allow stays of up to 30 days. LIAT's ticketing office (☎ 82421) is on King George V St in Roseau.

Air Guadeloupe flies to Dominica from Guadeloupe at 6.40 am daily except Sunday and every afternoon. In Dominica, the bookings are handled by Whitchurch Travel (☎ 82181), Old St, Roseau.

Air Caraibes (☎ 91416), formerly Nature Island Express, flies between Dominica and St Martin daily for US$125 one way, US$174 for a seven-day excursion and US$205 for a 21-day excursion. There's also a Saturday and Sunday flight to and from

Antigua that costs US$75 one way, US$137 for a 21-day excursion.

Air Caraibes and Caribbean Air Services (☎ 91748) provide air charter services.

### Airport Information

Dominica has two airports: Canefield, just outside Roseau, and Melville Hall, on the secluded north-east side of the island.

Most LIAT flights land in Canefield, but at least one flight a day to and from Antigua and Martinique lands at Melville Hall. On LIAT's printed schedule the letters C and M after the departure time indicate which airport is being used.

**Canefield Airport** There's a very helpful tourist information booth that's closed between 1 and 2 pm but is otherwise open whenever a flight is scheduled. A small gift shop, a snack bar with inexpensive sandwiches and drinks, rest rooms and coin, card and USA Direct phones make up the facilities. If you plan on renting a car, it's usually quicker to get your local licence at airport immigration even though you may have to wait until incoming passengers are cleared.

**To/From the Airport** While there are no car rental agencies at Canefield Airport, some agencies will provide customers with free airport pick-up. Taxis are readily available but if you're travelling light you could also walk out to the road and catch a bus into town.

**Melville Hall Airport** Sitting in the midst of the countryside, this airport looks all but abandoned except at flight time. There's a gift shop, tourist information booth, rest rooms and coin and card phones.

### SEA

#### Catamaran

The *Caribbean Express* connects Dominica with Guadeloupe and Martinique via a modern catamaran that seats about 300 passengers.

The boat leaves Pointe-à-Pitre, Guadeloupe, at 7.45 am on Monday, Wednesday,

Friday and Saturday, arriving in Roseau at 10.15 am. It departs Roseau at 10.45 am, arriving in Fort-de-France, Martinique, at 12.35 pm. It returns the same day, leaving Martinique at 1.25 pm, arriving on Dominica at 3.15 pm, departing Dominica at 3.45 pm and arriving in Guadeloupe at 6 pm.

The cost in French francs is 305F one way to Dominica from either Martinique or Guadeloupe, but it's only 10F more to make the one-way trip between Martinique and Guadeloupe with a free stopover on Dominica. From either Martinique or Guadeloupe there's an excursion fare to Dominica for 450F, valid for stays of up to seven days. From Dominica, the one-way fare is EC$106 to Guadeloupe, EC$124 to Martinique.

There are discounts of 50% for children aged two to 11 and 10% for passengers under 26 or older than 59. Reservations are made on Dominica through Whitchurch Travel (☎ 82181), Old St, Roseau. For information in Martinique call ☎ 60 12 38, in Guadeloupe ☎ 91 13 43, or check with any travel agent.

The *Madikera*, a 352-passenger catamaran, also has passenger service between Pointe-à-Pitre and Fort-de-France that stops in Roseau on Wednesday, Friday, Saturday and Sunday. There's also a sailing on Monday between Pointe-à-Pitre and Roseau. Arrival and departure times vary, but the boat is about 15 minutes faster than the *Caribbean Express*.

Fares from either Martinique or Guadeloupe to Roseau are 285F one way, 420F return (130F/285F for children). Reservation numbers are ☎ 91 60 87 on Guadeloupe and ☎ 73 35 35 on Martinique. On Dominica, book through Trois Pitons Travel (☎ 86977), 5 Great Marlborough St, Roseau.

### Yacht
Yachts can clear immigration and customs at Woodbridge Bay, north of Roseau, and in Portsmouth, and get a coastal permit that allows visits at other ports and anchorages along the coast. Mooring in Soufriere Bay, now a marine reserve, is no longer permitted.

### Cruise Ship
A number of cruise lines call on Dominica, most docking at Woodbridge Bay, the deepwater harbour just north of Roseau that serves as the island's main commercial port. Handicraft sellers and lines of taxis are on hand at the harbour whenever a ship docks.

In hopes of encouraging cruise ship visitors to spend more time in the northern part of the island, a smaller cruise ship berth has been opened at Cabrits National Park, a scenic setting, and the site of historic Fort Shirley.

### TOURS
LIAT offers a day tour to Dominica from Antigua that costs US$150 including airfare, lunch at Papillote and a sightseeing tour that takes in the botanical gardens, Trafalgar Falls, Carib Territory, Emerald Pool and Layou River.

Antilles Trans Express (☎ 83 12 45) operates a day tour from Guadeloupe that leaves Pointe-à-Pitre with the 7.45 am sailing of the *Caribbean Express* and returns with the 3.45 pm sailing from Dominica. It includes a minibus tour of Roseau that incorporates the botanical gardens, Emerald Pool and lunch at the Layou River Hotel. The cost is 640F adults and 500F for children.

### LEAVING DOMINICA
Visitors aged 12 and older who have stayed more than 24 hours must pay EC$25 (or US$10) departure tax when flying out of Dominica.

# Getting Around

Dominica is a visitor-friendly island. Road signs mark most towns and villages, and major intersections are clearly signposted.

Primary roads are usually narrow but in very good shape – most are newly paved and nearly all are pothole free. Secondary roads vary and while some are quite rutted it's possible to explore the island thoroughly by car. Be careful of deep rain gutters that run

DOMINICA

along the side of many roads – a slip into one could easily bring any car to a grinding halt.

## BUS

Buses, which are mostly minivans, run regularly along the coastal routes between Roseau and both Scotts Head and Canefield; the farther north you go past Canefield the less frequent they become. There's no Sunday bus service along most routes.

In Roseau you can catch buses heading south for Scotts Head (EC$3) from the Old Market. The same bus will drop you in the Castle Comfort area for EC$1.50. Buses heading to Canefield (EC$1.50), the Carib Territory (EC$7) and Portsmouth (EC$7.50) leave from the east side of the Roseau River near the public market. Buses to Trafalgar (EC$2.25) and Laudat (EC$3) leave from the north side of the police station.

## TAXI

From Canefield Airport, the fares for one taxi (up to four people) are EC$20 to Roseau, EC$25 to the Castle Comfort area, EC$65 to Scotts Head, EC$40 to Castaways Beach Hotel, EC$75 to the Layou River Hotel and EC$110 to Portsmouth.

From Melville Airport, the fare per person in a shared taxi is EC$42 to Roseau, EC$44 to Castle Comfort and EC$30 to Portsmouth.

## CAR & MOTORBIKE
### Road Rules

Dominicans drive on the left-hand side of the road. Visiting drivers must be aged between 25 and 65 and have a valid driving licence and at least two years' driving experience to drive in Dominica. In addition, a local driving licence (EC$20) is required, which can be picked up from immigration at either airport any day of the week. Licences can also be obtained Monday to Friday at the Traffic Department, High St, Roseau. Hours are from 8.30 am to 1 pm and 2 to 3 pm (to 4 pm on Monday), although when there's a queue (and they move slowly!) the office door is commonly shut 10 to 15 minutes before closing time. As a courtesy, car rental

agencies will usually pick you up and take you to get your licence.

There are petrol stations in larger towns around the island, including Canefield, Portsmouth and Marigot. Petrol costs about EC$6.50 a gallon.

### Rental

The nearest car rental agency to Canefield Airport, and the island's only international affiliate, is Budget (☎ 92080) at the south side of the village of Canefield. It opens at 8 am and provides free airport pick up. Rates begin at US$48 a day.

Wide Range Car Rentals (☎ 82198) on Bath Rd in Roseau has about 30 vehicles, many quite aged, but rates begin at US$35 for cars, US$40 for jeeps. If you arrange it in advance, staff can drop you at Canefield Airport when you return the car.

There are many other car rental agencies on the island, including Valley Rent-A-Car, which has offices in both Roseau (☎ 83233) and Portsmouth (☎ 55252), and STL Rent-A-Car (☎ 82340) on Goodwill Rd in Roseau. Both have competitive rates and provide free pick up around town and at Canefield Airport.

In addition to rental fees, most companies charge US$6 to US$8 a day for an optional collision damage waiver.

Francis' Scooter Rentals (☎ 85295), 5 Cross St, Roseau, and DeA's Rent-A-Bike (☎ 85075) at 21 Winston Lane in the Goodwill area of Roseau, rent scooters for about US$25 a day.

### HITCHING

Hitching is quite popular among islanders. While some islanders walk out into the street a metre or so and attempt to wave drivers down, the most acceptable stance is to stand at the side of the road and hold out an open hand. The usual safety precautions apply.

### TOURS

There are a number of small companies that provide standard sightseeing tours, wilderness hiking tours or both. For vehicle tours you might try Mally's Tour and Taxi Service

(☎ 83114) or Whitchurch Travel (☎ 85787), and for hiking tours Ken's Hinterland Adventure Tours (☎ 84850) or Antours Dominica (☎ 86460). Hiking guides can also be arranged through many hotels and guesthouses or at the tourist office in Roseau, where it's common to find a tour guide or two hanging out.

Most taxis can also be hired for sightseeing tours at a rate of EC$45 per hour for up to four people.

# Roseau

Roseau is a colourful West Indian capital, its streets lined with old stone-and-wood buildings. Some are strikingly picturesque with jalousied windows, gingerbread trim and overhanging balconies, while others are little more than weathered shells leaning precariously out over the sidewalks. Many of the buildings are two-storey structures with shops below and living quarters above. There are modern cement structures too, but for the most part walking around Roseau feels like stepping back a hundred years.

While Roseau is one of the region's poorer capitals, it's not one of the grimmer ones. Shopkeepers wash down the sidewalks every morning, police walk their beats with a rhythmic stride and most people are quite friendly.

Roseau's waterfront, which was severely damaged by Hurricane David, has undergone a decade-long reclamation and now has a new promenade with a good view of Scotts Head to the south.

Roseau, incidentally, is pronounced 'rose-oh' and is named after a local reed.

## Information
**Tourist Office** The tourist office at the Old Market plaza is open from 8 am to 1 pm and 2 to 4 pm weekdays, and from 9 am to 1 pm on Saturday.

**Money** Barclays Bank on Old St is open from 8 am to 3 pm Monday to Thursday and from 8 am to 1 pm and 3 to 5 pm on Friday. There's a Royal Bank of Canada near the Old Market, a Scotiabank and a National Commercial Bank of Dominica on Hillsborough St and a Banque Française Commerciale on Queen Mary St.

**Post & Telecommunications** The post office on Long Lane is open from 8 am to 4 pm Tuesday to Friday, and until 5 pm on Monday. Cable & Wireless, on Hanover St, open from 7 am to 8 pm Monday to Saturday, has coin and card phones outside the building.

**Bookshops** Paperbacks on King George V St is a good place to browse if you're looking for books on the island.

## Old Market
The cobblestone plaza and small covered arcade of the Old Market is the site of a former slave market. A wrought iron Victorian-style memorial marks the old block where the auctions took place. In addition to the tourist office, there are a few stalls selling baskets and other handicrafts.

## Public Market
The public market, along the riverfront at the west end of Bay St, is open from sunrise to about 4 pm daily, except Sunday. You can find fresh fruit, vegetables and herbs – if you hear the blowing of a conch shell then there's also fresh fish for sale. For a refreshing drink (EC$1), look for the coconut vendor near the river.

## Churches
Roseau's Catholic cathedral, on Virgin Lane above the Methodist Church, is an old stone edifice with an expansive interior. The windows are of typical Gothic shape but only the upper part is stained glass; the lower sections are wooden shutters which open to catch cross breezes. While the church is not a must-see sight, it's nicely maintained and worth a peek if you're in the area.

The Anglican Church, opposite the Fort Young Hotel, is a rather attractive grey stone-

DOMINICA

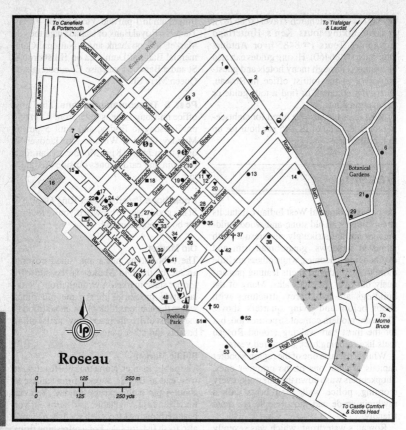

**Roseau**

```
0        125        250 m
0        125        250 yds
```

block church. It was left with only its shell standing in 1979 after Hurricane David ripped off the roof, which has been replaced with tin.

### Library
The public library on Victoria St was built in 1905 with funding from US philanthropist Andrew Carnegie. It has a nice old verandah with a sea view and a grand streetside cannonball tree that blooms in late spring. Government House, the white mansion with the expansive lawn, and a new Assembly building are opposite the library.

### Botanical Gardens
The botanical gardens, which date from 1890, are on the north side of town below Morne Bruce hill. It's a pleasant place to take a stroll. There are big banyan trees, flowering tropical shrubs and an aviary housing the Jaco and Sisserou parrots, the two parrot species found in Dominica's rainforests.

Brochures describing the island's parks and trails are sold at the park headquarters. Nearby you'll find a monument of sorts to hurricane David – a school bus crushed under the weight of a huge baobab tree that fell during the 1979 hurricane.

PLACES TO STAY

| 10 | Continental Inn |
| 11 | Vena's Guest House |
| 15 | Wykie's La Tropical Guest House |
| 18 | Cherry Lodge |
| 26 | Kent Anthony Guest House |
| 40 | Bon Marché Guest House |
| 48 | The Garraway |
| 51 | Fort Young Hotel |

PLACES TO EAT

| 2 | Pina Colada Bar |
| 12 | World of Food |
| 20 | Bakery |
| 25 | Whitchurch Grocery Store |
| 27 | Guiyave |
| 28 | The Orchard |
| 32 | Country Life Natural Foods |
| 34 | La Tropicale |
| 36 | A C Shillingford Grocery Store |
| 39 | Raffoul's Snackette |
| 43 | Cartwheel Cafe |
| 46 | Cathy's Pizzeria |
| 47 | La Robe Creole & Mousehole |

OTHER

| 1 | Government Offices |
| 3 | National Commercial Bank of Dominica |
| 4 | Buses to Trafalgar & Laudat |
| 5 | Police Station |

| 6 | Parrot Aviary |
| 7 | Buses to Canefield, Portsmouth & CaribTerritory |
| 8 | Scotiabank |
| 9 | Banque Francaise Commerciale |
| 13 | LIAT |
| 14 | Wide Range Car Rentals |
| 16 | Public Market |
| 17 | British Consulate |
| 19 | Caribana Handcrafts |
| 21 | Forestry Office |
| 22 | Cable & Wireless |
| 23 | Dominica Handicrafts |
| 24 | Whitchurch Travel |
| 29 | Bus under Baobab Tree |
| 30 | Post Office |
| 31 | Barclays Bank |
| 33 | Pharmacy |
| 35 | Photoworld 1-hour Lab |
| 37 | Roman Catholic Cathedral |
| 38 | Tropicrafts |
| 41 | Paperbacks |
| 42 | Methodist Church |
| 44 | Royal Bank of Canada |
| 45 | Old Market & Tourist Office |
| 49 | War Memorials |
| 50 | Anglican Church |
| 52 | Government House |
| 53 | Library |
| 54 | Assembly Building |
| 55 | Traffic Department |

DOMINICA

You can drive into the gardens from entrances off Bath Rd or Trafalgar Rd until 10 pm or walk in any time. Admission is free.

## Places to Stay

**Town Centre** The *Kent Anthony Guest House* (☎ 82730; fax 87559), 3 Great Marlborough St, is rather cheerless with sloping floors, peeling linoleum and furniture to match, but the rates are hard to beat at US$11/19 for singles/doubles. Add US$8 for a room with a private bath and another US$4 for one with air-con.

*Cherry Lodge* (☎ 82366), PO Box 138, on Kennedy Ave, is popular with backpackers. This small family-run West Indian guesthouse occupies an interesting wooden building that looks timeless but was actually built in 1946. The rooms are rather simple; the upper section of wall between them is

open to allow air (and consequently noise) to circulate. Some rooms have balconies and private showers and toilets. Singles/doubles cost US$20/30.

*Vena's Guest House* (☎ 83286), on a noisy street corner at 48 Cork St, is at the site of author Jean Rhys' birthplace, but the guesthouse is on the shabby side and the rooms are uninviting. Rates begin at US$20 for a single room with shared bathroom.

*Wykie's La Tropical Guest House* (☎ 88015; fax 87665), 51 Old St, has six small rooms above a little local bar, all a bit ramshackle. The rooms are very basic, essentially a foam mattress and, upon request, a fan, but the place certainly has character and the manager is friendly. Rates are from US$25/35 for singles/doubles.

*Continental Inn* (☎ 82214; fax 87022), 37 Queen Mary St, has a dozen rooms, most quite small and straightforward, but it's clean and overall probably the most comfortable of Roseau's budget accommodation. The four rooms with shared bathroom cost US$30/40 for singles/doubles, while those with private bath cost US$40/50. Master Card, Discover Card and American Express are accepted, and there's a small inexpensive restaurant.

*Bon Marché Guest House* (☎ 82083), 11 Old St, is a newer guesthouse on a relatively quiet street. The four rooms are smallish with foam mattresses, portable fans and private showers and toilets. The louvred windows are not screened, which on hot nights leaves guests with the choice of sweltering or warding off mosquitoes. There's a shared kitchen and a living room with cable TV. Rooms cost from US$32 to US$35 and overall are good value for this price range. The office is in the store below the guesthouse. On Sunday and after 5 pm you can reach the owners at ☎ 84194.

*Fort Young Hotel* (☎ 85000; fax 85006; in the USA ☎ (800) 223-1588) is on Victoria St, a few minutes' walk from the centre of town. This 1st-class hotel incorporates the walls of the 18th-century Fort Young, which once guarded the eastern flank of the capital. The 33 rooms are nicely appointed with hardwood floors, tiled baths, louvred windows with screens, ceiling fans, air-con, cable TV and phone. The deluxe rooms, which are on the 2nd floor, also have private ocean-view balconies, king-size beds and cathedral ceilings. Rates, the same year-round, are US$85/95 for singles/doubles in standard rooms. The larger deluxe rooms, which are arguably the best on the island, cost US$115/135 for singles/doubles.

*The Garraway* (☎ 83247) is a new hotel at the east end of the renovated bayfront. There are 31 modern rooms with fans, air-con and TV. Singles/doubles cost US$85/105.

**Around Castle Comfort** The following four hotels are all in a row on a rocky shoreline in the Castle Comfort area, a mile (1.6 km) south of Roseau.

The *Sisserou Hotel* (☎ 83111; fax 83130), PO Box 134, has 20 older, faded rooms with air-con, TV and phone. Rates are US$50 and US$65 for singles, and US$65 and US$85 for doubles; the higher rates are for upstairs rooms.

The *Anchorage Hotel* (☎ 82638; fax 85680), PO Box 34, has 32 rooms with air-con, cable TV, phone and private balconies. Standard rooms have one double and one single bed and cost US$60/80 for singles/doubles. The superior rooms are larger, have two double beds and cost US$75/100. Add US$15 more for a third person. Rooms on the top floor have better views at no extra cost. There's a small pool, a squash court, a pricey restaurant and a dive shop. Reservations can be made by calling ☎ (800) 223-6510 in the USA, ☎ (416) 484-4864 in Canada and ☎ (0628) 477088 in the UK.

The *Evergreen Hotel* (☎ 83288; fax 86800), PO Box 309, is an appealing little hotel with a tropical atmosphere. The buildings incorporate native woods and stonework, and the rooms are comfortable, each with air-con, cable TV, a phone and screened windows. The 2nd-floor rooms in the new wing have wonderful ocean-front balconies. Rates include breakfast and dinner and are one of the island's better deals at US$85/110 a single/double for standard rooms and US$95/130 for ocean-view rooms. A third person is US$30 more. There's a small pool.

*Castle Comfort Lodge* (☎ 82188; fax 86088), PO Box 63, caters to divers. There are 10 simple rooms that vary quite a bit in size and amenities, but all have air-con and ceiling fans and some have TVs. Rates are on the high side at US$80/115 for singles/doubles, breakfast included.

**Places to Eat – cheap**
The *Mousehole*, downstairs from La Robe Creole restaurant, has inexpensive rotis, fish & chips, sandwiches and pastries. You can get a nice slab of banana bread for EC$1.25 and a large glass of fresh, creamy papaya or guava juice for EC$3.50. While most people order takeaway, there's also a small counter

where you can chow down. It's open from 8 am to 9.30 pm daily, except Sunday.

The *Cartwheel Cafe* on Bay St is a pleasant little eatery in an historic waterfront building with thick stone walls. Ham, eggs and coffee cost EC$9, and sandwiches EC$4. It's open weekdays from 7.30 am to 3.30 pm and Saturday from 8 am to 1 pm.

*Guiyave*, 15 Cork St, has small tables on a 2nd-floor balcony that offer a bird's-eye view of the street scene below. This cheery little restaurant serves breakfast from 8 to 11.30 am. French toast, ham and eggs and omelettes, all served with juice or coffee, cost EC$10 to EC$20, but there are also cheaper pastries. At lunch, sandwiches and burgers cost EC$5 to EC$10. On Saturday, local dishes such as rotis, goat water and souse are available. Guiyave closes at 4 pm and is not open on Sunday. There's a bakery downstairs with reasonably priced though rather average quiches, pastries and sweet potato pudding.

The *Orchard*, on the corner of King George V and Great George Sts, is a pleasantly simple restaurant decorated with island paintings. Sandwiches, rotis and good callaloo and pumpkin soups cost under EC$10. You can also order a complete meal of the day, choosing from chicken leg (EC$20), fish (EC$30) or lambi (conch; EC$45), accompanied by rice, plantain, pickled beets, salad and yam pie. The servings are generous and the food is quite good. It's open weekdays from 10 am to about 10 pm, and on Saturday to 4 pm.

One of the few central places open on Sunday is *Cathy's Pizzeria*, opposite the Old Market, which serves pizza, inexpensive rotis and calzones.

*World of Food*, 48 Cork St at Vena's Guest House, is an open-air courtyard restaurant that's a popular spot for an after-work drink. Sandwiches cost around EC$5, while lambi and fish dishes average EC$40.

*Raffoul's Snackette*, 13 King George V St, is essentially a bread outlet but also makes inexpensive sandwiches. *Country Life Natural Foods* on Cork St, a very small shop with vitamins and a few packaged health foods, sells locally baked loaves of wholewheat bread, with or without raisins. *La Tropicale*, on a 2nd-floor balcony on King George V St, sells frozen yoghurt and cheap snacks.

There are a number of grocery stores around town, the largest being A C Shillingford on King George V St and Whitchurch on Old St. Hours are from 8 am to 5 pm Monday to Friday, to 2 pm on Saturday. The public market is the place to get fruit and vegetables.

Eric's Bakery, in the orange and white building opposite the Woodbridge Deepwater Harbour, supplies much of the island's bread and makes tasty raisin slices (EC$1) and other pastries.

## Places to Eat – expensive

*La Robe Creole*, 3 Victoria St, is one of the island's best dining spots. It has good Creole food and an engaging setting with stone walls and highback chairs. The waitresses wear traditional Creole dress. The excellent callaloo soup has a creamy coconut base and costs EC$7. The fish of the day or chicken breast Creole are tasty main dishes priced at a reasonable EC$35 and are accompanied by plantain, dasheen and sweet potato. The restaurant makes a powerful rum punch (EC$4.50) and good fresh fruit juices and desserts. There's also a varied snack menu and an inexpensive kids' menu. It's open from 11.30 am, with the last order from the main menu at 9.30 pm and from the snacks menu at 10.30 pm.

The *Fort Young Hotel* has a large restaurant incorporating the stone wall of the fort, however, it's too hall-like to make for an intimate dining experience. There's a varied menu, with main courses averaging about EC$40.

The *Evergreen Hotel* (☎ 83288) in the Castle Comfort area has a very pleasant seaside terrace dining room that's open for dinner to non-guests by reservation. A full soup-to-dessert dinner, with a choice of main dishes that commonly includes fish, shrimp, chicken and lamb, costs EC$50. While not

DOMINICA

as good value, the nearby *Anchorage* and *Sisserou* hotels also have restaurants.

# Around Dominica

## MORNE BRUCE

Morne Bruce is a rather exclusive hillside suburb south-east of Roseau. It has a couple of places to stay but most people who venture up this way do so for the panoramic hilltop view of Roseau and its surroundings. One way to get to the viewpoint is to drive up and park below the president's office. You can also hike up from the botanical gardens; the trail begins just east of the parrot aviary and takes about 10 to 15 minutes to walk.

### Places to Stay & Eat

*Itassi Cottages* (☎ 84313; fax 83045), PO Box 319, is in an exclusive hillside neighbourhood with a view of Roseau and Scotts Head. These self-catering cottages have cooking facilities, phone and TV, and there's a tennis court. The cost is US$60 for one or two people, US$90 for three or four and US$110 for five or six. There's also a studio unit that costs US$40 for one or two people.

*Reigate Hall Hotel* (☎ 84031; fax 84034) is a 16-room hotel in the Reigate area on a hill above Morne Bruce. It has the subdued feel of a small mountain inn and a superb view of Roseau two km below. The 16 rooms are rather simply appointed but are modern and have air-con and private balconies. Single rooms, which are quite small, cost US$75, while doubles cost US$95 and larger, more comfortable suites begin at US$150. There's a small pool, sauna and tennis court. The hotel is at the end of an unmarked and rather tortuous one-lane road.

Breakfast and lunch at Reigate Hall are moderately priced, while dinner is a bit more upscale, featuring dishes such as fish Creole, fillet steak bearnaise or mountain chicken for around EC$50.

## CANEFIELD AREA

Canefield, a 10-minute drive north of Roseau, is half suburbia, half industrial, and the site of the main inter-island airport. While Canefield isn't much of a tourist area there are a few places to stay, and as it's on a main bus route, getting into Roseau is fairly easy without a car.

**Pringles Bay**, just south of the airport, is a popular swimming spot for local residents despite being in an industrial setting with a commercial loading dock nearby. There are a couple of diving wrecks to explore in the area: a tugboat in about 20 metres of water near the river mouth and a barge a few metres below the surface at the side of a reef.

The **Old Mill Cultural Centre**, half a mile (800 metres) south of the airport, is in an attractive stone building with gearworks from the old mill rusting on the grounds. It has been undergoing renovation and is expected to reopen as a museum and cultural performance centre.

In **Massacre**, a small village north of the airport, a mural along the main road commemorates the 1674 Carib massacre after which the town is named.

### Places to Stay

*Canefield Overnighter* (☎ 91378), PO Box 412, is on the main road about a five-minute walk south of the airport. There are three simple but clean rooms each with screened

---

**Massacre**

Philip Warner, son of the St Kitts governor, was responsible for the widespread massacre of Carib Indians on Dominica in 1674, as well as for the murder of 'Indian' Warner, his half-brother.

Indian Warner, whose mother was a Dominican Carib, left his English upbringing on St Kitts to return to Dominica where he became a Carib chief. Philip Warner, leading a contingent of British troops intent on seeking vengeance for Carib raids on St Kitts, tricked Indian Warner into meeting on the west coast of Dominica in the village now known as Massacre, where he then ambushed his half-brother along with his entire tribe. ∎

louvred windows, a fan and sink. The price is US$15 for a room with a single bed, US$25 for a double bed and US$30 for two twin beds. The bathroom is shared. The congenial elderly woman who runs the guesthouse speaks fluent French. The *Ambassador Hotel* (☎ 91501), PO Box 413, is a newish but rather lacklustre place a couple of minutes' walk from Canefield Overnighter. It has about a dozen rooms with foam mattresses, private bath, fan, phone and shared balconies. Singles/doubles cost US$40/55. There's a dining room in the hotel and the village grocer is across the street.

The *Hummingbird Inn* (☎ 91042; fax 85778), PO Box 20, on the main road midway between Canefield and Roseau, is 250 metres up a steep driveway just south of the West Indies petrol station. All in all, it's not a terribly convenient location. There are 10 rather simple rooms, each with a private bathroom, which in some cases is outside the room. Rates begin at US$50/55 for singles/doubles with advance reservations, US$5 more without.

*Shipwreck Bar & Restaurant* (☎ 91059; fax 91042) at Pringles Bay has three rather wear-worn cottages that cost US$55 per night for a studio-style unit and US$85 for a two-bedroom unit with four-poster bed, a bathtub and TV.

*Springfield Plantation Guest House* (☎ 91401; fax 92160), PO Box 456, is a winding 10-minute drive inland from Canefield. This scenic mountain retreat, perched on a 370-metre cliff, is part of the 92-hectare Archbold Tropical Research Station, a holding of the Clemson University of South Carolina. The former plantation is now used to house visiting scientists studying tropical ecosystems and as a centre for nature tourism. The old plantation house is a bit weathered but quite atmospheric, and has large rooms with hardwood floors, eclectic furnishings, a smattering of antiques and grand verandah views. Summer rates are US$40 and US$50 for singles, US$55 and $65 for doubles; winter rates are US$15 higher. Breakfast and dinner can be included for an additional US$25 per person.

Springfield Plantation also has a few one and two-bedroom apartments in an adjacent annexe. These vary in size and have a mountain cabin decor, but they are quite adequate, have cooking facilities, phone, shower and private verandah, and rate as one of the island's best value places to stay at US$150 to US$225 a week. There are also a few two-bedroom cottages for US$225 to US$300 a week.

### Places to Eat

*Shipwreck Bar & Restaurant* (☎ 91059; fax 91042), a beachside bar at Pringles Bay, is open daily. At lunch, snacks like chicken and chips for EC$12 are served, but it's most popular as a place to come for a sunset drink. The dinner menu changes daily, with choices like pork chops, baked chicken or fresh tuna, all with a green salad and rice for EC$20 to EC$30.

### LAYOU RIVER AREA

The Layou River, Dominica's longest, empties into the sea just south of St Joseph, at the centre of the west coast. The river basin is a peaceful rural area, with bamboo leaning over the river banks and banana and coconut trees at the side of the road. When it's not running strong, the river is a popular place for freshwater swimming.

**St Joseph**, a simple fishing village of 2600 people, rises up the slope from a small black-sand beach, but the area's best beach is farther north at the Castaways Beach Hotel in Mero. There's good swimming in front of Castaways and fair snorkelling along the rock formations at the southern end of its beach – with a little luck you might even spot stingrays or octopus.

Just north of Mero, on the inland side of the coast road, is the **Macoucherie Rum Distillery**. The distillery crushes sugar cane grown in the surrounding fields using an old-fashioned water wheel. You can view the operation from 7 am to 3 pm Monday to Friday. This rum is very popular on Dominica, with some islanders claiming it has aphrodisiac qualities.

The coastal road continues north along the

DOMINICA

leeward side of Dominica's highest mountain range, an effective rain screen that makes this region one of the driest on the island.

## Places to Stay

The *Layou River Hotel* (☎ 96281; fax 96713), PO Box 8, is at the north side of the Layou River, 1.25 miles (two km) inland from the coastal road. The 34 air-con rooms, which are in two identical buildings, have a bath, phone and either a double bed or two twin beds. Some of the furnishings are faded and the rooms could use a fresh coat of paint but they are otherwise adequate. The river setting is quite pleasant and there's a pool. Rates are US$50/60 for singles/doubles; some rooms have a nice river view at no extra cost. The hotel is about a 20-minute drive from the Canefield Airport, and if you have a car and intend to explore the island it could make a reasonably convenient base. The hotel's Taiwanese owners have plans to build a 250-room resort, the *Caribbean Shangrila Hotel*, on the land across the road.

The *Castaways Beach Hotel* (☎ 96246; fax 96246), PO Box 5, is an inviting place on a long, attractive grey-sand beach fronted by calm waters. There are 27 rooms in two wings. Those in the south wing have one double bed, while those in the north wing have two single beds, are a bit bigger and have TVs. All are pleasant enough and have ceiling fans, shower, phone and ocean-fronting balconies. Singles/doubles cost US$72/96. There's a dive operation on site (room/dive packages available), a small dock and a tennis court.

## Places to Eat

The *Castaways Beach Hotel* restaurant has a casual open-air setting overlooking the water and makes a nice place to stop for breakfast on your way north. There are set Haitian, Creole and continental breakfasts for EC$18, but the à la carte French toast at EC$6.50 is also a generous dish.

The restaurant at the *Layou River Hotel* has a less interesting setting and more stan-dard fare, including pancakes (EC$8), continental (EC$11) and American (EC$20) breakfasts. Both restaurants also serve lunch and dinner at moderate prices.

## NORTHERN FOREST RESERVE

The Northern Forest Reserve is a huge area that encompasses 22,000 acres of land in the interior of the island, including the 1447-metre Morne Diablotin, the island's highest peak. The main habitat of Dominica's two endangered parrot species is in the eastern section of the reserve.

The government plans to turn a quarter of the reserve into a national park, complete with an interpretation centre and a nature trail and viewing station in the parrot sanctuary. For the latest on the park status, check with the tourist office or the forestry office at Roseau's botanical gardens.

To get to the reserve, turn east on the signposted road that begins just north of the village of Dublanc and continue to the Syndicate Estate, about 4.5 miles (7.2 km) inland. There you'll find a path to a parrot observatory platform as well as the start of the trail leading up Morne Diablotin, a rugged hike that's best done with a guide (see Tours in the Getting Around section earlier in this chapter). The best times for sighting parrots are in the early morning and late afternoon, when they're most active.

## PORTSMOUTH

Portsmouth, Dominica's second-largest town, sits on the banks of Prince Rupert Bay. Columbus entered the bay during his fourth voyage to the New World in 1504, and three decades later the Spanish established a supply station here for their galleons. It was visited by 16th-century buccaneers Sir Francis Drake and his rival John Hawkins, as well as Prince Rupert of the Rhine.

In 1607, Captain John Smith and his followers stopped for a couple of days before heading north to establish Jamestown, North America's first permanent English settlement. Indeed, the harbour was so important

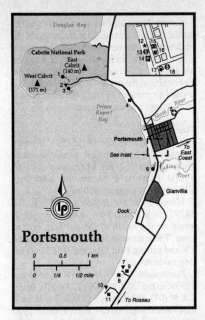

**Portsmouth**

| 0 | | 0.5 | | 1 km |
|---|---|---|---|---|
| 0 | 1/4 | | 1/2 mile | |

1 Fort Shirley
2 Snack Bar
3 Cruise Ship Complex
4 Mamie's on the Beach
5 Hospital
6 Indian River Boats
7 Le Flambeau
8 Portsmouth Beach Hotel
9 Picard Beach Cottage Resort
10 Coconut Beach Restaurant
11 Coconut Beach Hotel
12 Police Station
13 National Commercial Bank of Dominica
14 Parking Lot
15 Cable & Wireless
16 Douglas Guest House & Restaurant
17 Petrol Station
18 Barclays Bank

to the British that they intended to make Portsmouth the island's capital until outbreaks of malaria and yellow fever thwarted the plan.

Cabrits National Park on the north side of town and Indian River to the south are the area's noteworthy attractions. Although Portsmouth centre doesn't have any sights per se, there are a couple of oddities you might want to take a look at: the small but colourful monument at the bus stop dedicated to Lord Cathcart 'who died of the bloody flux off Dominica in 1741' and the nearby line of shipwrecks piled up in the shallow waters at the back of the police station.

Prince Rupert Bay is a lovely harbour whose grand scale is most easily appreciated when seen from the hills at Cabrits National Park. There are stretches of black sand along much of the bay, but the nicest beach fronts Portsmouth Beach Hotel. Snorkelling is reasonable along the north side of the hotel pier.

Douglas Bay, a few km north of Portsmouth, also has a black-sand beach and decent snorkelling. A good paved road leads to Douglas Bay, but the area remains a bit of a backwater that's well off the tourist track.

**Information**
The police and immigration office is on Bay Rd, the main road that runs through the centre of town. The National Commercial Bank of Dominica is south of the police station and south of that is a small parking lot where you can pick up the bus to Roseau.

**Indian River**
Just south of town you can expect to be met by a handful of rowers ready and willing to take you on a boat ride up the Indian River. The boats wind up the shady river through tall swamp bloodwood trees whose buttressed trunks rise out of the shallows, their roots stretching out laterally along the river banks. This river trip can be a fascinating outing, taking you into an otherwise inaccessible habitat and offering a close-up view of the creatures that live at the water's edge.

The rowers, who set up shop along the coastal road at the river mouth, charge about EC$20 per person for a tour that goes up the river for about a mile (1.6 km) and takes about an hour.

DOMINICA

## Cabrits National Park

Cabrits National Park, on a scenic peninsula 1.2 miles (two km) north of Portsmouth, is best known as the site of Fort Shirley. In addition to the peninsula the park encompasses the surrounding coastal area and the island's largest swamp, which links Cabrits to the mainland. The Cabrits Peninsula, formed by two extinct volcanoes, separates Prince Rupert Bay from Douglas Bay. The coral reefs and waters of Douglas Bay are also part of the park.

While the British built a small battery on Cabrits in 1765, it wasn't until 1774 that they began constructing the main elements of Fort Shirley. In 1778, the French captured the island and continued work on the fort. Between the two vying powers, a formidable garrison was built. France's effort proved to be counterproductive, as Dominica was returned to the British under the 1783 Treaty of Paris and the fort was subsequently used to repel French attacks.

Fort Shirley had more than 50 major structures, including seven gun batteries, quarters for 600 officers and soldiers, numerous storehouses and a hospital. Following the cessation of hostilities between the British and French, the fort gradually slipped into disrepair and in 1854 was abandoned.

Today Cabrits is a fun place to explore. Some of the stone ruins have been cleared and partially reconstructed, while others remain half-hidden in the jungle. The powder magazine to the right of the fort entrance has been turned into a small museum with exhibits on the restoration and a display of artefacts unearthed during the work. From the nearby ruins of the Officer's Quarters there's a fine view of Prince Rupert Bay.

The fort is home to scores of ground lizards (*Ameiva fuscata*) that scurry about the ruins and along the hiking trails that lead up to the two volcanic peaks. The trail up the 171-metre West Cabrit begins at the back side of Fort Shirley and takes about 30 minutes. Most of the walk passes through a wooded area but there's a panoramic view at the top.

Cabrits National Park is open free to the public. There's a parking lot at the end of the road next to the new cruise ship complex, where there's a handicraft centre, rest rooms, an auditorium and a dock. The path up to the fort begins at the nearby snack shop; it takes about five minutes to reach the main cluster of buildings and the museum.

### Places to Stay

*Douglas Guest House* (☎ 55253), in town opposite the bus stop, has nine very basic rooms – essentially just a bed, not even a fan – that share two bathrooms and cost US$12/24 for singles/doubles.

*Mamie's on the Beach* (☎ 54295; fax 54295) is a small, tidy, two-storey guesthouse on the beach at the northern end of town. There are seven plain rooms with fans, TV and private bath that cost US$30/40 for singles/doubles.

*Portsmouth Beach Hotel* (☎ 55142; fax 55599; in the USA ☎ (800) 223-6510, in the UK ☎ (01) 287-1555), PO Box 34, is on a nice black-sand beach half a mile (800 metres) south of town. While there are 96 rooms in all, one wing of the hotel is rented out to foreign students who attend the nearby Ross University medical school. However the choicest wing, the one nearest the beach, has rooms that are available on a daily basis. Rooms are clean and straightforward with shower, phone, ceiling fans and screened louvred windows. Overall it's a pleasant place and at US$30/40 for singles/doubles it's also the best value in the area. Ask for a room facing the water. There's a pool, pier, restaurant and dive shop.

*Picard Beach Cottage Resort* (☎ 55131), which is next to Portsmouth Beach Hotel and shares the same management, has 16 nicely rustic cottages with big ocean-front porches. Each has a separate bedroom with a double bed, a small kitchenette, a dining/living room with two single beds and a table for four. Cottages right on the beach cost US$120/140 for singles/doubles, while those a little farther back are US$100/120. It's US$20 more for each additional person.

*Coconut Beach Hotel* (☎ 55393; fax

55693), PO Box 37, is on the beach a mile (1.6 km) south of town. Good-sized rooms with kitchenettes on the terrace cost US$55/65 for singles/doubles and there are larger bungalows for US$90 a double. While the rooms are nice enough, overall the hotel is not a terribly welcoming place.

### Places to Eat

*Douglas Snackette & Restaurant*, on the ground floor of Douglas Guest House, is a large, hall-like eatery with rotis (EC$6), chicken and chips (EC$7.50) and other simple inexpensive dishes.

*Le Flambeau* at the Portsmouth Beach Hotel is a pleasant al fresco restaurant on the beach, open from 7 am to 10 pm (to about 11 pm for sandwiches). French toast or an omelette costs EC$10 and sandwiches and burgers are about the same price. Other dishes include a vegetarian platter or eggplant marinara for EC$16, fresh fish for EC$25 and Creole pork chops with rice for EC$35.

*Mamie's on the Beach*, on the north side of Portsmouth, has a small restaurant serving sandwiches for about EC$5 and chicken or fresh fish for around EC$25, while the *Coconut Beach Hotel*, south of town, has a moderately priced seaside restaurant serving three meals a day.

### PORTSMOUTH TO THE EAST COAST

The route that cuts across the northern neck of the island from Portsmouth to the east coast is a delightful drive through mountainous jungle. The road is winding and narrow, the terrain is all hills and valleys, and the landscape is lush with tropical greenery. Once you reach the coast there are some fine ocean vistas, a couple of one-lane bridges and plantations with seemingly endless rows of coconut palms. The road is newly paved, but be cautious of the deep gutters on the mountain side and steep drops on the cliff side.

### CALIBISHIE TO PAGUA BAY

Calibishie, the first sizeable village you'll reach on the east coast, is a good place to grab a bite to eat. In the centre of the village is the *Almond Beach Restaurant & Bar*, a pleasant local seaside spot that serves lunch all afternoon, including a good inexpensive chicken palau and tangy freshly squeezed ginger beer.

There are a few small villages as you continue south but the area is made up predominantly of coconut and banana plantations. Occasionally the road winds from the jungle out to the coast. There are brown-sand beaches at **Woodford Hill Bay** and near Melville Hall Airport at **Londonderry Bay**. Both bays have rivers emptying into them where women gather to wash clothes; at Londonderry the airport fence doubles as a clothesline.

Surrounded by lush green hills, **Marigot**, the largest town on the east coast, is a pretty village of brightly painted houses, some of them built up on stilts. If you come by during the late afternoon there's a good chance you'll see villagers bringing in their fishing boats and sorting the day's catch.

### CARIB TERRITORY

The 3700-acre Carib Territory, which begins around the village of Bataka and continues south for 7.4 miles (12 km), is home to most of Dominica's 3000 Caribs. It's a predominantly rural area with cultivated bananas, breadfruit trees and wild heliconia growing along the roadside. Many of the houses are traditional wooden structures on log stilts, but there are also simple cement homes and, in the poorer areas, shanties made of corrugated tin and tarpaper.

The main east coast road runs right through the Carib Territory. Along the road there are several stands where you can stop and buy intricately woven Carib baskets, mostly ranging in price from US$4 to US$30.

**Salybia**, the main settlement, has a couple of noteworthy buildings. One is the carbet, an oval-shaped community centre designed in the traditional Carib style with a high-pitched ribbed roof; in pre-western times, these buildings served as collective living quarters. The Saint Marie of the Caribs

DOMINICA

church in Salybia, which also has a sharply pitched roof, has exterior murals of Caribs encountering the early Europeans and an altar made from an overturned dugout canoe.

At Sineka a sign points oceanward to **L'Escalier Tête Chien**, a stairway-like lava outcrop that seems to climb out of the turbulent ocean. This unique natural formation was thought by the Caribs to be the embodiment of a boa constrictor and is significant in Carib legends.

After leaving the Carib Territory the road offers glimpses of the rugged coastline.

There's an intersection half a mile (800 metres) south of Castle Bruce; take the road marked Pont Casse to continue to the Emerald Pool and Canefield. This road takes you through a scenic mountain valley with a luxuriant fern forest and lots of rushing rivers.

### Places to Stay & Eat
The *Carib Territory Guest House* (☎ 57256) at Crayfish River consists of five rooms in the home of Charles Williams, who also has a basket shop at the side on the property. Accommodation is simple, essentially a bed and a fan with a shared bathroom. Singles/doubles cost US$20/35. There's a local café with simple fare, *Cafe Woch La*, which is 1.25 miles (two km) to the south.

*Floral Gardens* (☎ & fax 57636), PO Box 192, is in the village of Concord, on the road leading inland from Pagua Bay. It has rooms with fans that cost US$35/40, apartments for US$80 and a restaurant with a varied menu at moderate prices. Credit cards are accepted.

### EMERALD POOL
Emerald Pool, which takes its name from its lush green setting, is a little basin below a gentle 12-metre waterfall which is good for a dip. The pool is reached via a five-minute walk through a rainforest of ferns and tall trees. The path is well defined and easy to follow, although it can get a bit slippery in places. There are a couple of covered picnic tables which could make a nice spot to break for lunch. Emerald Pool is generally a nice quiet area, although on cruise ship days

(Wednesday is the big one) one minivan after another can pull up to the site.

Emerald Pool is on the road that runs between Canefield and Castle Bruce, a nice winding drive with thick jungle vegetation, mountain views and lots of beep-as-you-go hairpin turns. It's about a 30-minute drive from Canefield; the trailhead is marked with a roadside forestry sign.

### Places to Stay & Eat
*Emerald Pool Hotel* is on the Castle Bruce Rd about a mile (1.6 km) north-east of Emerald Pool. It has a handful of straightforward rooms with private baths that cost US$25/40 for singles/doubles, breakfast included, and there is a moderately priced restaurant and bar.

*Emerald Bush Hotel* (☎ 84545; fax 87954), PO Box 277, has eight rooms in simple Carib-style cottages. This is a very rustic place with no electricity, phones or other modern distractions. Single rates range from US$14 for a cottage without a bath to US$30 for a room with shower and toilet. It's US$4 more for a second person. It's about half a mile (800 metres) down a rough dirt road that continues inland from the Emerald Pool Hotel. It's a good idea to call in advance; if you can't reach anyone at the above number call the proprietor, Peter Kaufmann, at home ☎ 86900).

### TRAFALGAR FALLS
Trafalgar Falls, on the eastern edge of the Morne Trois Pitons National Park, is both spectacular and easily accessible. The 10-minute walk to the falls begins at Papillote Wilderness Retreat, about a mile (1.6 km) beyond the village of Trafalgar.

Start the walk at the bottom of the inn's driveway, where you'll find a cement track leading east. Follow the track until you reach a little snack bar, take the footpath that leads downhill from there and in a couple of minutes you'll reach a viewing platform with a clear view of the falls in a verdant jungle setting.

There are two separate waterfalls. Water from the upper falls crosses the Titou Gorge before plunging down the sheer 60-metre rockface that fronts the viewing platform. At the base of the waterfall are hot sulphur springs with a couple of basins that bathers can sit in – look for the yellow streaks on the rocks.

The lower falls flow from the Trois Pitons River, which originates in the Boiling Lake area. This waterfall, which is gentler and broader than the upper falls, has a pool at its base that's deep and wide enough for an invigorating swim.

Young men hang out at the start of the trail and tout their services as guides. Getting to the viewing platform is straightforward and doesn't require a guide, so if you plan to go only that far, save yourself the 'tip' (roughly EC$20), as the guides call their negotiable fee.

Going beyond the platform is trickier, as getting to the base of the falls requires crossing a river. Depending on how sure-footed you are, a guide could be helpful in climbing down the boulders to the lower pool and even more so in clambering over to the hot springs.

Guide or not, be very careful with your footing as the rocks get moss covered and can be as slippery as ice. This is a serious river, and during spells of severe rain it may be too high to cross. Flash floods are also a potential danger, as heavy rains in the upper slopes can bring a sudden torrent – if you're in the river and the waters start to rise, get out immediately.

### Places to Stay & Eat
*Papillote Wilderness Retreat* (☎ 82287; fax 82285), PO Box 67, is a delightful little inn nestled in the mountains above Trafalgar village. American owner Anne Baptiste, a naturalist who has been living on Dominica for many years, has planted the grounds with nearly 100 types of tropical flowers and trees. The rustic inn blends nicely with its environment. It has eight simple units with private bathrooms, wooden plank floors, straw mats and patchwork bed quilts made at the local women's co-op. Singles cost US$45, doubles US$50 to US$60, plus an optional US$30 per person for breakfast and dinner. There's also a two-bedroom, two-bath cottage near a waterfall that costs US$120, which can be divided into two sections for US$70 with the kitchenette, US$50 without.

Papillote's lunch menu is limited but the food is quite good and there's a lovely jungle setting, complete with the sound of running water. When available, the flying fish plate (EC$20) is a good choice. There's also a nice green salad for EC$15 and a chicken plate for EC$23. Bring a bathing suit and top off lunch by sitting in the inn's little hot springs pool. Lunch, served from 10 am to 3 pm, is currently the only meal available to non-guests, but a new restaurant is under construction so that may change.

### Getting There & Away
To get to Trafalgar from Roseau, take King George V St north from the town centre. After crossing the Roseau River, continue up the Roseau Valley road for 2.3 miles (3.7 km), at which point the road forks; take the right branch. From here it's a 10-minute drive along a narrow potholed road to Papillote, two miles (3.2 km) away.

Buses go from Roseau to the village of Trafalgar (EC$2.25), from where it's a 15-minute walk to Papillote. Taxis from Canefield Airport to Papillote cost EC$45.

### MORNE TROIS PITONS NATIONAL PARK
This national park, in the southern half of the island, encompasses 17,000 acres of Dominica's mountainous volcanic interior.

Most of the park is primordial rainforest, varying from jungles thick with tall, pillar-like gommier trees to the stunted cloud forest cover on the upper slopes of Morne Trois Pitons (1372 metres), Dominica's second-highest mountain. The park has many of the island's top wilderness sites including Boiling Lake, Boeri Lake, Freshwater Lake and Middleham Falls. Hikes to all four start at Laudat (elevation 600 metres), a small hamlet with fine mountain views.

The Emerald Pool, at the northernmost tip

of the park, is described earlier in this chapter.

## Middleham Falls

The trail to Middleham Falls, one of Dominica's highest waterfalls, is a nice rainforest walk. More than 60 species of trees, including the tall buttressed chataignier, form a leafy canopy that inhibits undergrowth and keeps the forest floor relatively clear. The treetops provide a habitat for light-seeking plants, including climbing vines, bromeliads and other air plants. The forest is also home to numerous bird species and a tiny tree frog.

There are often guides available at the trailhead; they charge about EC$45 to EC$55 to accompany up to four people on this hike, which takes about 1.25 hours each way. If you don't use a guide, carry a compass and be careful not to stray off the main trail, as it would be easy to lose your bearings in the surrounding wilderness.

## Boiling Lake

A rugged day-long hike leads to Boiling Lake, the world's second-largest actively boiling lake (the largest is in New Zealand). Geologists believe the 63-metre-wide lake is a flooded fumarole, a crack in the earth that is allowing hot gases to vent from the molten lava below. The eerie-looking lake sits inside a deep basin, its greyish waters veiled in steam, its centre emitting bubbly burps.

En route to the lake the hike passes through the Valley of Desolation, a former rainforest destroyed by a volcanic eruption in 1880. Today it's an active fumarole area with a barren-looking landscape of crusted lava, steaming sulphur vents and scattered hot springs. The hike follows narrow ridges, snakes up and down mountains and runs along hot water streams. Expect to get wet and muddy.

This strenuous six-mile (9.6 km) hike, which begins at Titou Gorge, requires a guide. The cost is generally about US$20 to US$30 if you sign up with a tour. It's about EC$80 (plus EC$25 for a second person) if you arrange your own guide in Laudat,

double that if you hire a guide to take you from Roseau.

## Other Trails

The walk to **Freshwater Lake**, the island's largest lake, is a straightforward hike that skirts the southern flank of Morne Macaque. As the 2.5-mile (four km) trail up to the lake is along a well-established 4WD track, this hike doesn't require a guide. It's a relatively gradual walk and takes about 2½ hours return.

Hikers can continue another 1.2 miles (two km) from Freshwater Lake to **Boeri Lake**, a scenic 45-minute walk that passes mountain streams and both hot and cold springs. The 40-metre-deep Boeri Lake occupies a volcanic crater that's nestled between two of the park's highest mountains. En route there's a nice range of flora that includes ferns, heliconia and various epiphytes, as well as the mossy trees of the elfin woodlands that surround the lake.

For a short walk and a dip there's the trail to **Titou Gorge**, where a deep pool is warmed by a hot spring. Just above the pool the gorge narrows and when the water's calm it's possible to swim upriver to a small cascading waterfall. Whenever there's any brown water being kicked up there's also a dangerous current and you should stay out of the pool. To get to the trail turn at the pay phone in Laudat and follow the short road to the utility station. The trail follows a narrow canal that feeds water to the hydroelectric plant. The walk takes about 15 minutes.

Serious hikers could also hire a guide to tackle **Morne Trois Pitons**, the park's tallest peak. The trail begins at Pont Casse at the north side of the park.

### Places to Stay

*Roxy's Mountain Lodge* (☎ & fax 84845), PO Box 265, in the village of Laudat, makes a great base if you're planning to do a lot of hiking. This friendly family-run place has six clean, simple rooms with shared bathroom. There's a TV room, a small bar and a restaurant with meals priced from EC$22 to EC$40 at lunch and from EC$30 to EC$50 at dinner.

DOMINICA

In season the menu includes mountain chicken and crayfish. Valerie Rock, who runs the guesthouse with her brother, can arrange reliable trail guides and is a fine source of information on the island. Room rates are US$20 to US$28 for singles, US$23 to US$32 for doubles. There are plans to add six new rooms with private bath, a three-room cottage and a swimming pool in the near future.

### Getting There & Away

To get to Laudat, take King George V St north from Roseau. After crossing the Roseau River, continue up the Roseau Valley for 2.3 miles (3.7 km), at which point the road forks; take the left fork, marked Laudat. The road is narrow and a bit potholed, but passable. The trail to Middleham Falls begins on the left 2.5 miles (four km) up; the trail to Freshwater and Boeri lakes begins opposite the shrine, half a mile (800 metres) farther.

There's regular but limited bus service. Buses (EC$3) to Laudat leave from the Roseau police station at 6.30 am and 1.15 pm, except Sunday, and also at 12.15 pm on Monday, Wednesday and Friday; buses return to Roseau from Laudat 30 minutes later. Taxis from Roseau to Laudat cost about EC$50.

## SOUTH OF ROSEAU

The coastal road south of Roseau is a delightful 30-minute drive that takes you through a couple of attractive little seaside villages and ends at Scotts Head. Most of the road skirts the water's edge, although there's a roller coaster section just before Soufriere that winds up the mountain and gives a nice coastal view before dropping back down to Soufriere.

**Soufriere** (population 950) has a picturesque old stone church on the north side of the village. There are steaming sulphur springs in the hills above Soufriere, including one about a mile (1.6 km) inland on the road that leads east from the village centre.

### Scotts Head

Scotts Head (population 800), on the southernmost tip of Dominica's west coast, is a picturesque fishing village and a fun place to kick around.

The village has a gem of a setting along the gently curving shoreline of Soufriere Bay, the rim of a sunken volcanic crater. Mountains form a nice inland backdrop. At the southern tip of the bay is a promontory, also called Scotts Head, which is connected to the village by a narrow, rocky neck of land. It's a short, easy walk to the top of the promontory, where there's a fine coastal view.

The centre of village activity is the waterfront, where brightly painted fishing shacks and snack shops line the shore and colourful fishing boats are hauled up onto the sand.

The bay offers good swimming and snorkelling conditions, as well as some of the island's best diving.

**Places to Stay** If you're tempted to stay at Scotts Head, a couple of people in town rent out small, furnished houses, generally for about US$25 to US$50 a day or US$150 to US$200 a week. Two such places are *Castille Apartment* (☎ 82926) and *Lydiaville* (☎ 84313).

DOMINICA

# Grenada

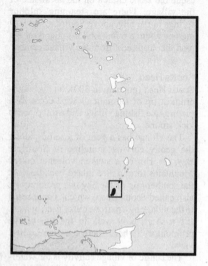

Grenada is colourful, robust and rough around the edges. Dubbed the 'Spice Island', it is the Caribbean's leading producer of nutmeg and mace, and also grows cinnamon, ginger and cloves. The Carib Indians called the island Camerhogne and Columbus, in passing, named it Concepción. However, Spanish explorers soon began calling the island Granada, after the city of the same name in Spain. When the French moved in they called it Grenade, which the British later changed to Grenada.

Pronounce it Gre-NAY-duh, with a long 'a' to rhyme with 'say'.

The island has a mountainous interior of rainforests and waterfalls and an indented coastline with protected bays and beaches. The capital, St George's, has one of the prettiest harbour settings in the Caribbean and takes its character from the 19th-century stone and brick buildings that slope down to the waterfront.

Although a couple of larger hotels have

recently been constructed on Grenada, most places to stay and eat are small locally owned businesses that offer a nice balance between comfort and price. Almost all of the accommodation and tourist facilities are concentrated at the south-west tip of the island, leaving the rest of Grenada with an unspoiled West Indian nature.

The nation is comprised not only of the island of Grenada, which has 90% of the land and population, but also of several Grenadine islands, a couple of which are inhabited. The largest of these, Carriacou, has the relaxed pace of an overlooked backwater. It makes a nice off-the-beaten-path destination and can easily be visited en route between Grenada and the St Vincent Grenadines.

## ORIENTATION

The airport is at the south-western tip of the island, 5.5 miles (nine km) from the capital of St George's. Midway between the two lies Grand Anse Beach, Grenada's main tourist area. It's possible to tour most of the island in a full-day outing. The most common sightseeing route is up the scenic Grand Etang Rd and north to Sauteurs via Grenville, Pearls and Bathways Beach, returning to St George's via the west-coast road.

Grenada is divided into six parishes. From north to south they are St Patrick, St Mark, St Andrew, St John, St George and St David.

# Facts about the Islands

## HISTORY

In 1498, during his third voyage to the New World, Christopher Columbus became the first European to sight Grenada, but didn't land on the island. The first European attempt to settle Grenada was made in 1609 by a party of 208 English settlers who planned to establish tobacco plantations on the island. Within a year most of the colonists

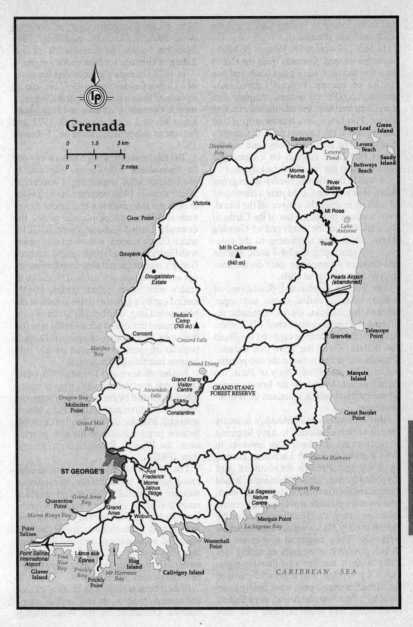

# Grenada

| 0 | 1.5 | 3 km |
| 0 | 1 | 2 miles |

Duquesne Bay

Sauteurs

Sugar Loaf

Green Island

Levera Beach

Morne Fendue

Levera Pond

Bathways Beach

Sandy Island

River Sallee

Victoria

Mt Rose

Gros Point

Lake Antoine

Gouyave

Mt St Catherine ▲ (840 m)

Tivoli

Dougaldston Estate

Pearls Airport (abandoned)

Fedon's Camp ▲ (765 m)

Concord

Concord Falls

Grenville

Telescope Point

Halifax Bay

Grand Etang

Marquis Island

Annandale Falls

Grand Etang Visitor Centre

GRAND ETANG FOREST RESERVE

Dragon Bay

Molinière Point

Etang

Constantine

Great Bacolet Point

Grand Mal Bay

St GEORGE'S

Fort Frederick

Morne Jaloux Ridge

Crochu Harbour

Quarantine Point

Grand Anse Bay

Grand Anse

Woburn

La Sagesse Nature Centre

Requin Bay

Morne Rouge Bay

Marquis Point

La Sagesse Bay

Point Salines

Westerhall Point

Point Salines International Airport

Lance aux Épines

True Blue Bay

Prickly Bay

Hog Island

Mt Hartman Bay

Caligny Island

CARIBBEAN SEA

Glover Island

Prickly Point

GRENADA

had fallen victim to raiding Caribs and the settlement was abandoned.

In 1650, Governor Du Parquet of Martinique 'purchased' Grenada from the Caribs for a few hatchets, some glass beads and two bottles of brandy. Parquet immediately moved in 200 French settlers, complete with a prefabricated fort, and established a trading station, Port Louis, on a narrow strip of land that separated the Lagoon from St George's Harbour. (The land eventually sank and the site of Port Louis is today on a submerged sand spit near the mouth of the Lagoon.)

In 1651, the French, weary of ongoing skirmishes with the Caribs, sent a contingent of soldiers to drive the natives off the island. French troops routed the last of the Caribs to Sauteurs Bay at the north end of Grenada where, rather than submitting to the colonists, the remaining Caribs – men, women and children – jumped to their deaths from the precipitous coastal cliffs.

The French established plantations of indigo, tobacco, coffee, cocoa and sugar, worked by African slaves. Grenada remained in French control until 1762, when Admiral George Rodney captured the island for Britain. Over the next two decades Grenada see-sawed between the two powers, but in 1783, under the Treaty of Paris, the French ceded Grenada to the British, under whose colonial rule it remained until independence.

British colonists and Grenada's minority French settlers continued to have lingering animosities towards each other however. In 1795 a group of French Catholics, encouraged by the French Revolution and supported by comrades in Martinique, armed themselves for a revolt. Led by Julien Fedon, who owned a plantation in Grenada's central mountains, they launched their assault on the British in early March with a brutal attack on Grenville. They managed to capture the British governor, eventually executing him along with a number of other hostages. Fedon's guerrillas, who controlled much of the island for over a year, were finally overcome by a fleet from the British navy. Fedon, incidentally, was never captured – he may

have escaped to Martinique or drowned while attempting to get there, although some islanders believe he remained a recluse hiding in Grenada's mountainous jungles.

In 1877 Grenada was accorded the status of a Crown Colony and in 1967 became an associated state within the British Commonwealth. Grenada, Carriacou and Petit Martinique adopted a constitution in 1973 and became an independent nation on 7 February 1974.

The road to independence was a rocky one for Grenadians. Eric Garity, who rose to prominence after organising a successful labour strike in 1950, became a leading voice in both the independence and labour movements. When independence came, the Grenada United Labour Party (GULP), which Garity headed, was swept into power with Garity as Grenada's first prime minister. Garity's regime gained notoriety for patronage and corruption. It attempted to silence its critics with secret police tactics, largely carried out by a group of thugs known as the Mongoose Gang, who brutally attacked antigovernment critics and occasionally went on their own little looting campaigns. Garity's popular support evaporated as his rule became increasingly dictatorial.

Just before dawn on 13 March 1979, while Garity was overseas, a small group of armed rebels supported by the opposition party, the New Jewel Movement (NJM), led a bloodless coup. Maurice Bishop, head of the NJM, became prime minister of the new government, the People's Revolutionary Government (PRG).

The 34-year-old Bishop, a London-educated lawyer, immediately reinstated a measure of human rights and promised a resolution of the country's economic problems. Bishop had widespread public support and proved a charismatic leader but his policy of nonalignment and socialist leanings didn't settle well with the USA and some of Grenada's more conservative Caribbean neighbours like Barbados.

Bishop built schools and medical clinics and created credit unions and farmers' cooperatives. Ostracised by the West, Bishop turned for aid to the Cubans, who undertook the construction of a new airport on Grenada. In the meantime divisions developed in the PRG between Bishop and those military leaders who wanted to take a more authoritarian approach.

In October 1983, a struggle between Bishop and the military hardliners resulted in Bishop's overthrow. On 19 October 1983, after learning of Bishop's house arrest, 30,000 supporters – the largest spontaneous crowd to ever gather in Grenada – forced his release. Together they marched to Fort George. At the fort the military opened fire on the crowd, killing an estimated 40 protesters. Bishop and several of his followers were taken prisoner and summarily executed in the courtyard.

In the turmoil that followed, the US government convinced a handful of Caribbean nations to pledge support to a US invasion of the island. On 25 October US troops, accompanied by symbolic forces from half a dozen Caribbean states, invaded Grenada. During the fighting that followed, 70 Cubans, 42 American and 170 Grenadians were killed, including 18 who died when the US forces mistakenly bombed the island's mental hospital. Most US forces withdrew in December 1983, although a joint Caribbean force and 300 US support troops remained on the island for two more years.

When elections were held again, in December 1985, Herbert Blaize and his newly formed New National Party won 59% of the vote and 14 of the 15 House seats. In July 1991 the death sentences for the 14 people who had been condemned to hang for the murder of Maurice Bishop and his supporters were commuted to life in prison.

## GEOGRAPHY

The three-island nation of Grenada, Carriacou and Petit Martinique has a total land area of 344 sq km. Grenada, with 310 sq km, measures 19 km in width and 34 km in length. The island is of volcanic origin, although part of the northern end is comprised of limestone. Grenada's rainy interior is rugged, thickly forested and cut by valleys and streams. The highest point is the 840-metre Mt St Catherine, an extinct volcano in the northern interior.

The south side of Grenada has a markedly indented coastline of jutting peninsulas, deep bays and small nearshore islands, making it a favourite haunt for yachters.

Carriacou, at 30 sq km, is the largest of the Grenadine islands that lie between Grenada and St Vincent.

## CLIMATE

In St George's in January the average daily high temperature is 29°C (84°F) while the low averages 24°C (75°F). In July the average daily high is 30°C (86°F) while the low averages 25°C (77°F).

During the rainy season, June to November, rain falls an average of 22 days a month in St George's and the mean relative humidity is 78%. In the driest months, January to April, there's measurable rainfall 12 days a month and the humidity averages 71%.

Annual rainfall is about 152 cm (60 inches) in St George's and 406 cm (160 inches) in the Grand Etang rainforest. Carriacou is substantially drier than Grenada, averaging 102 to 152 cm (40 to 60 inches) of rain a year.

---

**Nutmeg**

The nutmeg tree (Myristica frangrans), originally from East India, was commercially introduced by the Dutch in the mid-19th century. It thrived so well that Grenada now produces a third of the world's nutmeg.

A fragrant evergreen with glossy leaves and small yellow flowers, the nutmeg tree produces two spices: nutmeg and mace. The tree's yellow fruit, called the pericarp, splits open when ripe to reveal a brown nut, the nutmeg, which is covered with a lacy, orange-red webbing of mace.

Nutmeg is used to flavour baked goods, drinks, sauces and preserves. Mace is used as a seasoning and in cosmetics. The pericarp is used in nutmeg syrup. ∎

GRENADA

## FLORA & FAUNA

Grenada has a varied ecosystem of rainforests, montane thickets, elfin woodlands and lowland dry forests. Breadfruit, immortelle, flamboyant and palms are some of the more prominent trees.

About a dozen troops of Mona monkeys, introduced from West Africa centuries ago, live in Grenada's wooded areas. Other mammals are nine-banded armadillos (tatou), opossum (manicou), mongoose and a few agouti, the latter recently reintroduced to the island. Birdlife includes hummingbirds, pelicans, brown boobies, osprey hawks, endangered hook-billed kites and hooded tanagers.

There are no poisonous snakes, but the island does have tree boas. These nocturnal serpents spend their daytimes wound around branches many metres above the ground, however, so human contact with the creatures is quite limited.

## GOVERNMENT

Grenada, a member of the British Commonwealth, has a parliamentary government headed by a prime minister. The Governor-General, who represents the British Queen, has a largely advisory role but is responsible, on the advice of majority and opposition party leaders, for appointing the 13-member Senate. The 15-member House of Representatives is elected by universal suffrage.

The country's political parties are noted for their frequent splintering. The current prime minister, Nicholas Brathwaite, is a member of the National Democratic Congress, which was formed by the union of splinter groups from GULP and a rival party, the NNP. Brathwaite, incidentally, led the interim government appointed by the Governor-General following the US invasion of Grenada.

## ECONOMY

Grenada is the world's second-largest producer of nutmeg. It also exports mace, cloves, cinnamon, cocoa and bananas. Although agriculture remains the most important sector of the economy, since the 1980s the government has been attempting to boost tourism, which now rates second as a source of gross domestic product (GDP). The island averages 325,000 visitors annually, about a third of whom are cruise ship passengers. The unemployment rate, estimated at 32%, is one of the highest in the Eastern Caribbean.

## POPULATION & PEOPLE

The population of Grenada is 91,000, nearly a third of whom live in St George's. Another 6000 people live on Carriacou and about 600 live on Petit Martinique. Approximately 82% of Grenadians are Black, of African descent, while 13% have mixed origins. The other 5% is comprised of people of East Indian and European descent.

## ARTS & CULTURE

Grenadian culture is a mix of British, French, African and West Indian influences. A resurgence of Black pride is visible in the

### Sea Turtles
Sea turtles nest along some of Grenada's sandy beaches. All sea turtles are endangered, but that doesn't stop them from making it onto the menu at a few restaurants around the island. Travellers should give pause before eating at any restaurant that serves turtle meat. ■

GRENADA

widespread use of African names given to Grenadian children.

Steel band and calypso music are popular. Cricket and soccer are the most common sports; matches are held in St George's at Queen's Park and the Tanteen.

### Dress Conventions
Dress is casual on Grenada and simple cotton clothing is suitable attire for any occasion. In the more upmarket restaurants men will need to wear long pants but not ties. To avoid offence and unwanted attention, swimwear should be restricted to the beach.

### RELIGION
Almost 60% of all Grenadians are Roman Catholic. There are also churches for Anglicans, Seventh Day Adventists, Methodists, Christian Scientists, Presbyterians, Scots Kirk, Baptists, Jehovah's Witnesses and the Baha'i faith.

### LANGUAGE
The official language is English; a French-African patois is also spoken by some people.

# Facts for the Visitor

### VISAS & EMBASSIES
Passports are not required of citizens of the USA or Canada for stays of less than three months, as long as they have proof of citizenship, such as an official birth certificate or an expired passport, as well as a photo ID, such as a driving licence. Citizens of all other countries must have a valid passport.

As immigration officials generally stamp in the exact number of days you tell them you intend to stay, be sure to include any time you plan to spend in Carriacou in your calculations. They also ask where you're staying, so it's best to have some place in mind to smooth the process – in the end you can stay anywhere.

### Foreign Embassies & Consulates
The following embassies and consulates are found in Grenada:

Guyana
    Consulate of the Cooperative Republic of Guyana, Gore St, St George's (☎ 440-2189)
Netherlands
    Consulate of the Netherlands, Huggins Building, Grand Etang Rd, St George's (☎ 440-2031)
UK
    British High Commission, 14 Church St, St George's (☎ 440-3536)
USA
    US Embassy, Ross. Point Inn, Point Salines (☎ 444-1173)
Venezuela
    Venezuelan Embassy, Archibald Ave, St George's (☎ 440-1721)

### CUSTOMS
Visitors can bring in 200 cigarettes and a quart (one litre) of spirits duty free.

### MONEY
The official currency is the Eastern Caribbean dollar (EC$2.70 equals US$1). Most hotels, shops and restaurants will accept US dollars, but you'll generally get a better exchange rate by changing to EC dollars at a bank and using local currency. Major credit cards are accepted by most hotels and upper-end restaurants as well as some car rental agencies. Make sure it's clear whether prices are being quoted in EC or US dollars, particularly with taxi drivers.

An 8% tax and a 10% service charge is added to most hotel and restaurant bills. If no service charge is added, a 10% tip is generally expected.

### TOURIST OFFICES
When requesting information by mail, write to: Grenada Board of Tourism (☎ 440-2279; fax 440-6637), The Carenage, PO Box 293, St George's, Grenada, West Indies.

There's a tourist office booth at the airport, just before immigration, where you can pick up tourist literature and brochures; the staff can also help you book a room. Current

GRENADA

operating hours are from noon to 10 pm. A smaller tourist office booth is at the cruise ship dock in St George's.

## Overseas Reps

Tourist offices abroad include:

Canada
> Grenada Board of Tourism, 439 University Ave, Suite 820, Toronto, Ontario M5G 1Y8 (☎ (416) 595-1339; fax (416) 595-8278)

Germany
> Marketing Services International, Walter Stohrer und Partner GmbH, Liebigstrabe 8, D-6000 Frankfurt/M1 (☎ (496) 972-7770; fax (496) 972-7714)

UK
> Grenada Board of Tourism, 1 Collingham Gardens, Earls Court, London SW5 0HW (☎ (071) 370-5164/5; fax (071) 370-7040)

USA
> Grenada Board of Tourism, 820 Second Ave, Suite 900D, New York, NY 10017 (☎ (212) 687-9554, (800) 927-9554; fax (212) 573-9731)

## BUSINESS HOURS

Shops are generally open from 8 am to noon and 1 to 4 pm Monday to Friday and 8 am to noon on Saturday, although some larger shops stay open through the lunch hour.

Banking hours are generally from 8 am to 2 pm Monday to Thursday (some banks close at 1 or 3 pm) and 8 am to 1 pm and 2.30 to 5 pm on Friday.

## HOLIDAYS

Public holidays are:

| | | |
|---|---|---|
| *New Year's Day* | – | 1 January |
| *Independence Day* | – | 7 February |
| *Good Friday* | – | late March/early April |
| *Easter Monday* | – | late March/early April |
| *Labour Day* | – | 1 May |
| *Whit Monday* | – | eighth Monday after Easter |
| *Corpus Christi* | – | ninth Thursday after Easter |
| *Emancipation Days* | – | first Monday & Tuesday in August |
| *Thanksgiving Day* | – | 25 October |
| *Christmas Day* | – | 25 December |
| *Boxing Day* | – | 26 December |

## CULTURAL EVENTS

Carnival, held on the second weekend in August, is Grenada's big annual festival. It includes calypso and steel band competitions, all sorts of costumed revellers, a pageant and a big grand finale jump-up on Tuesday. Many of the events occur at Queen's Park at the north side of St George's.

Carriacou's four-day Carnival usually takes place in February. The island also has a major sailing event, the Carriacou Regatta, held in late July or early August. The regatta features races to Grenada, Union Island and Bequia, various sporting events from volleyball competitions to donkey races, and plenty of music and dancing.

## POST

Grenada's general post office is in St George's and there are sub-post offices in most villages. The cost to mail an aerogramme is EC$.50, an airmail letter is EC$0.75.

When addressing a letter, include the street name or box number, the village and 'Grenada (or Carriacou), West Indies'.

## TELECOMMUNICATIONS

Grenada has both coin and card phones. Coin phones take 25-cent coins (either EC or US) or EC$1 coins; each 25 cents allows three minutes on a call within the country. Card phones accept the same Caribbean Phonecard used on other Eastern Caribbean islands; cards are sold at the airport, at Grenada Yacht Club in St George's and at Sugar & Spice at Grand Anse, among other places.

International phone calls can be made and faxes and telexes sent from the Grenada Telecommunications (Grentel) office at the Carenage in St George's from 7 am to 6 pm weekdays, until 1 pm on Saturday and from 10 am to noon on Sunday. Expect long queues.

Local phone numbers have seven digits; when calling from outside the Caribbean add the area code 809. More information on phonecards and making international phone calls is in the Telecommunications section in the introductory Facts for the Visitor chapter.

## ELECTRICITY

The electrical current is 220 volts AC, 50 cycles.

## WEIGHTS & MEASURES

Grenada uses the imperial system.

## BOOKS & MAPS

A good book to pick up if you want to learn more about geology, flora and fauna is *A Natural History of the Island of Grenada* by John R Groome, a past president of the Grenada National Trust.

*The Mermaid Wakes: Paintings of a Caribbean Isle*, published by Macmillan, is a hardcover book featuring paintings by Carriacou artist Canute Caliste, with text about island life by Lora Berg.

*Revolution in Reverse* by James Ferguson, Monthly Review Press, presents a critical account of Grenada's development since the US invasion.

The best road map of Grenada is the Ordnance Survey's 1:50,000 map, which can be bought for EC$13 at the Grenada National Museum in St George's.

## MEDIA

Grenada has two local TV and four radio stations. Most hotels also have satellite or cable TV, which brings in numerous off-island stations, including major US network broadcasts.

The *Grenadian Voice*, *Grenada Today* and *The Barnacle* are the local newspapers. The *Miami Herald* and *USA Today* can be found in bookshops and large grocery stores.

The tourist office dispenses the 100-page magazine *The Greeting* and the pocket-sized *Discover Grenada*, both free and with lots of visitor-related ads and general information on Grenada and Carriacou.

## HEALTH

St George's General Hospital (☎ 440-2051), the island's main medical facility, is in St George's near Fort George. There's a small hospital on Carriacou. The quality of medical care on Grenada is not highly regarded and for serious health issues medical evacuation to Miami (or Barbados) is fairly common.

## DANGERS & ANNOYANCES

Safety precautions are warranted in Grenada. There have been muggings of tourists in the Grand Anse area, mostly along the beach at night, and the Lagoon area on the south side of St George's. Avoid walking in isolated areas after dark and don't carry an exposed camera bag or anything else that might make you stand out as a target. Yachters should have everything as secure as possible and belongings shouldn't be left unattended, especially in St George's.

Women travelling alone can expect to hear the occasional 'hey darlin' and other catcalls.

## EMERGENCY

For police and fire emergencies, dial ☎ 911.

## ACTIVITIES

### Beaches & Swimming

Grenada's most popular beach, Grand Anse, is a fine sweep of white sands. For somewhere less frequented, Morne Rouge Bay on the other side of Quarantine Point is both secluded and protected.

Some nice beaches can be found off the southern tip of the island, including True Blue just south-east of the airport runway and along much of Lance aux Épines.

Calivigny Island, east of Lance aux Épines, has a couple of pretty beaches, some walking tracks and the remains of an old hotel. If you don't have your own boat, The Moorings at Secret Harbour shuttles people over for US$15 per person, or for even less you can arrange with fishers at Woburn Pier to drop you off on the island.

### Diving

The waters around Grenada have extensive reefs, with a wide variety of corals, fish, turtles and other marine life. There are shallow reef dives, wall dives, drift dives and shipwrecks.

Perhaps the most challenging dive is to the wreck of the *Bianca C* ocean liner. Because of strong currents, coupled with a depth of

GRENADA

over 30 metres, it's strictly for experienced divers; dive shops usually require at least one check-out dive in advance.

Other popular sites include the *Buccaneer*, a deliberately sunk schooner about 25 metres deep; Bose Reef and Dragon Bay, which both have rich marine life, including manta rays; and Grand Mal Point, a reef and wall dive.

The islands between Grenada and Carriacou are also popular dive spots. These include Kick 'em Jenny, which has pristine waters and great visibility, and Sisters islands, a sheer wall dive.

**Dive Shops** All the dive shops on Grenada and Carriacou charge US$40 for a regular one-tank dive. They include:

Dive Grenada, PO Box 441, St George's (☎ 444-4371; fax 444-4800); at the Ramada Renaissance Hotel on Grand Anse Beach. Dive Grenada has dives to the *Bianca C* for US$55, night dives for US$45, a resort course that includes a reef dive for US$55 and open-water PADI certification for US$375 (US$325 if there are two or more people).

Grand Anse Aquatics, Grand Anse Beach (☎ 444-4129; fax 444-4808); at the Coyaba Beach Resort. This operation has dives to the *Bianca C* for US$60, night dives for US$50, two-tank dives for US$65, resort courses for US$70 and open water PADI certification for US$350 (or US$300 if more than one person).

Silver Beach Diving, Carriacou (☎ & fax 443-7882); at the Silver Beach Resort. This operation gives instruction in PADI and CMAS.

### Snorkelling

Molinière Point, north of St George's, has some of the best snorkelling on Grenada, although land access is difficult. Grand Anse Aquatics offers two-hour snorkelling trips to Molinière Point at 10 am and 2 pm daily for US$20 and Dive Grenada goes out at 2 pm for US$18.

### Windsurfing

Grenada is not particularly known for its windsurfing, but you can rent boards at a couple of places. At Grand Anse, Dive Grenada at the Ramada Renaissance Hotel and Grand Anse Aquatics at Coyaba Beach Resort both rent windsurfing gear for US$15 an hour and give lessons for US$10 an hour. The Moorings rents windsurfing gear at Secret Harbour for the same price.

### Sailing

Sail Grenada (☎ 444-2000), PO Box 308, St George's, has a two-day workshop with instruction in sailing, rigging, anchoring, docking, steering and compass and chart reading. The cost of US$200 includes lunches and hotel pick up.

For information on day sails see Tours in the Getting Around section.

### Fishing

Grenada offers good game fishing for blue marlin, white marlin, sailfish and yellowfin tuna. Winter is the best season. Tropix Professional Sport Fishing (☎ 440-4961) and Evans Chartering Services (☎ 443-7542) are two reputable fishing charterers. Expect a boat to cost about US$500 a day.

The Spice Island Billfish Tournament, held yearly in January, attracts anglers from North America and around the Caribbean with prize money of $100,000. Information is available from the Grenada Billfish Association (☎ 440-2018), PO Box 14, St George's.

### Hiking & Walking

The most popular hiking area in Grenada is the Grand Etang rainforest, where trails wind through a forest of mahogany and ferns and lead to a crater lake, waterfalls and mountain ridges. For details on specific trails, see the Grand Etang National Park, La Sagesse Nature Centre and Concord Falls sections.

The Hash House Harrier's Club sponsors a 'hash' on alternate Saturday afternoons, walking a different course each time. The trail is marked with scraps of paper and the object is to follow the route without getting lost. Visitors are welcome to join; schedules are posted at Rudolf's restaurant in St George's.

## Tennis

Several hotels have tennis courts for guests' use. The Coyaba Beach Resort in Grand Anse charges non-guests EC$25 an hour.

## Golf

The Grenada Golf Club (☎ 444-4128) near Grand Anse has a nine-hole course open to visitors from 8 am to 7 pm daily. Green fees are US$12 for nine holes, US$20 for 18 holes, and clubs can be rented.

## Yoga

If you're interested in yoga or meditation, you could check out the Amanda Marga Yoga Centre (440-5880), PO Box 303, St George's, near the Tanteen playing field.

## People to People Tours

New Trends Tours (☎ 444-1236; fax 444-4836) arranges a 'People to People' programme which offers visitors the opportunity to meet Grenadians of similar interests. There's no fee for the service.

Write to New Trends Tours, PO Box 438, St George's, and tell them a little about yourself, whether you'd like to meet a Grenadian family or someone with a specific profession, what you'd like to do (chat over lunch, go for a walk etc) and the dates you'll be on the island. The company maintains a list of islanders interested in meeting visitors and will attempt to make an introduction. Don't expect a reply to your letter. When you arrive in Grenada call New Trends to see if arrangements have been made. The office hours are from 8.30 am to 4.30 pm Monday to Saturday.

## HIGHLIGHTS

On Grenada, don't miss a drive through the scenic Grand Etang National Park, with a dip at the Annandale Falls on the way. A stop at one of the island's nutmeg stations can be interesting. In St George's, walk up to Fort George for a great harbour view.

Carriacou offers an appealing portion of the West Indies still undisturbed by tourism – it's peaceful and a fun place to get away from everything. From Carriacou either a trip to White Island for an afternoon of snorkelling and swimming or a boat trip to Petit Martinique can make a nice excursion.

## ACCOMMODATION

The main tourist areas are Grand Anse Beach and Lance aux Épines; both have some good-value moderate and top-end places to stay. The island's handful of budget guesthouses are not on the beach, but are concentrated in St George's. In the Point Salines area there are a couple of moderately priced hotels and two new beachside resorts. Beyond that, there are only a few scattered inns around the rest of Grenada.

Carriacou, which gets far fewer overnight visitors, has a number of good-value guesthouses.

In addition to booking direct, about two dozen hotels can be booked through the Grenada Hotel Association (☎ 444-1353; fax 444-4847; from the USA ☎ (800) 322-1753), PO Box 444, St George's.

## Camping

Camping is officially allowed in Grand Etang National Park but there are no established facilities and the park is in one of the rainiest parts of the island. Arrangements should be made through the park visitor centre (☎ 442-7425); because so few people camp, the fee seems to be set at whim, but it should be modest. The park also has a lake house that can be rented, although it's often booked long term by visiting forestry officials.

## FOOD

You'll find Italian and French food and plenty of seafood and West Indian dishes. Popular local dishes include fish stew, curried lambi (conch) and the ubiquitous roti. Pigeon peas with rice, plantains, yams and callaloo soup are common side dishes.

Grenadians have a nice sense of how a water view can add to a dining experience and many restaurants have good harbour and ocean views.

GRENADA

## DRINKS

The official word is that water is safe to drink from the tap, although some expatriates boil their drinking water as a precaution. Bottled water is available in grocery stores.

Carib beer is brewed on Grenada. Several rums are made using imported sugar, including Westerhall, a reasonably smooth rum that sells for about EC$12 a bottle.

Local nonalcoholic drinks worth a try are sorrel juice, mauby and ginger beer.

## ENTERTAINMENT

Entertainment is limited on Grenada, although there's usually a steel band or other dinner entertainment in Grand Anse a few nights a week. Most entertainment is at the Ramada Renaissance Hotel, Spice Island Inn, Flamboyant Hotel and Coyaba Beach Resort.

Fantazia 2001, a disco on Morne Rouge Beach, has dancing from 9 pm to 2 am four nights a week with a modest cover charge. Wednesday is oldies night, Thursday is reggae night and there are live bands on Friday and Saturday.

Le Sucrier, in the Old Sugar Mill at the airport/Grand Anse roundabout, has music and dancing on weekends from 9 pm until the wee hours of the morning. Music includes oldies, jazz and top-40 hits.

St George's is very quiet in the evening, although the Regal Cinema shows a double feature each evening for EC$5.

## THINGS TO BUY

Spices make nice, lightweight souvenirs. A good place to pick up quality spices at good prices is the Marketing & National Importing Board in St George's, which also sells local hot sauces, sorrel, nutmeg syrups and nutmeg and guava jams, some items gift-boxed.

White Cane Industries, at the south end of Wharf Rd in St George's, is a workshop for the blind where straw and cane baskets, placemats and serving trays are made and sold. The calibre of the work is high and the proceeds provide an income for the craftspeople working there.

For a general gift shop, Tikal on Young St in St George's has a quality collection of local handicrafts, batiks and wood carvings. Tikal also sells Rainforest Jewelry's locally crafted earrings made from the rock-solid, jet-black nuts of the gru-gru palm tree. The earrings make a nice alternative to black coral products, which they resemble in appearance.

There are also a few craft shops near the BWIA office on the inner Carenage in St George's and in the Grand Anse area.

# Getting There & Away

## AIR

Airline reservation numbers on Grenada are:

| | | |
|---|---|---|
| Aereotuy | – | ☎ 444-4732 |
| Airlines of Carriacou | – | ☎ 440-8251 |
| American Airlines | – | ☎ 444-2222 |
| British Airways | – | ☎ 440-2796 |
| BWIA International | – | ☎ 440-3818, |
| airport | – | ☎ 444-4134 |
| LIAT | – | ☎ 440-2796 |
| reservations | – | ☎ 444-4121 at Point |
| | | Salines Airport |
| | – | ☎ 443-7362 on Carriacou |

## To/From the USA

American Airlines has a daily flight to Grenada from San Juan, Puerto Rico, which connects with flights to the USA. Excursion tickets to Grenada from the US east coast typically begin around US$400 in the low season, US$500 in the high season.

BWIA International flies daily from New York and Miami, with fares that are competitive with American Airlines.

## To/From the UK

British Airways has a weekly Sunday flight direct from London to Grenada and BWIA has London-Grenada flights on Saturday, Sunday and Monday. Both charge £685 for an excursion ticket with a seven-day minimum stay, a six-month maximum stay and a 21-day advance purchase.

## To/From South America

Aereotuy flies from Grenada and Carriacou to Margarita Island in Venezuela two to three times a week, departing from Grenada around 8 am and returning in the late afternoon. The flights are geared for one-day outings and cost EC$504 return.

## Within the Caribbean

LIAT has daily nonstop flights between Grenada and Barbados, Carriacou, Trinidad, Tobago and St Vincent, with connecting flights to the rest of its Caribbean network.

The one-way/return fare to Grenada is US$116/152 from Barbados, US$111/173 from St Lucia, US$275/360 from St Martin and US$64/124 from St Vincent. A free stopover is allowed in either Carriacou or Union on flights between Grenada and St Vincent. The one-way fare from Tobago to Grenada is US$80. Grenada can also be included as a free stopover on flights between Trinidad (or Tobago) and points north.

LIAT has some good-value fares for flights that leave Grenada in the morning and return in the late afternoon. The airfare from Grenada for one-day outings is US$86 to Union Island, US$93 to Barbados and US$94 to St Vincent.

BWIA has daily flights to Grenada from Trinidad and Barbados; an excursion ticket, good for two to 21 days, costs US$104 between Trinidad and Grenada, US$155 between Barbados and Grenada. BWIA also has a one-way flight from Tobago to Grenada, that allows a stopover in Trinidad, for US$91.

Helenair (☎ 444-4101) has charter flights throughout the Caribbean.

## Airport Information

Point Salines International Airport has car rental offices, pay phones and a reasonably priced 2nd-floor restaurant. There's a tourist office booth in the arrivals section *before* you reach immigration. Between immigration and customs you can find a courtesy phone that rings direct to a number of car rental agencies, hotels and guesthouses.

The departure lounge has a duty-free liquor store and gift shop but you shouldn't count on them being open.

**To/From the Airport** There are no buses operating from Point Salines Airport but taxis are readily available at flight times. See Taxis in the Getting Around section for fares.

## SEA

For boats between Carriacou and Union Island, see the Getting There & Away in the Union Island section of the St Vincent & the Grenadines chapter. For boats between Grenada and Carriacou, see the Getting Around section of this chapter.

## Yacht

Customs and immigration can be cleared at St George's or Prickly Bay on Grenada and at Hillsborough on Carriacou. There are no port charges for yachters. In St George's, customs is at the Grenada Yacht Club (GYC) and most yachts anchor between GYC and Grenada Yacht Services. Customs and immigration is open from 8 am to 4 pm weekdays; outside those hours officials are available on an overtime basis.

The most frequented anchorages are along the south-west side of Grenada, including Prickly Bay, Mt Hartman Bay, Hog Island and True Blue Bay.

The Moorings (☎ 444-4439) bases its yacht charter operation at Secret Harbour and Sea Breeze Yacht Charters (☎ 444-4924) is at Prickly Bay, both in Lance aux Épines.

## Cruise Ship

Grenada is a port of call for a fair number of cruise ships. Ships dock at the south-east side of St George's centre; at the dock there's a tourist office, waiting taxis and a line of souvenir shops. It's only a 10-minute walk to the opposite side of the harbour, where most of St George's sights and shops are situated.

Cruise ship passengers can expect to encounter young men touting their services as guides. It's not a good idea to follow an unknown person around and a guide is unnecessary anyway as St George's is easy to explore. You're better off strolling around the town with a few friends or arranging an island tour with one of the taxi drivers.

## LEAVING GRENADA

There's an EC$25 departure tax for stays of longer than 24 hours (EC$12.50 for children aged five to 12). In addition there's an EC$10 (EC$5 for children) security charge. Children under five are exempt from both fees.

There are no taxes or fees on flights between Grenada and Carriacou.

# Getting Around

## AIR

Airlines of Carriacou has an average of four flights a day between Grenada and Carriacou. The first usually leaves Grenada at 6.30 am, the last returning from Carriacou at 5.30 pm. LIAT has two daily flights from Grenada to Carriacou, one at 9.30 am and the other at 4.45 pm. From Carriacou, flights leave for Grenada at 8.45 am and 4.15 pm. The cost on either airline is EC$82 one way, EC$130 return.

You could also check with Helenair (☎ 444-4101), a charter airline that sometimes has scheduled flights between Grenada and Carriacou.

## BUS

Buses on Grenada are privately operated minivans. Using the bus is a good way to experience the rhythms of daily life on Grenada – most blast calypso and reggae music and provide a hair-raising ride. Most buses leave St George's from the Esplanade bus terminal at the west end of Granby St. Signs mark some of the routes and it's all fairly orderly. If you're not sure who's going where, any of the drivers can point you in the right direction. Generally you're better off hopping into an almost-full bus, as most buses leave only after they fill. You can catch buses bound for St David parish from the public market.

Fares in the greater St George's area, including to Grand Anse Beach, are EC$1. From St George's fares are EC$2 to La Sagesse, EC$3 to Gouyave or Grand Etang and EC$5 to Grenville or Sauteurs. Although it depends on how many passengers are picked up and dropped off, it takes about 45 minutes from St George's to Grenville, 1½ hours to Sauteurs.

Buses begin running around 7 am. Times for the last buses vary with location, but it's hard to catch any bus after 6 pm; head back early enough so as not to get stuck. There are very few buses on Sunday.

You can flag down a passing bus from the side of the road by sticking out your hand. To get off the bus, yell out 'drop one'.

## TAXI

Taxi fares are regulated by the government. From the airport to Grand Anse or Lance aux Épines costs EC$25, to St George's or Woburn it's EC$30. From central St George's it's EC$8 to other parts of the city, EC$20 to Grand Anse or Morne Rouge and EC$32 to Lance aux Épines.

For trips elsewhere on Grenada, taxis charge EC$4 per mile for the first 10 miles and EC$3.50 per mile after that. The waiting charge is EC$15 per hour. For sightseeing purposes, taxis can be hired at a flat rate of EC$40 per hour. Fares are higher between 6 pm and 6 am.

## CAR & MOTORBIKE

### Road Rules

Vehicles drive on the left-hand side. Many roads are narrow and curving and a few bus drivers seem a bit hellbound. For safety, slow down when approaching blind curves and toot your horn liberally. There are few road signs on the island, so a good road map and a measure of patience is essential for self-touring.

You'll need to buy a local driving licence for EC$30 to drive in Grenada. You can get it from most car rental companies or from the fire station on the east side of the Carenage in St George's.

The larger towns, including Grenville,

Sauteurs and Victoria, have petrol stations; a gallon of unleaded costs EC$5.70.

There are a lot of one-way streets in St George's but some of them are not marked, so be careful and watch the traffic flow; better yet, try to avoid driving around the town centre, especially on the north side of the Carenage.

### Rental

There are a number of local car rental agencies but many of them have very small fleets and a three-day minimum rental period. For the most part, you're better off dealing with international companies – not that that will necessarily be smooth either. Budget (☎ 444-1620) has an office at the airport (if no-one's at the booth, ask around – there's a good chance the agent's nearby) and on Melville St in St George's. Avis (☎ 440-3936), at the Shell station on the corner of Paddock and Lagoon roads in St George's, will pick you up at the airport or your hotel at no charge.

Avis rents cars for US$45 a day, jeeps for US$60. Budget has slightly cheaper rates but is unreliable with reservations – at least at their St George's office – and can be difficult to reach.

David's Car Rentals (☎ 444-4310) and Zamba's Car Rentals (☎ 444-4101) are two local companies with booths at the airport.

A collision damage waiver (CDW) is US$6 a day extra. Without the CDW you're responsible for the full value of any damages to the car; even if you do take it, you're usually responsible for at least the first US$500 – check with the car rental company.

### BICYCLE

Cosy Corner Cottages (☎ 444-1157), Petite Valley, Lance aux Épines, rents 15-speed mountain bikes.

### BOAT

There's a scheduled passenger/cargo boat service between Grenada and Carriacou which takes three to four hours.

The *Adelaide B* and the *Alexia I* depart from Grenada at 9.30 am Wednesday and Saturday and leave Carriacou at 9.30 am Monday and Thursday.

The *Alexia III* departs from Grenada at 9.30 am Tuesday, 11 am Friday and 7 am Sunday, and leaves Carriacou at 1 pm on Wednesday and Saturday, and 8.30 pm Sunday.

The fare is EC$20 one way; buy your ticket on the boat. On Grenada the boat docks at the north side of the Carenage in St George's and on Carriacou at Hillsborough's town pier.

### TOURS
### Land Tours

Several small Grenadian-owned companies provide land tours of Grenada at competitive prices. Arnold's Tours (☎ 440-0531; fax 440-4118) offers a seven-hour round-the-island tour for US$35 that includes Grand Etang National Park, Grenville, lunch at the Morne Fendue Plantation House, Sauteurs, the nutmeg station in Gouyave, Concord Falls and the Dougaldston Estate.

Sunsation Tours (☎ 444-1656; fax 444-2836) travels a similar route but tours the Grenville nutmeg station, Pearls Airport and the River Antoine Rum Distillery, stopping to swim at Bathways Beach before returning via the west coast. The tour is by 4WD vehicle and lunch is either at Morne Fendue Plantation House or picnic-style on Levera Beach. The cost is US$40. Sunsation has both English and German-speaking guides.

If you want to trek into the interior, Henry's Safari Tours (☎ 444-5313; fax 444-4847) offers hiking tours. There's a seven-hour US$45 tour that includes a hike to the Seven Sisters Falls and another for US$65 which is essentially a one-way five-hour trek to Fedon's Camp that begins in the national park and returns from the village of Mt Qua Qua via a minibus. The prices are per person, with a minimum of two people.

Some companies, including Sunsation, do a nicely packaged half-day triangle tour that takes in Concord Falls, the nutmeg station in

GRENADA

Gouyave and Dougaldston Estate before turning inland to cut down through the Grand Etang National Park on the return. The cost is US$20.

La Sagesse Nature Centre (☎ 444-6458) offers a tour that includes hotel pick up, an hour-long guided nature walk through the nature centre, time on the beach, lunch and return transportation for US$26. Arnold's Tours has a half-day tour that includes a shorter stop at La Sagesse, but also takes in Grand Etang National Park, Grenville and the Annandale Falls for US$20.

### Boat Tours

Several boats in Grenada offer trips to nearshore islands as well as sails through the Grenadines, often including snorkelling time. Tour frequency depends on demand and most require a minimum of four to six passengers. For details, look for flyers, ask at your hotel or flip through *The Greeting* tourist magazine. Expect to pay about US$20 for a sunset cruise, US$30 for a half-day sail and US$50 for a full-day sail. Some of the companies offering boat tours include Starwind Enterprise (☎ 440-3678), Sunshine Cruises (☎ 444-1852) and Arnold's Tours (☎ 440-0531).

If you want to plan your own itinerary, The Moorings at Secret Harbour arranges yacht charters, with a skipper, for half-day (US$25) and full-day (US$40) sails. Rates are per person, with a minimum of four people.

The *Rhum Runner* (☎ 440-2198) is Grenada's version of a party boat, with all-you-can-drink rum punches, steel band music and limbo dancing. The cruise includes some snorkelling and beach time and costs US$20.

### Day Tours to Other Islands

Fun Tours (☎ 444-3167) offers day-trips to Carriacou for US$150; to Union Island, Palm Island, Mayreau and the Tobago Cays for US$180; to Mustique and Bequia for US$250; and to Tobago for US$225. Rates include airfare, lunch and sightseeing.

# St George's

St George's is a picturesque hillside town surrounding a deep horseshoe-shaped harbour called the Carenage. The main sights can easily be seen in a couple of hours. There's a small museum, two old forts offering fine views, a few churches, a colourful public market and a bustling waterfront.

You won't find wooden houses, which were banned in St George's following two catastrophic fires that swept through the town in the late 18th century. Instead, there's a predominance of 19th-century structures of brick and stone, many of them roofed with orange fishscale tiles brought over as ballast on ships from Europe.

The head of the Carenage makes a good place to begin a stroll of the town. Opposite

---

### The *Bianca C*

At 200 metres in length, the Italian liner *Bianca C* is the largest shipwreck in the Eastern Caribbean. In the early morning of 22 October 1961 the ship was anchored in St George's outer harbour preparing to sail when an explosion ripped through the engine room, setting off a fire that quickly engulfed the vessel.

A flotilla of yachts, fishing vessels and inter-island schooners came to assist in the rescue efforts and all 400 passengers escaped without loss of life, although three of the 300 crew members died of fire injuries. A few days later a British warship towed the smouldering vessel out of the harbour and into deeper waters where it broke away and sank. Today the *Bianca C*, with its upper decks 30 metres below the surface, is the region's best known dive wreck.

The cause of the fire remains unknown. ■

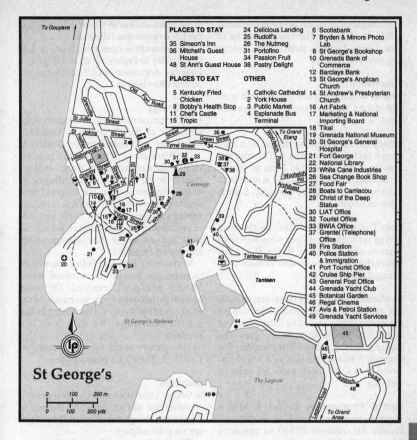

**St George's**

| PLACES TO STAY | | OTHER | | |
|---|---|---|---|---|
| 35 | Simeon's Inn | 1 | Catholic Cathedral | |
| 36 | Mitchell's Guest House | 2 | York House | |
| 48 | St Ann's Guest House | 3 | Public Market | |
| | | 4 | Esplanade Bus Terminal | |

PLACES TO STAY
35 Simeon's Inn
36 Mitchell's Guest House
48 St Ann's Guest House

PLACES TO EAT
5 Kentucky Fried Chicken
9 Bobby's Health Stop
11 Chef's Castle
15 Tropic

24 Delicious Landing
25 Rudolf's
26 The Nutmeg
31 Portofino
34 Passion Fruit
38 Pastry Delight

OTHER
1 Catholic Cathedral
2 York House
3 Public Market
4 Esplanade Bus Terminal

6 Scotiabank
7 Bryden & Minors Photo Lab
8 St George's Bookshop
10 Grenada Bank of Commerce
12 Barclays Bank
13 St George's Anglican Church
14 St Andrew's Presbyterian Church
16 Art Fabrik
17 Marketing & National Importing Board
18 Tikal
19 Grenada National Museum
20 St George's General Hospital
21 Fort George
22 National Library
23 White Cane Industries
26 Sea Change Book Shop
27 Food Fair
28 Boats to Carriacou
29 Christ of the Deep Statue
30 LIAT Office
32 Tourist Office
33 BWIA Office
37 Grentel (Telephone) Office
39 Fire Station
40 Police Station & Immigration
41 Port Tourist Office
42 Cruise Ship Pier
43 General Post Office
44 Grenada Yacht Club
45 Botanical Garden
46 Regal Cinema
47 Avis & Petrol Station
49 Grenada Yacht Services

the LIAT office is Christ of the Deep, a life-size bronze statue put up by Costa Cruise Line in honour of their ship, the *Bianca C*, which went up in flames inside the harbour in 1961. The Carriacou boats, mostly wooden schooners painted bright red, are loaded nearby, on the west side of the Carenage. Farther along Wharf Rd are some 19th-century warehouses, including one restored building housing the National Library.

The winding maze of streets on the west side of the Carenage can be fun to wander through. At Scott and Lucas Streets a smartly

uniformed police officer (locally dubbed 'cop in a box') directs traffic at a busy blind corner.

On congested Young St, women sell cloth dolls and spice baskets along the pavement and there are some interesting craft shops and art galleries – you can watch batik being made on site at Art Fabrik.

There's a modest botanical garden and a neglected little 'zoo' (one monkey and a few mislabelled birds) at the south-east side of town, a 10-minute walk from the post office, but it's not worth going out of your way to see.

A couple of irregular water taxis shuttle across St George's Harbour and down to Grand Anse. Look for them at the Carenage opposite The Nutmeg.

## Information

**Tourist Office** The tourist office, at the north side of the Carenage, is open weekdays until 4 pm.

**Money** Barclays Bank, on Halifax St, is open from 8 am to 2 pm Monday to Thursday and 8 am to 1 pm and 2.30 to 5 pm on Friday. Scotiabank, also on Halifax St, is open from 8 am to 3 pm Monday to Thursday, 8 am to 5 pm on Friday.

**Post** The general post office, on the south side of the harbour, is open weekdays from 8 am to noon and 1 to 3.30 pm. If you just want to buy stamps, a window remains open during the lunch hour.

**Bookshops** St George's Bookshop on Halifax St has a fairly good collection of Caribbean books, including island flora and fauna. Sea Change Book Shop, below The Nutmeg, sells local and US newspapers. The Grenada National Museum sells a few historical books. All these places sell maps of Grenada.

**Film & Photography** Bryden & Minors Photo Lab, on the corner of Granby and Halifax Sts, charges EC$40 to process a 24-print roll of film; one-hour service costs 10 cents more per print.

## Grenada National Museum

The Grenada National Museum, on the corner of Young and Monckton Sts, incorporates an old French barracks dating from 1704. The building served as a prison from 1766 to 1880 and as the island's first hotel in the 1900s.

The hodgepodge of exhibits includes Amerindian pottery fragments, an old rum still and a rather grubby marble bathtub that once belonged to the Empress Josephine. There's also a display on the events leading to the assassination of Maurice Bishop and the US invasion that followed.

The museum is open from 9 am to 4.30 pm Monday to Friday, 10 am to 1.30 pm on Saturday. Admission is EC$2.50 for adults, 50 cents for children.

## Fort George

Fort George, on the hilltop promontory at the west side of the Carenage, is Grenada's oldest fort, established by the French in 1705. While many of the fort buildings are used by the national police, the grounds are open to the public and offer some fine views of the surrounding area. The lookout opposite the police station provides one of the best vantages – a sweeping view of the west side of the city with its church spires and red-tile roofs and out across the Carenage to the hilltop Fort Frederick.

In the inner fort, just below the row of cannons, you'll find the courtyard where Maurice Bishop was executed. The bullet holes in the basketball pole were made by the firing squad and the spot is marked by fading graffiti that reads 'No Pain No Gain Brother'.

The entrance to the fort is at the end of Church St. There's no admission fee.

## Churches

St George's boasts a number of 19th-century churches that add an appealing element to the skyline, though the churches themselves are not extraordinary.

The most interesting is **St George's Anglican Church** on Church St. Built in 1825, it has a four-sided clock tower that doubles as the town's official timepiece; floor tiles in West Indian hues of red, black and yellow; and a marble tablet commemorating the English colonists killed in the French-inspired 1795 Fedon uprising.

The Catholic cathedral, the largest of the lot, has a brightly painted interior. It's opposite York House, a building of early Georgian architecture which holds the Supreme Court, House of Representatives and the Senate.

The yellow brick church immediately north of Fort George is St Andrew's Presbyterian church, which dates from 1833. It has a spired four-sided clock tower.

The doors of all three churches are usually open for viewing.

### Fort Frederick

Fort Frederick, atop Richmond Hill, 1.2 miles (two km) east of St George's, was constructed by the French in 1779 after wresting control of the island from the British. After 1783, when the French were forced by treaty to return Grenada to the British, the fort served to guard against the threat of French attacks. The cessation of hostilities between the two powers led to the fort's abandonment in the 1850s. The fort provides a fine panoramic view that includes Quarantine Point, Point Salines and Grover Island. Grover Island, incidentally, was used until 1927 as a Norwegian whaling station.

Fort Frederick remains well intact, in part due to a targeting blunder made during the US invasion of 1983. The US intended to hit Fort Frederick, then in use by the Grenadian military, but instead mistakenly bombed Fort Matthew, just a few hundred metres to the north, which was being used as a mental hospital at the time of the attack.

On cruise ship days there's often a steel band playing at the Fort Frederick entrance. Admission is free.

### Places to Stay

*St Ann's Guest House* (☎ 440-2717), 16 Paddock Rd, is on the south-east side of town, a 20-minute walk from the centre but on a main bus route. The management are friendly, the dozen rooms straightforward but clean. Each room has a sink. Singles/doubles cost US$16/23 for rooms with shared baths, US$20/31 with private baths. Rates include breakfast. There's a TV room and access to a phone and a refrigerator.

*Mamma's Lodge* (☎ 440-1623), on Lagoon Rd at the south side of the Lagoon, is a bit out of the way, in an area that's not terribly safe to stroll in at night. It is on a main bus route and offers the newest rooms around St George's. Rooms have twin beds, portable fans, private baths and balconies.

Singles/doubles cost US$30/42 including tax, service charge and breakfast – some days eggs, other days saltfish cakes. There's a bit of a view of the harbour from the patio and a TV in the front room.

*Mitchell's Guest House* (☎ 440-2803) is an older place on Tyrrel St in central St George's. The 11 rooms have table fans, washbasins and either a double or two single beds. Bathrooms are in the hall. There's a shared sitting room with a TV, phone and small refrigerator. Singles/doubles cost US$21/34. A full breakfast can be arranged for an extra EC$15.

*Simeon's Inn* (☎ 440-2537), on Green St opposite the Jehovah's Witnesses hall, is a simple guesthouse with nine rooms that share two toilets and showers. Rooms are basic with two twin beds; some have sinks, and table fans are available on request. There's a nice harbour view from the shared balcony. Singles/doubles cost US$20/35 including a full breakfast.

### Places to Eat – cheap

*Pastry Delight* on the inner Carenage makes a nice place for a cheap snack on the run. In the morning you can get a fish bake for a mere EC$1.50 and during the day there are inexpensive sandwiches to order. Other items include coconut turnovers, whole wheat bagels and various breads. It's open from 7 am to 6 pm weekdays, until noon on Saturday.

It's hard to believe, but the longest queues in town are at the *Kentucky Fried Chicken* on Granby St, where two pieces of chicken and fries cost EC$10. It's open from 10.30 am to 10 pm Monday to Saturday, from 1 to 10 pm on Sunday.

*Chef's Castle* on the corner of Halifax and Gore Sts is a modern fast-food restaurant with ice cream, hot dogs, burgers, fried chicken and rotis, all for EC$10 or under. It's open from 9 am to 10 pm Monday to Saturday, from 5 to 10 pm on Sunday.

For something in the same price range but a bit more holistic there's *Bobby's Health Stop*, a small 2nd-floor eatery on Gore St, serving vegie burgers, tofu dishes, crab backs, fresh juices and both chicken and vegetarian rotis. On Saturday there's cow heel soup as well! It's open from 10 am to 5.30 pm Monday to Saturday.

*Tropic*, a small eatery on Young St with a counter and a few stools, has reasonably priced local food including good fish rotis for EC$7 and plate lunches for EC$12. It's open from 8 am to 5 pm Monday to Saturday.

The *Passion Fruit* on Tyrrel St is a popular spot with Peace Corps volunteers. It has fish sandwiches for EC$3, chicken rotis for EC$5 and inexpensive juices. Hours are 9 am to 4.30 pm Monday to Friday.

*Delicious Landing* has an enviable waterfront location but the restaurant changes management frequently and it's a better spot for having a drink than a meal. It's open to 11 pm daily.

Foodland on Lagoon Rd is the island's largest supermarket and the best place to find imported Western foods. On the west side of the Carenage, there's Food Fair for groceries.

Local fruits and vegetables are sold at the public market, although foreigners generally do better at the Marketing & National Importing Board on Young St, a farmers' cooperative with set prices and no haggling.

### Places to Eat – middle

Casual and with a nice harbour view, *The Nutmeg*, on the west side of the Carenage, is one of the capital's most popular dining spots. At lunch and dinner, there are sandwiches and burgers for around EC$10, fish and rather oily chips for EC$18 and a good curried conch and salad for EC$30. Specialities include a nice spicy callaloo soup and a potent nutmeg rum punch. It's open Monday to Saturday from 9 am to 1 pm and Sunday from 5 to 11 pm.

*Portofino* (☎ 440-3986), next to the tourist office, has good pizzas from EC$12, various pasta dishes from around EC$20 and a few pricier meat dishes. The catch of the day (EC$30) is often a generous slab of tuna. At dinner there's recorded jazz and New Age music, making for one of the area's mellower dining scenes. Ask for a window table to enjoy a harbour view. It's open from noon to 11 pm on weekdays and 6 to 11 pm on Saturday.

*Rudolf's* on Wharf Rd is a casual pub-style restaurant with hot fish sandwiches for EC$6.50, flying fish, dolphin (mahimahi) or chicken and chips for around EC$20 and seafood brochettes or lambi for a few dollars more. It's open from 10 am to midnight Monday to Saturday.

# Around Grenada

## GRAND ANSE

Grenada's main resort area is along Grand Anse Beach, a long lovely sweep of white sand fronted by turquoise blue waters. The beach has lots of vendors selling T-shirts and spice baskets, others offering to braid hair, but overall the activity is fairly low-key.

There are numerous places to eat and stay around Grand Anse. The most expensive hotels front the beach, while rates tend to drop proportionally as you get farther away. Grand Anse Beach is backed by hills and consequently many of the hotels and restaurants are terraced along the hillside and have good views.

### Information

The Grand Anse Shopping Centre, opposite the Ramada hotel, has a Scotiabank; a nice gift shop called Imagine; and Food Fair, a large modern grocery store that's open from 9 am to 5.30 pm Monday to Thursday, to 7 pm on Friday and Saturday.

There's a Barclays Bank, travel agency, photo lab, drugstore and fruit stand in the Cellar Shopping Centre a few hundred metres to the west.

Tangie's Laundry, at the airport/Grand Anse roundabout, will wash and dry a load of clothing for EC$20. It's open from 8 am to 8 pm Monday to Saturday, 9 am to 2 pm on Sunday.

### Places to Stay – bottom end

*Palm Grove Guest House* (☎ 444-4578), PO

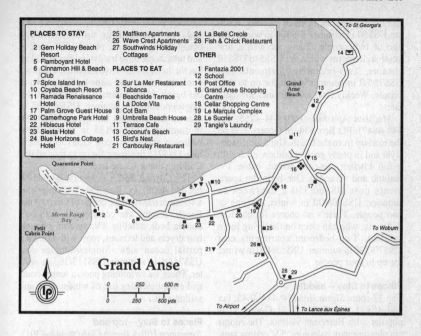

PLACES TO STAY

2 Gem Holiday Beach Resort
5 Flamboyant Hotel
6 Cinnamon Hill & Beach Club
7 Spice Island Inn
10 Coyaba Beach Resort
11 Ramada Renaissance Hotel
17 Palm Grove Guest House
20 Camerhogne Park Hotel
22 Hibiscus Hotel
23 Siesta Hotel
24 Blue Horizons Cottage Hotel
25 Maffiken Apartments
26 Wave Crest Apartments
27 Southwinds Holiday Cottages

PLACES TO EAT

2 Sur La Mer Restaurant
3 Tabanca
4 Beachside Terrace
6 La Dolce Vita
8 Cot Bam
9 Umbrella Beach House
11 Terrace Cafe
13 Coconut's Beach
15 Bird's Nest
21 Canboulay Restaurant
24 La Belle Creole
28 Fish & Chick Restaurant

OTHER

1 Fantazia 2001
12 School
14 Post Office
16 Grand Anse Shopping Centre
18 Cellar Shopping Centre
19 Le Marquis Complex
28 Le Sucrier
29 Tangie's Laundry

**Grand Anse**

Box 568, St George's, is uphill from the Grand Anse Shopping Centre, about a five-minute walk from the beach. The guesthouse is popular with French and German travellers and makes a good low-end option for the Grand Anse area. The nine rooms are simple but clean with one or two twin beds, private baths and ceiling fans. Some also have small tables and at least one of the double rooms has a TV and radio. There's access to a phone and shared kitchens and there are a few hammocks strung out the back. Singles/doubles cost US$25/35 and the rate drops US$5 for stays of more than two days.

*Southwinds Holiday Cottages* (☎ 444-4310; fax 444-4404), PO Box 118, St George's, has 21 apartments in boxy two-storey buildings about 10 minutes' walk from the beach. The units are straightforward with kitchens, phones and radios. One-bedroom apartments cost US$50 with a ceiling fan, US$55 with air-con. Two-bedroom apartments, which have air-con,

cost US$80 for up to four people. Rates are US$10 less during summer. Children under the age of 12 are free, while extra adults pay US$5 more.

The *Camerhogne Park Hotel* (☎ 444-4587), a block from the beach, has 21 rooms in a few two-storey apartment-like buildings. The rooms are straightforward and a bit wear-worn, with two twin beds, air-con, TV and phone. Singles/doubles cost US$45/55 in summer, US$55/65 in winter. There are also self-contained apartments which can accommodate from three to six people that cost from US$90 to US$150 in winter, US$15 less in summer. The hotel has a restaurant and bar with moderately priced breakfasts and sandwiches.

*Wave Crest Apartments* (☎ 444-4116), PO Box 278, St George's, is a good-value 15-unit apartment complex about 10 minutes' walk from the beach. The one-bedroom apartments each have a double or two twin beds, air-con, TV, phone, a separate kitchen

GRENADA

and dining area and a small balcony. Rates are US$50 in summer, US$60 in winter, for one or two people. There are also a few hotel-style rooms which are US$5 to US$10 cheaper. Two-bedroom apartments cost US$70/80 in summer/winter for up to four people. Weekly rates are six times the daily rate.

*Maffiken Apartments* (☎ 444-4255; fax 444-4847), PO Box 534, St George's, is on the road up from the beach. Units are condo-style and in pretty good condition, each with a full kitchen, air-con, phone, cable TV, bathtub and verandah. One-bedroom apartments cost US$60/350 a day/week in summer, US$70/400 in winter, for one or two people. There's no charge for children under six, who can sleep on the living room sofabed. Two-bedroom apartments cost US$70/390 in summer, US$85/450 in winter for up to four people.

### Places to Stay – middle

The 37-room *Siesta Hotel* (☎ 444-4645; fax 444-4647), PO Box 27, St George's, is popular with European visitors. The rooms are pleasant with balconies, TV, ceiling fans, air-con, bathtubs and tile floors. While it's not on the beach, it's only a few minutes' walk away, the location is quiet and there's a pool. Singles/doubles cost US$50/60 in summer, US$70/80 in winter. Add an extra US$10 for a room with a small kitchenette. There are also roomy one-bedroom apartments that cost US$80/95 in summer, US$105/120 in winter.

*Hibiscus Hotel* (☎ 444-4233; fax 440-6632), PO Box 279, St George's, has 10 rooms in attractive duplex-style cottages spread out on a landscaped lawn. The rooms are modern and clean, each with one or two double beds, a TV, a small table, a bathtub and a balcony. A footpath leads to Grand Anse Beach, a few minutes' walk away, and the hotel has a pool. Singles/doubles cost US$55/70 in summer, US$65/80 in winter.

The *Flamboyant Hotel* (☎ 444-4247; fax 444-1234), PO Box 214, St George's, is a pleasant, sprawling hillside complex at the west end of Grand Anse Beach. The hotel has a variety of accommodation, mostly in buildings of two to four units. All have ocean-facing terraces, phones, TV, air-con and tubs; some have hardwood floors and all but the hotel rooms have kitchens. There's a pool, fine views and steps leading down to the beach. Hotel rooms cost US$65/80 for singles/doubles in summer, US$95/105 in winter; one-bedroom suites cost US$80/90 in summer, US$115/135 in winter. Two-bedroom apartments cost US$130 in summer, US$215 in winter, for up to four adults. Children under 12 are free.

The *Coyaba Beach Resort* (☎ 444-4129; fax 444-4808), PO Box 336, St George's, is a 40-room resort on the centre of Grand Anse Beach. Rooms are comfortable with two double beds, satellite TV, air-con, phones, hair dryers and terraces, most with at least a partial ocean view. Singles/doubles cost US$75/95 in summer, US$115/165 in winter. There's a swimming pool, a tennis court and complimentary use of windsurfing and sailing gear.

### Places to Stay – top end

*Cinnamon Hill & Beach Club* (☎ 444-4301), PO Box 292, St George's, has 20 units in two-storey Mediterranean-style buildings. The units are very large – all have full kitchens, big balconies and at least four beds and two bathrooms – although the decor is dated and they're not overly spiffy. The 2nd-floor apartments are best, as they have beam ceilings. Rates for one or two people are US$77/121 in summer/winter for a one-bedroom apartment, US$114/153 in the two-bedroom apartments. It's US$17 each for a third and fourth person. There's a pool and an Italian restaurant on site.

*Blue Horizons Cottage Hotel* (☎ 444-4316; fax 444-2815), PO Box 41, St George's, just a few minutes from Grand Anse Beach, is one of the island's most popular villa-style hotels. The 32 suites and apartments are spread out in Mediterranean-style buildings and units are attractive and spacious with kitchens, tile floors, ceiling fans, air-con, TV, phones and verandahs. Suites cost US$90/130 in summer/winter;

one-bedroom apartments with two twin beds cost US$95/140; deluxe units, which are very large and have two double beds, are US$10 more. There's a pool, restaurant and bar.

*Ramada Renaissance Hotel* (☎ 444-4371; fax 444-4800), PO Box 441, St George's, is Grand Anse's largest hotel, with 186 rooms in a sprawling, low-rise complex of beachside buildings. The rooms are standard Ramada fare, comfortable with air-con, TV, and phone, but without much West Indian influence. The hotel has a beachfront pool and lighted tennis courts. Rates, which are the same for singles or doubles, begin at US$100 in summer, US$158 in winter.

Grenada's most expensive property is the *Spice Island Inn* (☎ 444-4258; fax 444-4807), PO Box 6, St George's, an all-inclusive beachfront resort. The 56 cottage-style rooms have a casual, tropical elegance with rattan furnishings, tile floors, ceiling fans, air-con, minibars and radios. In winter, singles/doubles cost US$355/460 for a beachfront unit with a whirlpool bathtub, US$460/585 for a larger unit, set back from the beach, with its own plunge pool. Rates include meals, drinks, sports and entertainment and are about 20% cheaper in summer.

### Places to Eat – cheap

*Sugar & Spice* in the Grand Anse Shopping Centre has frozen yoghurt and ice cream in traditional and tropical flavours (the mango is good!) for EC$3 a cone. The shop also sells inexpensive sandwiches, burgers, pizza and juices. It's open from 11 am to 9.30 pm Tuesday to Saturday, from 4 pm on Sunday.

*Hooters* in the Le Marquis Complex features beef or chicken burgers for EC$7, rotis, fresh juices and Carib beer on tap. It's open from 11 am to 10 pm Tuesday to Saturday, from 5 to 10 pm on Sunday.

*The Little Bakery & Coffee House* in the Le Marquis Complex has simple bakery items and a daily lunch special such as chicken wings, fried rice and salad for EC$12. It's open Monday to Saturday from 7 am to 8 pm.

*Bobby's Health Stop* in the Le Marquis

Complex is a simple shop with good fish rotis (EC$7), crab backs, vegetarian pizzas, yoghurt, juices and teas. It's open from 11.30 am to 6.30 pm Monday to Saturday.

*Cot Bam*, a large open-air bar and restaurant on Grand Anse Beach, has inexpensive rotis and sandwiches, chicken or fish & chips for EC$13 and a few more substantial fish or goat dishes for around EC$30. It's open from 9.30 am to at least 9 pm.

The *Umbrella Beach House*, the small white and red eatery just east of Cot Bam, is a friendly family-run place with good inexpensive food. A fish or chicken sandwich is EC$4, a tasty roti is EC$6 and a bottle of Carib beer costs a mere EC$1.75. It's open from 9 am to about 6 pm weekdays, from 11.30 am on Saturday.

The *Fish & Chick Restaurant*, at the Old Sugar Mill on the airport/Grand Anse roundabout, has pretty good fish and chicken at fast-food prices. You can eat in or takeaway.

### Places to Eat – middle

The *Bird's Nest* (☎ 444-4264) is a moderately upscale Chinese restaurant opposite the Ramada hotel. At lunch there are inexpensive sandwiches and various combination plates, such as sweet and sour chicken with fried rice, for EC$18. À la carte Chinese dishes average EC$15 for chicken, EC$20 for fish and EC$35 for shrimp and beef. It's open from 9.30 am to 11 pm daily except on Sunday when it opens at 6 pm.

*Coyaba Beach Resort* has an open-air restaurant with bamboo and rattan decor. From 7 to 10 am there's a continental breakfast for EC$15 and a full breakfast for EC$20. Lunch, served until 3 pm, includes sandwiches for around EC$10 and salads or fish & chips for about double that. At dinner there's an à la carte menu daily, except Tuesday and Saturday when there's a fixed price menu (EC$60) and a steel band.

The *Beachside Terrace*, a casual open-air restaurant at the Flamboyant Hotel, is open from 7.30 am to 10.30 pm daily. It has a range of Western breakfast offerings and daytime snacks such as fish & chips or rotis for around EC$20; fresh tuna salad or chef's salad cost a few dollars more. At dinner, main dishes range from EC$33 for Grenadian fish stew to EC$60 for lobster. On Sunday there's a barbecue beach brunch from 10.30 am to 5 pm, and on Monday and Wednesday an EC$65 buffet dinner from 7 pm.

*Tabanca*, opposite the office of the Flamboyant Hotel, has a fine water view and good food. Sandwiches, omelettes and other simple lunch offerings cost from EC$10 to EC$30. At dinner, a chalkboard menu of main dishes ranges from fresh fish for around EC$30 to steak for EC$50. It's open daily from 11 am to 10 pm.

The Ramada's *Terrace Cafe* is an open-air restaurant that features a lunch barbecue from noon to 2 pm daily. It's buffet style with chicken, fish, hamburgers, hot dogs, pork chops and a selection of salads. The price depends on what you select, but is roughly EC$15 to EC$35. The hotel's more formal dinner restaurant can be a bit stuffy.

The place to go for Italian food is *La Dolce Vita* (☎ 444-4301) at the Cinnamon Hill hotel. They make their own pastas and have a variety of dishes such as lasagne, ravioli and tagliatelle from EC$25 to EC$55. It's open for dinner daily except Monday from 7 to 11 pm.

### Places to Eat – expensive

*Coconut's Beach* (☎ 444-4644), known locally as the French Restaurant, is on the water at the east side of Grand Anse Beach. The food is predominantly French Creole. At lunch you can get a sandwich, a cheese and tomato crêpe or quiche lorraine for under EC$20. At dinner, à la carte main courses range from curried lambi or fresh catch of the day for EC$40 to lobster thermidor for EC$60. The food is quite good and the restaurant is rustic and informal. You can dine indoors or right out on the sand under thatched umbrellas. There's a barbecue with live music a few nights a week and free transportation can be arranged. It's open from 10 am to 10 pm daily.

For a splurge dinner out, the *Canboulay Restaurant* (☎ 444-4401) is a popular spot with good creative food. This hillside restau-

rant has a panoramic view clear out to St George's and features a contemporary Caribbean cuisine combining West Indian, African and European influences and using local fruits and spices. Dinners with a choice of starter, a salad or sorbet, main course, dessert and coffee cost from EC$70 to EC$90, while the à la carte menu starts at EC$30. It's open for dinner from 6.30 to 10 pm nightly except Sunday; reservations are recommended.

*La Belle Creole* (☎ 444-4316) at the Blue Horizons Cottage Hotel is a well-regarded restaurant serving a blend of Grenadian and continental food. There's a fixed-price dinner (EC$95) that changes nightly; it includes a starter, a salad or West Indian soup, a choice of three main dishes (generally chicken, red meat and seafood) accompanied by island-grown vegetables, dessert and coffee. Dinner is served from 7 to 9 pm nightly.

## MORNE ROUGE

If Grand Anse seems a bit busy, you could follow the road to its end at Morne Rouge, a lovely little U-shaped bay that's fringed by white sand and backed by green hills. Undeveloped except for one small resort, Morne Rouge Bay is but a 15-minute walk over the hill from Grand Anse. Only when the *Rhum Runner* party boat drops off passengers for an hour or so do vendors even bother coming over to this sleepy beach.

The long thin peninsula that separates Morne Rogue Bay from Grand Anse Beach was once a leper colony. For those who care to explore, a dirt road leads a few hundred metres out to the site, called Quarantine Point. While there's little to see in terms of the old colony, there's a good view of the coast in both directions. To the south you can see Point Salines, to the north as far as Molinière Point.

### Places to Stay

*Gem Holiday Beach Resort* (☎ 444-4224; fax 444-1189), PO Box 58, St George's, has an enviable beachfront location on the north side of Morne Rouge Bay. This pleasant family-run place has 17 units, all with terraces, TVs, phones and kitchenettes; the upper-storey units have high ceilings as well. The only problem is getting in, as it books up quite heavily between November and March. One-bedroom units cost from US$55 to US$80 for singles, US$65 to US$95 for doubles, depending on the view. Two-bedroom units cost US$110 for two people, US$125 for four people. Summer rates are about 15% cheaper. There's no charge for one child under 12 in the one-bedroom unit or for two children under 16 in the two-bedroom unit. It's US$15 for an extra adult.

## Places to Eat

The *Sur La Mer Restaurant* on the beach has a nice water view and moderately priced lunch and dinner offerings, with an emphasis on seafood and West Indian dishes. Adjacent is the Fantazia 2001 nightclub, which has dancing until 2 am from Wednesday to Saturday.

## POINT SALINES

The Point Salines area is dry and scrubby. Although there are a couple of remote beaches on either side of the airport runway, there's not much activity in the area. There are, however, a couple of reasonably priced places to stay on the airport road and two new beach resorts. Keep in mind you'll probably want to spend most of the day elsewhere and thus will be dependent on some sort of transportation. Passing taxis are plentiful but bus traffic becomes lighter as you get closer to the airport.

Incidentally, St George's Medical School, a private med school serving foreign students, is at the eastern tip of the airport runway. Former US president Reagan used the safety of the students at this small American-run facility as a rationale for invading Grenada following the 1983 military coup.

## Places to Stay & Eat

*No Problem Apartments* (☎ 444-4634; fax 444-2803), PO Box 280, St George's, on the main road midway between the airport and Grand Anse, compensates for its no-beach location with numerous amenities. The 20 apartments are spacious and modern, each with a kitchen, living room, separate bedroom with two twin beds, air-con, satellite TV and phone. There's a pool, a help-yourself coffee bar, free airport transport and four free shuttles a day to and from Grand Anse. The shuttle bus can also drop you in St George's a couple of times a day (take a minibus back for EC$1.50). Singles/doubles cost US$55/65 in summer, US$75/85 in winter. There's a small moderately priced restaurant serving three meals a day; dinner, which is available by reservation, costs about EC$35.

The *Fox Inn* (☎ 444-4123), PO Box 205, St George's, a mile (1.6 km) east of the terminal, is the closest place to the airport. It has 16 standard motel-style rooms for US$55/65 for singles/doubles in summer, US$60/70 in winter, and there are six air-con studios for US$80/85. Rooms have TVs and phones and there's a pool and restaurant. Despite the fact that the US Embassy is in the same area, the location is quite remote with no other facilities nearby.

New as of 1994 are the all-inclusive *La Source* (☎ 444-3777) on Pingouin Beach, which has 102 rooms priced from US$280/480 for singles/doubles, and the 212-room *Grenadian Hotel* (☎ 444-3333) on Magazin Beach, which has fan-cooled rooms from US$145, and air-con rooms from US$170.

## LANCE AUX ÉPINES

Lance aux Épines, a peninsula that forms the southernmost point on the island, is a rather affluent and quiet area with fine coastal views and some good-value places to stay, most with their own little beaches.

The west side of Lance aux Épines, where most of the activity is centred, fronts Prickly Bay, one of the island's most popular yachting anchorages. Lance aux Épines (pronounced 'lance-a-peen') is sometimes spelled L'Anse aux Épines, from the original French.

## Information

Spice Island Marine Services (☎ 444-4257;

GRENADA

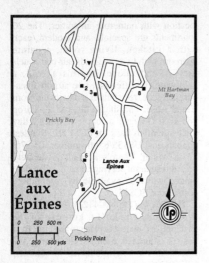

1   Red Crab
2   Calabash Hotel
3   Lance Aux Epines Cottages
4   Spice Island Marine Services & The
    Boatyard (restaurant)
5   Twelve Degrees North
6   Horse Shoe Beach Hotel
7   Coral Cove
8   Secret Harbour Hotel

VHF 16), a full-service marina on Prickly Bay, has a customs and immigration office, stern-to berths for 30 boats, a chandlery, fuel, water, electricity, showers (EC$2.50), a pay phone, taxis and a daily bus service to St George's.

### Places to Stay – bottom end
*Coral Cove* (☎ 444-4422; fax 444-4718; in the USA ☎ (800) 322-1753), PO Box 487, St George's, is a delightful little place set on a quiet knoll at the east side of Lance aux Épines. It has an expansive view across Mt Hartman Bay to a run of peninsulas and islets. There are six large apartments and five cottages, all modern with full kitchens, high ceilings, screened louvred windows, tile

floors and phones. The two-bedroom apartments (ask for the 2nd floor) have huge dining areas, balconies and two twin beds in each bedroom. This place is a bargain at US$60/90 in summer/winter for a one-bedroom cottage, US$80/110 for a two-bedroom cottage. There's a swimming pool, a tennis court and a small beach.

*Horse Shoe Beach Hotel* (☎ 444-4410; fax 444-4844), PO Box 174, St George's, is a very pleasant place whose 22 rooms are comparable to those in other hotels that charge twice the price. Most rooms are in duplex and fourplex buildings; each building has a shared kitchen. All rooms have private balconies, air-con, TVs, phones and bathtubs; some have mahogany four-poster beds. Try for room No 26 – a large 2nd-floor corner room at no extra charge. Singles/doubles cost US$70/85 in summer, US$100/110 in winter. The Mediterranean-style main building also has lovely rooms, which cost US$85/95 in summer, US$115/125 in winter. The beach isn't great here, but it's good enough for a swim. The hotel has a pool and restaurant.

*Lance Aux Épines Cottages* (☎ 444-4565; fax 444-2802), PO Box 187, St George's, is a small cottage complex on a peaceful tree-shaded cove with a nice sandy beach. There are 14 modern, large apartments, most in duplex cottages, all with full kitchens, screened windows, ceiling fans and TVs. It's a good value and quite popular with return visitors. Summer/winter rates are US$55/80 for two people in a one-bedroom apartment, US$70/100 for up to four people in a two-bedroom apartment.

### Places to Stay – top end
*Twelve Degrees North* (☎ & fax 444-4580), PO Box 241, St George's, is a small exclusive beachside resort on the west side of Lance aux Épines. There are just eight apartments, each with its own housekeeper to do the cooking and cleaning. The apartments all have ocean-view balconies and are comfortable but not luxurious. There's a pool, tennis court and small beach. One-bedroom apartments cost US$115/150 in summer/winter

for up to two people. Two-bedroom apartments cost US$185/240 for up to four people. Children under 12 are not allowed.

The *Calabash Hotel* (☎ 444-4334; fax 444-4804; in the UK ☎ (0502) 513112), PO Box 382, St George's, is a pleasant, up-market, British-managed, beachside resort. The 28 suites have ceiling fans, air-con, sitting areas and generous terraces. Tile floors, rattan furnishings and wicker decor create a refreshing West Indian touch. Eight suites have their own private pools. Singles/doubles, which include breakfast and dinner, begin at US$150/190 in summer, US$265/295 in winter.

The *Secret Harbour Hotel* (☎ 444-4448; fax 444-4819; in the USA and Canada ☎ (800) 334-2435), PO Box 11, St George's, is a Club Mariner resort owned by The Moorings yacht charter operation. Perched above Mt Hartman Bay, it has a pool, a restaurant and a swank Mediterranean ambience. There are 20 suites, all with balconies, two four-poster double beds, phones, refrigerators and air-con. Summer/winter rates are US$125/208 for one or two people. The resort is the site of a small marina that's home base for The Moorings yacht charter operation on Grenada.

### Places to Eat

*The Boatyard* at Spice Island Marine Services is open from 11.30 am to 11 pm every day but Monday. At lunch there are sandwiches for EC$12, burgers, fish & chips, curries and an EC$25 spaghetti plate. Dinner is mainly seafood priced from EC$30 to EC$40. A steel band plays on Friday from 8 pm to 4 am.

The marina mini-mart has good banana bread (EC$2.50) and is open from 9 am to 6 pm Monday to Saturday.

The *Red Crab* (☎ 444-4424), near the Calabash Hotel, has consistently good food and a following with foreign residents, many of whom come here specifically for the steaks. The most popular dish at lunch is the seafood platter at EC$24 and there are also salads, hamburgers, omelettes and seafood crêpes, all under EC$30. Dinner is à la carte, with a 'light bites' menu starting at EC$30 and other main dishes ranging from EC$40 for fish to EC$69 for lobster newburg. It's open Monday to Saturday from 11 am to 2 pm and 6 to 11 pm.

## LA SAGESSE NATURE CENTRE

La Sagesse Nature Centre fronts a deep coconut-lined bay with protected swimming and a network of hiking trails. The centre occupies the former estate of the late Lord Brownlow, a cousin of Queen Elizabeth II. His beachside estate house, built in 1968, has been turned into a small inn, while the agricultural property is now operated by the government as a banana plantation. The beach has a nice sandy bottom and waters that are calm year-round. Just outside the gate there's a water faucet where bathers can rinse off.

The centre is about a 25-minute drive from St George's on the Eastern Main Rd. The entrance is opposite an old abandoned rum distillery and sugar mill, from where it's half a mile (800 metres) through banana fields to La Sagesse Bay. St David's bound buses can drop you at the old distillery.

### La Sagesse Trails

A trail to the north-east begins opposite the water faucet, outside Brownlow's Gate (see

---

**Brownlow's Gate**

Lord Brownlow gained notoriety in the early 1970s when he built a gate at the entrance to La Sagesse, blocking public access to the area's best beach. The New Jewel Movement, the opposition party, gained momentum by targeting 'Brownlow's Gate' as a symbol of lingering colonialism and provoking islanders to tear the gate down. When the People's Revolutionary Government gained control of the island in 1979, the estate was taken over and turned into a public agricultural campus. After the military coup of 1983 the property was abandoned until 1986, when it was set aside and restored as the La Sagesse Nature Centre. ■

---

GRENADA

box), and leads 20 minutes through scrubby terrain to Marquis Point, where there are good coastal views, including that of a sea arch. Don't get too close to the edge of the point, which is eroded and crumbly.

Another trail leads west from the centre to a mangrove swamp and salt pond that's a habitat for herons, egrets and other shore-birds. It takes less than 10 minutes to reach the swamp.

### Places to Stay & Eat
*La Sagesse Nature Centre* (☎ 444-6458; fax 444-4847; in the USA ☎ (800) 322-1753), PO Box 44, St George's, has four airy rooms with private bathrooms, ceiling fans and double beds. Two of the rooms have kitchens and satellite TV and cost US$50/60 for singles/doubles in summer, US$70/80 in winter. The two smaller rooms have refrig-erators but no kitchens or TV and cost US$40/50 in summer/winter for either singles or doubles.

The beachside restaurant, open daily, has fish sandwiches and burgers for EC$15 and fresh seafood dishes for about double that. There's also a vegetarian plate of tofu, brown rice, quinoa (a grain similar to rice) and amaranth for EC$28. At breakfast, served from 8 to 10 am, there's reasonably priced Western fare. Lunch is from 11 am to 3.30 pm, dinner from 7 to 9 pm and light snacks, smoothies (fruit shakes) and bar drinks are available at other times.

### GRAND ETANG RD
The Grand Etang Rd cuts across the moun-tainous centre of the island through the Grand Etang Forest Reserve, taking in an easily accessible waterfall and a number of forest trails. To get started, you can take River Rd or Sans Souci Rd out of St George's, and when you reach the Mt Gay roundabout, take the road north. Don't expect too many directional signs en route.

While the road can be tortuously narrow and twisting (beware of deep roadside ditches), it's an otherwise delightful drive through the rainforest. There are lots of ferns, bamboo, heliconia and buttressed kapok trees and roadside plantations of nutmeg, cocoa and bananas.

### Annandale Falls
Annandale Falls is an idyllic little waterfall with a 10-metre drop, surrounded by a grotto of lush vegetation. There's a pool beneath the falls that's deep enough for a refreshing swim.

In the village of Constantine, about four miles (6.5 km) north-east of St George's, turn left on the road that leads downhill im-mediately past the yellow Methodist church. After three-quarters of a mile (1.2 km) you'll reach the Annandale Falls visitor centre, which is on the left side of the road. From the visitor centre the falls are just a two-minute walk along a begonia-lined path. At the falls, a short trail leads up the hillside to the right where a modest botanical garden is being developed.

The visitor centre is open from 8 am to 4 pm Monday to Saturday and also on Sunday when cruise ships are in port. Its little gift shop sells spices at reasonable prices; pro-ceeds benefit the park. The falls can be visited whether the centre is open or closed. There's no entrance fee.

### Grand Etang National Park
Two and a half miles (four km) north of Constantine, after winding steeply up to an elevation of 580 metres, a roadside sign welcomes visitors to Grand Etang National Park. Near the sign there's a little turn-off with a sweeping view of the west coast, clear out to Grand Anse Beach and Point Salines.

Half a mile (800 metres) after entering the park you'll reach the visitor centre, which overlooks Grand Etang Lake, a crater lake that forms the centrepiece of the park. The visitor centre, which is open from 8.30 am to 4 pm daily, has displays on flora and fauna and sells trail maps. Near the parking lot there are a couple of Mona monkeys in a cage and stalls selling soft drinks, fruit, sand-wiches and souvenirs.

Heading north from the park, the road hairpins down, offering views into valleys

Top Left: Route de la Trace, Martinique (NF)
Top Right: St Pierre, Martinique (TW)
Bottom Left: Birth place of Empress Josephine, Martinique (GB)
Bottom Right: Saint-Louis Cathedral, Fort-de-France, Martinique (NF)

Top Left: Plymouth, Montserrat (NF)
Top Right: Produce seller, public market, Plymouth, Montserrat (NF)
Bottom Left: Abandoned sugar mill at Galways Plantation, Montserrat (GB)
Bottom Right: Limin' in Plymouth, Montserrat (NF)

thickly forested with immortelle trees, which bloom bright red-orange in winter.

**Park Trails** The visitor centre is the starting point for several trails that lead into the forest. Easiest is the **Morne LaBaye Trail,** an interpretive walk that starts behind the visitor centre, takes in a few viewpoints and passes through native vegetation, including the Grand Etang fern, whose sole habitat is in this area. The walk takes about 30 minutes return.

The **Grand Etang Shoreline Trail** is a 1½-hour loop walk around the Grand Etang Lake. Whilst this is a gentle hike, the going can get muddy as much of it is at shoreline elevation and it doesn't offer the same sort of views as the higher trails. The **Mt Qua Qua Trail** is a moderately difficult three-hour (return) hike that leads to the top of a ridge offering some fine views of the interior forest.

Serious hikers could branch off shortly before Mt Qua Qua to pick up the **Concord Falls Trail** for a long trek to Concord Falls, which takes about five hours one way from the visitor centre. From Concord Falls, it's possible to walk about another 1.5 miles (2.5 km) to the village of Concord on the west coast, where you can pick up a bus back to St George's. This hike shouldn't be done alone; see the Concord Falls section for safety precautions.

A long, arduous hike leads deep into the forested interior to **Fedon's Camp,** the site where Julien Fedon, a rebel French plantation owner, hid out after a 1795 uprising in which he and his followers massacred the British governor and 47 other people.

One of the area's nicest hikes is to the **Seven Sisters Falls,** a series of seven waterfalls in the forested interior east of the Grand Etang Rd. The main hiking track is from the tin shed used by the banana association 1.25 miles (two km) north of the visitor centre, on the right side of the Grand Etang Rd. The hike from the shed takes about an hour; there's a charge of EC$10 per person. Also see Tours in the Getting Around section earlier in this chapter.

## GRENVILLE

Grenada's second-largest city, Grenville is the main port on the east coast and a regional centre for collecting cocoa, nutmeg and other crops. The town, known as La Baye by the French, was established in 1763.

The centre of town is just a couple of blocks, one of which runs along the waterfront. Within a few minutes' walk from the bus terminal there's a Barclays Bank, police station, post office, supermarket and public market. Near the public market is a nutmeg processing station, said to be the island's largest.

While the town doesn't have a lot of interest for most visitors, there are a few older buildings of some note, including the Grenville Court House (circa 1886) near the market, the old police station and a couple of churches.

Grenville is fairly easy to get to by bus and the ride (EC$5) from St George's is the island's most scenic.

### Pearls Airport

Perhaps Grenville area's best known site is Pearls Airport, two miles (3.2 km) north of town, which was the island's airfield until the Cubans built the Point Salines Airport in 1983. The runway at Pearls still has an abandoned Russian biplane and a Cubana aircraft, hastily left here after the US invasion in October 1983. The Grenada Defense Force has a barracks at the airstrip, but it's no problem driving into the site.

Because of Grenada's proximity to South America, it was one of the first islands to be settled by migrating Amerindians, and the airport area was a major settlement and burial ground. Thousands of pottery shards, adornos and grinding stones have been collected over the years, both by archaeologists and souvenir hunters. The construction of the airport in the 1940s damaged much of the site, although the area north of the runway still has significant Amerindian remains. Recent government regulations have made it illegal to remove artefacts.

To get to the airport, head north out of Grenville and follow the signs to Seamoon

Industrial Park. On the way you'll also pass a former horse race track, a river used to wash laundry and the ruins of an old sugar mill.

### Places to Stay & Eat

*Sam's Inn* (☎ 442-7853), Dunfermline, St Andrew, is north of Grenville, just west of the old Pearls Airport. This two-storey, motel-like place has 16 rather simple rooms with portable fans, private baths, balconies and either two twin beds or a twin and a double. Singles/doubles cost US$23/29. Meals can be arranged.

*Rainbow Inn* (☎ 442-7714), PO Box 923, Grenville, is a 15-room local hotel on the east side of town, about a 10-minute walk from the centre. Rooms are basic and straight-forward, with double beds and private bathrooms. Singles/doubles cost US$30/45. You can also get meals, snacks and fresh juices here.

In town, you can get reasonably priced rotis and seafood dishes at the *Waterfront Restaurant*, just south of the bus terminal. It's open from 8 am to 6 pm Monday to Saturday, from 10 am to 5 pm on Sunday. There are also a number of little restaurants around the centre where you can get a quick snack, or you could pick up fruit at the public market.

### NORTH OF GRENVILLE

As the road continues north from Grenville, it passes through a run of small towns with the occasional stone church and abandoned mill and lots of old wooden homes, some on stilts. Shortly after passing the large church in the village of Tivoli, turn right to continue north to Mt Rose. When you reach the post office at the north end of Mt Rose, bear left to continue to Sauteurs or take the sharp right to get to River Sallee and Bathways Beach.

**Lake Antoine**, a crater lake in an extinct volcano, is along a rough dirt road a mile (1.6 km) south of River Sallee. The **River Antoine Rum Distillery**, which has been producing rum since the 18th century and claims to have the oldest working water mill in the Caribbean, is south of the lake and

most easily accessed from the Tivoli direction. Call ☎ 442-7109 for details on touring the distillery.

### BATHWAYS BEACH

From River Sallee, a good road leads to undeveloped Bathways Beach, where there's a beach of speckled white coral sands. At the north side of the beach a rock shelf parallels the shoreline, creating a very long, 10-metre wide 'pool' that's deep enough for swimming. The pool is protected, with a gentle current, while outside the shelf there are strong currents and rough Atlantic seas. The government is constructing a visitor facility opposite the beach which will have changing rooms and a snack bar.

There are three islands off Bathways Beach. From west to east they are Sugar Loaf, a privately owned island with a cottage on its south shore; Green Island, which has a few abandoned buildings but no beach; and Sandy Island, an uninhabited island with a freshwater cistern. Sandy Island also has an abandoned hotel, crystal clear waters and a beautiful beach on its leeward side with fine swimming and snorkelling. It's possible to arrange for a boat in Sauteurs to take you to Sandy Island; make enquiries with the fishers on Sauteurs Beach – expect to pay about EC$150 per boat for the return trip.

### LEVERA BEACH

Levera Beach is a wild beautiful sweep of sand backed by eroded sea cliffs. Just offshore is the high, pointed Sugar Loaf (also called Levera Island), while the Grenadine Islands dot the horizon to the north. The beach, the mangrove swamp and the nearby pond have been incorporated into Grenada's national park system and are an important waterfowl habitat and sea turtle nesting site. The road north from Bathways Beach to Levera Beach is rough and usually passable only in a 4WD vehicle, so most visitors end up hiking in. The walk from Bathways Beach takes about 25 minutes; stick to the road, as sea cliffs and rough surf make it impossible to walk along the coast between the two beaches.

## SAUTEURS

Sauteurs, the largest town on the north side of Grenada, takes its name from the French word for 'jump' and its place in history as the site where, in 1651, Carib families jumped to their deaths upon their final retreat from approaching French soldiers. Today the town's main tourist sight is Caribs' Leap, the name given to these 40-metre-high coastal cliffs.

The cliffs are on the north side of the cemetery next to St Patrick's Roman Catholic church. You may well be approached by someone wanting to be your guide, but this is an unnecessary service. Simply walk through the cemetery to get to the ledge, a couple of minutes away.

From the ledge you can look down on the fishing boats along the village beach and get a view of the offshore islands. The largest is Isle de Ronde, home to a few fisher families. The small islets to the left are called The Sisters; to the right, and closer to shore, is London Bridge, an arch-shaped rock.

### Places to Stay & Eat

*Mrs Brown's Roti Shop*, in the town centre below the Catholic church, makes Sauteurs' best rotis.

The *Morne Fendue Plantation House* (☎ 442-9330), 1.5 miles (2.4 km) south of Sauteurs, is a popular lunch spot for people touring the island. Octogenarian Betty Mascoll, whose father built this plantation house in 1908 with river stones and a mortar of lime and molasses, serves a West Indian buffet on the verandah. Dishes include pepperpot, chicken fricassee, sweet potato casserole, pigeon peas and rice, christophene and plantain. Lunch, available from 12.30 to 3 pm Monday to Saturday, costs EC$40. Reservations are advised.

The three guest rooms upstairs have creaky floors and are in a bit of disrepair, but are loaded with character. The large front room has a mountain view, a brass double bed, a twin bed and a private bathroom and costs US$75 a double. Another has two twin beds, a wash basin and ageing furnishings

and costs US$60 a double, while a smaller third room costs US$30 for a single; these last two rooms share a bathroom. Rates include breakfast and dinner.

The house, marked by a small sign, is in the village of Morne Fendue at the end of a drive lined with palm trees and taro.

## VICTORIA

The west-coast road can be a bit rough in places, as sections of it are along eroded cliffs that occasionally release a few falling rocks. One of the larger of the fishing villages that dot the west coast is Victoria, which has churches, schools, a post office, market, police station and health clinic. Grass Roots, at the Victoria Bridge at the south end of town, sells quality crafts.

While Victoria certainly isn't a tourist destination, it does have a nice place to stay if you want to be merged in village life and totally away from the tourist scene. Buses to St George's cost EC$3.50 and take about 40 minutes.

### Places to Stay & Eat

*Victoria Inn* (☎ 444-9367), Queen St, Victoria, is a new and quite pleasant 10-room hotel on the beach in the centre of the village. The rooms, which are above a restaurant and bar, are tastefully decorated and have high ceilings, fans, satellite TV and either a double or two single beds. Rooms are good value at US$30/40 for singles/doubles. At lunch, available from 11.30 am to 2.30 pm, there are fish, chicken and mutton dishes with rice and vegetables for EC$15 to EC$20; breakfast, from 7.30 to 10 am, costs half that. Dinner, from 7.30 to 9 pm, generally includes pasta, fish and meat dishes for EC$20 to EC$40.

There's a grocery store in Fletcher's Shopping Complex opposite the inn and a few other places in town where you could grab a bite.

## GOUYAVE

Gouyave is the main town in the parish of St John. Many of the people here make a living from fishing and you can see their boats pulled up along the beach at the north end of town, which is called The Lance. The main sight in town is the nutmeg processing station. There's a market, a bank and a couple of snack shops on the main road.

Just south of the bridge on the south side of Gouyave, a dirt road leads inland half a mile (800 metres) along the river to the **Dougaldston Estate**, where cocoa and spices are processed. Though it's not particularly set up for visitors, if you're curious you could drive up and look around.

### Nutmeg Station

On the north side of Gouyave, there's a large roadside nutmeg processing station. One of the workers is usually available to take visitors on a tour and explain the process. It can be quite interesting with its fragrant vats of curing nuts and various sorting operations. Tickets are sold at the office for US$1 and a tip to the guide of about the same amount is the norm. The station is open from 8 am to 4 pm weekdays, to noon on Saturdays.

### CONCORD FALLS

There are a couple of scenic waterfalls along the Concord River. The lowest falls, a picturesque cascade of about 30 metres, can be viewed by driving to the end of Concord Mountain Rd, a side road leading 1.5 miles (2.4 km) inland from the village of Concord. The trail to the upper falls begins at the end of the road and takes about 30 minutes each way. The falls are on private property and the owner usually charges visitors US$1 to visit them. However, unless you're with a group, it's recommended that you only go as far as the lower waterfall as there have been muggings and at least one rape at the falls in recent times.

Back on the main road, just south of the turn-off to Concord Mountain Rd, there's a small roadside monument dedicated to nine people killed when a dislodged boulder crushed the minibus they were travelling in.

There's a lovely view of Halifax Bay as the road continues south to St George's.

# Carriacou

Carriacou, 27 km north-east of Grenada, is a rural island with small villages, good beaches and a delightfully slow pace. It's a hilly island, about 12 km long and a third as wide. The landscape is dry and scrubby and dotted with cactus and acacia, although dryland flowering plants such as bougainvillea add a splash of colour. Carriacou has 6000 people and about as many goats and sheep.

While the island's low-key character and natural harbour have long attracted yachters, few other Caribbean visitors have Carriacou on their itinerary. Consequently the beaches are uncrowded, finding a room is seldom a problem and islanders are quite friendly to visitors.

Carriacou has fantastic views of the neighbouring Grenadines and of its own nearshore islets, a few of which can readily be visited for picnicking, snorkelling and diving.

The island has a unique folk troupe that performs the African-influenced Big Drum Dance, which centres around the playing of drums made of small rum kegs covered with goatskin.

### HILLSBOROUGH

Hillsborough, the administrative and commercial centre of Carriacou, is an unspoiled and unhurried place – a mix of colourful wooden shops, cement buildings, and ramshackle tin structures. Main St, which parallels the beach, has a few interesting 19th-century buildings with ground floors of stone and upper floors of wood that once served as seaside warehouses; three of them can be found near Barclays Bank.

Much of the town's activity is centred around the pier where the ferries dock. The customs and immigration offices, public market, tourist office, post office, museum and bakery are all within a two-minute walk of the pier.

For a nice view of Hillsborough Bay and

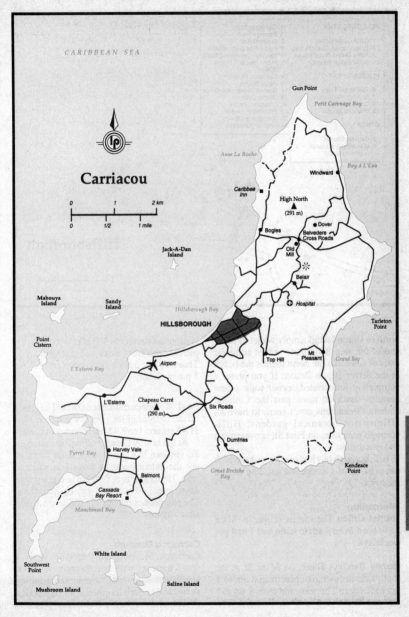

CARIBBEAN SEA

**Carriacou**

0        1        2 km

0    1/2      1 mile

Gun Point

Petit Carenage Bay

Anse La Roche

Bay á L'Eau

Windward

Caribbee
Inn

High North
(291 m)

Bogles

Dover

Belvedere
Cross Roads

Old
Mill

Jack-A-Dan
Island

Belair

Mabouya
Island

Sandy
Island

Hospital

Hillsborough Bay

**HILLSBOROUGH**

Tarleton
Point

Point
Cistern

L'Esterre Bay

Airport

Top Hill

Mt
Pleasant

Grand Bay

L'Esterre

Chapeau Carré
(290 m)

Six Roads

Dumfries

Tyrrel Bay

Harvey Vale

Belmont

Great Bretche
Bay

Kendeace
Point

Cassada
Bay Resort

Manchineel Bay

White Island

Southwest
Point

Mushroom Island

Saline Island

**GRENADA**

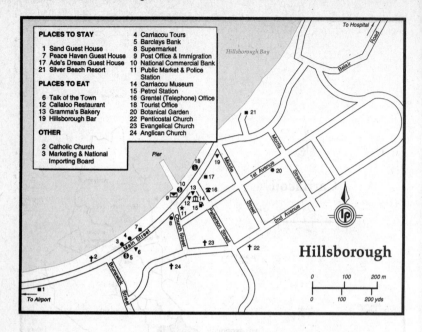

PLACES TO STAY

1 Sand Guest House
7 Peace Haven Guest House
17 Ade's Dream Guest House
21 Silver Beach Resort

PLACES TO EAT

6 Talk of the Town
12 Callaloo Restaurant
13 Gramma's Bakery
19 Hillsborough Bar

OTHER

2 Catholic Church
3 Marketing & National
  Importing Board

4 Carriacou Tours
5 Barclays Bank
8 Supermarket
9 Post Office & Immigration
10 National Commercial Bank
11 Public Market & Police
   Station
14 Carriacou Museum
15 Petrol Station
16 Grentel (Telephone) Office
18 Tourist Office
20 Botanical Garden
22 Penticostal Church
23 Evangelical Church
24 Anglican Church

Hillsborough

north to Union Island simply walk out to the end of the pier. Swimming is best at the far ends of town. To the north there's the beach at the Silver Beach Resort; if you prefer a completely untouristed scene, walk a few minutes south of town past the Catholic church. Grenadians don't seem to have an affinity for botanical gardens; Hillsborough's version, on First St, is overgrown and gated shut.

Hillsborough has lots of stray dogs, which can put a bit of a damper on strolling around the town.

## Information

**Tourist Office** The tourist office, on Main St, is open from 8 am to noon and 1 to 4 pm weekdays.

**Money** Barclays Bank, on Main St at the south side of town, is open from 8 am to 1 pm Monday to Thursday and from 8 am to 1 pm and 2.30 to 5 pm on Fridays. The National Commercial Bank, opposite the pier, is open from 8 am to 2 pm Monday to Thursday and from 8 am to noon and 1.30 to 5 pm on Fridays.

**Post & Telecommunications** The post office, in front of the pier, is open from 8 to 11.45 am and 1 to 3.45 pm Monday to Friday.

At the nearby Grentel office, on Patterson St, you can buy phonecards, send faxes or use the indoor booth to make international calls. Hours are from 7.30 am to 6 pm weekdays, from 7.30 am to 1 pm on Saturdays. The pay phones outside the office are accessible any time.

## Carriacou Museum

Carriacou Museum, on Patterson St, is a small museum with a collection of island artefacts that includes Amerindian grinding stones and pottery fragments, a hodgepodge of colonial-era items from clay pipes to

China dishes and a few works of local artists, including Canute Caliste.

It's open from 9.30 am to 3.45 pm weekdays. Admission is EC$5 for adults, EC$2.50 for children, and your support will help keep this community-run museum in operation.

### Activities

Diving can be arranged through Silver Beach Diving (☎ 443-7882), a German-run dive shop at the Silver Beach Resort. The shop also rents windsurfing gear for US$15 an hour.

### Places to Stay

*Ade's Dream Guest House* (☎ 443-7733; fax 443-7317), Main St, in the centre of Hillsborough, has 16 good-value rooms in a new three-storey building and seven rooms in an older wing. The older rooms, which cost US$19 for singles or doubles, are small and simple with shared bathrooms but they have fans, are clean and there's a large group kitchen. The new rooms, which have kitchenettes, private baths, small balconies and fans, cost US$24 on the 2nd floor, US$26 on the 3rd floor. There's a grocery store on the ground floor of the hotel and the family operating the guesthouse plans to open a restaurant on the ocean side of the road.

*Peace Haven Guest House* (☎ 443-7475), Main St, is a recommendable family-operated guesthouse with six units, all fan-cooled and spotlessly clean. Rates range from US$23 for a straightforward room with private bath to US$55 for a new flat with full kitchen, two double beds and a balcony perched over the beach. The flats are very comfortable, if not the nicest on the island. Ask for flats No 1 or 2, which have ocean-fronting balconies and lovely views of Sandy Island. Rates include tax.

*Sand Guest House* (☎ 443-7100) is in a quiet area opposite the beach, a 10-minute walk west of Hillsborough centre. This small two-storey guesthouse has six simple rooms with shared baths and kitchen, costing US$25 for singles or doubles.

*Silver Beach Resort* (☎ 443-7337; fax 443-7165), on a nice grey-sand beach at the north side of town, has 18 units. The 'oceanfront' cottages – which face the main building, not the ocean – are ageing and neglected, with shower drains that block up and louvred windows with missing slats. Some of the rooms in the main building have balconies with pleasant ocean views but are otherwise ordinary. Rates for either begin at US$70/85 for singles/doubles in summer, US$80/95 in winter.

### Places to Eat

*Gramma's Bakery*, in the town centre, is a large modern bakery with good bran muffins and mouth-watering loaves of raisin sweet bread (EC$2) that come warm from the oven in the late morning. You can also get microwaved cheese sandwiches (EC$1.75), chicken rotis (EC$5.75) and drinks throughout the day. There are a few café-style streetfront tables. Gramma's is open Monday to Saturday from 6 am to 7 pm.

*Callaloo Restaurant* (☎ 443-8004) is a pleasant little 2nd-floor restaurant with lunch sandwiches for under EC$10 and fish or chicken & chips for a few dollars more. At dinner, chicken or nicely grilled fresh fish costs EC$20, garlic shrimp is EC$35. Meals are accompanied with fried plantains, rice and peas. For another EC$10 you can add soup or salad, dessert and coffee to the meal. It's open Monday to Saturday from 10 am to 2 pm and 6 to 10 pm.

*Silver Beach Resort* has an ocean-fronting al fresco restaurant serving three meals a day. At lunch, rotis, burgers and sandwiches are priced from EC$8 to EC$13. Dinner main courses include curried lambi or fresh fish for around EC$30 and sirloin steak for EC$55. The restaurant occasionally has a Big Drum performance or steel band at dinner.

*Talk of the Town* on Main St has rotis and other inexpensive local food. The *Hillsborough Bar*, at the opposite end of Main St, also has food and drinks.

You can find island fruits and vegetables at the small public market and get spices at

GRENADA

the Marketing & National Importing Board, both on Main St.

## NORTH OF HILLSBOROUGH
The northern section of Carriacou offers some of the island's finest scenery, a couple of secluded beaches and a glimpse of rural areas that were formerly planted in sugar cane.

From the hilltop hospital, there's a splendid view of Hillsborough Bay and the offshore islands. Take Belair Rd, which begins about a third of a mile (500 metres) north of Silver Beach Resort, follow it uphill for half a mile (800 metres) and then bear right on the side road leading into the hospital. In addition to the view you'll find a couple of cannons on the hospital grounds, vestiges from the colonial era when a British fort occupied the site.

If you continue north after leaving the hospital, the road follows the crest of Belvedere Hill, providing some fine views of the east coast and the islands of Petit St Vincent and Petit Martinique. You'll then pass the remains of an old stone **sugar mill** just before reaching the Belvedere Cross Roads. From there, the route going north-east (called the High Rd) leads down to **Windward**, a small windy village backed by gentle hills that's home to the Scottish descendants of shipwrights brought to Carriacou to build inter-island boats for the planters.

From Windward it's possible to continue another mile (1.6 km) to **Petit Carenage Bay** at the north-eastern tip of the island, where there's a good beach and views of the northern Grenadines.

If instead you were to go west from the Belvedere Cross Roads you'd soon come to the village of **Bogles**. There's a lovely secluded beach north of the village, at **Anse La Roche Bay**. Buses can drop you at Bogles, from where it's about half an hour's walk to the beach.

### Places to Stay & Eat
The *Caribbee Inn* (☎ 443-7380; fax 443-8142), Prospect, between Bogles and Anse La Roche Beach, is a relaxed place to stay if you're looking for rural seclusion. Owned and operated by British couple Wendy and Robert Cooper, this pleasantly informal inn has eight bedrooms furnished with four-poster beds, ceiling fans, mosquito nets and private baths. Large louvred windows open to the tradewinds and views. There's a small cove good for swimming and snorkelling below the inn. Winter room rates are US$100 a single or double, with a two-day minimum stay. There's also a detached villa with a kitchen and two bedrooms that rents by the week for US$1000 for up to four people. Summer rates are 20% less. Breakfast and a home-cooked dinner can be included for an extra US$30 per person. Non-guests interested in coming up for dinner (US$24) should call ahead to enquire about the day's set meal and to make reservations.

There are no guesthouses or restaurants in Windward or Bogles but there are shops where you can buy cold drinks and snacks.

## L'ESTERRE
L'Esterre is a small village south-west of the airport that retains a bit of French influence,

---

### Boat Building
Carriacou islanders have long made their living from the sea, as fishers, mariners and boat builders. Until recent times, it was possible to see wooden schooners being built along the beach in Windward, with boat builders using the same handcrafting techniques that the early Scottish settlers brought with them in colonial times. However, a penchant for steel hulls has undermined traditional boat building and, save for the occasional small fishing boat, little boat construction is done on Carriacou these days. The situation is similar on the more northerly Grenadine island of Bequia, which also has a sizeable settlement of Scottish descendants. ∎

most noticeably in the French patois that many of the older villagers still speak.

The village's main sight is the home of Carriacou artist Canute Caliste, who paints uncomplicated visions of mermaids and sailing vessels. After many decades, his folk art is now gaining a bit of an international following and is the subject of a recent book *The Mermaid Wakes: Paintings of a Caribbean Isle*. To get to his shop, follow the road west at the main village T-junction rather than turning south towards Tyrrel Bay.

### Places to Stay & Eat

*Hope Inn* (☎ 443-7457) is a fairly new guesthouse on a pleasant sandy beach midway between the airport and L'Esterre village. There are six clean, straightforward rooms with fans and shared baths. Guests have use of two shared kitchens and a little sitting area. Singles/doubles cost US$25/28. You can pick up groceries at Alexis Mart, a 10-minute walk south of the guesthouse.

### TYRREL BAY

Tyrrel Bay is a deep protected bay with a sandy beach and the small low-key village of Harvey Vale. This is a popular anchorage for visiting yachters, the nearest thing Carriacou has to a beach hang out. The deep, narrow lagoon at the north end of the bay is known by yachters as Hurricane Bay, because it's a safe harbour during severe storms, and to local fishers as Oyster Bed, because of the oysters that grow on the roots of the lagoon's mangrove trees.

Opposite the beach are a couple of places to stay and eat, including a popular restaurant run by a young French couple. A relatively frequent bus route operates from Hillsborough to Belmont via Tyrrel Bay.

### Places to Stay

*Constant Spring* (☎ 443-7396), a small guesthouse at the south side of Tyrrel Bay, has three simple rooms with shared baths and a shared kitchen. Singles/doubles cost US$17/30.

*Scraper's Cottages* (☎ 443-7403), adjacent to the restaurant of the same name,

consists of four apartments in two simple duplex cottages. Each has a refrigerator, stove, bedroom with a double bed and private bathroom. Singles/doubles cost US$22/33; rates are negotiable for longer stays.

*Alexis Apartment Hotel* (☎ 443-7179) is a new place with a dozen rooms with private baths, opposite the beach at the centre of Tyrrel Bay. Singles/doubles cost US$65/85 for rooms with kitchenettes, US$45/55 for those without.

The British-run *Cassada Bay Resort* (☎ 443-7494; fax 443-7672; VHF 68), between Tyrrel Bay and Belmont, about a 20-minute walk from either, has 14 hillside rooms and a splendid view. The weathered wooden duplex cottages have quite a bit of character, and were once part of a marine biology school, 'Camp Carriacou', which catered to wealthy North American. The roomy cottages are pleasantly simple with wooden floor boards, ocean-view decks, screened louvred windows, a table, couch and two single beds. There's a pier and guests are shuttled over to the beach at White Island across the bay free of charge. Singles/doubles cost US$75/90 in winter, US$10 less in summer.

### Places to Eat

*Poivre et Sel* (☎ 443-8207, VHF 16), an open-air restaurant above Alexis Supermarket, is an energetic place serving good French food. Starters range from pumpkin soup (EC$8) to lobster crêpes (EC$25); main courses include fresh fish (EC$25) and steak (EC$40). It's open from 8 am to 2 pm and from 5.30 pm to around midnight, with drinks available all day. Occasionally there's live entertainment.

*Scraper's Restaurant* has a varied menu that includes fish sandwiches or hamburgers for EC$7 and main dishes ranging from spaghetti for EC$16 to lobster for EC$45. They also do a good barbecued chicken. It's open Monday to Saturday from 9 am to 11 pm and on Sunday from 11 am to 11 pm.

*Turtle Dove* (☎ 443-7194, VHF 16), at the south side of Tyrrel Bay, has good fresh island fish, lambi and lobster at moderate prices. You can also get inexpensive meals at a couple of local eateries and bars opposite the beach, including *Al's*.

For groceries and liquor there's Alexis Supermarket near the centre of the beach and Barba's Supermarket closer to the dockyard.

*Cassada Bay Resort* has an open-air verandah restaurant and bar with a fine view and good food. At lunch either a burger or chicken with fries costs EC$20. At dinner, chicken or the catch of the day is EC$35, sirloin steak is EC$75.

## NEARSHORE ISLANDS

The little islet, **Sandy Island**, off the west side of Hillsborough Bay, is a favourite daytime destination of snorkellers and yachters. It's the epitome of the reef island cliche, nothing but glistening sands dotted with a few coconut palms and surrounded by turquoise waters. Snorkellers take to the shallow waters fronting Sandy Island, while the deeper waters at the far side are a popular dive site. Unfortunately, the island's easy accessibility has resulted in it being 'loved to death', with the surrounding coral gardens heavily damaged by dropped and dragging anchors.

A speedboat for up to two people costs EC$70 (EC$10 more for additional passengers) through the tourist office or you can make arrangements directly with one of the boaters at the jetty. Be clear as to when you want to be picked up – as the island takes only a couple of minutes to walk around, a whole afternoon here could tick by very slowly.

Although it's often overlooked by travellers, **White Island** makes for a nice little outing. It has a good sandy beach for bathing and a pristine reef for snorkelling. This small hat-shaped island, 1.5 km off the southern tip of Carriacou, is also easy to get to.

Cassada Bay Resort will shuttle day trippers over to White Island, just a five-minute ride from the resort's pier, for EC$30. You can also make boat arrangements through Scraper's or Turtle Dove in Tyrrel Bay.

## GETTING THERE & AWAY

Carriacou's airport, 1.2 miles (two km) west of Hillsborough, is such a modest facility that the island's main road cuts clear across the centre of the runway, with traffic yielding to planes!

The terminal has a tiny souvenir shop, a bar, pay phones and a single check-in counter for LIAT, Air Carriacou and Helenair. For details on flights, see the Getting Around section at the beginning of this chapter.

## GETTING AROUND
### Bus & Taxi

Buses, which are privately owned minivans, charge EC$2 to go anywhere on the island. The two main routes run from Hillsborough, one south to Tyrrel Bay, the other north to Windward. Minibuses start around 7 am and stop around 4.30 pm – they're easiest to catch in the early morning when people are going to school and work and are less frequent during the late morning and early afternoon.

You can get a cheap island tour by hopping on a minibus departing Hillsborough and either breaking en route or staying on for the return ride. The Windward-bound buses usually take the High Rd one way and the Low Rd the other, making for a good loop tour.

Some minibuses double as taxis and usually a couple of them will swing by the airport when a flight comes in. Taxis from the airport charge EC$20 to Tyrrel Bay or Cassada Bay, EC$10 to Hillsborough.

### Car

There are a few car rentals available on Carriacou, with rates typically around US$50 a day. Barba Gabriel (☎ 443-7454) at Barba's Supermarket in Tyrrel Bay rents cars and 4WD Suzukis. Martin Bullen (☎ 443-7204) and Silver Beach Resort (☎ 443-7337) can also arrange car rentals.

### Tours

Carriacou Tours (☎ 443-7134), on Main St in Hillsborough, arranges land tours of Carriacou for US$45 per taxi, although you can sometimes join a scheduled tour for around US$10 per person. A boat to either White Island or Sandy Island for up to six passengers costs US$30 and a catamaran tour to the Tobago Cays costs US$60 per person. Day tours of Grenada from Carriacou, or day tours of Carriacou from Grenada, can be arranged for US$140, airfare included.

# Petit Martinique

Petit Martinique, five km north-east of Carriacou, is a near-circular island, about 1.5 km in width, with a volcanic cone rising 227 metres.

Most of Petit Martinique's 600 inhabitants make a living from the sea – largely from fishing, although a fair number of men work as mariners on regional ships. The islanders have a reputation for their independent character as well as a bit of notoriety for smuggling. The island has no police, customs or bank. There is a school, a church and a grocer that doubles as the local bar and snack shop. The island has footpaths instead of roads, homes are tidy and residents of Petit Martinique enjoy one of the region's highest per capita incomes.

Although most visitors are yachters, it's possible to get over without your own boat. The easiest way is to arrange through the tourist office for a speedboat to zip you over from Windward; it'll cost about EC$100 for the boat. Alternatively you could go down to the dock at Windward and try to arrange a boat directly with one of the villagers. Or for just EC$2 you could catch the local cargo boat *(Adelaide B)* that goes from Hillsborough to Petit Martinique on Wednesday and Saturday afternoons and returns on Thursday and Monday mornings.

## Places to Stay
At *Sea Side View Holiday Cottages* (☎ 443-9210; evenings ☎ 443-9113), Mrs Emma Logan rents out a couple of one and two-bedroom cottages, about 50 metres from the beach, for EC$55/75/95 for singles/doubles/triples.

# Guadeloupe

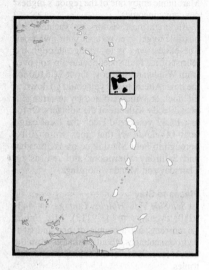

Guadeloupe, the centre of the Caribbean's Creole culture, boasts a spirited blend of French and African influences. The island archipelago is largely provincial in nature and remains as well known for its sugar and rum as for its beaches and resorts.

Guadeloupe's shape inevitably invites comparison to a butterfly, as it has two abutting wing-shaped islands. While the outline of the two islands is somewhat symmetrical, the topography is anything but. Grande-Terre, the eastern wing, has a terrain of gently rolling hills and level plains, much of which is cultivated in sugar cane.

Basse-Terre, the western wing, is dominated by rugged hills and mountains which are wrapped in a dense rainforest of tall trees and lush ferns. The interior of Basse-Terre has been set aside as a huge (17,300-hectare) national park, which includes trails through the rainforest, the Eastern Caribbean's highest waterfalls and the island's highest peak, La Soufrière, a smouldering volcano.

The centre of the island and its principal city is the bustling Pointe-à-Pitre, while the sleepy capital of Basse-Terre is on the remote south-western side. Virtually all of the resort hotels, as well as the larger marinas, are along the southern shore of Grande-Terre.

Guadeloupe's surrounding offshore islands make interesting side excursions. The most visited, Terre-de-Haut, is a delightful place with a quaint central village and harbour, good beaches and restaurants and some reasonably priced places to stay. The other populated islands – Terre-de-Bas, Marie-Galante and La Désirade – have very little tourism development and offer visitors a glimpse of a rural French West Indies that has changed little in recent times.

## ORIENTATION

The airport is at the north side of Pointe-à-Pitre, a five-minute drive from the city centre and 15 minutes from Gosier, the largest tourist area. Roads are good and the island can readily be explored in a series of day trips, with a day given to circling Grande-Terre, another day to northern Basse-Terre and the Route de la Traversée and a third day to southern Basse-Terre.

Ferries link Guadeloupe to the islands of

---

**Big Land, Flat Land**
At first glance, the names given to the twin islands that make up Guadeloupe proper are perplexing. The eastern island, which is smaller and flatter, is named Grande-Terre, which means 'big land', while the larger, more mountainous western side is named Basse-Terre, meaning 'flat land'.

The names were not meant to describe the terrain, however, but the winds that blow over them. The tradewinds, which come from the north-east, blow *grande* over the flat plains of Grande-Terre but are stopped by the mountains to the west, ending up flat *(basse)* on Basse-Terre. ∎

GUADELOUPE

228

Terre-de-Haut, Marie-Galante and La Désirade, with schedules that allow you to get over to any of these islands in the morning and return to Guadeloupe in the late afternoon.

# Facts about the Islands

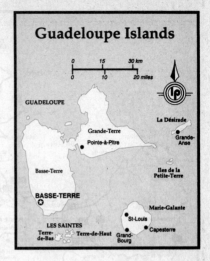

## Guadeloupe Islands

### HISTORY

When sighted by Columbus on 14 November 1493, Guadeloupe was inhabited by Carib Indians, who called it Karukera, 'Island of Beautiful Waters'. The Spanish made two attempts to settle Guadeloupe in the early 1500s but were repelled both times by fierce Carib resistance and finally in 1604 abandoned their claim to the island.

Three decades later, French colonists sponsored by the Compagnie des Iles d'Amérique, an association of French entrepreneurs, set sail to establish the first European settlement on Guadeloupe. On 28 June 1635 the party, led by Charles Liénard de l'Olive and Jean Duplessis d'Ossonville, landed on the south-eastern shore of Basse-Terre and claimed Guadeloupe for France. The French drove the Caribs off the island, planted crops and within a decade had built the first sugar mill. By the time France officially annexed the island in 1674, a slavery-based plantation system was well established.

The English invaded Guadeloupe several times and occupied it from 1759 to 1763. During this time they developed Pointe-à-Pitre into a major harbour, opened profitable English and North American markets to Guadeloupean sugar and allowed the planters to import cheap North American lumber and food. Many French colonists actually grew wealthier under the British occupation and the economy expanded rapidly. In 1763 British occupation ended with the signing of the Treaty of Paris, provisions of which relinquished French claims in Canada in exchange for the return of Guadeloupe.

Amidst the chaos of the French Revolution, the British invaded Guadeloupe again in 1794. In response to that invasion, the French sent a contingent of soldiers lead by Victor Hugues, a Black nationalist. Hugues freed and armed Guadeloupean slaves. On the day the British withdrew from Guadeloupe, Hugues went on a rampage and killed 300 Royalists, many of them plantation owners. In all Hugues was responsible for the deaths of over 1000 colonists and as a consequence of his attacks on US ships, the USA declared war on France.

In 1802 Napoleon Bonaparte, anxious to get the situation under control, sent General Antoine Richepance to Guadeloupe. Richepance put down the uprising, restored the pre-revolutionary government and reinstituted slavery.

Guadeloupe was the most prosperous island in the French West Indies and the British continued to covet it, invading and occupying the island for most of the period between 1810 and 1816. The Treaty of Vienna restored the island to France, which has maintained sovereignty over it continuously since 1816.

Slavery was abolished in 1848, following a campaign led by French politician Victor Schoelcher. (His contribution to the aboli-

GUADELOUPE

Guadeloupe

tion movement is commemorated on Schoelcher Day, a public holiday in July.) In the years that followed, planters brought labourers from Pondicherry, a French colony in India, to work in the sugar cane fields. Since 1871, Guadeloupe has had representation in the French parliament and since 1946 has been an overseas department of France.

## GEOGRAPHY

Guadeloupe proper is comprised of twin islands divided by a narrow mangrove channel called the Rivière Salée. The islands are volcanic in origin with a total land area of 1434 sq km. Grande-Terre, the eastern island, has a limestone cover, the result of having been submerged during earlier geologic periods. Basse-Terre, the larger western island, is rugged and mountainous. Guadeloupe's highest point is La Soufrière, a 1467-metre active volcano.

Of the nearby offshore islands, Les Saintes (14 sq km) are high and rugged, Marie-Galante (158 sq km) is relatively flat and La Désirade (22 sq km) has an intermediate topography with hills that rise 273 metres.

## CLIMATE

Pointe-à-Pitre's average daily high temperature in January is 28°C (83°F) while the low averages 19°C (67°F). In July the average daily high is 31°C (88*\F) while the low averages 23°C (74°F).

The annual rainfall in Pointe-à-Pitre is 1814 mm (71 inches). February to April are the driest months, when measurable rain falls an average of seven days a month and the average humidity is around 77%. The wettest months are July to November, when rain falls about 14 days a month and the average humidity reaches 85%.

Because of its height, the Basse-Terre side is both cooler and rainier than Grande-Terre. Its highest point, the Soufrière volcano, averages 9900 mm (390 inches) of rain a year.

The tradewinds, called *alizés*, often temper the climate.

## FLORA & FAUNA

Guadeloupe's diverse vegetation ranges from mangrove swamps to mountainous rainforest. Basse-Terre has an abundance of tropical hardwood trees, including lofty *gommiers* and large buttressed *chataigniers*, and thick fern forests punctuated with flowering *heliconia* and ginger plants.

Birds found on Guadeloupe include various members of the heron family, pelicans, hummingbirds and the endangered Guadeloupe wren.

The raccoon, whose main habitat is in the forests of Basse-Terre, is the official symbol of the Parc National de la Guadeloupe. You can expect to see drawings of raccoons on park brochures and in Guadelopean advertising as a means of projecting a 'natural' image.

Guadeloupe has mongooses aplenty, which were introduced long ago in a futile attempt to control rats in the sugar cane fields. Agoutis, a short-haired rabbit-like rodent with short ears that looks a bit like a guinea pig, is found on La Désirade. There are iguanas on Les Saintes and La Désirade.

## GOVERNMENT

Guadeloupe is an overseas department of France and has a status on par with the 96 *départements* on the French mainland. The department of Guadeloupe, which also encompasses St Barts and St Martin, is represented in the French parliament by four elected deputies and two senators.

A prefect, who is appointed by the French Minister of the Interior and assisted by two general secretaries and two *sous-préfets* (sub-prefects), represents the central government and oversees island authorities. There are two locally elected legislative bodies, the Conseil Général and the Conseil Régional, each with about 40 members. Guadeloupe is further divided into three districts and 34 communes (towns). Each town has a municipal council elected by popular vote and a mayor elected from the council.

## ECONOMY

Agriculture remains a cornerstone of Guadeloupe's economy. Although the importance of sugar is diminishing, 40% of Guadeloupe's cultivable land is still planted in cane and the industry is responsible for about 16,000 jobs. Much of the sugar is used in the production of rum, a leading export. The other important export crop is bananas, the bulk of which grow along the southern flanks of the Soufrière volcano. Two thirds of all bananas eaten in France are from Guadeloupe.

In the industrial sector, Guadeloupe has about 150 small-scale enterprises including food processing, cement, plastics and furniture.

Tourism accounts for about 10,000 jobs and is the fastest growing sector of the economy. Of the island's 330,000 annual visitors about 70% come from France, 13% from other parts of Europe and a little over 10% from the USA.

## POPULATION & PEOPLE

The population of Guadeloupe (Basse-Terre and Grande-Terre) is about 334,000. In addition, about 3000 people live on Les Saintes, 1600 on La Désirade and 13,000 on Marie-Galante.

About three-quarters of the population is

of mixed ethnicity, a combination of African, European and East Indian descent. There's also a sizeable population of White islanders who trace their ancestry to the early French settlers, as well as a number of more recently arrived French from the mainland.

## ARTS & CULTURE

Guadeloupean culture draws on French, African, East Indian and West Indian influences. The mix is visible in the architecture, which ranges from French colonial to Hindu temples; in the food, which merges all the cultures into a unique Creole cuisine; and in the local creole language that predominates in the home.

Guadeloupe is one place where you're more apt to see women wearing traditional Creole dress, predominantly at festivals and cultural events. The typical costume consists of a full, brightly coloured skirt, commonly a madras-type plaid of oranges and yellows, with a matching headdress, a white lace-trimmed blouse and petticoat and a scarf draped over the shoulder.

The island's most renowned native son is Saint-John Perse, the pseudonym of Alexis Léger, who was born in Guadeloupe in 1887 and who won the Nobel Prize for Literature in 1960 for the evocative imagery of his poetry. One of his many noted works is *Anabasis*, which was translated into English by T S Eliot.

### Dress Conventions

Except for fine dining, dress is casual but generally stylish. Topless bathing is common on the island, particularly at resort beaches. Swimwear is not appropriate away from the beach.

## RELIGION

The predominant religion is Roman Catholicism. There are also Methodist, Seventh Day Adventist, Jehovah's Witness and Evangelical denominations, as well as a sizeable Hindu community, the descendants of 19thC indentured workers from Pondicherry.

## LANGUAGE

French is the official language, but islanders commonly speak a local creole dialect among themselves.

While English is not widely spoken, most desk clerks in larger hotels speak English and a fair number of other people in tourist-related areas are willing to communicate in a combination of slow French and broken English. If you don't speak French, bring a French-English dictionary and phrase book.

# Facts for the Visitor

## PASSPORT & VISAS

US, Canadian and Japanese citizens can stay up to three weeks by showing proof of citizenship in the form of an expired (up to five years) passport or an official birth certificate accompanied by a driver's licence or other government-authorised photo ID. For stays of over three weeks a valid passport is necessary.

Citizens of the EC need an official identity card, passport or valid French *carte de séjour*. Citizens of most other foreign countries, including Australia, need a valid passport and visa for France.

Visitors officially require a return or onward ticket.

## CUSTOMS

Citizens of EC countries are allowed to bring in 300 cigarettes, 1.5 litres of spirits and four litres of wine duty free. Non-EC citizens are allowed to bring in 200 cigarettes, a bottle of spirits and two litres of wine duty free. All visitors are allowed to bring in 'large allowances of rum' as well.

Yachts are allowed to have firearms on board, but must declare them.

## MONEY

The French franc is the island currency. Hotels, larger restaurants and car rental agencies accept MasterCard (Eurocard) and Visa (Carte Bleue). For most other situations, you'll need to use francs. Avoid changing money at hotel lobbies, where the rates are worse than at exchange offices or banks. More information is under Money in the Facts for the Visitor chapter at the front of the book.

## TOURIST OFFICES

The mailing address for the central tourist office on Guadeloupe is: Office Départemental du Tourisme de la Guadeloupe (☎ 82 09 30; fax 83 89 22), 5 Square de la Banque, 97100 Pointe-à-Pitre, Guadeloupe, French West Indies.

There are also regional tourist offices in the towns of Basse-Terre (☎ 81 24 83) and Saint-François (☎ 88 48 74) and local information bureaus *(syndicat d'initiative)* in some smaller towns.

### Overseas Reps

For addresses of overseas tourist offices, see the Facts for the Visitor section of the Martinique chapter.

## BUSINESS HOURS

Although they vary, typical shop hours are from 9 am to 1 pm and 3 to 6 pm Monday to Friday. Many shops are also open on Saturday mornings.

Bank hours are commonly from 8 am to noon and 2 to 4 pm weekdays, with a few branches open on Saturday mornings as well. During the summer, many banks change their hours to 8 am to 3 pm. Banks close at noon on the day before a public holiday.

## HOLIDAYS

Public holidays in Guadeloupe are:

| | | |
|---|---|---|
| New Year's Day | – | 1 January |
| Labor Day | – | 1 May |
| VE Day (Allied WWII Victory in Europe) | – | 8 May |
| Easter Sunday | – | late March/early April |
| Easter Monday | – | late March/early April |
| Ascension Thursday | – | 40th day after Easter |
| Pentecost Monday | – | eighth Monday after Easter |
| Slavery Abolition Day | – | 27 May |
| Bastille Day | – | 14 July |
| Schoelcher Day | – | 21 July |
| Assumption Day | – | 15 August |
| All Saints Day | – | 1 November |
| Armistice Day | – | 11 November |
| Christmas Day | – | 25 December |

## CULTURAL EVENTS

Carnival celebrations, held during the traditional five-day Mardi Gras period which ends on Ash Wednesday, features costume parades, dancing, music and other festivities.

The Fête des Cuisinières (Festival of Women Cooks) is a colourful event held in Pointe-à-Pitre in early August. Women in Creole dress, carrying baskets of traditional foods, parade through the streets to the cathedral where they are blessed by the bishop. It's followed by a banquet and dancing.

The Tour de la Guadeloupe, a 10-day international cycling race, is also held in early August.

## POST

There are post offices in Pointe-à-Pitre, Basse-Terre, Gosier, Saint-François and other major towns. It costs 2.50F to send a postcard to France, 3.20F to the UK, 2.70F to the USA or Canada and 4.20F to Australia. This rate also covers letters up to 10 grams.

Postage stamps can be purchased at tobacco shops *(tabacs)* and some hotels in addition to post offices.

Mail addressed to Guadeloupe should end with the postal code, town name and 'Guadeloupe, French West Indies'.

## TELECOMMUNICATIONS

Public phones in Guadeloupe accept French phonecards *(télécarte)*, not coins. The cards cost 36F or 87F, depending on the calling time, and are sold at post offices and at shops marked *télécarte en vente ici*. Public phones can be found at most post offices.

When calling Guadeloupe from elsewhere in the French West Indies (or vice versa), dial just the six-digit local number. When calling Guadeloupe from outside the French West Indies, add the 590 area code to the six-digit local number.

More information on phonecards and making long-distance calls is under Telecommunications in the Facts for the Visitor chapter in the front of the book.

## ELECTRICITY
Electricity is 220 volts AC, 50 cycles, as in France. Some hotels can provide adaptor plugs and transformers.

## WEIGHTS & MEASURES
Guadeloupe uses the metric system and the 24-hour clock.

## BOOKS & MAPS
There are several books about Guadeloupe and its flora and fauna in French, but English-language books are harder to find. A good place to look is at the Boutique de la Presse in the Centre Saint-John Perse in Pointe-à-Pitre.

The best known contemporary novelist in the French West Indies is Guadeloupe native Maryse Condé, whose best-selling epic novel *Tree of Life* has recently been translated into English (Random House, 1992). The story centres around the life of a Guadeloupean family, their roots and the identity of Guadeloupean society itself.

The bilingual French/English *A Cruising Guide to Guadeloupe*, part of the Guide Trois Rivières series (Edition Caripress, 30 Rue Montesquieu, 97200 Fort-de-France, Martinique), is a comprehensive sailing manual for cruising Guadeloupe and the offshore islands.

The best map of Guadeloupe is the No 510 (1:100,000) map published by the Institut Géographique National (IGN), which is sold at bookshops around the island for about 40F.

## MEDIA
The island's local daily is the *France-Antilles*. Other French-language newspapers, such as *Le Monde*, are flown in daily from the mainland. Larger newsstands in Pointe-à-Pitre and major tourist areas sell the *International Herald-Tribune* and a few other English-language newspapers.

Radio France Outre-Mer (RFO) provides public radio and TV broadcasting. Guade-loupe also has two private TV stations and a number of independent FM radio stations.

## HEALTH
The main hospital is the Centre Hospitalier (☎ 89 10 10) in Pointe-à-Pitre, at the east end of Faubourg Victor Hugo. There's also a hospital (☎ 80 54 54) in Basse-Terre and a number of smaller medical facilities around Guadeloupe.

Bilharzia (schistosomiasis) is found throughout Grande-Terre and in much of Basse-Terre, including Grand Étang lake. The main method of prevention is to avoid swimming or wading in fresh water. More information can be found in the Health section in the introductory Facts for the Visitor chapter.

## DANGERS & ANNOYANCES
Guadeloupe's crime rate is relatively low compared to other large islands in the Eastern Caribbean. There are poisonous manchineel trees on some of the beaches, usually marked with a warning sign.

## EMERGENCIES
In an emergency, dial ☎ 17 for police and ☎ 18 for the fire department. For more routine police assistance dial ☎ 82 00 17 in Pointe-à-Pitre, ☎ 81 11 55 in Basse-Terre.

## ACTIVITIES
### Beaches & Swimming
There are white-sand beaches in the resort towns of Gosier, Sainte-Anne and Saint-François. At the north side of the peninsula leading to Pointe des Châteaux there are a couple of nice remote beaches, including Anse Tarare, a nudist beach. While most of Grande-Terre's east coast has rough surf, there is a swimmable beach at Le Moule and a little protected cove at Porte d'Enfer. On the west side of Grande-Terre, Port-Louis is the most popular swimming spot, with a broad sandy beach that attracts weekend crowds.

On Basse-Terre, the nicest beaches are along the north side of the island; the finest of them, Grande Anse, is a lovely golden-sand beach just north of Deshaies. There are a handful of black-sand beaches along Basse-Terre's southern shore.

## Diving

Guadeloupe's top diving site is the Réserve Cousteau at Pigeon Island off the west coast of Basse-Terre. Spearfishing has long been banned in this underwater reserve and consequently the waters surrounding Pigeon Island, which is just a km offshore, are teeming with colourful tropical fish, sponges and corals.

The following dive shops are in the Réserve Cousteau area; they all go out daily at 10 am, 12.30 and 3 pm:

Les Heures Saines, Rocher Malendure, 97132 Pigeon (☎ 98 86 63; fax 95 50 90); popular with English speakers, this well-regarded site has modern equipment and uses both NAUI and CMAS programmes. It costs 200F for a single dive, 850F for a five-dive package.

Aux Aquanautes Antillais, Plage de Malendure, 97125 Bouillante (☎ 98 87 30); right on Malendure Beach, this friendly local operation charges 150F per dive, 100F to go along as a snorkeller.

Chez Guy et Christian, Plage de Malendure, 97132 Pigeon (☎ 98 82 43; fax 98 82 84); this operation has dives for 150F, a six-dive package for 780F.

## Snorkelling

Guadeloupe's most popular snorkelling spot is Pigeon Island; there's a regular glass-bottom boat tour from Malendure Beach that includes snorkelling. On Grande-Terre, there's good snorkelling off Ilet du Gosier, which can be reached by boat from Gosier. Snorkelling equipment can be hired at many beachside tourist resorts.

## Other Water Sports

Le Moule, Port-Louis and Anse Bertrand commonly have good surfing conditions from around October to May. In summer, Sainte-Anne, Saint-François and Petit-Havre can have good wave action.

Windsurfing is quite popular on Guadeloupe, with much of the activity centred around the resort areas along the south side of Grande-Terre and on the island of Terre-de-Haut. Windsurfing gear can be rented

from beach huts for about 50F an hour. UCPA, the Union des Centres de Plein Air (☎ 88 64 80), 97118 Saint-François, has week-long windsurfing/hotel packages in both Saint-François and Terre-de-Haut.

Deep-sea fishing can be arranged with Caraïbe Pêche (☎ 90 97 51), Evasion Exotic (☎ 90 94 17) and other boats at the Bas du Fort Marina.

## Hiking

Guadeloupe has wonderful trails that take in waterfalls, primordial rainforest and botanical gardens. A number of them are simple 10 to 30-minute walks that can be enjoyed as part of a tour around the island.

Serious hikers will find many longer, more rigorous trails in the national park. The most popular are those leading to the volcanic summit of La Soufrière, the island's highest point, and to the base of Chutes du Carbet, the Eastern Caribbean's highest waterfalls. Both can make for scenic half-day treks and are in the rainforest, so be prepared for wet conditions and wear good hiking shoes. More information is found under individual sights in this chapter.

## Horse Riding

Le Criolo (☎ 84 04 86), a riding school in Saint-Félix near Gosier, offers horse-riding lessons and excursions.

## Tennis

Many resort hotels have tennis courts for their guests. Two private tennis clubs open to visitors for a fee are the Marina Club (☎ 90 84 08) in Pointe-à-Pitre and the Centre Lamby-Lambert (☎ 90 90 97) in Gosier.

## Golf

Guadeloupe's only golf course is the 18-hole Golf de St François (☎ 88 41 87), designed by Robert Trent Jones, in Saint-François. Green fees are 250F a day.

## HIGHLIGHTS

The national park on Basse-Terre has most of Guadeloupe's top attractions including the Route de la Traversée, a road that cuts across

GUADELOUPE

the park's rainforest; the majestic Chutes du Carbet waterfalls; and La Soufrière volcano, with its sulphur vents and hiking trails. Guadeloupe also has some nice sandy beaches and good diving and windsurfing.

Whatever you do, don't miss a visit to the charming little island of Terre-de-Haut, whether as a day excursion or for a longer stay.

## ACCOMMODATION

There are 4200 hotel rooms in Guadeloupe, most in small to mid-sized hotels. The bulk of the accommodation is along the south coast of Grande-Terre, between Pointe-à-Pitre and Saint-François. There are another 100 rooms on Les Saintes, 15 on La Désirade and a couple of dozen on Marie-Galante.

Many hotels have a three-night minimum stay in winter and as that's a busy season, advance reservations are a good idea.

As in France, taxes and service charges are included in the quoted rate; many hotels also include a breakfast.

### Gîtes de France

Some of the best value places to stay are not hotels but small family-run facilities. Gîtes de France Guadeloupe (☎ 82 09 30), BP 759, 97171 Pointe-à-Pitre, is an association of home-owners who rent private rooms and apartments. Most of the gîtes are quite comfortable; all are rated on a scale of one to three by the association, the higher the number the higher the standard. The gîtes are spread around Guadeloupe, with the largest collection in the Gosier, Sainte-Anne and Saint-François areas. Generally they're booked by the week and arrangements can be made in advance through the association. Most hosts do not speak English, so a working knowledge of French is often essential. A full list of gîtes can be obtained from the association or at the tourist office.

### Camping

Guadeloupe has two established seaside camping grounds, both on the north-west side of Basse-Terre. Les Sables d'Or (☎ 28 44 60) is a congested little place on Grande Anse Beach north of Deshaies and La Traversée (☎ 98 21 23) is in a garden-like setting south of Pointe-Noire.

Vert'Bleu (☎ 28 51 25) in Deshaies rents equipped campervans that sleep four people from 650/3700F a day/week and will provide free transport to and from the airport. Campervans can also be rented from Antilles Locap Soleil (☎ 90 95 72) in Gosier.

## FOOD

Guadeloupe has many restaurants with fine French and Creole food, the latter known for its savoury flavours. Island cuisine draws upon a wide range of seafood including crayfish (ouassous), octopus (chatrou), conch (lambi) and more traditional fishes such as red snapper. Some typical Guadeloupean dishes include accras (cod fritters), crabes farci (spicy stuffed land crabs), colombo cabris (curried goat), rice and beans, and breadfruit gratin. Another popular Creole dish is blaff, a seafood preparation poached in a spicy broth.

At the lower end, Guadeloupe has a number of pizza restaurants, pâtisseries selling hearty inexpensive sandwiches and roadside snack wagons.

If you just want something quick while you're touring, petrol stations along major roads often have convenience stores.

## DRINKS

Tap water is safe to drink. There are lots of local rums and many distilleries have tasting rooms. Homemade flavoured rums made by adding fruit are also popular; in bars and restaurants you'll commonly see these in large glass jars behind the counter. A common restaurant drink is ti-punch, where you're given white rum, cane sugar and fresh limes to mix to your own proportions.

## ENTERTAINMENT

Most night time entertainment, including discos and dinner shows, is found in the resort areas, especially at Bas du Fort, Gosier, Sainte-Anne and Saint-François.

Guadeloupe has two casinos, one in Gosier and one in Saint-François. On a more local level, cockfighting is held on Saturday afternoons and Sunday from November to April in galledromes (cockfighting pits) around the island and there are horse races at Hippodrome Saint-Jacques (☎ 22 11 08) in the northern part of Grande-Terre.

## THINGS TO BUY

The most popular island souvenir is a bottle of Guadeloupean rum.

The harbourfront market in Pointe-à-Pitre is a good place to buy island handicrafts, including straw dolls, straw hats and primitive African-style wood carvings. It's also a good spot to pick up locally grown coffee and fragrant spices.

# Getting There & Away

## AIR
### To/From the USA
American Airlines (☎ 83 62 62) has twice-daily flights to Guadeloupe from San Juan, Puerto Rico, which connect with mainland USA flights. In summer, the lowest midweek return fares to Guadeloupe begin at around US$330 from Miami, US$398 from New York; in winter fares begin at US$370 from Miami, US$440 from New York.

Air France (☎ 82 61 61) has a flight from Miami to Guadeloupe on Sunday. The fare for a one-month excursion ticket is around US$500.

### To/From Canada
Air Canada (☎ 83 62 49) has a Saturday flight from Montreal; fares depend on the season, beginning at around C$500 return.

### To/From Europe
Air France (☎ 82 61 61) flies to Guadeloupe from Paris at least once daily, with connections throughout Europe.

Air Outre Mer or AOM (☎ 83 12 12), Air Liberté/Minerve (☎ 90 00 08) and Corsair Nouvelles Frontières (☎ 90 36 36) also have flights from Paris, with the frequency depending on the season.

Return fares from Paris to Pointe-à-Pitre generally begin around 3700F.

### To/From South America
Air Guadeloupe and Air France have scheduled flights from Pointe-à-Pitre to Cayenne, French Guiana. Air Guadeloupe charges 1870F return. Air France also goes on to Caracas, Venezuela.

### Within the Caribbean
Air Guadeloupe (☎ 82 28 35) has at least four flights daily from Pointe-à-Pitre to St Barts (520F one way, 710F for a three-day excursion fare) and flights five days a week to Grand Case on St Martin (560F one way, 780F for a 21-day excursion). Air Guadeloupe has three to five flights daily between Guadeloupe and Martinique; the one-way fare is 305F to 466F, depending on the time of day (noon flights are the cheapest), and there's a 632F 21-day excursion fare. There are also daily flights to Dominica and twice-weekly flights to St Lucia. Air Guadeloupe offers student discounts; the age cut off, either 18 or 25, depends on the flight.

Air Martinique (☎ 90 28 25) has daily flights between Pointe-à-Pitre and Fort-de-France, with fares comparable to Air Guadeloupe's.

Air Saint-Barthelemy (☎ 91 74 59) flies to Pointe-à-Pitre from St Barts at 3 pm daily except on Wednesday. The return flight to St Barts is at 4.30 pm. The fare is 536F one way, 840F return.

LIAT (☎ 82 12 26) has four daily nonstop flights to and from Antigua and Dominica and two daily flights to Martinique. LIAT allows Guadeloupe to be included as a free stopover on a 30-day excursion ticket between Antigua and Martinique; the cost is US$204 return. LIAT's Dominica-Guadeloupe fare is US$81 one way, US$136 return.

Air Caraibes (☎ 83 13 38) and Air St-Martin (☎ 82 96 63) provide charter flights around the Caribbean.

### Airport Information
Aéroport Raizet is at the north side of Pointe-à-Pitre, three km from the city centre on N5.

The terminal has a travel agency, car rental booths, a restaurant and gift shops. Karuki Souvenirs sells the detailed IGN map of Guadeloupe. You can exchange money at the Crédit Agricole bank next to the post office. The departure lounge has an overpriced snack stand, a duty-free shop and card phones.

**To/From the Airport** There are car rentals and a taxi stand at the airport. An airport bus runs about twice an hour to Pointe-à-Pitre on weekdays until about 7 pm.

## SEA
### To/From France
Compagnie Générale Maritime (☎ 83 04 43) operates weekly 'banana boats' that carry passengers between the French West Indies and mainland France. Information is in the Getting There & Away chapter in the front of the book.

### Within the Caribbean
There are two companies providing regular boat service between Guadeloupe, Martinique and Dominica. Schedules are occasionally adjusted a little so they should be verified in advance.

**Catamaran** *Caribbean Express* operates modern 300-seat catamarans between Martinique and Guadeloupe that stop en route in either Terre-de-Haut or Dominica. The boats have air-conditioned and open-air decks and a snack bar. They leave Pointe-à-Pitre at 7.45 am on Monday, Wednesday, Friday and Saturday, arriving in Dominica at 10.15 am and in Fort-de-France at 12.35 pm. The boat returns the same day, leaving Martinique at 1.25 pm, arriving in Dominica at 3.15 pm and in Guadeloupe at 6 pm.

On Thursday and Sunday the boat leaves Pointe-à-Pitre at 7.45 am, stops in Terre-de-Haut at 8.45 am and arrives in Fort-de-France at noon. It departs Fort-de-France at 12.45 pm, arrives in Terre-de-Haut at 3.45 pm and in Pointe-à-Pitre at 5 pm.

The Martinique-Guadeloupe fare (either direction) costs 315F one way, with a free stopover allowed in either Dominica or Terre-de-Haut, or 450F for an excursion fare allowing stays of up to seven days but no en-route stopover.

There are discounts of 50% for children aged two to 11 and 10% for passengers under 26 or older than 59. For reservations in Martinique call ☎ 60 12 38, in Guadeloupe ☎ 91 13 43, or check with any travel agent.

The *Madikera*, a 352-passenger catamaran, also has passenger service between Pointe-à-Pitre and Fort-de-France that stops in Dominica on Wednesday, Friday, Saturday and Sunday. There's a Monday sailing between Pointe-à-Pitre and Dominica only. Arrival and departure times vary, but the boat is about 15 minutes faster than the Caribbean Express service.

Fares from either Martinique or Guadeloupe to Dominica are 285F one way, 420F return (130/285F for children). Fares between Martinique and Guadeloupe are comparable to those offered by Caribbean Express. Reservation numbers are ☎ 91 60 87 in Guadeloupe, ☎ 73 35 35 in Martinique and ☎ 86977 in Dominica.

### Yacht
Guadeloupe has three marinas. Marina de Bas du Fort (☎ 90 84 85), between Pointe-à-Pitre and Gosier, has 700 berths, 55 of which are available for visiting boats. It can handle craft up to 39 metres in length and has full facilities including fuel, water, electricity, sanitation, ice, chandlery and a maintenance area.

Marina de Saint-François (☎ 88 47 28), in the centre of Saint-François, has about 250 moorings, fuel, water, ice and electricity.

Marina de Rivière-Sens (☎ 81 77 61), on the southern outskirts of the town of Basse-Terre, has about 200 moorings, fuel, water and ice.

There are customs and immigration offices in Pointe-à-Pitre, Basse-Terre and Deshaies; hours are from 8 am to 4 pm weekdays.

The yacht charter companies The Moorings (☎ 90 81 81) and ATM (☎ 90 92 92) are based at the Bas du Fort Marina.

## Cruise Ship

Cruise ships dock right in the city at Centre Saint-John Perse, Pointe-à-Pitre's new port complex, which has shops, restaurants and a hotel. In 1992, 200 cruise ship visits brought 136,000 visitors to Guadeloupe.

## LEAVING GUADELOUPE

There's no departure tax.

# Getting Around

## AIR

Air Guadeloupe has daily flights between Pointe-à-Pitre and Marie-Galante, La Désirade and Terre-de-Haut; see those island sections for details.

## BUS

Guadeloupe has a good public bus system that operates from about 5.30 am to 6.30 pm, with fairly frequent service on main routes. On Sunday, service is much lighter and there's no operation on most secondary routes.

Many bus routes terminate in Pointe-à-Pitre. Schedules are a bit loose and buses generally don't depart Pointe-à-Pitre until they're near capacity. Jump seats fold down and block the aisle as the bus fills, so try to get a seat near the front if you're not going far.

The bus from Pointe-à-Pitre to Gosier costs 5.50F and takes about 15 minutes. If you're going to the Bas du Fort Marina, you can take this bus and get off just past the university. Other fares from Pointe-à-Pitre are 5.50F to the airport, 10F to Sainte-Anne and 30F to Basse-Terre.

Pay the driver as you get off the bus. Having the correct fare is not essential, although larger notes could be problematic.

Destinations are written on the buses. Bus stops have blue signs picturing a bus; in less developed areas you can wave buses down along their routes.

## TAXI

Taxis are plentiful but expensive. There are taxi stands at the airport, in Pointe-à-Pitre and in Basse-Terre. Larger hotels commonly have taxis assigned to them with the drivers waiting in the lobby.

The fare from the airport is about 50F to Pointe-à-Pitre, 80F to Gosier and 225F to Saint-François. Fares are 40% higher from 9 pm to 7 am and on Sunday and holidays. You can call for a taxi by dialling ☎ 82 00 00 or 82 13 67 in the Pointe-à-Pitre area, ☎ 81 79 70 in Basse-Terre.

## CAR & MOTORBIKE
### Road Rules

In Guadeloupe drive on the right; your home driving licence is valid.

Roads are excellent by Caribbean standards and almost invariably hard surfaced, although secondary and mountain roads are often narrow. Around Pointe-à-Pitre there are multi-lane highways, with traffic zipping along at 110 km per hour. Outside the Pointe-à-Pitre area most highways have a single lane in either direction and an 80 kmh speed limit.

Traffic regulations and road signs are of European standards. Exits and intersections are clearly marked and speed limits are posted.

### Rental

**Car** Several car rental companies have offices at the airport and in major resort areas. Some agents will let you rent a car near your hotel and drop it off free of charge at the airport, which can save a hefty taxi fare.

Companies generally drop their rates the longer you keep the car, with the weekly rate working out to be about 20% cheaper than the daily rate. Note that many companies have both an unlimited-km rate and a cheaper rate with a per-km charge; as the island is big, fees on the latter can rack up quite quickly.

Rates for small cars with unlimited km are advertised for as low as 190F a day, although the best walk-in rate we found was 230F (including CDW and tax) for a little Opel Corsa from Budget.

Car rental companies, with their airport phone numbers given first, include:

| | |
|---|---|
| Avis | – ☎ 82 33 47;<br>☎ 90 46 46 in Gosier;<br>☎ 88 60 60 in Saint-François |
| Budget | – ☎ 82 95 58;<br>☎ 84 24 24 in Gosier |
| Citer | – ☎ 82 10 94 |
| Europcar | – ☎ 82 50 51;<br>☎ 84 45 84 in Gosier;<br>☎ 88 69 77 in Saint-François |
| Hertz | – ☎ 82 00 14;<br>☎ 84 23 23 in Gosier |
| Nad In Car | – ☎ 91 60 60;<br>☎ 84 19 17 in Gosier;<br>☎ 88 32 45 in Sainte-Anne |
| Thrifty | – ☎ 91 42 17;<br>☎ 90 86 32 in Bas du Fort;<br>☎ 84 51 26 in Gosier |

**Motorbike** Equateur Moto (☎ 84 59 94) in Gosier rents Peugeot 50s and 80s for 180F a day and has bigger bikes, up to 750 cc, for 440F a day. Motorbikes can also be rented from Vespa Sun (☎ 82 17 80), 29 Rue Bébian, Pointe-à-Pitre, and from Rent A Bike (☎ 88 51 00) in Saint-François.

### BICYCLE
Equateur Moto (☎ 84 59 94) in Gosier rents mountain bikes for 95F a day, 565F a week.

### HITCHING
Hitching is fairly common on Guadeloupe. The proper stance is to hold out an open palm at a slightly downward angle. All the usual safety precautions apply.

### BOAT
Ferries to Les Saintes leave from Pointe-à-Pitre, Saint-François, and Trois-Rivières. Ferries to Marie-Galante leave from Pointe-à-Pitre and Saint-François. Ferries to La Désirade leave from Saint-François.

Schedule and fare information is given under individual islands.

### TOURS
Emeraude Guadeloupe (☎ 81 98 28) puts together 'green tourism' sightseeing outings with an emphasis on nature and hiking.

# Pointe-à-Pitre

In 1654 a merchant named Peter, a Dutch Jew who settled in Guadeloupe after being exiled from Brazil, began a fish market on an undeveloped harbourside jut of land. The area became known as Peter's Point and eventually grew into the settlement of Pointe-à-Pitre.

Pointe-à-Pitre, Guadeloupe's largest municipality, is a conglomerate of old and new, and is largely commercial in appearance. There are a couple of museums, but other than that the most interesting sight is the bustling harbourside market.

The hub of town is the Place de la Victoire, an open green space punctuated with tall royal palms that extends north a few blocks from the inner harbour. There are pavement cafés opposite its west side, a line of big old mango trees to the north and some older buildings along with the sous-préfecture office at the park's east side.

All visitors can expect to at least pass through Pointe-à-Pitre as it's the main port for ferries to Guadeloupe's outer islands and a major bus terminal.

Central Pointe-à-Pitre is quite compact and nothing is more than a five or 10-minute walk from Place de la Victoire.

### Information
**Tourist Office** The tourist office (☎ 82 09 30), opposite the north-west end of the harbour, at 5 Square de la Banque, is open from 8 am to 5 pm Monday to Friday, 8 am to noon on Saturday. A second office in the Centre Saint-John Perse, next to the police booth, is open when cruise ships are in port.

Pick up a copy of *Bonjour Guadeloupe* and the monthly *Living in Guadeloupe*, both free general-info tourist magazines published in English, and *Ti Gourmet*, a pocket-sized bilingual restaurant guide

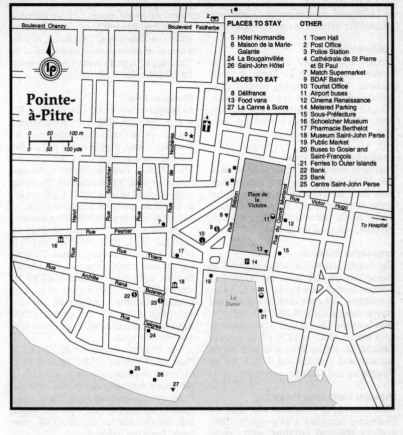

**Pointe-à-Pitre**

PLACES TO STAY
5 Hôtel Normandie
6 Maison de la Marie-Galante
24 La Bougainvillée
26 Saint-John Hôtel

PLACES TO EAT
8 Délifrance
13 Food vans
27 La Canne à Sucre

OTHER
1 Town Hall
2 Post Office
3 Police Station
4 Cathédrale de St Pierre et St Paul
7 Match Supermarket
9 BDAF Bank
10 Tourist Office
11 Airport buses
12 Cinema Renaissance
14 Metered Parking
15 Sous-Préfecture
16 Schoelcher Museum
17 Pharmacie Berthelot
18 Museum Saint-John Perse
19 Public Market
20 Buses to Gosier and Saint-François
21 Ferries to Outer Islands
22 Bank
23 Bank
25 Centre Saint-John Perse

which offers a free drink or appetiser at many restaurants.

**Money** The BDAF bank next to the tourist office is open weekdays from 8 am to noon and 2 to 4 pm; there are a few more banks nearby on Rue de Noziéres.

You can also change major currencies (notes only) to francs or get credit card advances at the Crédit Agricole automatic teller at the ground level of the Centre Saint-John Perse. The machine operates 24 hours a day but you need a credit card to enter the booth between 10 pm and 6 am.

**Post & Telecommunications** The post office, a block north of the cathedral on Blvd Faidherbe, has very few windows and long, slow-moving queues. There's a row of card phones outside the entrance.

**Bookshops** The Boutique de la presse in the Centre Saint-John Perse sells English and French-language newspapers and Institut Géographique National maps of Guadeloupe, Pointe-à-Pitre and other French West Indies islands. It also sells a rather good selection of French-language books on the French West Indies. The tobacco shop next

GUADELOUPE

to Délifrance sells maps of Guadeloupe, phonecards and international newspapers.

### Public Market

There's a lively and colourful open-air market running along La Darse, the inner harbour. Women wearing madras cloth turbans sell island fruit, vegetables, flowers, pungent spices, handicrafts and clothing while a few fishing boats docked at the edge of the harbour sell fresh fish.

### Centre Saint-John Perse

This large new port complex is on the west side of the harbour, less than five minutes' walk from the Place de la Victoire. It has cruise ship docks, port authority offices, a tourist booth, numerous boutiques, shops, galleries, cafés and restaurants.

### Schoelcher Museum

The Musée Schoelcher, which occupies an interesting period building at 24 Rue Peynier, is dedicated to abolitionist Victor Schoelcher. The main exhibits are personal objects belonging to Schoelcher and artefacts from the slave period. The museum is open from 8.30 am to 12.30 pm Monday to Saturday as well as from 2 to 5.30 pm on Monday and Tuesday and 2 to 6 pm on Wednesday and Thursday.

### Museum Saint-John Perse

This municipal museum, at 9 Rue de Noziéres, occupies a two-storey 19th-century colonial building with ornate wrought-iron balconies. The museum is dedicated to the renowned poet and Nobel laureate Alexis Léger, better known as Saint-John Perse. The house offers both a glimpse of a period Creole home and displays on Perse's life and work. Perse was born a bit farther down the same street, in house No 54. The museum is open from 9 am to 5 pm on weekdays, from 8.30 am to 12.30 pm on Saturday. Admission is 10F.

### Cathédrale de St Pierre et St Paul

Rather than the traditional arches, this weathered sand-coloured church, nick-named the 'Iron Cathedral', is supported by iron girders intended to brace it against earthquakes and hurricanes. The church, which is a couple of minutes' walk north-west of the Place de la Victoire, doesn't get any points for aesthetics but it is a curiosity.

### Places to Stay

*Le Bougainvillée* (☎ 90 14 14; fax 91 36 82), 9 Rue Fréboult, 97110 Pointe-à-Pitre, a block from the Centre Saint-John Perse, is a four-storey hotel with 36 rooms and a rather old-fashioned ambience. It's not fancy but it's sufficient, clean and better maintained than other small hotels in the area. The rooms are good-sized with air-con, TV, phones and small private balconies. Singles/doubles cost 335/400F in summer, 450/525F in winter.

*Maison de la Marie-Galante* (☎ 90 10 41; fax 90 22 75), 12 Place de la Victoire, 97110 Pointe-à-Pitre, is centrally located. There are nine air-con rooms, some with TV, phones, showers and toilets that cost 320/400F for singles/doubles. A couple of others are more spartanly furnished with private showers, but toilets in the hall, and cost 260/350F. Breakfast is included and it's good value for a bottom-end hotel.

The *Hôtel Normandie* (☎ 82 37 15), 14 Place de la Victoire, 97110 Pointe-à-Pitre, has seven rooms upstairs above a bar. It's an older place with rather dreary, air-con rooms. A shower is separated from the sleeping space by a curtain and the toilet is down the hall. Singles/doubles are 250/300F year-round, breakfast included.

The new *Saint-John Hôtel* (☎ 82 51 57; fax 82 52 61), Centre Saint-John Perse, 97110 Pointe-à-Pitre, a member of the Anchorage chain, is centrally located in the cruise ship complex. It has 44 very compact but otherwise comfortable rooms with air-con, room safes, satellite TV, phones and small shared balconies overlooking the harbour. Singles/doubles cost 350/450F in summer, 400/500F in winter, breakfast included.

If you need to be near the airport, there's *Relais Bleus du Raizet* (☎ 90 03 03; fax 90 00 26), 97139 Abymes, a two-storey motel at the intersection of the airport drive and the main road, 700 metres from the terminal. The 60 rooms are standard motel fare with TV, phone and air-con and there's a pool. Singles/doubles start at 330/430F in summer, 490/535F in winter.

### Places to Eat

**Place de la Victoire** *Délifrance*, on the west side of Place de la Victoire, is a great place for breakfast. For 28F you can get juice, coffee and hot crispy bread with butter and jam. Good croissants and pastries cost 5F to 12F and there are meat pies, quiches, sandwiches and a few steamer trays of warm dishes that could make for a reasonable lunch at modest prices. It's a very popular local spot and there are pavement café tables. It's open from 6.30 am to 7 pm Monday to Friday, to 2 pm on Saturday.

The *Maison de la Marie-Galante* hotel, 12 Place de la Victoire, has indoor and outdoor dining and a menu du jour with dessert for 60F. The nearby *Hôtel Normandie* has pizza from 40F, fish dishes from 60F to 85F, and there's usually a good-value menu du jour.

If you're catching a ferry, there are a couple of snack bars near the harbourside ticket offices with sandwiches, snacks and drinks. In the evening you can find a line of food vans on the east side of the Place de la Victoire that sell inexpensive crêpes, sandwiches, fried food and barbecued chicken. There's a Match supermarket a minute's walk west of the tourist office.

**Centre Saint-John Perse** *La Canne à Sucre* (☎ 82 10 19), widely regarded as Pointe-à-Pitre's finest French/Creole restaurant, is on the waterfront at the south-east side of the complex. The restaurant has two sections. The ground level is open air and casual, with fish and meat dishes from 70F to 95F, large and varied salads including seafood, crab and Mexican for around 60F and a special lunch of the day for 70F. It's open from 12.30 to 11 pm. The air-conditioned 2nd-floor dining room is quite elegant with unobstructed harbour views and main dishes in the 110F to 180F range. It's open from noon to 2.30 pm and 7.30 to 10.30 pm. Both sections are closed on Sunday.

The *Pâtisserie St-John*, at the side of the Saint-John Hôtel, has great sandwiches, quiches and raspberry tarts priced around 15F. The *l'As de Trèfle*, nearby in the courtyard, opens at 7 am and has a 20F breakfast of juice, coffee and a croissant, as well as sandwiches from 10F, omelettes from 20F and a plat du jour for 40F.

*St John's Restaurant* on the hotel terrace opens at noon and has a weekday lunch special complete with salad for 49F as well as pizza and other moderately priced dishes. It's open for dinner on Sunday only.

### Getting There & Away

**Bus** Buses to Gosier, Sainte-Anne and Saint-François leave from the east side of the harbour, while buses to places in Basse-Terre leave from the north-west side of town near Bergevin Stadium, which is about a 15-minute walk from the centre along Boulevard Chanzy. The airport bus leaves from the east side of the Place de la Victoire about every half hour on weekdays.

**Car** On weekdays traffic in the centre is congested and parking can be quite tight. There's a car park on the south-west side of Place de la Victoire that charges 4F an hour, 20F for eight hours (the maximum time allowed); buy the ticket from the machine near the entrance. The lot is heavily patrolled and violators are ticketed. There are also parking meters on some side streets that charge the same fees as the car park.

# Grande-Terre

The southern coast of Grande-Terre, with its reef-protected waters, is Guadeloupe's main resort area. The eastern side of the island is largely open Atlantic with crashing surf and a decidedly rural character. In the interior there's a mix of rolling hills and flat plains, the latter still largely given over to sugar cane.

## BAS DU FORT

Bas du Fort, on the southern outskirts of Pointe-à-Pitre, has Guadeloupe's largest marina, a university and some new condo and hotel developments. The main hotel stretch is a couple of km by road south of the marina. Bas du Fort takes its name from its location at the base *(bas)* of Fort Fleur-d'Épée.

### Marina Bas du Fort

This expansive marina has full yachting facilities, shops, restaurants and a Photo Express lab.

Crédit Agricole has a 24-hour change machine next to Restaurant Shangai that changes US and Canadian dollars, British pounds and a number of other major currencies to French francs; it also gives cash advances on major credit cards. The adjacent Crédit Agricole bank is open from 8.45 am to 12.45 pm and 2.15 to 5.40 pm Tuesday to Friday (to 5 pm on Thursday), from 8.45 am to 12.45 pm on Saturday.

### Fort Fleur-d'Épée

This small 18th-century hilltop garrison offers fine views of Gosier and the island of Marie-Galante. Much of the coral block walls and some of the buildings stand intact and there are rusting cannons and flowering flamboyant trees on the grounds. A discreet sign near the discotheque Elysées Matignon marks the side road that leads 800 metres up to the fort.

### Aquarium de la Guadeloupe

This harbourside aquarium (☎ 90 92 38), rated as France's fourth best, has 60 species of tropical fish as well as turtles and sharks. To get there turn off highway N4, east of the roundabout, between the Elf and Esso petrol stations. The aquarium is open from 9 am to 7 pm daily and costs 20F for children, 35F for adults.

### Places to Stay

The cheapest of the half dozen hotels in the Bas du Fort area is the *Sprimhotel* (☎ 90 82 90; fax 82 87 63), Bas du Fort, 97190 Gosier,

which has 19 older studio units with kitchenettes priced from 300/345F in summer, 490/600F in winter.

A good mid-range place is the *Village Viva* (☎ 90 98 98; fax 90 96 16), Bas du Fort, 97190 Gosier, on a point near the mouth of the marina. The 76 units, in contemporary four-storey buildings, have air-con, TV, phone, balconies and kitchenettes. The shoreline is rocky, but there's a large pool. Singles/doubles begin at 480/580F in summer.

At the top end is *Fleur d'Épée Novotel* (☎ 90 40 00; fax 90 99 07), Bas du Fort, 91790 Gosier, an older but popular resort hotel. The 191 rooms are in three-storey buildings and have all the standard amenities including room safes and balconies. There's a pool, tennis courts, a white-sand beach and a couple of restaurants and bars. Singles/doubles cost 670/776F in summer, 885/1130F in winter. For reservations phone ☎ (800) 221-4542 in the USA, ☎ (1) 60 77 27 27 in France, ☎ (071) 724-1010 in the UK.

### Places to Eat

There's a cluster of cafés and restaurants all within a few minutes' walk of each other at the marina. *Le Fregate* is a simple open-air harbourside restaurant with fresh fish dishes and daily chalkboard specials for around 65F. It opens for breakfast from 5.30 am and closes around midnight.

Nearby and also on the waterfront, the pizzeria *La Sirène* has pizza or a quarter chicken with fries and salad for 50F, grilled fish for 60F and a tank of live lobsters priced at around 35F per 100 grams.

You can get pizza a bit cheaper at *Michelangelo*, which also offers a range of other Italian dishes. There's a bakery on the corner of the complex, next to Thrifty car rental, which has good pastries and makes excellent baguette sandwiches for 15F to 18F.

For Chinese food, the nearby *Restaurant Shangai* has a soup-to-dessert plat du jour for 90F, vegetarian main dishes for 45F and pork and chicken dishes for 55F.

North of the parking area is a supermarket

and across the road a couple of vendors sell fruit and flowers.

## GOSIER

Guadeloupe's largest tourist area is Gosier, eight km south-east of Pointe-à-Pitre. On the west side of Gosier there's a tourist strip with a run of resort hotels, a casino, car rental agents and restaurants. The beach forms a series of scalloped sandy coves, with a hotel backing each cove. The water is generally calm, the swimming good and there's a nice view across the channel to Basse-Terre.

Gosier's village centre, about a 15-minute walk away, lacks the fine beaches found in the main hotel area but retains an appealing local character. On the west side of the village centre there's a park with flamboyant, white cedar and tropical almond trees, a small but swimmable beach and a good view across to the Ilet du Gosier. The village's Catholic church is modernistic with a cement steeple and there's a cemetery with above-ground vaults and tombs opposite the post office.

In the evening birdwatchers can find scores of white egrets roosting on the bare trees in the roadside swamp west of the casino.

### Information

La Gazette in the village centre sells the IGN map of Guadeloupe, local newspapers, the *International Herald-Tribune, USA Today*, other international papers and a wide variety of French magazines.

Laverie du Gosier, near the post office, is a coin laundry open from 8 am to 12.30 pm and 2 to 7.30 pm Monday to Saturday. It costs 53F to wash and dry a load of clothes.

Ambiance Photos on Route des Hôtels does one-hour photo processing. It costs 124F to process a roll of 24 prints.

Beach huts in front of the resort hotels rent windsurfing equipment for about 50F an hour, Sunfish boats for 80F an hour, larger Hobie Cat boats for 200F an hour as well as fun boards, pedal boats and other water activities gear.

### Ilet du Gosier

Just 600 metres off Gosier village is Ilet du Gosier, a little undeveloped island surrounded by turquoise waters. It's a relaxed place with an old lighthouse, nice white sand and lots of coral. This is a good spot to snorkel, sunbathe or just have a peaceful picnic.

The water sports hut (open from 9 am to 12.30 pm and 2 to 5 pm) in front of the Callinago Hotel shuttles passengers back and forth to the island on demand for 50F return and also rents snorkelling gear for 40F a day.

### Places to Stay – bottom end

*Les Flamboyants* (☎ 84 14 11; fax 84 53 56), Chemin des Phares et Blaises, 97190 Gosier, is on a hilltop about a km east of the village centre and a five-minute walk from a bus stop. This small hostelry has a nice view of Ilet du Gosier, a small pool, a TV lounge and personable management. There are 14 rooms, including a couple of bungalows with kitchenettes. The rooms are essentially just a place to sleep, small and simple with air-con and private bathrooms. It's popular with budget travellers, so reservations, particularly in the high season, are advisable. Phone reservations generally require a command of French. Singles/doubles cost 215/280F in summer, 260/360F in winter, plus 40F to 60F more for a kitchenette. Breakfast is included in the rates and there's a discount of about 15% for weekly stays.

*Bungalows Village* (☎ 84 04 47; fax 84 55 34), Montauban, 97190 Gosier, is conveniently located between Gosier's main hotel strip and the village centre. Set back from the main road there are 16 studio apartments and simple bungalows on grounds that resemble a botanical garden. All have kitchenettes and showers; some are fan cooled, others air-conditioned. In summer, doubles range from 190F to 270F per day and in winter from 1540F to 1820F per week. There's an apartment for up to six people that costs 350F a day, 2240F a week.

There are numerous Gîtes de France private guesthouses in the Gosier area,

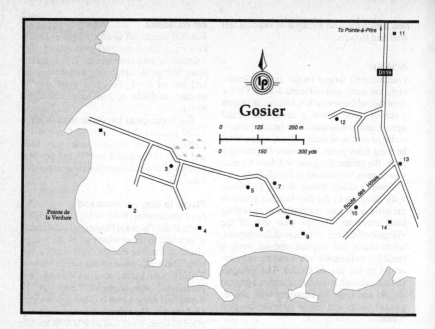

**To Pointe-à-Pitre**

**Gosier**

0      125      250 m

0      150      300 yds

Pointe de
la Verdure

Route des Hôtels

D119

including a few places on a short side road that begins about 50 metres west of Bungalows Village. Mme Pierrette Montout (☎ 84 22 89), 8 Lot Montout, Montauban, 97190 Gosier, has six air-con rooms that range from 1320F per week for a double to 3300F for a place big enough for six. Mme Eugénie Coudair (☎ 84 01 64) also has a couple of rooms on this road that rent for 1430F to 1980F per week, while Mme Marguerite Joachim (☎ 84 17 92) has five rooms similarly priced.

### Places to Stay – middle

*Callinago Hotel & Village* (☎ 84 25 25; fax 84 24 90; in the USA ☎ (800) 223-6510), BP No 1, 97190 Gosier, has two separate wings: the 'hotel' with 40 rooms and the 'village' with 93 studios. The village units are spacious with kitchenettes and small balconies, while the hotel units have no cooking facilities but the rooms are a bit spiffier, have larger balconies and a buffet breakfast is

included in the rate. Both wings have air-con and phones. There's a beachside pool and a courtesy luggage room and shower for late checkouts. The Callinago is not one of the area's newest hotels but the standards are fine and the rates, particularly in the low season, are good value. In the hotel section, singles/doubles cost 474/564F in summer, 728/924F in winter. In the village section, it's 366/450F in summer, 646/790F in winter; ask for a 3rd-floor unit to get an ocean view at no extra cost.

*Canella Beach Residence* (☎ 90 44 00; fax 90 44 44; in the USA ☎ (800) 223-9815), Pointe de la Verdure, BP 73B, 97190 Gosier, has 150 modern and comfortable air-con units in two three-storey buildings. Studios have rattan furniture, a queen-size or two twin beds, a little sitting area with a sofabed, a room safe, TV, phone and a balcony with a kitchenette. Singles/doubles cost 420/530F in summer, 570/730F in winter, plus 50F for an ocean view. There are also suites and

GUADELOUPE

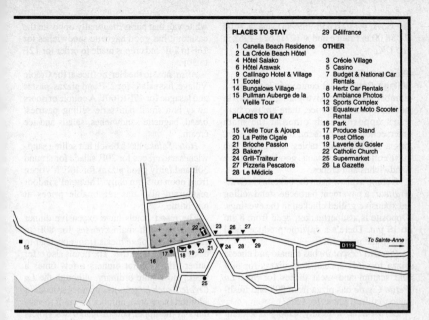

PLACES TO STAY
1 Canella Beach Residence
2 La Créole Beach Hôtel
4 Hôtel Salako
6 Hôtel Arawak
9 Callinago Hotel & Village
11 Ecotel
14 Bungalows Village
15 Pullman Auberge de la
  Vieille Tour

PLACES TO EAT
15 Vielle Tour & Ajoupa
20 La Petite Cigale
21 Brioche Passion
23 Bakery
24 Grill-Traiteur
27 Pizzeria Pescatore
28 Le Médicis

29 Délifrance

OTHER
3 Créole Village
5 Casino
7 Budget & National Car
  Rentals
8 Hertz Car Rentals
10 Ambiance Photos
12 Sports Complex
13 Equateur Moto Scooter
  Rental
16 Park
17 Produce Stand
18 Post Office
19 Laverie du Gosier
22 Catholic Church
25 Supermarket
26 La Gazette

duplex apartments. Four studios on the ground level are handicapped-accessible. There's a pool and rates include the use of tennis courts, paddle boats, canoes and snorkelling gear.

**Places to Stay – top end**
The following are all modern beachside resorts with standard 1st-class amenities including swimming pools, activity centres, restaurants and well-appointed rooms with balconies.

*La Créole Beach Hôtel* (☎ 90 46 46; fax 90 46 66), BP 19, 97190 Gosier, is a 321-room complex with three adjacent sections that are different in design but are all contemporary and somewhat condo-like in appearance. The Yucca Residence is the best value, with singles/doubles costing from 440/500F in summer, 620/680F in winter; add another 100F for an ocean view. Breakfast is not included, but units have kitchenettes.

*Hôtel Salako* (☎ 84 22 22; fax 84 38 15), BP 8, 97190 Gosier, is a 120-room hotel starting at 515/680F for singles/doubles for the lower three floors, 580/720F for the top three floors. In winter, singles/doubles start at 780/832F. A member of the Holiday Inn chain, reservations are made in the USA by calling ☎ (800) 465-4329.

The *Hôtel Arawak* (☎ 84 24 24; fax 84 38 45; in France ☎ 47 23 75 13), BP 396, 97162 Pointe-à-Pitre, is an eight-storey hotel with 160 rooms that cost 600/700F for singles/doubles in summer, 960/1180F in winter.

*Pullman Auberge de la Vieille Tour* (☎ 84 23 23; fax 84 33 43), Montauban, 97190 Gosier, is a very popular 160-room hotel. It has an interesting lobby that incorporates an 18th-century windmill although most of the rooms are in modern, motel-like, two and three-storey buildings. Standard rooms cost 782/814F for singles/doubles in summer, 1115/1205F in winter. To make reservations from overseas phone ☎ (800) 223-9862 in

GUADELOUPE

the USA, ☎ (800) 638-9699 in Canada, ☎ 05 28 88 00 in France and ☎ (071) 621-1962 in the UK.

## Places to Eat

**Village Centre** The centre of Gosier has a number of inexpensive eating options. In addition to a *Délifrance*, there are two bakeries opposite each other at the main intersection. One of them, *Brioche Passion*, has a few sidewalk tables where you can have coffee and croissants, good inexpensive sandwiches and crêpes.

A stone's throw from the bakeries is *Grill-Traiteur*, a pavement barbecue stand selling inexpensive grilled chicken in the evenings. Opposite is a supermarket, open from 8 am to 10 pm. There's a daytime produce stand next to the post office.

*Pizzeria Pescatore* has tomato and cheese pizza for 36F, special-item pizzas for 50F and scampi and meat dishes for 90F. *La Petite Cigale* has pizza from 50F and fresh-squeezed fruit juices for 15F.

*Le Médicis*, a trendy Creole restaurant with streetside terrace dining, has fish and meat dishes for 80F to 100F, crêpes from 40F and homemade ice cream. Food is served daily from 11.30 am to 3 pm and again from 7 pm. There's often live music on the weekends.

West of the village centre, the *Vieille Tour* in the Pullman Auberge de la Vieille Tour hotel is Gosier's most popular fine dining restaurant, serving traditional French and Creole cuisine. Open only for dinner, main courses range from lamb chops for 74F to a Caribbean seafood plate of conch, octopus, crabs and sea urchins for 119F. Salads and starters begin around 50F.

The Pullman hotel's beachside restaurant, *Ajoupa*, has a nice open-air seaside setting and a quality 70F breakfast buffet, available from 7 to 10 am, that includes croissants, pastries, fresh fruit, cereal and juice. At lunch it serves grilled fare at moderate prices.

**Main Hotel Area** In the evening you can find a couple of roadside food vans west of the Callinago Hotel. The best is the yellow and white van that parks diagonally opposite the casino; it has good baguette sandwiches for 16F to 24F and crêpes made to order for 12F to 30F.

*Alisa*, next to the Hertz office at the Créole Village, has salads for 25F and pizzas, pastas and lasagne for 45F to 60F. A couple of doors away is a small pâtisserie selling pastries, bread, baguette sandwiches, salads and ice cream.

*Hôtel Salako* has a beach hut selling sandwiches and crêpes for 20F, salads for around 30F and fairly good pizzas for 40F. It's open from noon to 5 pm daily. The hotel's indoor restaurant also has reasonable prices at lunchtime.

The resort hotels have expensive dinner restaurants with main courses for 80F to 100F, and complete meals from appetiser to dessert about twice that. The hotels also offer rather pricey buffet dinners a few times a week, most quite ordinary, although the *La Créole Beach Hôtel* puts on a nice spread. In addition there are a number of small restaurants at the upper end of Route des Hôtels that feature lobster dinners for around 175F.

## Entertainment

There's a casino with roulette and black jack open from 9 pm daily except Sunday in the resort area. The nearby Hôtel Salako has a nightclub that's open nightly. There's often music in the bar at the Pullman Auberge de la Vieille Tour hotel and on weekends at Le Médicis restaurant in Gosier village.

## SAINTE-ANNE

The village of Sainte-Anne has a pleasantly unspoiled French West Indian character. There's a seaside promenade along the west side of town and a fine white-sand beach stretching along the east side. The beach, which is shaded by sea grape trees, is a popular swimming spot for both islanders and tourists.

Also worth a visit is the town square, which is flanked by the Catholic church and town hall and has a statue of abolitionist Victor Schoelcher. It's a particularly nice scene in the evening when people stroll to the square to buy homemade sorbet from street vendors.

## Places to Stay

**Town Centre** The *Motel Sainte-Anne* (☎ 88 22 40) is on the main road on the west side of town, next to the Esso petrol station. This two-storey motel has 10 good-sized air-con rooms, some with kitchenettes. Singles/ doubles begin at a reasonable 285/320F in summer, 385/520F in winter. It's about a 10-minute walk to the beach and there's a restaurant on site.

*Auberge du Grand Large* (☎ 88 20 06; fax 88 16 69), Route de la Plage, 97180 Sainte-Anne, is opposite Sainte-Anne Beach on the corner of the beach access road. It has 10 straightforward concrete bungalows with kitchenettes that rent for 350F to 500F.

The *Mini Beach Hôtel* (☎ 88 21 13; fax 88 19 29), BP 77, 97180 Sainte-Anne, on the east end of Sainte-Anne Beach, has six rooms above its restaurant and three bungalows with kitchens. The nicest of the lot is No 1, a large airy room with tile floors, air-con, a double bed, a balcony with a fine sea view, a sitting area and a bathroom with tub and bidet; it costs 500/700F in summer/ winter. Other rooms rent from 350/500F and vary in size, but all are handsomely furnished and the place has a nice colonial-style atmosphere. Breakfast is included and the prices are the same for singles and doubles.

**Around Sainte-Anne** If you have a car an interesting option is the rural gîte *Les Hesperides* (☎ 85 73 12), Beau Manoir, 97190 Gosier, located in the hills between Gosier and Sainte-Anne, nine km from both. This attractive country home is in a tropical setting with lots of flowering bushes and the helpful proprietor, A Henry-Counannier, speaks English and welcomes foreign visitors. Rooms, which have private baths and cooking facilities, begin at 1320F a week for doubles.

*Relais du Moulin* (☎ 88 23 96; fax 88 03 92), Chateaubrun, 97180 Sainte-Anne, has a picturesque old sugar mill used as a reception area and nicely planted grounds. Accommo-

dation is in 40 rather rustic, free-standing, one-bedroom bungalows with phones, porches and refrigerators. There are four beds in each, but the two in the common area are best suited for kids. The hotel has a country setting on the south side of N4, about a five-minute drive east of Sainte-Anne. There's a pool, tennis court and children's playground. Singles/doubles begin at 330/ 480F in summer, 670/820F in winter.

*La Toubana* (☎ 88 25 78; fax 88 38 90; in Paris ☎ 42 56 46 98, in the USA ☎ (407) 777-2207), BP 63, 97180 Sainte-Anne, is on a quiet coastal cliff above a beach on the Caravelle Peninsula. There are 32 comfortable bungalows terraced down the hillside and surrounded by oleander and other flowering plants. Each has a kitchenette, air-con and a porch. There's a pool and tennis court. Singles/doubles begin at 480/610F in summer, 770/960F in winter, breakfast included. While the hotel's location, about two km west of Sainte-Anne centre, is wonderfully private, it could prove inconvenient without a car.

*Le Club Méditerrannée*, or *Club Med* (☎ 88 21 00; fax 88 06 06; in the USA ☎ (800) 258-2633), is a secluded 310-room all-inclusive hotel on Caravelle Peninsula, two km west of Sainte-Anne. It has a nice white-sand beach, its own dock and all the standard Club Med amenities. Weekly rates, which include meals and an array of water sports activities, are US$900/1500 for singles/doubles in summer, US$1340/2060 in winter.

## Places to Eat

Opposite Sainte-Anne Beach there's a row of simple open-air restaurants with tables in the sand and barbecue grills at the side. Most popular are *Chez Monique*, a friendly place offering big servings of straightforward food including chicken (40F) and grilled fish (70F), and *Chez Jose*, which has crêpes and sandwiches for around 15F as well as reasonably priced fish, chicken and beef dishes.

For fine dining there's the *Mini Beach Restaurant*, at the east side of the beach, which has a pleasantly relaxed verandah dining room and specialises in fresh seafood. Most main courses are in the 80F to 100F range but there's usually a daily special that includes an appetiser, main dish and dessert for 120F. It's open from 7.30 pm to midnight daily except on Wednesday.

The hotels outside town also offer fine dining. The restaurant at *La Toubana* specialises in lobster with prices beginning at 130F. The restaurant at the *Relais du Moulin* features French nouvelle cuisine and Creole dishes with main courses from 80F to 130F.

## SAINT-FRANÇOIS

Saint-François is a former fishing village that has boomed into Guadeloupe's second-largest tourist area. The west side of town is largely provincial in character while the east side has been given over to tourism development. The centre of the action is the deep U-shaped harbour, which is lined with restaurants, hotels, car rental offices, boutiques

and marina facilities. Just north of the marina there's an international-class golf course.

A small beach fronts Le Méridien hotel but the best beaches in the area, if not the whole island, are a 10-minute drive east of town in the direction of Pointe des Châteaux.

### Information

At the south side of the marina is the dock for boats to La Désirade, Marie-Galante and Les Saintes. (See the individual island sections for details.) The post office and a BNP bank are a block west of the harbour. The Banque Populaire has an exchange office on the north side of the marina. It doesn't charge commissions and is open from 7.30 am to noon and 2 to 4.45 pm weekdays, 7.30 am to 12.30 pm on Saturday.

The offices of Dollar, Budget, National/Europcar, Hertz and a couple of local car rental agencies are in a line on the north side of the marina, a little west of the entrance to Le Méridien hotel.

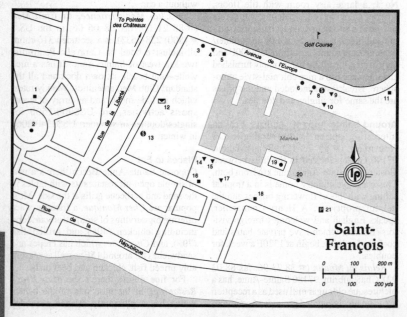

Saint-François

## Diving & Snorkelling

The beach hut at Le Méridien organises scuba diving and rents windsurfing equipment and snorkelling gear.

## Places to Stay

*Chez Honoré* (☎ 88 40 61) is an older local hostelry in the centre of town opposite the market, about a 15-minute walk from the marina and beach. The 10 rooms, upstairs above the Chez Honoré restaurant, are quite simple with single beds, very soft mattresses, louvred windows (no screens), tiny balconies, phones and air-con. Singles/doubles cost 240/320F all year round, breakfast included.

*Hotel Kayé La* (☎ 88 77 77; fax 88 74 67), BP 204, 97118 Saint-François, at the marina, has 75 modern rooms with waterfront balconies, phones, TVs, air-con and bathtubs. Singles/doubles start at 455/610F in summer, 685/860F in winter, breakfast included.

The Kayé La also books the adjacent *Hotel Residence Port Marina*, a modern three-storey apartment building with 33 air-con studios that cost 480/620F in summer/winter.

A third sister hotel, the *Golf Marine Club* (☎ 88 60 60), on the north side of the harbour, has 74 straightforward but modern rooms with TV, air-con, phones and balconies. There's a pool. Singles/doubles begin at 455/610F, breakfast included.

The new *Anse des Rochers Anchorage* (☎ 93 90 00; fax 93 91 00; in Paris ☎ 47 53 99 80), a 10-minute drive west of Saint-François, is a large resort complex with a colonial facade and splashy lime and aqua colours. It's on a nice little secluded beach with calm waters and there are water sports rentals, tennis courts, restaurants, a seaside café, pool, boutique, laundrette etc. The 356 rooms are spacious and have balconies or porches with kitchenettes, air-con and phones. Rates for one or two people are 600F in the low season, 1100F during the Christmas and New Year holidays and 900F from mid-January to mid-May. A third person is 100F more.

*Le Méridien St-François* (☎ 88 51 00; fax 88 40 71; in France ☎ 40 68 34 41, in the USA ☎ (800) 543-4300), BP 37, 97118 Saint-François, is a modern five-storey hotel with lots of flowering plants and a little white-sand beach. The 267 rooms are 1st-class but not posh. Each has a TV, phone, air-con and a small balcony. There's a pool, tennis courts and water sports hut. For standard rooms with breakfast, singles/doubles cost 1150/1525F in summer, 1400/1700F for most of the winter, jumping to 2500F around New Year's.

## Places to Eat

On the south-west corner of the marina, there's a line of inexpensive harbourside eateries selling pastries, sandwiches and ice cream. For more substantial fare, *West Indies* has quiche lorraine with a salad for 40F and Mexican enchiladas for 70F while *Le Bistro du Port*, at the end of the row, has omelettes for 30F, spaghetti for 45F and grilled fish for

---

**PLACES TO STAY**

| 1 | Chez Honoré |
|---|---|
| 5 | Golf Marine Club |
| 11 | Le Méridien St-François |
| 16 | Hotel Residence Port Marina |
| 18 | Hotel Kayé La |

**PLACES TO EAT**

| 4 | Pâtisserie/Sandwich Shop |
|---|---|
| 9 | Les Folie's Pâtisserie |
| 10 | Restaurant des Artistes |
| 11 | La Balaou |
| 14 | Le Bistro du Port |
| 15 | West Indies |
| 17 | La Printania |

**OTHER**

| 2 | Public Market |
|---|---|
| 3 | Match Supermarket |
| 6 | Casino |
| 7 | Car Rental Offices |
| 8 | Banque Populaire Exchange Office |
| 12 | Post Office |
| 13 | BNP Bank |
| 19 | Ferry Ticket Office |
| 20 | Ferries to Outer Islands |
| 21 | Parking |

GUADELOUPE

75F. Just to the east is *La Printania*, a snack bar and pizzeria with omelettes and burgers for around 20F and pizzas from 40F.

On the north side of the marina, near the car rental booths, *Restaurant des Artistes* has a nice waterfront setting and simple Italian fare. Pizza starts around 40F, while spaghetti is priced from 45F to 60F. Meals are served from noon to 2.30 pm and 7 to 10.30 pm daily, but the bar is open straight through.

Next door is *Les Folie's Pâtisserie*, which has inexpensive pastries, sandwiches for about 12F and salads from 20F to 35F. You can get takeaway food or eat at one of their café tables.

Near the Golf Marine Club hotel there's a second Italian restaurant, another pâtisserie/sandwich shop and a large Match supermarket.

The Méridien hotel has an informal beachfront restaurant and bar with moderately priced sandwiches that's open until 5 pm. The hotel's upmarket *La Balaou* restaurant has a different theme buffet dinner nightly from 7.30 pm at a cost of 195F; weekends generally feature Creole and French fare.

One of the area's more highly regarded restaurants is *La Louisiane* (☎ 88 44 34), in the Sainte Marthe quarter, up the hill from the airstrip. The cuisine is French with Creole hints; dishes include the likes of crayfish with fennel, saffron shark and sea egg pâté. Dinner for two will cost around 500F.

### Entertainment
The Méridien's Lele Bar has live bands most evenings from 8 to 11 pm and there's a casino with blackjack and roulette on the north side of the marina.

### POINTE DES CHÂTEAUX
It's just a 10-minute drive from Saint-François to Pointe des Châteaux, the easternmost point of Grande-Terre. This intriguing coastal area has white-sand beaches, limestone cliffs and fine views. From the end of the road you can make a couple of short hikes, including a 10-minute walk to the hilltop cross where there's a good view of the

jagged nearshore bird islets and the island of La Désirade. The beach at the end of the point has rough surf and a steep shoreline, but there are more protected white-sand beaches to the north-west.

Anse Tarare is a nudist beach on a sheltered cove a couple of km west of the road's end. The dirt road north of the main road is signposted 'Plage Tarare'.

A few minutes' drive to the west, a signposted side road leads a km north to Anse à la Gourde, a lovely sweep of white coral sands. The waters are good for swimming and snorkelling, but be careful of sharp nearshore coral shelves.

### Places to Eat
A simple beach restaurant at the end of the road at Pointe des Châteaux sells ice cream and sandwiches for 15F and local juices for 10F.

*Chez Honoré* (☎ 88 40 61), an open-air restaurant facing the beach at Anse à la Gourde, specialises in seafood. A complete dinner that includes crab farci, grilled fish and dessert costs 90F; the same dinner with grilled lobster instead of fish costs 150F.

### LE MOULE
Le Moule served as an early French capital of Guadeloupe and was an important Amerindian settlement in pre-colonial times. Consequently, major archaeological excavations have taken place in the area and Guadeloupe's archaeological museum is located on the outskirts of town.

Although the town itself is not a must-see sight, the centre is worth a stroll if you've come this way. The town square has a few historic buildings, including the town hall and a neoclassical Catholic church. Along the river there are some discernible waterfront ruins from an old customs building and a fortress dating back to the original French settlement.

There's a beach with calm reef-protected waters at l'Autre Bord, about a km east of town, while Baie du Moule on the west side of town is popular with surfers.

### Edgar Clerc Archaeological Museum

This modern museum (☎ 23 57 57), on a coastal cliff in the Rosette area, has Amerindian petroglyphs, pottery shards, tools made of shells and stone and an exhibition on local excavations. It's closed on Wednesday but is otherwise open from 9 am to 12.30 pm and 2 to 5.30 pm; on Saturday and Sunday it remains open until 6.30 pm. Admission is free for children under 12, 5F for children aged 12 and older and 10F for adults. The museum is about a km north on La Rosette Rd (D123) on the western outskirts of Le Moule.

### Places to Stay & Eat

The *Tropical Club Hotel* (☎ 93 97 97; fax 93 97 00) BP 121, 97160 Le Moule, is a 72-room hotel on a nice white-sand beach about a km east of Le Moule. Rooms have two single beds and two bunk-style beds, balcony kitchenettes, TV, air-con and phones. There's a pool, a moderately priced French/Creole restaurant, a bar, a Hertz car rental office, an activities desk and a water sports centre. Singles/doubles cost 470/590F in summer, 785/880F in winter, breakfast included.

There are a few restaurants in town including *Restaurant Le Madras* on the waterfront at the west end of Rue St Jean. In the Baie du Moule area there's a bakery on N5 just west of the beach.

### NORTHERN GRANDE-TERRE

The northern half of Grande-Terre is a rural area of grazing cattle, cane fields and abandoned roadside sugar mills. The main sights are Porte d'Enfer and Pointe de la Grande Vigie, about a 40-minute drive north of Le Moule. The road can be a bit narrow, but it's in good condition and paved all the way.

From Le Moule, drive up past the museum in Rosette, then turn right on D120 and follow that road north. As you get closer to Porte d'Enfer the route will be signposted.

### Porte d'Enfer

Despite its name, Porte d'Enfer ('Gate of Hell') is a lovely sheltered cove surrounded by cliffs and backed by a small beach. Inside the cove the water is shallow but deep enough for swimming, while the entire coastline outside of the cove is tumultuous, with pounding surf and strong currents. There are picnic tables and sea cotton trees near the beach – it would make a fine spot to break for a picnic lunch.

As you continue north there's a nice viewpoint about a km beyond Porte d'Enfer that looks back at the beach and the area's craggy coastal cliffs. About a km farther along if you look to the east you'll see a series of seven coastal points, the second of which has a blowhole.

### Pointe de la Grande Vigie

Pointe de la Grande Vigie, the island's northernmost point, offers scenic views from its high sea cliffs. On a clear day you can see Antigua to the north and Montserrat to the north-west, both about 75 km away. There's a nice view of Grande-Terre's east side from the parking lot and you can take a short walk out to the farthest point for a view of the west side of the island.

### Anse Bertrand

Anse Bertrand is a modest coastal town, a mix of concrete homes and simple wooden structures. The coastal section still shows signs of damage from hurricane Hugo in 1989.

At Anse Laborde, about a km north of town, there's an attractive little beach with a seaside restaurant, *Folie Plage*, that serves fish for 75F, grilled lobster for 100F, and also rents out a few rooms (*Chez Prudence*, ☎ 22 11 17) at 200F.

### Port-Louis

Port-Louis is a sleepy fishing village full of character, from its ageing wooden houses splashed in bright colours to the main street lined with turn-of-the-century iron lampposts.

At the north side of town is La Plage de Souffleur, a nice, long bathing beach that's especially popular on weekends. The beach is backed by white cedar trees (*poui*) that drop delicate pink flowers twice a year (*souffleur* means 'blowing flowers').

**Places to Eat** There are a couple of snack wagons selling crêpes, sandwiches, hamburgers and hot dogs on the beach. Down by the boat harbour at the south end of town there are some small unpretentious Creole restaurants, including the friendly *La Corrido du Sud* which offers fresh fish meals with dessert and wine for 60F.

*Le Poisson d'Or*, in the centre of town opposite the Catholic church, has waterfront dining, a pleasant local ambience and a changing chalkboard menu featuring seafood dishes from 65F to 100F. It's open from noon to 3 pm daily and for dinner by reservation.

### South to Morne-à-l'Eau
South of Port-Louis the road passes inland through a couple of agricultural towns, while the coast is largely mangrove swamp.

The main sight in Morne-à-l'Eau, the largest town in central Grande-Terre, is its cemetery, at the intersection of roads N5 and N6. Guadeloupe's most elaborate burial ground, it's terraced with raised vaults and tombs, many decorated in chequered black and white tiles.

### Grands Fonds
The central part of Grande-Terre, known as the Grands Fonds, is an undulating landscape of mounded hills and deeply creviced valleys (*fond* means valley). It's a pretty rural area that's given over to small farms and lush green pastures and crossed by narrow winding roads.

The northern section of Grands Fonds is settled by the descendants of the Blancs Matignon, a group of White colonists who retreated to the hills following the abolition of slavery in the mid-19th century. Unlike people on the rest of the island, they have largely kept to themselves and not married outside the region.

Grands Fonds is a fun place to drive – expect to get lost in the criss-cross of roads,

but as long as you head in a southerly direction, you'll eventually come out to the coast.

To get into the heart of Grands Fonds simply take N5 east one km from Morne-á-l'Eau and then turn south on D109.

# Basse-Terre

Shortly after entering Basse-Terre island from Pointe-à-Pitre, you have a choice of three main routes: north along the coast, south along the coast, or along the Route de la Traversée across the interior through the national park.

### ROUTE DE LA TRAVERSÉE
The road that heads across the centre of the island, Route de la Traversée (D23), slices through the Parc National de la Guadeloupe, the huge forest reserve that occupies the interior of Basse-Terre. It's a lovely mountain drive that passes fern-covered hillsides, thick bamboo stands and enormous mahogany and gum trees. Other rainforest vegetation en route includes orchids, heliconia and ginger.

Route de la Traversée begins off N1 about 15 minutes west of Pointe-à-Pitre and is well signposted. There are a few switchbacks but driving is not tricky if you don't rush and it's a good two-lane road all the way. Although

Orchid

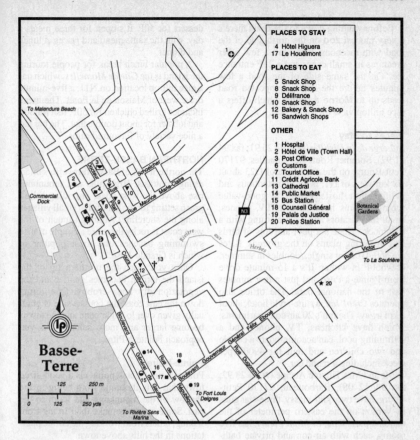

**PLACES TO STAY**

4  Hôtel Higuera
17  Le Houëlmont

**PLACES TO EAT**

5  Snack Shop
8  Snack Shop
9  Délifrance
10  Snack Shop
12  Bakery & Snack Shop
16  Sandwich Shops

**OTHER**

1  Hospital
2  Hôtel de Ville (Town Hall)
3  Post Office
6  Customs
7  Tourist Office
11  Crédit Agricole Bank
13  Cathedral
14  Public Market
15  Bus Station
18  Counsell Général
19  Palais de Justice
20  Police Station

**Basse-Terre**

To Malendure Beach

Commercial Dock

Botanical Gardens

To La Soufrière

To Fort Louis Delgres

To Rivière Sens Marina

0   125   250 m
0   125   250 yds

the road could easily be driven in an hour, give yourself double that to stop and enjoy the scenery – more if you want to do any hiking or break for lunch.

Don't miss **Cascade aux Ecrevisses**, a pretty little jungle waterfall that drops into a broad pool. From the parking area the waterfall is just a three-minute walk on a well-beaten but lushly green trail. The roadside pull-off is clearly marked on D23, two km east of Maison de la Forêt.

At **Maison de la Forêt** there's a staffed roadside exhibit centre with a few simple displays on the forest (in French only), open

from 9 am to 5 pm daily. A map board and the trailhead for three hikes is at the back of the centre. The shortest walk takes 10 minutes while the longest is an hour-long jaunt through the rainforest. There are covered picnic tables about 50 metres west of the centre and in roadside spots along the stream.

Continuing west, if the weather's clear you'll find a nice view of Pointe-à-Pitre from the rear of Gîte de Mamelles, a hilltop restaurant on the north side of the road. The restaurant takes its name from the smooth double-mounded hills to the south.

Before winding down to the coast there's a very modest **zoo** on the north side of the road with raccoons, birds and a few other creatures in small cages and a 25F entrance fee. On the same side of the road a few minutes before the zoo a signposted road leads up to **Morne á Louis** which offers a nice hilltop view on a clear day.

### Places to Stay

*Auberge de la Distillerie* (☎ 94 25 91; fax 94 11 92), Sommet Route de Versailles, 97170 Petit-Bourg, on the north side of D23 about six km west of N1, is an unpretentious and inviting little hostelry with 14 good-value rooms. Rooms have air-con, TV, phones, small refrigerators and a patio strung with a hammock. There's a pool and lots of birds and flowering plants on the grounds. Rates are 360/410F for singles/doubles in summer, 450/650F in winter. It's a 15-minute drive from Pointe-à-Pitre and just a few minutes east of the national park. The office also operates *Creol' Inn*, a suite-style hotel, about a km away. The inn's 20 air-con apartments, which have kitchens, TV, phones and a swimming pool, can accommodate a couple and two children and rent for 4900F per week including a rental car.

Mr and Mrs Tiburce Accipe (☎ 94 23 92; fax 94 12 08), Barbotteau, 97170 Petit-Bourg, have two quite classy, three-star gîtes in Vernou on the eastern perimeter of the national park. One, *Le Mont Fleuri*, has five rooms, each with air-con and private bathroom, plus a shared kitchen and pool. They cost 1470F per week for two people. At the other, *Les Alpinias*, there are eight air-con apartments with kitchenettes, balconies and TV that rent for 3080F a week for up to four people.

### Places to Eat

If you want to grab something to eat on the way into the national park, the *Auberge de la Distillerie* has a small bakery with crispy baguettes, croissants and sandwiches. The hotel has a restaurant with a varied menu with many offerings in the 60F to 75F range as well as a full children's meal including dessert for 50F. It's open for three meals a day, with the same menu and prices at lunch and dinner.

A popular lunch break for people touring the island is the *Gîte de Mamelles*, which has a nice hilltop location on N11; a five-minute drive west of Maison de la Forêt. The menu includes grilled chicken for 50F, fish for 80F and lobster for about double that. The bar has a nice variety of flavoured rums.

## NORTHERN BASSE-TERRE

The northern half of Basse-Terre offers interesting contrasts. High hills and mountains rise above the west coast providing a lush green setting for the handful of small villages along the shoreline. Although much of the west coast is rocky there are a couple of nice swimming beaches, the most popular of which is Grande Anse.

Once you reach the northern tip of the island the terrain becomes gentler and the vegetation dry and scrubby. Continuing down the east coast the countryside is gradually given over to sugar cane and the towns become larger and more suburban as you approach Pointe-à-Pitre.

### Pointe-Noire

Pointe-Noire ('black point') is a good-sized town that gets its name from being in the shadow of the mountains that loom to the east. Some residents make their living from fishing, others from working the coffee plantations in the hills above town.

The area is best known for its furniture and cabinet-making industries. Just off N2, at the south side of town, is **Maison du Bois**, a small museum of traditional woodworking tools and products (admission 5F). There's also a showroom selling furniture made of mahogany and other native woods harvested from the surrounding forests. Labels identify many of the trees on the grounds.

**Places to Stay** *Camping Traversée* (☎ 98 21 23) is a camping ground at Anse de la Grande Plaine, on the coast a few km south of Pointe-Noire. It has a garden-like setting that attracts lots of hummingbirds and there

GUADELOUPE

are well-equipped facilities including hot showers and a laundry. Setting up a tent costs 50F per day for one person, 20F for each additional person, and there are also some rustic cabins with little porches that rent for 180F a double. Breakfast is available for 30F.

### Deshaies

Deshaies is an appealing little harbourside village surrounded by lofty hills. It has a deep sheltered bay and is a rather popular stop with yachters; there's a customs office at the southernmost end of town.

Grande Anse, just two km north of Deshaies, is an absolutely beautiful beach with no development in sight. There are scenic hills at either end of the beach and mounds of glistening ochre-hued sands along the shore. While it's arguably the finest beach in Basse-Terre, with the exception of weekends it's usually not crowded.

**Places to Stay** *Les Sables d'Or* (☎ 28 44 60), on Grande Anse beach adjacent to the Karacoli restaurant, is a tiny and not very neat camping area that charges 60F for one person (80F for two) for a tent. It also has a few rundown bungalows for 140F a double.

There are a handful of gîtes on the road that leads inland from Grande Anse beach towards Caféière. One of the larger and better priced ones is *Jacky Location* (☎ 28 43 53; fax 28 50 95), Plage de la Grande Anse, 97126 Deshaies, which has seven rooms that rent from 1260F to 2860F per week, with the most expensive accommodating six people. It's about a 10-minute walk from the beach and has a swimming pool.

*Fort Royal Touring Club* (☎ 25 50 00; fax 25 50 01), Pointe du Petit Bas-Vent, 97126 Deshaies, is on a nice sandy stretch a couple of km north of Grande Anse. The hotel, which was formerly a Club Med, has 194 rooms and bungalows with TVs and phones. There are tennis courts, complimentary windsurfing equipment and two beaches, one of which is clothing-optional. Room prices are 590/850F for singles/doubles from 11 January to 15 March, 485/680F from 16 March to 11 May and 420/600F the rest of

the year. A buffet breakfast costs 40F more per person.

**Places to Eat** In the village of Deshaies there are a handful of restaurants that cater mostly to beachgoers, sailors and weekend visitors. *Le Madras* is a quaint little moderately priced restaurant opposite the waterfront on the north side of town. *Le Mouillage* is a dockside restaurant specialising in seafood and Creole dishes, most priced around 100F. *La Note Bleue*, at the south side of town, is a large restaurant with a harbourside patio and fish or ribs for around 80F.

In the parking area fronting Grande Anse beach you'll find a couple of food stalls selling inexpensive crêpes and sandwiches. One of them, *Cuisine Locale*, also has salads from 15F to 30F.

A nice place to try traditional Creole food is *Le Karacoli* (☎ 28 41 17), a family-run restaurant in a covered garden setting right on Grande Anse beach. An excellent starter is the crab farci while main courses include lobster, some nicely spiced colombo dishes and red snapper with cloves. Side dishes include the likes of breadfruit gratin and various sweet potato and plantain preparations. Main courses are priced from 50F to 120F, while starters are half that and there's also a good-value menu du jour for 75F. Karacoli is open daily for lunch only, from noon to about 4 pm.

### Sainte-Rose

In days past Sainte-Rose was a major agricultural town and while sugar production has declined and a number of the mills have closed, sugar cane is still an important crop in this area. There are a couple of rum-related tourist sights on the outskirts of town.

**Musée du Rhum** This museum, dedicated to the history of sugar and rum production, is at the site of the former Reimonenq Distillery, about 500 metres inland from N2 in the village of Belleuve, just south-east of Sainte-Rose. Exhibits include an old still, cane extraction gears and a vapour machine dating from 1707. It's open from 9 am to 5 pm Monday to Saturday, from 10 am to 1 pm and 3 to 5 pm on Sunday. Admission is 30F for adults, 15F for children.

**Domaine de Séverin** A fun place to stop is Domaine de Séverin, a working mill and distillery, which has a nice country setting, doesn't charge an entrance fee and has exhibits in English explaining the distillation process. Visitors are free to go out the back and get a close-up look at the distillery works. The tasting room offers samples of their rums, including a nice light citron-flavoured one. Domaine de Séverin is near the village of Cadet, which is off N2 midway between Sainte-Rose and Lamentin. The turn-off from N2, as well as the five-minute drive up to the site, is well signposted. It's open to 5 pm.

## SOUTH TO CAPESTERRE-BELLE-EAU

N1, the road that runs along the east coast of Basse-Terre, is for the most part pleasantly rural, a mix of sugar cane fields, cattle pastures, banana plantations and small towns.

**Valombreuse Floral Parc**, in the hills west of Petit-Bourg, is a pleasant 14-hectare botanical garden. Trails wind through thick growths of flowering heliconias and gingers and there are lots of orchids, anthuriums and other tropical plants. Inside the park is a simple open-air restaurant above a little stream with a few Creole dishes like colombo cabris for around 70F. The park is open from 9 am to 6 pm daily; admission is 35F for adults, 20F for children, including a drink. The road leading off N1 to the park, five km inland, is well signposted.

In the centre of the village of **Sainte-Marie** a bust of Columbus and two huge anchors comprise a modest roadside monument, honouring the explorer who landed on this shore in 1493. If you're up for a dip there's a brown-sand beach, **Plage de Roseau**, on the south side of town.

Two km farther south and visible from the roadside is a bone-white **Hindu temple** adorned with the colourfully painted figures of Shiva and other Hindu gods, followed

shortly by a **galledrome** where cockfights take place.

The road is lined with flamboyant trees on the north side of **Capesterre-Belle-Eau**, a good-sized town that has a Match supermarket, some local eateries and a petrol station.

On the south side of Capesterre-Belle-Eau is the **Allée Dumanoir**, a stretch of N1 bordered on both sides by majestic century-old royal palms.

## CHUTES DU CARBET

Unless it's overcast, the drive up to the Chutes du Carbet lookout will reward you with a view of two magnificent waterfalls plunging down a sheer mountain face.

Starting from Saint Sauveur on N1, the road runs 8.5 km inland, a beautiful 15-minute drive up through a lush green rainforest. It's a good hard-surfaced road all the way, although it's a bit narrow and twisting. Three km before the end of the road there's a marked stop at the trailhead to **Grand Étang**, a placid lake circled by a loop trail. It's just a five-minute walk from the roadside parking area down to the edge of the lake and it takes about an hour more to stroll the lake's perimeter. (Due to the danger of bilharzia infection, this is not a place for a swim.)

The road ends at the **Chutes du Carbet lookout**. You can see the two highest falls from the upper car park, where a signboard marks the trailhead to the base of the falls. The well-trodden walk to the second-highest waterfall (110 metres) takes 30 minutes; it's about a two-hour hike to the highest waterfall (115 metres). It's also possible to hike from the lookout to the summit of La Soufrière, a hardy three-hour walk with some wonderfully varied scenery.

There are picnic facilities at the lookout along with a few food stalls selling plate lunches of simple barbecue fare. This is a very popular spot for outings and can get quite crowded on weekends and holidays.

A nice stop on the way back is the flower nursery **Les Jardins de Saint-Eloi**, where there's a short path through a garden of ginger, heliconia and anthuriums. It's at the side of the road (parking opposite the entrance) about 1.5 km south of Grand Étang and there's no admission charge.

## TROIS-RIVIÈRES

Most visited as a jumping-off point to Les Saintes, Trois-Rivières has a sleepy town centre of old leaning buildings with delicate gingerbread and rusting tin roofs. The town is surrounded by lush vegetation and has fine views of Les Saintes, just 10 km offshore to the south.

Signs at the west side of the town centre point the way from N1 to the dock, one km away, where the ferry leaves for Terre-de-Haut. The restaurant La Roche Gravée, a few minutes' walk from the dock, provides parking for ferry passengers at a cost of 12F a day.

There's a black-sand beach good for swimming at Grande Anse, a few km west of Trois-Rivières.

### Parc Archéologique des Roches Gravées

This lovely park contains both a botanical garden and some impressive petroglyphs that date to around 300 AD. There are huge banyan trees, flowering tropical plants, scampering lizards and paths that wind up and around boulders, some of which are covered with Arawak carvings of human faces and simple designs thought to represent animals.

The park is on the road to the ferry dock, 200 metres north of the waterfront. It's open daily from 9 am to 4.30 pm and admission is a bargain at 4F. You can get a brochure in English upon request.

### Places to Stay

Le Joyeux (☎ 92 74 78), Faubourg, 97114 Trois-Rivières, is a pleasant little place in the village of le Faubourg, about a km west of Trois-Rivières. It has six straightforward air-con rooms with cooking facilities that rent for 280F a double and there's a moderately priced restaurant.

The Grand Anse Hôtel (☎ 92 92 91), Route Vieux Fort, 97114 Trois-Rivières, on the main beach road about three km west of town, has 16 air-con rooms with balconies, phones and kitchenettes that rent from 400/500F for singles/doubles, breakfast included. It's just a short walk to the beach and there's also a pool.

### Places to Eat

There are a few snack bars and restaurants on the waterfront near the ferry dock. La Terrasse du Park, in town near the town hall, serves moderately priced Creole food.

West of town, the Grand Anse Hôtel has a Creole restaurant with a menu du jour for 70F. La Paillote du Pêcheur, a popular waterfront restaurant about 400 metres south of the Grand Anse Hôtel, has a menu that ranges from pizza to lobster.

## LA SOUFRIÈRE

From Trois-Rivières there are a couple of ways to get to La Soufrière, the active volcano that looms above the southern half of the island.

If you have extra time you could take the D6 coastal road through Vieux-Fort, a town known for its eyelet embroidery, and then turn north to La Soufrière from Basse-Terre.

However, the most direct route to La Soufrière is to follow D7 north-west from Trois-Rivières, turn west on N1 for a few km and then follow the signs north to Saint-Claude. This is a nice jungly drive into the mountains; you'll cross some small streams and pass banana plantations before reaching the village of Saint-Claude, just south of the national park boundaries. If you want to grab a bite to eat (there's no food available in the park), Saint-Claude has a couple of local restaurants and small grocers.

From Saint-Claude signs point to La Soufrière, six km to the north-east on D11. The steep road up into the park has a few beep-as-you-go hairpin turns and narrows in places to almost one lane but it's a good solid road all the way. If it's fogged in, proceed slowly as visibility can drop to just a few metres.

**Maison du Volcan**, on the right about two km after entering the park, has a small exhibit centre with displays on vulcanology and La Soufrière's last eruption in July 1976. The centre is also the trailhead for a couple of hour-long walks, including one to Chute de Galleon, a scenic 40-metre waterfall on the Galleon River.

There are a couple of viewpoints and picnic areas as the road continues up the mountain for the 15-minute drive to **La Savane à Mulet**, a parking area at an elevation of 1142 metres. From here, there's a clear-on view straight up La Soufrière (when it's not covered in clouds or mist) and you can see and smell vapours rising from nearby fumaroles.

If you're up for a hardy 1½-hour hike to La Soufrière's sulphurous, moonscape-like summit, a well-beaten trail starts at the end of the parking lot along a gravel bed and continues steeply up the mountain through a cover of low shrubs and thick ferns. In addition to a close-up view of the steaming volcano the hike offers some fine vistas of the island. It's also possible to make a four-hour trek from La Savane à Mulet to the Chutes du Carbet lookout.

The road continues east another 1.75 km, taking in a lookout and views of sulphur vents before it dead-ends at a relay station.

---

**Precautions at La Soufrière**

The higher you go into the La Soufrière rainforest, the cooler it gets and the more likely you are to encounter rain. Even when it's sunny below it's a good idea to bring along rain gear if you plan to do any hiking. Hikers should also bring along a light jacket or sweater and a full canteen.

Young children and people with heart conditions or respiratory ailments should be cautious near the sulphur vents. ∎

---

## BASSE-TERRE

Basse-Terre, the administrative capital of Guadeloupe, is home to a population of 14,000.

The south side of town, along the Blvd Félix Eboué, has a couple of rather imposing government buildings including the Palais de Justice and the sprawling Conseil Général, the latter flanked by water fountains.

At the north side of town, opposite the commercial port, is the old town square. It's bordered by the ageing Hôtel de Ville (town hall), the tourist office, customs and some older two and three-storey buildings that overall are more run-down than quaint. There's also a pharmacy on the square, a Crédit Agricole bank and a central parking area.

There's an unadorned cathedral near the river about five minutes' walk south of the square and a modest little botanical garden on the west side of town about 250 metres beyond the police station.

The bus station is on the shoreline at the west end of Blvd Félix Eboué. Opposite the north end of the station is the public market.

Fort Louis Delgres, which dates from 1643, is at the south side of town, as is the Rivière Sens Marina.

### Places to Stay

The *Hôtel Higuera* (☎ 81 11 92), on the main square a stone's throw from the town hall, is a quite basic little local hotel run by a friendly woman who speaks good English. Rooms cost from 110F.

*Le Houëlmont* (☎ 81 35 96), 34 Rue de la République, 97100 Basse-Terre, opposite the Conseil Général, has eight very simple rooms, with either a double or two twin beds, a private bathroom and air-con. Doubles cost 310F, plus 30F for breakfast.

### Places to Eat

Opposite the bus terminal there are a handful of cheap, if somewhat scruffy, snack shops serving sandwiches from around 7F. There's a *Délifrance* a block west of the town square on Rue Docteur Pitat, with good breads, pastries and sandwiches. There are other snack shops nearby on Rue Schoelcher.

For something more substantial, *Le*

*Houëlmont* at 34 Rue de la République is a well-regarded restaurant with a menu of the day for about 100F.

## MALENDURE BEACH/PIGEON ISLAND

The road up the west coast from Basse-Terre (N2) follows the shoreline much of the way, passing fishing villages, small towns and a few black-sand beaches. The landscape gets drier as you continue north into the lee of the mountains. There's not much of interest for visitors until Malendure Beach, a rather popular dark-sand beach that's the departure point for snorkelling and diving tours to nearby Pigeon Island.

Jacques Cousteau brought Pigeon Island to international attention a couple of decades ago by declaring it to be one of the world's top dive sites. The waters surrounding the island are now protected as the Reserve Cousteau, an underwater park.

There are a few dive shops (see the Diving section earlier in this chapter) and a tourist information booth on Malendure Beach. Nautilus (☎ 98 89 08) has a glass-bottom boat tour from Malendure Beach daily at 10.30 am, noon, 2.30 and 4 pm. It takes 1¼ hours and costs 80F for adults, 40F for children; snorkelling gear is provided for those who want to jump in for a closer look.

It's a five-km drive from Malendure Beach to the beginning of Route de la Traversée (D23) for the scenic 45-minute drive back to Pointe-à-Pitre.

### Places to Stay

In the centre of the village of Pigeon, just south of Malendure Beach, there are several private room for rent and gîte signs. One is for Guy Yoko (☎ 98 71 42), a member of the Gîte de France network, who has 12 rooms that rent weekly from 1650F a double to 4290F for a flat that can accommodate eight people.

The restaurant *Le Rocher de Malendure* (☎ 98 70 84; fax 98 89 92), Malendure, 97125 Bouillante, has a couple of bungalows with nice sea views that rent for 350F a night.

### Places to Eat

There are huts on Malendure Beach selling cheap sandwiches and snacks and a couple of simple open-air beachside restaurants with more substantial meals.

For something more upmarket, most people head south to the village of Pigeon. *Le Rocher de Malendure*, on a headland between Pigeon and Malendure Beach, has a nice seaside setting and features a good-value meal of ti-punch, accras, fish brochettes or barbecued chicken and coffee for 110F. It's open for lunch until about 3.30 pm daily as well as for dinner on Friday and Saturday.

*Le Pigeonnier*, in the centre of Pigeon, is an unpretentious restaurant with a water view. The chalkboard menu features French/Creole food, with starters priced around 50F and main dishes such as grilled parrotfish or coconut land crab from 70F to 100F. It's open for lunch from noon to 2.30 pm, for dinner from 6.30 to 9.30 pm.

Jacques Cousteau

# Terre-de-Haut

Lying 10 km off Guadeloupe is Terre-de-Haut, the largest of the eight small islands that make up Les Saintes. The island was too hilly and dry for sugar plantations and most islanders still trace their roots to the early seafaring Norman and Breton colonists.

Terre-de-Haut is quaint and unhurried, quite French in nature and almost Mediterranean in appearance. Although it's a tiny package it's got a lot to offer, including a strikingly beautiful landscape of volcanic hills and deep bays. The island has fine protected beaches with good swimming and windsurfing, a fort with a botanical garden, good restaurants and a range of places to stay at reasonable prices. In all, it's one of the most appealing little islands in the Eastern Caribbean.

Although tourism is growing, many islanders still rely on fishing as a mainstay. You can often find the fishers mending their nets along the waterfront and see their locally made boats, called *saintoises*, lined along the shore.

Terre-de-Haut is only five km long and about half as wide. If you don't mind uphill walks you can get around on foot, although many people opt to rent motorbikes. Ferries to Guadeloupe and Terre-de-Bas dock right in the centre of Bourg des Saintes, the island's only village. The airstrip is to the east, a 10-minute walk from the village centre.

## BOURG DES SAINTES
Home to most of the island's residents, Bourg des Saintes is a picturesque village with a decidedly Norman accent. Its narrow streets are lined with whitewashed red-roofed houses with shuttered windows and yards of flowering hibiscus.

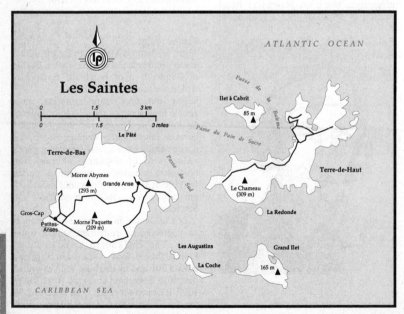

GUADELOUPE

The ferry is met by young girls peddling *tourment d'amour* ('agony of love') cakes with a sweet coconut filling – an island treat that makes for a tasty light breakfast.

At the end of the pier there's a small courtyard with a gilded column commemorating the French Revolution; it's a bustling place at ferry times, quiet at others. Turn right and in a minute you'll be at the central town square, flanked by the *mairie* (town hall) and an old stone church.

It's a fun town to kick around. There are small restaurants, ice-cream shops, scooter rentals, art galleries and gift shops clustered along the main road, which is pedestrian-only during the day. Galerie Martine Cotten, opposite the pier, has some nice island paintings. Most shops close from noon to 2 pm.

### Information

**Money** It's best to bring along sufficient francs to cover your stay as the island's bank, Crédit Agricole, is only open on Tuesday and Friday from 9 am to 2.30 pm. Credit cards are accepted at hotels (but not bottom-end guesthouses) and by the motorbike rental companies.

**Post & Telecommunications** There are card phones at the pier. You can buy phonecards nearby at Digemar Vad, a souvenir shop. The post office is on the main road a few minutes' walk south of the town hall. When writing to any hotel simply follow the hotel name with Terre-de-Haut, 97137 Les Saintes, Guadeloupe, French West Indies.

### Diving

Club Nautique des Saintes (☎ 99 54 25), south of the village, arranges diving around the island.

### Places to Stay

**In Town** There are room for rent signs

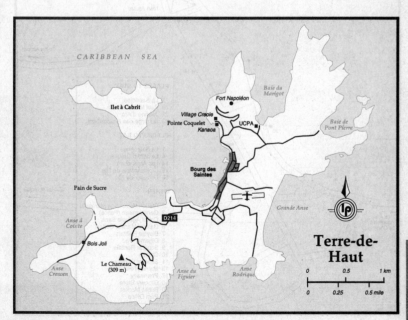

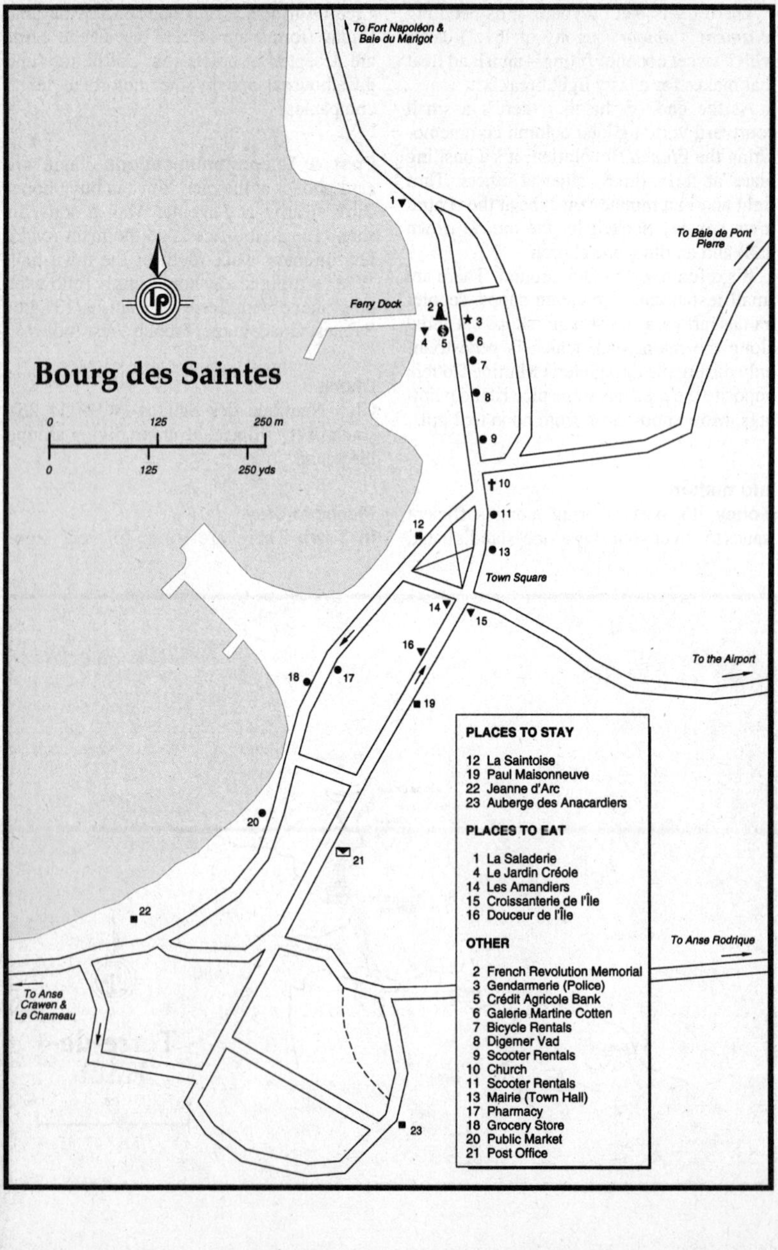

**Bourg des Saintes**

0    125    250 m
0    125    250 yds

To Fort Napoléon &
Baie du Marigot

To Baie de Pont
Pierre

Ferry Dock

Town Square

To the Airport

To Anse Rodrique

To Anse
Crawen &
Le Chameau

**PLACES TO STAY**
12  La Saintoise
19  Paul Maisonneuve
22  Jeanne d'Arc
23  Auberge des Anacardiers

**PLACES TO EAT**
1   La Saladerie
4   Le Jardin Créole
14  Les Amandiers
15  Croissanterie de l'Île
16  Douceur de l'Île

**OTHER**
2   French Revolution Memorial
3   Gendarmerie (Police)
5   Crédit Agricole Bank
6   Galerie Martine Cotten
7   Bicycle Rentals
8   Digemer Vad
9   Scooter Rentals
10  Church
11  Scooter Rentals
13  Mairie (Town Hall)
17  Pharmacy
18  Grocery Store
20  Public Market
21  Post Office

GUADELOUPE

around the island and it's usually not difficult to find a room in a small guesthouse, though things can get a bit tight in winter.

One good-value place is *Paul Maisonneuve* (☎ 99 53 38), on the main road just south of the town hall. The three rooms are simple but bright, with comfortable foam beds, standing fans, glass louvred windows and a rate of 150F for doubles. The bathroom is shared and kitchen facilities are available. English is not spoken, but the owners are friendly and accommodating and there shouldn't be any problems if you don't speak French.

*Jeanne d'Arc* (☎ 99 50 41) is a popular hotel on the waterfront about 500 metres south of the town centre. It has 10 straightforward rooms, each with a private bathroom, two beds and a fan, and there's a terrace with a good ocean view. Singles or doubles cost 290F with breakfast.

*La Saintoise* (☎ 99 52 50), a 10-room hotel on the square opposite the town hall, has no particular charm but the rooms are clean and good-sized and have private bathrooms, air-con and phones. Singles/doubles cost 250/350F, breakfast included.

*Auberge des Anacardiers* (☎ 99 50 99; fax 99 54 51) is an eclectic hillside inn south-east of the town centre, about a 15-minute walk from the pier. There are 12 smallish but comfortable rooms with a few antiques, tropical decor, air-con and phones; some have balconies and TVs. Singles/doubles cost 350/400F in summer and 400/500F in winter for rooms with shared showers and 450/500F in summer and 650/700F in winter for nicer rooms with private bathroom. Rates include breakfast. There's a French restaurant specialising in seafood (120F for a three-course meal) and a nice pool with a great view of the harbour.

**North of Town** *Village Creole* (☎ 99 53 83; fax 99 55 55), Pointe Coquelet, about a km north of the pier, consists of 22 very comfortable, contemporary, duplex apartments. Each is split level; there's a fully equipped kitchen and a living/dining room downstairs and two bedrooms with skylights upstairs.

Each apartment has two bathrooms, two phones and a small safe. The coast is predominantly rocky, but there's a bit of a beach out front and the area is peaceful. The management is pleasant and speaks English. Rates are a reasonable 460F a double in summer, plus 100F each for a third or fourth person. In winter it costs 640/840/960F for two/three/four people. For waterfront units add 100F in summer, 150F in winter. There's a 20% surcharge during the Christmas holidays and from mid-February to mid-March.

*Kanaoa* (☎ 99 51 36; fax 99 55 04), adjacent to Village Creole, has 14 simple seaside rooms and bungalows. Singles/doubles rent from 380/440F in summer, 495/630F in winter, breakfast included. There's a restaurant on site serving Creole and French dishes at moderate prices.

## Places to Eat

There are lots of casual restaurants around town that cater to day trippers and offer a meal of the day in the 60F to 90F range.

On the right as you step off the boat is *Le Jardin Créole*, which has a pleasant 2nd-floor balcony overlooking the harbourside courtyard and a menu heavy on crêpes, coffees and ice cream. A breakfast of juice, bread and coffee costs 35F and the daily lunch dish is around 70F.

*Douceur de l'Île*, south of the town hall, is a popular, unpretentious restaurant with good prices. You can get a simple breakfast for 20F, sandwiches for 15F and a plat du jour with the likes of colombo cabrit or lambi for 45F. It's closed on Monday.

*Les Amandiers* is a nice place on the town square with both indoor and outside dining. There's a good-value lunch that includes accras or salad, fish, rice and banana flambé for 60F; otherwise, main dishes are in the 40F to 50F range.

A good place for salads and light seafood dishes is *La Saladerie*, a few minutes' walk north of the pier on the main road. Most dishes are in the 50F to 75F range. It's closed on Tuesday.

*Restaurant Plongée*, a km south of town, is a simple beachside open-air restaurant with salads and starters for around 30F and a range of main dishes for 45F to 70F.

*Croissanterie de l'Île*, opposite the town hall, sells croissants, breads and pastries.

## FORT NAPOLÉON

Fort Napoléon, built in the mid-19th century and never used in battle, stands intact and well preserved on the north side of the harbour. There's a fine hilltop view of Bourg des Saintes and you can look across the channel to Fort Josephine, a small fortification on the Ilet à Cabrit. On a clear day you can also see Marie-Galante and La Désirade.

The grounds surrounding the fort are planted in cacti gardens. The fort's barracks contain a small museum with a few simple historical displays in both French and English and some minor exhibits of local contemporary art. You can walk through on your own or join a 30-minute guided tour conducted in French. The fort is open daily, from 9 am to noon only, and admission is 15F. Fort Napoléon is 1.5 km north of the centre of Bourg des Saintes; simply turn left as you come off the pier and follow the road uphill.

## BAIE DU MARIGOT

Baie du Marigot is a pleasant little bay with a calm protected beach about a km north of Bourg des Saintes. Even though it's just a 15-minute walk from town there's very little development in the area and the beach doesn't get crowded. It's fairly close to Fort Napoléon so you could combine a visit to the two; after visiting the fort turn left at the bottom of the winding fort road and bear left again a few minutes later as you near the bay.

### Places to Stay

*UCPA* (☎ 99 54 94; fax 99 55 28), Baie du Marigot, has 60 rooms in free-standing duplex and fourplex buildings. It sits alone above Baie du Marigot with its own jetty and a fine sea view. Geared for windsurfing holidays, UCPA offers week-long packages that include accommodation, meals, lessons and unlimited use of sailboards and Hobie Cat catamarans.

## BAIE DE PONT PIERRE

Baie de Pont Pierre is a lovely reef-protected beach with light brown sand and a splendid setting. This deep horseshoe-shaped bay is backed by sea grape trees and flanked on both sides by high cliffs, while an offshore islet at its mouth gives the illusion of closing the bay off as a complete circle. It's a very gentle place, with a nice mix of tourists and locals; there are even tame goats that mosey onto the beach and lie down next to sunbathers. The beach is an easy 1.5 km walk north-east of Bourg des Saintes.

## EAST COAST BEACHES

The long sandy beach **Grande Anse**, immediately west of the airport runway, has rough seas and water conditions that are more suitable for surfing than swimming. The north side of this windy beach is backed by clay cliffs.

South of Grande Anse beach and about two km from town is **Anse Rodrique**, a nice beach on a protected cove that usually has good swimming conditions.

## SOUTH-WEST BEACHES

Two km south-west of Bourg des Saintes, **Anse à Cointe** is a good beach for combining swimming and snorkelling. The snorkelling is best at the north side of the beach. There's also good snorkelling and a sandy beach at **Pain de Sucre**, the basalt 'Sugarloaf' peninsula that's about 700 metres to the north.

**Anse Crawen**, 500 metres south of the Bois Joli hotel, is a secluded clothing-optional beach just a couple of minutes' walk down a dirt path that starts where the coastal road ends. Anse Crawen has golden sands and a natural setting backed by trees.

### Places to Stay

*Bois Joli* (☎ 99 50 88; fax 80 07 75), Anse à Cointe, the island's only resort-like hotel, has 29 rooms fronting a golden-sand beach. Most accommodation is bungalow-style with small porches, air-con, showers, toilets and bidets; the cost is 1050F a double, plus 160F for a third or fourth person. There are also some small straightforward rooms with good views that rent for 550/710F for singles/doubles. Rates include breakfast and dinner. The hotel's poolside restaurant has a fine sea view and features steak and seafood dishes priced around 100F, about twice that if you add a starter, wine and dessert.

## LE CHAMEAU

A winding cement road leads to the summit of Le Chameau, which at 309 metres is the island's highest point. There are picture-perfect views of Bourg des Saintes and the Ilet à Cabrit on the way up and sweeping views of the other Les Saintes islands, Marie-Galante, Basse-Terre and Dominica from the top of the hill. The summit is capped by an old stone sentry tower that's deteriorated but still has metal steps leading to the top where there's an unobstructed view as far as the eye can see.

To get to Le Chameau turn south from the Bourg des Saintes pier and continue one km on the coastal road. At Restaurant Plongée turn inland on D214; 500 metres later, turn left on the cement road and follow it up 1.75 km where it ends at the tower. From town it's a moderately difficult hour-long walk to the top or a fun five-minute motorbike ride.

## GETTING THERE & AWAY
### Air
Air Guadeloupe (☎ 99 51 23) flies to Terre-de-Haut from Pointe-à-Pitre at 8 am Monday to Saturday and at 5 pm daily, returning 15 minutes later. The fare is 180F one way (135F for students) and 269F for a one-day excursion.

### Sea
Antilles Trans Express (☎ 83 12 45) leaves from the east side of Pointe-à-Pitre harbour at 8 am daily, returning from Terre-de-Haut at 3.45 pm. The crossing takes 50 minutes.

From 1 December to 30 April, Antilles Trans Express (☎ 88 48 63) also has boat service from the Saint-François Marina, leaving at 8 am on Tuesday and Thursday and returning from Terre-de-Haut at 4 pm.

The crossing takes 80 minutes, as the boat stops at Marie-Galante en route.

Brudey Frères (☎ 90 04 48) leaves Pointe-à-Pitre at 8 am daily for Terre-de-Haut, departing Terre-de-Haut at 3.45 pm. There's also a Wednesday boat from Saint-François, with the same departure times.

The return fare with either company, from either Guadeloupean port, is 160F for adults, 85F for children.

The *Princesse Caroline* (☎ 86 95 83) departs from Trois-Rivières at 8 am daily for the 20-minute crossing to Terre-de-Haut, returning in late afternoon. The return fare is 80F.

## GETTING AROUND
With advance reservations, most hotels will pick guests up free of charge at the airport or pier.

### Motorbike
Motorbikes are a great way to tour the island. Although roads are narrow there are only a few dozen cars (and no car rentals) on Terre-de-Haut, so you won't encounter much traffic. With a motorbike you can zip up to the top of Le Chameau and Fort Napoléon, get out to the beaches and explore the island pretty thoroughly in a day. The motorbikes are capable of carrying two people but, because the roads are so winding, unless you're an accomplished driver it's not advisable to carry a passenger.

There are lots of rental locations on the main road leading south from the pier, but the ones that set up dockside seem as good as any. Most charge 180F a day and require a 1500F to 2000F deposit or an imprint of a major credit card. Motorbikes come with gas but not damage insurance, so if you get in an accident or spill the bike the repairs will be charged to your credit card.

Motorbike riding is prohibited in the centre of Bourg des Saintes from 9 am to noon and 2 to 4 pm. Although you'll see people flaunting the law, if you run into a gendarme expect to get stopped.

## Bicycle

A couple of the motorbike rental booths in town also rent bicycles. The rate is 60F for a standard bicycle, 70F for a mountain bike, plus a 500F deposit.

## Tours

There are a few taxi minivans that provide two-hour tours of the island for about 50F per person, if there are enough people, or 350F for the whole van. Look for them parked along the street between the pier and the town hall right after the ferry arrives.

# Terre-de-Bas

Terre-de-Bas, just a km to the west of Terre-de-Haut, is the only other inhabited island in Les Saintes.

A bit less craggy than Terre-de-Haut, Terre-de-Bas once had small sugar and coffee plantations and is largely populated by the descendants of African slaves.

It's a quiet rural island and tourism has yet to take root, but there is a regular ferry service between the islands, making it possible for visitors to go over and poke around on a day excursion.

The main village, Petites-Anses, is on the west coast. It has hilly streets lined with trim houses, a small fishing harbour and a quaint church with a graveyard of tombs decorated with conch shells and plastic flowers.

Grande Anse, diagonally across the island on the east coast, is a small village with a little 17th-century church and a nice beach.

One-lane roads link the island's two villages: one of the roads cuts across the centre of the island, passing between the two highest peaks, and the other goes along the south coast. If you enjoy long country walks it's possible to make a loop walk between the two villages (about a nine-km round trip) by going out on one road and returning on the other. Otherwise there's usually an inexpensive jitney bus that runs between the villages.

There are shops and a couple of local eateries in the villages where you can pick up something for lunch.

## GETTING THERE & AWAY

The boat *L'Inter* shuttles between Terre-de-Haut and Terre-de-Bas (25F) four to five times a day between 8 am and 4 pm.

# Marie-Galante

Marie-Galante, 25 km south-east of Guadeloupe proper, is the largest of Guadeloupe's outer islands. Compared to the archipelago's other islands, Marie-Galante is relatively flat, its dual limestone plateaus rising only 150 metres. It is roughly round in shape with a total land area of 158 sq km, much of which is planted in sugar cane. The island is exceedingly rural in character and totally untouched by mass tourism. It offers visitors lovely uncrowded beaches and some pleasant country scenery. Very few English-speaking tourists come this way and few islanders speak any English at all.

Marie-Galante has a population of about 13,000, half of whom live in Grand-Bourg, on the south-west coast. Most of the rest are evenly divided between its two smaller towns, Saint-Louis and Capesterre.

In the early 1800s Marie-Galante boasted nearly 100 sugar mills and the countryside is still dotted with the scattered ruins of most of them. Today sugar production is concentrated at one mill, while cane is distilled into rum at three distilleries. Most of the cane is still cut by hand and hauled from the fields using ox carts.

The distilleries are among the island's main 'sights'. The Distillerie Poisson, midway between Saint-Louis and Grand-Bourg, bottles the island's best known rum under the Père Labat label. Distillerie Bielle, between Grand-Bourg and Capesterre, offers tours of its age-old distillery operation. Both places have tasting rooms and sell rum.

## GRAND-BOURG

Grand-Bourg is the commercial and admin-

Marie-Galante

istrative centre of the island. The town was levelled by fire in 1901 and its architecture is a mix of turn-of-the-century buildings and more drab concrete structures. The ferry dock is at the centre of town. Opposite the dock are a handful of local cafés and restaurants and the post office, customs office and town hall are all within a couple of blocks of the waterfront.

**Château Murat**, about two km from Grand-Bourg on the north side of the road to Capesterre, is an 18th-century sugar estate that's undergone extensive restoration and is reopening as a museum.

### Places to Stay & Eat

*Philippe Bavarday* (☎ 97 83 94; fax 97 81 90), 97112 Grand-Bourg, is a member of the Gîtes de France network and head of the local tourist information office. His gîte has four three-star air-conditioned rooms that cost 1650F per week for up to two people. It's near the coast, a few km east of town in the section of Les Basses, between the airport and Grand-Bourg centre.

If you want to be in the centre of town, there's *Auberge de l'Arbre à Pain* (☎ 97 73 69), Rue Jeanne d'Arc, 97112 Grand-Bourg, a few minutes' walk from the dock. It has

GUADELOUPE

seven small, straightforward rooms that rent for 250F with breakfast. It also has a good Creole restaurant.

There are a handful of local cafés and restaurants opposite the dock, most specialising in seafood. There's a bakery and a supermarket about two blocks inland.

## SAINT-LOUIS

Saint-Louis, a fishing village of about 4000 residents, is the island's main anchorage for yachters and a port for ferries from Guadeloupe. There's a little market at the end of the dock and a couple of restaurants and the post office are just east of that.

Although there are beaches along the outskirts of Saint-Louis, some of the island's most beautiful strands lie a few km to the north. The golden sands of Plage de Moustique, Anse Canot and Anse du Vieux-Fort unfold one after the other once you round the point that marks the north end of Saint-Louis Bay.

### Places to Stay & Eat

The island's largest hotel, *Le Salut* (☎ 97 02 67), 97134 Saint-Louis, has 15 simple rooms starting around 400F, including breakfast and dinner in the hotel restaurant.

*Chez Henri*, south of the dock and opposite Le Salut, is quite popular for seafront dining and has good local food at moderate prices.

## CAPESTERRE

Capesterre (population 4100), on the southeast coast, is a seaside town backed by hills. There are sea cliffs and hiking trails to the north of the village.

On the south side of town there's a beautiful beach, Plage de la Feuillère, and a second nice beach, Petite Anse, is about a km to the south-west. Fun Evasion (☎ 97 35 21) rents windsurfing equipment and gives lessons at Plage de la Feuillère.

### Places to Stay & Eat

The *Hôtel Hajo* (☎ 97 32 76), 97140 Capesterre, which has a Mediterranean decor and six ocean-view rooms, is about two km

south-west of Capesterre and a short walk from the beach. Rooms, which have fans and private bathrooms, cost 270F a double and there's a reasonably priced French/Creole restaurant on site.

*Le Touloulou* (☎ 97 32 63; fax 97 33 59), 97140 Capesterre, on the beach at Petite Anse, has a few simple bungalows from 250F and an open-air beachside restaurant serving traditional Creole and French food such as sea urchin blaff, colombo and conch dishes at moderate prices.

## GETTING THERE & AWAY
### Air

Air Guadeloupe flies to Marie-Galante from Pointe-à-Pitre at 7 am, 1 and 6 pm Monday to Saturday and at 7.30 am and 6 pm on Sunday. Flights return from Marie-Galante 20 minutes later. The fare is 180F one way (136F for students) and 289F for a one-day excursion. The airport is midway between Grand-Bourg and Capesterre, about five km from either.

### Boat

The inter-island crossing from Grande-Terre to Marie-Galante can be a bit rough, so if you're not used to bouncy seas it's best to travel on a light stomach and sit on deck.

There are two boat companies that make the run. On both, the return fare on all boats (except the car ferry) between the two islands is 160F for adults, 85F for children.

**Antilles Trans Express** Antilles Trans Express (☎ 83 12 45) leaves from the east side of Pointe-à-Pitre Harbour at 8 am, 12.30 and 5 pm Monday to Saturday and at 8 am, 5 and 7 pm on Sunday. The 12.30 pm boat goes via Saint-Louis, but all other sailings are to Grand-Bourg only. The boat leaves Grand-Bourg at 6 and 9 am and 3.45 pm Monday to Saturday and at 6 am, 3.45 and 6 pm on Sunday. The crossing takes 35 minutes.

In winter, Antilles Trans Express (☎ 88 48 63) has boat service to Saint-Louis from the Saint-François Marina, leaving at 8 am on Tuesday and Thursday and returning from

Marie-Galante at 4.45 pm. The trip takes 45 minutes. There's sometimes a Thursday crossing in summer as well.

In addition, Antilles Trans Express operates the *Amanda Galante* car ferry, which leaves Saint-François for Saint-Louis at 7.45 am on Tuesday and Sunday. The return departure from Saint-Louis is at 4 pm. The cost is 140F return for adults plus 265F return for a car. The crossing takes 90 minutes and car reservations should be made a day in advance.

Antilles Trans Express also offers day tours of Marie-Galante that include the boat crossing, a land tour and lunch for 325F, but require a 10-person minimum.

**Brudey Frères** Brudey Frères (☎ 90 04 48) sails to Grand-Bourg, leaving Pointe-à-Pitre at 8 am, 2 and 5 pm weekdays; at 8 am, 12.30 and 5 pm on Saturday; and at 8 am, 4.45 and 6 pm on Sunday. The ferry departs Grand-Bourg at 6 and 9 am and 3.45 pm Monday to Saturday and at 6 am, 3.45 and 6 pm on Sunday.

Also, Monday only, there's a boat from Saint-François to Saint-Louis that leaves at 8 am and makes a return departure from Saint-Louis at 5.45 pm.

### GETTING AROUND
### Bus
During the day, except for Sunday, inexpensive minibuses make regular runs between the three villages.

### Car, Motorbike & Bicycle
Cars, motorbikes and bicycles can be rented from Caneval (☎ 97 97 76) at the Shell station in Grand-Bourg. Other agents include Magauto (☎ 97 98 75) on Rue Savane, a couple of blocks east of the dock in Grand-Bourg, and Stamag (☎ 97 02 15) and La Somat (☎ 97 07 33) in Saint-Louis. Bicycles can also be rented from the Bureau Touristique de Marie-Galante (☎ 97 77 48), 51 Rue du Presbytère, Grand-Bourg.

Cars generally cost from 250F to 300F a day, motorbikes 170F and bicycles about half that.

# La Désirade

La Désirade, about 10 km off the eastern tip of Grande-Terre, is the archipelago's least developed and least visited island. Looking somewhat like an overturned boat when viewed from Guadeloupe, La Désirade is 11 km long and two km wide, with a central plateau that rises 273 metres at its highest point, Grand Montagne.

The terrain is desert-like, with coconut and sea grape trees along the coast and scrub and cactus on the hillsides. It's too dry and arid for extensive agriculture and though some people raise sheep, most of La Désirade's 1600 inhabitants make their living from fishing and boat building.

The uninhabited north side of the island has a rocky coastline with rough open seas, while the south side has sandy beaches and reef-protected waters.

La Désirade's harbour and airport are on the south-west side of the island in **Grande Anse** (also called Le Bourg), the main village. The island's town hall, post office and library are also in Grande Anse. There are smaller settlements at **Le Souffleur** and **Baie Mahault**. La Désirade's main road runs along the south coast, joining the villages.

In 1725 Guadeloupe established a leper colony on La Désirade and for more than two centuries victims of the dreaded disease were forced to make a one-way trip to the island. The **leprosarium**, which was run by the Catholic Sisters of Charity, closed in the mid-1950s. Its remains, a chapel and a cemetery are just east of Baie Mahault.

There are white-sand beaches near all three villages and for a good view of the island there's an hour-long hike up Grand Montagne.

### Places to Stay & Eat
The 10-room *L'Oasis* (☎ 20 02 12) hotel and restaurant and the *Hôtel Le Mirage* (☎ 20 01 08), both in the Desert Saline quarter of Grand Anse, have simple rooms at 180/200F for singles/doubles. There are also a few

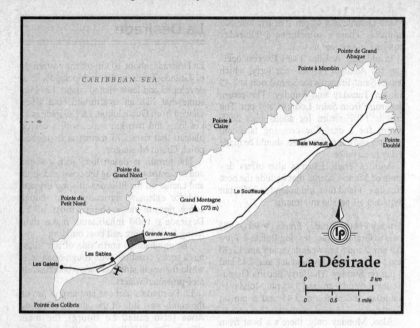

rooms in private homes around Grande Anse for 150F to 200F.

There are a handful of both moderately priced seafood restaurants and cheaper snack bars in Grande Anse and Baie Mahault.

## GETTING THERE & AWAY
### Air
Air Guadeloupe flies to La Désirade from Pointe-à-Pitre at 7 am daily except on Sunday and at 4 pm daily except on Saturday; return flights depart from La Désirade 25 minutes later. The fare is 180F one way (135F for students) and 289F for a one-day excursion.

### Boat
There are two ferries to La Désirade, *Mistral* (☎ 88 48 63) and *Sotramade* (☎ 20 02 30). They leave from Saint-François daily at 8.30 am and 4 or 4.30 pm. The ferries depart from La Désirade for Saint-François at 6.15 am and 3.30 pm. The ride takes about 45 minutes and the return fare is 100F. The ferry companies also offer day-tour packages that include the boat ride and a land tour of La Désirade for around 200F.

## GETTING AROUND
Bicycle, scooter and car rentals are all available from Loca Sun (☎ 20 01 11) at the marina.

# Martinique

Martinique is a slice of France set down in the tropics. Its shops are full of Paris fashions, every village has a corner pâtisserie selling freshly baked baguettes and croissants, and its resorts are crowded with holiday-makers from mainland France.

The capital, Fort-de-France, is a bustling city of 100,000, the largest in the French West Indies. Most of the island's other large towns are modern and suburban-like, linked to the capital by multi-lane highways and fast-moving traffic.

Nevertheless, nearly a third of Martinique is forested and other parts of the island are given over to pineapples, bananas and sugar cane fields. You can still find sleepy fishing villages untouched by development, remote beaches and lots of hiking tracks into the mountains.

Martinique is volcanic in origin, topped by the 1397-metre Mont Pelée, an active volcano. Pelée last erupted in 1902, gaining an infamous place in history by wiping out the then-capital city of Saint-Pierre, along with its entire population. Today the ruins of Saint-Pierre are Martinique's foremost tourist sight.

## ORIENTATION

Martinique's only commercial airport is in Lamentin, nine km east of Fort-de-France. The main resort areas are on Martinique's south-west coast, from Pointe du Bout to Sainte-Anne. Roads on the island are good and despite the island's large size, no place is more than a two-hour drive from Fort-de-France.

# Facts about the Island

## HISTORY

When Columbus sighted Martinique it was inhabited by Carib Indians who called the island Madinina, 'Island of Flowers'. Three decades passed before the first party of French settlers, led by Pierre Belain d'Esnambuc, landed on the north-west side of the island. There they built a small fort and established a settlement that would become the capital city, Saint-Pierre. The next year, on 31 October 1636, King Louis XIII signed a decree authorising the use of slaves in the French West Indies.

The settlers quickly went about colonising the land and by 1640 had extended their grip down to Fort-de-France, where they constructed a fort on the rise above the harbour. As forests were cleared to make room for sugar plantations, conflicts with the native Caribs escalated into warfare and in 1660 those Caribs that had survived the fighting were finally forced off the island.

The British took a keen interest in Martinique, invading and holding the island for most of the period from 1794 to 1815. The island prospered under British occupation; the planters simply sold their sugar in British

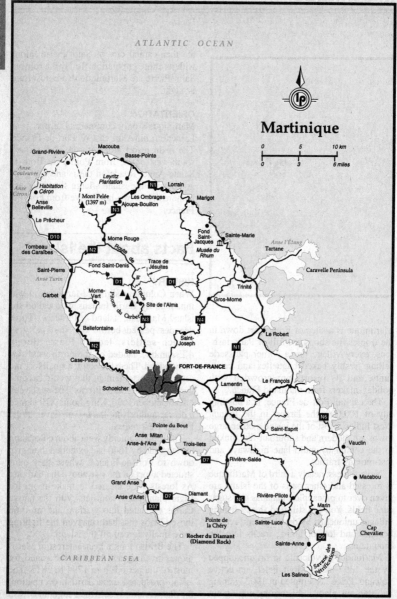

**Martinique**

ATLANTIC OCEAN

CARIBBEAN SEA

markets rather than French. Perhaps more importantly, the occupation allowed Martinique to avoid the turmoil and bloodshed of the French Revolution. By the time the British returned the island in 1815, the Napoleonic Wars had ended and the French empire was again entering a period of stability.

Not long after the French administration was re-established on Martinique, the golden era for sugar cane began to wane, as glutted markets and the introduction of sugar beets on mainland France eroded prices. With less wealth, the aristocratic plantation owners lost much of their political influence and the abolitionist movement, led by Victor Schoelcher, gained momentum.

It was Schoelcher, the French cabinet minister responsible for overseas possessions, who convinced the provisional government to sign the 1848 Emancipation Proclamation that brought an end to slavery in the French West Indies.

On 8 March 1902, in the most devastating natural disaster in Caribbean history, the Mont Pelée volcano erupted violently, destroying the city of Saint-Pierre and claiming the lives of its 30,000 inhabitants. Shortly thereafter, the capital was moved permanently to Fort-de-France. Saint-Pierre, which had been regarded as the most cultured city in the French West Indies, was eventually rebuilt, but it has never been more than a shadow of its former self.

In 1946 Martinique became an overseas department of France, with a status similar to those of metropolitan departments, and in 1974 it was further assimilated into the political fold as a region of France.

## GEOGRAPHY
At 1080 sq km, Martinique is the second-largest of the French West Indies. Roughly 65 km long and 20 km wide, it has a terrain punctuated by hills, plateaus and mountains.

The highest point is the 1397-metre Mont Pelée, an active volcano at the northern end of the island. The centre of the island is dominated by the Pitons du Carbet, a scenic mountain range reaching 1207 metres.

Martinique's irregular coastline is cut by deep bays and coves while the mountainous rainforest in the interior feeds numerous rivers.

## CLIMATE
Fort-de-France's average daily high temperature in January is 28°C (83°F) while the low averages 21°C (70°F). In July the average daily high is 30°C (86°F) while the low averages 23°C (74°F).

The annual rainfall in Fort-de-France is 1840 mm (72 inches). Measurable rain falls an average of 13 days a month in April, the driest month, and about twice as often in September, the rainiest month. Martinique's average humidity is high, ranging from 80% in March and April to 87% in October and November.

The mountainous northern interior is both cooler and rainier than the coast.

## FLORA & FAUNA
Martinique has lots of colourful flowering plants, with the type of vegetation varying with altitude and rainfall. Rainforests cover the slopes of the mountains in the northern interior, which are luxuriant with tree ferns, bamboo groves, climbing vines and hardwood trees like mahogany, rosewood, locust and gommier.

The drier southern part of the island has brushy savanna vegetation such as cacti, frangipani trees, balsam, logwood and acacia shrubs.

Martinique has *Anolis* lizards, manicous (opossums), mongoose and venomous fer-de-lance snakes. Endangered birds include the Martinique trembler, white-breasted trembler and white-breasted thrasher.

## GOVERNMENT
Martinique, an overseas department of France, is represented in the French Parliament by four elected deputies and two senators.

A prefect, who is appointed by the French Minister of the Interior, represents the central government and oversees the execution of French law by island authorities. There are two island-wide legislative bodies, the Conseil Général and the Conseil Régional, each with about 40 members who are elected by universal suffrage.

Martinique is further divided into 34 *communes*; each has an elected municipal council which in turn appoints a mayor. Quite a bit of political diversity and power rests at the municipal level.

## ECONOMY
Agriculture accounts for many of the jobs in Martinique, with sugar cane, bananas and pineapples the leading crops. The cane is used by Martinique's 14 distilleries to produce rum, the island's best known export item. Tourism is the leading growth sector of the economy and in a drive to encourage more investment the government has been subsidising the construction of new hotels. About 325,000 tourists visit the island annually.

## POPULATION & PEOPLE
The population of Martinique is 359,600, of which nearly one-third live in the Fort-de-France area. The majority of residents are of mixed ethnic origin. The earliest settlers were from Normandy, Brittany, Paris and other parts of France; shortly after, African slaves were brought to Martinique; later, smaller numbers of immigrants came from India, Syria and Lebanon.

## ARTS & CULTURE
French and Creole influences are dominant in Martinique's cuisine, language, music and customs.

The Black Pride movement known as *négritude* emerged as a philosophical and literary movement in the 1930s largely through the writings of Martinican native Aimé Césaire, a poet and long-time (and current) mayor of Fort-de-France.

The *biguine* (or beguine), a dance with a bolero rhythm, originated in Martinique in the 1930s.

### Dress Conventions
Except for fine dining, dress is casual but generally stylish. Topless bathing is common on the island, particularly at resort beaches.

## RELIGION
More than 90% of all islanders are Roman Catholic. There are also Seventh Day Adventist, Baptist and Evangelical Christian denominations as well as Hindus, Bahai's and a small Jewish community.

## LANGUAGE
French is the official language but islanders commonly speak creole when chatting among themselves. English is spoken at larger hotels but is understood rather sporadically elsewhere so if you don't have a fair command of French, a dictionary and phrasebook will prove quite useful.

# Facts for the Visitor

## VISAS & EMBASSIES
US and Canadian citizens can stay up to three weeks by showing proof of citizenship in the form of a current passport, an expired (up to five years) passport, or an official birth certificate accompanied by a driving licence or other government-authorised photo ID. For stays of over three weeks, a valid passport is required. Citizens of the EU (European Union) need an official identity card, valid passport or French *carte de séjour*. Citizens of most other foreign countries, including Australia, need a valid passport and a visa for France.

A return or onward ticket is officially required of visitors.

### Consulates
The US Consulate (☎ 63 13 03) is at 14 Rue Blénac and the British Consulate (☎ 61 56 30) is on Route du Phare, both in Fort-de-France.

There are also consulates in Fort-de-France for Belgium, Denmark, Germany, Haiti, Italy, Mexico, the Netherlands, Norway, Spain, Sweden, Switzerland and Venezuela.

## CUSTOMS

Citizens of EU countries are allowed to bring in 300 cigarettes, 1.5 litres of spirits and four litres of wine duty free. Non-EU citizens are allowed to bring in 200 cigarettes, a bottle of spirits and two litres of wine duty free. All visitors are allowed to bring in 'large allowances of rum' as well.

Yachts are allowed to have firearms on board, but must declare them.

## MONEY

The French franc is the island currency. Hotels, larger restaurants and car rental agencies accept MasterCard (Eurocard) and Visa (Carte Bleue). For most other situations, you'll need to use francs. Avoid changing money at hotel lobbies, where the rates are worse than at exchange offices or banks. More information is under Money in the Facts for the Visitor chapter at the front of the book.

## TOURIST OFFICES

Martinique's main tourist office is the Office Départemental du Tourisme (☎ 63 79 60; fax 73 66 93), Blvd Alfassa, 97206 Fort-de-France, Martinique, French West Indies.

There is also a tourist information booth at the airport that usually stays open until the last flight comes in.

There are local information bureaus (syndicats d'initiative) in several towns including Sainte-Anne (☎ 76 73 06), Diamant (☎ 76 40 11), Saint-Pierre (☎ 78 15 02), Le Prêcheur (☎ 52 02 57) and Grand-Rivière (☎ 55 72 74). Most information distributed by the syndicats d'initiative is in French only.

### Overseas Reps

Martinique, like the other French West Indies, is represented in most countries by the French Government Tourist Office. Some of these overseas offices are:

Australia
 French Government Tourist Office, BNP Building, 12th Floor, 12 Castlereagh St, Sydney, NSW 2000 (☎ (02) 231-5244; fax (02) 221-8682)

Canada
 French Government Tourist Office, 30 St Patrick St, Suite 700, Toronto, Ontario M5T 3A3 (☎ (416) 593-4723; fax (416) 979-7587)
 French Government Tourist Office, 1981 Ave McGill College, Suite 490, Montreal, Quebec H3A 2W9 (☎ (514) 288-4264; fax (514) 845-4868)
France
 Office du Tourisme des Antilles Françaises, 2 Rue des Moulins, 75001 Paris (☎ (1) 44 77 86 00; fax 40 20 01 14)
Germany
 French Government Tourist Office, Westendstrasse 47, Postfach 100128, D6000 Frankfurt am Main 1 (☎ 69 75 60 83; fax 69 75 32 87)
UK
 French Government Tourist Office, 178 Piccadilly, London W1V OAL (☎ (071) 491-7622; fax (071) 493-6594)
USA
 French West Indies Tourist Board, 610 Fifth Ave, New York, NY 10020 (☎ (900) 420-2003 – a toll call which costs 50 cents per minute; fax (212) 247-6468)
 French Government Tourist Office, 676 N Michigan Ave, Chicago, IL 60611 (☎ (312) 751-7800)
 French Government Tourist Office, 9454 Wilshire Blvd, Beverly Hills, CA 90212 (☎ (310) 271-7838)

## BUSINESS HOURS

Although hours vary, many shops are open from 8.30 am to 6 pm Monday to Friday and until 1 pm on Saturday. Banks, and many other offices, are typically open from 7.30 am to 4.30 pm, with a two-hour lunch siesta beginning at noon. Note that banks close at noon on the day before a public holiday.

## HOLIDAYS

Public holidays on Martinique are:

| | | |
|---|---|---|
| *New Year's Day* | – | 1 January |
| *Labor Day* | – | 1 May |
| *Easter Sunday* | – | late March/early April |
| *Easter Monday* | – | late March/early April |
| *Ascension Thursday* | – | 40th day after Easter |
| *Pentecost Monday* | – | eighth Monday after Easter |
| *Slavery Abolition Day* | – | 22 May |
| *Bastille Day* | – | 14 July |
| *Schoelcher Day* | – | 21 July |
| *Assumption Day* | – | 15 August |
| *All Saints Day* | – | 1 November |
| *Armistice Day* | – | 11 November |
| *Christmas Day* | – | 25 December |

## CULTURAL EVENTS

Martinique has a spirited Mardi Gras Carnival during the five-day period leading up to Ash Wednesday. The streets spill over with revellers, rum-fuelled partying, costume parades, music and dancing. Much of the activity is centred around La Savane in Fort-de-France.

On a smaller scale, every village in Martinique has festivities to celebrate its patron saint's day.

Saint-Pierre commemorates the 8 May eruption of Mont Pelée with live jazz and a more sombre candlelight procession from the cathedral.

The Tour de la Martinique, a week-long bicycle race, is held in mid-July. The Tour des Yoles Rondes, a week-long race of traditional sailboats, is held in early August. A 22-km semi-marathon around Fort-de-France is held in November. The biennial week-long Martinique Jazz Festival is held in December on odd-numbered years, while a guitar festival is held on even-numbered years.

## POST

There are post offices in all major towns. It costs 2.50F to send a postcard to France, 3.20F to the UK, 2.70F to the USA or Canada and 4.20F to Australia. This rate also covers letters up to 10 grams. You can buy postage stamps at some tobacco shops *(tabacs)*, hotels and souvenir shops in addition to post offices.

With the exception of Fort-de-France, where street addresses are given, the mailing address for each hotel in this chapter is simply the hotel name followed by the postal code, town and 'Martinique, French West Indies'. The postal code for Pointe du Bout, Anse Mitan and Anse-à-l'Ane is 97229, for Diamant 97223, for Sainte-Anne 97227 and for Saint-Pierre 97250.

## TELECOMMUNICATIONS

Public phones in Martinique accept French phonecards *(télécartes)*, not coins. The cards cost 36F or 87F, depending on the calling time, and are sold at post offices and at shops

marked *télécarte en vente ici*. Card phones can be found at post offices, the airport and larger parks, among other public places. For directory assistance, dial 12.

When making a local call, or when calling Martinique from elsewhere in the French West Indies (or vice versa), dial just the six-digit local number. When calling Martinique from outside the French West Indies, add the 596 area code in front of the six digits.

More information on phonecards and making long-distance calls is under Telecommunications in the Facts for the Visitor chapter in the front of the book.

## ELECTRICITY

Electricity is 220 volts AC, 50 cycles, and plugs have two round prongs.

## WEIGHTS & MEASURES

Martinique uses the metric system, with elevations noted in metres, speed limit signs in km and weights in grams. Time is given using the 24-hour clock.

## BOOKS & MAPS

The bilingual French/English *A Cruising Guide to Martinique*, part of the Guide Trois Rivières series (Édition Trois Rivières, BP 566, 97242 Fort-de-France, Martinique), is a comprehensive sailing manual for cruising around Martinique.

*Texaco*, a novel by Patrick Chamoiseau which won the prestigious Prix Goncourt, recounts the social history of a shanty town in Martinique.

*Le Quatrième Siècle* (1962) and *Malemort* (1975) by Martinican native Édouard Glissant examine contemporary West Indian life against the backdrop of slavery and colonial rule.

The best road map of Martinique is the Institut Géographique National's No 511 map, which is sold around the island for 45F. However, this same map (on glossy paper, dotted with ads and labelled 'Carte Routière') is distributed free by car rental agencies at the airport.

## MEDIA

The daily *France-Antilles* has island news. Other French-language newspapers, such as *Le Monde*, are flown in from the mainland. Larger newsstands in Fort-de-France and major tourist areas sell a few English-language newspapers including the *International Herald-Tribune*.

Radio France Outre-Mer (RFO) has radio frequencies at 92 and 94.5. The Martinique TV network RFO (Channel 1) carries a lot of local programming, while a couple of other stations air standard programming from mainland France.

For tourist information these free publications are useful: the English-language *Martinique Info*, a 50-page booklet of general information; the bilingual *Ti Gourmet*, a pocket-size restaurant guide offering a complimentary drink at many island restaurants; and *Choubouloute*, a weekly French-language publication listing events, entertainment and other current information.

## HEALTH

Medical care is of high quality by Caribbean standards. There are a number of general hospitals on the island, including Hôpital de la Meynard (☎ 55 20 00) on D13 at the north-east side of Fort-de-France.

There is a risk of bilharzia (schistosomiasis) infection throughout the island; the main precaution is to avoid wading or swimming in fresh water. More information on this disease is under Health in the Facts for the Visitor Chapter.

## DANGERS & ANNOYANCES

The fer-de-lance, a large pit viper, can be found on Martinique, particularly in overgrown and brushy fields. The snake's bite is highly toxic and sometimes fatal. Hikers should be alert for the snakes and stick to established trails.

Beware of manchineel trees on some beaches, as rainwater dripping off them can cause skin rashes and blistering.

## EMERGENCY

Emergency telephone numbers include:

| | |
|---|---|
| Ambulance – | ☎ 75 22 80 |
| Fire | – ☎ 18 |
| Police | – ☎ 17 |
| Sea rescue – | ☎ 63 92 05 |

## ACTIVITIES
### Beaches & Swimming

The beaches in the southern half of the island have white or tan sands while those in the northern half have grey or black sands. Many of Martinique's nicest beaches are scattered along the south-west coast from Grand Anse to Les Salines. In the Trois-Ilets area, Anse-à-l'Ane and Anse Mitan are both good sandy beaches that attract a crowd. Popular east-coast beaches include Cap Chevalier and Macabou to the south and the Caravelle Peninsula beaches of Anse l'Étang and Tartane. Beaches along the north-east side of the island can have very dangerous water conditions and have been the site of a number of visitor drownings.

### Diving

Saint-Pierre is one of the island's top dive sites with wrecks, coral reefs and plenty of marine life. More than a dozen ships that were anchored in the harbour when the 1902 volcanic eruption hit now lay on the sea bed, most in 10 to 50 metres of water; they include a 50-metre sailing ship, cargo ships and a tug.

Grand Anse, with its calm waters and good coral, is a popular diving spot for beginners. Cap Enragé, north of Case-Pilote, has underwater caves harbouring lots of fish and lobster. Rocher du Diamant (Diamond Rock) also has interesting cave formations but trickier water conditions. Ilet la Perle, a rock off the north-west coast, is a good place to see groper, eels and lobster when water conditions aren't too rough.

**Dive Shops** Dive shops on Martinique include:

Centre de Plongée (☎ 66 01 79); at the Méridien hotel in Pointe du Bout, the Centre de Plongée charges 250F a dive.

Okeonos Club (☎ 76 21 76); at the Village du Diamant in Diamant this club dives Diamond Rock and charges 200F a dive.

Planète Bleue (☎ 66 08 79); a dive boat that docks at the marina at Pointe du Bout.

Tropicasub (☎ 78 38 03); does the Saint-Pierre wreck dives at 9.30 am and 3 pm and charges 200F a dive.

Most of the larger resort hotels around the island also have dive operations.

### Snorkelling

Snorkelling is good around Grand Anse, Sainte-Anne and Case-Pilote. Most larger hotels rent snorkelling gear and many provide it complimentary to their guests. Some of the dive shops offer snorkelling trips, others let snorkellers tag along with divers.

### Windsurfing

Most beachfront hotels have beach huts and rent windsurfing gear. Rentals generally cost 80F to 100F an hour for non-guests, but are often complimentary to hotel guests.

### Hiking

Martinique has numerous hiking tracks. From Route de la Trace a number of signposted trails lead into the rainforest and up and around the Pitons du Carbet. Also popular is the moderate three-hour hike to the ruins of Château Dubuc on the Caravelle Peninsula.

There are strenuous trails leading up both the northern and southern flanks of Mont Pelée. The shortest and steepest begins in Morne Rouge and takes about four hours return. The hike up the northern flank is eight km long and takes about 4½ hours one way; two trails begin just east of Grand-Rivière and converge halfway up the mountain.

A bit less strenuous but still moderately difficult is the 20-km hike around the undeveloped northern tip of the island between Grand-Rivière and Anse Couleuvre. An easy way to do this trail is to join one of the guided hikes organised by the syndicat d'initiative (☎ 55 72 74) in Grand-Rivière. They're conducted on Sunday about twice a month.

Hikers leave from the town hall at 8 am, arrive at Anse Couleuvre around 1 pm and return to Grand-Rivière by boat. The cost of 150F includes lunch.

Other syndicats d'initiative organise hikes in other parts of the island and the Parc Naturel Regional (☎ 73 19 30), 9 Blvd du Général de Gaulle, Fort-de-France, leads guided hikes several times a week. You can find hiking (randonnée) schedules for both groups in the weekly tourist magazine Choubouloute.

### Horse Riding

Ranch Black Horse (☎ 66 00 04) in Trois-Ilets offers three-hour rides daily except Monday for 180F. Horse riding is also available at Ranch Jack (☎ 68 63 97) near Anse d'Arlet, La Cavale (☎ 76 22 94) in Diamant and Ranche Val d'Or (☎ 76 70 58) in Sainte-Anne.

### Cycling

Mountain bike tours, as well as other organised outdoor activities, can be arranged with V T Tilt (☎ 66 01 01) in Pointe du Bout.

### Golf

Martinique has one golf course, the 18-hole Golf de l'Impératrice Joséphine (☎ 68 32 81) in Trois-Ilets. It has a pro shop, a restaurant and a bar.

### Tennis

Most of the larger resort hotels have tennis courts for their guests and there are three lighted tennis courts at the golf course in Trois-Ilets. For information on other courts open to visitors for a fee, contact La Ligue Régionale de Tennis (☎ 51 08 00) in Lamentin.

### HIGHLIGHTS

Be sure to visit the town of Saint-Pierre, with its ruins from the 1902 volcanic eruption. The most scenic drive is the Route de la Trace, up the mountainous interior of the island. Fort-de-France can be a fun town to wander through; don't miss the Bibliothéque Schoelcher (Schoelcher Library), the cathedral and the surrounding back streets with their French colonial architecture.

## ACCOMMODATION

Martinique has about 85 hotels with a total of 4000 rooms. While the French shun the mega-resorts found elsewhere in the Caribbean, Martinique has about a dozen mid-size resorts with 100 rooms or more. Most of the island's other hotels range from 12 to 40 rooms. By Caribbean standards rates are moderate, with upper-end hotels averaging US$250, mid-range US$125 and the lower end about US$65. As in France, taxes and service charges are included in the quoted rate.

There's been a rush of construction in the past couple of years and some of the better deals are in these newer hotels. Anse Mitan in particular has a good selection of moderately priced rooms in recently opened places.

Gîtes de France (☎ 73 67 92; fax 73 66 93), BP 1122, 97209 Fort-de-France, offers rooms and apartments in private homes, with weekly rates ranging from 1200F to 5500F.

Centrale de Réservation (☎ 63 79 60; fax 63 11 64; in Paris ☎ 44 77 86 11), BP 823, 97208 Fort-de-France, opposite the tourist office, books both villas and rooms in private homes, with weekly rates ranging from 1200F to 7200F.

### Camping

There are established camping grounds with facilities at Camping de Sainte-Anne (☎ 76 72 79), BP 8, 97227 Sainte-Anne; Tropicamp (☎ 62 49 66), Gros Raisins Plage, Sainte-Luce; Le Nid Tropical (☎ 68 31 30) in Anse-à-l'Ane; and in Pointe-Marin (☎ 76 72 79), Vauclin (☎ 74 43 11) and Diamant (☎ 76 40 11).

Camping is also allowed along the beach at Les Salines and in a few other areas on weekends and during school holidays. Check with the tourist office for more details.

Fully equipped campervans that sleep four can be rented from West Indies Tours (☎ 54 50 71), Quartier Beauregard, Le François,

for about US$575 to US$750 per week, depending on the season.

To rent a tent, try T S Autos (☎ 63 42 82), 38 Ave Maurice Bishop, Fort-de-France, or MAB Location (☎ 71 98 95), 3.5K Route Châteauboeuf, Fort-de-France.

## FOOD

Most restaurants serve either Creole or French food with an emphasis on local seafood. Red snapper, conch, crayfish and lobster are popular, although the latter is very pricey at about 40F per 100 grams. The best bet at many restaurants is the fixed-price menu, sometimes labelled *menu touristique*, which is a three or four-course meal that usually runs from 90F to 160F, depending on the main course.

For more moderately priced meals there are a number of Italian restaurants and pizzerias on the island. Bakeries make good low-end places to grab a quick meal, as most of them make sandwiches to go and some have a few café tables out the front.

Martinique grows much of its own fruit and produce, including some very sweet pineapples.

## DRINKS

Water is safe to drink from the tap. In restaurants, if you ask for water you'll usually get served bottled water; if you don't want to pay extra for that, ask for *l'eau du robinet* to get tap water.

The legal drinking age is 18. The local beer is Lorrain but island rums are far more popular than beer. Martinique's de rigueur apéritif is ti-punch, which is white rum, sugar cane juice and a squeeze of lemon. Planteur punch is essentially a rum punch, a mix of rum and fruit juice.

## ENTERTAINMENT

The larger hotels in southern Martinique offer a range of entertainment, including steel bands, discos, dancing, limbo shows etc. The most popular tourist show on the island is the performance by the 30-member folk troupe Ballets Martiniquais, which does a dinner show at a different hotel each night.

There are nightclubs and cinemas in Fort-de-France. For current entertainment schedules, see the weekly *Choubouloute*.

Martinique's sole casino, at Le Méridien in Pointe du Bout, offers roulette and blackjack.

Cockfights are locally popular at various 'pitts' around the island.

## THINGS TO BUY

The best place for shopping is Fort-de-France, where air-conditioned shops sell the latest Paris fashions, French perfumes, leather handbags, crystal, silk scarves etc. The main boutique area is along Rue Victor Hugo, particularly from Rue de la République to Rue Schoelcher. The department store Merlande, near the cathedral, has a little of everything. Foreigners who pay with travellers' cheques or a credit card get 20% off the posted price at Merlande and many of the fancier shops.

Local handicrafts such as wicker baskets, dolls in madras costumes, wooden carvings and T-shirts are sold by vendors at the northwest corner of La Savane and at craft shops around the island.

Island pottery at reasonable prices can be purchased directly from craftspeople at the potters village near Trois-Ilets.

Local rum makes a popular souvenir and sells from about 25F to 200F a litre, depending on the quality.

# Getting There & Away

## AIR

Following are the airline reservation numbers on Martinique:

| | |
|---|---|
| Air France | – ☎ 55 33 00 |
| Air Guadeloupe | – ☎ 59 09 90 |
| Air Martinique | – ☎ 60 00 23 |
| American Airlines | – ☎ 51 12 29 |
| AOM | – ☎ 51 74 85 |
| Corsair | – ☎ 51 26 21 |
| LIAT | – ☎ 51 10 00 |

## To/From the USA

American Airlines has a daily service except on Monday to Martinique via San Juan, Puerto Rico, which connect with American's mainland US flights. In the off-season, the lowest midweek fares begin at US$330 from Miami, US$398 from New York. In the high season, they're US$370/440 from Miami/New York. These fares allow a 30-day stay and generally require a two-week advance purchase.

Air France flies to Martinique from Miami on Sunday only. The fare is US$552 with no advance purchase requirement and a 30-day maximum stay.

## To/From France

Air France and AOM have daily flights between Paris and Martinique, while Air Martinique and Corsair have a few flights weekly. The cheapest fares begin at around 3700F return.

## To/From South America

Air France has flights from Fort-de-France to Caracas, Venezuela, on Thursday and Sunday and to Cayenne, French Guiana, every day but Wednesday. The least expensive fare to Caracas requires a 14-day advance purchase, allows a 17-day stay and costs 1550F (US$273). To Cayenne, there's a 14-day excursion ticket which costs 1700F (US$300) return, with no advance purchase required.

## Within the Caribbean

Air Martinique flies to Martinique daily from Guadeloupe, St Martin, St Lucia, St Vincent and Barbados. Return fares from Fort-de-France are US$97 to St Lucia (minimum two-day stay; ticket must be purchased at time of reservation if departure is within seven days); US$164 to Guadeloupe (no restrictions); US$210 to Barbados (four to 21-day excursion) and US$245 to St Vincent (no restrictions).

Air France flies between Martinique and Guadeloupe for US$164 return with no restrictions.

There are discounts of about 25% on both

Air France and Air Martinique for people under 25, students aged 26 to 31, senior citizens 60 or older and families (including husband and wife) travelling together.

Air Guadeloupe has three to five flights daily between Guadeloupe and Martinique. The 21-day excursion fare is 632F and the one-way fare is 305F to 466F, depending on the time of day.

LIAT connects Martinique with the rest of the Caribbean. A return ticket to Martinique allowing a 30-day stay and two intermediate stopovers costs US$204 from Antigua, US$294 from St Kitts and US$320 from St Martin.

### Airport Information

The Lamentin International Airport has a friendly tourist information booth where you can get maps and brochures in English, car rental booths, snack bars, souvenir shops, duty-free liquor stores, a newsstand and a pharmacy. The public phones take phonecards, which can be bought at the airport post office. The post office is open from 7 am to 2.30 pm and 3 to 9.30 pm daily. You can change money at the Change Caraïbes office daily from 7.30 am to 10 pm.

**To/From the Airport** The airport is just a 10-minute ride from Fort-de-France, traffic permitting, and about 20 minutes from the Pointe du Bout resort area. Taxis are readily available at the airport but are expensive (about 80F), so if you plan to rent a car during your stay consider picking it up at the airport upon arrival.

Because of the taxi union, there's no direct bus service from the airport. However, on the return it's possible, if not terribly practical, to take a bus from Pointe Simon in Fort-de-France heading to Ducos (8.70F) and ask to be dropped off on the highway outside the airport.

Returning a rental car at the airport can be quite confusing. While Budget and Hertz have offices just outside the airport entrance, the return lot for most other companies is immediately before the pay parking lot in the area marked 'Eurocar P'.

### SEA

Compagnie Générale Maritime (☎ 55 32 00), BP 574, Ave Maurice Bishop, Fort-de-France, has a weekly cargo/passenger boat between the French West Indies and mainland France. Information is in the Getting There & Away chapter in the front of the book.

Both Caribbean Express (☎ 60 12 38) and Madikera (☎ 73 35 35) operate modern catamaran ferries between Martinique, Guadeloupe and Dominica. Detailed information on these boats is in the Getting There & Away section of the Guadeloupe chapter.

### Yacht

The main port of entry is in Fort-de-France, but yachts may also clear at Saint-Pierre or Marin.

Yachting is very popular in Martinique and there are numerous yacht charter companies operating on the island. ATM (☎ 74 98 17) and The Moorings (☎ 74 75 39) are based at the marina in Marin and Star Voyage (☎ 66 00 72) is based at the Pointe du Bout Marina.

### Cruise Ship

Cruise ships land at Pointe Simon in Fort-de-France, at the west side of the harbour and within easy walking distance of the city centre and main sights.

### LEAVING MARTINIQUE

There's a 35F security tax when flying out of Martinique.

# Getting Around

### BUS

Although there are some larger public buses, most buses are minivans, marked 'TC' (for *taxis collectifs*) on top. Destinations are marked on the vans, sometimes on the side doors and sometimes on a small sign stuck in the front window. Bus stops are marked *arrêt autobus* or with signs showing a picture of a bus.

Fort-de-France's busy main taxi collectifs terminal is at Pointe Simon, on the west side of the harbour. Buses to Saint-Pierre leave frequently on weekdays, less frequently on Sunday, take 45 minutes and cost 17F. Other bus fares from Fort-de-France are: 16F to Trois-Ilets, 18F to Diamant, 30F to Sainte-Anne and 39F to Grand-Rivière. You can pick up buses to the Balata Gardens and Morne Rouge alongside the cemetery south of the Parc Floral; they leave about every 30 minutes during the day, Sunday excepted.

## TAXI

The taxi fare from the airport is about 80F to Fort-de-France, 270F to Sainte-Anne and 160F to Pointe du Bout or Anse Mitan. The fare from Pointe du Bout is 50F to Anse-à-l'Ane and 210F to Fort-de-France.

There's a 40% surcharge on all fares between 8 pm and 6 am and on Sunday and holidays. To call a taxi, dial ☎ 63 63 62.

## CAR & MOTORBIKE
### Road Rules

In Martinique, drive on the right. Your home driving licence is valid. Traffic regulations and road signs are the same as in Europe, speed limits are posted, and exits and intersections are clearly marked.

Roads are excellent by Caribbean standards and there are multi-lane freeways (and rush-hour traffic) in the Fort-de-France area.

### Car Rental

There are numerous car rental agencies at the airport; the daily rate for an economy car with unlimited km ranges from 180F with Union to 230F with Hertz. During the sluggish summer season many agencies will discount an additional 20%, while at the height of winter you might not find anything available at the lower range without advance reservations.

Be aware that some companies such as Europcar also offer a rate that adds on an extra charge for every km you drive; for example, an economy car from Europcar at the plus-km rate would be 144F a day plus 1.44F per km, versus their unlimited-km rate of 183F a day.

Optional Collision Damage Waiver (CDW) insurance that covers collision damage to the car, after a 2000F excess (a fixed payment in the event of an accident), costs another 50F to 60F a day for an economy-class car. The minimum age to rent a car is 21 and to purchase the CDW is 25 years.

Car rental companies, with the airport phone numbers given first, include:

| | | |
|---|---|---|
| Avis | – | ☎ 51 26 86; |
| | | ☎ 70 11 60 in Fort-de-France; |
| | | ☎ 66 04 27 in Pointe du Bout |
| Budget | – | ☎ 51 22 88; |
| | | ☎ 63 69 00 in Fort-de-France; |
| | | ☎ 66 00 45 in Pointe du Bout |
| Citer | – | ☎ 51 65 75; |
| | | ☎ 72 66 48 in Fort-de-France; |
| | | ☎ 76 74 12 in Sainte-Anne |
| Europcar | – | ☎ 51 20 33; |
| | | ☎ 73 33 13 in Fort-de-France; |
| | | ☎ 66 04 29 in Pointe du Bout |
| Eurorent | – | ☎ 51 55 44; |
| | | ☎ 60 43 62 in Fort-de-France |
| Hertz | – | ☎ 51 28 22; |
| | | ☎ 60 64 64 in Fort-de-France; |
| | | ☎ 66 06 59 in Pointe du Bout |
| Thrifty | – | ☎ 51 29 6; |
| | | ☎ 66 09 59 in Pointe du Bout |
| Union/Ozier- | – | ☎ 51 64 67; |
| Lafontaine | | ☎ 76 79 66 in Sainte-Anne |

**Motorbike & Bicycle** Motorbikes and bicycles can be rented from Funny (☎ 63 33 05) or T S Autos (☎ 63 42 82) in Fort-de-France, Discount (☎ 66 54 37) in Pointe du Bout, Scootonnerre (☎ 76 41 12) in Diamant and Centrale du Cycle (☎ 50 28 54) in Lamentin.

## HITCHING

Hitching is fairly common on Martinique, although the usual precautions apply.

## BOAT

There are a couple of regular ferries (vedettes) between main resort areas and Fort-de-France that provide a nice alternative to dealing with heavy bus and car traffic, allow you to avoid city parking hassles and are quicker to boot. In Fort-de-France the ferries dock at the quay fronting La Savane.

Schedules are posted at the docks; the ferries leave promptly and occasionally even a few minutes early.

### Fort-de-France to Pointe du Bout

Somatours Vedettes (☎ 73 05 53) runs a ferry between Fort-de-France and the Pointe du Bout Marina. It's quite a pleasant way to cross and takes only 15 minutes. The boat runs daily from early morning to around midnight, with 22 crossings on weekdays, 15 on weekends. The fare is 16/24F one way/return for adults, 6/10F one way/return for children aged two to seven.

### Fort-de-France to Anse Mitan & Anse-à-l'Ane

Madinina Vedettes (☎ 63 06 46) makes a triangle route between Fort-de-France, Anse Mitan and Anse-à-l'Ane. The boats run daily, every 30 to 60 minutes from about 6 am (8.30 am on Sunday) to about 6 pm.

The Franck Perret Vedette (☎ 71 82 28) runs from Fort-de-France to Anse Mitan from Monday to Saturday, leaving Fort-de-France on the hour from 8 am to 5 pm and Anse Mitan on the half-hour from 8.30 am to 4.30 pm.

The fare between Fort-de-France and Anse Mitan for either boat is 15F one way or 22F return (10F return for children). The fare between Anse Mitan and Anse-à-l'Ane is 5F.

### Fort-de-France to Grand Anse

Trou Au Chat (☎ 66 01 44) has a boat service from Fort-de-France to Grand Anse via Anse-à-l'Ane. The boat doesn't run daily; call for schedule information.

### TOURS

Taxi tours cost about 220F an hour, or about 600F for a half-day tour which includes a drive up the Route de la Trace, a visit to Saint-Pierre and a return to Fort-de-France down the west coast.

There are various catamaran tours and boat charters operating around the island. For the latest information check with the tourist office, ask at your hotel desk or leaf through the tourist magazines.

# Fort-de-France

Fort-de-France, the island capital, is the largest and most cosmopolitan city in the French West Indies. It has a pretty harbourfront setting with the Pitons du Carbet rising up beyond, a view best appreciated when approaching the city by ferry.

The narrow, bustling streets opposite La Savane, the harbourfront central park, are lined with a mix of ordinary offices and interesting turn-of-the-century buildings housing French cafés and designer boutiques. It has as much the flavour of the side streets of Paris as it does that of the Caribbean. Give yourself a few hours to wander around and take in the handful of historic sites and museums the city has to offer, longer if you want to shop or enjoy a meal.

### Information

**Tourist Office** The tourist office (☎ 63 79 60), on Blvd Alfassa, is open from 7.30 am to 12.30 pm and 2.30 to 5.30 pm on weekdays (to 5 pm on Friday) and from 8 am to noon on Saturday.

**Money** Change Caraïbes, 4 Rue Ernest Deproge, is open from 7.30 am to 6 pm on weekdays and 8 am to 12.30 pm on Saturday. Change Point, a block away, is open from 8 am to 6 pm on weekdays, until 1 pm on Saturday. Both exchange major currencies and don't charge commissions for most transactions.

A BFC bank is a couple of doors away from Change Caraïbes, on Rue Ernest Deproge. Other banks can be found along Rue de la Liberté, opposite La Savane.

**Post & Telecommunications** You can send faxes, buy phonecards, use a card phone or pick up mail sent poste restante at the central post office on the corner of Rue Antoine Siger and Rue de la Liberté. It's open from 7 am to 6 pm Monday to Friday, to noon on Saturday; expect long lines.

Other public card phones can be found in

MARTINIQUE

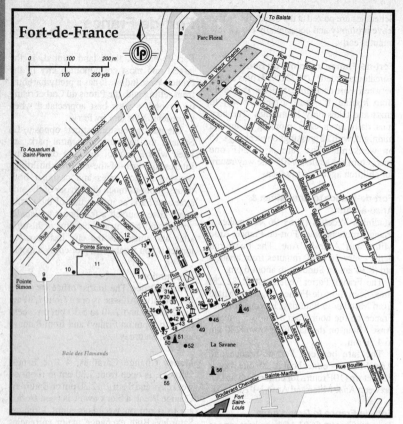

La Savane, opposite the post office, and around the city.

**Bookshops** The newsstand at the west corner of La Savane sells the *International Herald-Tribune* and numerous French-language newspapers and magazines.

Centrale Catholique, 57 Rue Blénac, sells books in French about Martinique (history, flora and fauna etc) and the Institut Géographique National's map of Martinique.

**Laundry** There's a self-service laundrette on

the 2nd floor behind La Bodega restaurant. The entrance is off Rue Victor Hugo; just follow the signs for 'Laverie Automatique' and look for the stairs.

**Pharmacy** There are several pharmacies around town, including Pharmacy de l'Impératrice on the corner of Rue de la Liberté and Rue Antoine Siger.

**Parking** Parking is not a problem on weekends and holidays, but is quite a challenge on weekdays. There's a car park off Blvd Alfassa between the tourist office and the

## PLACES TO STAY

| 33 | Le Balisier |
|----|-------------|
| 37 | Hôtel Central |
| 41 | L'Impératrice |
| 43 | Lafayette |
| 44 | Hôtel Malmaison |
| 54 | Un Coin de Paris |

## PLACES TO EAT

| 4 | Délifrance |
|----|-------------|
| 5 | Marie-Sainte |
| 6 | Le Coq d'Or |
| 12 | Délifrance |
| 13 | Burger King |
| 14 | Café des Îles |
| 18 | Pâtisserie |
| 23 | McDonald's |
| 24 | Le Second Souffle |
| 26 | Délifrance |
| 30 | La Bodega |

## OTHER

| 1 | Farmers' Market |
|----|-------------|
| 2 | Fish Market |
| 3 | Buses to Balata |
| 7 | Produce Market |
| 8 | Match Supermarket |
| 9 | Cruise Ship Terminal |
| 10 | Immigration & Customs |
| 11 | Minibus Terminal |
| 15 | Centrale Catholique Bookshop |
| 16 | Saint-Louis Cathedral |
| 17 | Palais de Justice |
| 19 | Parking |
| 20 | Merlande Department Store |
| 21 | Quick Photo 1-hr |
| 22 | Europcar & Budget Car Rental |
| 25 | US Consulate |
| 27 | Bank |
| 28 | Bibliothèque Schoelcher |
| 29 | BNP Bank |
| 31 | Laundrette |
| 32 | Hertz Car Rental |
| 34 | Change Point |
| 35 | Tourist Office |
| 36 | Centrale de Réservation |
| 38 | Musée Départemental d'Archéologie |
| 39 | Post Office |
| 40 | Pharmacy de l'Impératrice |
| 42 | Change Caraïbes |
| 45 | Taxi Stand |
| 46 | Statue of Empress Josephine |
| 47 | Air France |
| 48 | Avis Car Rental |
| 49 | Public Toilets |
| 50 | Newsstand |
| 51 | Statue of Belain d'Esnambuc |
| 52 | Souvenir Stands |
| 53 | Cinema |
| 55 | Ferries to Pointe du Bout |
| 56 | War Memorial |

minibus terminal which costs 8F an hour, 80F for 12 hours. There's also metered parking along many of the side streets running off Rue de la Liberté for 5F an hour, with a two-hour limit, and along La Savane on Ave des Caraïbes with a four-hour (18F) limit. Streetside parking is free in the evenings and on Sunday and holidays.

### La Savane

This large central park sports grassy lawns, tall trees, clumps of bamboo and lots of benches. The harbour side of La Savane has souvenir stalls, a newsstand and statues dedicated to early settlers and fallen soldiers.

At the north side of the park, near the bustling Rue de la Liberté, there's a statue of the Empress Josephine holding a locket with a portrait of Napoleon – although in recent times her own head was lopped off the statue. Despite all the Josephine hoopla, the Empress is not highly regarded among islanders, many of whom believe she was responsible for convincing Napoleon to continue slavery so her family plantation in Trois-Ilets wouldn't suffer.

Opposite the south side of the park is Fort Saint-Louis. The original fort, built in the Vauban style, dates from 1640, although most of the extensive fort which stands today is the result of subsequent additions. The fort is still an active military base and is off limits to visitors.

### Musée Départemental d'Archéologie

This archaeological museum, at 9 Rue de la Liberté, displays Amerindian artefacts, including stone tools, ritual objects and pottery. Most engaging are the 100 or so clay *adornos*, the decorative figurines used to adorn vases and bowls. There are also illustrations of the Caribs and a diorama of thatched huts. Overall the presentation is simple, if not a bit dry, and you can walk through it all in about 20 minutes. Most signs are in French only. It's open from 8.30 am to 1 pm and 2.30 to 5 pm Monday to Friday, from 9 am to noon on Saturday. Admission is 15F for adults, 5F for children under 12.

### Bibliothèque Schoelcher

The Bibliothèque Schoelcher (Schoelcher Library), on Rue de la Liberté, is an elaborate and colourfully painted building with a Byzantine dome. The work of architect Henri Pick, a contemporary of Gustave Eiffel, the library was built in Paris in 1887, then dismantled, shipped to Fort-de-France and reassembled on this site. The interior is also interesting; it's open from 8.30 am to noon and 2.30 to 6 pm on weekdays, mornings only on Saturday.

### Saint-Louis Cathedral

With its Roman Byzantine style and 57-metre-high steeple, the Saint-Louis Cathedral on Rue Schoelcher, a block northwest of La Savane, is one of the city's most distinguished landmarks. Built in 1895 by Henri Pick, the church fronts a small square and is picturesquely framed by two royal palms. The interior is bright and ornate and well worth a look.

### Palais de Justice

The Palais de Justice, a neoclassical courthouse built in 1906, is two blocks north-east of the cathedral. The design resembles a French railroad station, as the plaque out front unabashedly points out. The square fronting the courthouse has a statue of French abolitionist Victor Schoelcher.

### Parc Floral & Public Markets

The Parc Floral is a public park at the north side of the city; it's worth a stroll through if you're already in the area.

A farmers' market runs along the west side of the Parc Floral and spills over into the street along the Rivière Madame. In addition to island-grown fruits and vegetables, this open-air market sells drinking coconuts (5F) and cut flowers. The fish market is a block to the south, while a second and larger public produce market is on the north side of Rue Isambert.

### Aquarium de la Martinique

This aquarium (☎ 73 02 29), promoted as 'one of Europe's largest', is 1400 sq metres in size, contains 2000 fish, sharks and turtles and includes an 18-metre-long tropical river display. It's on Blvd de la Marne, one km west of the city centre, and is open from 9 am to 7 pm daily. Admission is 38F for adults, 24F for children aged under 12.

### Places to Stay

**City Centre** *Un Coin de Paris* (☎ 70 08 52; fax 63 69 51), 54 Rue Lazare Carnot, 97209 Fort-de-France Cédex, has 14 austere rooms with private bathrooms and air-con but little else. However, unlike other small hostelries in this neighbourhood it's geared towards budget travellers more than local boarders, and the singles/doubles rate is just 210/250F with breakfast.

*Le Balisier* (☎ & fax 71 46 54), 21 Rue Victor Hugo, 97200 Fort-de-France, has 32 rooms in a couple of buildings. Best are the small but adequate rooms in the main hotel, which have TV, phones and private bathrooms. Ask for a room at the rear of the hotel, as they're quieter and some have partial ocean views. In an apartment building on the same street are studios which are a bit run-down but OK for the price, each with a refrigerator, hot plate, TV, phone, air-con and a double and single bed. Hotel rooms cost 290/340F a single/double, studio apartments cost 340F.

The *Hôtel Malmaison* (☎ 63 90 85), 7 Rue de la Liberté, 97200 Fort-de-France, has 20 rooms that vary in size and amenities. All have air-con and private bathrooms and most have TV. Although a few of the rooms have saggy mattresses and at least one has no windows, they are clean and the desk clerk will usually let you look around and pick one to your liking. Singles/doubles cost 260/290F for smaller rooms, 330/360F for larger rooms.

*Hôtel Central* (☎ 70 02 12; fax 63 80 00), 3 Rue Victor Hugo, 97200 Fort-de-France, is a small hotel with 18 very small rooms that are a little on the claustrophobic side. The rooms, which have TV, air-con and private bathrooms, cost 300/330F for singles/doubles in summer, 375/415F in winter.

*Lafayette* (☎ 73 80 50; fax 60 97 75), 5 Rue de la Liberté, 97200 Fort-de-France, is a good central hotel with rooms that are clean and quite pleasant for this price range. This three-storey hotel has 24 rooms with air-con, phones, TV, minibars and private bathrooms. Singles/doubles cost 330/380F in summer, 380/420F in winter.

Another popular central hotel is *L'Impératrice* (☎ 63 06 82; fax 72 66 30), 15 Rue de la Liberté, 97200 Fort-de-France, which has 24 air-con rooms that are clean and adequate. Some have balconies facing La Savane. In summer, singles/doubles begin at 300/350F. In winter, the cheapest rooms cost 320/415F, while those with a TV and a view of La Savane cost 375/460F. Breakfast is included in the rates.

**Around Fort-de-France** The *Squash Hotel* (☎ 63 00 01; fax 63 00 74), 3 Blvd de la Marne, 97200 Fort-de-France, is one km west of the town centre, near the aquarium. This modern, mid-priced hotel, part of the PLM Azur chain, has 108 comfortable rooms with air-con, phones, TVs and minibars. There's also a pool, restaurant, fitness centre and three squash courts. Singles/doubles start at 480/570F year-round.

*La Batelière* (☎ 61 49 49; fax 61 70 57; in France ☎ 47 23 75 13; in the USA ☎ (800) 223-6510), 97233 Schoelcher, a couple of km west of central Fort-de-France, is a modern luxury hotel that caters in part to businesspeople. The hotel has a beach, pool, gym, dive shop, disco, tennis courts and restaurants and recently underwent a US$22 million renovation which turned its casino into a conference centre. The 200 rooms and suites have all the expected amenities – heavy curtains, four-poster beds, marble baths and the like. Rates for doubles range from 780F for a standard room to 2500F for a suite in summer, from 900F to 3500F in winter.

**Places to Eat**
There are a number of cafés and small res-

taurants opposite La Savane on Rue de la Liberté. If you want to eat cheaply you can easily find takeaway food and freshly baked bread for a picnic in the park. Bakeries selling inexpensive sandwiches are scattered throughout the city. In the evenings food vans selling sandwiches, crêpes and other cheap local food park along the Blvd Chevalier Sainte Marthe at the south side of La Savane.

There are a couple of fast food chains in the centre, including *Burger King* and *McDonald's*, both open to at least 11 pm daily. Burgers at either range from 13F to 25F. A nice local alternative in the same price range is the *Délifrance* on Rue Antoine Siger, which has sandwiches from 15F and inexpensive plate lunches.

*Café des Îles*, Rue Victor Hugo, is a small owner-run café with freshly squeezed orange juice (12F), omelettes and salads for 30F to 40F and inexpensive sandwiches.

*Le Second Souffle*, diagonally opposite the cathedral at 27 Rue Blénac, is a good vegetarian restaurant. Salads are priced from 15F to 38F and the plat du jour is 50F. It's open weekdays, for lunch until 3 pm and for dinner from 7.30 to 10 pm.

*La Bodega*, on Rue Ernest Deproge near the car rental agencies, is a pleasant pub-style restaurant with a variety of salads, pizzas and pasta dishes from 40F to 50F, a vegetarian plate for 45F and a three-course menu du jour for 75F. It's open from 10 am to 11.30 pm, closed on Sunday.

If you're near the river, *Marie-Sainte*, 160 Rue Victor Hugo, is a popular little hole-in-the-wall serving good inexpensive Creole food such as accras, lambi (conch) and grilled fish. It's open for lunch only, from noon to 3 pm Monday to Saturday. Also in that neighbourhood is *Le Coq d'Or* on Rue François Arago, which has simple local fare and fresh sugar cane juice.

Match supermarket on Rue Antoine Siger is a good place to buy groceries (it also has a drugstore). It's open from 8 am to 6.30 pm on weekdays, to 1.30 pm on Saturday. For vegetables and fruits, the produce market a block away is the best bet.

MARTINIQUE

# Northern Martinique

Several roads head north from Fort-de-France. The most interesting sightseeing routes are the coastal road (N2) to Saint-Pierre and the Route de la Trace (N3), which crosses the lush mountainous interior before ending in Morne Rouge. The two routes can be combined to make a nice loop drive whose highlights can be seen in a half day or which could be stretched into a leisurely full-day outing.

## FORT-DE-FRANCE TO SAINT-PIERRE

N2, the coastal road north to Saint-Pierre, passes along dry, scrubby terrain and goes through a line of small towns, a merging of modern suburbia and old fishing villages. If you were to drive without stopping, it would take about 45 minutes to reach Saint-Pierre from Fort-de-France.

It's worth swinging off the highway at **Case-Pilote** to take a peek at the old village centre. Turn south off N2 at the Total petrol station and you'll immediately come to a quaint stone church, one of Martinique's oldest. Just 75 metres south is a pleasant town square with a water fountain, an historic town hall and a nice moderately priced café. In Case-Pilote, as well as in the next village, **Bellefontaine**, you can find brightly painted wooden fishing boats called *gommiers* (after the trees they're constructed from) lined up along the shore.

The town of **Carbet** fronts a sandy beach and has a few tourist amenities, including a couple of restaurants, a dive shop and a rather forlorn little zoo.

**Anse Turin**, a long grey-sand beach that attracts a crowd on weekends, is along the highway 1.5 km north of Carbet. Opposite the beach is the **Paul Gauguin Museum**, marked by a very small sign. Gauguin (1848-1903), one of the great post-impressionists of Europe, is best known for his paintings of Polynesian women, which were painted in the 1890's after he moved to Tahiti. Like his close friend Van Gogh, Gauguin's work was largely ignored in his time and gained respect and monetary value only after his death. This interesting museum contains Gauguin memorabilia, letters from the artist to his wife and reproductions of Gauguin's paintings including *Bord de Mer I* and *L'Anse Turin – avec les raisiniers*, which were painted on the nearby beach during Gauguin's five-month stay on the island in 1887. The museum is open daily from 10 am to 5.30 pm. Admission is 15F.

Half a km north of the museum is the driveway up to **La Vallée des Papillons** (☎ 78 18 07), where the scattered stone ruins of one of the island's earliest plantations have been enhanced with gardens and a butterfly farm. It's open from 9.30 am to 4.15 pm daily. Admission is 38F for adults, 28F for children, and there's a restaurant on site.

## SAINT-PIERRE

Saint-Pierre is on the coast seven km south of Mont Pelée, the still-active volcano that laid the town to waste at the turn of the century. It's a fascinating town to wander around. There are ruins throughout Saint-Pierre, some of which are little more than foundations, others partially intact. Many of the surviving stone walls have been incorporated into the town's reconstruction, forming the base for the buildings that replaced them. Even these newer buildings have a nice period feel, with shuttered doors and wrought-iron balconies.

The centre of town is long and narrow, with two parallel one-way streets running its length. All of the major sights have signs in both French and English and you can explore the area thoroughly in a few hours. You could also take the *Cyparis Express* (☎ 55 50 92), a 40-minute guided tram tour of the main sights, which runs at 9.30 am and 1, 2.30 and 5.30 pm Monday to Friday; it costs 40F for adults, 20F for children. The tram leaves from the ruins below the museum (Ruines du Figuier), on the coastal road Rue Isambert. Note that most of the tours are narrated in French only.

These days Saint-Pierre has 6000 residents, which is one-fifth of the pre-eruption population. The central gathering spot is the waterfront town park, next to the market. A nice beach of soft black sand fronts the town and extends to the south.

## Musée Vulcanologique

This small but very interesting museum, founded in 1932 by American vulcanologist Franck Perret, gives a glimpse of the devastating 1902 eruption of Mont Pelée. On display are items plucked from the rubble, including petrified rice, a box of nails melted into a sculpture-like mass, glass cups fused together by heat and the cast iron bell from the cathedral tower squashed like a saucer. There are also historic photos of the town before and immediately after the eruption. The displays are in both English and French.

There's free parking on both sides of the museum, which occupies the site of an old hillside gun battery. From the old stone walls along the parking lot you can get a nice

perspective of the harbour and city, and look down upon a line of ruins on the street below. The museum, on Rue Victor Hugo, is open from 9 am to 5 pm daily. Admission is 10F.

## Ruins

The most impressive ruins are those of the old theatre, just 100 metres north of the museum. While most of the theatre was destroyed, enough remains to give a sense of the former grandeur of this building, which once seated 800 and hosted theatre troupes from mainland France. A double set of stairs still leads up to the partial walls of the lower storey.

On the north-east side of the theatre you can look over the wall to the tiny, thick-walled jail cell that housed Cyparis, the town's sole survivor.

Another area rich in ruins is along Rue Bouillé, directly below the vulcanology museum.

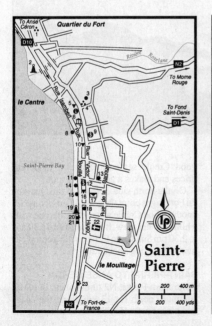

**Saint-Pierre**

**MARTINIQUE**

## The Eruption of Mont Pelée

At the turn of the century Saint-Pierre, the capital of Martinique, was a flourishing port city, so cosmopolitan it was dubbed the 'Little Paris of the West Indies'. Mont Pelée, the island's highest mountain, provided a scenic backdrop to the city.

In the spring of 1902, sulphurous steam vents on Mont Pelée began emitting gases, and a crater lake began to fill with boiling water. Authorities dismissed it all as the normal cycle of the volcano, which had had periods of activity in the past without dire consequences.

But in late spring the lake broke and spilled down the mountainside in Rivière Blanche, just north of the city, burying a plantation and its workers in hot mud. On 25 April the volcano spewed a shower of ash onto Saint-Pierre. Up until this point the volcanic activity had largely been seen as a curiosity, but now people became apprehensive and some sent their children to stay with relatives on other parts of the island. The governor of Martinique, hoping to convince residents that there was no need to evacuate the city, brought his family to Saint-Pierre.

At 8 am on Sunday, 8 May 1902, Mont Pelée exploded into a glowing burst of superheated gas and burning ash, with a force 40 times stronger than the nuclear blast over Hiroshima. Between the suffocating gases and the fiery inferno, Saint-Pierre was laid to waste within minutes.

When rescuers from the French navy landed ashore that afternoon, they found only three survivors among the city's 30,000 inhabitants. Two of them had received fatal injuries, but the third, a prisoner named Cyparis, survived with only minor burns – ironically, he owed his life to having been locked in a tomb-like solitary confinement cell at the local jail. Following the commutation of his prison sentence by the new governor, Cyparis joined the P T Barnum circus where he toured as a sideshow act.

Pelée continued to smoulder for months, but by 1904 people began to resettle the town, building among the crumbled ruins. ∎

## Places to Stay & Eat

The only in-town hotel is the ageing *Novelle Vague* (☎ 78 14 34), which has five very simple rooms for 200/250F a single/double and a waterfront restaurant that's open for lunch daily except on Monday.

There's an '8 à Huit' grocery store in the centre of town; a pâtisserie, *Plateau du Théâtre*, opposite the theatre ruins; a very simple snack shop a few doors down from that; and a pizza place, *Pizzaria de Musée*, about 100 metres south of the museum.

*Le Central*, opposite the town park, serves good Creole seafood dishes at moderate prices and makes a good lunch spot.

On the north side of town in the Quartier du Fort, signs point the way to *La Factorerie*, another good Creole restaurant, this one with a hilltop water view. It's open from 11.30 am to 2.30 pm Sunday to Friday, with a complete lunch averaging about 120F.

## SAINT-PIERRE TO ANSE CÉRON

From Saint-Pierre, N2 turns inland but D10 continues north for 13 km along the coast and makes a scenic side drive, ending in 20 minutes at a remote beach. The shoreline is rocky for much of the way and the landscape is lush, with roadside clumps of bamboo.

The limestone cliffs four km north of Saint-Pierre, called **Tombeau des Caraïbes**, are said to be the place where the last Caribs jumped to their deaths rather than succumb to capture by the French.

The road goes through the town of **Le Prêcheur**, where green and orange fishing boats dot the shoreline, and **Anse Belleville**, a village so narrow that there's only room for a single row of houses between the cliffs and the sea.

Just half a km before the end of the road is **Habitation Céron** (☎ 52 94 53), a former sugar plantation open to visitors from 9.30 am to 5 pm Tuesday to Saturday. Admission is 30F for adults, 15F for children aged five to 12.

The road ends at **Anse Céron**, a beautiful black-sand beach in a wild, jungle-like setting. Anse Céron is backed by coconut palms and faces Ilet la Perle, a rounded off-shore rock that's a popular dive site. Despite the remote location, the beach has a shower, toilets, picnic tables and a snack shop.

A very steep one-lane drive continues for 1600 metres beyond the beach. This is the start of a six-hour, 20-km hike to Grand-Rivière.

## ROUTE DE LA TRACE

The Route de la Trace (N3) winds up into the mountains north from Fort-de-France. It's a beautiful drive through a lush rainforest of tall tree ferns, anthurium-covered hillsides and thick clumps of roadside bamboo. The road passes along the eastern flanks of the pointed volcanic mountain peaks of the Pitons du Carbet. Several well-marked hiking trails lead from the Route de la Trace into the rainforest and up to the peaks.

The road follows a route cut by the Jesuits in the 17th century; islanders like to say that the Jesuits' fondness for rum accounts for the twisting nature of the road.

Less than a 10-minute drive north of Fort-de-France, you'll reach the **Balata Church**, a scaled-down replica of the Sacré-Coeur Basilica in Paris. This interesting domed church has a stunning hilltop setting – the Pitons du Carbet rise up as a backdrop and there's a view across Fort-de-France to Pointe du Bout below.

The **Jardin de Balata**, on the west side of the road 10 minutes' drive north of the Balata Church, is a mature botanical garden in a rainforest setting. Walkways wind past tropical trees and flowers including lots of ginger, heliconia, anthuriums and bromeliads. Many of the plants are numbered; you can pick up a free corresponding handout listing 200 of the specimens with their Latin and common French names. This pleasant garden takes about 30 to 45 minutes to stroll through and is a great place to photograph flowers and hummingbirds. It's open from 9 am to 5 pm daily. Admission is 35F for adults, 15F for children aged three to 12.

After the garden, N3 winds up into the mountains and reaches an elevation of 600 metres before dropping back down to **Site de l'Alma**, where a river runs through a lush green gorge. There are riverside picnic tables, trinket sellers and a couple of short trails into the rainforest.

Four km later N3 is intersected by D1, a winding scenic drive that leads west 14 km via Fond Saint-Denis to Saint-Pierre. Just beyond this intersection, N3 leads through a cobblestone tunnel and a km beyond that, on the east side of the road, is the signposted trailhead for **Trace des Jésuites**. This popular hike is five km long and takes about three hours one way. It winds up and down through a variety of terrain, ranging in elevation from 310 metres at the Lorrain River crossing to 670 metres at its termination on D1.

Continuing north on N3, the Route de la Trace goes past banana plantations, flower nurseries and the Mont Pelée juice factory before reaching a T-junction at Morne Rouge, on the southern slopes of Mont Pelée. From here, N2 winds west eight km down to Saint-Pierre, while N3 heads east to Ajoupa-Bouillon.

**Morne Rouge** was partially destroyed by Mont Pelée in August 1902, several months

MARTINIQUE

after the eruption that wiped out Saint-Pierre. At 450 metres it has the highest elevation of any town on Martinique and enjoys some nice mountain scenery.

About 2.5 km east of the T-junction, a road signposted to L'Aileron leads three km up the slopes of Mont Pelée, from where there's a rugged trail (four hours return) up to the volcano's summit.

## LES OMBRAGES

Les Ombrages (☎ 53 31 90) is a naturalised botanical garden at the site of a former rum distillery. A trail passes stands of bamboo, tall trees with buttressed roots, torch gingers and the ruins of the old mill. It's a nice jungle walk.

The garden opens at 9 am daily, closing at 4 pm in winter and 5.30 pm in summer. Tour guides lead 45-minute walks, in French only. Admission is 15F for adults and 5F for children aged five to 11. Les Ombrages is 250 metres east of N3, immediately north of the town of Ajoupa-Bouillon and a third of a km south of the Falaise River.

## BASSE-POINTE

As N3 nears the Atlantic it meets N1, which then runs along the coast both north and south. The northern segment of the road edges the eastern slopes of Mont Pelée and passes through banana and pineapple plantations before reaching the coastal town of Basse-Pointe.

### Leyritz Plantation

Leyritz Plantation, dating from the early 18th century, is a former sugar plantation that now houses a hotel and restaurant.

It's an interesting place with a park-like setting. You can stroll around the grounds at leisure and explore some of the old buildings. Most intriguing is the former plantation house, a weathered two-storey building with period furnishings. If you arrive after the lunch crowd has cleared out, the house is often deserted, which adds a nice element.

Inside the gift shop near the entrance is a 'museum' that's essentially a small collec-

tion of Victorian-style dolls made of dried plants and fibres.

If you're not eating at the plantation it costs 15F to explore the grounds and visit the museum; a drink is included in the ticket price. There's no charge for children under 12. It's open every day from 9 am to 5 pm. The plantation is on D21, two km south-east of Basse-Pointe.

### Places to Stay & Eat

The *Leyritz Plantation* (☎ 78 53 92; fax 78 92 44), 97218 Basse-Pointe, has 68 guest rooms spread across its grounds, many in the old plantation quarters. Rooms vary, but most are comfortable and full of atmosphere. Some of the nicer ones are in the renovated stone cottages that once served as dwellings for married slaves. All rooms have air-con, TVs and phones, some have minibars, and there's a pool and a tennis court. It's a popular place with returning retirees from mainland France, but its secluded country setting may prove too remote for first-time visitors intent on exploring the entire island. Singles/doubles cost 408/558F in summer, 570/732F in winter, breakfast included.

The Leyritz Plantation dining room, within the old stone walls of the refinery, has an engaging setting despite the rush of tour buses that arrive at lunchtime. Servings are generous and considering the volume the kitchen puts out, the food is fine. There's a 115F lunch that includes crab farci, blood pudding, your choice of conch or goat fricassée, rice, vegetables and either coconut cake or fresh pineapple. Otherwise, main dishes range from 60F for chicken to 185F for grilled lobster, starters from 22F to 50F. It's open for lunch from noon to 2.30 pm and for dinner from 7 to 9 pm.

In the centre of Basse-Pointe, along the main road, *Chez Mally Edjam* is a pleasant little family restaurant serving home-cooked food at honest prices. Grilled fish costs 55F, colombo is 65F, and there's a daily set meal for 60F with dessert. If you're heading towards Grand-Rivière it's on the right, just before the cultural centre, at Ruelle Saint-Jean.

## GRAND-RIVIÈRE

From Basse-Pointe it's a nice 20-minute drive to Grand-Rivière along a winding, but good, sealed road. En route you'll go through the coastal village of Macouba, where there's a rum distillery, pass two trails leading up the northern flank of Mont Pelée, cross a couple of one-lane bridges and finally wind down into Grand-Rivière.

Grand-Rivière is an unspoiled fishing village scenically tucked beneath coastal cliffs at the northern tip of Martinique. Mont Pelée forms a rugged backdrop to the south while there's a fine view of neighbouring Dominica to the north.

The road dead-ends at the sea where there's a fish market and rows of bright fishing boats lined up on a little black-sand beach. The waters are sometimes good for surfing at the west side of town. The syndicat d'initiative, in the town centre, has local tourist information and organises guided hikes in the region.

While there's no road around the tip of the island there's a 20-km hiking trail leading to Anse Couleuvre, on the north-west coast. The trailhead begins on the road opposite the quaint two-storey *mairie* (town hall), just up from the beach. For information on this hike, as well as the nearby hike up Mont Pelée, see the Hiking section of this chapter.

### Places to Stay & Eat

If you want something on the run there's a snack shop opposite the town hall and sometimes a sidewalk vendor making hand-cranked ice cream nearby.

*Chanteur Vacances* (☎ 55 73 73), 97218 Grand-Rivière, is a restaurant and hotel with friendly management. There are seven straightforward rooms on the 3rd floor that cost 140/190F for singles/doubles, breakfast included. The 2nd-floor restaurant has fixed-price meals with soup or salad, Creole rice and ice cream or fruit. The cost depends on the main dish, ranging from 71F for fish blaff to 100F for crayfish, the house speciality. Lunch is from noon to 4.30 pm.

*Chez Tante Arlette* (☎ 55 75 75), about 50 metres from the syndicat d'initiative, is another Creole restaurant with three-course meals (from 80F for mutton to 150F for lobster) and a handful of simple rooms (200F with breakfast) on the floor above. Meals are served from noon to 9 pm.

*Chez Vava*, on the outskirts of town near the river, is slightly more upmarket and has fine Creole fare with an emphasis on seafood. A full meal will cost from 110F to 170F. It's open from noon to 5 pm.

### BASSE-POINTE TO LAMENTIN

The highway (N1) from Basse-Pointe to Lamentin runs along relatively tame terrain and is not one of the island's most interesting drives, although there are a few worthwhile sights. The communities along the way are largely modern towns that become increasingly more suburban as you continue south.

**Fond Saint-Jacques** (☎ 69 10 12), two km north of Sainte-Marie, is the site of an old Dominican monastery and sugar plantation dating from 1660. One of the early plantation managers, Father Jean-Baptiste Labat, created a type of boiler (the *père labat*) that modernised the distilling of rum. During the French Revolution, the plantation was confiscated by the state and it's now under the domain of the local government, which is developing it as a cultural centre. The chapel and most of the living quarters are still intact and there are many ruins on the grounds including those of the mill, distillery basins, boiling house and sugar factory. This site, which is about 500 metres inland from N1, is open from 8.30 am to 5 pm Monday to Friday and by appointment on weekends.

The **Museé du Rhum**, at the site of Saint-James Plantation's working distillery, is a fun place to stop. The plantation is 200 metres west of N1, signposted on the northern outskirts of Sainte-Marie. There are both indoor and outside displays of old sugar-making equipment including steam engines, rum stills, cane-crushing gears and trains. There's also a tasting room where you can sample different rums and if you don't get too heady you might want to go out the back to check out the sugar mill and distillery. Admission is free. It's open from 9 am to 5 pm weekdays, to 1 pm on Saturday and Sunday.

The road continues south through cane fields and passes the **Caravelle Peninsula**, which can make an interesting side trip if you have extra time. On the north side of the peninsula there are a couple of nice protected beaches, Tartane and Anse l'Étang. Out at the tip of the peninsula are the deteriorated ruins of Château Dubuc, an old 17th-century estate whose master gained notoriety by using a lantern to lure ships into wrecking off the coast and then gathering the loot.

# Southern Martinique

The southern part of Martinique has many of the island's best beaches and most of its hotels. The largest concentration of places to stay is in the greater Trois-Ilets area, which encompasses Pointe du Bout, Anse Mitan and Anse-à-l'Ane. Other important resort areas are in Diamant and Sainte-Anne.

The interior of the southern half of the island is largely a mix of agricultural land and residential areas. Lamentin, the site of the international airport, is Martinique's second-largest city but like other interior towns has little that is targeted for tourists.

## TROIS-ILETS

Trois-Ilets is a pretty little village with a central square that's bordered by a small market, a quaint town hall and the church where Empress Josephine was baptised in 1763. Despite its proximity to the island's busiest resort area, the village retains a delightful rural charm that's unaltered by tourism.

Pointe du Bout and Anse Mitan (both of which use Trois-Ilets as their postal address) are a few km west of the village centre, as are the island's golf course, the birthplace of Josephine and a small botanical park. The area's other chief attractions, a sugar museum and a pottery village, are both east of Trois-Ilets.

### Musée de la Pagerie

This former sugar estate was the birthplace of Marie Joseph Rose Tascher de la Pagerie, better known as Empress Josephine. A picturesque stone building, formerly the family kitchen, has been turned into a museum containing Josephine's childhood bed and other memorabilia. Multilingual interpreters relate tidbits of Josephine's life, such as the doctoring of the marriage certificate to make Josephine, six years Napoleon's elder, appear to be the same age as her spouse.

A couple of other buildings on the museum grounds contain such things as the Bonaparte family chart, old sugar cane equipment, and love letters to Josephine from Napoleon. One, dated 21 July 1796, reads in part:

...Don't you know that you are the soul of my life and the love of my heart? ... far from you, the nights are long, dull and sad. When I am close to you I wish the night would never end. Goodbye beautiful and kind, unrivalled, and divine creature. A thousand loving kisses all over, everywhere.

The road leading up to the museum, one km inland, begins opposite the golf course entrance. The museum is open from 9 am to 5.30 pm daily except Monday and admission is 20F.

You can poke around in the ruins of the old mill directly opposite the museum for free.

### Parc des Floralies

Parc des Floralies, halfway up the road to the Musée de la Pagerie, is a rather modest botanical park with a pond, picnic tables, a few birds in cages and identified plants and trees. It's open until 5 pm daily, except on public holidays, and admission is 10F for adults, 5F for children.

### Maison de la Canne

This worthwhile sugar cane museum occupies the site of an old sugar refinery and distillery. Artefacts include an old locomotive once used to carry cane from the fields to the distillery, antique cane crushers and period photos. Displays are in both French and English. It's open from 9 am to 5.30 pm daily except Monday. Admission is 15F for adults, 5F for children aged five to 12. The museum is on D7, 1.5 km east of Trois-Ilets centre.

### Pottery Village

There's an interesting brick kiln and pottery village on the north side of D7 one km east of Maison de la Canne. Look for the roadside sign 'Poterie Artisanale' marking the red clay road that leads into the village, 0.75 km from the highway.

The main workshop is International Atelier Caraïbe, but there are a few other potters in the village as well, all working out of old brick buildings. You can watch them at work making cups, vases, figurines and jewellery. The wares are quite nice and the prices are reasonable.

## POINTE DU BOUT

Pointe du Bout has Martinique's most frequented yachting marina and three of its largest resort hotels. The point is a U-shaped peninsula, with the hotels fringing the coast and the marina in the middle. All roads intersect south of the marina and traffic can get congested.

The three resorts (Bakoua, Méridien and Carayou) have each created their own little sandy beaches but the best beach is the Plage de l'Anse Mitan which runs along the western side of the neck of the peninsula between Pointe du Bout and Anse Mitan.

### Information

Ferries to and from Fort-de-France leave from the west side of the marina, where a money changing office, a laundrette, the port bureau and marine supply shops are all clustered together. Also at the marina is a newsstand, souvenir shops, boutiques and a Crédit Agricole bank, open from 7.30 am to 12.30 pm Tuesday to Saturday and from 2.15 to 4 pm Tuesday to Friday.

Thrifty, Budget, Hertz and Avis car rental agencies have offices at or near the peninsula's main intersection. There's a pharmacy near Bora Bora grocery store.

### Places to Stay

The harbourside *Davidiana* (☎ 66 00 54; fax 66 00 70) is a 14-room hotel above a restaurant and bar. Rooms are lacklustre although each has air-con and a private bathroom. Singles/doubles cost 250/300F in summer, 350/450F in winter.

*Karakoli* (☎ 66 02 67) is a pleasant little hotel in a quiet neighbourhood, 100 metres uphill from the busy heart of Pointe du Bout. The 18 studios and apartments have air-con, phones and kitchenettes; most have nice ocean views. There's a TV room and a garden courtyard with a small pool. Studio rates for up to two people are 310/430F in summer/winter. Apartments that hold up to four people cost 440F in summer, 495F in winter. Breakfast is available for an additional 40F.

The PLM Azur *La Pagerie* (☎ 66 05 30; fax 66 00 99; in France ☎ (1) 60 77 27 27, in the USA and Canada ☎ (800) 221-4542) is tucked between a busy intersection and the inner harbour. The hotel's 98 modern, comfortable rooms are reasonably priced for Pointe du Bout. Each has a balcony, air-con, TV, phone and a small refrigerator; many also have kitchenettes at no extra cost. Overall the atmosphere is similar to that of an apartment complex and services are minimal but there's a pool and it's within walking distance of the beaches at neighbouring resorts. Singles/doubles cost 406/436F in summer, 670/820F in winter. Breakfast is available for 57F more.

The 197-room PLM Azur *Hôtel Carayou* (☎ 66 04 04; fax 66 00 57) is a moderately priced resort hotel on the peninsula that forms the north-east side of the marina. This popular place has good-sized rooms with air-con, phones, TV, bathtubs, minibars and balconies. Rooms are in a series of three-storey buildings and many have sea views at no extra cost. Rates include a full buffet breakfast; there's a water sports centre, complimentary windsurfing, snorkelling and kayaking equipment, a pool and tennis

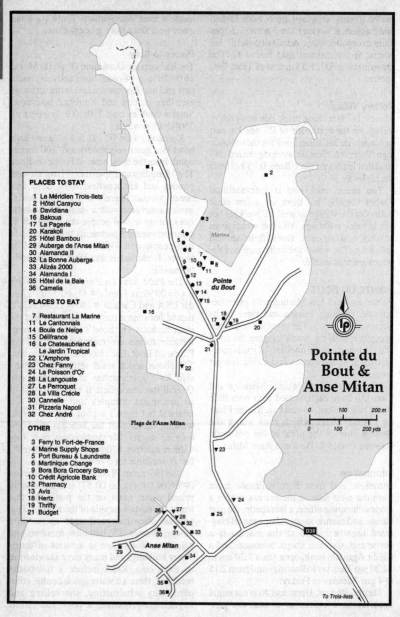

PLACES TO STAY
1 Le Méridien Trois-Ilets
2 Hôtel Carayou
8 Davidiana
16 Bakoua
17 La Pagerie
20 Karakoli
25 Hôtel Bambou
29 Auberge de l'Anse Mitan
30 Alamanda II
32 La Bonne Auberge
33 Alizés 2000
34 Alamanda I
35 Hôtel de la Baie
36 Camelia

PLACES TO EAT
7 Restaurant La Marine
11 Le Cantonnais
14 Boule de Neige
15 Délifrance
16 Le Chateaubriand &
   Le Jardin Tropical
22 L'Amphore
23 Chez Fanny
24 Le Poisson d'Or
26 La Langouste
27 Le Perroquet
28 La Villa Créole
30 Cannelle
31 Pizzeria Napoli
32 Chez André

OTHER
3 Ferry to Fort-de-France
4 Marine Supply Shops
5 Port Bureau & Laundrette
6 Martinique Change
9 Bora Bora Grocery Store
10 Crédit Agricole Bank
12 Pharmacy
13 Avis
18 Hertz
19 Thrifty
21 Budget

Marina

Pointe
du
Bout

Plage de l'Anse Mitan

Anse Mitan

To Trois-Ilets

Pointe du
Bout &
Anse Mitan

0        100       200 m
0        100       200 yds

courts. It's a particularly good value in summer, when it costs 517/650F for singles/doubles. Winter rates are 870/1034F.

The *Bakoua* (☎ 66 02 02; fax 66 00 41; in France ☎ 40 60 30 39, in the USA ☎ (800) 221-4542) is the area's most exclusive resort. Each of the 132 rooms and suites are comfortably furnished with either a king-size or two twin beds, air-con, TV, phone, minibar, room safe and a terrace or balcony. The grounds are spacious and there's a nice pool, tennis courts and complimentary water sports. Singles/doubles begin at 868/986F in summer, 1212/1424F in winter. These rates are for garden views; ocean-view rooms are on average about 15% more.

*Le Méridien Trois-Ilets* (☎ 66 00 00; fax 66 00 74; in the USA ☎ (800) 543-4300), with 295 rooms, is the area's largest and busiest resort. It has tennis courts, a pool and a water sports centre. Rooms have the usual 1st-class amenities and cost from 1150/1525F for singles/doubles in summer, 1400/1700F in winter.

### Places to Eat

Bora Bora, a small grocery store just north of the La Pagerie hotel, is open from 8 am to 1 pm daily and from 3.30 to 7.30 pm Monday to Saturday.

The nearby *Délifrance*, open from 7 am to 7.30 pm, has good breads, croissants, pastries and sandwiches.

Next door is *Boule de Neige*, a simple café with crêpes from 12F to 40F, salads from 40F to 45F and ice cream.

*Le Cantonnais* at the marina has the usual Chinese fare with a wide range of dishes from 55F to 60F, including five vegetarian offerings. It's open from 6.30 to 11 pm nightly except on Tuesday.

*Chez Fanny*, on the neck of the peninsula, is one of the cheaper restaurants in the area and thus quite popular. The changing chalkboard menu includes half a dozen starters such as crab farci priced around 25F and an equal number of main dishes, such as couscous or fried fish, from 40F to 55F. Food is served from steamer trays, cafeteria style.

*Restaurant La Marine* is a very popular open-air pizzeria and bar fronting the marina. Thin-crust pizzas cost 38F to 50F and there are some good seafood dishes with tasty sauces for around 75F. In the morning there's a simple buffet-style breakfast with bread, pineapple, eggs and coffee for 40F.

For fine dining the Bakoua hotel's *Le Chateaubriand* features French and continental food with main courses in the 70F to 100F range, while the hotel's less formal *Le Jardin Tropical* offers a four-course Creole dinner for 165F.

There's a fine water view of Anse Mitan Bay from *L'Amphore*, which has a rather romantic setting. Lobster is the speciality but the menu includes other Creole and French fare as well. A three-course dinner averages about 200F. It's open for dinner from 7 to 10 pm daily except Sunday and for lunch from noon to 2 pm Tuesday to Saturday. To get there take the road between the Budget office and the entrance to the Bakoua hotel.

**Hotel Breakfast Buffets** The *Hôtel Carayou*'s open-air restaurant has a nice breakfast spread with fresh fruit, cereals, juices, croissants, pastries, yoghurt, bacon and eggs. There are views across the bay to Fort-de-France and if you get a waterfront table it's quite a nice experience for 65F. *Le Méridien* puts on a similar spread with the addition of crêpes to order and charges 100F. The buffet at the *Bakoua* is not quite as extensive as the other two but the food is good, the atmosphere is pleasant and there's a fine sea view; it costs 75F. All serve breakfast from 7 to 10 am.

### ANSE MITAN

Overall, the small seaside tourist area of Anse Mitan is cheaper and more casual than neighbouring Pointe du Bout, a km to the north. There are no large resorts, but rather a number of smaller moderately priced hotels and guesthouses. Anse Mitan has good restaurants and a pleasant view across the bay to Fort-de-France, to which it's connected by ferry. The sandy Plage de l'Anse Mitan beach extends north from the village.

## Places to Stay – bottom end

*La Bonne Auberge* (☎ 66 01 55; fax 66 04 50) is a three-storey hotel on the main road, with 32 rooms that open onto a small garden courtyard. Rooms are very simple, with private bathrooms, phones and either air-con or a ceiling fan. Singles/doubles cost 180/280F in summer, 250/350F in winter, breakfast included.

*Hôtel de la Baie* (☎ 66 06 66; fax 63 00 70), on a hillside a few minutes' walk from the main road, has a dozen straightforward but comfortable rooms with air-con, private bathrooms, kitchenettes and phones. Summer rates are 250F for a standard room, 350F for a room with a balcony, some of which have lovely views of Fort-de-France. In winter rates range from 280F to 580F.

*Auberge de l'Anse Mitan* (☎ 66 01 12) is on the water at the south end of Anse Mitan. This older inn has 20 rooms with phones and air-con and six studios with kitchenettes. The rooms can be mosquito infested and the overall value is poor. For standard rooms, singles/doubles cost 280/330F in summer, 330/420F in winter. The studios cost 300F in summer, 400F in winter.

## Places to Stay – middle

The first three listings (Alamanda I & II and Camelia) are part of the Archipel Group, a small chain that is constructing moderately priced hotels on Martinique. Bookings for all three hotels can be made through a central reservation system (in Fort-de-France ☎ 63 13 72, fax 73 20 75; in Paris ☎ 43 25 25 16, fax 43 29 12 34), 26 Rue Perrinon, 97200 Fort-de-France.

*Alamanda I* (☎ 66 06 66) has 24 self-contained studios in an older three-storey building on a hillside a few minutes' walk from Anse Mitan centre. The units have TV, phones, air-con, kitchenettes and large balconies. While not fancy the accommodation is comfortable enough and the price is a good deal at 265/ 330F for singles/doubles in summer, 410/490F in winter.

*Alamanda II* (☎ 66 03 66) is a new 30-room hotel opposite the waterfront in the village centre. The rooms and suites vary in size and decor; the cheapest are on the small side but otherwise comfortable. Rooms have air-con, TV and phones; some have bathtubs, others just showers. A few have views and small balconies. Rates for singles or doubles begin at 330F in summer, 490F in winter. Breakfast is an additional 50F per person.

If you don't mind the five-minute uphill walk, a good-value place to stay is the new *Camelia* hotel, which has 49 compact but quite sufficient rooms with air-con, TV and phones. About half the units also have balcony kitchenettes for the same rate: 330F in summer, 490F in winter. Ask for a 2nd or 3rd-floor room as they have nice views of Fort-de-France.

*Alizés 2000* (☎ 66 05 55; fax 66 01 04), on the main road, is a clean and cosy place with 18 modern, air-con rooms. Each has a phone, TV, a small balcony and a kitchenette. Two of the rooms are handicapped-equipped. Singles/doubles cost from 335/380F in summer, 505/540F in winter. Breakfast is an additional 30F per person.

*Hôtel Bambou* (☎ 66 01 39; fax 66 05 05), at the south end of the road between Anse Mitan and Pointe du Bout, is a sprawling complex with 118 cabin-like duplex bungalows surrounded by neatly clipped lawns. These simple units have rustic knotty pine interiors, air-con, phones and private bathrooms. The complex is set back from the beach and there's a pool and a large restaurant. Singles/doubles start at 380/440F in summer, 580/640F in winter, breakfast included.

## Places to Eat

*Pizzeria Napoli*, in the village centre, attracts a crowd with a menu that includes a range of good pizzas and pastas from 38F to 65F and a handful of meat dishes, heavy on the veal, for around 85F. It's open from noon to 3 pm and 7 to 11.30 pm daily in the high season, closed on Tuesday in the low season.

*Chez André* is à pleasant little restaurant at the side of the La Bonne Auberge hotel. There's a fixed three-course meal of the day for 100F and à la carte fish and meat main dishes from 80F.

*Cannelle*, at the Alamanda II hotel, has the area's cheapest lobster, at 30F per 100 grams, and a variety of other main courses for around 60F to 90F.

*La Langouste*, next to the pier, is a popular bar and restaurant and the only place right on the water. It has a nice atmosphere and view, although the food is average and the service leisurely. The 100F menu touristique includes accras, blood sausage, a main course of grilled fish or chicken colombo and fresh fruit or ice cream for dessert. Otherwise, the spicy fish blaff with rice for 70F is a good choice; conch and beef dishes are similarly priced. Lobster is available at market prices. It's open from about 12.30 to 3 pm and 7.30 to 10 pm daily.

*La Villa Créole*, a French/Creole restaurant, features three fixed menus at 150F, 190F and 240F. The cheapest includes a drink, accras, grilled fish, rice, beans and coconut flan, while the most expensive pairs salmon pâté with half a lobster. There's also an à la carte menu with main dishes averaging about 90F and a fixed children's menu for 75F. It's open for dinner from 7 to 10 pm daily except on Sunday and for lunch from noon to 2 pm Tuesday to Saturday.

Closer to the pier, *Le Perroquet* is another restaurant with a three-course menu touristique featuring a starter, grilled fish and ice cream for 120F. It's open daily for lunch and dinner.

*Le Poisson d'Or*, on the road between Pointe du Bout and Anse Mitan, has a friendly Creole atmosphere and moderate prices. The menu du jour includes a lambi appetiser, Creole fish, rice and banana flambé for 100F. It's open from noon to 2.30 pm and 7 to 10 pm daily except on Monday. There's a guitarist in the evenings.

## ANSE-À-L'ANE

Anse-à-l'Ane is a modern seaside village with a nice beach of light grey sand. The north side of the village is largely residential, while the south side is developed for tourism; it's quite compact and nothing is more than a few minutes' walk from anywhere else. The bay, which is generally calm,

is a rather popular anchorage for yachts. At night you can see the lights of Fort-de-France twinkling across the water.

Anse-à-l'Ane is connected to Fort-de-France by ferry and on weekends the beach attracts a crowd. The ferry dock is in the centre of the beach, near Chez Jojo.

### Places to Stay

*Le Nid Tropical* (☎ 68 31 30) has simple bungalows and camping along the beach. Rates range from 70F for tenting with own tent to 220F for a studio.

*Le Tulipier* (☎ 68 41 21), family run and good value, consists of five modern studio units and a one-bedroom apartment in a quiet residential area, about a five-minute walk from the beach. The studios rent for 300/1617F a night/week for two people, the apartment for 350/2260F for up to four people, with about a 10% drop in the low season. Not much English is spoken, but the hosts are amiable and patient with non-French speakers.

The *Frantour* (☎ 62 31 67; fax 68 37 65) is a pleasant contemporary resort hotel conveniently located in the centre of the beach. The 77 rooms have air-con, ceiling fans, TV, minibars, safes and small balconies or terraces. There's a disco, pool, tennis courts and a water activities centre. Singles/doubles begin at 440/600F in summer, 665/1020F in winter.

### Places to Eat

There are a number of places to eat on or near the waterfront, ranging from simple beachside snack bars to fine Creole restaurants. At the lower end, *Chez Jojo*, a popular local hangout near the Texaco petrol station, has sandwiches, fried chicken and a range of coffees and beers.

There's a modest pizza bar, *La Gondola*, a block inland from the beach. The village also has a couple of grocery stores.

*Pignon sur Mer* is a good Creole restaurant on the beach, with dishes that include chicken brochettes (54F), grilled fish (70F) and lobster (160F). It's open from noon to 2 pm and 7 to 9 pm; closed on Monday and on Sunday evenings.

*Le Calalou* at the Frantour hotel has a daily salad-to-dessert meal for 165F; otherwise main courses begin at around 100F. The best deal is at lunch, noon to 2 pm daily, when there's a buffet of rice dishes, cold salads, luncheon meats, fruit, pâtés, marinated fish and bread for 77F.

## GRAND ANSE

Grand Anse, on Grand Anse d'Arlet Bay, is a scenic beach that's lined with brightly painted fishing boats and weathered beachside restaurants. On weekends the area is packed with urbanites from Fort-de-France, yachters and other tourists.

Grand Anse is a popular swimming beach and there's good snorkelling along the south end of the bay just off Morne Champagne, the volcanic peninsula that separates Grand Anse from Anse d'Arlet. A trail at the south end of the beach leads up to the top of Morne Champagne.

### Places to Eat

The beachfront road has a score of unpretentious restaurants with reasonably priced meals, and it's easy to stroll along the beach and compare menus. A number of places offer a three-course menu du jour for 70F to 85F. There are a few cheaper places as well, including *Délices des Anses*, which has pizzas and chicken dishes from around 35F, and *Chez Gaby*, a pleasant spot at the south end of the beach whose varied menu includes sandwiches (15F), half a roasted chicken and fries (45F) and fish with vegetables and rice (65F).

For something more upmarket, the popular *Ti'Sable*, at the more private north end of the beach, has a selection of fixed-price meals from 135F to 260F as well as a Sunday Creole buffet lunch for 165F. It's open from noon to 2.30 pm daily for lunch and on Friday and Saturday for dinner. Ti'Sable is on a fine section of the beach, has a line of lounge chairs and rents Hobie Cat boats and jet-skis.

## GRAND ANSE TO DIAMANT

The coastal road south of Grand Anse passes through **Anse d'Arlet** and **Petit Anse**, two seaside villages off the tourist track, and then winds around the south side of **Morne Larcher** (477 metres). As you come around a curve, the offshore islet Rocher du Diamant (Diamond Rock) pops into view before the road drops down to the town of Diamant. Beware of tortuously high speed bumps near the beach on the western outskirts of Diamant.

### Places to Eat

On a rise at the south end of Anse d'Arlet is *Le Flamboyant des Isles*, a moderately priced Creole restaurant perched right above the water. There are lots of seafood dishes such as fish blaff and squid fricassée priced around 75F and a three-course fixed meal for 90F (50F for children). It's open from noon to 2.30 pm and 7 to 9.30 pm; closed on Sunday evenings and Tuesday.

## DIAMANT

Diamant is a small seaside town facing Diamond Rock. The centre of Diamant is far more local than touristy in character and even though a number of hotels list Diamant as their address, most are on the outskirts of town, with the biggest resorts a couple of km to the east.

A long and narrow grey-sand beach extends nearly two km along the west side of Diamant. Despite being less than 100 metres from D37, the beach has a delightfully natural setting with a wooded strip of seagrape, coconut and tropical almond trees providing a buffer between the waterfront and the road. The whole beach is quite popular and there are several pull-offs along the main road that provide beach access.

### Places to Stay

*Hôtel Diamant les Bains* (☎ 76 40 14; fax 76 27 00) is a small in-town hotel with a pleasant West Indian character. It has a big pool, lots of flowering plants on the grounds and a nice beachfront view, although the beach itself is narrow and not terribly appealing.

**Diamond Rock**

The 176-metre-high Rocher du Diamant, or Diamond Rock, is a gumdrop-shaped volcanic islet three km off the south-western tip of Martinique. It is a haven for sea birds and favoured by scuba divers, but most intriguing of all is its history.

In 1804 the British landed 120 sailors on Diamond Rock who quickly established barracks and warehouses within the rock's caves and cliffs, reinforcing it all with cannons. In one of the more unusual moments of British military history, the Royal Navy then registered the rock as a fighting ship, the unsinkable HMS *Diamond Rock*, and for the next 17 months used it to harass French ships trying to navigate the passage. French attacks proved unsuccessful until French Admiral Villaret de Joyeuse devised a plan to catch the enemy off balance. According to the French account, the admiral cut loose a skiff loaded with rum in the direction of Diamond Rock, the isolated British sailors chugged down the hooch and the French forces retook the island. ■

The rooms are small and straightforward, but not uncomfortable, and have air-con, twin beds and phones, while the bungalows also have refrigerators. In summer, rooms cost 310/380F for singles/doubles, bungalows cost 380/450F. In winter, rooms cost 380/500F for singles/doubles, bungalows cost 480/600F. Rates include breakfast.

The beachside *Village du Diamant* (☎ 76 28 93), La Dizac, is a new three-storey hotel 2.5 km west of Diamant centre. The 59 modern studio-style rooms have air-con, balconies, kitchenettes and phones. This hotel, popular with divers, has its own dive shop, a pool and a TV lounge. Singles/doubles cost 360/420F in summer, 500/600F in winter, plus an optional 40F for breakfast.

The *Marine Hôtel* (☎ 76 46 00; fax 76 25 99), Pointe de la Chéry, is a pleasant, new 150-room resort hotel on a predominantly rocky shoreline about two km east of Diamant centre and on the same peninsula as the Novotel hotel. Rooms have air-con, phones, both a king-size bed and a sofabed, room safes, kitchenettes on the balconies and nice ocean views. There's a restaurant and snack bar, a large pool, tennis courts and complimentary snorkelling and windsurfing gear. Diving, deep-sea fishing and motor boat rentals are also available. Singles/doubles are a reasonable 460/550F in summer, 570/755F in winter.

The *Novotel Diamant* (☎ 76 42 42; fax 76 22 87), Pointe de la Chéry, has a secluded location at the end of the peninsula that forms the eastern edge of Diamant Bay. This is the area's largest and most exclusive resort; the 180 rooms have air-con, TVs, phones and room safes. There are a couple of restaurants, a car rental agency, a pool, a white-sand beach and complimentary water activities including canoes, snorkelling and pedal boats. Singles/doubles cost 685/870F in summer, 970/1125F in winter.

**Places to Eat**

For cheap eats in the town centre, there's a snack shop with sandwiches, burgers, and fried chicken on the waterfront opposite the church. For pizza there's *Pizza Pépé*, a couple of minutes' walk south-east of the town hall, by the Esso station.

There are half a dozen small restaurants on either side of the town hall. All are moderate to slightly expensive, though a few have a meal du jour for around 85F. In the same neighbourhood is the *Hôtel Diamant Les Bains* restaurant, which has good reasonably priced Creole food with fish and other main dishes from 70F to 80F.

**MARIN**

Marin, at the head of a deep protected bay, is one of the island's two sub-prefectures and the regional commercial centre. There's a large marina on the west side of town that has full yachting services and is home port to the island's yacht charter industry.

In the centre of town there's a lovely stone church that dates from 1766. To get there turn south off the main road at the disco; it's on the plaza just 200 metres down.

## SAINTE-ANNE

Sainte-Anne, the southernmost village on the island, has an attractive seaside setting. There are several good beaches in the area including the magnificent Les Salines, just a 10-minute drive away. Despite the number of visitors that flock to the town on weekends and during the winter season, Sainte-Anne remains a casual, low-key place.

The area waters have abundant near-shore reef formations that make for good snorkelling. If you want to see the underwater world without getting your feet wet, Aquascope, a semi-submerged vessel with transparent viewing windows, operates daily at 9.30 and 11 am, 2 and 3.30 pm and charges 110F for adults, 60F for children.

### Information

The post office is at the north end of town. There's a laundrette on Rue du Calvaire, open from 7 am to 6.30 pm weekdays, to 3 pm on Saturday.

### Places to Stay

There's camping at *Vivre & Camper* (☎ 76 72 79; fax 76 97 82), BP 8, Pointe Marin, on a nice beach near Club Med, about a 30-minute walk north of the village centre. You can rent an equipped tent for a week for 700F or set up your own tent and pay 40F a day.

*Georges III Hôtel* (☎ 76 73 11) in the village centre is a bit shoddy but clean enough and has very straightforward rooms with bathrooms (no towels) and kitchenettes at 250F per room.

The in-town *La Dunette* hotel (☎ 76 73 90; fax 76 76 05) has 18 modern rooms with air-con, TV, hair dryers and phones. Some of the rooms look out over the water and there's a beach fronting the hotel. Singles/doubles cost 300/400F in summer, 500/600F in winter, breakfast included.

*Hameau de Beauregard* (☎ 76 75 75; fax 73 20 75; in France ☎ 43 25 25 16) is a modern condo-like hotel on D9, about 500 metres south-east of the village centre. Part of the Archipel hotel chain, it has 90 studio and one-bedroom units with kitchenettes, air-con, TV, phones and balconies. Rates

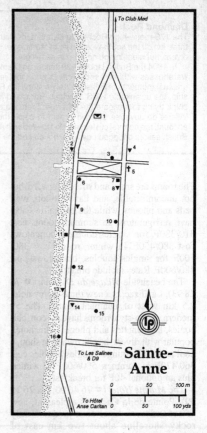

Sainte-Anne

| | |
|---|---|
| 1 | Post Office |
| 2 | Poi et Virginie |
| 3 | Pharmacy |
| 4 | Les Tameriniers |
| 5 | Church |
| 6 | Town Hall |
| 7 | Georges III Hôtel |
| 8 | Délifrance |
| 9 | Athanor & Crêperie |
| 10 | Le Gallerie Newsstand |
| 11 | La Dunette |
| 12 | Grocery Store |
| 13 | L'Epi Soleil |
| 14 | Snack Shop |
| 15 | Public Market |
| 16 | Esso Petrol Station |

start at 370F in summer, 660F in winter. There's a pool.

*Hôtel Anse Caritan* (☎ 76 74 12; fax 76 72 59) has a secluded location one km south of the village centre. This modern hotel has 96 contemporary rooms with kitchenettes, air-con, phones and terraces or balconies. There's a restaurant, a pool and a white-sand beach. Singles/doubles cost 464/645F in summer, 690/950F in winter, breakfast included.

*Club Med's Buccaneer's Creek* (☎ 76 76 13) is at the end of the peninsula that juts out north of Sainte-Anne. It's fronted by a nice white-sand beach and is virtually a little village unto itself. There are 300 rooms with air-con, queen-size or twin beds and the usual amenities. Weekly rates for doubles, including meals, begin at US$1400 in summer, US$1600 in winter.

### Places to Eat

There's a local snack bar on the coastal road in front of the public market and a grocery store a minute's walk to the north. In the same area, *L'Epi Soleil* sells pastries, bread and sandwiches and has a small dining area. For crispy baguettes and croissants try the *Délifrance* on the Rue de l'Église, a little south of the church.

*Athanor* is a simple restaurant with an adjacent crêperie. The food, other than the crêpes, is pretty good although the service is erratic. Salads and starters cost 25F to 35F, grilled fish is 65F and lobster is 38F per 100 grams. It opens for dinner at 7 pm.

The restaurant at *La Dunette* hotel has open-air waterfront dining and a menu featuring seafood. Fish soup costs 32F, lambi or grilled fish is 65F and lobster is about 200F.

*Poi et Virginie* has an intimate waterfront setting. Starters and a whole menu page of desserts are priced from 30F to 40F, while main courses range from chicken colombo for 60F to lobster for 180F.

*Les Tameriniers*, immediately north of the church, has salads and appetisers from 28F to 60F and main courses ranging from grilled Creole fish for 52F to lobster for 140F.

### LES SALINES

Les Salines, at the undeveloped southern tip of the island, is a long, gently curving beach with golden sands. Shaded by coconut palms and tropical almond trees, it is widely regarded as Martinique's finest beach. As the area is arid, Les Salines is often sunny when other parts of the island are not. The beach attracts scores of visitors on weekends and holidays, but it's big enough to accommodate everyone without feeling crowded.

Les Salines is five km south of Sainte-Anne at the end of D9. There are showers and food vans near the centre of the beach and about 500 metres farther south you'll find snack shops selling reasonably priced sandwiches, burgers and chicken. Camping is allowed at the west side of the beach on weekends and during school holidays.

Les Salines gets its name from Étang des Salines, the large salt pond that backs it. Beware of poisonous manchineel trees (most marked with red paint) on the beach, particularly at the south-east end.

### Savane des Pétrifications

From the end of D9 at Les Salines, the road continues south-east along the beach for another two km to the site of a petrified forest that unfortunately has been heavily scavenged by decades of souvenir hunters. There's a blazed trail through the former forest, which begins at the end of the road. It's also possible to continue walking up the coast; the track continues all the way to Macabou, about 25 km away.

# Montserrat

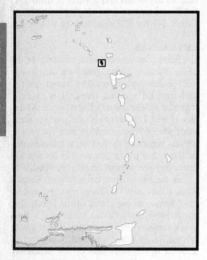

Small and lightly populated, Montserrat is one of the least developed and least touristed islands in the Eastern Caribbean. It is pleasantly rural and green, with a countryside of rolling hills, mountains and valleys.

The old stone sugar mills that dot the countryside stand as reminders of Montserrat's colonial past. Early Irish immigrants, in particular, have had an indelible influence. Green shamrocks show up in business logos, atop the governor's residence and stamped into visitors' passports. There are nearly 100 families on Montserrat with the surname Ryan and dozens of O'Briens, Galloways and Sweeneys, while village names include the likes of Blakes, Kinsale and Cork Hill.

Plymouth, the island's only real town, is an appealing West Indian capital of narrow curving streets lined with period buildings. Like the rest of the island, it's a throwback to another era, lending credibility to Montserrat's promotional claim of being 'The Way the Caribbean Used to Be'.

There are hikes into the mountainous interior, a couple of historic sites, a crater with steaming sulphur vents and a few black-sand beaches, but the island is mainly notable for its relaxed, unhurried character. Many people, including a sizeable number of retirees, return year after year with the express purpose of doing nothing at all.

In September 1989 Montserrat was ravaged by Hurricane Hugo, which struck the island head-on with winds that reached more than 150 mph. Eleven people died, 90% of the population was left homeless and damages were estimated at US$300 million. While the island has largely recovered, bare trees on some hillsides are testimony to the storm's fury.

## ORIENTATION

The airport is on the east coast, seven miles (11.2 km) north-east of Plymouth. A loop road connects the upper half of the island while the island's other main road runs south from Plymouth towards the sightseeing area at Galways Soufrière. Virtually all of Montserrat's villages, sights and accommodation are on the west side of the island. It's a small island that can easily be toured in a day.

# Facts about the Island

## HISTORY

Amerindians called this island Alliouagana, meaning 'Land of the Prickly Bush'. When Columbus sighted the island in 1493, he named it Montserrat, as its craggy landscape reminded him of the serrated mountains above the Monastery of Montserrat near Barcelona, Spain.

The first European settlers were Catholics, mainly Irish, who moved to Montserrat in 1632 to escape persecution from Protestant rule on neighbouring St Kitts. In the years that followed Montserrat continued to attract

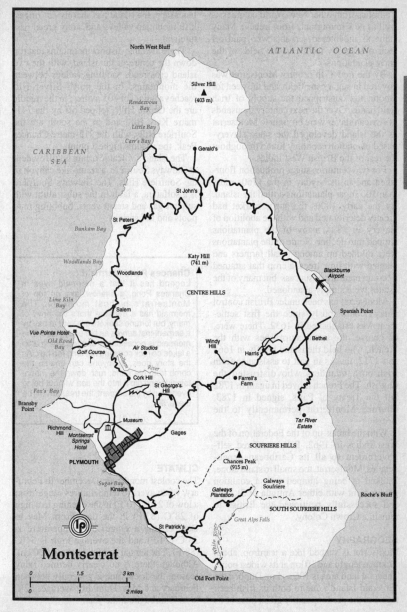

North West Bluff

ATLANTIC OCEAN

Silver Hill
(403 m)

Rendezvous
Bay

Little Bay

Carr's Bay

CARIBBEAN
SEA

Gerald's

St John's

St Peters

Bunkum Bay

Woodlands Bay

Katy Hill
(741 m)

Blackburne
Airport

Woodlands

CENTRE HILLS

Lime Kiln
Bay

Salem

Spanish Point

Vue Pointe Hotel
Old Road
Bay

Air Studios

Windy
Hill

Bethel

Golf Course

Belham River

Harris

River

Cork Hill

Farrell's
Farm

Fox's Bay

St George's
Hill

Gages

Tar River
Estate

Bransby
Point

Museum

Richmond
Hill

Montserrat
Springs
Hotel

SOUFRIERE
HILLS

PLYMOUTH

Chances Peak
(915 m)

Sugar Bay

Kinsale

Galways
Plantation

Galways
Soufriere

Roche's Bluff

SOUTH SOUFRIERE HILLS

White River

Great Alps Falls

St Patrick's

**Montserrat**

0       1.5      3 km

0    1       2 miles

Old Fort Point

Catholics from other New World colonies as well as new immigrants from Ireland. Many came as indentured servants who paid off their passage by toiling in the fields of the early plantations.

By the mid-17th century Montserrat was covered in sugar cane fields and the need for labour had outstripped the supply of Irish field hands. Over the next century thousands of African slaves were brought to Montserrat as the island developed the same slavery-based plantation economy found throughout the rest of the British West Indies.

For two centuries sugar production flourished and in its heyday in the 1760s more than 100 sugar plantations dotted the island. By the early 1800s the sugar market had greatly deteriorated and with the abolition of slavery in 1834 many of the plantations slipped into decline. Some of the plantations were divided up among small farmers and planted with lime trees, a crop that attained a certain measure of success, but many of the estates were simply abandoned.

Montserrat has been under British control almost continuously since the first settlement was established in 1632. There were, of course, the usual skirmishes with the French, who held the island briefly in 1665 and 1712, thanks in part to assistance from Irish-born islanders who distrusted the English. The French moved in again in 1782 but the Treaty of Paris, signed in 1783, returned Montserrat permanently to the British.

With the break-up of the Federation of the West Indies in 1962, Britain offered self-government to all its Caribbean dependencies. Montserrat, too small to stand alone, baulked at being lumped into a coalition government with either Antigua or St Kitts and successfully petitioned the British to remain a Crown Colony.

### GEOGRAPHY

Montserrat is shaped like a teardrop, about 17 km in length and 10 km at its widest point. The total land area is 106 sq km. Dubbed the 'Emerald Island', due to both its Irish heritage and the predominantly green hues of its landscape, the island has sharply cut ridges, lush mountain valleys and stony green pastureland.

There are three distinct mountains that run down the centre of the island, with the two island crossroads saddling valleys between the mountains. In the north Silver Hill reaches a height of 403 metres; in the middle are the Centre Hills, topped off by the 741-metre Katy Hill; and in the south are the Soufrière Hills, with the 915-metre Chances Peak, the island's highest point.

The island's volcanic origin is still evident at Galways Soufrière, a crater-like canyon in the Soufrière Hills. The Galways Soufrière is a solfatara, a fault in the substratum with sulphur gas and steam vents, bubbling mud pools and hot springs.

**Chances Pond Mermaid**
Legend has it that a mermaid lives in Chances Pond, a shallow lake on top of Montserrat's highest mountain. The mermaid has a treasure that's the envy of many, but fortune seekers are kept at bay by a serpent that serves as her bodyguard. The mermaid is occasionally spotted sitting atop a lakeside rock combing her long red hair. As the story goes, if anyone can snatch the comb from her hand, rush down the mountainside and dip it into the sea without being overtaken by the serpent, the treasure will be theirs. ■

### CLIMATE

The coolest months are December to February, when average temperatures range from a low of 21°C (70°F) in the evening to a high of 28°C (83°F) in the day. From May to October, the average low temperature is 23°C (74°F) and the average high is 31°C (88°F). The annual rainfall is about 150 cm. Although there is no clearly defined rainy season, the driest time is generally between February and May. Humidity averages 62% to 69% throughout the year.

## FLORA & FAUNA

About 90 species of birds have been sighted on Montserrat, a third of which breed on the island. The national bird, the endemic Montserrat oriole, is a pretty black and yellow bird that survives solely in Montserrat's mountains with only about 500 pairs remaining.

The crapaud, a large frog which appears on restaurant menus as 'mountain chicken', is found only at higher elevations on Montserrat and Dominica. Montserrat also has iguanas, agouti and seven bat species.

There are rainforests, tree fern forests, montane thickets and elfin woodland on Montserrat. Mango, breadfruit, heliconia, ginger, elephant ears and other tropical plants are abundant along the roadsides.

## GOVERNMENT

Montserrat is a British Crown Colony. The resident governor, David Taylor, who represents the Queen, presides over both the executive council and the legislative council. Seven members of the legislature are elected in general elections while four others are appointed. The chief minister is Reuben Meade.

## ECONOMY

Montserrat is self-sufficient in fruit and vegetable production, and some small-scale export crops, including the growing of herbal teas, are being promoted. Some of the more abundant island crops include sweet potatoes, Irish potatoes, tomatoes, cabbages, lettuce, hot peppers, limes, papayas and bananas.

About 10% of the labour force works in small-scale industries, manufacturing such things as electronic components and leather goods. Despite the fact that only about 30,000 tourists visit Montserrat annually,

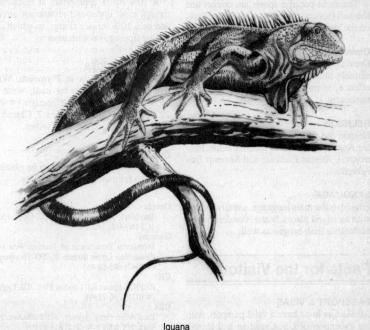

Iguana

tourism accounts for roughly 25% of the island's GNP.

## POPULATION & PEOPLE

The population is about 11,000, of which 3500 live in Plymouth. Most islanders are black, the descendants of African slaves, although there is an admixture of Irish blood.

## ARTS & CULTURE

While the island's African heritage is strong, it blends uniquely with Irish influences. For instance, island folk dances incorporate Irish steps enlivened with an African beat. And although Montserrat is the only island in the Caribbean to observe St Patrick's Day, the most spirited celebrations are seen at Carnival, the quintessential West Indian festival.

Probably the Montserratian best known throughout the Caribbean is Alphonsus Cassell, otherwise known as Arrow, whose tune *Hot! Hot! Hot!* is a soca classic.

The most popular sports are cricket and football (soccer), both played at Sturge Park, on the north side of Plymouth.

### Dress Conventions

Dress is casual and simple cotton clothing is suitable attire for any occasion. To avoid offence, swimwear should be restricted to the beach.

### RELIGION

Despite the Irish legacy, most of the people are Anglican, the rest of are Methodist, Pentecostal, Roman Catholic and Seventh Day Adventist.

### LANGUAGE

English is the main language, usually spoken with an island patois. Some islanders have a noticeable Irish brogue as well.

# Facts for the Visitor

## PASSPORT & VISAS

All visitors must have a valid passport, with the exception of US, Canadian and British citizens who may instead present an official ID, such as a birth certificate, as proof of citizenship.

Entry visas may be required of visitors from Haiti, Cuba and former Soviet bloc countries. British consulate offices can issue visas and provide information.

Officially all travellers must have an onward or return ticket.

## CUSTOMS

Visitors may bring in 40 ounces of alcoholic beverages, 200 cigarettes and six ounces of perfume duty free.

## MONEY

The Eastern Caribbean dollar (EC$) is the official currency, but US dollars are widely accepted. The exchange rate is US$1= EC$2.70. Major credit cards are accepted by hotels and a few of the larger restaurants.

A 10% tip is appropriate at restaurants, though most upper-end restaurants already add on a 10% service charge, in which case further tipping is not necessary.

## TOURIST OFFICES

The tourist office is in Plymouth. When requesting information by mail, write to: Montserrat Department of Tourism (☎ 491-2230; fax 491-7430), PO Box 7, Church St, Plymouth, Montserrat, West Indies.

### Overseas Reps

Information on Montserrat can be obtained from the following overseas offices:

Canada
   TravMark, 33 Niagara St, Toronto, Ontario M5V 1C2 (☎ (416) 362-3900)
Germany
   Montserrat Department of Tourism/West India Committee, Lomer Strasse 28, 2000 Hamburg 70 (☎ (040) 695-88-46)
UK
   RBPR, 3 Epirus Rd, London SW6 7UJ, England (☎ (071) 730-7144)
USA
   Pace Advertising Agency, 485 Fifth Ave, New York, NY 10017 (☎ (212) 818-0100)

## BUSINESS HOURS

Government and business offices are typically open from 8 am to noon and 1 to 4 pm Monday to Friday. Shop hours vary, but stores are generally closed on Sunday and many also close at noon on Wednesday and Saturday.

## HOLIDAYS

Public holidays on Montserrat are:

| | | |
|---|---|---|
| *New Year's Day* | – | 1 January |
| *St Patrick's Day* | – | 17 March |
| *Good Friday* | – | late March/early April |
| *Easter Monday* | – | late March/early April |
| *Labour Day* | – | first Monday in May |
| *Whit Monday* | – | eighth Monday after Easter |
| *Queen's Birthday* | – | second Saturday in June |
| *August Monday* | – | first Monday in August |
| *Christmas Day* | – | 25 December |
| *Boxing Day* | – | 26 December |
| *Festival Day* | – | 31 December |

## CULTURAL EVENTS

Montserrat observes 17 March not only for its Irish connection but also to commemorate a rebellion by island slaves in 1768. The village of St Patrick's is the main focal point, with festivities that include music, street dancing and traditional food.

Montserrat's Carnival festivities start in mid-December and culminate on New Year's Day with a parade through Plymouth and street jump-ups (mass dancing and merry-making). The most festive day is 31 December, when music and costume competitions begin in the afternoon at Plymouth's Sturge Park and partying continues until after midnight.

## POST

The main post office is in Plymouth; there are sub-post offices in major villages. All post office boxes are in Plymouth, so when writing to Montserrat box numbers should be followed by 'Plymouth' (if there's no box number just put the village name), ending with 'Montserrat, West Indies'.

## TELECOMMUNICATIONS

You can purchase phonecards, make long-distance phone calls and send fax, telex and telegrams at the Cable & Wireless office in Plymouth. MasterCard and Visa are accepted.

Both coin and card phones are easily found around the island. For directory assistance, dial 118 (toll free).

Montserrat phone numbers begin with 491 followed by a four-digit number; you only need to dial the final four digits when making a local call. When calling from overseas add the area code 809 to the seven-digit number.

For more information, see Telecommunications in the front of the book.

## ELECTRICITY

The electric current is 220 volts AC, 60 cycles, but most hotels and villas also have a 110-volt adaptor outlet in the bathroom.

## WEIGHTS & MEASURES

Montserrat follows the British imperial system: highway signs and car odometers are in miles, survey map elevations are in feet and weights are generally in pounds and ounces.

## BOOKS & MAPS

The Montserrat National Trust has published several books about the island including *Birds of Montserrat* (EC$10) by Allan Siegel, *Wildlife of Montserrat* (EC$30) by Jay Blankenship and *Montserrat, West Indies, a Chronological History* (EC$20) by Marion Wheeler. They can be purchased at the Sea Wolf Diving School and the Montserrat National Trust office, which are both in Plymouth.

The best map of the island is the Ordnance Survey's *Tourist Map of Montserrat* (scale 1:25,000). It sells for about EC$18 at the airport gift shop and in Plymouth at Jus Looking, the Sea Wolf Diving School and the Lands & Surveys department.

## MEDIA

There are two local papers, *The Montserrat Reporter* and *The News*, both published on Friday.

Radio Antilles, one of the Caribbean's most powerful networks, has a central broadcasting station on Montserrat. The island's other major radio station is the government-owned Radio Montserrat. TV programming is relayed from other Caribbean islands.

## HEALTH

Glendon Hospital (☎ 491-2552) in Plymouth is a 68-bed government-run facility that handles emergencies; the most serious cases are usually air-lifted to Guadeloupe or Barbados.

There's a risk of bilharzia on Montserrat's east coast, in the villages surrounding the airport, where it's advisable to avoid wading or swimming in freshwater. More information is under Health in the introductory Facts for the Visitor chapter.

## DANGERS & ANNOYANCES

Montserrat has very little crime, although the usual safety precautions still apply.

## EMERGENCIES

In case of a police or fire emergency dial 999; for medical emergencies dial 911.

## ACTIVITIES
### Beaches & Swimming

While no one comes to Montserrat for its beaches, there are some reasonable places to swim. The west coast of the island is generally calm and the east coast turbulent.

All Montserrat's beaches have volcanic grey or black sand, with the exception of Rendezvous Bay on the north-west coast, which has golden-brown sand. Rendezvous Bay and adjacent Little Bay are both nice, secluded beaches that can be reached by boat or by foot.

Popular beaches that can be reached by car include Fox's Bay, just north of Plymouth; Old Road Bay, below the Vue Pointe Hotel; and Woodlands Bay, the only spot with beach facilities. Bunkum Bay, about a five-minute walk from the road in the village of St Peter's, is also a nice beach.

Sugar Bay, at the south side of Plymouth, is not a great beach but it's a popular swimming spot for local kids. There's also a beach at the north side of Plymouth that continues up to the Montserrat Springs Hotel.

### Diving

Diving is relatively new to Montserrat. The island has coral that is still pristine, giant sponges, varied marine life and good visibility.

O'Garros, at the southern end of the island, is a popular spot that has both shallow and deep-water diving. The water is very clear and there are schools of barracuda and other big fish. There's a drop-off at 20 metres with some rather spectacular marine scenery that often includes sharks, turtles and rays.

A good advanced dive is the Pinnacle, about 800 metres off Woodlands Bay in an area that's being considered for a national marine park. The reef here drops from about 20 metres to a depth of over 100 metres and has abundant fish, huge colourful sponges and brain corals. Woodlands Bay is also good for shore dives and has some nice coral at about seven metres, lobster, barracuda and lots of other fish.

Another popular shore dive is Lime Kiln Bay, a rather shallow area that drops to about 15 metres. It has a good variety of sponges, coral and fish and you can sometimes spot stingrays.

Other dive spots on the west coast include Colby's, which is good for beginners, and Little Bay. When the water is calm it's also possible to dive off the east coast.

**Dive Shops** Sea Wolf Diving School (☎ 491-7807 or 491-6859), PO Box 400, on George St in Plymouth, is run by a friendly German couple who know the island well.

Sea Wolf does shore dives for US$40, one-tank boat dives for US$50, two-tank trips for US$70 and night dives for US$45. PADI open-water dive certification courses are available for US$375. The shop is open from 9 am to noon daily except Wednesday and Sunday.

### Snorkelling

Woodlands Bay is a good choice for snorkellers, as there's lots of fish and coral.

Sea Wolf Diving School offers snorkelling lessons at Woodlands Bay for EC$50, gear included. Another easy-to-reach spot that can be snorkelled is Old Road Bay.

You can also snorkel at Little Bay and it's possible for confident swimmers to snorkel around Rendezvous Bluff from Little Bay to Rendezvous Bay.

Danny's Water Sports at Old Road Bay rents snorkel sets for EC$20 a day. Sea Wolf rents snorkel sets for EC$26 a day and also sells quality masks and snorkels at moderate prices.

### Windsurfing & Other Water Sports

Danny's Water Sports (☎ 491-5210), on the beach at Old Road Bay, rents windsurfing gear from US$10 an hour and gives windsurfing lessons for US$10 an hour. Owner Danny Sweeney is an easy-going guy whose windsurf students have included Sting and members of Dire Straits.

Danny also rents Sunfish sailing boats for US$10 an hour, gives sailing lessons for US$10 an hour and offers water skiing for US$15 a run, boat excursions to Rendezvous Beach for US$20 per person and fishing trips for US$40 an hour per boat.

### Hiking

The most popular hikes on Montserrat are the short trails at Fox's Bay, the hike to the Great Alps Falls, the walk into Galways Soufrière and the hike that continues on through the Bamboo Forest. All are detailed in their respective sections.

Some hikes are best done with a guide; they can usually be hired near trailheads or through the tourist office. For short hikes, some taxi drivers are also willing to act as guides. If you want to go somewhere remote, the tourist office can arrange for a forestry officer to guide you – no doubt a good opportunity to get insights into the island's flora and fauna.

**Chances Peak** One hardy hike that doesn't require a guide is the trail up Chances Peak, Montserrat's highest point, which offers a 360° view of the island. The trailhead begins at Broderick's Estate, which is inland up a steep road just south of Kinsale.

The trail consists of nearly 2000 wood and gravel steps set in place by Cable & Wireless, which maintains an antenna on the mountaintop. It's a nonstop vertical haul all the way to the summit, so this strenuous hike is best done in the early morning; in the heat of the day it can be quite unbearable. The hike takes about 90 minutes going up, a bit less coming down. There are a couple of viewing platforms on the way up but the main reward is at the top. When it's clear you can see Redonda, Nevis and St Kitts in a line to the north-west, Antigua to the north-east and Guadeloupe to the south. On cloudy days spare your knees as it's the view that makes it all worthwhile.

### Golf

The Montserrat Golf Club (☎ 491-5220) in Belham Valley, the island's only golf course, has 11 holes that can be played as two nine-hole courses, with different tees and shot directions for each nine. Green fees are EC$60 a day, half price after 4 pm. Clubs and carts can be hired. It's open from 6.30 am to 7 pm daily.

### Tennis

There are two lighted tennis courts at both the Vue Pointe Hotel and the Montserrat Springs Hotel. Both places are open to the public and charge EC$10 an hour per court. If you don't have your own racket, you may be able to rent one at Vue Pointe, which loans them free to guests.

### HIGHLIGHTS

Be sure to spend some time poking around historic Plymouth, including the market, the area around the clock tower and Parliament St.

Must-see sights beyond Plymouth are the Galways Plantation and the lookout at Galways Soufrière. Fox's Bay, just a short ride north of Plymouth, is a fun spot where you can make a short birdwatching hike, see lots of scurrying iguanas and take in a swim.

## ACCOMMODATION

Montserrat has only two 1st-class hotels: the Vue Pointe, which is favoured by holiday-makers, and the Montserrat Springs, which is a bit more business oriented. In addition, there are two rather basic little in-town hotels and a few guesthouses and apartment complexes to choose from. All are on the west side of the island and prices are generally reasonable by Caribbean standards.

The other accommodation options on Montserrat are private villas can be rented for a minimum of one week and are booked through real estate agents. There are about a hundred rental villas in all, the majority in the countryside north of Plymouth. Most are quite comfortable, with private swimming pools and grand views. Some are very exclusive and cater to the same wealthy clientele year after year.

Rates are per villa, not per person, so prices can be reasonably economical, particularly for a family or group. As an example, a simply furnished two-bedroom, two-bath home with a pool might cost around US$500 a week from 1 May to 31 October, US$650 from 1 November to 14 December and US$800 from 15 December to 15 April. The island's ritziest homes go for four or five times this price. All accommodation is subject to a 7% room tax and hotels add on a 10% service charge as well.

The following agencies handle villa rentals and will send listings of their properties:

Caribbee Agencies, PO Box 223 (☎ 491-7444; fax 491-7426)
Montserrat Estates, PO Box 58 (☎ 491-2431; fax 491-3257)
Neville Bradshaw Agencies, PO Box 270 (☎ 491-5270; fax 491-5069)

## FOOD

There are a handful of recommendable places to eat in Plymouth, but very few restaurants elsewhere on the island other than those in the hotels. A favourite island dish is goat water, essentially a spicy goat-meat stew that's often flavoured with cloves and rum. It's popular on special occasions and is available at island restaurants on Friday and Saturday.

The other island speciality is 'mountain chicken', the legs of a large mountain frog (called crapaud in Creole) which taste a bit like chicken. They are commonly sautéed in garlic butter or deep fried.

## DRINKS

Water is safe to drink from the tap and bottled water is sold in stores.

Perks, a rum-based liqueur that tastes something like apricot brandy, is made on Montserrat. You can get a free sample (or pick up a bottle for EC$14) at Perks' outlet, J W R Perkins on Chapel St in Plymouth.

## ENTERTAINMENT

In Plymouth, the Inn on Sugar Bay, opposite the Yacht Club, has live music and dancing on Saturday nights and no cover charge; Casuarina, a lively 2nd-floor bar above the Oasis restaurant, is a popular evening hangout for students from the medical college; and La Cave, in Evergreen Drive, is the island's weekend disco.

The Vue Pointe and Montserrat Springs hotels have bars and occasionally live entertainment.

## THINGS TO BUY

There are several interesting stores in Plymouth. Montserrat Sea Island Cotton on George St is still weaving a bit of island cotton left over from pre-Hurricane Hugo days. (Hurricane Hugo destroyed the cotton fields in 1989, effectively ending the once profitable industry on Montserrat.) Items range from inexpensive napkins to quality stoles that sell for a few hundred dollars.

Another popular shop is Tapestries of Montserrat on Parliament St, which sells island-made wall hangings and rugs. It's open from 8.30 am to 3 pm on Tuesday, Thursday and Friday, to noon on Wednesday. It's often possible to watch weavers at work.

Jus Looking on George St sells quality clothing by Caribelle Batiks, books and other souvenirs. Montserrat Shirts on Parliament St has a good selection of T-shirts with island prints.

Montserrat Philatelic Bureau, in a historic building immediately south of the Fort Ghaut bridge, sells commemorative stamps depicting Montserrat's flora, fauna and history.

# Getting There & Away

### AIR
The only scheduled flights to the island are from Antigua. LIAT makes the 15-minute flight to Montserrat five times a day. The fare is US$33 one way, US$66 return.

From St Martin to Montserrat there's a 21-day excursion fare for US$113 that includes a free optional stopover in Antigua; the equivalent Anguilla-Montserrat fare is US$147.

LIAT's (and BWIA's) agent on the island is Montserrat Aviation Services (☎ 491-2533 or 491-2362), PO Box 257, on Lower George St in Plymouth.

Montserrat Airways (☎ 491-5342) and Carib Aviation (☎ 462-3147 on Antigua) provide charter services to the island.

### Airport Information
Blackburne Airport, the island's only airport, has a small (1036-metre) runway that's capable of handling night flights. Services at the terminal are pretty much limited to card and coin phones, a small gift shop and a little snack shop that's not recommended.

**To/From the Airport** Taxis meet the flights; if there's not one waiting ask the immigration officer to call for one. For fares to various destinations on the island, see Taxi in the Getting Around section of this chapter. There are no car rental agencies at the airport but some agents will provide airport pick-up. Buses from Plymouth come only as close as Harris or Bethel, about 1.8 miles (three km) to the south.

### SEA
Plymouth Harbour is the island's only port of entry. Hurricane Hugo destroyed the deepwater pier in 1989 but a new pier capable of handling cruise ships is nearing completion and it's expected that a number of cruise ship lines will be adding Plymouth as a port of call.

In the past there's been an off and on boat service from Guadeloupe to Montserrat; call Brudey Frères (☎ 90 04 48 in Pointe-à-Pitre) for current information.

Yachts can anchor at Old Road Bay after checking in at Plymouth. The customs office, near the Plymouth dock, is open from 8 am to 4 pm on Monday, Tuesday, Thursday and Friday and from 8 to 11.30 am on Wednesday and Saturday.

### TOURS
Caribrep (☎ 462-0818 on Antigua) arranges day trips from Antigua to Montserrat for US$125, which includes airfare, a sightseeing tour and lunch at the Vue Pointe Hotel.

LIAT (☎ 462-0700 on Antigua) offers a variety of specialised day trips (US$150 to US$165) to Montserrat, featuring either a mountain bike tour, a round of golf, or a guided hike to the Bamboo Forest and the Great Alps Falls.

Both Caribrep and LIAT tours leave Antigua at 9.20 am and return at 4.45 pm.

### LEAVING MONTSERRAT
There's a departure tax of EC$20 (US$8) for visitors aged 12 years and older who have spent more than 24 hours on Montserrat.

# Getting Around

Montserrat's roads are not in great shape – they tend to be narrow and a bit potholed. Outside of Plymouth most roads are also twisting and quite hilly but on the plus side there's very little traffic once you get beyond the town. Most villages and sights are clearly marked with road signs.

Taxis and buses can be identified by the letter 'H' (for hire) on their licence plates.

## BUS

Buses on the island are privately owned minivans. They operate Monday to Saturday, starting around 6 am and continuing until early evening. The farther you get from Plymouth the less frequent the buses, and there's no service at all on the eastern side of the island between St John's and Harris.

In Plymouth, catch buses heading north (to St John's) at Papa's Supermarket, buses heading south (to St Patrick's) along Parliament St by the Royal Bank of Canada and buses going east (to Harris) on George St just above Suntex Bakery.

Fares from Plymouth are EC$2 to St Patrick's, EC$2.50 to Harris, $2.75 to Cudjoe Head or Bethel and EC$3 to St John's.

## TAXI

Taxi fares are set by the government and are the same for up to four people. A fare list is available at the tourist office.

Sample fares from the airport are: EC$29 to Plymouth, EC$35 to Montserrat Springs Hotel and EC$42 to Vue Pointe Hotel. From Plymouth it costs EC$5.50 to Kinsale, EC$10.50 to St George's Hill or St Patrick's, EC$13 to the Vue Pointe Hotel and EC$34 to St John's.

## CAR & MOTORBIKE
### Road Rules

Driving is on the left. You'll need a temporary Montserrat driving licence (EC$30), which you can get from the immigration officer at the airport or at the traffic desk in the Treasury Building, opposite the clock tower in Plymouth. The traffic desk is open from 8.30 am to noon and 1 to 2.30 pm Monday to Friday.

There are a couple of petrol stations in Plymouth, one in St John's and another on the west side of Harris. The latter is the closest to the airport and is open on Sunday.

### Rental

As we go to print no international car rental agencies are represented in Montserrat, but in the past Budget has had an affiliate here.

Local rental agencies, all in Plymouth, include:

Pauline's Car Rentals, Church Rd (☎ 491-2345)
Edith's Car Rental, George St (☎ 491-6696)
Ethelyne's Car Rental, Weekes Rd (☎ 491-2855)
Neville Bradshaw Agencies, Parliament St
    (☎ 491-5270)
Reliable Car Rental, Marine Drive (☎ 491-6990)
Montserrat Enterprises, Marine Drive (☎ 491-2431)
Bernadette Roach Realty Co Parliament St
    (☎ 491-3844)

In the low season older cars rent from about US$25, while newer cars average US$40 a day; in winter rates generally run a bit higher.

With advance reservations, many agencies will pick renters up and drop them back off at the airport. Try to make reservations during weekday business hours as many agents are hard to reach on weekends and after hours.

### BICYCLE

Island Bikes (☎ 491-4696), on Harney St in Plymouth, rents mountain bikes for EC$25 for two hours, EC$54 a day, and also leads cycling tours.

### TOURS

Sightseeing tours by taxi cost EC$30 an hour, with a tour of the island averaging about EC$130. Taxis will take you from Plymouth to Soufrière and back for EC$60, including waiting time.

# Plymouth

Plymouth, the island's political and commercial centre, is a compact and quite likeable West Indian town. Its streets are lined with two-storey period buildings, many of them constructed of discarded ballast stones brought over in British ships in the 18th and

19th centuries. Though styles vary, the buildings commonly have stone lower storeys and brightly painted wooden upper storeys complete with shuttered windows and overhanging balconies. In places the town has a rather English look, save for the ubiquitous tin roofs.

Down by the waterfront there's a small square that's flanked by half a dozen cannons, the post office and the island's main taxi stand. The chief landmark in the square is a clock tower dedicated to the seven Montserratians who died in WW I and the seven who died in WW II. The square is essentially the town centre and gathering spot of sorts, particularly for the taxi drivers who polish their cars and make small talk while waiting for customers.

The south side of Plymouth spills across the Fort Ghaut bridge, where you'll find the town's best restaurants and a beach that's popular with local kids.

### Information

**Tourist Office** The friendly tourist office (☎ 491-2230), on Church Rd, is open from 8 am to 4 pm Monday to Friday.

**Money** Barclays Bank on Church Rd and the Royal Bank of Canada on Parliament St are open from 8 am to 3 pm Monday to Thursday, to 5 pm on Friday. The Bank of Montserrat on Parliament St has the same hours except that it closes at 1 pm on Wednesday and is open until 12.30 pm on Saturday.

**Post & Telecommunications** The post office, on Marine Drive, is open from 8.15 am to 3.55 pm on Monday, Tuesday, Thursday and Friday and from 8.15 to 11.25 am on Wednesday and Saturday.

The Cable & Wireless office, on Houston St, is open from 7.30 am to 6 pm Monday to Saturday (to 8 pm on Friday). There are card and coin phones next to Barclays Bank and near the post office.

**Laundry** Allen's 1-Stop Laundry on Church Rd is open from 8 am to 4 pm Monday to Wednesday, to 6 pm Thursday to Saturday. It costs about EC$13 to wash and dry a load of clothes.

**Other Information** Lee's Pharmacy on Evergreen Drive is open from 9 am to 7 pm Monday to Saturday. Next door is 3D's, which sells newspapers from Montserrat, Antigua, Barbados and Trinidad, plus the *New York Times* and a good range of magazines.

The public library, on Church Rd, is open from 9 am to 4.30 pm Monday to Friday, to 1 pm on Saturday.

### Public Market
Montserrat's colourful market, on Strand St, is open from about 6 am every day but Sunday, although it's at its liveliest on Saturday mornings when street preachers set up opposite the market and half the island come out to do their shopping. Island fruits, vegetables, spices and meats are sold at booths marked with the owner's names – you can choose between 'Alice the Farmer' and 'Alice the Busy Bee' or from S Furlonge who posts the motto 'When days are dark, friends are few'.

### Government House
Government House, the governor's residence, is a pretty 18th-century Victorian house on a hill at the south side of Plymouth. It embodies a certain British element with fanciful gingerbread trim, gabled roof and tidy lawns and gardens. Government House is currently undergoing renovations but once they're complete it's expected that the grounds will once again be open to the public on weekday mornings.

### St Anthony's Anglican Church
On the north side of town is St Anthony's, the island's largest and oldest church. The original rectory was built in 1636, but French invasions, earthquakes and hurricanes have all taken their toll and the church has been

MONTSERRAT

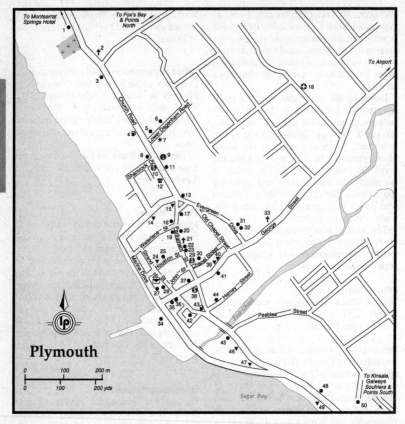

## Plymouth

```
0        100       200 m
0        100       200 yds
```

*Sugar Bay*

To Montserrat Springs Hotel

To Fox's Bay & Points North

To Airport

To Kinsale, Galways Soufriere & Points South

rebuilt many times. A handsome stone-block edifice, the church contains memorial tablets from the early colonial days and silver plates and chalices given by former slaves in tribute for their emancipation.

### Sugar Mill Museum

The Montserrat National Trust operates a small museum of island history in a restored sugar mill 100 metres west of the main road in the Richmond Hill area. It's only open from 2.30 to 5 pm on Wednesday and Sunday. Admission is free, but donations are appreciated.

### St George's Hill

At the top of St George's Hill are the remains of Fort St George, built by the French in 1782 during their brief occupation of the island. The fort, which never saw battle, once had two gun batteries surrounded by trenches and earthworks, but only three cannons and a small reconstructed powder magazine remain. The hilltop here also offers a fairly good, albeit distant, view of Plymouth, which is a 15-minute drive away. From Plymouth, take the airport road through Gages and turn left at the Cedar Valley Rasco All Nation Klub. Continue up past the wind-

**PLACES TO STAY**

5   Flora Fountain Hotel
17  Oriole Plaza Hotel
19  Lime Court Apartments

**PLACES TO EAT**

14  The Attic
15  Evergreen Cafe
24  Harbour Court
39  Suntex Place
40  Suntex Bakery
46  Emerald Cafe
47  Oasis & Casuarina
49  Yacht Club

**OTHER**

1   Sturge Park
2   St Anthony's Anglican Church
3   Allen's 1-Stop Laundry
4   Texaco Petrol Station
6   Ram's Emdee Supermarket
7   Police & Immigration
8   Papa's Supermarket & Buses to the North
9   Tourist Office
10  Barclays Bank
11  Library
12  Pay Phones
13  La Cave
16  Land & Surveys Department & Montserrat
    National Trust
18  Glendon Hospital
20  Court House & Parliament
21  Methodist Church
22  Montserrat Shirts
23  Tapestries of Montserrat
25  Cable & Wireless
26  Post Office
27  Taxi Stand
28  Clock Tower
29  Bank of Montserrat
30  J W R Perkins
31  3D's
32  Lee's Pharmacy
33  St Patrick's Roman Catholic Church
34  Port Authority
35  Montserrat Aviation Services
36  Montserrat Sea Island Cotton
37  Jus Looking
38  Royal Bank of Canada
41  Sea Wolf Diving School
42  Public Market
43  Texaco Petrol Station
44  Island Bikes
45  Philatelic Bureau
48  Inn on Sugar Bay
50  Government House

mills; the fort is 1.5 miles (2.4 km) from the airport road.

## Places to Stay

**Town Centre** The eight apartments at *Lime Court Apartments* (☎ 491-3656), PO Box 250, on Parliament St, are not overly cheery but are adequate and good value, particularly if you want to do your own cooking. They range from a studio for US$25/115 a day/week to a two-bedroom 'penthouse' with a harbour view for US$45/225. The four one-bedroom units, which cost US$30/150, vary in size and layout but are all OK. Request one of the upstairs units which get more light and have balconies, as the ones downstairs can feel a bit dungeon-like. All units have TVs, standing fans and kitchens with hot plates and microwave ovens. Rates are the same year-round. For advance reservations, a non-refundable deposit of one week's rent is required. During business hours rooms can be booked through the office out front, at other times check with the desk at the Oriole Plaza, across the street.

The *Oriole Plaza Hotel* (☎ 491-6982; fax 491-6690), PO Box 250, on Parliament St, is a local 12-room hotel with straightforward rooms and friendly management. Most rooms have twin or double beds, a desk and chair, ceiling fan, phone and TV and cost US$40/50 for singles/doubles in summer, US$55/65 in winter. 'Super double' rooms have two double beds and a private balcony and cost US$65 in summer, US$85 in winter. Children under 12 don't pay; a third adult pays US$15 more. When there's a cricket match in town the hotel can be booked solid with visiting players, but at other times there's seldom a problem getting a room.

The *Flora Fountain Hotel* (☎ 491-6092; fax 491-2568), PO Box 373, on Lower Dagenham Rd, is an older business hotel. While the 18 rooms are large enough and the mattresses are comfortable, overall the place has an air of neglect. Rooms have air-con, phones and small balconies. Singles/doubles cost US$50/70 in summer, US$60/85 in winter. If you want a TV in the room, it's US$15 more.

MONTSERRAT

**Around Plymouth** *Marie's Guest House* (☎ 491-2745), in a residential area on the northbound road, is about a 10-minute walk from Plymouth centre. There are three bedrooms with private bathrooms and guests have use of a kitchen, dining room and TV lounge. Singles/doubles cost US$20/30 all year round.

*Niggy's Guest House* (☎ 491-7489) is at the restaurant of the same name in Kinsale, about a mile (1.6 km) south of Plymouth. The four rooms are small and basic, with little more than a bed, but the mattresses are comfortable. There are louvred windows but no screens or fan; bathrooms are shared. Singles/doubles/triples cost US$15/20/25.

*Moose Guest House* (☎ 491-3146) has five rooms above Ida's Restaurant on the ocean side of the coastal road in Kinsale. Rooms are quite simple and not exactly spotless, but they're fairly large and have two beds, private bathrooms and shared balconies. If you're not too demanding, these rooms are good value at US$20/25 for singles/ doubles.

The *Montserrat Springs Hotel* (☎ 491-2481; fax 491-4070; in the USA ☎ (800) 253-2134), PO Box 259, is on a knoll above Sturge Park, about a 20-minute walk north of Plymouth centre. The 46 rooms are modern and quite nice, each with two double beds, air con, ceiling fans, cable TV and bathrooms with tubs. The 1st-floor rooms have patios and cost US$80/110 for singles/ doubles in summer, US$110/140 in winter. The 2nd-floor units are larger, have balconies and high ceilings and cost US$20 more. There are also one-bedroom suites with kitchenettes and washing machines that cost from US$115/145 in summer, US$170/ 200 in winter, and a few rather expensive two-bedroom suites. Children under 12 are admitted free; a third adult is US$30 more. The hotel has a large swimming pool, tennis courts, a nearby black-sand beach and a whirlpool bath fed by natural hot springs.

*Shamrock Villas* (☎ 491-2431), PO Box 221, is a condominium complex in the Richmond Hill area, between Montserrat Springs Hotel and Sturge Park. The 50 units, in stark white two and three-storey buildings, each have kitchens, ceiling fans and patios or balconies. Rentals are on a weekly basis, with one/two bedroom units costing US$350/ 400 a week in summer, and US$450/550 in winter. There's a pool and a nearby black-sand beach.

### Places to Eat – cheap
The popular *Evergreen Cafe* on upper Marine Drive has fast food such as burgers (EC$5), chicken & chips (EC$8.50), pizza (from EC$12) and ice cream. It's open from 7 am to at least 8 pm Monday to Saturday and from 4 to 8 pm on Sunday. There's a bakery adjoining the restaurant.

*The Attic*, a simple 2nd-floor eatery on upper Marine Drive, has sandwiches from EC$4 and chicken rotis, cheeseburgers and conch water for around EC$8. It's open from 8 am to 3 pm Monday to Saturday and from 6 to 9.30 pm on Friday.

*Harbour Court*, which despite its name is a block east of the harbour on Houston St, is an unpretentious local bar and restaurant. Sandwiches and burgers cost EC$4 to EC$7, chicken & chips are EC$10 and there are a few full meals, including mountain chicken for EC$40. It's open for lunch and dinner from Monday to Saturday.

One of the larger of the numerous grocery stores in the centre is Ram's Emdee Supermarket on Lower Dagenham Rd. It's open from 8 am daily except Sunday and closes at 4.30 pm on Wednesday and Saturday, at 6 pm other days.

You can find good inexpensive pastries and bread at *Suntex Bakery* on George St from 7 am to 9 pm daily except Sunday. For coffee to go (EC$2.50) and cheap fast food there's *Suntex Place*, just down the street.

### Places to Eat – middle & expensive
The *Emerald Cafe*, at the south side of the Fort Ghaut bridge, has a nice open-air setting and is one of the most popular restaurants in Plymouth. Sandwiches and burgers served with fries and salad cost from EC$10 to EC$15. Main dishes range from baked chicken or omelettes (EC$16) to lobster or

mountain chicken (EC$55) and come with rice, vegetables and salad. It's open for lunch and dinner daily except Sunday.

The *Oasis* is an open-air terrace restaurant at a 200-year-old stone building a minute's walk south of the Emerald Cafe. It's run by a couple from England who make authentic English-style fish and chips for EC$20 and sub sandwiches (including vegetarian) for EC$12 to EC$23. On Friday and Saturday nights there's also pizza in the same price range. In addition there are slightly more expensive chicken and steak dishes. Servings are generous and the food and atmosphere are good. The Oasis is open from noon to 1.30 pm Tuesday to Saturday and from 6.30 to 10 pm daily except Monday.

The *Yacht Club* has an attractive waterfront setting on Sugar Bay, just south of town. Omelettes and burgers cost EC$10, and a chef's salad is double that. The wide and varied menu also includes a fresh tuna sandwich for EC$8, a jumbo shrimp with garlic sandwich for EC$12 and catch of the day or curried conch with rice and salad for EC$25. For dessert there are tempting chocolate truffle and mango-ginger cheesecakes. It's open on Saturday for dinner only, Sunday for lunch only and on weekdays (closed Wednesday) from noon to 3 pm and 6 to 11 pm.

*Niggy's Bistro* (☎ 7489), south of Plymouth in the village of Kinsale, has good food and is a popular dinner spot. Starters include gazpacho soup (EC$7) and smoked salmon (EC$14). Main dishes include vegetable pasta for EC$20 and scampi, tenderloin bordelaise or snapper Provençale with bread, salad and pasta for around EC$40. It's open from 7 to 10 pm daily except Wednesday; the piano bar is open until midnight. Niggy's is about 100 metres up the road that leads inland from Ebenezer Methodist Church in Kinsale.

The poolside restaurant at the *Montserrat Springs Hotel* (☎ 2481) is one of the more upscale options in the Plymouth area. It serves inexpensive breakfast fare from 7.30 to 10.30 am. Lunch, which is from noon to 3 pm, includes sandwiches and omelettes

from EC$12 and grilled chicken and various salads for around EC$20. A fixed dinner that includes salad, dessert and coffee, is served from 7.30 to 10.30 pm and costs from EC$30 to EC$50, depending on the main course. On Sunday there's a barbecue lunch from 12.30 to 2 pm.

# North of Plymouth

## FOX'S BAY

Fox's Bay is a delightful place to spend some time. It has a nice swimming beach and there are short walks around a bird sanctuary and out to Bransby Point, the site of a former coastal fortification.

To get to the trails, walk a minute south from the beach along the tree line until you see the 'Bird Sanctuary' sign, cross a little wooden bridge and you're on the path. Scores of lizards scurry across the sandy trail – most are quite small but a few reach nearly a metre in length and splash like little alligators into the pond. After about five minutes the trail forks. The right fork leads 500 metres up to Bransby Point, a coastal bluff with good views, where a few cannons and a bit of a retaining wall are all that remain of the old battery. The left fork continues through the sanctuary's 15 acres, skirting the swampy pond and leading to a small viewing platform.

A picture-board near the start of the trail identifies swamp and marsh birds that might be seen here: belted kingfishers, solitary sandpipers, yellow warblers, blue-winged teals, soras, common gallinules and various members of the heron family. The sanctuary is magical at dusk when hundreds of cattle egrets fly in to roost.

The waters at Fox's Bay are generally calm, but non-swimmers should be cautious as it drops off rather suddenly. There's a current near Bransby Point. Fox's Bay has a faucet with fresh water that can be used to wash off after swimming.

Taxis to Fox's Bay from Plymouth cost EC$8 each way (arrange a time with the driver to come back and pick you up) or you could take a bus to Richmond Hill and walk the 1.2 miles (two km) from the main road. From the Vue Pointe Hotel, there's a hike along an old cart road to Fox's Bay; get a trail map from the front desk.

## PLYMOUTH TO CARR'S BAY

The road that runs north from Plymouth along the west side of the island passes through little hillside villages and offers nice views of Montserrat's green, mountainous interior. It is not a coastal drive, although there is the occasional hilltop ocean vista and side roads lead down to beaches along the way.

**Old Road Estates**, a former plantation a few miles north of Plymouth, is the site of the golf course, many of the island's private villas and the Vue Pointe Hotel, Montserrat's only beachside resort. **Old Road Bay**, the black-sand beach at the Vue Pointe Hotel, is a popular spot for swimming, snorkelling, windsurfing and sailing. It has a water sports hut, a beach bar and a small dock.

On a ridge just above the golf course is the white compound of **Air Studios**, a state-of-the-art recording studio which over the years has attracted top rock music identities including Mick Jagger, Duran Duran and Eric Clapton. Owned by George Martin, who produced most of the Beatles' albums, at the time of writing Air Studios was being used by the governor while his in-town residence was being restored.

A mile (1.6 km) north of the village of Salem is the marked turn-off to **Woodlands Bay**, a small grey-sand beach with good swimming and snorkelling and beach facilities that include showers, toilets and picnic tables.

The main road continues through the village of **St Peter's** and from there it runs into the mountains offering, some fine views before dropping down to Carr's Bay.

### Places to Stay

The *Belham Valley Apartments* (☎ 491-5553), PO Box 409, are three hillside cottages beside the Belham Valley Restau-

rant. The cottages are comfortable and charming, each with a bathroom, kitchen, phone, cable TV, stereo and patio. The Frangipani cottage has a bedroom with a double bed, a living/dining room and screened windows. It can be rented by the week for US$325/475 in summer/winter. Weekly rates are US$250/350 for a smaller studio adjacent to the restaurant and US$375/525 for a newer two-bedroom apartment. When the units aren't booked out by the week they can be rented on a daily basis for about US$50/75 in summer/winter. The manager is friendly, the surroundings are scenic and the beach at Old Road Bay is a 10-minute walk away.

The *Vue Pointe Hotel* (☎ 491-5210; fax 491-4813; in the USA ☎ 800) 235-0709), PO Box 65, has a nice hillside location at the north end of Old Road Bay. There are 28 cottages called 'rondavels', each with a high pitched ceiling, a little sitting area and lots of screened windows to catch the sea breeze. In addition, there are 12 smaller hotel rooms. Both types of accommodation are quite comfortable and have cable TV, phones, mini-refrigerators and either two twins or a king-bed. In summer, singles/doubles cost US$60/80 for a room, US$80/105 for a cottage. In winter, rooms cost US$109/126, cottages US$150/166. The hotel is above one of the island's better beaches and has a pool, tennis courts and a gift shop. A complimentary shuttle bus goes into Plymouth at 9.30 am daily, returning at 12.30 pm.

*Woodsville Condominiums* (☎ 491-5119), PO Box 319, is in the countryside above Belham Valley north of the Cork Hill area. While the mountain scenery is fine this condo complex is otherwise ordinary. Summer/winter rates for one-bedroom units with cooking facilities, cable TV and telephone are US$50/80 by the day, US$250/450 by the week. There's a pool.

Tony and Marlene Glasner run *Providence Estate House* (☎ 491-6476), a B&B in a restored plantation home near the village of St Peter's. There are two guest bedrooms, each with a private bathroom. Singles/doubles cost US$35/60 in the 'cosy' room,

US$45/80 in the 'spacious' room, including a full breakfast complete with fruit from the garden. There's no room tax or service charge added on, local phone calls are free and guests have access to the swimming pool, TV and a kitchenette with refrigerator.

**Places to Eat**

One of the island's finer dining spots is the *Belham Valley Restaurant* (☎ 491-5553), a pleasant hillside restaurant with fine views. Main dishes range from EC$35 for fettuccine Alfredo to EC$65 for Caribbean crawfish and include a green salad, vegetables and rice. The menu also has mountain chicken (when available), steak, chicken and fish dishes. Starters include conch fritters or escargots for EC$15, while desserts such as coconut cream cheesecake or mango mousse cost about half that. Dinner is served from 6.30 to 8.30 pm Tuesday to Sunday; call for reservations. Lunch is available in winter only, from noon to 2 pm Tuesday to Friday, with fish & chips for EC$20, omelettes and sandwiches a bit less. The restaurant is about 500 metres east of the Vue Pointe Hotel.

The dining room at the *Vue Pointe Hotel* (☎ 5210) has windows all around, affording a panoramic view. Continental breakfast costs EC$14, while a full breakfast with a lobster omelette costs EC$30. At lunch there are sandwiches, quiche, chicken salad or fresh fruit with yoghurt for EC$15. The dinner menu changes nightly but generally includes chicken, seafood and steak dishes priced from EC$30 to EC$55. There's a West Indian barbecue with a steel band on Wednesday evenings and in the high season a Sunday buffet barbecue lunch; reservations are requested.

The *Village Place*, a local bar and restaurant in Salem, features inexpensive fried chicken, goat water and fish dishes and sometimes has music on Friday nights.

**CARR'S BAY & LITTLE BAY**

Carr's Bay is a sleepy fishing village that's thought to have been the landing site of the first Irish settlers. It has a roadside black-sand beach with a view of uninhabited

Redonda Island to the north-west and on a clear day you can also see Nevis beyond.

At the north end of Carr's Bay, where the road turns sharply inland to cut across the island, a secondary road leads 0.6 mile (one km) north to Little Bay, a nice secluded black sand beach backed by hilly pastures. The road to Little Bay gets rougher as it goes along and if it hasn't been graded recently you may have to park halfway in and walk the last part.

**RENDEZVOUS BAY**

From Little Bay you can hike north to the even more secluded Rendezvous Bay, which has broad golden sands. The quickest route is via a hardy 30-minute walk directly over the 100-metre-high bluff that separates the two bays. In addition there's a gentler 50-minute hike that heads inland, circling around the eastern flank of the bluff. Both these scenic trails start at the north end of Little Bay.

The other option for reaching Rendezvous Bay is by boat. Danny's Water Sports will provide transportation from Old Road Bay to Rendezvous Bay and come back to pick you up at a pre-arranged time for US$20 per person.

Neither Little Bay nor Rendezvous Bay have any facilities, so bring water.

**CARR'S BAY TO THE AIRPORT**

From Carr's Bay the main road cuts across the island between Silver Hill and the Centre Hills. Midway is the village of **St John's**, where there's a little local bar, *Mrs Morgan's*, run by a colourful West Indian woman who serves up a good goat water (EC$8) on most weekends. Once you get past St John's, the road winds in and out of uninhabited valleys until you reach the airport.

**AIRPORT TO PLYMOUTH**

The drive from Blackburne Airport to Plymouth is along a narrow, winding road that cuts between Montserrat's two highest mountain masses, the Centre Hills and the Soufrière Hills. This scenic road passes abandoned

MONTSERRAT

plantation ruins and a run of small hillside villages.

Two minutes south of the airport there's a deserted farm that grew sea island cotton until Hurricane Hugo flattened the cotton fields. You'll also pass a couple of attractive stone churches along the way, an old Methodist one in **Bethel** and the turn-of-the-century St George's Anglican Church in **Harris**. One of the more picturesque roadside estates is **Farrell's Farm**, just west of Harris, which once distilled sugar into one of the island's top rums. As the road continues on to Plymouth, native vegetation – ginger, ferns and elephant ears – gives way to banana patches and vegetable fields.

# South of Plymouth

It's about a 20-minute ride south from Plymouth to Galways Plantation and Galways Soufrière, the island's top sightseeing spots.

The rock-strewn slopes of the Soufrière Hills were favoured by Irish planters in part because they so resembled the green terrain back in Ireland. From the village of St Patrick's, there's a signposted road that winds up the mountain slopes for just over a mile (1.6 km) to Galways Plantation and then continues a mile more to end at Galways Soufrière. On the way you'll pass a couple of abandoned sugar mills, get some nice views down to the coast and, if it's clear, see the island of Guadeloupe to the south-east. The road is paved but bumpy and narrow, and forms just a single lane for the final third of a mile (500 metres).

If you were to follow the coastal road south without turning inland at St Patrick's, it would end 4.5 miles (7.2 km) from Plymouth at a quarry at Old Fort Point. The hike up to the Great Alps Falls begins at the river crossing a little before the road's end.

### GALWAYS PLANTATION

Galways Plantation, once a thriving sugar estate, sits at an elevation of 335 metres on the green slopes of the Soufrière Hills. It was started in the 1660s by David Galway, an Irishman from Cork who gained favour with the powers of the day by crossing partisan lines and siding with English colonial bureaucrats. The Irish indentured servants that Galway brought over to work the fields were in time replaced by African slaves. At its peak, in the mid-1700s, the plantation encompassed 1300 acres and 'employed' 150 people. The abolition of slavery in 1834 marked the end of the plantation era and Galways Plantation was eventually abandoned.

Today some of the ruins stand partially restored in a clearing near the roadside. The Montserrat National Trust, which has spearheaded the restoration, encourages visitors to explore the site. It's always open and there's no admission fee.

The old stone windmill, whose sails once powered rollers that crushed the sugar cane, and a nearby stone warehouse are the most intact buildings, but there are other foundations as well. You can also wander across the road where a bit of the old walls and steps of the former Great House are nearly hidden by overgrown vegetation.

### GALWAYS SOUFRIÈRE

The road ends at a car park where two short paths lead to lookouts perched above the rim of Galways Soufrière, an impressively deep volcanic valley. In contrast to the lush green Soufrière Hills that surround it, Galways Soufrière appears as a sharply cut canyon with barren earth walls in hues of yellow, grey and rust. Warm sulphuric springs flow out of the side of the mountains and feed the small streams that cut across the valley floor, while steam rises out of vents circled by bright yellow sulphur crystals.

You can get a nice overview of it all from the lookouts, both of which take only two minutes to reach. The main lookout is at the end of the path that begins near the buttressed-trunked tree in the upper car park. This lookout also has a view of the island's highest point, Chances Peak, just over 0.6 miles (one km) to the north.

The path to the second lookout starts a

little to the right of the main one. If you want a closer look you can walk from here down into the base of the canyon, which takes about 15 minutes to reach. The slope is rather steep, the trail is crumbly in places and some sections can get quite slippery when wet, so good shoes are a must if you intend to hike down. Stick to the trail and beware of bubbly vents and springs that release very hot water.

### Bamboo Forest Trail

This hike goes up the east side of Galways Soufrière and then leads into a thick forest of bamboo whose stalks measure half a metre in diameter and stand a good 10 metres high. The bamboo creates a jungle canopy as it leans over the trail and tree ferns drape the surrounding mountainsides, so that it all looks quite primordial – you almost expect a dinosaur to step out and complete the scene.

The hike begins at the lower lookout, goes down into the crater and then climbs out on the opposite side. Only the first part of the walk is steep – after that the trail levels off and passes between two peaks. While most hikers take about 90 minutes to walk in and then backtrack out the same way, with some planning it would be possible to continue on the trail all the way to Tar River Estate at the end of the east coast road.

At the crossroads in St Patrick's you'll probably find young men who'll want to be your guide into the Bamboo Forest (about EC$100 to EC$120 for two people).

Although some people do hike on their own with just a topographic map and compass, it becomes quite jungle-like after you leave the crater area, so a guide might be a good investment.

### GREAT ALPS FALLS

A relatively easy hike winds 1.2 miles (two km) up a lush canyon to the base of the Great Alps Falls, a 21-metre drop down a sheer rockface. There's a pool beneath the falls that's deep enough to stand and splash in but too shallow for swimming.

The trail up to the falls follows the White River which, despite its name, is more of a rocky stream than a river and flows muddy yellow with the sulphuric waters that run down from Galways Soufrière.

The trailhead, which is marked by a sign, is at the inland side of the road about 0.6 miles (one km) south of St Patrick's. There's a parking area, a pay phone and a little yellow hut where you'll usually find guides willing to take you up to the falls for EC$15 for one person, EC$25 for two. While the trail is not terribly difficult to follow, a good guide can identify trees and plants along the route and make an interesting walking companion.

It takes about 45 minutes to reach the waterfall. Wear shoes with good traction as there are numerous stream crossings en route.

# Saba

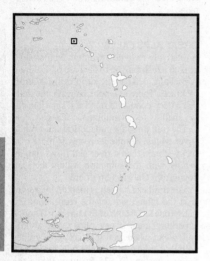

Dubbed the 'Unspoiled Queen', Saba is both the smallest and loftiest of the islands that comprise the Netherlands Antilles. This ruggedly steep island has beautiful scenery, good hiking, pristine diving and strikingly little tourism.

At first glance Saba appears more like a misplaced Alpine community than part of the West Indies. As the tip of an immense underwater mountain, the island looms out of the sea, with no pause for lowlands or beaches. Saba's central volcanic peak, Mt Scenery, is cloaked in clouds. The slopes are dotted with quaint white houses with green shutters, red roofs and gingerbread trim, while tiny vegetable plots sprout between rock-strewn hillsides.

The island has four villages, all spotlessly neat. Although The Bottom is the island's capital, Windwardside is the largest village and the most popular base for visitors. The villages of St John's and Hell's Gate are largely residential areas.

With just over 1000 inhabitants, everyone on Saba knows everyone else and it's certainly one of the gentlest and friendliest places in the Caribbean.

## ORIENTATION

It's virtually impossible to get lost on Saba. There is only one main road, which runs from the airport at the north-east side of the island, through the villages of Hell's Gate, Windwardside, St John's and The Bottom, and continues down to Fort Bay, the island's main port. A second road connects The Bottom with Well's Bay, on the island's north-west side.

# Facts about the Island

## HISTORY

Because of the island's rugged terrain, Saba was probably not heavily settled in pre-Columbian times. However, recent artefacts uncovered in the Spring Bay area indicate the existence of a small Arawak settlement at that site about 1300 years ago.

---

**The Road That Couldn't Be Built**
Up until a few decades ago, Saba's villages were connected solely by footpaths. For years engineers from low-lying Holland had declared that the island's steep terrain made road construction impossible.

One sceptical islander, Josephus Lambert Hassell, enrolled in an engineering correspondence course and then organised a local construction team. In the 1940s his 20-man crew constructed the first section of the concrete road from Fort Bay to The Bottom and over the next 20 years gradually extended the road to Hell's Gate. They built the entire road by hand and while it may be narrow and twisting, it's free of the patchwork potholes that characterise roads elsewhere in the Caribbean. ■

---

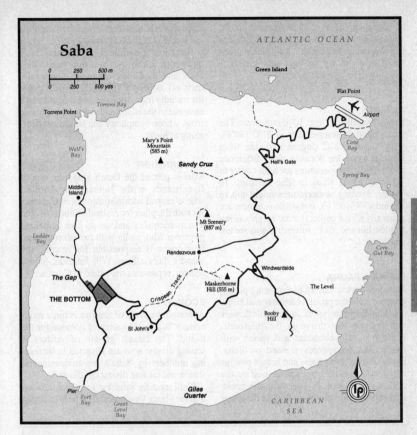

Saba

During his second trip to the New World, on 13 November 1493 Christopher Columbus became the first European to sight Saba. The Dutch laid claim to the island in 1632 and sent a party of colonists from St Eustatius in 1640 to form a permanent settlement. These early colonists originally lived at Middle Island and Mary's Point, where bits of a few cisterns and stone walls can still be found, but soon moved to The Bottom, which still remains the administrative centre of the island.

As the steep topography precluded large-scale plantations, colonial-era slavery was quite limited on Saba. Those colonists who did own slaves generally had only a few and often worked side by side with them in the fields, resulting in a more integrated situation than on larger Dutch islands.

## GEOGRAPHY

Saba's land area is just 13 sq km but, because of its topography of folding mountains, Saba is far more substantial than any mere area measurement would indicate. The island is the emerged peak of an extinct volcano that rises to 877 metres at Mt Scenery, Saba's highest point.

There are no rivers or streams on the island. The leeward western side is quite dry, the windward eastern side has thicker green vegetation and the mountainous interior is given over to lush jungle growth.

## CLIMATE

Saba's rainfall averages 1070 mm a year. The mean monthly temperature is 27°C (80°F), with about a 2°C degree variance from summer to winter. Because of the difference in elevation, temperatures are a bit cooler in Windwardside than in The Bottom. In winter, evening temperatures might dip to around 17°C (63°F), and while summers are generally a little cooler than on neighbouring islands, hot and sticky summer nights are not unknown.

## FLORA & FAUNA

Saba has a wide variety of flowering plants, ranging from the prolific oleander and hibiscus that decorate yards to the wildflowers and orchids that thrive in the rainforest. Birdlife is also abundant and varied with more than 60 species sighted on Saba. Bridled terns, sooty terns and brown noddys breed on the island, tropicbirds nest on the cliffs and frigatebirds soar near the coast. Red-tailed hawks can be spotted on the lower slopes, while thrashers and hummingbirds are found at higher elevations.

Saba has a harmless racer snake that's quite common to spot as it suns itself along trails and roadsides, although it generally darts off as people approach. Expect to see the friendly little *Anolis sabanus* lizard that's endemic to the island and to hear the tiny tree frogs whose symphony can be almost deafening at night.

## GOVERNMENT

Saba is part of the Dutch kingdom, one of five islands in the Netherlands Antilles, whose central administration is in Curacao. As with the other four islands, Saba is treated as a municipality and has its own lieutenant governor who, along with two elected commissioners, is responsible for running the island's daily affairs. Will Johnson, Saba's senator, represents the island in Curacao.

## ECONOMY

Although the scale of tourism is quite moderate, it is a major source of revenue for the island. The largest growth of visitors is among divers, who are attracted in increasing numbers by Saba's pro-environmental stance and its fine diving conditions.

Until recently Saba was a popular destination for young Dutch who flew here to obtain

---

### Saba Marine Park

The Saba Marine Park was established in 1987 and encompasses all the waters surrounding the island from the highwater mark to a depth of 71 metres. The park has established zones for different marine uses. For example, it limits anchoring to the Fort Bay and Ladder Bay areas and sets aside the waters between the two bays exclusively for diving. Fishing is allowed in most other waters but there are restrictions and quotas for at-risk creatures such as conch.

The marine park was established with funding from the World Wildlife Fund and the Saba and Dutch governments. It is administered by the nonprofit Saba Conservation Foundation. ■

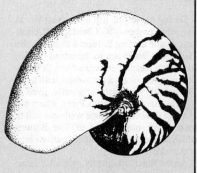

their drivers licences and escape strict and costly regulations in Holland. It was a thriving business for a handful of driving schools that arranged licensing package tours and for guesthouses that catered to them, but new regulations put an end to the practice in 1992. One of the old driving schools in The Bottom is now being converted into a small medical school for overseas students.

Sabans grow much of their own food, from Irish potatoes and taro to hydroponically grown lettuce. Potatoes and locally caught fish and lobster are exported to neighbouring islands.

## POPULATION & PEOPLE

Saba's permanent population is about 1100. It's fairly evenly divided between descendants of African slaves and descendants of the early Scottish, Irish and Scandinavian settlers. Most people can trace their lineage to one of half a dozen families, and just two names, Hassell and Johnson, account for almost a third of the phonebook listings. Incidentally, despite its Dutch government, Saba has very few people of Dutch descent.

## ARTS & CULTURE

The craft most associated with the island is Spanish work, or Saba lace, a drawn threadwork first introduced to Saba in the 1870s by a woman who learned the stitching technique in a convent in Venezuela. While this lacelike embroidery work is quite fine, the market for it is so limited that the craft is not being practised by the younger generation and appears to be a dying art. Saba has attracted a number of good contemporary artists whose paintings and drawings take their inspiration from the island's natural scenery. One of the best known is Heleen Cornet, who has a gallery at her home in The Bottom. Her work, along with that of most other island artists, can also be seen at the Breadfruit Gallery in Windwardside.

As for sports, there's not enough flat land for soccer and cricket fields, so basketball, volleyball and tennis are local favourites.

## RELIGION

Catholicism is the predominant religion on Saba, but the island's eight churches also include Anglican, Wesleyan Holiness and Seventh Day Adventist denominations.

## LANGUAGE

Although Dutch is the 'official' language, English is the primary language of the island and the language most commonly spoken in the home. To accommodate this reality the Dutch government recently allowed the Saban school system to switch from Dutch to English as the principal classroom language. Schoolchildren now study Dutch as a second language.

# Facts for the Visitor

## PASSPORT & VISAS

Valid passports are required of all visitors except for US and Canadian citizens, who need only proof of citizenship, such as a birth certificate or voter's registration card.

A return or onward ticket is officially required.

## CUSTOMS

Saba is a free port and there are no customs regulations.

## MONEY

The official currency is the Netherlands Antilles guilder or florin, but US dollars are accepted everywhere. Islander-geared businesses such as grocers and shops post prices in guilders while visitor-related businesses such as hotels, restaurants and dive shops post prices in US dollars. The exchange rate is 1.77 guilders to US$1. Generally there's no advantage in changing to guilders unless you're planning a lengthy stay. For more information see Money in the Facts for the Visitor chapter.

The island's two banks, Barclays and the Commercial Bank, are both in Windwardside.

Credit cards are not as widely accepted on

Saba as on other islands. MasterCard and Visa are accepted by a few hotels and restaurants in Windwardside, including Juliana's, the Captain's Quarters and Brigadoon, and also by Sea Saba dive shop.

## TOURIST OFFICES

The Saba Tourist Bureau (☎ 62231; fax 62350), PO Box 527, Windwardside, is a helpful office that provides general information on the island, sells books about Saba and keeps a list of cottages and homes for rent.

### Overseas Reps

Overseas tourism representatives include:

Canada
New Concepts in Canada, 410 Queens West Suite 303, Toronto, Ontario M5V 2Z3 (☎ (416) 362-7707; fax (416) 368-7818)
Netherlands
Antillen Huis (Kabinet van de Gevolmachtigde Minister van de Nederlandse Antillen), Badhuisweg 173-175, 2597JP's-Gravenhage (☎ (70) 3512811; fax (70) 3512722)

## BUSINESS HOURS

Shops and offices are commonly open from 8 or 9 am to noon and from 1 to 5 pm.

## HOLIDAYS

Public holidays on Saba are:

| | | |
|---|---|---|
| *New Year's Day* | – | 1 January |
| *Good Friday* | – | Friday before Easter |
| *Easter Sunday* | – | late March/early April |
| *Easter Monday* | – | late March/early April |
| *Queen's Day* | – | 30 April |
| *Labor Day* | – | 1 May |
| *Ascension Thursday* | – | 40th day after Easter |
| *Christmas Day* | – | 25 December |
| *Boxing Day* | – | 26 December |

## CULTURAL EVENTS

The Saba Summer Festival, held in late July, is the island's Carnival. The Hill Climb, a one-at-a-time car race from the airport to the church in Hell's Gate, begins a week-long series of festivities that includes jump-ups, a talent show, a queen contest, a calypso king competition and a parade around The Bottom with floats and costumes.

Saba Days, held in early December, features sporting events, steel bands, dancing, donkey races and barbecues.

## POST

Saba's two post offices are in Windwardside and The Bottom. When writing to Saba from abroad, just address mail with the individual or business name, followed by the town and 'Saba, Netherlands Antilles'.

From Saba, it costs Fls 0.55 to mail a postcard and Fls 1.75 to mail a 10-gram letter to either North America or the Netherlands and Fls 0.90 to mail a letter within the Caribbean.

## TELECOMMUNICATIONS

Local phone numbers have five digits. The area code, which must be added when calling Saba from overseas, is 599-4.

You can make phone calls from the Landsradio office in The Bottom, but other than that there are no public pay phones on the island. Visitors generally make calls from their hotel. If you're at the airport there's a courtesy phone on the wall that can be used to make local calls.

## ELECTRICITY

Electricity is 110 volts AC, 60 cycles, and a flat two-pronged plug is used, the same as the type used in the USA.

## WEIGHTS & MEASURES

Saba uses the metric system, although most rental car odometers register in miles.

## BOOKS

*Guide to the Saba Marine Park* by marine biologist Tom van't Hof (Saba Conservation Foundation, 1991) is an authoritative guide to underwater Saba. Van't Hof, who spearheaded the development of the Saba Marine Park, gives detailed descriptions of each of Saba's 26 dive sites and the 102-page book includes lots of colour photos illustrating coral and marine life. It can be purchased at the Saba Tourist Bureau in Windwardside for US$14.

*Saban Cottages*, a hardcover book by

artist Heleen Cornet, contains lovely water-colour drawings of scores of the island's quaintest buildings. It can be purchased in shops and galleries on the island and makes a nice souvenir.

## MAPS
The tourist office has a free, simple island map that's suitable for most needs and a slightly more detailed colour map that costs US$1.

## MEDIA
As Saba has no newspaper, local news and announcements are posted on bulletin boards in each village. St Martin newspapers can be purchased at Big Rock market or Scout's Place in Windwardside.

## HEALTH
The A M Edwards Medical Center (☎ 63289) in The Bottom is the island's medical facility.

There's a decompression chamber for divers at Fort Bay, which also serves divers who get the bends on neighbouring islands.

## ACTIVITIES
### Beaches & Swimming
Saba is not the place to go if you want to lay out on sandy strands. The main swimming spot is Well's Bay at the north-western side of the island, which has a small, rocky beach.

Some hotel swimming pools are open to the public, including those at Scout's Place, which charges US$2, and at Captain's Quarters, which charges US$5.

### Diving & Snorkelling
Saba's stunning scenery extends beneath the surface, with steep wall drops just offshore and some varied nearshore reef dives. Most of the island's 26 dive spots are along the calmer leeward side, between Tent Bay and Diamond Rock.

Some of the more exciting dives include Tent Reef Wall, which has colourful tube sponges and corals and lots of fish activity; Third Encounter and Twilight Zone, adjacent

sponge and coral-encrusted pinnacles that rise about 30 metres from the ocean floor; and Diamond Rock, which has a great variety of fish, including stingrays, black-tip sharks and bull sharks.

For snorkellers, Well's Bay and the adjacent Torrens Point are popular spots and there's even a marked underwater trail.

**Dive Shops** Saba has three dive shops. Rates include a US$2 per-dive fee which helps cover the Saba Marine Park's operating expenses.

Sea Saba (☎ 62246; fax 62362), based in Windwardside, has 11 and 12-metre boats, and generally does a 10 am and noon dive daily and night dives on request. Single-tank dives cost US$45, double-tank dives US$75 and night dives US$55. Masks and fins can be rented for US$8. Sea Saba also does a resort course (which includes an open-water dive) for US$85 and a five-day certification course for US$350. There's a three-person minimum for courses. The shop, which also sells snorkelling equipment and film, is open from 8 am to 5 pm daily.

Saba Deep (☎ 63347) at Fort Bay goes out at 9 and 11 am and 1 pm, taking no more than eight divers per boat. The first dive of the day is a deep dive, the second intermediate and the last a shallow dive. Rates are US$45/80/105 for single/double/triple tank dives and US$60 for a night dive. They do an open-water certification course for US$375 inclusive and a resort course for US$50.

Wilson's Dive Shop (☎ 23248; fax 63410), the smallest operation, is also at Fort Bay.

**Live-Aboard Boats** The live-aboard dive boat M/V *Caribbean Explorer* generally starts and ends its week-long trips in St Martin, but spends much of its time around Saba. For more information see Tours in the Getting There & Away chapter.

### Hiking
Saba has some excellent and varied hiking opportunities. There are seven signposted and maintained hikes, ranging from a 15-minute walk to tide pools just beyond the

airport to a steep climb up through cloud forest to the top of Mt Scenery, Saba's highest point. Interpretive plaques describing natural history and trail-side bird and plant life have been erected along the trails by the Saba Conservation Foundation.

As the trails cross private property, hikers should stick to established paths and, as always, be careful not to litter. There are no poisonous creatures on Saba and it's one of the safest places in the Caribbean, so this is one island where you can feel free to concentrate all your attention on the environment.

Some of the trails, such as the Crispeen Track between The Bottom and Windwardside, follow the old footpaths that linked the villages before the first roads were built. A simple trail brochure and map is available free at the tourist office.

## HIGHLIGHTS

Diving is a highlight on Saba, as is hiking, especially the walk to the top of Mt Scenery. Strolling around Windwardside is always a pleasant experience – chat with the lacemakers, wander into the art galleries and enjoy the serenity of the island.

## ACCOMMODATION

Though the latest trend is towards more upscale development, most of Saba's accommodation falls solidly in the moderate price range and all but a couple of places have the same rates all year round.

In addition to the hotels listed in this chapter, there are a couple of dozen cottages and apartments for rent on the island. Prices range from US$40 to US$100 nightly, US$200 to US$500 weekly. The Saba Tourist Bureau office will send out an annually updated list with descriptions, rates and contact numbers. While you could book these cottages on your own, you could also do it through the tourist office and generally that's an easier route to take, as the tourist office staff know which cottages are available at any given time.

To all rates given in this chapter add a 5% government room tax. Most hotels also add a 10% service charge (15% at Scout's).

## FOOD

Food in Saba has continental and Creole influences, with an emphasis on fish and seafood, though popular local dishes also include goat meat, johnny cakes and barbecued ribs. A variety of fruit is grown on the island, including bananas, papayas, mangoes, avocados, and soursop.

## DRINKS

Water is by catchment, but generally fine to drink from the tap – although you should enquire first.

Be sure to try Saba Spice, a rum-based liqueur spiced with a 'secret concoction' that varies depending on whose liquor you buy. It can be purchased in bars for US$1 a drink or US$10 a 750ml bottle.

## ENTERTAINMENT

On weekends from 9 pm to 2 am, Guido's Restaurant pushes the pool tables aside and turns into the Mountain High Club, a 'private membership disco' that admits visitors for US$3.

Foxie's in Lower Hell's Gate, in the white building with triple red gables, is another popular weekend disco.

Otherwise the island is generally quiet at night, with only a bit of action at the hotel bars.

## THINGS TO BUY

Saba lace handwork in the form of handkerchiefs, table runners, placemats, bun warmers, purses, aprons and other clothing items are available at quite reasonable prices from craftswomen, some of whom have small shops in their homes in Windwardside and The Bottom. However, the best selection is at the community centre in Hell's Gate.

The same women also sell (and give samples of) homemade Saba Spice. Most varieties have a liquorice-like flavour, as one of the common ingredients is the fennel that's planted at the side of some Saban homes.

# Getting There & Away

## AIR

The only scheduled flight service to Saba is with Winair (☎ 62212 or 62255), which has three to five flights a day from St Martin, a 15-minute hop. Winair also has a daily flight from St Eustatius and a flight a couple of times a week from St Barts. There's also an off-and-on flight from St Kitts.

The one-way fare to Saba is US$33 from St Martin and US$20 from St Eustatius. Return fares are double. To Saba from St Barts the fare is US$56 one way, US$79 for a one-day excursion ticket and US$92 for a 30-day excursion ticket.

### Airport Information

Saba's seaside airstrip is a mere 400 metres long, the region's shortest. It's similarly narrow, with the plane touching down just metres away from a sheer cliff, all of which makes for a thrilling landing.

The small airport has a Winair booth, restrooms, a courtesy telephone, a stall with beer and soda and the Saba Artisan's Boutique, which sells T-shirts, cloth dolls and Saba Spice liqueur.

**To/From the Airport** Taxis meet the flights. See Taxi in the following Getting Around section for relevant fares. There are no car rentals at the airport.

## SEA

The ferry MV *Style*, which once ran between Saba and St Martin, caught fire in late 1992 and there is currently no ferry service to Saba.

### Yacht

Saba has two designated anchorages: the harbour at Fort Bay and the area from Well's Bay to Ladder Bay. Under normal conditions, Well's Bay is the best anchorage and offers excellent holding in sand. Ladder Bay also has good holding but has some tricky downdrafts as well as boulders in the shal-

lower waters. There are five yellow buoys in the Ladder and Well's Bay anchorage area that can be used by visiting yachts; however, the white and orange buoys are reserved for dive boats.

People arriving by boat should first clear immigration at the harbour office at Fort Bay. The office monitors channels 16 and 11. If there's no-one at the harbour office, check in at the Saba Marine Park office, which is also at Fort Bay.

To help support the Saba Marine Park, there is a yacht visitor fee of US$2 per person aboard boats less than 30 metres long and 10 cents per gross register tonne for boats longer than 30 metres. The fee is payable at the marine park office and is valid for seven days.

### Cruise Ship

Saba does not have a deepwater port capable of handling large cruise ships. However, Windjammer Barefoot Cruises and a few other small ships stop over at Saba by anchoring in Fort Bay and bringing passengers ashore by dinghy.

## TOURS

Most package tours to Saba are day trips from St Martin run by Irish Travel Tours,

SABA

whose St Martin office (☎ 53663) is in the Safari Building, Airport Rd, Simpson Bay. The cost of US$100 (US$70 for children under 12) includes return airfare on Winair, a sightseeing tour and lunch at Scout's Place, with the afternoon free for hiking, snorkelling etc.

Irish Travel Tours arranges a weekday tour that squeezes Saba and St Eustatius into a day trip for US$180, including airfare, sightseeing tours on both islands, a drink and lunch, and also has a one-day dive package on Saba that costs US$145 for a single dive and US$180 for a double dive.

Dive packages that include accommodation and airport transfers can be arranged from all three dive shops. Prices average about US$500 per person for a five-night package, based on double occupancy.

### LEAVING SABA

The departure tax, for people aged two and older, is US$2 if leaving for a Netherlands Antilles island, US$5 for day trippers from St Kitts, St Barts or other non-Dutch islands and US$10 for those who have stayed overnight and are going to non-Dutch islands. Passengers connecting with an international flight from St Martin pay US$10; be sure to pick up a transit pass at your airline check-in counter in St Martin which exempts you from paying an additional departure tax there.

# Getting Around

There are no public buses and no bicycles for rent on Saba.

### TAXI

Taxi fares are set by the government. The price from the airport is US$7 to Windwardside and US$10 to The Bottom for up to four people, plus 50 cents for each piece of luggage.

From Windwardside it costs US$5 to The Bottom, US$7.50 to Fort Bay and US$10 to Well's Bay. A sightseeing tour, which lasts 1½ to two hours and covers most of the island, costs US$35 per taxi.

### CAR & MOTORBIKE

Saba has narrow and very steep roads that may intimidate some drivers. However, traffic is quite light and stone walls line most of the roads so they're not unduly hazardous.

### Road Rules

Drive on the right side of the road. Your home driving licence is valid for driving on Saba. The island's sole petrol station is in Fort Bay; it's open from 9 am to 2 pm Monday to Friday and to noon on Saturday.

### Rental

Johnson's Rent a Car (☎ 62269) at Juliana's in Windwardside rents small cars for US$40 a day and Daihatsu jeeps for US$45. If you're just renting for one day to cruise the island, there's no charge for petrol. Scout's Place (☎ 62205) in Windwardside rents cars for US$40 a day and Daihatsu jeeps for US$50. Steve's Scooter Rentals (☎ 62507), also known as Rent A Scoot, rents Peugeot scooters for US$10 an hour or US$35 a day. The office is near the Brigadoon restaurant in Windwardside.

### HITCHING

Hitchhiking is relatively safe on Saba and is a common means of transport, however, the usual safety precautions apply. In Windwardside, the main hitching spot is near the wall by the Corner Deli and in The Bottom it's by the Department of Public Works.

# Around Saba

### HELL'S GATE

When you stand at the airport and look up the mountain, you see the village of Hell's Gate, whose houses seem to cling precariously to the side of the mountain slopes. The road from the airport to Windwardside passes directly through the village.

The main landmark in Hell's Gate is the

Holy Rosary Church, a seemingly old stone church that was built just three decades ago. Behind the church is the Hell's Gate Community Centre, which sells the best collection of Saba lace on the island, as well as bottles of homemade Saba Spice liqueur. The community centre is usually open from 9 to 11 am and whenever a cruise ship comes in.

The ride from Hell's Gate to Windwardside is steep and winding. It passes through a variety of terrains and offers some fine scenic views of Saba itself as well as glimpses of the neighbouring islands of St Eustatius, St Kitts, Nevis and St Barts.

## WINDWARDSIDE

The island's largest hamlet, Windwardside has curving alleyways lined with picturesque cottages and flower-filled gardens. Being on the windward side of the island, just below Mt Scenery, this hillside village is pleasantly green and a tad cooler than other parts of the island. It's a delightfully unhurried and friendly place.

Windwardside makes the best base for visitors as it has the most hotels, restaurants and shops, as well as the tourist office, the museum, a good art gallery and the trailhead for the island's most popular hike. While walking around you'll probably notice that many homes have Dutch doors. The top half of these doors are commonly kept open in the evening, allowing people to chat from their living rooms with neighbours strolling by.

### Information

**Tourist Office** The Saba Tourist Bureau (☎ 62231) is at the north-west side of town and is open from 8 am to noon and 1 to 5 pm Monday to Friday.

**Money** Barclays Bank, near the crossroads, is open from 8.30 am to 2 pm Monday to Friday. Barclays exchanges money, cashes travellers' cheques for a 1% fee and can provide cash advances to MasterCard, Visa and Discover card holders. The island's only other bank, the Commercial Bank, is opposite the post office.

**Post** The Windwardside post office is open from 8 am to noon and from 1 to 3 pm Monday to Friday.

**Library** The library, next to the post office, is open from 8 am to noon on Monday, 2 to 5 pm on Tuesday and Thursday and 7 to 9 pm on Saturday.

### Saba Museum

The Saba Museum is in a garden-like setting surrounded by wildflowers, including some black-eyed susans, the official island flower. The museum is in a typical Saban home, whitewashed with green-shuttered windows, and recreates the living quarters of a 19th-century Dutch sea captain. There's a four-poster bed with period decor, a collection of pottery fragments and lots of memorabilia. Check out the cushion-like grass at the back where Sabans play croquet each Sunday. Curiously, there's also a bust of the South American revolutionary Simon Bolivar in the grounds, which was presented to Saba by the Venezuelan government. The museum is open from 10 am to noon and 1 to 3.30 pm Monday to Friday. Admission is US$1.

### Breadfruit Gallery

The Breadfruit Gallery, in the same building as the tourist office, has a high quality collection of local artwork that makes for good browsing. It's open from 10 am to 12.30 pm and 2 to 5.30 pm.

### Maskehorne Hill Trail

For a quick sense of what Saban wilderness is like, take this 45-minute round-trip hike that starts on the Mt Scenery trail out of Windwardside. After about 10 minutes of climbing old stone steps through a forest thick with tall elephant ears and birdsong, you'll reach a small taro (dasheen) farm. At the farmer's hut, turn left off the Mt Scenery Trail onto the Maskehorne Hill Trail, a dirt path through the forest that continues to nearby Maskehorne Hill and a view of Windwardside.

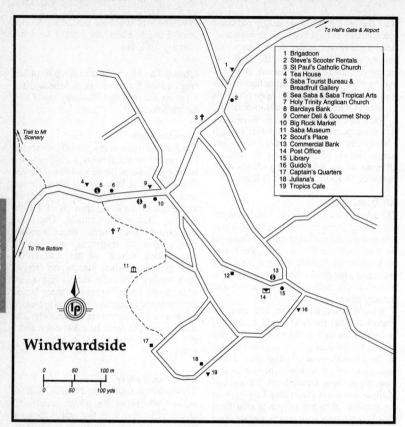

1  Brigadoon
2  Steve's Scooter Rentals
3  St Paul's Catholic Church
4  Tea House
5  Saba Tourist Bureau &
   Breadfruit Gallery
6  Sea Saba & Saba Tropical Arts
7  Holy Trinity Anglican Church
8  Barclays Bank
9  Corner Deli & Gourmet Shop
10 Big Rock Market
11 Saba Museum
12 Scout's Place
13 Commercial Bank
14 Post Office
15 Library
16 Guido's
17 Captain's Quarters
18 Juliana's
19 Tropics Cafe

Trail to Mt Scenery

To The Bottom

**Windwardside**

SABA

## Mt Scenery Trail

The island's premier hike is to the top of Mt Scenery, a strenuous climb up a virtual nonstop run of stairs (1064 in all!) that ends at the highest point in the Kingdom of the Netherlands. The trail, which is clearly marked and easy to follow, begins at the side of the road a couple of minutes' walk west of the tourist office. Hiking time is about 2½ hours return.

As ample reward for a good workout you'll get a close-up view of an elfin forest with its lush growth of ferns, tropical flowers and epiphyte-covered mahogany trees and,

if clouds don't roll in, the summit provides panoramic views of Saba and neighbouring islands. There are four interpretive sign-boards along the trail which describe some of the prolific flora and fauna and a couple of shelters erected by Cable & Wireless, which maintains the trail.

If you get an early start the two mainte-nance men who hike to work at the summit antenna tower may pass you on the way up. After reaching the summit be sure to con-tinue along the left side of the radio tower to reach the unmarked scenic lookout 100 metres beyond.

The trail can be very slippery in places; wear shoes with good traction, watch your footing and be especially careful where there are fallen leaves. This hike is only partially shaded and can get very hot at noon. Bring water; most hotels will provide guests with canteens.

### Places to Stay

*Captain's Quarters* (☎ 62201, in the USA ☎ (800) 365-8484) has 10 rooms, a cliffside pool and a popular open-air bar and restaurant. The main building, which was once the home of sea captain Henry Hassell, has two guest rooms, while the rest of the rooms are in two newer adjacent buildings. Most of the rooms are quite large, each has a private bath and some are furnished with antique four-poster beds. Rates, which include continental breakfast, are US$80/95 for singles/doubles in summer, US$95/125 in winter.

*Juliana's* (☎ 62269, fax 62389; in the USA ☎ (800) 365-8484) is a friendly family-run operation with eight rooms, each with private bath and a terrace with a distant ocean view. The rooms are good-sized, cheerful and spotlessly clean. Each has a coffee-maker, ceiling fan and screened windows to keep mosquitoes out. There's a common room with TV, a pool, a reasonably priced restaurant and a prize collection of flowering hibiscus on the grounds. Rates are US$60/75 for singles/doubles in summer, US$75/95 in winter. Juliana's also has a two-bedroom cottage and an apartment, both with kitchens, which rent for US$100 in summer and US$125 in winter.

*Scout's Place* (☎ 62205) has two sections, an older original wing with four rooms, two of which have private bath (cold water only) and two smaller rooms that share a bath. Rooms are quite basic; there are no fans and the louvred windows have no screens, a combination that can make for long nights during mosquito season. Rates are US$35/55 for singles/doubles. There are also 10 newer rooms, though they too are simple with the primary nod to creature comforts being hot water. Rates for the newer section are US$65/85 for singles/doubles, breakfast included.

### Places to Eat

A good-value breakfast and lunch spot is *Tropics Cafe*, next to the pool at Juliana's. From 7 to 9.30 am, French toast costs US$4, a cheese omelette with muffin US$5, both served with coffee. At lunch, from noon to 2.30 pm, a big cheeseburger with fries is US$5, while a hardy chef's salad with locally grown produce costs US$6. They'll also prepare reasonably priced box lunches, with a sandwich and an apple or potato chips. Tropics is closed on Sundays.

*Captain's Quarters* has good food, a pleasant open-air setting and reasonable prices. From 7.30 to 9 am a continental breakfast costs US$3.50, and a full breakfast is US$6. At lunch, soup, salads and sandwiches are in the same price range. At dinner, a changing chalkboard menu is featured, with dishes like fresh catch of the day with Creole sauce for US$14, shrimp or steak a few dollars more. Add US$4 for a green salad or lobster bisque.

*Scout's Place* has nice views and a pleasant setting for either a drink or meal. At lunch, sandwiches are around US$5, while a few hot dishes, including fresh fish, cost US$12. Reservations are required for dinner, which starts at 7.30 pm and is a set three-course meal, usually priced at US$16.50. The bar is a popular hangout.

*Scout's Snack & Shop*, a simple snack bar in front of Scout's Place, has hot dogs and burgers for US$3 and ice-cream cones for US$1.50.

*Guido's* is the Windwardside party place, serving as the island's pool hall during the week and a disco on weekends. At lunch and dinner, Guido's has burgers and fries for US$3.50 and thick-crusted pizzas from US$7.

*Brigadoon* is considered by many the best restaurant on the island. Salads and starters are around US$5, while main courses include Cajun meat loaf at US$14 and Saba fish pot, a combination of fish, clams and shrimp in a spicy sauce, for US$18. There's

SABA

also a special on most nights that features a generous cut of fresh fish for US$17 and local lobster at market price. It's open for dinner only, from 6 to 9 pm nightly.

*Saba Chinese Restaurant* is in the large hillside building topped with the satellite TV antenna on the north side of town. It's about a five-minute walk from Brigadoon, although a couple of ill-tempered dogs along the way may dissuade you from making the walk at night. The restaurant offers typical Cantonese dishes at moderate prices.

*Corner Deli & Gourmet Shop* is an authentic New York-style deli that makes good sandwiches and sells salads, cold cuts, breads, desserts and coffees. It's open from 7 am to 1 pm and 2 to 6 pm Monday to Saturday.

*Tea House*, behind the tourist office, is open from 9.30 am to 6 pm Monday to Saturday. The speciality is the pastries, which are homemade daily by the owner and might include raspberry cake, banana bread and cinnamon-raisin rolls, all under US$2. The Tea House also has hot and cold drinks, ice-cream, hot dogs and sandwiches. There's a small farmers' market with fresh produce and flowers behind the Tea House.

Big Rock Market, a rather large supermarket in the centre of town, also has produce, including hydroponically grown lettuce plucked fresh from its tub. It's open from 8 am to noon and 1 to 6 pm Monday to Saturday.

## ST JOHN'S

The road from Windwardside to The Bottom passes by the village of St John's. The most notable site is the roadside plaque to Josephus Lambert Hassell, the man responsible for constructing the island's road, a nearby section of which bears a striking resemblance to China's Great Wall.

From St John's you can see the secluded section of the coast to the south that has been earmarked by Dutch developers for Saba's first beach resort; plans call for a marina, golf course, country club and villa hotel. Island conservationists are challenging the project,

however, and there's some question as to whether it will ever be built.

St John's has Saba's only school, which provides all island children with primary and secondary education.

There is a lovely view of The Bottom as you drive down from St John's. The trailhead for the Crispeen Track begins at the side of the main road 500 metres before reaching The Bottom. This rural track leads to Windwardside, connecting with the Mt Scenery trail after about an hour.

### Places to Eat

*Lollipop's* (☎ 63330), on the road between St John's and The Bottom, is popular for its island dishes, which include stuffed land crabs, curried goat and fresh fish and lobster. Located about 800 metres up from The Bottom, it has a nice hillside view. Prices are moderate, it's open for lunch and dinner and diners are provided with free transport to and from the restaurant.

## THE BOTTOM

The Bottom, Saba's capital, is on a 250-metre plateau surrounded by hills and is the island's lowest town. As you first enter The Bottom you'll come upon the Department of Public Works, a quaint former schoolhouse flanked by three-metre-high night-blooming cacti that give off a wonderful scent in the evening. On the next corner is the Anglican church, a picturesque stone structure more than 200 years old. The church is followed by the police and fire station, in front of which you'll find a bell that was rung every hour on the hour until just a few years ago.

The Bottom also has a couple of cobble-stone streets lined with old stone walls, a public library that opens for a few hours most weekdays and the island's government offices.

As you stroll around, you may be approached by women selling Saba lace, and there are handicraft booths, which have rather irregular hours, at the south-west side of the government centre. At the northern end of the same street is Saba Artisans Foundation, open from 8 am to noon and 1 to 5 pm weekdays and on weekend mornings. The 'governor's house' (actually home to the lieutenant governor) is on the left as you leave The Bottom for Well's Bay. The gate is marked with orange balls, for the House of Orange, which rules the Netherlands.

## Information

The post office, at the government centre, is open from 8 am to noon and 1 to 5 pm Monday to Friday. Next door is Landsradio, where you can make overseas phone calls from 6 am to midnight daily. Saba's small rural hospital is at the north-west end of the village.

## Places to Stay

*Caribe Guesthouse* (☎ & fax 63259), on the south-east side of the hospital, has five simple but clean rooms. Guests have access to a shared kitchen and a living room with cable TV. One room has air-con for the same price as the others, which is US$45/60 for singles/doubles all year round.

*Cranston's Antique Inn* (☎ 63208) is an old-fashioned and neglected inn in the centre of town. It has six rooms, hardwood floors, a smattering of antiques and a murky pool. There are no fans or window screens. The best bet here is the downstairs room with private bath, which has a high four-poster bed with a canopy and mosquito net, a large armoire and a couple of tarnished oil lamps. The other five rooms share two washrooms and vary in quality and size, with room No 1, which is upstairs and fairly large, being a reasonable second choice. The rate is the same for all the rooms: US$44/58 for singles/doubles all year round, including tax and service charge.

*Queen's Gardens Resort* (☎ 63440; fax 63441), PO Box 34, The Bottom, is a new 40-unit luxury condo resort 800 metres east of town. Accommodation is in four-storey buildings, with each unit having cable TV, a phone, a fully equipped kitchen, a separate living room and its own little plunge pool. The facility has a fitness centre, tennis court and restaurant. The rate is US$200 a double.

## Places to Eat

The Bottom has a few eateries serving local food in simple surroundings. The largest is the *Sunset Bar & Restaurant*, which serves goat, fish and chicken dishes with potatoes and salad for about US$7 to US$10. It's open for lunch and dinner.

*Lime Time*, down by the governor's house, is essentially a bar that serves cheap local food such as chicken legs or stew from noon to 2 pm Monday to Saturday.

*My Store*, immediately south of the government centre, is a well-stocked grocery store that sells fresh pastries from Windwardside's Tea House. It's a good spot to stop and pick up a snack, and is open from 8 am to noon and 2 to 6 pm Monday to Saturday.

*Earl's Snack Bar* at the side of My Store, sells burgers and snack foods but has limited and irregular hours.

## LADDER BAY

Before Fort Bay was enlarged as a port, Saba's supplies were commonly unloaded at Ladder Bay. They were then hauled up to The Bottom via the Ladder, a series of hundreds of steps hewn into the rock. Everything from building materials and school books to a Steinway piano entered the island via the Ladder.

These days there's not much at Ladder Bay, other than an abandoned customs house and the coastal views, but the curious can still walk the route, which takes about half an hour down and a bit longer back up. The road to the bay leads steeply downhill to the left after the last house in The Bottom, not far from Nicholson's store.

## FORT BAY

The main road continues south from The Bottom to Fort Bay, the island's commercial port. This winding section of road, which is 1.2 km long, leads down through dry terrain punctuated by Turk's-head cacti. Fort Bay has two dive shops, a small restaurant, the marine park office, the island's power station and Saba's only petrol station. A water desalination plant is being built here, and the road to the proposed resort begins at the east side of the harbour.

The Saba Marine Park office has a few brochures to give away and books on diving and flora and fauna for sale. For US$5 you can purchase a plastic laminated card designed to guide you underwater along the snorkelling trail at Well's Bay. If you don't wish to keep the card you can return it to the office and have your US$5 refunded. The office is open from 8 am to noon and 1 to 5 pm on weekdays, Saturday morning and Sunday afternoon.

### Places to Eat

*In Two Deep* is a cosy little restaurant and bar above the Saba Deep dive shop. A full breakfast or lunchtime sandwiches and salads cost US$6.50 to US$8. It's open for dining from 8 am to 4 pm daily and for drinks (Fosters on tap) until 6 pm.

There's also a snack shop, *Pop's Place*, next to Wilson's Dive Shop, which sells hot dogs, soda and beer.

### WELL'S BAY

Saba's newest stretch of road runs from The Bottom to Well's Bay, where it terminates at the island's only beach. Just before the road nose-dives for Well's Bay there's a fine view of the coast that's worth having a camera ready for.

The beach at Well's Bay has a small patch of chocolate-coloured sand, though the amount of sand varies the season and the shoreline is generally quite rocky. For shade there's a small shelter at the south end of the beach. Those thinking of sunbathing on the shoreline might pause to look up at the cliffs towering above the beach – an eroding conglomerate of sand and boulders with many rocks hanging precariously directly overhead.

The bay, which is part of the Saba Marine Park, offers good swimming and snorkelling. You can find some coral-encrusted rocks in shallow waters along the north side of the bay, but the best snorkelling is near **Torrens Point** at the north-east end of the bay, about a 15-minute swim from the beach. About 50 metres short of the point a partially emerged sea tunnel cuts through the rock leading to deeper waters where there's good coral, schools of larger fish and an occasional sea turtle and nurse shark.

Off Torrens Point is glistening **Diamond Rock**, the tip of an underwater pinnacle and a bird nesting site. All that glitters, in this case, is simply guano.

There are no facilities at Well's Bay and you should bring water.

### COVE BAY

Although the waters off Saba's east coast are often turbulent, Cove Bay, near the airport, has a little boulder-protected pool that provides a safe spot for cooling off on a hot day. The bay is reached after a five-minute walk along the side road that begins just outside the terminal.

Along the road into Cove Bay there's a signposted trail that begins at the old leather factory and goes out along coastal bluffs to some nice tidal pools at **Flat Point**, behind the airport. The hike takes about 15 minutes one way.

To the south of Cove Bay is **Spring Bay**, which was named after a freshwater spring and was the site of an Arawak settlement.

# St Barthélemy (St Barts)

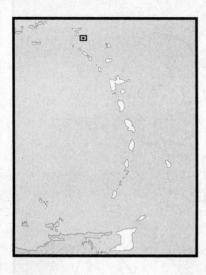

St Barthélemy, more commonly called St Barts, is the smallest of the French West Indies, a mere 10 km long and at its widest just four km across.

St Barts has lovely beaches and a relaxed pace. The island is hilly and dry, with a landscape that includes rock-strewn pastures, deeply indented bays and villages of trim white houses with red-tiled roofs. There's such a quintessential French flavour to the place that it's easy to forget you're in the Caribbean and to instead imagine little St Barts as some Mediterranean isle off the coast of France. The architecture, lifestyles, culture and food are all solidly French.

St Barts' low-key character has long appealed to wealthy escapists. Decades ago the Rockefellers and Rothchilds built estates here and in more recent times the island has become a chic destination for the well-heeled, attracting royalty, rock stars and Hollywood celebrities.

Although the island has a reputation for being an expensive destination, it's possible to get by in reasonable comfort on a moderate budget. St Barts can also be visited inexpensively as a day trip aboard one of several catamaran shuttles from St Martin.

## ORIENTATION
The airport is at the western end of St Jean, just a km from Gustavia. As there aren't many roads on the island and most destinations are signposted, it isn't difficult to find your way around.

# Facts about the Island

## HISTORY
Carib Indians made fishing expeditions to St Barts but the absence of a reliable freshwater source on the island hindered the establishment of permanent Amerindian settlements. During his second New World voyage in 1493, Christopher Columbus sighted the island and named it after his brother Bartholomew.

The first European attempt to settle the island was not until 1648 when a party of French colonists arrived from St Kitts. After Caribs raided the island in 1656 and massacred the entire colony, St Barts was abandoned. In 1673 Huguenots from Normandy and Brittany established the first permanent settlement. The island's prosperity didn't come from fishing and farming, however, but from the booty captured by French buccaneers who used St Barts as a base for their raids on Spanish galleons.

Conditions on St Barts didn't favour the development of sugar plantations so unlike other Caribbean islands, where large numbers of slaves were brought in, the population remained predominantly European.

In 1784, King Louis XVI ceded the island to his friend King Gustaf III of Sweden in exchange for trading rights in the Swedish

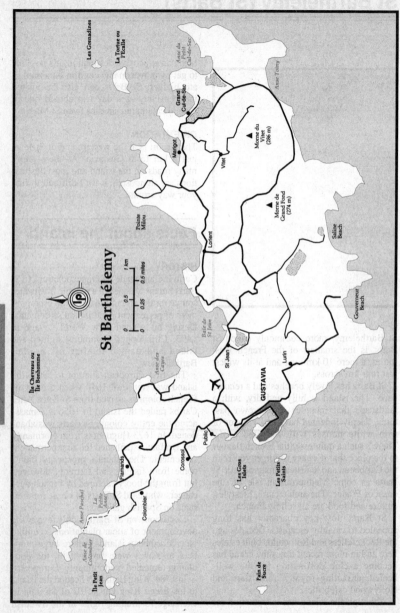

Les Grenadines

La Tortue ou l'Ecaille

Anse du Petit Cul-de-Sac

Anse Toiny

Grand Cul-de-Sac

Morne du Vitet (286 m)

Margot

Vitet

Morne de Grand Fond (274 m)

Pointe Milou

Lorient

Saline Beach

St Barthélemy

Île Chevreau ou Île Bonhomme

1 km

0.5 miles

0.5

0.25

0

0

Gouverneur Beach

Baie de St Jean

Anse des Cayes

St Jean

GUSTAVIA

Lurin

Public

Corossol

Les Gros Islets

Les Petits Saints

Flamands

Anse Paschal

La Petite Anse

Colombier

Anse de Colombier

Île Petit Jean

Pain de Sucre

ST BARTHÉLEMY

port of Gothenburg. The Swedes changed the name of St Barts' port from Carenage to Gustavia, built a town hall and constructed three small forts named Gustaf, Octave and Karl. Hoping to make money on their new outpost, the Swedes turned St Barts into a duty-free port and by 1800 the population had swelled to 6000.

In 1852 a catastrophic fire swept across much of Gustavia. By this time a change in European-American trade routes had led to a decline in both trade and population and most of the city was not rebuilt. In 1878 the Swedes, anxious to cut their losses on St Barts, sold the island back to France for the sum of 320,000F. Although today St Barts is decidedly French, traces of the Swedish era, evident in a few period buildings and Swedish street names, and the island's duty-free status, still remain.

## GEOGRAPHY
St Barts' total land area is a mere 21 sq km, although its elongated shape and hilly terrain makes it seem larger. The island lies 25 km south-east of St Martin.

St Barts has numerous dry and rocky offshore islets. The largest, Île Fourchue, is a half-sunken volcanic crater whose large bay is a popular yacht anchorage and a destination for divers and snorkellers.

## CLIMATE
The island is dry; the temperature averages 26°C (79°F) in winter, 28°C (82°F) in summer. The water temperature averages about one degree warmer than the air temperature.

## FLORA & FAUNA
St Barts has an arid climate with dryland flora such as cacti and bougainvillea. Reptiles include lizards, iguanas and harmless grass snakes. From April to August sea turtles lay eggs along the beaches on the north-west side of the island. The numerous islets off St Barts support seabird colonies, including those of frigatebirds.

## GOVERNMENT
St Barts, together with St Martin, is a sub-prefecture of Guadeloupe, which in turn is an overseas department of France. While the sub-prefect resides in St Martin, St Barts has its own mayor who is responsible for administering local affairs.

## ECONOMY
Some islanders still make a living from fishing, but tourism is the mainstay of the economy these days. St Barts gets about 160,000 visitors annually; a little over half come by boat, mostly on day trips from St Martin. In winter the majority of visitors come from the USA, in the summer from France.

## POPULATION & PEOPLE
St Barts has a population of nearly 5000. While most native islanders trace their roots to the 17th-century Norman and Breton settlers, the island is also home to the descendants of latter-day Swedish merchants and more recent arrivals from mainland France.

## CULTURE
The island's culture is very French, with a

St Barts' coat of arms

rural character that's manifested in the local dialect, the architecture and the slow-paced lifestyle of the islanders.

### Dress Conventions

Although topless bathing is de rigueur, nudity is officially banned on St Barts. Still, on some of the more secluded beaches, such as Saline, the restriction is not strictly adhered to. While the island has some very exclusive restaurants, jackets and ties are not required for dining

### RELIGION

Catholicism is the dominant religion. There are Roman Catholic churches in Gustavia and Lorient and an Anglican church in Gustavia.

### LANGUAGE

French is the official language, although the type spoken by many islanders is heavily influenced by the old Norman dialect of their ancestors.

Many people speak some English, particularly those in hotels and restaurants. A French-English dictionary and phrasebook will come in handy, but a working knowledge of French is not essential.

# Facts for the Visitor

### PASSPORT & VISAS

US and Canadian citizens can stay up to three weeks by showing proof of citizenship in the form of a current passport, an expired (up to five years) passport, or an official birth certificate accompanied by a driver's licence or other government-authorised photo ID. For stays of over three weeks, a valid passport is required. Citizens of the EU need an official identity card, valid passport or French *carte de séjour*. Citizens of most other foreign countries, including Australia, need both a valid passport and a visa for France.

A return or onward ticket is officially required of visitors.

### CUSTOMS

St Barts is a duty-free port and there are no restrictions on items brought in for personal use.

### MONEY

The French franc is the official currency and most transactions are calculated in francs. US dollars are readily accepted everywhere, though each shop sets its own exchange rate, so if you're going to be on the island any length of time you'll probably be better off paying in francs. Major credit cards are widely accepted in shops and at most hotels and restaurants.

More information can be found under Money in the introductory Facts for the Visitor chapter.

### TOURIST OFFICES

The St Barts Tourist Office (☎ 27 87 27; fax 27 74 47) is on the harbourfront in Gustavia at Quai du Général de Gaulle. When requesting information by mail, write to: Office du Tourisme, BP 113, Gustavia, 97098 Cedex, St Barthélemy, French West Indies.

Overseas tourist representatives are listed under Tourist Offices in the Facts for the Visitor section of the Martinique chapter.

### BUSINESS HOURS

While business hours vary, offices and shops are generally open weekdays from about 8 am to 5 pm, with most taking a lunchtime siesta. Some tourist-geared shops are open until 7 pm and have Saturday hours as well.

Banking hours are from 8 am to noon and 2 to 3.30 pm Monday to Friday.

### HOLIDAYS

Public holidays on St Barts are:

| | |
|---|---|
| *New Year's Day* | – 1 January |
| *Labor Day* | – 1 May |
| *Easter Sunday* | – late March/early April |
| *Easter Monday* | – late March/early April |
| *Ascension Thursday* | – 40th day after Easter |
| *Pentecost Monday* | – seventh Sunday after Easter |
| *Bastille Day* | – 14 July |
| *Assumption Day* | – 15 August |
| *All Saints Day* | – 1 November |

| *All Souls Day* | – 2 November |
|---|---|
| *Armistice Day* | – 11 November |
| *Christmas Day* | – 25 December |

## CULTURAL EVENTS

A number of festivals are celebrated on St Barts throughout the year. Some of these include:

*St Barts Music Festival* Held in mid-January, this two-week festival features jazz, chamber music and dance performances.

*Carnival* Carnival is held for four days before Lent and includes a pageant, costumes and street dancing, ending with the burning of a King Carnival figure at Shell Beach, Gustavia. Many businesses close during Carnival.

*Festival of St Barthélemy* This festival, celebrated on 24 August, the feast day of the island's patron saint, includes fireworks, a public ball, boat races and other competitions.

St Barts is the setting for several regattas: the St Barth's Cup, a three-day yachting race sponsored by the St Barth's Yacht Club, held in late January; the St Barth Regatta, a colourful four-day regatta in mid-February; the International Regatta of St Barthélemy, held for three days in mid-May; and La Route du Rosé, a transatlantic regatta of tall ships transporting the latest vintage of rosé wines from St Tropez to Gustavia. The latter is held in mid-December and ends with a yacht race around the island.

## POST

There are post offices in Gustavia, St Jean and Lorient. It costs 2.50F to send a postcard to France, 3.20F to the UK, 2.70F to the USA or Canada and 4.20F to Australia. This rate also covers letters up to 10 grams.

To address mail to the island, follow the business name (and the post office box number – BP – when there is one) with the town or beach name and '97133 St Barthélemy, French West Indies'.

## TELECOMMUNICATIONS

Most pay phones are card phones although there's one coin phone at the airport and another at Crédit Agricole in Gustavia. *Télécartes* for card phones are sold at post offices and at the petrol station near the airport. The area code for St Barts is 590. To call between St Barts and French St Martin, Martinique or Guadeloupe, simply dial the six-digit phone number direct.

More information can be found under Telecommunications in the introductory Facts for the Visitor chapter.

## ELECTRICITY

The electric current is 220 volts AC, 50/60 cycles. Many hotels have dual voltage (110/220) shaver adaptors.

## WEIGHTS & MEASURES

St Barts uses the metric system and the 24-hour clock.

## BOOKS & MAPS

Two popular souvenir-type books are the *History of St Barth*, a 64-page book (150F) by Stanislas Defize and *Architecture St Barth*, a 48-page book (100F) by J L Cailleux, N Herard & P Hochart. They're both hardcover books with bilingual (French/English) text and are published by Editions du Latanier on St Barts.

There are several free tourist maps of the island that are suitable for most purposes. For something more detailed, there's the Institut Géographique National's Serie Bleue map 4608-G (1:25,000), which includes both St Martin and St Barts. This map shows both roads and topography, but is easier to find on St Martin than on St Barts.

## MEDIA

The free monthly *St-Barth Magazine* newspaper has local news in French and tourist information in both English and French. *Le Journal de St Barth* is a free weekly newspaper in French that's published on Thursday.

The local radio station is Radio St-Barth at 98 MHz.

## HEALTH

There's a small medical facility, Bruyun Hospital (☎ 27 60 35), in Gustavia, and there are pharmacies in Gustavia and St Jean.

## EMERGENCIES

For police emergencies dial ☎ 27 60 12.

## ACTIVITIES

### Beaches & Swimming

St Barts, with its numerous bays and coves, boasts nearly two dozen beaches. For 'in-town' beaches, St Jean, Flamands, Lorient and Shell Beach all have beautiful sandy strands. For more secluded spots, Colombier, Saline and Gouverneur beaches are all fine choices.

### Diving & Snorkelling

The most popular diving spots are off the islets surrounding St Barts, which are rich in marine life and coral.

Two of the largest dive shops are St-Barth Diving Center at Marine Service (☎ 27 70 34) and Rainbow Dive (☎ 27 91 79; fax 27 91 80) at the Ocean Must Marina, both in Gustavia. Single dives average about 250F, resort courses are 600F and a four-day open-water certification course is 2400F.

Popular snorkelling spots include Anse de Colombier, La Petite Anse and Lorient. For snorkel/sail day trips see Tours in the Getting Around section of this chapter.

Snorkelling gear can be rented for about 60F a day from Hookipa Surf Shop (☎ 27 71 31) or the Mistral School (☎ 27 64 84) in St Jean and from Marine Service (☎ 27 70 34) in Gustavia.

### Windsurfing

Grand Cul-de-Sac, the main windsurfing centre, has a large protected bay that's ideal for beginners and some nice wave action beyond the reef good for advanced windsurfers. Wind Wave Power (☎ 27 62 73) at St Barts Beach Hotel in Grand Cul-de-Sac gives windsurfing lessons for 300F and rents equipment for 100F to 120F an hour.

There's also good windsurfing at St Jean, where the St Barth Wind School (☎ 27 71 22), next to Chez Francine, rents beginners' equipment for 75/225F per hour/day and advanced gear for 100/300F. Lessons are available as well. Windsurfing equipment

can also be rented at the Mistral School (☎ 27 64 84) at Filao Beach Hotel in St Jean.

### Surfing

The main surfing spots are at Lorient, Anse des Cayes and Toiny. Hookipa Surf Shop (☎ 27 71 31) in St Jean rents surfboards for 110F a day and bodyboards for 100F. The store is open from 9 am to 7 pm (to 2 pm on Sunday). The Reefer Surf Club (☎ 27 78 74) in Lorient organises surfing events and gives lessons to those wanting to take up the sport.

### Fishing & Boating

Tuna, dorado, marlin and wahoo are caught in the waters off St Barts. Marine Service (27 70 34) and La Maison de la Mer (☎ 27 81 00), both members of the Big Game Fishing Club of France, can arrange charter boats. The cost is about 4000F for a full day with drinks and lunch, 2500F for a half day, including fishing gear for four people. These two agencies also rent motorboats and sailing boats.

If you're just looking to rent a little Sunfish or Hobie Cat boat, try the windsurf shops or beachside water sports centres, which generally rent them from about 85F per hour.

Game fish

## Horse Riding

The Ranch de Flamands (☎ 27 80 72) offers two-hour excursions for beginning and experienced riders for 200F, departing at 9 am and 3 pm daily except Monday.

## HIGHLIGHTS

St Barts' beaches are certainly a highlight. A favourite is Anse de Colombier – not only for the beach itself, which is lovely and secluded, but also for the hike to it which offers wonderful views of the north coast. The island is also a special place for wind-surfers, with Grand Cul-de-Sac and St Jean the two main haunts. And then there's the classy French ambience, chic boutiques, villa hotels and fine restaurants with Parisian chefs.

## ACCOMMODATION

Accommodation on St Barts is all small scale. The island has about 40 hotels, with a combined capacity of only 650 rooms. Virtually all accommodation is in the moderate to high range; there are none of the local-style guesthouses which shore up the bottom range on many other Caribbean islands. Some hotels set prices in US dollars, others quote them in French francs. As the exchange rate between the two currencies can fluctuate rather substantially, we've listed rates in the currency quoted by each hotel.

Most hotels include the tax and service charge in their quoted rates, although a few places add 5% to 10% onto the bill.

## Villas

In addition to hotels, St Barts has numerous villas for rent. The biggest agent is Sibarth (☎ 27 62 38; fax 27 60 52), Rue du Général de Gaulle, BP 55 Gustavia, 97098 St Barthélemy, which handles around 200 villas and apartments. Weekly rates range from US$800/1150 in summer/winter for a one-bedroom apartment to US$7000/12,000 for a four-bedroom four-bath villa with a pool.

Sibarth's representative in the USA is WIMCO (☎ (401) 849-8012, ☎ (800) 932-3222; fax (401) 847-6290), PO Box 1461, Newport, RI 02840. In France, Sibarth can be reached toll free on ☎ 05 90 16 20.

Other villa rental agencies on St Barts are Villas St Barth (☎ 27 74 29) and Ici & Là (☎ 27 78 78).

## FOOD

St Barts has many fine French restaurants and if money is no object you can eat very well indeed. There are also moderately priced places to eat but as most of the island's food is imported the only inexpensive options are pretty much limited to grocery stores and bakeries.

## DRINKS

St Barts lacks a freshwater source. The island has a desalination plant but water prices are so high that many places maintain their own rainwater catchment systems. If your tap water is from catchment, the best policy is to boil it before drinking. You can buy inexpensive bottled water at grocery stores.

Wine is the drink of choice on St Barts and French wines and champagnes can be purchased from grocery stores around the island at duty-free prices, which make them one of the best buys to be found on St Barts. Restaurants generally have extensive wine lists, although their prices are much higher.

## ENTERTAINMENT

In terms of entertainment on St Barts, an evening out is most commonly a dinner affair. However, there are a few places where you can find dancing, including Le Pelican in St Jean which has live bands (pop, rock, reggae) on weekends from 10.30 pm. In Lorient, there's a disco as well as a French follies-type revue at La Banane hotel. For the latest in entertainment information, pick up a copy of *St-Barth Magazine*.

## THINGS TO BUY

There are plenty of shops in Gustavia selling duty-free perfumes, French and Italian designer clothing, Swiss watches and jewellery. You can pick up duty-free alcohol in grocery stores.

ST BARTHÉLEMY

The most traditional island-made crafts are the straw products from the lantania palm made and sold in Corossol. A popular line of natural cosmetics, called 'M', is made in Lorient using island flowers.

# Getting There & Away

## AIR
The landing strip at St Barts can't handle anything larger than 20-seater STOL aircraft and is not equipped for night landings. While there are no long-distance direct flights to St Barts, there are numerous daily flights from St Martin and Guadeloupe.

Air Guadeloupe (☎ 27 64 44) flies to St Barts four times daily from Guadeloupe; the fare is 520F (390F student) one way, 710F for a three-day excursion ticket. It also flies to St Barts three times daily from French St Martin for 180F each way.

Air Saint-Barthélemy (☎ 27 71 90) flies to St Barts daily from both French and Dutch St Martin and from Guadeloupe. The fare from Guadeloupe is 536F one way, 840F return. From French St Martin the fare is 200F one way, 400 return, and from Dutch St Martin the fare is US$50.

Virgin Air (☎ 27 71 76) flies to St Barts from Puerto Rico twice daily, from St Thomas three times a day and from Virgin Gorda once a day. The one-way fare from San Juan is US$115 from Monday to Thursday, US$141 from Friday to Sunday. The fare from the Virgin Islands is US$80 from Monday to Thursday, US$100 from Friday to Sunday. Return tickets cost double the one-way fare.

Winair (☎ 27 61 01) flies at least half a dozen times a day from Dutch St Martin. The flight, which takes only about 15 minutes, costs US$40 one way. There's also a one-day excursion fare of US$70.

## Airport Information
St Barts' modest airport terminal has a liquor store, a gift shop selling souvenirs and T-shirts and a magazine stand that sells the *International Herald-Tribune* and a good selection of French magazines and newspapers.

**To/From the Airport** Many hotels will provide free transportation from the airport with advance notice. There are usually taxis parked in front of the airport, though occasionally it's necessary to wait a few minutes for one to show.

## SEA
Several boats sail daily between St Martin and St Barts. Details are under Sea in the Getting There & Away section of the St Martin chapter.

### Yacht
Those arriving by yacht can clear immigration at the port office (VHF: 16 or 10), on the east side of the Gustavia Harbour. It's open from 7 am to 6 pm (9 am to noon on Sunday) during the high season; in the low season, it siestas from noon to 3 pm and is closed on Sunday.

Loulou's Marine (☎ 27 62 74), behind the port office in Gustavia, is a well-stocked chandlery that sells charts and has a useful bulletin board with yachting information. Boats can fuel up at the Jeanne d'Arc dock in Public from 8 am to noon and 2 to 5 pm daily except Saturday afternoons and Sunday.

Gustavia Harbour has mooring and docking facilities for about 40 yachts. Popular anchorages can be found up the coast at Public, Corossol and Colombier.

For bareboat charters check with Marine Service (☎ 27 70 34) and for crewed yachts contact Stardust Marine (☎ 27 79 81), both in Gustavia.

## LEAVING ST BARTS
The departure tax is 16F, but it's generally added on to the airfare when you purchase your ticket.

# Getting Around

St Barts has no public bus system so hiring a vehicle is essential to thoroughly explore the island.

## TAXI

In addition to the taxi terminal at the airport, there's one in Gustavia near the tourist office. To call for a taxi dial ☎ 27 66 31.

A taxi from the airport to either St Jean or Gustavia costs about US$8. For US$40 day trippers can get a one-hour tour of the island, be dropped off at a beach or in town and be picked up at a pre-arranged time and driven back to the airport.

## CAR & MOTORBIKE

The most popular rental vehicle on the island is the open-air Mini Moke (see under Rental below), although small cars can be rented for about the same price. Mopeds and motorcycles are also available; however, this option is best suited to experienced motorcycle drivers as the island's roads have a cement surface that can get slippery when wet and many roads are narrow, winding and very steep. There are two petrol stations on the island: one in Lorient and the other opposite the airport. The airport station accepts major credit cards at the pump, making it possible to get petrol 24 hours a day as long as the system's not down. Otherwise it's staffed from 7.30 am to noon and 2 to 6 pm Monday to Saturday. The Lorient station is open from 7.30 am to 12.30 pm Monday to Saturday and from 2 to 5 pm on some afternoons. Both are closed on Sunday.

## Road Rules

Drive on the right. Your home driving licence is valid in St Barts. The speed limit is 45 km/h unless otherwise posted.

## Rental

A dozen car rental companies have booths at the airport, including Hertz, Avis, Budget and Europcar/National. Cars can also be rented from most hotels and in Gustavia. There's a lot of competition and prices fluctuate but in summer you can generally get a Mini Moke or a small car for about US$35 per day, in winter for about US$50.

Ouanalao (☎ 27 88 74) at the side of the airport Shell station and Rent Some Fun (☎ 27 70 59) behind the Catholic church in Gustavia rent scooters and motorbikes for about US$25 per day.

## HITCHING

Hitching is legal and fairly common on the island. The usual safety precautions apply.

## TOURS

### Glass-Bottom Boat

*Aquascope*, which can be booked through Marine Service (☎ 27 70 34), is a 10-passenger glass-bottom boat which offers a one-hour tour of coral gardens and the wreck of the 63-metre yacht *Non Stop*. It costs 160F for adults, 80F for children aged five to 12, free for children under five. A similar excursion is offered by the *Aquarius* (☎ 27 81 00).

### Sailing/Snorkelling Tours

Marine Service offers a full-day sail aboard the 12.6-metre catamaran *Ne Me Quitte Pas* that takes in Île Fourchue and Anse de Colombier for 450F. Snorkel gear is included, as is an open bar and lunch. Marine Service also has a half-day snorkel sail to Anse de Colombier for 270F and a 1½-hour sunset sail for 230F.

Saint Barth Yachting Service (☎ 27 65 79) in St Jean and the 12.6-metre ketch *Zavijava* (☎ 27 62 38) offer similar outings at similar prices.

### Sightseeing Tours

The tourist office organises minibus tours that depart from their Gustavia office. There's a 45-minute tour (150F) of the western side of St Barts, an hour tour (200F) of the eastern side and a 90-minute tour (250F) of the whole island. The cost covers up to three people; it's 50F extra for each additional passenger.

# Gustavia

Gustavia, the island's capital and main port, is an appealing horseshoe-shaped town built up around a deep harbour. It has streetside

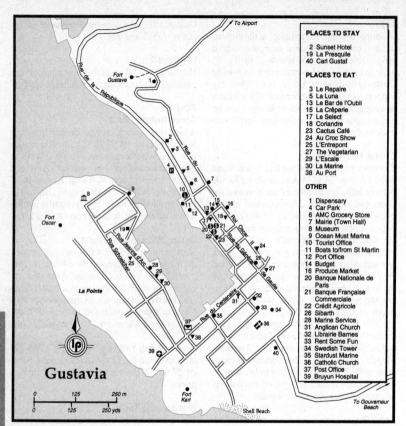

**PLACES TO STAY**

2  Sunset Hotel
19  La Presquile
40  Carl Gustaf

**PLACES TO EAT**

3  Le Repaire
5  La Luna
13  Le Bar de l'Oubli
15  La Crêperie
17  Le Select
18  Coriandre
23  Cactus Café
24  Au Croc Show
25  L'Entrepont
27  The Vegetarian
29  L'Escale
30  La Marine
38  Au Port

**OTHER**

1  Dispensary
4  Car Park
6  AMC Grocery Store
7  Mairie (Town Hall)
8  Museum
9  Ocean Must Marina
10  Tourist Office
11  Boats to/from St Martin
12  Port Office
14  Budget
16  Produce Market
20  Banque Nationale de
      Paris
21  Banque Française
      Commerciale
22  Crédit Agricole
26  Sibarth
28  Marine Service
31  Anglican Church
32  Librairie Barnes
33  Rent Some Fun
34  Swedish Tower
35  Stardust Marine
36  Catholic Church
37  Post Office
39  Bruyun Hospital

Gustavia

cafés where day visitors linger the afternoon away, a couple of historic sites worth a stroll and a nice beach within walking distance. As Gustavia is a duty-free port, there are also numerous jewellery shops and exclusive boutiques, with the highest concentration along the Quai de la République.

The old *mairie* (town hall), built during the Swedish period, is at the end of Rue Couturier. There's a small fruit and vegetable market 100 metres east of the mairie and adjacent to that is a little war memorial. In the same area there's also a small market selling locally made arts and crafts. As you walk around, you'll notice that some of the street signs in this neighbourhood still bear Swedish names ending in the suffix '-gaten'.

At the inner harbour, in the area around Rue du Centenaire, you'll find a stone Anglican church dating from 1855 and the town's landmark Swedish tower which houses an antique clock that is still hand-wound daily.

### Information

**Tourist Office** The tourist office (☎ 27 87 27) is on the east side of the harbour at Quai du Général de Gaulle. Be sure to pick up *Tropical St Barth* and *St-Barth Magazine*, two free French/English publications filled with tourist info and ads.

The office is open from 8.30 am to 12.30 pm and from 3 to 7 pm Monday to Thursday, from 8.30 am to 3 pm on Friday. It's closed on weekends and holidays.

**Money** Crédit Agricole, on Rue du Bord de Mer, exchanges money without charging commissions. The counter is open from 8 am to 1 pm and 2.30 to 5 pm on weekdays and from 8 am to 1 pm on Saturday. If you have notes rather than travellers' cheques, there's also an automatic money exchange dispenser that can convert major currencies to French francs or US dollars. The dispenser is open from 7 am to 10 pm daily but can be accessed 24 hours a day using a major credit card.

There are also two banks in the same area, the Bank Nationale de Paris on Rue du Bord de Mer and the Banque Française Commerciale on Rue du Général de Gaulle.

**Post** The Gustavia post office, on the corner of Rue Jeanne d'Arc and Rue du Centenaire, is open from 8 am to noon Monday to Saturday and from 2 to 4 pm on Monday, Tuesday, Thursday and Friday.

**Bookshops** Librairie Barnes on Rue Courbet has a small selection of books about the Caribbean, mostly in French, as well as many French newspapers and the *International Herald-Tribune*. It's open from 7.30 am to 5.30 pm Monday to Saturday.

### Le Musée de St-Barth
The Municipal Museum of St-Barthélemy, at the north-west side of La Pointe, is a modest museum, established in 1989. It has period photo exhibits, engravings and some simple displays that give a glimpse into the island's history. Opening hours are from 8.30 am to noon and 1.30 to 5.30 pm weekdays (to 5 pm on Friday) and from 8.30 am to noon on Saturday. Admission is 10F.

### Shell Beach
Shell Beach, the common name for Anse de Grand Galet, is a nice sandy beach with a shoreline packed high with tiny shells. Only a 10-minute walk from the harbour the beach makes a fine swimming spot.

To get there go south on Rue Gambetta, turn right and go past the Catholic church and continue on that road until you reach the beach.

### Fort Gustave
The site of old Fort Gustave has a couple of cannons and a milk-bottle-shaped lighthouse, but most people come here for the fine view of Gustavia and the harbour. An interpretive plaque points out local sights and landmarks. Across the harbour to the south is Fort Oscar, which is still used as a military installation, and on a clear day you can see the islands of St Kitts and St Eustatius.

To get there, take the Gustavia road 700 metres from the airport crossroads and then as the road curves left down to Gustavia, pull off to the right where there's space for a couple of cars. The fort isn't marked, but you'll see a Meteo France sign here. It's just a minute's walk up the hill to the fort.

### Places to Stay
*La Presquile* (☎ 27 64 60; fax 27 72 30), on Rue Avaler at Le Pointe, has 14 good-value rooms. While they're not fancy, they're clean and all have refrigerators, air-con and private baths – some also sport nice harbourview balconies. There's a pleasant young manager and singles/doubles cost 220/330F.

*Sunset Hotel* (☎ 27 77 21; fax 27 83 44), Rue de la République, is an unpretentious older hotel with nine good-sized rooms, clean and simple but not austere. From its

3rd-floor balcony there are nice views of the harbour and Gustavia. Rates are US$55 to US$75 for singles and US$70 to US$90 for doubles in summer, US$10 to US$20 more in winter.

*Carl Gustaf* (☎ 27 82 83; fax 27 82 37), Rue des Normands, on a hillside overlooking the harbour, is a modern luxury hotel with 14 suites, each with a video, fax, a couple of phones and a private plunge pool. Rates begin at about US$550 in the low season, US$800 in the high season, for up to four people.

### Places to Eat
**Central Gustavia** *Au Croc Show*, a friendly pâtisserie with a few café tables, is a good place to get an inexpensive bite to eat. Slices of pizza or quiche are about 10F, as are some wonderful desserts, including fresh strawberry tarts. There's also takeaway roast chicken, beer and wine. It's open from 6.30 am to 7 pm Monday to Saturday and from 7.30 am to 1 pm on Sunday.

The outdoor patio of *Le Select*, on the corner of Rue de France and Rue du Général de Gaulle, resounds with reggae music and is the place to hang out and down a few drinks. You can get inexpensive cheeseburgers and sandwiches from 10.30 am to 2 pm and 6.30 to 10 pm. It's closed on Sunday and holidays.

A quieter crowd sips drinks opposite Le Select at *Le Bar de l'Oubli*, where there's a reasonably priced chalkboard snack menu at lunchtime.

*La Crêperie* on Rue du Roi Oscar II has a variety of main-course crêpes and sandwiches from about 25F and dessert crêpes ranging from 12F to 40F. The crêpes are on the small side, but the atmosphere is pleasant. It's open from 7 am to 10 pm Monday to Friday, to 6 pm on Saturday.

*Cactus Café*, a natural food café of sorts, serves deli food such as quiche and salads and usually has a couple of chalkboard meals for around 55F. There's a breakfast special of two croissants, fresh orange juice and coffee for 30F. They also have fresh juices, Haagen-Dazs ice cream, cakes and pies. It's

open from 7.30 am to about 8.30 pm Monday to Saturday.

*Le Repaire* is a good streetside restaurant opposite the harbour with lunchtime sandwiches for 25F to 30F. At both lunch and dinner you can get grilled steak with fries for 70F, grilled fish for 85F and a range of salads and warm starters from 40F to 70F. It's closed on Sunday.

*La Luna* (☎ 27 72 63), off Rue de la République, is a large new restaurant with a 2nd-floor harbour view. At lunch, there's a barbecue with prices ranging from 45F for chicken to 85F for fish. At dinner, main courses are mostly in the 75F to 100F range.

*Coriandre* (☎ 27 93 84) is a small Thai restaurant on Rue du Roi Oscar II. Prices average 50F to 70F for dishes that include the likes of lemongrass soup, goat cheese salad and spicy chicken with fresh basil and Thai rice. It's open from 11 am to 11 pm daily, except on Sunday when it's open for dinner only.

During the winter season you can get fresh juice and vegetarian lunches and dinners at *The Vegetarian*, a Rastafarian stand at the south end of Rue du Roi Oscar II.

*AMC* is a large grocery store opposite the harbour on Rue de la République that sells everything from pastries and wine to deli foods. It's open from 8 am to at least 5 pm on weekdays, except for Wednesday when it closes at 1 pm.

**La Pointe** The following restaurants are at La Pointe, the large peninsula-like land area that comprises the west side of the harbour.

*L'Entrepont* (☎ 27 90 60), operated by an Italian family, has good Italian food and open-air dining. Pizza ranges from 45F to 70F, pastas from 60F to 90F and meat dishes a bit more. It's open daily for lunch and dinner.

*L'Escale* (☎ 27 81 06) is a popular, reasonably priced seaside eatery with offerings ranging from pizza and pasta to seafood. It's open daily for lunch and dinner but is commonly closed during the low season.

*La Marine* (☎ 27 68 91) is a harbourfront restaurant open for lunch and dinner Monday to Saturday. Burgers and omelettes cost 30F to 60F, fish and meat dishes start around 100F. The restaurant is packed on Thursday nights (reserve early) when they serve mussels which are flown in from France and prepared in a delectable wine broth.

*Au Port*, opposite the post office, is a pretty good choice for a classic French dinner at moderate prices. Main dishes include colombo of lamb (95F), fillet of duck (120F) and a number of seafood offerings. Add another 60F for a mixed salad.

*Carl Gustaf* has a piano bar and is a good place for a sunset cocktail. There's also an exclusive French restaurant where dinner for two can easily add up to 1000F.

**Around Gustavia** Two popular, although rather expensive, restaurants are just a few minutes' drive from Gustavia. *Maya's* (☎ 27 73 61) on the beach at Public, to the north-west of Gustavia, has very good Creole food. It's open from 4.30 pm for sunset drinks and for dinner nightly except on Sunday. It closes in summer.

*Castelets* (☎ 27 78 80) in Lurin, east of Gustavia, has a nice hilltop view and features fine French food. It's open for lunch during the holiday season, and for dinner nightly; reservations are recommended.

# Around St Barts

## COROSSOL

About two km north-west of Gustavia is Corossol, one of the island's most traditional fishing villages. The brown-sand beach is lined with blue and orange fishing boats and stacks of lobster traps. Women here still weave the leaves of the lantania palm into straw hats, baskets and placemats, which they line up on the walls in front of their homes to attract buyers.

On the south-east end of the beach, just 50 metres down a dirt road, is the Inter Oceans Museum (☎ 27 62 97), a collection of 7000 seashells in the home of Ingenu Magras, who started the museum half a century ago. It's open from 9.30 am to 5 pm daily except holidays and has an admission fee of 20F.

## FLAMANDS

Flamands, a small village on the north-western side of the island, borders a curving bay that's lined with a long, broad strand of white sand. The waters are clear and blue and it's a popular bathing beach, backed in places by low-growing coconut trees and sea-grapes. Despite a handful of small beachside hotels, the area still retains a pleasantly rural character. There's easy beach access with streetside parking at the westernmost end of Flamands Bay.

The peninsula on the west side of the beach separates Flamands from nearby La Petite Anse, where rocky waters afford good snorkelling. To get there, continue west past Flamands for about 200 metres and take the short spur that curves down to the right before the main road reaches a dead end.

### Places to Stay

*Auberge de la Petite Anse* (☎ 27 64 60; fax 27 72 30), BP 117, has 16 condo-like units above a rocky coastline. It's within walking distance of Flamands Beach and right at the trailhead to Anse de Colombier. Each unit has a bedroom with two beds, a kitchenette, ocean-facing terraces and air-con. Rates are a reasonable 440F in summer, 700F in winter.

*White Sand Beach Cottages* (☎ 27 82 08; fax 27 70 69) consists of four pleasant duplex beach cottages, two of which are ocean fronting. These modern units have fans, air-con, kitchenettes and sun decks. Rates are US$55 to US$75 for singles and US$80 to US$110 for doubles in summer, US$125 to US$140 for singles and US$180 to US$200 for doubles in winter. There's also a separate three-bedroom, two-bath villa that rents by the week for US$2550 in summer, US$3400 in winter.

*Baie des Flamands* (☎ 27 64 85; fax 27 83 98), BP 68, is an older two-storey hotel with 24 rooms. Each room fronts the beach and has air-con, TV and a refrigerator; superior rooms have kitchenettes on their balconies.

ST BARTHÉLEMY

Summer rates are US$90 or US$110 for singles, US$116 or US$140 for doubles, with the higher rates for superior rooms. Winter rates are US$173 or US$219 for singles, US$195 or US$242 for doubles. There's a pool.

*Isle de France* (☎ 27 61 81), a new luxury hotel at the east end of the bay, has 30 spacious rooms and suites that cost US$240 to US$375 in summer, US$335 to US$540 in winter, breakfast included.

### Places to Eat

Most people staying in this area prepare their own meals and restaurant options are limited.

For something quick and cheap, there's *Epicerie Sainte Helen*, a small bakery on the village's main road about 50 metres before the beach.

A nice place to dine is at *Frégate* (☎ 27 66 51), a French restaurant at the Baie des Flamands hotel, which has both indoor and outdoor patio tables above Flamands Beach. The extensive menu includes main dishes such as grilled shark, duck with lychees and red snapper in coconut milk, each around 100F. It's open for lunch from noon to 3 pm and for dinner from 7 pm.

For Creole food, there's *Jardin Samba*, on a side road about a km south-east of Flamands – the route is marked with orange stars. Starters such as stuffed conch or hot goat cheese salad cost 45F while main dishes include chicken with lime or fish Creole for 75F and grilled lobster at market prices. It's open for dinner only.

### ANSE DE COLOMBIER

Anse de Colombier is a beautiful and secluded white-sand beach fronted by turquoise waters and backed by hills. It's reached by boat or via a scenic 20-minute walk that begins at the end of the road in La Petite Anse, just beyond Flamands.

The well-trodden trail, which is unmarked but easy to follow, leads through a fascinating desert-like terrain punctuated by organ pipe cacti and wildflowers. En route it provides some wonderful coastal views of La Petite Anse and the rugged shoreline of Anse Paschal before crossing a ridge and ending at the north side of Colombier Bay, where there are steps leading down to the beach.

The sandy bottom at the beach is ideal for swimming and there's fairly good snorkelling at the north side. Take water, as the trail is unshaded and there are no facilities.

### ST JEAN

St Jean, the island's most touristed area, is spread along a large curving bay lined with a white-sand beach.

St Jean has no real centre and from the road it can seem like a nondescript strip of small shopping complexes, hotels and restaurants. However, it's quite appealing once you're on the beach, where reef-protected turquoise waters provide good conditions for swimming, snorkelling and windsurfing. The beach is divided into two separate sections by a quartzite hill topped by the picturesque Eden Rock Hotel. The airport is at the west end of St Jean.

### Information

There are two shopping centres opposite the airport: Galeries du Commerce has a post office and petrol station and La Savane has a supermarket, bakery and pharmacy.

It costs 70F to wash and dry a load of clothes at the Lav'matic Laundromat, opposite the Sodexa grocery store. It's open from 8 am to noon Monday to Saturday and from 2 to 5 pm on Monday, Tuesday, Thursday and Friday.

### Places to Stay

*Village St Jean* (☎ 27 61 39; fax 27 77 96; in the USA ☎ (800) 633-7411), BP 23, is a very pleasant family-run hotel five minutes walk uphill from the beach. There are 20 modern cottages with kitchens, air-con, ceiling fans and private terraces. The deluxe cottages have some elegant touches and there's a small side room with a twin bed that would be ideal for a couple with a child. There's a nice pool with a view of the bay, a jacuzzi and a small 'honour store' with soft drinks, alcohol and snacks. Rates for the standard

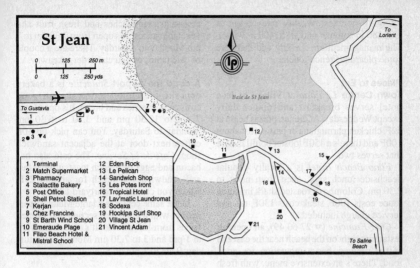

St Jean

| 0 | 125 | 250 m |
| 0 | 125 | 250 yds |

To Gustavia

To Lorient

*Baie de St Jean*

To Saline Beach

1 Terminal
2 Match Supermarket
3 Pharmacy
4 Stalactite Bakery
5 Post Office
6 Shell Petrol Station
7 Kerjan
8 Chez Francine
9 St Barth Wind School
10 Emeraude Plage
11 Filao Beach Hotel & Mistral School
12 Eden Rock
13 Le Pelican
14 Sandwich Shop
15 Les Potes Iront
16 Tropical Hotel
17 Lav'matic Laundromat
18 Sodexa
19 Hookipa Surf Shop
20 Village St Jean
21 Vincent Adam

cottages begin at US$105/155 in summer/winter, deluxe cottages begin at US$135/235. Rooms with ocean views are about 20% higher. There are also six hotel rooms, without kitchens but including breakfast, for US$75/135 in summer/winter.

The *Tropical Hotel* (☎ 27 64 87; fax 27 81 74), BP 147, on a hillside a couple of minutes' walk from the beach, has 20 air-con rooms with refrigerators, TV and balconies. Singles/doubles cost US$95/130 in summer, US$160/185 in winter, for garden-view rooms with breakfast included. Ocean-view rooms are 10% to 15% higher and there's a sizeable jump in prices over the Christmas holidays. It's closed in June and July.

*Emeraude Plage* (☎ 27 64 78; fax 27 83 08) is a pleasant beachfront hotel landscaped with lots of flowering oleanders and hibiscus. It has 25 bungalow-style units, each with a kitchenette that opens onto a terrace, TV, phone, air-con and ceiling fan. Rates vary depending on the size of the bungalow and its proximity to the beach, ranging from 650F to 850F in summer, 920F to 1500F in winter, for one-bedroom bungalows. There are also a few two-bedroom bungalows for 1150/1950F in summer/winter.

*Filao Beach Hotel* (☎ 27 64 84; fax 27 62 24), BP 167, has 30 rooms in one-storey duplex buildings. The hotel has attractive grounds, amiable staff and a nice beachfront location. Rooms are comfortably furnished with a TV, refrigerator, ceiling fan, air-con and a queen or king-sized bed. Rates which include breakfast are 900F to 1500F in summer, 1600F to 2900F in winter.

*Eden Rock* (☎ 27 72 94; fax 27 88 37), St Barts' first hotel, sits above the rocky promontory separating the two sandy strands of St Jean Beach. This six-room hotel is loaded with character. Each room is different, but all have good water views and most have balconies. There are four-poster beds, air-con, mosquito nets and a pleasant old-fashioned decor. You can even sleep in the same bed that Greta Garbo slept in. The only drawback is the price, which ranges from US$230 to US$395 depending on the season, breakfast included. Room No 5 is US$50 cheaper but it's by the street and gets traffic noise.

*Kerjan* (☎ 87 62 38) consists of five wooden bungalows right on the beach next to Chez Francine. Each has an air-con bedroom, kitchen, TV, radio and daily housekeeping service; some have nice little lounging porches. Weekly rates begin at US$880 in summer and US$1400 in winter. The management are friendly and there are some pleasant French touches.

## Places to Eat

**Town Centre** *Le Patio* at Village St Jean hotel serves breakfast and dinner daily except Wednesday. At dinner, pizzas begin at 52F, chicken parmigiana or pastas cost about 100F and there's a 450F lobster bouillabaisse that serves two.

*Filao Beach Hotel* is a locally popular beachside lunch spot, open from noon to 2.30 pm. Colombo or roasted shark in lemon sauce costs 100F, steak costs 130F, tax and service charge included.

*Chez Francine* (☎ 27 60 49), an open-air restaurant right on the beach near the east end of the runway, has a reputation for good food. There's an extensive menu, with fresh fish or chicken dishes beginning around 100F, lobster around 225F. It's open for lunch only.

The historic *Eden Rock* has al fresco seaview dining and is a nice atmospheric place for lunch. The speciality is lobster, fresh from their own pool, with preparations ranging from cold lobster in mayonnaise for 135F to lobster flambéed with whiskey for 160F.

*Vincent Adam* (☎ 27 93 22) features a 190F three-course French dinner with your choice of starter, main dish and dessert selected from a varied menu. Some of the main dishes are filet mignon, duck rolled in juniper berries, hunter's hare and lobster tail. The food is quite good and there's a pleasantly tranquil setting overlooking a salt pond.

At the triangle in the road opposite Le Pelican there's a little snack bar that sells moderately priced sandwiches, ice cream and frozen yoghurt. *Sodexa*, in the Centre Commercial St Jean, is a small grocery store with liquor and produce sections and a deli with a variety of cheeses and luncheon meats. It's open from 8 am to 8 pm daily.

*Les Potes Iront*, in the Espace Neptune centre east of Sodexa, has French bread, croissants, sandwiches and fresh fruit and vegetable juices. It's open from 7.30 am to 7 pm Monday to Saturday. There are a couple of café tables or you can order takeaway.

**Around the Airport** *Stalactite* is a bakery opposite the airport terminal with good croissants, pastries and bread. It's open from 7 am to 12.30 pm and 3.30 to 6.30 pm Monday to Saturday. You can pick up 10F coffee next door at the adjacent sandwich shop, *Café de la Savane*. The café also has bacon and eggs or French toast at breakfast and sandwiches at lunch for around 25F, which you can eat at courtyard tables.

In the same centre is a large Match supermarket with a good deli section and French wines from 12F a bottle. It's open from 8 am to 1 pm and 3 to 7.30 pm Monday to Saturday, 9 am to 1 pm on Sunday.

## LORIENT

Lorient, the site of the first French settlement (1648), is a small village fronted by a nice white-sand beach. When it's calm snorkellers take to the water but when the surf's up this is one of St Barts' best surfing spots. To get to the beach, turn left at the cemetery on the east side of the village. Don't confuse this with the cemetery at the intersection that fronts an attractive old church and tower.

Lorient has a postage-stamp-size post office, a petrol station and Jojo's grocery store with an attached burger shop, all on the main road.

### Places to Stay

Lorient has little of the commercial development found in St Jean, although there are some private rooms for rent – look for signs posted by the beach and near the church. In addition there are a couple of small hotels on the inland road within walking distance of the beach. The cheapest is *La Normandie Hôtel* (☎ 27 61 66), which has eight simple motel-style rooms that cost 250/320F for singles/doubles.

A very interesting option is *Le Manoir* (☎ 27 79 27; fax 27 65 75), near the old church. Accommodation is in 17th-century-style cottages that sit in a private garden surrounding a manor house which was built in Normandy in 1610 and reconstructed here in the 1980s. The brainstorm of Jeanne Audy-Roland, creator of the 'M' natural cosmetic line, Le Manoir was designed for visiting artists and other like-minded travellers. The cottages are rustic with small kitchens and private baths and rent for 200F per person.

### LORIENT TO GRAND CUL-DE-SAC

On the eastern outskirts of Lorient the road climbs up into the hills, offering some fine coastal views. The area encompasses the coastal headland of **Pointe Milou**; the hamlet of **Vitet**, at the foothills of 286-metre Morne du Vitet; and **Marigot**, a small bay with a couple of hotels and restaurants.

### Places to Stay & Eat

Hubert Delemotte, a New Age astrologer and chef, operates *Hostellerie des 3 Forces* (☎ 27 61 25; fax 27 81 38) in Vitet. The site has a dozen simple rooms, each named for a sign of the Zodiac; all have private bathrooms and balconies, mosquito nets and mini-refrigerators. Fan-cooled singles/doubles cost US$65/75 in summer, US$120/140 in winter. Air-con rooms are about 20% higher. The restaurant serves French and Creole food. At lunch offerings range from omelettes (50F) to beef brochette (105F), while dinner features a 230F three-course meal with a choice of fish, vegetarian or red meat main dishes.

Sofitel's *Christopher Hôtel* (☎ 27 63 63, in the USA ☎ (800) 221-4542), BP 571, on Pointe Milou, is a new upscale resort with 40 luxurious rooms. Each has an ocean-view patio, separate bathtub and shower, silent air-con, ceiling fan, a minibar, room safe, TV and phone. While the beach is rocky, the hotel has a large, free-form swimming pool and a fitness centre. Rates are from US$215 in summer, US$325 in winter, full breakfast included. For guests staying more than a couple of nights, there are often some good-value package deals that cut the rates by a third. The hotel's seaside restaurant,

*L'Orchidée,* offers a three-course dinner of the day for 220F.

*Marigot Bay Club* (☎ 27 75 45), a six-room hotel in Marigot, has a waterview restaurant that's very popular with islanders for its Creole dishes, fresh fish and lobster. It's open from November to the end of May and prices are moderately expensive.

### GRAND CUL-DE-SAC

Grand Cul-de-Sac has a sandy beach and a reef-protected bay with good water sports conditions. The area attracts an active crowd that includes lots of windsurfers. The beach is along a narrow strip of land that separates the bay from a large salt pond (sand fleas can be a nuisance). Fronting the bay are a couple of hotels and restaurants, along with a windsurfing school and water sports centre.

### Places to Stay

*St Barths Beach Hotel* (☎ 27 60 70; fax 27 75 27), BP 581, is right on the beach with 36 rooms in two-storey buildings, each with air-con, a balcony, phone and minibar. There are volleyball and tennis courts. Singles/doubles cost US$78/112 in summer, US$185/254 in winter. There are also packages for stays of three nights or longer which include a rental car and usually work out as a better deal.

*Hôtel de la Plage* (☎ 27 60 70) shares a pool and front office with neighbouring St Barths Beach Hotel. This is a cluster of 16 older but adequate beachside bungalows, some with kitchenettes on the porch. Summer rates are US$63 to US$76 for singles and US$88 to US$112 for doubles, and winter rates are about double.

At the north end of the beach is the *El Sereno Beach Hotel* (☎ 27 64 80; fax 27 75 47), which has 20 rooms surrounding a central courtyard garden. While each has a TV, small refrigerator, air-con and room safe, the rooms are small for the price, beginning at US$130/155 for singles/doubles in summer, US$245/310 in winter. There's a pool. This hotel also has nine modern villas on the main road, a five-minute walk from the beach. Each has an air-con bedroom with twin beds, a kitchen, a living room with a double sofabed, TV, phone and safe. The rate is US$120 in summer, US$200 to US$245 in winter. El Sereno adds a steep 15% service charge at both facilities.

### Places to Eat

*Le Rivage* at St Barths Beach Hotel is a casual beachfront restaurant serving lunch and dinner. Sandwiches start at 40F and main dishes range from Creole chicken for 68F to curried shrimp for 94F. It's open daily from noon to 2.30 pm and from 7 to 9.30 pm.

*La Gloriette*, next to El Sereno Beach Hotel, features Creole food. Goat curry or grilled fish in Creole sauce cost 80F, a chef's salad is 65F. It's open for lunch and dinner, but closed on Monday.

El Sereno's *La Toque Lyonnaise* (☎ 27 64 80) has a good reputation for gourmet French cuisine, with fish and meat main dishes starting around 130F and complete fixed-price meals from 240F. It's open daily for dinner only.

At lunchtime, El Sereno's *Le Lagon Bleu* has moderately priced seafood, salads and sandwiches.

### BEYOND GRAND CUL-DE-SAC

From Grand Cul-de-Sac the road makes a curving sweep around the base of the 286-metre Morne du Vitet and the 274-metre Morne de Grand Fond, the island's highest mountains. It's a nice country drive, passing grassy green slopes, handsome stone walls, grazing cows and the occasional farmer, creating a scene that's often compared to rural Normandy.

### SALINE BEACH

Anse de Grande Saline is a long lovely beach, broad and secluded, named after the large salt pond that backs it. Stilts and other waterbirds flock to the pond, but so do biting gnats which sometimes can be an obstacle to enjoying the beach. Saline Beach is off the main tourist track but is considered a special place by islanders and return visitors.

The cement road into Saline Beach ends about half a km before the beach, but you can often continue to drive along the south side of the salt pond on a rutted dirt road that will take you within a two-minute walk of the beach.

For an enjoyable lunch *Le Tamarin*, on the way to the beach, has a pleasant setting and offers a melange of good Creole and French food at moderate prices. It's open for lunch only, to 3.30 pm daily except Monday.

### GOUVERNEUR BEACH

Anse du Gouverneur is a gorgeous sandy beach lining a U-shaped bay that's embraced by high cliffs at both ends. The beach is broad and secluded and makes a nice spot for sunbathing and picnics. There are no facilities.

To get there from Gustavia, head southeast past the Carl Gustaf hotel. The road becomes increasingly steep until you reach the mountain crest in Lurin, where you turn right and wind down a narrow cement road that will test your brakes (use low gear). There are some spectacular glimpses of the coast en route. Upon reaching a 'private property' sign turn into the dirt drive on the left. The beach, hidden by foliage, is just 100 metres away.

# St Eustatius (Statia)

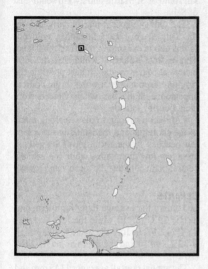

St Eustatius – spelled Sint Eustatius in Dutch and usually called Statia for short – is a tranquil little outpost with an intriguing colonial history. Part of the Netherlands Antilles, the island has interesting historical sites and some good hiking and diving opportunities.

Just a few km wide, Statia is essentially a one-town island, with the airport and a few residential neighbourhoods on the town's outskirts.

While only a 20-minute flight from St Martin, Statia is one of the most overlooked destinations in the Leeward Islands, partly because it has none of the tourist-luring beaches that St Martin's closer neighbours boast. Of course the lack of crowds is part of the appeal for travellers who do come this way. In many ways landing in Statia is a bit like stepping back into a little niche of the Caribbean from the 1950s – islanders enjoy striking up a conversation, stray chickens and goats mosey in the streets and the pace is delightfully slow. Little Statia offers a nice, quiet break for those looking to get away from the more touristed islands.

## ORIENTATION
Statia has few roads and is easy to get around. Oranjestad, the island's town, is 1.5 km south of the airport. It is divided by a cliff into Upper Town and Lower Town, and the two sections are connected by a footpath and a vehicle road.

# Facts about the Island

## HISTORY
The Caribs called the island Alo, which means cashew tree, while Columbus named the island after St Anastasia. Although the French began construction of a fort in 1629, the first permanent settlement was established by the Dutch in 1636 after they routed the small French contingent off the islands. The island subsequently changed hands 22 times between the Dutch, French and British.

In the 18th century, as the British and French buried their colonies in taxes and duties, the Dutch turned St Eustatius into a duty-free port. As a result, West Indian and North American colonies were able to circumvent duties by shipping goods via Statia, which boomed into a thriving entrepôt and a major trade centre between the Old and New worlds.

During its heyday in the 1770s, as many as 300 trading ships pulled into port each month and the island's population swelled to 20,000. The resulting prosperity earned Statia the nickname 'Golden Rock of the Caribbean'.

Many of the goods destined for the rebellious North American colonies passed through Statia. Along with 'legal' cargoes of molasses and slaves, the merchant ships sailing from Statia also smuggled in arms and gunpowder to New England, much to the ire of British officials, whose protest to the mercantile Dutch drew little response.

One event that particularly irritated the British took place on 16 November 1776 when Statia, rather inadvertently, became the first foreign land to recognise the American colonies' Declaration of Independence by returning a cannon salute to the passing American war brig *Andrew Doria*. Unfortunately for Statia, another American vessel went on to capture a British ship in nearby waters, adding an element of significance to the gesture.

In 1781, British admiral George Rodney settled the score by launching a naval attack on Statia, ransacking the warehouses, exiling the island's merchants and auctioning off their goods. The Dutch regained possession of the island a few years later but the British invasion marked the end of Statia's predominance as a trade centre.

Ironically, US independence, and the signing of a peace treaty between the USA and Britain in 1783, allowed the former North American colonies to establish more direct trade routes and bypass Statia altogether. To this day Statia remains well off the beaten path.

## GEOGRAPHY

St Eustatius is eight km long and three km wide, with 21 sq km of land. The island is 61 km south of St Martin and 27 km south-east of Saba.

The Quill (whose name is derived from the Dutch word *kwil*, meaning volcano) looms above the southern half of the island. This extinct volcano, which reaches 600 metres at Mazinga, the highest point on the rim, is responsible for the high conical appearance Statia has when viewed from neighbouring islands.

Cliffs drop straight to the sea along much of the shoreline and the island has precious few beaches. At the north side of Statia there are a few low mountains, while the island's central plain contains the airport and town.

## CLIMATE

In January the average daily high temperature is 29°C (85°F) while the low averages 22°C (72°F). In July the average daily high is 32°C (90°F) and the average low is 24°C (76°F).

The annual rainfall averages 1145 mm and is fairly evenly dispersed throughout the year. Humidity is in the low 70s from March to December and in the mid-70s in January and February.

## FLORA & FAUNA

Most of the island is dry, with scrubby vegetation, although oleander, bougainvillea, hibiscus and chain of love flowers add a splash of colour here and there. The Quill collects enough cloud cover for its central crater to harbour a rainforest, with ferns, elephant ears, bananas and tall trees.

Most animal life is limited to goats, cows and donkeys. White-tailed tropicbirds nest on the cliffs along the beach north of Lower Town.

## GOVERNMENT

St Eustatius is part of the Dutch kingdom, one of five islands in the Netherlands Antilles, whose central administration is in Curaçao. As with the other four islands,

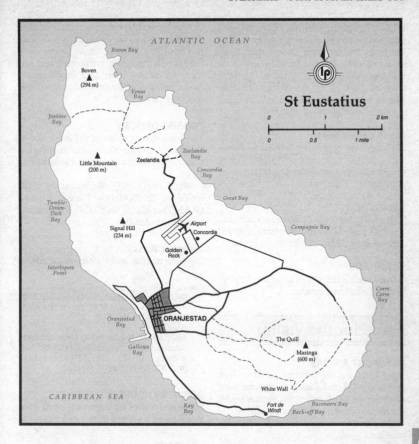

**St Eustatius**

Statia is treated as a municipality and has its own lieutenant governor, Irwin E Temmer, appointed by Queen Beatrix of the Netherlands. The lieutenant governor and two elected commissioners are responsible for running Statia's daily affairs.

## ECONOMY
The island's economy is dependent upon a mix of fishing, small retail businesses, and a bit of tourism. A large proportion of the island's population is employed in government administration. There are large oil tanks on the north-west side of the island where oil is off-loaded and stored for transhipment to other islands.

## POPULATION & PEOPLE
The population of Statia is about 1600. The majority of the people are Black, largely the descendants of African slaves brought to Statia to work in the warehouses in Lower Town and on a handful of long-vanished plantations.

## ARTS & CULTURE
The culture is a mix of African and Dutch heritage, similar to that found on other Dutch

islands. The island's wealth of historic buildings and its pivotal place as a major trading centre in colonial times make it stand apart from the other Dutch islands. Many of its buildings have been set aside as historical treasures, including the Simon Doncker House, which has been turned into one of the region's finest historical museums.

### Dress Conventions
Bathing suits should be limited to beach areas; people wandering into Upper Town, Oranjestad, in a swimsuit can expect to be confronted by the police.

### RELIGION
There are Methodist, Roman Catholic, Seventh Day Adventist, Anglican, Baptist, Apostolic and Baha'i churches on Statia.

### LANGUAGE
While Dutch is the official language, English is most commonly spoken.

# Facts for the Visitor

### PASSPORT & VISAS
Valid passports are required of all visitors except for US and Canadian citizens, who need only proof of citizenship, such as a birth certificate or voter's registration card.

A return or onward ticket is officially required.

### CUSTOMS
Statia is a free port and there are no customs regulations.

### MONEY
The Netherlands Antilles guilder or florin (Fl) is the official currency, but US dollars are accepted everywhere. Hotel, car rental and dive shop prices are given in dollars, while islander-geared businesses post prices in guilders. The exchange rate is officially 1.77 guilders to US$1. For more information see Money in the Facts for the Visitor chapter.

Avis and Rainbow car rentals and the dive shop Dive Statia accept MasterCard, Visa and American Express, as do Oranjestad's three hotels; however, credit cards are not accepted for any other accommodation on Statia. Some establishments also accept the Discover card.

### TOURIST OFFICES
The main tourist office is in Upper Town, Oranjestad, and there's a tourist information booth opposite the dinghy dock in Lower Town.

When requesting information by mail, write to: St Eustatius Tourist Bureau (☎ 82433 or 82209; fax 82324), St Eustatius, Netherlands Antilles.

### Overseas Reps
Overseas tourism representatives include:

Canada
    New Concepts in Canada, 410 Queens West Suite 303, Toronto, Ontario M5V 2Z3 (☎ (416) 362-7707; fax (416) 368-7818)
Netherlands
    Antillen Huis (Kabinet van de Gevolmachtigde Minister van de Nederlandse Antillen), Badhuisweg 173-175, 2597 JP's-Gravenhage (☎ (70) 3512811; fax (70) 3512722)

### BUSINESS HOURS
Shops and offices are commonly open from 8 or 9 am to noon and from 1 to 5 pm.

### HOLIDAYS
Public holidays on St Eustatius are as follows:

| | |
|---|---|
| *New Year's Day* | – 1 January |
| *Good Friday* | – Friday before Easter |
| *Easter Sunday* | – late March/early April |
| *Easter Monday* | – late March/early April |
| *Queen's Day* | – 30 April |
| *Labor Day* | – 1 May |
| *Ascension Thursday* | – 40th day after Easter |
| *Christmas Day* | – 25 December |
| *Boxing Day* | – 26 December |

### CULTURAL EVENTS
The Statia Carnival, which is held during late July and culminates on a Monday, is the

island's biggest festival. Music, shows, games, contests and local food are the highlights.

Fort Oranje is the site of ceremonies held on Statia-America Day, 16 November, which commemorates the date in 1776 when Statia became the first foreign land to salute the US flag.

## POST
Statia's only post office is in Oranjestad on Cottageweg. When writing to Statia from abroad, if a post office box number is not listed, simply address mail with the individual or business name, followed by 'St Eustatius, Netherlands Antilles'.

It costs Fls 0.55 to mail a postcard and Fls 1.75 to mail a 10-gram letter to either North America or Europe and Fls 0.90 to mail a letter within the Caribbean.

## TELECOMMUNICATIONS
To call Statia from overseas add the area code 599-3 in front of the five-digit local number.

## ELECTRICITY
Electricity is 110 volts AC, 60 cycles, and a flat two-pronged plug is used, the same type as in the USA. The electricity supply is generally quite reliable, although during elections and other disputed events it sometimes goes dark without warning!

## WEIGHTS & MEASURES
Statia uses the metric system.

## MEDIA
*The Gem*, the island's paper, is published weekly. Daily St Martin newspapers are sold on the island.

## HEALTH
Statia's hospital, the Queen Beatrix Medical Center (☎ 82211), is at Prinsesweg 25 on the east side of Oranjestad.

## DANGERS & ANNOYANCES
There is little crime on Statia, although it's best not to leave things unattended on the beach – snorkelling gear sometimes seems to wander off. Appropriate clothing should worn around town. See Dress Conventions in the Arts & Culture section earlier in this chapter.

## ACTIVITIES
### Beaches & Swimming
No-one visits Statia for its beaches, which are few in number and undistinguished. The island's best beach for swimming is Oranje Beach in Lower Town, while the other popular beach is Zeelandia Bay on the east coast.

### Diving & Snorkelling
Statia has about 30 dive sites, the majority of which are coral formations on old lava flows. There are also a few wrecks of colonial trading ships, although the remains are basically piles of ballast stones as the ships themselves have disintegrated. To protect the island's historical remains from souvenir hunters, all divers are required to be accompanied by a guide.

The *Stingray* wreck (1768), a few minutes from Lower Town in 15 metres of water, is near a ledge with a rich concentration of marine life, including stingrays, spotted eels and octopuses.

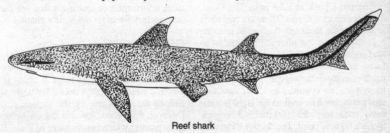

Reef shark

Caroline's Reef is a popular medium-depth dive with coral-encrusted lava flows and a series of ledges harbouring lobsters, nurse sharks and sea turtles.

For a deep dive, Doobie Crack, a large cleft in a reef, has black-tip sharks and schools of large fish. At the other end of the spectrum there's Kim's Coral, a nice shallow dive with lots of bottom time.

For snorkellers, Jenkins Bay on the north-west side of the island is the favourite spot, with calm waters sheltering coral formations and lots of reef fish.

**Dive Shop** Statia's only dive shop, Dive Statia (☎ 82435; fax 82539), PO Box 158, in Lower Town, is open from 8.30 am to 4 pm daily. The operation is Statian scale, small and friendly. Divers go out in either a nine-metre cabin boat or inflatables, and all dives are within a 15-minute boat ride.

In addition to regular dives, which cost US$55, Dive Statia has a US$45 introductory course that includes a shallow dive at the old city wall, a US$80 resort course with both a beach and boat dive and a full five-day certification course for US$325. Dive Statia rents snorkelling gear for US$8 and takes snorkellers out to Jenkins Bay for US$20, including gear. Yachters receive a 10% discount on dives.

### Hiking

The tourist office has a free hiking brochure with descriptions of 12 different trails and should be able to provide information on current trail conditions. Most of the trails are signposted and some are marked with orange ribbons.

The most popular hike is to The Quill, Statia's extinct volcano. There are two trails leading up the mountain that merge into one before reaching the summit. The easiest to find and to walk starts at the end of Rosemary Laan in Oranjestad and takes about 45 minutes to reach the edge of the crater. From there you can continue in either direction along the rim. The trail to the right (south-east) ends atop the 600-metre Mazinga, Statia's highest point. The shorter Panorama

Track to the left offers spectacular views and takes about 15 minutes. A third option is the steep track leading down into the crater, where there's a thick rainforest of tall trees, some with huge buttressed trunks. This track, which takes about 30 minutes each way, can be quite slippery when wet so sturdy shoes are essential.

### HIGHLIGHTS

Statia has several interesting historical sights and rambling around the town to take them all in is certainly a must – don't miss the exceptional museum, the fort and a stroll along the waterfront in Oranjestad. A nice drive is the one to Fort de Windt, where there's a fine view of St Kitts.

### ACCOMMODATION

Most accommodation is either in Oranjestad or near the airport. All places are quite modest in scale and prices are moderate by Caribbean standards.

There's a 7% government tax on accommodation in St Eustatius and hotels tack on a 10% to 15% service charge.

### FOOD & DRINKS

Considering its size, Statia has a reasonable number and variety of restaurants; most are moderately priced. There are several small grocery stores in Oranjestad. The Windward Islands Supermarket on Heilligerweg is one of the better stocked and is open from 8 am to 6.30 pm Monday to Friday, to 9 pm on Saturday.

Most tap water comes from individual rainwater catchment systems and should therefore be boiled before drinking. For more information on treating water, see the introductory Facts for the Visitor chapter.

### ENTERTAINMENT

The hottest entertainment is Saturday night at *Gerald's* in Upper Town, when the local steel drum band takes the stage at about 10 pm. The band also plays on Friday night at *Talk of the Town*, out by the airport. *Exit Disco* on Faeschweg has dancing on weekends, usually with a cover charge of Fls 3. If you just want to have a drink, the bar at the *Old Gin House* in Lower Town has a nice old world character.

## THINGS TO BUY
Mazinga Gift Shop on Fort Oranje Straat in Upper Town sells a little bit of everything, including T-shirts, jewellery and other souvenirs. The Park Place gallery, opposite Cool Corner bar and restaurant, sells island artwork and crafts.

# Getting There & Away

## AIR
The only scheduled flights to Statia are with Winair (☎ 82381 or 82362), which has four flights a day (three on Sunday) from St Martin.

Statia can be easily visited as a day trip. The first flight from St Martin leaves at 8.45am on Sunday, 7 am on Tuesday, Thursday and Saturday and 8 am on Monday, Wednesday and Friday. The last flight to St Martin leaves Statia at 5.10 pm daily. The fare is US$33 one way, US$66 return.

Winair also makes the 10-minute hop from Saba to Statia every afternoon, as well as a couple of mornings a week, for US$20 each way.

It's also possible to fly with Winair from St Kitts to Statia on Monday and Saturday afternoon and from Statia to St Kitts on Saturday morning.

### Airport Information
**To/From the Airport** There are usually one or two taxis on hand to meet flights; they charge US$3.50 per person to take passengers to a hotel in town. If you miss the taxis, look for Rosie, the cheery ex-St Martiner who owns Rainbow Car Rental, as she'll drop you off in town for the same rate.

## SEA
Statia has just completed a 210-metre L-shaped breakwater at the south end of Lower Town, constructed with 10-tonne rocks brought in from Norway. The breakwater is the cornerstone of a new harbour, which includes an anchorage for fishing boats and some space for visiting yachts. Yachters should check in with the harbour master upon arrival.

### Cruise Ships
Statia does not have a deepwater port capable of handling large cruise ships, but the island is visited by the Windjammer Barefoot Cruises' schooner S/V *Polynesia* and a few other small cruise ships.

## TOURS
Irish Travel Tours (☎ 53663) in the Safari Building on Airport Rd, Simpson Bay, St Martin, operates day-trips to Statia. The cost of US$100 (US$70 for children under 12) includes return airfare on Winair, a sightseeing tour, lunch at the Old Gin House and use of the hotel pool. They also offer a one-day dive package on Statia that costs US$160 for a single dive, US$180 for a double dive.

On weekdays, Irish Travel Tours squeezes Statia and Saba into a US$180 day trip which includes airfare, sightseeing tours on both islands and lunch.

Dive Statia, PO Box 158, St Eustatius, offers diving packages for US$450 that include five nights at Talk of the Town or Golden Era, breakfast, six dives and airport and dive transfers. The rates are based on double occupancy, but it's possible for the second person to be a non-diver and pay half-price. There are also rates for singles and week-long packages.

## LEAVING ST EUSTATIUS
There's a departure tax of US$2 for flights within the Netherlands Antilles, US$5 to other Caribbean islands.

# Getting Around

Taxis are relatively expensive and not terribly plentiful. There are no buses. Renting a car is a near necessity if you want to explore the island properly, which could be done in a day. If you're staying on in Oranjestad, you probably won't need a car for most of your stay but expect to do some serious walking as the town is spread out. If you only want a quick glimpse of the island, your hotel can arrange a two-hour taxi tour for US$40.

Statia's only petrol station is in Lower Town opposite the pier. It's closed on Sunday but is usually open from 7 am to 7 pm on other days.

### CAR
### Road Rules
Drive on the right-hand side of the road. Your home driving licence is valid for driving on Statia.

By Caribbean standards Statia's roads are good, albeit sometimes narrow, and you need to watch out for stray animals on the road. Surprisingly, Oranjestad has quite a few one-way streets.

### Rental
Rainbow Car Rental (☎ 82586) rents air-conditioned Hyundai Excels for US$35 and charges an additional US$5 for collision damage waiver (CDW) coverage.

Avis (☎ 82421) rents Daihatsu Charades for US$40 a day and 4WD vehicles for US$50, and charges US$9 for CDW.

Other companies include Brown's Car Rental (☎ 82266) and Lady Ama's Services (☎ 82451). Rainbow and Avis are the only car rental agencies at the airport.

### HITCHING
Hitching is practised on Statia, but traffic is light to the more distant parts of the island, and, of course, the usual precautions apply.

# Oranjestad

Oranjestad, the island's capital and its only town, is a pleasant place with a fine sense of history. It consists of Lower Town, which is the area down along the waterfront, and Upper Town, which is on the bluff above.

Lower Town was the location of the original port town. Although most of the colonial-era buildings have succumbed to storms, Lower Town still has some ruins from that era as well as two hotels, the island's best beach and Statia's port. Upper Town is the main commercial and residential area. It has numerous historical sites, all of which can easily be explored on foot in a few leisurely hours. Bay Rd, a steep cobbled lane that was once used to march Africans from the slave ships, provides a pedestrian route up the coastal cliff to link the two parts of town.

You can pick up a useful historical walking tour book and map of Oranjestad for US$2 at the museum.

### Information
**Tourist Office** The St Eustatius Tourist Bureau (☎ 82433 or 82209; fax 82324) is behind Government Guesthouse in an old stone building that once served as a debtor's prison. It's open from 8 am to noon and 1 to 5 pm Monday to Friday. The office hands out a few brochures, including an accommodation sheet listing apartments that are sometimes available for rent.

**Money** The island's only bank, Barclays, is between the library and museum. It's open from 8.30 am to 2 pm Monday to Friday. Barclays provides cash advances to Master-Card, Visa and Discover card holders.

**Post & Telecommunications** The post office is on Cottageweg, behind Landsradio, the telephone office.

**Library** The public library is open from 1 to 5 pm on Monday and from 8 am to noon and 1 to 5 pm Tuesday to Friday.

### Fort Oranje
Right in the centre of town, Fort Oranje is an intact fort complete with cannons, triple bastions and a cobblestone courtyard. It's perched on the cliffside directly above Lower Town and offers a broad view of the waterfront below. The French erected the

**PLACES TO STAY**

8  Old Gin House
9  Golden Era Hotel
27  Daniel's Guesthouse

**PLACES TO EAT**

1  Kings Well
7  Old Gin House Restaurant
10  Cool Corner
20  Chinese Restaurant
22  Franky's

**OTHER**

2  School
3  Post Office
4  Telephone Office
5  Police Station
6  Dive Statia
11  Sint Eustatius Museum
12  St Eustatius Tourist Bureau
    & Government Guesthouse
13  Barclays Bank
14  Library
15  Mazinga Gift Shop
16  Windward Islands
    Supermarket
17  Exit Disco
18  Synagogue Ruins
19  Dutch Reformed Church
21  Queen Beatrix Medical
    Centre
23  Methodist Church
24  Tourist Information Booth
25  Petrol Station
26  Harbour Office

**Oranjestad**

first rampart here in 1629 but most of the fort was built after the Dutch took the island from the French in 1636. They added to the fort a number of times over the years, enlarging it into the largest fortress on Statia.

The courtyard has a couple of memorials, including a plaque presented by US president Franklin Roosevelt to commemorate the fort's fateful 1776 salute of the American war vessel *Andrew Doria*. The fort is always open and there's no admission fee.

### Sint Eustatius Museum

This museum, operated by the Sint Eustatius Historical Foundation, gives visitors a glimpse of upper-class colonial life on Statia and is one of the Eastern Caribbean's finest historical museums.

It occupies the Simon Doncker House, a restored 18th-century Dutch merchant's home that's decorated with period furnishings and holds collections of nautical artefacts, china and hand-blown bottles. The house's history includes a stint as the headquarters of Admiral George Rodney following the British invasion of the island in 1781. The museum is open from 9 am to 5 pm weekdays and admission is US$2.

## Government Guesthouse

The Government Guesthouse is the handsome 18th-century stone and wood building opposite Barclays Bank. It was thoroughly renovated in 1992 with funding from the EU and is now the government headquarters, with the offices of the lieutenant governor and commissioners on the ground floor and the courtroom on the upper floor.

The building, which once served as the Dutch naval commander's quarters, derived its name from its 1920s spell as a guesthouse. The basement, formerly a wine cellar, houses the museum's pre-Columbian collection. There are plans to add an arts and crafts centre.

## Synagogue Ruins

The roofless and slowly decaying yellow-brick walls of the Honen Dalim, an abandoned synagogue that dates from 1739, can be found 30 metres down the alleyway opposite the south side of the library. The synagogue is the second oldest in the western hemisphere.

With Statia's rising influence as a trade centre, there was a large influx of Jewish merchants to the island beginning in the early 1700s. However, most Jews, whose livelihoods were closely linked to trade, left Statia around the turn of the 19th century as Statia's importance as a port declined.

About half a km east of the synagogue ruins is a Jewish cemetery with gravestones dating from 1742 to 1843.

## Dutch Reformed Church

The thick stone walls (600 cm) of the old Dutch Reformed Church, built in 1775, remain perfectly intact, but the roof collapsed during a 1792 hurricane and the building has been open to the heavens ever since. The church tower, also damaged by the hurricane, was renovated in 1981 and offers a nice view of the surrounding area from the top, should you catch it when it's open.

Also noteworthy are the old tombstones in the churchyard, including that of Jan de Windt, a former governor of St Eustatius, Saba and St Martin, who died in 1775. The church is on Kerkweg, a few minutes' walk south of the Government Guesthouse.

## Lower Town

Lower Town is a narrow coastal area backed by steep cliffs. High seas and hurricanes have taken their toll on the historic waterfront; however, the remains of the old foundations from some of the 18th-century warehouses that once lined the coast can still be seen jutting into the water along the shore. Submerged sections of the old seawall that once protected the harbourfront can be explored by donning a mask and snorkel. On both sides of the coastal road you'll see a handful of brick warehouses from the period; a few are still in use, including one housing the dive shop.

With a little imagination, the fading ruins can help conjure up an image of the past, when the area was bustling with traders and merchants and the bay was chock full of ships.

Oranje Beach, at the north end of Lower Town, has grey sands and generally calm waters. Modest as it may be, it's the island's best all-round beach and a popular swimming spot for Statian families. There's a new harbour at the south end of Lower Town.

## Places to Stay – bottom end

*Airport View Apartments* (☎ 82299), a two-minute walk from the airport terminal, has simple apartments with cooking facilities and private bath from US$30/40 for singles/doubles. Manager Carine Henriquez also has a few rooms in a large house on Prinsesweg, just west of the hospital, that cost US$20/30 for singles/doubles.

There are a handful of other small apartments and guesthouses that rent rooms and studios. On Rosemary Laan, on the south side of town, there's *Daniel's Guesthouse* (☎ 82358), which has rooms for US$25/35 for singles/doubles and *Sugar Hill Apartments* (☎ 82305), which has rooms for US$30.

*Country Inn* (☎ 82484) in Concordia, near the airport, has four apartments with air-con and cable TV that cost US$35/50 for singles/doubles.

## Places to Stay – top end

*Talk of the Town* (☎ 82236) is half a km south of the airport on LE Saddlerweg, which is the first side street to the right as you drive from the airport towards Oranjestad. The hotel's original section, which is above the restaurant, has eight rooms that are quite sufficient. The new poolside wing has nine modern, comfortable rooms with king-size beds and high ceilings that easily rate as the island's best hotel rooms. Rooms in both sections have air-con, private bath, a phone and multichannel cable TV. Year-round rates are US$49/62 for singles/doubles in the older section, US$59/74 in the newer section, both including breakfast. There's a small discount for stays of three nights or longer.

*Golden Era Hotel* (☎ 82345; fax 82445; in the USA ☎ (800) 365-8484), in the centre of Lower Town on a rocky shoreline, is a two-storey hotel with 20 rather ordinary rooms, each equipped with a TV, phone, refrigerator and air-con. There's an ocean-front pool. Rates are US$60/75 for singles/doubles in summer, US$70/88 in winter.

The popular *Old Gin House* (☎ 82319; fax 82555; in the USA ☎ (800) 223-9832) in Lower Town has 20 good-sized rooms. While there are some antique furnishings, overall the rooms are rather simple. The more atmospheric rooms are the six in the weathered oceanfront building, with room No 3 being the nicest. The rest of the rooms are in a newer poolside wing that's on the inland side of the street behind the converted cotton gin mill. Rooms are fan-cooled and have neither phones nor TV. Rates are US$85/100 for singles/doubles in summer, US$110/150 in winter. Children under 10 are not accepted.

## Places to Eat

*Franky's*, a popular eatery on De Ruyterweg,

has ice cream, sandwiches and simple West Indian food. The best chocolate milkshakes on the island are at *Super Burger* on De Graafweg. *Sunny's Place* in the centre of town on Oranje Straat is a cheap spot for lunch and dinner.

*Cool Corner*, a bar and restaurant in the centre of town, offers good Chinese-Caribbean style food, with curries, chop suey and similar dishes from about US$10. It's open daily from 10 am to midnight. For more conventional Chinese food, there's the *Chinese Restaurant* on Prinsesweg.

The *Kings Well*, on the road between Upper Town and Lower Town, has light lunches such as sandwiches or a chef's salad for around US$6. At dinner you can get chicken for US$10 or fresh fish for US$15.

*Talk of the Town*, between the airport and Upper Town, is run by a Dutch family and has straightforward food. Breakfast, from 7 to 11 am, is a simple Dutch-style buffet that includes cold cuts, eggs, cornflakes and orange juice for US$6. At lunch, burgers and sandwiches are around US$5. Dinner ranges from US$9 for chicken to US$20 for lobster thermidor, including rice or fries. There's also a bar.

The *Old Gin House* (☎ 82319) in Lower Town is the most romantic dinner spot on the island, with old brick walls, high-backed chairs and pewter plates. The changing menu is predominantly steak and seafood. The food is good and the prices are surprisingly moderate, averaging US$12 to US$20 for main dishes with a salad. Wine costs US$2 by the glass and starts at US$10 by the bottle.

Lunch, served until 2 pm on the terrace across the street, includes good burgers for US$4 and a variety of salads for around US$7. On Sunday there's a pleasant brunch from 10.30 am to 2.30 pm for US$9 and an evening barbecue that costs US$11 for chicken or US$15 for fish.

The restaurant at the *Golden Era Hotel* in Lower Town has an attractive seafront setting. At lunch you can get sandwiches for US$5, while standard chicken, meat and seafood dishes are US$10 to US$16 at dinner.

ST EUSTATIUS

# Around Statia

## FORT DE WINDT

The road south from Oranjestad ends abruptly at Fort de Windt, where a couple of rusty cannons sit atop a cliffside stone wall. While there's not much else to this small 18th-century fort, you'll be rewarded with a fine view of St Kitts to the south-east. The most interesting geological feature in the area is the white cliffs to the east of Fort de Windt, a landmark readily visible from neighbouring islands.

To get there, take the road that runs past the old Dutch Reformed Church and follow it south, through a dry terrain of cacti and stray goats, to its end three km away.

## ZEELANDIA BAY

Zeelandia Bay, three km north-east of Oranjestad, has a dark-sand beach that collects a fair share of flotsam. It's not a good beach for swimming, as the Atlantic side of the island is turbulent and there are strong currents. It is a good strolling beach, however, and you can find private niches by walking south along the beach towards the cliffs.

If you're up for a longer walk, a track from the main road leads north to the semi-secluded Venus Bay. There's no beach, but it makes for a nice hike, taking about 45 minutes one way.

### Places to Stay & Eat

*La Maison Sur la Plage* (☎ 82256), the only development at Zeelandia Bay, has 10 rooms in five duplex cottages, each with private bath and TV. There's also a pool. The rate is US$55 in summer and US$75 in winter for either singles or doubles, including breakfast. Credit cards are not accepted. As this is an isolated area, you'll need a car.

La Maison Sur la Plage has one of the best restaurants on the island, serving traditional French cuisine for lunch and dinner. It is in an open-air setting above the beach with a view of The Quill. The prices are relatively expensive and reservations are required.

# St Kitts & Nevis

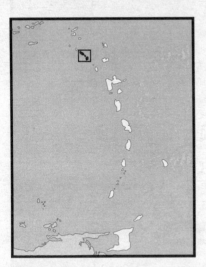

The islands of St Kitts and Nevis are linked by a daily ferry, making it easy to visit both halves of this two-island nation on a single trip. Most visitors to the islands fly into St Kitts, which on a clear day provides a wonderful introduction to that island. You'll get a glimpse of the mountainous interior, the patchwork of cane fields that carpets the lowlands and the curving south-east peninsula with its rugged hills, salt ponds and deeply indented bays.

While St Kitts has 80% of the population, both islands are small, rural and lightly populated. On both St Kitts and Nevis the colonial past is evident in the numerous old sugar mills and plantation estates found throughout the countryside. Many of the grander plantation houses have been converted into atmospheric inns.

The island known today as St Kitts was called Liamuiga, 'Fertile Island,' by its Amerindian inhabitants. When Columbus sighted the island on his second voyage to the New World in 1493, he named it St Christopher after his patron saint. St Kitts, the shortened name which came later, is today used by virtually everyone, including government offices.

Columbus used the Spanish word for snow, *nieves*, to name Nevis, presumably because the clouds shrouding its mountain reminded him of a snow-capped peak. Native Caribs knew the island as Oualie, 'Land of Beautiful Waters'.

These gentle islands can make for a nice quiet holiday, but keep in mind there's not a great deal of activity on either. Some people find the islands' relaxed nature ideal, while others get restless after a few days.

## ORIENTATION

St Kitts' shape resembles a cricket bat, with an oval road running around the perimeter of its main body and another extending down the spine of its southern arm. It would take about 1½ hours to make a nonstop loop around the northern road and about 30 minutes to drive from Basseterre, the capital, to the end of the south-east peninsula.

St Kitts' airport is on the northern outskirts of Basseterre, just a five-minute drive from the centre.

On Nevis the airport is in Newcastle at the north side of the island, about a 20-minute drive from Charlestown, the main town. A loop road circles the island, making exploring quite straightforward.

# Facts about the Islands

## HISTORY

St Kitts, settled by Sir Thomas Warner in 1623, was the site of the first British colony in the West Indies. The following year the French also settled part of St Kitts, a situation Warner tolerated in part to gain an upper

hand against the native Caribs living on the island.

After massacring the Caribs in a series of battles, the British and French turned on each other and St Kitts changed hands between the two colonial powers several times before the 1783 Treaty of Paris brought the island firmly under British control. During this era, sugar plantations thrived on St Kitts.

Nevis had a similar colonial history. In 1628 Sir Warner sent a party of about 100 colonists to establish a British settlement on the west coast of Nevis. Although their original settlement, near Cotton Ground, fell to

an earthquake in 1680, Nevis went on to prosper, developing one of the most affluent plantation societies in the Eastern Caribbean. As on St Kitts, most of the island's wealth was built upon the labour of African slaves who toiled in the island's sugar cane fields. By the late 18th century Nevis, buoyed by the attraction of its thermal baths, had become a major retreat for Britain's rich and famous.

In 1816 the British linked St Kitts and Nevis with Anguilla and the Virgin Islands as a single colony. In 1958 these islands became part of the West Indies Federation, a grand but unsuccessful attempt to combine all of Britain's Caribbean colonies as a united political entity. When the federation dissolved in 1962, the British opted to lump St Kitts, Nevis and Anguilla together as a new state.

In February 1967 the three islands were given independence from the Crown as an Associated State, with its capital in Basseterre. Within months Anguilla, fearful of domination by a larger St Kitts, rebelled and found its way back into the British fold as a colony.

Nevis was also wary of bonding with St Kitts and threatened to follow suit but after a period of unrest it agreed to the union with the stipulation that it be given a heightened measure of internal autonomy and the right to secede in the future if it so desired. With these conditions guaranteed to Nevis under a new constitution, in September 1983 St Kitts and Nevis were linked as a single federated state within the Commonwealth.

Hummingbird

## GEOGRAPHY
St Kitts is 37 km long and 10.5 km wide, with a land area of 168 sq km. It has a central mountain range dominated by the 1156-metre Mt Liamuiga, a dormant volcano. The higher mountain slopes are covered by rainforest, while the drier foothills and lowlands are largely planted with sugar cane.

Nevis, a few km south of St Kitts, is a nearly round island of 93 sq km that's dominated by a central volcanic peak, the 985-metre Nevis Peak.

## CLIMATE
In January the average daily high temperature is 27°C (81°F) while the low averages 22°C (72°F). In July the average daily high is 30°C (86°F) the average low 24°C (76°F).

Annual rainfall averages 1400 mm (55 inches) and is fairly consistent throughout the year. The driest months are February to June, when there's an average of 11 days of measurable rain a month and a mean relative humidity around 70%. The rest of the year

humidity averages 73%, with measurable rain falling an average of 16 days each month.

## FLORA & FAUNA
Vegetation ranges from grassy coastal lowlands to a rainforested interior of ferns and tall trees. Pelicans and frigatebirds are common along the coast, and you can spot hummingbirds wherever there are flowering plants.

Also plentiful is the mongoose, introduced to the islands for the purpose of controlling rats in the cane fields; these slender ferret-like creatures hunt during the day when the nocturnal rats sleep so the two seldom meet. Another exotic, the green vervet monkey, is found in the interior of both islands.

## GOVERNMENT
St Kitts and Nevis is a federation officially headed by the British monarch, who is represented by a Governor-General. Legislative power is vested in a unicameral 14-member National Assembly and in the Prime Minister, who is leader of the majority party.

St Kitts & Nevis Coat of Arms

Nevis has internal home rule and a separate legislature, and island administration that mirrors that of the federation.

## ECONOMY
St Kitts is heavily planted in sugar cane, which accounts for approximately 30% of the work force. Small-scale garment manufacturing, electronic assembly and a brewery and bottling plant account for 15% of the labour force, while tourism accounts for nearly 10%.

On Nevis, where the economy is more sluggish, sugar has long been abandoned, but honey and some vegetables are produced and attempts are being made to revive one traditional crop, sea island cotton. Tourism is Nevis' largest employer; the new Four Seasons Resort employs over 600 people – roughly a quarter of the island's labour force.

## POPULATION & PEOPLE
The population is approximately 45,000, with 35,500 on St Kitts and 9500 on Nevis. Over 90% are of African descent. The rest of the population is predominantly of European, or mixed European and African, descent

People on St Kitts are called Kittitians (Kit-TEE-shuns), and on Nevis they are called Nevisians (Nee-VEE-shuns).

## ARTS & CULTURE
Culturally the islands draw upon a mix of European, African and West Indian traditions. Architecture is predominantly British in style and cricket is the national sport.

The cultural mix is evident in island dance and entertainment. Masquerades, St Kitts' popular folk troupe, performs dances ranging from a traditional French quadrille to a spirited African war dance. The troupe wears colourful costumes of a unique West Indian design.

### Dress Conventions
Dress is very casual on both St Kitts and Nevis. Cotton clothing is suitable attire for any occasion; swimwear should be restricted to the beach.

## RELIGION
Just over one-third of all islanders are Anglican. The rest are Methodist, Roman Catholic, Baptist, Adventist, Moravian and Jehovah's Witness.

## LANGUAGE
The language of the islands is English.

# Facts for the Visitor

## PASSPORT & VISAS
Passports are required of all visitors except US and Canadian citizens, who may enter with proof of citizenship such as an official birth certificate and a photo ID.

Visas are not required of most visitors, including citizens of the UK, Western Europe and Commonwealth countries, for stays of up to six months. Visitors are required to be in possession of a return or onward ticket.

## CUSTOMS
One bottle of wine or spirits and 200 cigarettes can be brought in duty free.

## MONEY
The Eastern Caribbean Dollar (EC$) is the

official currency (EC\$2.70=US\$1). There's a Barclays Bank and a Scotiabank in both Basseterre and Charlestown.

Larger tourist-related charges, such as car rental and hotel bills, are generally billed in US dollars, although you can pay in either US or EC dollars. Most hotels, car rental agencies and restaurants accept major credit cards though there's not a great deal of consistency – the in-town pizza place accepts credit cards while a couple of the top-end plantation inns do not. Note that most businesses will use an exchange rate of EC\$2.65=US\$1 when converting a bill from EC to US dollars, a slight disadvantage if you're paying in US dollars.

Hotels and restaurants add a 7% tax and usually a 10% service charge. When a restaurant doesn't add a service charge, a 10% tip is appropriate.

## TOURIST OFFICES

St Kitts' main tourist office is in the Pelican Mall in Basseterre and there's also an information booth at the airport. The Nevis Tourist Office is on Main St in Charlestown.

When requesting information by mail, write to: St Kitts & Nevis Department of Tourism (☎ 465-2620; fax 465-8794), PO Box 132, Basseterre, St Kitts, West Indies.

### Overseas Reps

Overseas St Kitts & Nevis tourist offices include the following:

Canada
    11 Yorkville Ave, Suite 508, Toronto, Ontario M4W IL3 (☎ (416) 921-7717; fax (416) 921-7997)
UK
    10 Kensington Court, London W8 5DL (☎ (071) 376-0881; fax (071) 937-3611)
USA
    Presidents' Plaza II, 8700 West Bryn Mawr, Suite 800S, Chicago, IL 60631 (☎ (312) 714-5015, ☎ (800) 562-6208; fax (312) 714-4910)
    414 East 75th St, New York, NY 10021 (☎ (212) 535-1234; fax (212) 879-4789)

## BUSINESS HOURS

Business hours for offices and shops are generally from 8 am to noon and 1 to 4 or 4.30 pm Monday to Friday; however, on Thursday many shops close for the afternoon.

Most banks are open from 8 am to 3 pm weekdays and until 5 pm on Friday. The National Bank and the Bank of Nevis close at noon on Thursday but are open from 8.30 to 11 am on Saturday.

## HOLIDAYS

The following is a list of public holidays on St Kitts & Nevis:

| | | |
|---|---|---|
| *New Year's Day* | – | 1 January |
| *Good Friday* | – | late March/early April |
| *Easter Monday* | – | late March/early April |
| *Labour Day* | – | first Monday in May |
| *Whit Monday* | – | eighth Monday after Easter |
| *Queen's Birthday* | – | second Saturday in June |
| *August Monday* | – | first Monday in August |
| *Independence Day* | – | 19 September |
| *Christmas Day* | – | 25 December |
| *Boxing Day* | – | 26 December |

Many businesses are closed on St Kitts during Carnival, held from 26 December to 2 January.

## CULTURAL EVENTS

On St Kitts, the biggest event is the week-long Carnival held at the end of the year with calypso competitions, costumed street dances and steel band music. Nevis has a two-week 'Culturama' from late July to early August featuring music, crafts and cultural events.

## POST

The main post offices are in Basseterre and Charlestown. There are branch post offices on Nevis at Market Shop and on St Kitts at Cayon, Dieppe Bay Town, Old Road Town and Sandy Point Town.

Airmail postage costs EC\$0.50 for a postcard and EC\$0.80 for a 10-gram letter sent to Canada, the UK, the USA and most Caribbean countries. Postcards to Europe cost EC\$0.80, letters EC\$1.

When mailing a letter to the islands, follow the addressee's name with the town and then 'St Kitts, West Indies' or 'Nevis, West Indies'.

## TELECOMMUNICATIONS

St Kitts phone numbers start with 465, Nevis numbers with 469. To make a local call, dial all seven digits. When calling the islands from overseas, add the area code 809 to the local number.

The islands have both coin and card phones. To use a coin phone, insert a minimum of EC$0.25 (unused coins are returned), dial the number and as soon as the phone is answered push the pound (#) key. If you want to make another call push the 'follow-on call' button on the left under the hook, rather than hanging up the receiver.

Card phones, common in busier public places, take Caribbean Phonecards, which can be purchased at the airports, Skantel (telephone) offices and several shops. More details on phonecards can be found under Telecommunications in the introductory Facts for the Visitor chapter.

For an international operator dial ☎ 0, for directory assistance phone ☎ 411 and for USA Direct dial ☎ 111.

## ELECTRICITY

Most electric current is 230 volts, 60 cycles AC; however, some hotels supply electricity at 110 volts.

## WEIGHTS & MEASURES

St Kitts uses the imperial system of measurement. Speed limit signs are in miles and rental car odometers are usually in miles.

## BOOKS & MAPS

The best map is the Ordnance Survey's map of St Kitts & Nevis (1:50,000), which includes inset maps of Basseterre, Brimstone Hill Fortress and Charlestown. It can be purchased for EC$25 at Wall's Deluxe Record & Bookshop in Basseterre, which also has a good selection of books on the Caribbean, and at the gift shop at Brimstone Hill Fortress National Park.

## MEDIA

The government radio station, ZIZ, can be heard on 555 AM and 96 FM. The *Voice of Nevis* is on 895 AM and there's a gospel station at 825 AM. There's a government-operated TV station as well as US-network TV via cable.

There are two local newspapers: *The Democrat*, published on Saturday, and the twice-weekly *Labour Spokesman*.

The *Traveller Tourist Guide*, published biannually in spring and winter, is a good source of general tourist information and can be picked up from tourist offices and local hotels.

## HEALTH

The main hospital on St Kitts, the J N F General (☎ 465-2551), is at the west end of Cayon St in Basseterre. On Nevis, the small Alexandra Hospital (☎ 469-5473) is on Government Rd in Charlestown.

## DANGERS & ANNOYANCES

Manchineel trees, whose sap can cause a skin rash, grow along the coast, particularly on the leeward side of the islands.

## EMERGENCY

For police, fire and ambulance dial ☎ 911.

## ACTIVITIES
### Beaches & Swimming

The islands aren't known for their beaches, but there are reasonable strands on St Kitts and a couple of quite nice beaches on Nevis.

St Kitts' best beaches are on the south end of the island at Frigate Bay and in the sheltered bays along the south-east peninsula. Beaches along the main body of the island are mostly thin strands of black and grey sands.

On Nevis, Pinney's Beach, which runs north from Charlestown, is a long, lovely stretch of light grey-sands backed by coconut palms. There's a nice white-sand beach fronting the Nisbet Plantation Beach Club on the north shore in Newcastle.

All beaches on St Kitts and Nevis are public.

## Diving & Snorkelling

St Kitts has healthy, expansive reefs and varied marine life that includes rays, barracuda, garden eels, nurse sharks, sea turtles, sea fans, giant barrel sponges and black coral.

One popular dive spot is Sandy Point Bay below Brimstone Hill, which has a wonderful array of corals, sponges and reef fish as well as some coral-encrusted anchors from the colonial era. Among a handful of wreck dives is the 45-metre freighter *River Taw*, which sank in 15 metres of water in 1985 and now harbours soft corals and reef fish. Nevis has good diving off its west side, including some colourful caves at a depth of about 12 metres.

On St Kitts, Pro-Divers (☎ 465-3223) at Ocean Terrace Inn in Basseterre has single-tank dives for US$40, two-tank dives for US$60, night dives for US$50, an introductory resort course for US$75, a three-day PADI certification course for US$260 and a half-day snorkelling trip for US$25.

On Nevis, Scuba Safaris (☎ 469-9518) at Oualie Beach offers single-tank dives for US$45, two-tank dives for US$80, night dives for US$60, resort courses for US$80 and a half day of snorkelling for US$35.

## Windsurfing

On Nevis, windsurfing is good off Newcastle Bay, where winds typically blow cross-shore and there's a sheltered reef favourable for beginners. When the winds are strong, there are jumpable waves. Newcastle Bay Windsurfing (☎ 469-9615) on the beach at Newcastle Bay rents boards from US$12 an hour, US$50 for a full day. Two-hour lessons for beginners cost US$50.

## Other Water Sports

On St Kitts, R G Watersports (☎ 465-8050) on Frigate Bay Beach rents Sunfish sailing boats and windsurfing gear for US$20 an hour and snorkelling gear for US$15 a day; it also provides a shuttle to South Friar's Bay for US$5 return. Tropical Surf (☎ 469-9086), a beach hut at Turtle Beach, rents windsurfing gear, Sunfish boats and ocean kayaks.

On Nevis, Newcastle Bay Water Sports Centre (☎ 469-9395) at Newcastle Bay rents kayaks for US$5 to US$15 an hour (depending on the size) as well as snorkel sets and Sunfish boats. It's closed on Wednesday.

## Hiking

Tracks into the interior of St Kitts are not well defined, so it's advisable to do any major trekking with a guide.

Greg Pereira of Greg's Safaris (☎ 465-4121) leads a nice half-day hike into the rainforest of St Kitts. He moves at a comfortable pace that's suitable for all ages, identifies flora and fauna and stops to sample fruits along the way. The trip generally leaves around 8.30 am, returns to Basseterre around 2 pm and costs US$35 including lunch. You can also arrange a volcano tour through Greg's Safaris.

Kriss Berry of Kriss Tours (☎ 465-4042) is said to also do a nice job with guided hikes. A full-day trek which goes through the rainforest to the volcano costs US$40, lunch included.

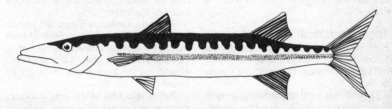

Barracuda

## Horse Riding

Horse riding is offered on St Kitts by Royal Stables (☎ 465-2222) and Trinity Stables (☎ 465-2922). On Nevis it's offered by Garners (☎ 469-5528) and Hermitage Plantation (☎ 469-3477). The latter also has carriage rides.

## Golf

The Four Seasons Resort on Nevis has an 18-hole golf course designed by Robert Trent Jones II. Green fees are US$75 for hotel guests, US$90 for non-guests, including cart rental.

On St Kitts, the 18-hole Royal St Kitts Golf Club (☎ 465-8339) at Frigate Bay has green fees of US$30. The green fees are waived for guests at many of Frigate Bay's hotels and condominiums, so if you're a golfer, you might want to enquire when booking a place to stay. Carts can be rented for another US$30.

Both courses offer club rentals and have lower rates for nine-hole play.

## HIGHLIGHTS

On St Kitts, plan a visit to Brimstone Hill Fortress National Park, both for its historic sites and its fine coastal views. The Amerindian petroglyphs at Old Road Town are some of the most easily viewed in the Eastern Caribbean; Romney Manor, just a couple of minutes' drive away, is also worthwhile. For some lovely scenery take the drive down the south-east peninsula.

Be sure to visit Nevis, at least on a day tour. The circle-island drive is pleasant, but if you don't want to rent a car, coconut-lined Pinney's Beach, which begins right in Charlestown, is a great beach on which to stroll.

## ACCOMMODATION

There are only two large resorts, the Jack Tar Village Beach Resort & Casino on St Kitts and the Four Seasons Resort & Golf Course on Nevis.

Beyond that most accommodation is in places with just a few dozen rooms, ranging from small hotels and condominiums to some fine inns in converted plantation estate homes. As there simply aren't very many rooms, St Kitts hotels can book up pretty solidly in winter, so early reservations are a good idea, particularly if you want to stay in one of the better-value places. Hotels add a 7% tax and a 10% service charge on top of their rates.

## FOOD

Reasonably priced local fresh fish and other seafood are plentiful on the islands and are generally the best bet. Beef and many other items are imported and tend to be expensive, particularly on Nevis. In Basseterre and Charlestown there are a few good inexpensive local restaurants, while the plantation inns on both islands offer some fine opportunities for romantic dining.

## DRINKS

Tap water is safe to drink on both islands. Cane Spirit Rothschild, more commonly known as CSR, is a clear sugar cane spirit distilled on St Kitts. CSR is often served on the rocks with Ting, a popular grapefruit soft drink. Ting, Ginseng Up and Carib beer are bottled on St Kitts.

## ENTERTAINMENT

Nightlife is not a highlight on St Kitts and Nevis, but there are a few options. On St Kitts, there's a casino and disco at Jack Tar Village Beach Resort, Frigate Bay; some low-key dinner entertainment at Ocean Terrace Inn, Basseterre; and occasional live entertainment at a few of the restaurants including Fisherman's Wharf, in Basseterre. Still, the busiest place is the cinema in the centre of Basseterre.

On Nevis, Caribbean Roots, the island's best band, usually plays at Four Seasons Resort, but they occasionally swing over to Oualie Beach Hotel where the crowd is less genteel and the band is free to hang a bit looser.

There's also a bit of weekend restaurant entertainment elsewhere on Nevis, including a Saturday night string band at Eddy's in

Charlestown and Friday dinner music and dancing at Mount Nevis Hotel.

## THINGS TO BUY

Caribelle Batik makes high-quality batik clothing, including T-shirts, pareos and skirts, and some pretty batik wall hangings of rainforest scenes. Items are sold at their Romney Manor factory and at Island Hopper shops in Charlestown, and at the Circus in Basseterre.

Spencer Cameron Gallery, on the north side of Independence Square in Basseterre, has some nice island artwork and prints at reasonable prices. There are duty free shops selling jewellery, watches and liquor at Basseterre's new Pelican Mall.

On Nevis, there's a handicraft co-op next to the tourist office on Main St in Charlestown. The Sand-box Tree, next to Super Foods on the south side of Charlestown, is a quality gift shop.

# Getting There & Away

See the Getting Around section for information on travelling between St Kitts and Nevis by air and boat.

## AIR

### To/From International Destinations

American Airlines (☎ 465-8490) flies from the USA to St Kitts daily via San Juan, Puerto Rico. The midweek fare for a 30-day excursion ticket is US$460 from Miami and US$500 from New York in the high season. It's about US$40 less in the low season.

There's currently no scheduled service to St Kitts from the UK, Europe or Canada and travel from those areas is via other Caribbean islands, most commonly Antigua, St Martin or San Juan.

### Within the Caribbean

**LIAT** LIAT has daily nonstop flights to St Kitts from Antigua and St Martin and connecting flights from those hubs to the rest of its Caribbean network.

The fare from St Martin to St Kitts is US$60 one way, US$73 for a one-day excursion and US$115 for a 30-day excursion.

LIAT's 30-day excursion ticket from Antigua to St Kitts or Nevis costs US$125. LIAT also has one-day excursion tours from Antigua to either St Kitts and Nevis that include a land tour (or rainforest hike), airfare and lunch and cost from US$125 to US$135.

**Winair** Winair (☎ 465-8010 on St Kitts, ☎ 469-7383 on Nevis) has daily flights from St Martin to St Kitts and Nevis. Fares to either are US$54 one way, US$63 for a one-day excursion, US$80 for a four-day excursion and US$100 for a 30-day excursion.

**Charters** Charter flights can be arranged with Air St Kitts Nevis (☎ 465-8571 on St Kitts, ☎ 469-9064 on Nevis), Carib Aviation (☎ 465-3055 on St Kitts, ☎ 469-9295 on Nevis, ☎ 462-3147 on Antigua) and Winair.

### Airport Information

St Kitts' Golden Rock Airport, on the outskirts of Basseterre, has limited facilities. The tourist office booth, which is just before immigration, distributes the standard tourist handouts and can help book accommodation.

**To/From the Airport** Taxis meet scheduled flights on both St Kitts and Nevis. If you're renting a car most rental agents will pick you up at the airport. On St Kitts, a taxi from the airport costs EC$16 to the west side of Basseterre, EC$25 to Frigate Bay, EC$42 to St Paul's. Phone ☎ 465-4253 to call a taxi.

### SEA

### Yacht

The two ports of entry are Basseterre and Charlestown. On both islands, customs is just north of the ferry dock and is open from 8 am to noon and 1 to 4 pm on weekdays. The entry charges range from EC$20 for 20 tonnes to EC$56 for 100 tonnes. Yachters will need cruising permits to visit other anchorages and a special pass to go between the two islands.

White House Bay, Ballast Bay and Major's Bay on St Kitts' south-east peninsula make good anchorages. On Nevis, Pinney's Beach is the most popular anchorage.

### Cruise Ship

Numerous cruise ships visit St Kitts, docking at the deep-water harbour at the east side of Basseterre. Nevis has traditionally been cool to cruise ship visits, but the current government is more receptive and a few small cruise lines have recently added Charlestown as a port of call.

### LEAVING ST KITTS & NEVIS

The departure tax is EC$20.

# Getting Around

### AIR

LIAT has three flights a day between St Kitts and Nevis, with an early morning, noon and late afternoon flight in each direction. The fare is US$31/39 one way/return.

### BUS

The buses are privately owned minivans. In Basseterre, most leave from the west side of the Treasury Building. From Basseterre it's EC$2 to Sandy Point Town, EC$2.50 to St Paul's and EC$3 to Dieppe Bay Town. The bus service is fairly sporadic and there's no schedule, although buses are most plentiful in the early morning and late afternoon. The last bus is generally around 6 or 7 pm. Frigate Bay is outside regular bus routes. For information on buses on Nevis see the end of the Nevis section.

### TAXI

From the Circus in Basseterre, the main taxi stand, it costs EC$8 to points within town, EC$18 to Frigate Bay and EC$30 to Brimstone Hill. Rates are 25% higher between 11 pm and 6 am. There's an EC$3 charge for each 15 minutes of waiting time. To call for

a taxi, dial ☎ 465-4253. Information on taxis on Nevis is at the end of the Nevis section.

### CAR & MOTORBIKE
#### Road Rules

Drive on the left. Speed limits are posted in miles per hour, and are generally between 20 and 40 m/h. Petrol costs about EC$5 a gallon (EC$1.10 a litre).

Basseterre has quite a few one-way streets, some of which are not clearly marked, so keep an eye out for signs and when in doubt simply follow the traffic.

#### Driving Licences

Foreign visitors must purchase a visitor's driving licence, which costs EC$30 (or US$12) and is valid for one year. The easiest place to get them is at the fire station on Pond Rd at the east side of Basseterre, which is open 24 hours and has a separate window designated for issuing visitor licences. If you're flying into St Kitts and renting a car, the rental agency will usually pick you up at the airport and then stop at the fire station on the way to their office.

During weekday business hours, driving licences can also be obtained at the Inland Revenue Office, above from the Basseterre post office on Bay Rd. However, this is not a good option in February and March, as all Kittitians renew their licences during those months and queues can be quite long.

In Nevis, visitor's driving licences can be obtained at police stations.

#### Rental

There are numerous car rental agencies on St Kitts. Rates begin at about US$30 a day with unlimited mileage for a Nissan March, Toyota Starlet or Austin Mini Moke. In addition, optional collision damage waivers cost from US$5 to US$10 a day. With some companies you're still responsible for the first few hundred dollars worth of damage, while with others the CDW waives all liability.

In Basseterre, three of the largest agents are Avis (☎ 465-6507) on South Independence Square, TDC Auto Rentals (☎ 465-2991) on West Independence Square and

Sunshine Car Rental (☎ 465-2193; in the USA and Canada ☎ (800) 621-1270) on Cayon St. All three provide free airport or hotel pick-up.

Other car rental agents include Delisle Walwyn & Co (☎ 465-8449), Liverpool Row, Basseterre; Caines Rent-A-Car (☎ 465-2366), Princes St, Basseterre; and Ken's Car Rental (☎ 465-3706), Crab Hill, Sandy Point Town.

Information on renting cars on Nevis is at the end of the Nevis section.

## BOAT

The government-run passenger ferry *Caribe Queen* runs between St Kitts and Nevis daily except Thursday and Sunday. The ferry docks are in central Basseterre and Charlestown, which for most people makes the ferry more practical than flying between the two islands.

From Basseterre the boat departs for Charlestown on Monday at 8 am and 4 pm; on Tuesday at 2 pm; on Wednesday at 7 am, 4 pm and 7 pm; on Friday at 8.30 am and 4 pm; and on Saturday at 8.30 am and 3 pm.

From Charlestown the boat departs for Basseterre on Monday at 7 am and 3 pm; on Tuesday at 7.30 am and 6 pm; on Wednesday at 8 am and 6 pm; on Friday at 7.30 am and 3 pm; and on Saturday at 7.30 am and 2 pm.

The ferry strictly enforces its 150-passenger limit and does not sell advance or return tickets. Dockside booths begin selling tickets about half an hour before the scheduled departure time. As sailings occasionally reach capacity, it's wise to arrive early. Also note that if a boat does reach capacity it sometimes sails a few minutes before its scheduled departure time – so don't stroll too far away after you've bought your ticket!

The fare is EC$10 each way. The ride, which takes about 45 minutes, is usually a smooth trip and offers good views of both islands, best from the small outdoor deck at the front of the boat.

Plying the same route on Thursday and Sunday is the *Spirit of Mt Nevis*, a private 70-passenger cruiser with both air-con indoor seating and an open-air upper deck. It

leaves Charlestown at 8 am and 3.30 pm and leaves Basseterre at 9 am and 4.30 pm. The cost is EC$16 one way.

## TOURS

On St Kitts, Tropical Tours (☎ 465-4167), Addy's Island Tours (☎ 465-8069) and Annie's Caribbean Tours (☎ 465-7043) all have half-day circle-island tours for US$12 to US$15. The same companies also offer catamaran cruises, deep-sea fishing and rainforest walks.

Taxis charge US$48 (for one to four people) for an island tour that takes 4½ hours, including time for lunch at one of the plantation inns. You can get a taxi to take you up to Brimstone Hill, wait while you look around and bring you back to town for US$30.

# Basseterre

Basseterre was founded and named by the French in the 17th century. A fire swept through the town in 1867, destroying the capital's early colonial buildings. Still, there are a fair number of Victorian-era stone block structures that are topped with wooden second storeys that are decorated with fancy latticework and gingerbread trim.

The town centre is the Circus, a roundabout featuring a four-sided clock tower. It's supposedly modelled on London's Piccadilly Circus, but the most noticeable similarity lies in a bit of traffic congestion. Most of the island's banks, airline offices and travel agents are in the streets radiating from the Circus, while taxis, coconut sellers and souvenir shops cluster at the roundabout. Almost all of the shops and places of interest are within a five-minute walk.

The nearby Independence Square, once the site of slave auctions, is a small public park with a central water fountain. The square is flanked by some of Basseterre's grander buildings including a few Georgian-style houses and the twin-towered

**Basseterre**

Basseterre Bay

*Ferry to Nevis*

Independence Square

Springfield Cemetery

To Airport
To Frigate Bay
To Hospital & Brimstone Hill

**PLACES TO STAY**

1 Fort Thomas Hotel
2 Ocean Terrace Inn
11 Glimbaro Guest House
11 Hôtel Canne à Sucre
18 Park View Guest House
22 On the Square

**PLACES TO EAT**

3 Fisherman's Wharf
10 Chef's Place
13 The New Pizza Place
13 American Bakery
25 Ballahoo Restaurant
34 Redi-Fried
39 Georgian House

**OTHER**

4 War Memorial
5 Public Market
6 National Supply
8 St George's Anglican Church
9 Shell Petrol Station
12 Government Offices
14 Wall's Deluxe Record & Bookshop
15 Delisle Walwyn Travel Agency & Car Rental
16 Ram's Supermarket
17 Bus Stop
20 Skantel (Telephone) Office
21 Parris Pharmacy
23 LIAT/BWIA Offices
24 Scotiabank
25 Island Hopper
26 The Circus
27 Museum
28 TDC Auto Rentals
29 Barclays Bank
30 Treasury Building
31 Post Office & Customs
32 Pelican Mall & Tourist Office
33 Ferry Ticket Booth
34 Cinema
35 Police Station
36 Spencer Cameron Gallery
37 Immaculate Conception Cathedral
38 Avis

ST KITTS

Immaculate Conception Cathedral which dates from 1927.

On the west side of town, Fort Thomas Hotel sits at the site of the old Fort Thomas. Though it's not a major sight, just below the hotel pool you can find a bit of the fort walls ringed with half a dozen cannons.

### Information
**Tourist Office** The tourist office, in Pelican Mall, is open from 8 am to 4.30 pm Monday and Tuesday, to 4 pm on Wednesday, Thursday and Friday.

**Money** Scotiabank, at the Circus, charges EC$2.50 per transaction plus five cents per cheque to cash travellers' cheques, while Barclays Bank nearby charges EC$1.50 per transaction plus 15 cents per cheque. Both are open from 8 am to 3 pm Monday to Thursday, to 5 pm on Friday.

**Post** The general post office on Bay Rd is open from 8 to 11 am on Thursday and 8 am to 3 pm on Monday, Tuesday, Wednesday, Friday and Saturday. You can get colourful commemorative stamps at the philatelic bureau in Pelican Mall.

**Telecommunications** You can make international phone calls and send faxes and telegrams from the Skantel office on Cayon St; credit cards are accepted. The office is open from 8 am to 6 pm Monday to Friday, 8 am to 1 pm on Saturday and 6 to 8 pm on Sunday and holidays.

**Bookshop** Wall's Deluxe Record & Bookshop on Fort St sells maps and a fairly good selection of books on the Caribbean.

### Museum
The St Christopher Heritage Society on Bank St, on the 2nd floor above the US Peace Corps office, hopes to eventually establish a substantial national museum. Meanwhile there's a small room with a few historic photos and a thin display of local flora and fauna. It's open from 8.30 am to 1 pm and 2 to 4 pm weekdays (mornings only on Wednesday) and 9 am to noon on Saturday. Admission is free, but donations are appreciated.

### Brewery & Sugar Factory
The St Kitts Breweries, which brews Carib beer, and the St Kitts Sugar Factory will both usually give visitors an informal tour during weekday business hours. The brewery is along the south side of the circle-island road just west of the hospital. The sugar factory is midway between Basseterre centre and the airport and is reached by taking Wellington St north-east from Independence Square. There's no fee for either, but a tip to the worker who gives you the tour is the norm.

### Places to Stay – bottom end
**Town Centre** *Hôtel Canne à Sucre* (☎ 465-2344) on Church St, opposite Chef's Place, mostly rents long-term but it does have a handful of very basic rooms that can be rented on a nightly basis. Expect chipped linoleum, saggy mattresses and no fans, but rooms do have private baths and cost just US$15/26 for singles/doubles, tax included.

*Park View Guest House* (☎ 465-2100), PO Box 64, on the corner of Victoria Rd and Losack St, is an older guesthouse with cheerless singles/doubles for US$25/50.

*Glimbaro Guest House* (☎ 465-2935; fax 465-9832), Cayon St, is a newly constructed guesthouse with 10 straightforward rooms, each with a ceiling fan and phone. For singles, the six rooms with private bath cost US$35/45 in summer/winter, while the four that share a bath cost US$25/35. For doubles, add US$10.

*On the Square* (☎ 465-2485; fax 465-7723), PO Box 81, centrally located on Independence Square, has simple but clean rooms, all with air-con, radio and private bath. Rates, which include tax and service, are US$30/35 for singles/doubles and US$53 for doubles with a kitchenette.

*Earle's Vacation Home* (☎ 465-7546), PO Box 604, is in the Shadwell neighbourhood at the north side of town and within walking distance of the centre. There are two one-bedroom and four two-bedroom apartments with kitchens, dining areas and cable TV. Rates are US$40/50 in summer/winter for one-bedroom units and US$70/80 for two bedrooms.

**Around Basseterre** *Trinity Inn Apartments* (☎ 465-2922), Palmetto Point, is a small apartment building on the coastal road four miles west of Basseterre. There are a couple of furnished flats that can be rented for US$40/200 a day/week. Ruth, the English woman who runs the place along with her husband Will, can be hard to reach so keep trying.

If you want to be closer to the water consider *Coral Reef Beach Cottages* (☎ 465-8154), c/o Mrs Zenaida Katzen, PO Box 323, Basseterre, which are at Conaree Beach, about a mile (1.6 km) north-east of the airport. These straightforward cottages each have two bedrooms, two bathrooms, a living room, kitchen, phone and verandah. Rates are US$30 a day with a three-day minimum stay, or US$200\680 a week\month, utilities included.

### Places to Stay – top end
**Town Centre** *Fort Thomas Hotel* (☎ 465-2695; fax 465-7518; in the USA ☎ (800) 851-7818, in the UK ☎ (081) 908-3348), PO Box 407, is a modern 64-room hotel on the quiet western side of town. It's the best hotel value on St Kitts, with large comfortable rooms, each with two double beds, air-con, phone, cable TV, bath and balcony for US$55/65 singles/doubles all year round. There's a moderately priced restaurant, an Olympic-sized pool and a free daily beach shuttle to Frigate Bay. The hotel often fills up, particularly in winter, and early reservations are advised – request an ocean-view room, as all rooms are currently priced the same.

*Ocean Terrace Inn* (☎ 465-2754; fax 465-1057; in the USA ☎ (800) 524-0512, in the UK (081) 367-5175), PO Box 65, is Basseterre's biggest hotel. Known locally as OTI, it's popular with both tour groups and business travellers. Accommodation is spread across three sites and varies greatly,

ranging from cramped streetside cottages and standard hotel rooms to commodious split-level ocean-view apartments perched above Fisherman's Wharf. All rooms have air-con, cable TV and phone. Winter rates vary from US$93/116 for the cheapest single/double rooms to US$195 for the split-level apartments. Summer rates average about 15% less. There are a couple of swimming pools and a complimentary shuttle to Turtle Beach.

**Around Basseterre** The *Bird Rock Beach Hotel* (☎ 465-8914; fax 465-1675; in the USA ☎ (800) 621-1270), PO Box 227, in the suburbs two miles (3.2 km) east of central Basseterre, has 36 pleasant, comfortable rooms. All are well appointed with cable TV, air-con, fan, phone, tub and cliffside ocean-view balcony. The studios and suites have kitchens as well. There's a moderately priced restaurant, tennis courts, a pool and a small black-sand beach. The units are spread across six contemporary two-storey buildings, the farthest two having the finest views. Summer/winter rates are US$70/120 for a room, US$80/140 for a studio and US$125/220 for a two-bedroom suite.

*Fairview Inn* (☎ 465-2472; fax 465-1056; in the USA ☎ (800) 223-9815), PO Box 212, is situated above a working cane field four miles (6.4 km) west of town, on the north side of the circle-island road. A former plantation estate, Fairview is quite ordinary in comparison to other plantation inns on the island. The main house serves as a restaurant, while accommodation is provided in 30 cottages, some nondescript and others more atmospheric with old stone walls. All have private bathrooms and some have tubs, TV and separate dining area. Superior rooms, which cost US$80/140 in summer/winter, have air-con, while moderate rooms (US$75/130) are fan cooled. Standard rooms (US$70/120) have neither air-con nor fans. There's a pool.

*Morgan Heights Condominiums* (☎ 465-8633; fax 465-9272), PO Box 536, is on the circle-island road in the Canada Estate area two miles (3.2 km) north-east of the airport.

Left: Rainforst, Mt Scenery trail, Saba (NF)
Top Right: Anglican Church, The Bottom, Saba (NF)
Bottom Right: Well's Bay, Saba (NF)

Top Left: Art Gallery, St Barts (NF)
Top Right: St Jean, St Barts (NF)
Bottom: Eden Rock Hotel, St Jean, St Barts (NF)

While the location is a bit out of the way, the units are large and modern and have full kitchen, air-con, cable TV, phone and patio. Summer/winter rates are US$65/125 for one-bedroom suites, US$95/175 for two-bedroom suites. You can also rent just a bedroom, hotel-style, for US$50/85. There's a restaurant and a pool.

### Places to Eat

The most popular spot in town for a quick cheap eat is *Redi-Fried*, a hole-in-the-wall next to the cinema on Bay Rd, where you can pick up two pieces of chicken with fries for EC$7.

There's pretty good pizza-by-the-slice for EC$5 at *The New Pizza Place* on Central St. Small, whole pizzas cost from EC$15 to EC$22, depending on the toppings, which include all the standards plus vegetarian and saltfish varieties. It's open from 11 am to 10 pm daily except Sunday.

*Chef's Place* on Church St in central Basseterre is a friendly spot with great food and generous servings. You can eat at picnic tables on the streetside patio or indoors under ceiling fans. Breakfast costs EC$15, with a wide range of offerings and is served until 10 am. For lunch and dinner there are four or five choices from the chalkboard, with such items as sweet and sour chicken, grilled fresh fish and butterfly shrimp, all EC$20 or less and served with rice, a good green salad and island vegetables such as squash and christophene. For a zingy drink, try the freshly squeezed ginger beer for EC$1.50. It's open from about 8 am to 11.30 pm daily except Sunday.

The popular *Ballahoo Restaurant* has a nice 2nd-floor balcony overlooking the Circus. Full breakfasts, including saltfish in Creole sauce or pancakes with bacon, cost EC$15. At lunch, rotis, burgers and sandwiches start at EC$7, while full meals average EC$20. Dinner offerings, which include vegetarian stuffed peppers, chicken kebabs, blue parrotfish fillet and lobster, range in price from EC$26 to EC$52. Conchs in garlic butter (EC$10) make a good starter and the banana-and-rum toasted sand-wich topped with vanilla ice cream is a delicious finale. It's open from 8 am to 11 pm daily except Sunday.

*Fisherman's Wharf* can be a fun place to eat, with dining at picnic tables on a waterfront dock below Ocean Terrace Inn. Dinners are cooked to order over an open grill and are accompanied by a self-service buffet of salad, rice, potatoes and local vegetables. The price depends on the main dish you select: various fresh fish (tuna is a good choice) cost EC$35, while meats range from barbecued chicken for EC$22 to sirloin steak for EC$55. It's good value, tax is included and there's no service charge. Fisherman's Wharf is open for dinner only, from 7 pm nightly.

The main restaurant at *Ocean Terrace Inn* has rather average fare and an undistinguished ambience but it does have a good view. There's a set full dinner that changes nightly for EC$88 or you can order à la carte with main dishes from EC$40 for fish to EC$55 for shrimp scampi or broiled lobster.

*The Lighthouse Restaurant* (☎ 465-8914), in the Bird Rock area above the cruise ship dock, is a rather upmarket place to go for dinner. Main dishes include East Indian lamb curry or shrimp linguini for EC$50, beef Wellington for EC$65, plus EC$8 for soup or salad. The wine list includes selections from France, Germany and California. It's open daily from 6 to 11 pm.

*The Georgian House* (☎ 465-4049) has romantic dining in a restored manor house on Independence Square. The restaurant is owned by American chef Roger Doche and is open from 6 pm daily except Monday. Main dishes range from chicken cacciatore on pasta or West Indian chicken with rice and peas for EC$39 to shrimp Marseillaise or steak for EC$57. Add another EC$10 for soup or salad. During the winter season, there's a barbecue with live music on Tuesday.

*American Bakery* has fresh bread and pastries and is open from 6 am to 6 pm weekdays, to 2 pm on Saturday and 7 pm on Sunday.

The green-walled, tin-roofed public

market on Bay Rd is the best place to pick up fruit and vegetables. There are two good-sized grocery stores between the public market and the post office: National Supply, open from 8 am to 9 pm Monday to Saturday and 8 am to 2 pm on Sundays, and Ram's Supermarket, open from 8 am to 6 pm Monday to Saturday.

# Around St Kitts

## FRIGATE BAY

Frigate Bay, three miles (4.8 km) south-east of Basseterre, is the main beach resort area for St Kitts. It has two beaches, North Frigate Bay (also called Atlantic Beach) and Frigate Bay Beach (also known as Caribbean Beach or Timothy Beach). It's a 15-minute walk between the two bays.

The calmer Frigate Bay Beach, on the south side of the peninsula, is the island's most popular bathing spot. The facilities at this grey-sand beach include water sports huts and a bustling open-air drinking spot, the Kittitian Monkey Bar, which attracts a crowd on weekends. The beach is backed by a salt pond while the nearshore waters are a common feeding ground for pelicans.

North Frigate Bay has waters that are a bit rough and a long stretch of golden sand – it's possible to walk north along the beach for several km. Most of the area's development is along North Frigate Bay, with condominiums and shops lined up along the beach and opposite the golf course and Jack Tar Village. Despite the fact that Jack Tar has the island's only casino, Frigate Bay is nonetheless a pretty low-key, uneventful area.

Buses generally don't run to Frigate Bay, so if you don't have your own rental car you'll have to plan on doing some hefty walking or rely on taxis.

### Information

Barclays Bank is open from 8.30 am to 1 pm Monday to Thursday and from 8.30 am to 1 pm and 3 to 4 pm on Friday. TDC Auto Rentals has an office inside the mini-mart next to PJ's Pizza Bar and there's a Tropical Tours hut at the south end of Jack Tar Village resort.

### Places to Stay

*Gateway Inn* (☎ 465-7155; fax 465-9322), PO Box 64, is off by itself at the side of the main road between Basseterre and Frigate Bay. This straightforward one-storey apartment complex has 10 furnished units each with a full kitchen, living room, a separate bedroom with air-con, phone and cable TV. Rates are US$50/80 in summer/winter. On weekly rentals the seventh day is free.

Despite its name, the modern 64-room *Frigate Bay Beach Hotel* (☎ 465-8935; fax 465-7050), PO Box 137, is not, on the beach but on a hillside above Frigate Bay. Rooms have tiled floor, ceiling fan, air-con, bathtub, phone and two double beds. They're rather pleasant but not fancy and the cheapest rooms, which have hillside views, are a reasonable deal in summer at US$60, but pricey in winter at US$145. There are also suites with kitchenettes from US$80/195 in summer/winter. There's a restaurant and a large pool. It's possible to walk down to Frigate Bay Beach via a path behind the hotel, but overall it's not a terribly convenient place for visitors without a car.

*SeaLofts* (☎ 465-8004; fax 465-8454), PO Box 139, a new townhouse condominium project, is one of Frigate Bay's best value places to stay. The two-bedroom units each have a living room with sofabed, wicker and rattan furnishings, a dining area, full kitchen, large balcony, cable TV and a washing machine and dryer. It's on the beach and there are two tennis courts and a pool. Rates are US$125 to US$155 in winter, depending on the view, US$90 to US$115 in summer. There's no housekeeping service and thus no service charge. Credit cards are not accepted.

*Leeward Cove* (☎ 465-8030; fax 465-3476; in the USA ☎ (800) 223-5695), PO Box 123, a small condominium opposite the golf course, has six pleasant apartments that are rented out when not owner-occupied. Units have full kitchen, living room with a sofabed and ceiling fan, air-con bedrooms,

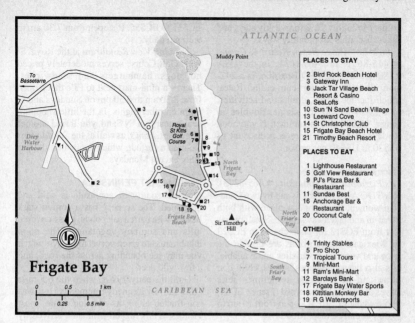

Frigate Bay

PLACES TO STAY

2  Bird Rock Beach Hotel
3  Gateway Inn
6  Jack Tar Village Beach
    Resort & Casino
8  SeaLofts
10  Sun 'N Sand Beach Village
13  Leeward Cove
14  St Christopher Club
15  Frigate Bay Beach Hotel
21  Timothy Beach Resort

PLACES TO EAT

1  Lighthouse Restaurant
5  Golf View Restaurant
7  PJ's Pizza Bar &
    Restaurant
11  Sundae Best
16  Anchorage Bar &
    Restaurant
20  Coconut Cafe

OTHER

4  Trinity Stables
5  Pro Shop
7  Tropical Tours
9  Mini-Mart
11  Ram's Mini-Mart
12  Barclays Bank
17  Frigate Bay Water Sports
18  Kittitian Monkey Bar
19  R G Watersports

dining area and patio. One-bedroom apartments cost US$110/155 in summer/winter, two-bedroom units cost US$155/250. For week-long apartment stays a free rental car is thrown in. Visitors can sometimes rent just a bedroom, hotel style, for US$45/75 in summer/winter for singles, US$55/110 for doubles.

*Timothy Beach Resort* (☎ 465-8597; fax 465-7723; in the USA ☎ (800) 858-5375), PO Box 81, is a small condominium development, which forms part of the Colony resort chain. The rooms are not special but the resort does have a good beachside location on the east side of Frigate Bay Beach. Mountain-view rooms are the cheapest; they have a tub, a tiny balcony, mini-refrigerator, air-con and phone and cost US$99/140 in summer/winter. Add another US$30/40 in summer/winter for an ocean-view room and US$10 more for a room with a kitchenette.

*Sun 'N Sand Beach Village* (☎ 465-8037; fax 465-6745; in the USA ☎ (800) 223-

6510), PO Box 341, has 18 fully equipped condo-style two-bedroom cottages and 32 motel-style studio apartments, with air-con, ceiling fan, cable TV and phone. The studios have toaster, refrigerator and microwave oven while the cottages have full kitchen. There's a pool and tennis courts. The studios cost US$80/160 in summer/winter for up to two people and the cottages cost US$130/260 for up to four people. The seventh night is free year-round.

*St Christopher Club* (☎ 465-4854; fax 465-6466), PO Box 570, is a condominium with 16 units, some of which are rented out on a short-term basis. Furnishings vary, but all have full kitchen, dining area, bathtub, cable TV, tiled floor and phone. The bedrooms have air-con and either one or two double beds. One-bedroom suites cost US$78/155 in summer/winter, two-bedroom suites US$105/205. You can sometimes rent a single bedroom, without kitchen and dining room, for US$60/100. There are discounts of roughly 20% for weekly stays and larger discounts for monthly stays.

*Jack Tar Village Beach Resort & Casino* (☎ 465-8651; fax 465-1031; in the USA ☎ (800) 999-9182), PO Box 406, is a 242-room all-inclusive resort-cum-casino. Rates, which include meals, drinks and activities, cost US$180/300 for singles/doubles in winter, US$20 less in summer. If you book 60 days in advance there is a discount of US$30 to US$40 per person.

**Places to Eat**

*PJ's Pizza Bar & Restaurant* (☎ 465-8373), near TDC Auto Rentals, is run by two Canadian women. It's a popular place with both an eat-in and takeaway service. Small pizzas cost from EC$13 for plain cheese to EC$23 for Mexican. Large pizzas are double the price and vegetarian varieties are available. PJ's also has sandwiches, salads, chilli con carne and lasagne and sometimes sells loaves of freshly baked bread (French EC$3, whole wheat EC$6). It's open from 10 am to 10.30 pm daily except Monday.

*Coconut Cafe* (☎ 465-3020), an open-air restaurant right on Frigate Bay Beach, has a fairly extensive menu. A continental breakfast costs EC$13, full Western fare is a bit more. At lunch, burgers, flying fish sandwiches and salads cost around EC$10, catch of the day is EC$30. The dinner menu concentrates on West Indian seafood dishes, most priced between EC$30 and EC$50. There's a buffet with steel band music on Saturday evening and live entertainment on Wednesday. It's open from 7.30 am to 11 pm daily and the bar stays open until 1 am.

The *Anchorage Bar & Restaurant*, at the west end of Frigate Bay Beach, is open from 8 am to midnight. It has a full breakfast for EC$17, moderately priced sandwiches and fish & chips for lunch, and chicken, fish and steak dishes priced from EC$25 to EC$40 for dinner.

The restaurant at the *Frigate Bay Beach Hotel* has breakfast fare and lunchtime sandwiches and salads priced from EC$14 to EC$22. At dinner there's West Indian and continental food, with main dishes from

EC$35 to EC$55. It's open from 7.30 am to 9.30 pm daily.

The *Golf View Restaurant* at the Royal St Kitts Golf Course serves moderately priced hot dogs, hamburgers and sandwiches. There's a mini-mart next to PJ's that's open from 8.30 am to 6.30 pm on Sundays and to 8 pm on other nights. In the little shopping centre near Sun 'N Sand, you'll find another mini-mart, *Ram's*, as well as the *Sundae Best* ice-cream parlour, which is open until 7 pm daily except Mondays.

## SOUTH-EAST PENINSULA

St Kitts' south-east peninsula is wild and unspoiled. The scenery has a certain stark beauty, with barren salt ponds, grass-covered hills and scrubby vegetation. The main inhabitants are green vervet monkeys, which you may see bounding across the road, and a few wild deer.

Until the early 1990s, when the 6.5-mile (10.5-km) Dr Kennedy Simmonds Hwy was constructed along its twisting spine, most visitors to this rugged peninsula arrived by boat. The highway signals grand plans to develop the peninsula for tourism and a couple of new resorts are now in the planning stages.

The new highway is the island's best road but be cautious of occasional deep V-shaped rain gutters at the edge, particularly if you're tempted to pull off quickly to enjoy the view. Also, it's not uncommon to encounter small landslides along the road.

The neck at the beginning of the peninsula has sandy beaches on both sides: **North Friar's Bay** and **South Friar's Bay**. South Friar's Bay, which has calmer waters and better swimming conditions, is reached via a dirt road about a mile (1.6 km) south of the start of the highway.

About 2.25 miles (3.6 km) from the start of the highway, you'll reach the crest of the peninsula, where there's an unmarked lookout that offers a good view of the salt ponds and coastline. There's another viewpoint about 1.5 miles (2.4 km) farther south. Soon after that a dirt road to the right leads to **White House Bay**, which has an old jetty and a couple of minor wrecks that should provide reasonable snorkelling.

The highway then passes the **Great Salt Pond**, which is rimmed with salt crystals and attracts plovers, stilts, whimbrels and other shorebirds. After that the road forks. The right fork leads to **Major's Bay**, which has a rocky shoreline and is earmarked for condo and hotel development. The left fork leads to **Cockleshell Bay**, which has a rather ordinary grey-sand beach and a wonderful view of Nevis. On the road to Cockleshell Bay, just past an old sugar mill, a sign points to **Turtle Beach**, which is a notch nicer than Cockleshell. Turtle Beach is used by Ocean Terrace Inn and has a restaurant, a water sports centre and a fine view of Nevis.

### Places to Eat

The only place to eat on the south-east peninsula is at the *Turtle Beach Bar & Grill* at Turtle Beach. The restaurant is open from 10 am to 6 pm daily (to 11 pm on Saturday) with simple offerings such as a chicken platter for EC$23 and fresh fish for EC$35.

### CIRCLE-ISLAND ROAD

The major sightseeing spot on St Kitts is Brimstone Hill Fortress, but the circle-island road passes a few other points of interest as well, including petroglyphs, a batik shop at Romney Manor and the crumbling stacks of abandoned sugar mills.

It's a pleasant rural drive with scenery dominated by fields of sugar cane, broken up here and there by scattered villages. The narrow gauge tracks of the sugar cane train run alongside the road and odds are good that you'll see these antique-looking trains hauling loads of freshly cut cane from the fields to the mill.

The villages themselves, with their weathered stone churches and old wooden houses with rusty tin roofs, offer a closer glimpse of island life. All have small stores or rum shacks that sell sodas, liquor and a few basic provisions.

The road is paved and in fairly good condition, though you'll have to slow down for potholes, rain gutters and the occasional stray goat. The circle-island tour can easily be done in half a day; however, giving yourself a few more hours would allow for a more leisurely exploration.

### Bloody Point

A little over four miles (6.4 km) west of Basseterre, at the north end of the village of Challengers, a fading sign marks Bloody Point, the site where more than 2000 Caribs were massacred by joint British and French forces in 1626.

Upon leaving the village there's a curve in the road and a small place to pull off – stop here for a scenic view of the coast and Brimstone Hill.

### Old Road Town

After Bloody Point the road swings down to the seaside village of Old Road Town, the landing site of the first British settlers in 1623. The rocky shoreline in this area is a good place to spot frigatebirds. In the centre of the village a sign pointing to Caribelle Batik marks Wingfield Rd.

**Petroglyphs & Caribelle Batik** Immediately after turning inland on Wingfield Rd, there's a yellow nursery school on the left. At the side of the road just past the school you'll find three large black stones; the middle one has two distinct human-like figures carved by Caribs. There are no fees to visit the site.

The road continues another 0.5 miles (800 metres) through corn and cane fields and up past the ruins of the mill, chimney and stone arches of the Wingfield Estate before reaching Romney Manor, the old estate house which now contains Caribelle Batik.

The estate is located at the edge of a rainforest and this drive makes a nice diversion from the more arid lowlands that edge the coast. Romney Manor is surrounded by lush vegetation and grand flowering trees; two notable specimens are the knobby-trunked guinip tree by the entrance and the giant saman tree in the front yard that supports colonies of spider-plant-like epiphytes.

Batiks are made and sold on site and you

can watch wax being painted on cloth in a small demonstration area. The shop sells batik clothing and wall hangings but there's no hard sell if you just want to look around. It's open from 8.30 am to 4 pm weekdays (and on weekends if a tour group is expected).

**Places to Eat** You can get good pizza at moderate prices at *Pizza Hot* on Main St in the centre of Old Road Town.

### Middle Island
The village of Middle Island is the site of the tomb of Sir Thomas Warner, the leader of the first British landing party on St Kitts, who died on 10 March 1648. His marble-topped tomb with its verbose epitaph is under a white wooden shelter fronting the ageing St Thomas church which sits on a rise in the middle of town.

### Brimstone Hill Fortress National Park
This rambling 18th-century compound, which in its day was nicknamed 'Gibraltar of the West Indies', is one of the largest forts in the Caribbean. As a major British garrison, Brimstone Hill played a key role in battles with the French, who seized the fort in 1782 but returned it the next year under terms of the Treaty of Paris. The treaty ushered in a more peaceful era and by the 1850s the fort was abandoned.

After the 1867 fire swept through Basseterre, some of the fort structures were partially dismantled and the stones used to rebuild the capital. In the 1960s major restoration was undertaken and much of the fortress has been returned to its earlier grandeur. Queen Elizabeth II inaugurated the fort as a national park during her visit to St Kitts in October 1985.

The main hilltop compound, the Citadel, is lined with 24 cannons and provides excellent views of St Eustatius and Sandy Point Town. Inside the Citadel's old barrack rooms are museum displays on colonial history which feature cannonballs, swords and other period odds and ends. There's also a small collection of Amerindian adzes, a few

pottery fragments and a rubbing of the Carib petroglyphs in Old Road Town. Another room contains a display on the American Revolution and the West Indian role in that revolt.

Also worthwhile is the short stroll above the cookhouse to the top of Monkey Hill which provides excellent coastal views. A small theatre next to the gift shop plays a brief video on the fort's history.

Brimstone Hill, upon which the fortress stands, is a 229-metre volcanic cone named for its odoriferous sulphur vents, which you'll undoubtedly detect as you drive past the hill along the coastal road.

The fortress is open from 9.30 am to 5.30 pm daily. Admission for foreign visitors costs US$5 for adults, US$2.50 for children.

**Places to Eat** Brimstone Hill Fortress has a small canteen that sells beer and burgers. Js' Restaurant, on the main road opposite the turn-off to the fort, is not recommended.

**Getting There & Away** Buses from Basseterre to Sandy Point Town can drop you off at the signposted road leading up to the fortress, from where it's a 1.25-mile (2-km) uphill walk on a narrow winding road. If you're driving up, be sure to beep your horn as you approach blind curves.

### North-East Coast
As you continue from Brimstone Hill Fortress, you'll pass through lowlands of cane while circling **Mt Liamuiga**, the 1156-metre volcano that dominates the interior of the island. The north side of the island has two exclusive resorts, Rawlins Plantation, in the hills east of St Paul's, and the Golden Lemon, on the coast at Dieppe Bay. **Dieppe Bay Town** is a seaside fishing village with the requisite stone mill but not much else of note.

At the south end of Sadlers, you'll spot an old stone church down in the cane fields and just beyond that a sign points to **Black Rocks**. A short drive down that side road ends at coastal cliffs and a view of some seaside lava rock formations. If the road proves too rough to drive on, the cliffs are only a five-minute walk from the circle-island road.

As the circle-island road continues south along the east coast, it passes more small towns, old sugar mills peeking above the cane fields and some stone churches, though there are no particular sights to stop for along the way. The villages on this side of the island are small and tidy. One of them, **Ottley's**, has a rather exclusive plantation estate.

**Places to Stay** *Rawlins Plantation* (☎ 465-6221; fax 465-4954; in the USA ☎ (800) 346-5358, in the UK ☎ (071) 730-7144), PO Box 340, a mile (1.6 km) inland from St Paul's, is a former sugar estate that nicely incorporates the historic plantation buildings. One of the stone mills has been turned into a romantic honeymoon suite, while other accommodation is in comfortable cottages with wooden floors, four-poster beds and large separate sitting rooms. There's a pool. Single/double rates for the 10 rooms, which include breakfast, afternoon tea and dinner, are US$165/235 in summer, US$250/375 in winter. Credit cards are not accepted.

The *Golden Lemon* (☎ 465-7260; fax 465-4019; in the USA ☎ (800) 633-7411) is on a stony black-sand beach right in Dieppe Bay Town. A 17th-century plantation house is the centrepiece of the complex; however, most rooms are in a modern condo-like facility next door. Rooms are very comfortable and artistically decorated. Singles/doubles begin at US$175/260 in summer, US$225/350 in winter, including breakfast, afternoon tea and dinner.

*Ottley's Plantation Inn* (☎ 465-7234; fax 465-4760; in the USA ☎ (800) 772-3039), PO Box 345, is a graceful 18th-century plantation house inland from Ottley's village. There are 15 air-con rooms in the main building and surrounding cottages. All are comfortably furnished, each with ceiling fan and queen or king-size beds, and some with antiques. Summer/winter rates range from US$120/170 for a twin room in the 'great house' to US$185/275 for the two-room English cottage where Princess Margaret once stayed. It's US$20 less for single occupancy and US$50 per person more for breakfast and dinner. There's a pool, a nice colonial atmosphere and a daily shuttle to the beach and town. Children under the age of 10 are not allowed.

**Places to Eat** *Rawlins Plantation* (☎ 465-6221), with its splendid view across cane fields to St Eustatius, is the choice place to have lunch on a circle-island tour. The West Indian lunch buffet, served daily on the patio from 12.30 to 2 pm, includes many dishes, such as chicken and breadfruit curry, beef brochettes, flying fish fritters and fresh fruit sorbet. The cost is EC$54, credit cards are not accepted and reservations are preferred. Dinner, a set four-course meal costing EC$94, is available at 8 pm by reservation only. The plantation is a mile (1.6 km) up a signposted cane road that begins half a mile (800 metres) east of St Paul's.

The *Golden Lemon* in Dieppe Bay Town serves lunch until 3 pm, offering salads, sandwiches and fish & chips for around EC$25 and a few hot main dishes for a bit more. The dinner menu changes daily but commonly includes a chicken, fish or lamb dish complete with appetiser, soup and dessert for around EC$100.

*Ottley's Plantation Inn* has good food and pleasant al fresco dining within the partial stone walls of a former sugar warehouse. At lunch, the menu commonly features dishes such as flying fish or Jamaican jerk chicken for around EC$22, and lobster quesadillas for EC$50. The restaurant is a particularly good spot for dinner. The changing menu usually includes a chicken, fish and meat main dish for about EC$55 to EC$85.

# Nevis

Despite the recent opening of its first resort hotel, Nevis is still a sleepy little backwater. It's a friendly island with a delightfully rural character and some reasonably good beaches.

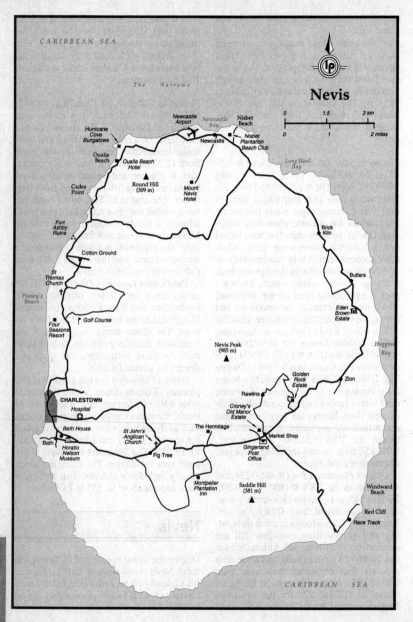

CARIBBEAN SEA

The Narrows

**Nevis**

0        1.5        3 km

0        1        2 miles

Newcastle
Airport

Newcastle
Bay

Nisbet
Beach

Hurricane
Cove
Bungalows

Newcastle

Nisbet
Plantation
Beach Club

Oualie
Beach

Oualie Beach
Hotel

Long Haul
Bay

Cades
Point

Round Hill
(309 m)

Mount
Nevis
Hotel

Brick
Kiln

Fort
Ashby
Ruins

Cotton Ground

Butlers

St Thomas
Church

Eden
Brown
Estate

Pinney's
Beach

Golf Course

Nevis Peak
(985 m)

Higgins
Bay

Four
Seasons
Resort

Golden
Rock
Estate

Zion

Rawlins

CHARLESTOWN

Hospital

Croney's
Old Manor
Estate

Bath House

St John's
Anglican
Church

The Hermitage

Market Shop

Bath

Horatio
Nelson
Museum

Fig Tree

Gingerland
Post
Office

Montpelier
Plantation
Inn

Saddle Hill
(381 m)

Windward
Beach

Red Cliff

Race Track

CARIBBEAN SEA

Sightseeing on Nevis is limited mainly to poking around the old stone churches and sugar plantation ruins scattered about the countryside. A good road circles the island and there are inexpensive car rentals, making it easy to explore Nevis on a day trip. The island has a forested interior rising to scenic Nevis Peak, which is often cloaked in clouds. The coastal lowlands, where the larger villages are located, are much drier and support bougainvillea, hibiscus and other flowering bushes that attract numerous hummingbirds.

While most visitors arrive on the St Kitts ferry for a one-day outing, Nevis has some interesting accommodation options for those seeking a quiet West Indian getaway.

## CHARLESTOWN

The ferry from St Kitts docks in Charlestown, the island's largest town and commercial centre. The town has a few buildings with gingerbread trim, some old stone structures and a centre that's marked by two tiny squares. Flanking one square is the tourist office, bank and taxi stand, while the second square, a block to the south, fronts the courthouse and library.

The greater Charlestown area can be readily explored on foot – the museums and the bath house are within walking distance. Just a 15-minute jaunt north of the centre will put you on a lovely stretch of Pinney's Beach that's lined with coconut trees and invites long strolls.

### Information

**Tourist Office** The Nevis Tourist Office (☎ 469-5521) is on Main St, a two-minute walk from the pier.

**Money** Barclays Bank on Main St will cash Barclays travellers' cheques free of commission and other travellers' cheques for an EC$2 commission.

**Post** The post office, on Main St, is open from 8 to 11 am on Thursday, 8 am to 3 pm other weekdays and 8 am to noon and 1 to 3 pm on Saturday. You can buy commemorative stamps at the Nevis Philatelic Bureau, which is near the public market and open from 8 am to 4 pm Monday to Friday.

**Telecommunications** You can make inter-

House with gingerbread trim

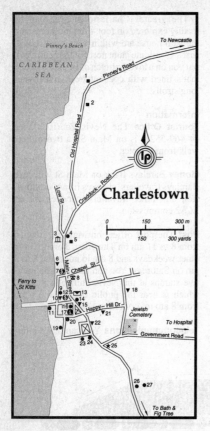

national phone calls and send faxes and telegrams from the Skantel office on Main St, which is open from 8 am to 5 pm on weekdays, to noon on Saturday.

**Laundry** There's a small laundrette next to Warner's market at the north end of town opposite the Museum of Nevis History.

### Museum of Nevis History

The Museum of Nevis History occupies a Georgian-style building at the site where American statesman Alexander Hamilton was born in 1757 (the original home was toppled by an earthquake in the mid-1800s). In addition to portraits of Hamilton, this pleasant little museum has period photos with interpretive captions and other bits and pieces of Nevis culture and history. It's open from 8 am to 4 pm Monday to Friday and from 10 am to noon on Saturday. Admission is free.

### Jewish Cemetery

A couple of minutes' walk up Government Rd from the town centre there's a small and largely forgotten Jewish cemetery, which consists of a grassy field of horizontal gravestones. The oldest stone dates from 1684 and quite a few others date from the early 1700s, when an estimated 25% of the non-slave population on Nevis were Jewish.

| PLACES TO STAY | | |
|---|---|---|
| 1 | Pinney's Beach Hotel | |
| 2 | Sea Spawn Guest House | |
| 5 | Lyndale Guest House | |

| PLACES TO EAT | | |
|---|---|---|
| 6 | Unella's | |
| 10 | Masy's Ice Cream | |
| 15 | Caribbean Confections | |
| 18 | Muriel's | |

| 21 | Nevis Bakery |
|---|---|
| 22 | Eddy's |

| OTHER | |
|---|---|
| 3 | Museum of Nevis History |
| 4 | Warner's Market & Laundrette |
| 7 | Scotiabank |
| 8 | Skantel (Telephone) Office |
| 9 | TDC Auto Rentals |

| 11 | Ferry Ticket Booth |
|---|---|
| 12 | Barclays Bank |
| 13 | Post Office |
| 14 | Customs |
| 16 | Handicraft Co-op |
| 17 | Tourist Office |
| 19 | Public Market |
| 20 | Philatelic Bureau |
| 23 | Library |
| 24 | Courthouse |
| 25 | Police Station |
| 26 | Super Foods |
| 27 | The Sand-Box Tree |

NEVIS

## Horatio Nelson Museum

The new Horatio Nelson Museum, on Building Hill Rd about 100 metres east of the old Bath House Hotel, contains memorabilia relating to Lord Nelson, who stopped off on this island in the 1780s, where he met and married Fanny Nisbett, the niece of the island's governor. This former private collection consists largely of mugs and dishes painted with Nelson's image, ceramic statues of the admiral and a few everyday items once used by Nelson. The museum is open from 9 am to 4 pm Monday to Friday and 10 am to 1 pm on Saturday. Admission is EC$5 for adults, EC$2 for children, EC$1 for senior citizens.

## Bath House

The Bath House, a 15-minute walk south of Charlestown centre, is a defunct hotel dating from 1778 that sits above thermal springs. Its mineral-laden waters, thought to have regenerative qualities, were the island's main attraction in colonial days, when wealthy visitors flocked here to soak in the baths. While its days of glory are long gone, the stone bath house just below the old hotel has reopened to the public and from 8 am to 4 pm you can soak in its shallow 42°C (108°F) waters for EC$5.

Some islanders skip the fees and simply bathe in the stream that runs below the bath house.

## Places to Stay

*Lyndale Guest House* (☎ 469-5412), PO Box 463, is behind Warner's market by the Museum of Nevis History. It has two rooms, each with two single beds, a ceiling fan and private bath. Kitchen facilities are available. Singles/doubles costs US$20/30. A dog with an intimidating bark greets guests, but he's usually tied up.

*Sea Spawn Guest House* (☎ 469-5239), Old Hospital Road, is a couple of minutes' walk from Pinney's Beach and a 10-minute walk from the Charlestown pier. This rather spartan 18-room guesthouse has small simple rooms, each with a private bathroom and portable fan. While the downstairs rooms are a bit dreary, the upstairs rooms are a tad bigger and brighter. There's a large common space that includes a TV room, kitchen and dining room. Rates are US$30/35 for singles/doubles downstairs and US$40 for the upstairs doubles.

The 55-room *Pinney's Beach Hotel* (☎ 469-5207), PO Box 61, is on the water at the south end of Pinney's Beach. The rooms, which have orange carpet and a standard motel ambience, are rather pricey for what you get. The cheapest, which cost US$60/75 for singles/doubles in summer and US$80/ 100 in winter, have one double and one single bed, air-con, phone, private bath and patio. Add about 20% more if you want a room with a TV.

## Places to Eat

If you're looking for breakfast, *Caribbean Confections* is the place to go after getting off the early-morning ferry from St Kitts. It has a quiet garden courtyard with white wrought-iron tables shaded by banana trees. Delicious warm ginger twists are EC$3, cinnamon and brown sugar crêpes are EC$9 and a full breakfast is double that. At lunchtime, sandwiches and burgers average EC$12. Dinner features soup-to-dessert meals ranging from a vegetarian platter for EC$32 to lamb curry for EC$53. It's open from 8 am to 3 pm and 5 to 11 pm Monday to Saturday.

*Eddy's*, run by a Canadian-West Indian couple, has a pleasant 2nd-floor verandah dining area that overlooks Main St. There's a homemade soup of the day for about EC$5, a flying fish sandwich or vegetarian burrito for EC$15 and conch fritters or stir fries for EC$20. It's open for lunch from noon to 3 pm and for dinner from 7.30 to 9.30 pm. There's a happy hour on Wednesday and the restaurant is closed on Thursday and Sunday.

There are three restaurants just north of the dock. For its waterfront view, *Unella's*, a 2nd-floor open-air restaurant, is the best choice, though the food is quite ordinary. You can get a burger for EC$6 and various hot meals for about EC$25.

For good local food without a view, there's *Muriel's*, an unpretentious little spot just

NEVIS

beyond Happy Hill Drive, at the back of the Lime Tree store. The menu includes chicken for EC$25, fish for EC$35 and lobster for EC$45, served with rice and peas, christophene and fried plantain. It's open for lunch and dinner except on Sunday.

*Nevis Bakery* on Happy Hill Drive has breads, pastries and good cinnamon rolls. *Masy's Ice Cream*, a hole-in-the-wall shop opposite the dock, has ice-cream cones from EC$2.

The best place to go for produce is the public market, which opens around 7 am daily except Sunday. There are a handful of small food markets in the town centre. Super Foods, which is about a five-minute walk south along Main St, is the island's biggest supermarket.

## SOUTH NEVIS

The circle-island road crosses the southern part of Nevis between Nevis Peak (985 metres) and Saddle Hill (381 metres), passing through the districts of Fig Tree and Gingerland. This area was the centre of Nevis' sugar industry in colonial days and there are many crumbling sugar mill stacks that evoke that era. A few of the former plantation estates have been converted into inns.

### St John's Anglican Church

St John's, on the main road in the village of Fig Tree, is a pretty stone church that dates from 1680. The register book from 11 March 1787 that records the marriage of Lord Horatio Nelson and Francis Nisbett is in a glass case at the rear of the church. If you peek beneath the red carpet in the centre aisle you'll find a continuous row of tombstones of island notables who died in the 1700s.

### Windward Beach

Windward Beach, also known as Indian Castle Beach, is the only easily accessible beach on the southern part of the island. Backed by beach morning glory and low scrubby trees, the beach has fine grey sand and fairly active surf. Unless it's a weekend, the odds are good that, with the exception of

a few rummaging goats, you'll have the beach to yourself.

To get there, turn south at the Gingerland Post Office in Market Shop and continue straight ahead for two miles (3.2 km). (Be aware of humps and dips in the road; just south of the church there's an especially bad dip that's not visible until you're on top of it.) Then turn left and follow the ribbon road for another 0.75 miles (1.2 km). After passing the race track (horse races on Sunday), the road turns to dirt and becomes somewhat rough but it should be passable unless it's been raining heavily. There are no facilities at the beach but you can get snacks and cold drinks at the Midway Bar & Grocery in the centre of Market Shop.

### Places to Stay

The following four plantation inns are all on the grounds of former sugar estates. All are within three miles (4.8 km) of each other and none is more than a few minutes' drive from the circle-island road. All four inns have meal plans available for about US$30 to US$50 more per person. A cooperative programme allows guests at any one inn to use the facilities of the others.

*The Hermitage* (☎ 469-3477; fax 469-2481), St John's Parish, about a mile (1.6 km) north-east of Fig Tree, is a quiet 11-room inn run by an American couple. The main plantation house, which is 250 years old and furnished with antiques, serves as a parlour and evening gathering spot. Accommodation is in one and two-storey cottages spread around the grounds. The cottages are pleasantly rustic with four-poster bed, hardwood floor, sitting room, ceiling fan, mini-refrigerator and lattice-shuttered windows. There's a pool and tennis court. Prices range from US$100 to US$180 in summer, US$195 to US$295 in winter; the higher priced cottages contain kitchens.

*Montpelier Plantation Inn* (☎ 469-3462; fax 469-2932), PO Box 474, 1.5 miles (2.4 km) south-east of Fig Tree, is an exclusive 16-room cottage-style English inn. The estate was the site of Horatio Nelson's marriage in 1787 and the inn retains a very proper British air – the recent guest list includes Princess Di. It has pleasant gardens, a beach shuttle and the island's nicest pool, which is scenically set next to the ruins of an old sugar mill. Singles/doubles cost from US$90/120 in summer, US$165/220 in winter, breakfast included. Credit cards are not accepted.

*Croney's Old Manor Estate* (☎ 469-3445; fax 469-3388; in the USA ☎ (800) 892-7093), PO Box 70, at the north side of Market Shop, is a relaxed inn run by an American family. The grounds are scattered with the remains of an 18th-century sugar plantation, including a mill stack, a nearly intact boiler and the huge steel rollers that until 1936 were used to crush the plantation's cane. The inn's 15 rooms, which occupy some of the estate's renovated buildings, are very large, cooled by ceiling fans and have either a king-size or two queen-size beds; some also have large separate sitting rooms. Singles/doubles cost US$85/115 in summer, US$130/175 in winter; there's a three-day minimum stay. There's a complimentary beach and town shuttle.

The 15-room *Golden Rock Estate* (☎ 469-3346; fax 469-2113), PO Box 493, is a casual family-run inn in the countryside between Market Shop and Zion. The main stone-block plantation house, circa 1815, has a bar, library and sitting room. Most accommodation is in cottages with four-poster beds and there's also an atmospheric stone sugar mill that's been converted into a two-bedroom, two-bathroom suite. There's a pool, tennis court, nature trails and a complimentary shuttle to the beach. Singles/doubles cost US$85/100 in summer, US$165/175 in winter, plus US$25 more for the sugar mill suite.

### Places to Eat

*The Hermitage* (☎ 469-3477) has pleasant, if pricey, open-air dining. Lunch selections include sandwiches, rotis and salads from EC$22 to EC$40. There's also a complete breakfast for EC$33 and a good four-course set dinner available by reservation from 8 pm for EC$108. A good night for dinner is Wednesday (during the winter season), when there's a string band and a hearty West Indian buffet for the fixed dinner price.

*Golden Rock Estate* (☎ 469-3346) makes a nice lunch stop (noon to 2.30 pm) offering outdoor dining on a cobblestone patio with a distant sea view. Lobster salad for EC$40 is a speciality and there are sandwiches from EC$10 and grilled fish for EC$29. There's also an afternoon tea, at which time you might see the green vervet monkeys, which come down from the hills in the morning, making their way back up the slopes. At dinner, which is a set meal for EC$81, reservations are preferred.

The *Cooperage Restaurant* (☎ 469-3445) at Croley's Old Manor Estate occupies the estate's old cooperage and serves good, moderately priced food. At dinner, from 7 to 9.30 pm, there's a wide range of main dishes including Jamaican jerk chicken or pork for EC$29 and grilled fresh fish or filet mignon for EC$46; soup or salad costs EC$8. Reservations are suggested. The restaurant is also open for breakfast (EC$25), but not for lunch.

### EAST NEVIS

As you continue around the circle-island road up the east coast, the villages become smaller and houses fewer. The area's main sight is the **Eden Brown Estate** on the inland side of the main road just south of Mannings. The estate house, built around 1740, has an interesting history.

On the eve of Julia Huggins' wedding in 1822, her groom and the best man got into a drunken duel and killed each other. After that Julia became a recluse in this house which she had inherited from her father. Following her death, the house was abandoned and has since been believed by islanders to be haunted by Julia's ghost. There are extensive stone ruins of the old plantation, including the remains of a mill behind the house. The estate, now owned by the government, is marked by a sign and free to explore.

### NEWCASTLE

Newcastle, at the north end of the island, has

Nevis' airport, a handful of places to stay and eat and a roadside pottery shop where traditional coal pots are made and sold.

Newcastle's biggest attractions are its beaches. The fine strand of white sand fronting the Nisbet Plantation Beach Club is Nevis' best. To get there follow the road that runs along the east side of the hotel down to the shore, where there's beachside parking. There's also a nice sandy stretch along Newcastle Bay, where there's a restaurant and a couple of water sports shops.

### Places to Stay

*Yamseed Inn* (☎ 469-9361) is a contemporary Mediterranean-style home on the north side of the airport. Owner Sybil Siegfried rents four comfortable airy rooms, each with private bath, ceiling fan, screened louvred windows and either a queen-size bed or two extra-long twin beds that can be converted into a king-size bed. It's on a small private beach with good swimming and a scenic view across the channel to St Kitts. Rooms cost US$75 in summer, US$100 in winter, including a full breakfast of fresh fruit, homemade granola, banana pancakes and other such goodies. There's a three-night minimum, and in winter it's best to book well in advance.

*Castle Bay Villas* (☎ 469-9490) is a small condominium development on the south side of the main road, opposite the airport. Two-bedroom, two-bath apartments rent for US$95/125 in summer/winter for one or two people, plus US$25 for each additional person aged 12 and over.

The *Mount Nevis Hotel* (☎ 469-9373; fax 469-9375; in the USA and Canada ☎ (800) 75-NEVIS), PO Box 494, a few minutes' drive inland past Cla-Cha-Del restaurant in Newcastle, is a new upmarket hotel on the slopes of Mt Nevis. The modern 32 rooms, which are in contemporary two-storey buildings, have full amenities, including cable TV, VCR, phone, ceiling fan, air-con, refrigerator and terrace. There's a fine view of St Kitts from the pool and from many of the rooms. The hotel has a complimentary beach shuttle. Double rooms cost US$120/170 in summer/ winter, while studios with cooking facilities cost US$150/210. There's no charge for children under 12.

*Nisbet Plantation Beach Club* (☎ 469-9325; fax 469-9864; in the USA ☎ (800) 344-2049) is a contemporary beach resort on the site of a former plantation. It's a pleasant place with cottages spread across an expansive lawn that fronts a white-sand beach. There are tennis courts, a beachside pool, a restaurant and a beach bar. The cheapest rooms, which cost US$190 for doubles in summer, US$315 in winter, are comfortable with wicker furnishings and tiled floors, two single beds, a screened porch, ceiling fan, phone and minibar. Larger rooms are US$50 to US$100 more. Rates include breakfast, afternoon tea and dinner.

### Places to Eat

*Cla-Cha-Del* (☎ 469-9640), run by a Nevisian family, has a view of St Kitts and a good reputation for local food. Fish or spareribs cost about EC$25, lobster EC$40, and include rice and peas, tannia (taro root) fritters and eggplant casserole. The restaurant is a minute's drive up the inland road that's just west of the Newcastle police station. It's open from 9 am to 4 pm and 6 pm until late, except Sunday, when it's open for dinner only, and Monday, when it's closed.

The *Mount Nevis Beach Club Restaurant* has al fresco dining on the beach at Newcastle Bay and good pizza, pastas and sandwiches at moderate prices. It's closed on Wednesday.

*Mount Nevis Hotel* has a chef who hails from New York, a great view and some of the best food on the island. The changing menu features West Indian and continental cuisine. At dinner, à la carte seafood and meat main dishes range from EC$35 to EC$70, while at breakfast and lunch there are simpler, moderately priced offerings.

The *Nisbet Plantation Beach Club* has a beachside café serving burgers, rotis and sandwiches for around EC$25, chef's or seafood salad for a couple of dollars more, and boiled lobster on a bed of ginger rice for EC$40. At dinner there's formal dining in the hotel's Great House (reservations required; ☎ 469-9325), which has an international menu priced around EC$150.

## OUALIE BEACH

Oualie Beach is a long, thin strip of grey sand fronted by waters that are shallow and generally calm. There are a couple of nice places to stay and a dive shop next to Oualie Beach Hotel.

### Places to Stay

*Oualie Beach Hotel* (☎ 469-9735; fax 469-9176; in the USA ☎ (800) 682-5431) is a pleasant little place right on the beach, with a dozen rooms split between duplex cottages and a two-storey building. The rooms are comfortable with two double beds, tiled floor, phone, ceiling fan, refrigerator and screened ocean-view patio. Singles/doubles cost US$70/90 in summer, US$110/130 in winter. A studio with a kitchen costs about US$35 more.

*Hurricane Cove Bungalows* (☎ & fax 469-9462) has a clifftop location at the north end of Oualie Beach and a nice view of St Kitts. Accommodation is in pleasantly rustic wooden cottages, each with a kitchen, porch and ceiling fans. The one-bedroom cottages have a queen-size bed and cost US$75/125 in summer/winter. The two-bedroom cottages have a queen-size bed and two twin beds and cost US$165/235 with a private pool, US$40 less without a pool. In spring and late autumn there's a mid-range rate, and in winter a minimum three-day stay is required.

### Places to Eat

*Oualie's Beach Hotel* has an open-air screened beachside restaurant with standard breakfast offerings and lunchtime sandwiches and burgers at moderate prices. At dinner there are dishes such as Creole dolphin or shrimp for EC$32, and lobster for EC$40. The restaurant also makes a pretty good thin-crust pizza and occasionally has beach barbecues and live music.

## PINNEY'S BEACH

Pinney's Beach is a long stretch of soft grey sand that runs along the west coast clear down to the north side of Charlestown. The beach, which is backed almost its entire length by tall coconut palms, has lovely views of St Kitts across the channel.

The site of **Fort Ashby**, which was built around 1702, is on the beach just north of Cotton Ground. It's the last of eight small fortifications that once extended along the coast north of Charlestown, but not much remains other than a few cannons and some partially reconstructed walls that now enclose a local restaurant and bar. This area was also the site of Jamestown, the island's original settlement, which was washed into the sea by an earthquake and tidal wave in 1680.

### Places to Stay & Eat

*Four Seasons Resort* (☎ 469-1111; fax 469-1112; in the USA ☎ (800) 332-3442, in Canada ☎ (800) 268-6282), PO Box 565, is on a nice stretch of Pinney's Beach. It has an 18-hole championship golf course, 10 tennis courts, a pool and various water sports. The posh 196 rooms have tiled floor, marble bathroom, terrace, ceiling fan, air-con, phone, TV and VCR. Rates are US$250 in summer and US$450 in winter for a golf course view, and US$50 more for an ocean-front room.

There are a couple of expensive restaurants at Four Seasons Resort and a few small local restaurants scattered along the coast. The *Fort Ashby Restaurant* at the old fort site serves moderately priced fish, curried lamb and barbecued chicken from 11 am to 2.30 pm Monday to Saturday.

See also Pinney's Beach Hotel under Places to Stay in the Charlestown section.

## GETTING THERE & AWAY
### Air

LIAT has 6 am, 12.30 and 5.20 pm flights daily from St Kitts to Nevis and a few daily flights from Antigua. For more information, see Getting There & Away at the beginning of this chapter.

**Airport Information** Nevis' airport, in Newcastle, is a very small operation with Winair, LIAT and a couple of charter desks.

***To/From the Airport*** Taxis meet scheduled flights. From Newcastle Airport, taxis cost EC$17 within the Newcastle area, EC$20 to Oualie Beach, EC$30 to Charlestown and EC$40 to Gingerland.

### Boat

Information on ferries between St Kitts and Nevis is in the Getting Around section at the beginning of this chapter.

### GETTING AROUND
### Bus

Buses are privately owned minivans. Those going up the west coast leave from the square in front of the tourist office in Main St. Some west-coast buses go only as far as Cotton Ground, others go to Newcastle and a few continue on to Butlers. Buses going east to Gingerland and Zion leave from the courthouse square. Note that there's rarely a bus between Butlers and Zion, and thus no circle-island bus route. Also, service is sketchy and it's risky relying on buses if you're trying to see Nevis on a day tour. Generally, buses don't leave Charlestown until they have a full load, which might be as often as every 15 minutes in the morning and late afternoon, or as infrequently as every hour or two during the middle part of the day. On Sunday there's virtually no service. The one-way fare to the farthest point is EC$3.

### Taxi

Taxis congregate by the pier and charge about EC$120 for a three-hour sightseeing tour. One-way taxi rates from Charlestown centre are EC$10 to Bath or Pinney's Beach, EC$23 to Oualie Beach and EC$36 to Newcastle.

### Car

There are no petrol stations on the east side between Fig Tree and Newcastle, so make sure you have sufficient petrol before heading off to explore the island.

**Rental** Parry's Car Rental (☎ 469-5917) is a friendly, locally owned operation. If you arrive by ferry, Parry will meet you at the harbour (give him a few minutes) and when returning the car you simply park it near the dock with the keys in the ignition. Rates begin at US$33, though for a few dollars more you can get a newer car with air-con and stereo.

TDC Auto Rentals (☎ 469-5690 on Nevis, 465-2991 on St Kitts) has an office opposite the Charlestown ferry dock. Rates are US$30 for a moke or a small manual-transmission car and US$40 for a jeep. If you rent for a minimum of three days their exchange programme allows use of vehicles on both St Kitts and Nevis with just one reservation and no extra costs.

In the Newcastle area, there's Nisbett Rentals (☎ 469-1913) and Skeete's Car Rental (☎ 469-4958), both of which rent cars and jeeps for about US$35. In the Fig Tree area, Avis (☎ 469-5604) has cars priced from US$30.

Most places charge about US$8 a day more if you want the collision damage waiver.

# St Lucia

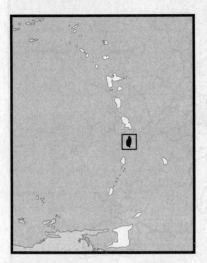

St Lucia is a high green island with a mountainous interior and a coastline pocketed with secluded coves and beaches. Its most dramatic scenery is in the south, where the twin peaks of the Pitons rise sharply from the shoreline to form one of the region's most distinctive landmarks.

In recent years, St Lucia has seen a spurt of new resort development and is fast becoming a trendy packaged tourism destination. Most hotels and visitor facilities are on the north-west coast, along the road that runs north from the capital city of Castries.

Still, the island is far from overdeveloped. Once you go south beyond Castries, St Lucia is markedly rural in nature, a mix of small fishing villages, sprawling banana plantations and untamed jungle. The interior rainforest is home to tall hardwood trees, climbing vines, tree ferns and one of the last remaining species of parrots in the Eastern Caribbean. See the aside in the Flora & Fauna section for more details.

## ORIENTATION

St Lucia has two airports: international flights land at Hewanorra, at the southern end of the island, while most inter-island flights land at the more conveniently located Vigie Airport near Castries, the capital.

# Facts about the Island

### HISTORY

Archaeological finds on the island indicate that St Lucia was settled by Arawaks between 1000 and 500 BC. Around 800 AD migrating Caribs conquered the Arawaks and established permanent settlements.

St Lucia was outside the routes taken by Columbus during his four visits to the New World and was probably first sighted by Spanish explorers during the early 1500s. The first attempt at European colonisation wasn't made until 1605, when a party of English settlers was quickly routed off the island by unreceptive Caribs. A second attempt by about 400 British colonists from St Kitts was made in 1638, but the settlement was abandoned within two years after most of the settlers were killed in Carib attacks.

After the British left, the French laid claim to the island and attempted to reach an agreement with the Caribs. The French established the island's first town, Soufrière, in 1746 and went about developing plantations. St Lucia's colonial history was marred by warfare, however, as the British still maintained their claim to the island.

In 1778 the British successfully invaded St Lucia and established naval bases at Gros Islet and Pigeon Island, which they used for attacks on the French islands to the north. For the next few decades St Lucia seesawed between the British and the French. In 1814 the Treaty of Paris finally ceded the island to the British, ending 150 years of conflict

St Lucia

0   2.5   5 km
0   1.5   3 miles

during which St Lucia changed flags 14 times.

Culturally the British were slow in replacing French customs and it wasn't until 1842 that English nudged out French as St Lucia's official language. Other customs linger, and to this day the majority of people speak a French-based patois among themselves, attend Catholic church services and live in villages with French names.

St Lucia gained internal autonomy in 1967 and full independence, as a member of the Commonwealth, on 22 February 1979.

## GEOGRAPHY

St Lucia is teardrop shaped, roughly 43 km in length and 23 km in width, with a land area of 616 sq km. The interior is largely mountainous, reaching its highest point at the 950-metre Mt Gimie in the south-west. Deep valleys, many of which are planted with bananas and coconuts, reach down from the mountains.

The Soufrière area has the island's best known geological features: the twin volcanic cones of the Pitons, which rise up from the shoreline (the Petit Piton at 750 metres and the Gros Piton at 798 metres), and the hot bubbling Sulphur Springs just inland from the town. Despite this little show of geological activity, there hasn't been a volcanic eruption on the island since 1766.

## CLIMATE

In January the average daily high temperature in Castries is 27°C (81°F) while the low averages 20°C (68°F). In July the average daily high is 29°C (85°F) while the low averages 22°C (72°F).

Annual rainfall ranges from 150 cm on the coast to 345 cm in the mountains. In Castries, measurable rain falls an average of 11 days a month from January to March, the driest months. The rainiest months, June to December, have an average of 18 days of rain. Humidity ranges from 76% in February to 83% in November.

## FLORA & FAUNA

St Lucia's vegetation ranges from dry and scrubby areas of cacti and hibiscus to lush jungly valleys with wild orchids, bromeliads, heliconia and lianas.

Under the British colonial administration much of St Lucia's rainforest was targeted for timber harvesting. In many ways the new St Lucian government has proved a far more effective environmental force and while only about 10% of the island remains covered in rainforest, most of it has recently been set aside as a nature reserve. The largest indigenous trees in the rainforest are the gommier, a towering gum tree, and the chatagnier, a huge buttress-trunked tree.

Island fauna includes the St Lucia parrot, St Lucian oriole, purple-throated Carib hummingbird, bats, lizards, iguana, tree frogs, introduced mongoose, the rabbit-like agouti and several snake species, including the venomous fer-de-lance and the boa constrictor.

---

**St Lucia Parrot**

The rainforest is home to the St Lucia parrot, *(Amazona versicolor)*, locally called the jacquot, the island's colourful endemic parrot. Despite the jacquot's status as the national bird and its appearance on everything from T-shirts to St Lucian passports, it has teetered on the brink of extinction in recent times.

However, a successful effort to educate islanders on the plight of the parrot and new environmental laws seem to be working to save the parrots, which occasionally made it onto island dinner tables in times past. Fines for shooting or capturing parrots have been increased a hundredfold while much of the parrots' habitat has been set aside for protection. The efforts have resulted in an increase in the population from about 100 birds in the late 1970s to around 300 today. Most of the birds are in the adjacent Edmond and Quilesse forest reserves, east of Soufrière. ∎

It's illegal to damage, collect, buy or sell any type of coral on St Lucia and nothing should be removed from any of the island's many marine reserves.

Tree frog

## GOVERNMENT

St Lucia is an independent state within the Commonwealth, with the British monarchy represented by an appointed Governor-General. The bicameral parliament has an 11-member Senate appointed by the Governor-General and a more powerful 17-member House elected by universal suffrage for five-year terms. The prime minister, a member of the majority party of the House, is the effective head of state.

## ECONOMY

Agriculture still accounts for nearly one-third of St Lucia's employment and gross national product (GNP). The leading export crop is bananas, followed by coconuts and cocoa. Tourism, which has been booming in recent years with the construction of new hotels and resorts, represents the fastest growing segment of the economy and either directly or indirectly accounts for about 15% of the labour force.

Some of the more upmarket resort projects are taking place in undeveloped and environmentally sensitive niches of the island, and consequently they have become quite controversial. One of the newest resorts, the exclusive Jalousie Plantation, was built smack between the twin Pitons, which have always stood as the very symbol of the island's unspoiled natural character. Prior to the construction, many islanders had hoped the land would be set aside for a new national park, a hope that had been spurred on by the discovery of Amerindian artefacts at the site.

## POPULATION & PEOPLE

The population is 157,000, one-third of whom live in Castries. Approximately 85% of all islanders are of pure African ancestry. Another 10% are an admixture of African, British, French and East Indian ancestry, while about 4% are of pure East Indian or European descent.

## ARTS & CULTURE

St Lucia has a mix of English, French, African and Caribbean cultural influences. They manifest themselves in many ways. If you walk into the Catholic cathedral in Castries, you'll find a building of French design, an interior richly painted in bright African-inspired colours, portraits of a Black Madonna and child, and church services delivered in English.

Derek Walcott, the renowned Caribbean poet and playwright, and winner of the 1992 Nobel Prize for Literature, is a native of St Lucia. Walcott, who teaches at Boston University, still maintains his connections with the island and is spearheading a movement to renovate the buildings on Rat Island, a former quarantine station off Choc Beach, and turn it into a retreat for writers and artists.

St Lucia's scenic landscape has been the backdrop for several foreign films, including the British movies *Water* (1985), with Michael Caine, and *Firepower* (1979), with Sophia Loren, and Hollywood's *Doctor Dolittle* and *Superman II*.

## RELIGION

About 85% of St Lucians are Roman Catholic. Anglican, Baptist, Christian Science, Methodist, Pentecostal and Seventh Day Adventist denominations are also represented on the island.

## LANGUAGE

The official language is English. When chatting among themselves islanders commonly speak a French-based patois that's spiced with African and English words.

# Facts for the Visitor

## VISAS & EMBASSIES

Citizens of the USA and Canada can enter St Lucia with proof of citizenship, such as an official birth certificate, and a photo ID, such as a driving licence. French citizens can enter with a national identity card. Citizens of the UK, Australia and most other countries must be in possession of a valid passport. For all foreign visitors, stays of over 28 days generally require a visa.

An onward or return ticket or proof of sufficient funds is officially required.

### Consulates in St Lucia

The British High Commission (☎ 452-2484) is at 24 Micoud St in Castries. Also in St Lucia are embassies or consulates for France (☎ 452-2462), Denmark (☎ 452-5332), Germany (☎ 452-2511), Italy (☎ 452-6319), the Netherlands (☎ 452-2811), Taiwan (☎ 452-0643) and Venezuela (☎ 452-4833).

## MONEY

The Eastern Caribbean dollar (EC$) is the island currency. One US dollar equals EC$2.70. US dollar travellers' cheques are the most convenient foreign currency to carry, but Canadian dollar and UK sterling cheques can also be changed without difficulty. Other currencies are more problematic – many banks, including Barclays, commonly tag on a US$30 fee per transaction to exchange French francs and US$20 to exchange Australian dollars, Dutch guilders or German marks.

The Royal Bank of Canada will cash US, UK and Canadian travellers' cheques for free if the transaction is under EC$200 or over EC$2500; otherwise, there's an EC$5 fee.

With prodding, Barclays will generally cash Barclays (Visa) travellers' cheques in US, Canadian and UK currencies free of the EC$2 service charge it normally tags on for transactions under EC$500 (there's no service charge on larger transactions). In addition, all banks charge a EC$0.25 government stamp fee per cheque.

Visa, MasterCard and American Express are the most commonly accepted credit cards and can be used for car rentals and at most mid-range and top-end restaurants and hotels.

An 8% tax and a 10% service charge are added onto the bill at all but the cheapest hotels and restaurants; there's no need for additional tipping.

## TOURIST OFFICES

The St Lucia Tourist Board has an office opposite the port police office on Jeremie St in Castries and booths at the two airports and the cruise ship dock in Pointe Seraphine.

When requesting information by mail, write to: St Lucia Tourist Board (☎ 452-4094), PO Box 221, Castries, St Lucia, West Indies.

## Overseas Reps

The St Lucia Tourist Board has the following overseas offices:

**Canada**
151 Bloor St West, Suite 425, Toronto, Ontario M5S 1S4 (☎ (416) 961-5608)
**France**
ANI, 53 Rue François 1er, 7th floor, Paris 75008 (☎ 47 20 39 66)
**Germany**
Postfach 2304, 6380 Bad Homburg 1 (☎ (06172) 30 44 31)
**UK**
10 Kensington Court, London W8 5DL (☎ (01) 937-1969)

**ST LUCIA**

**USA**
820 2nd Ave, 9th floor, New York, NY 10017
(☎ (212) 867-2950, ☎ (800) 456-3984)

## USEFUL ORGANISATIONS
The St Lucia National Trust (☎ 452-5005),
PO Box 525, Castries, can arrange tours to
the island's nature reserves, including the
Maria Island Nature Reserve, off the south-
east coast, and the Frigate Islands Nature
Reserve, off the east coast.

## BUSINESS HOURS
Government and business hours are generally from 8.30 am to 12.30 pm and 1.30 to
4.30 pm Monday to Friday. Many stores are
also open on Saturday mornings from 8 am
to noon. Bank hours are usually from 8.30 or
9 am to 3 pm on Monday to Thursday, and
to 5 pm on Friday. A few bank branches,
particularly in resort areas, are open on Saturday mornings as well.

## HOLIDAYS
St Lucia has the following public holidays:

| | | |
|---|---|---|
| New Year's Day | – | 1 January |
| New Year's Holiday | – | 2 January |
| Independence Day | – | 22 February |
| Good Friday | – | late March/early April |
| Easter Monday | – | late March/early April |
| Labour Day | – | 1 May |
| Whit Monday | – | eighth Monday after Easter |
| Corpus Christi | – | ninth Thursday after Easter |
| Emancipation Day | – | 3 August |
| Thanksgiving Day | – | 5 October |
| National Day | – | 13 December |
| Christmas Day | – | 25 December |
| Boxing Day | – | 26 December |

## CULTURAL EVENTS
Carnival takes place on the two days before
Ash Wednesday, with calypso tents, costume
parades, music contests and the like.

The four-day St Lucian Jazz Festival takes
place in late May and features musicians
such as Wynton Marsalis and Herbie
Hancock.

The Atlantic Rally for Cruisers (ARC),
one of the largest transatlantic yacht races, is
held in December, starting in the Canary

Islands and ending at Rodney Bay Marina,
St Lucia's largest yacht port.

## POST
There are post offices in major towns and
villages around the island. The general post
office, on Bridge St in Castries, is open from
8.30 am to 4 pm Monday to Friday.

When addressing mail to the island, the
town name should be followed by 'St Lucia,
West Indies'.

## TELECOMMUNICATIONS
There are both card and coin phones around
the island. Phonecards are sold at tourist
office booths, Cable & Wireless offices and
the Rodney Bay Marina office.

You can send international faxes, telexes
and telegrams and make phone calls from the
Cable & Wireless office on Bridge St in
Castries. It's open from 7 am to 7 pm
Monday to Friday, 7 am to 2.30 pm on Sat-
urday.

For local calls, dial all seven numbers.
When calling St Lucia from overseas, add
the area code 809. For more information on
phonecards and on making long-distance
calls see Telecommunications in the introductory Facts for the Visitor chapter.

## ELECTRICITY
Electricity is 220/240 volts AC, 50 cycles.
Most hotels have adaptor outlets in the bathrooms that allow 110-voltage shavers to be
used.

## WEIGHTS & MEASURES
St Lucia follows the imperial system: distances and car odometers are measured in
miles and survey maps note elevations in
feet.

## BOOKS & MAPS
Books are expensive on St Lucia. There's
commonly a good 30% mark-up over the list
price and selections are not very extensive.

In central Castries you'll find a modest
Caribbean section at the Book Salon, at the
corner of Laborie and Jeremie streets. North
of town, Sunshine Bookstore at the Gable-

woods Mall sells books on the Caribbean as well as US newspapers. Pieces of Eight at the Rodney Bay Marina has a small but select collection of books and sells Sunday newspapers from the UK.

The best island map is the 1:50,000 Ordnance Survey map of St Lucia, which can be obtained from the Department of Lands & Survey in Castries. A reduced black & white print of the map can be found in the *Tropical Traveller* (see below).

## MEDIA

St Lucia has three newspapers: the *Voice*, which is published three times a week, and the *Crusader* and the *Star*, both weeklies that hit the newsstand on Saturday. In addition there's a useful monthly tourist newspaper, the *Tropical Traveller*, that's loaded with general promotional articles, ads and visitor information. *Visions of St Lucia*, a 100-page glossy magazine published by the St Lucia Hotel and Tourism Association, has a similar format with the addition of detailed hotel and dining listings. Pick up both publications for free at the tourist office or in hotel lobbies.

Numerous radio stations, both in English and French, can be received on the island; 98.1 FM plays a lot of reggae. Cable TV has 19 channels with a combination of local, European and US programming.

## HEALTH

The island's two largest hospitals, Victoria Hospital (☎ 452-2421) in Castries and St Jude's Hospital (☎ 454-6041) in Vieux Fort, both have 24-hour emergency service. For more serious medical conditions people often obtain medical evacuation to Barbados or Miami.

Bilharzia (schistosomiasis) is endemic to St Lucia; the general precaution is to avoid wading or swimming in freshwater. St Lucia also has the fer-de-lance snake, a poisonous pit viper. More information on both the fer-de-lance and bilharzia is under Health in the introductory Facts for the Visitor section.

## DANGERS & ANNOYANCES

Around the Soufrière area, people wanting

to serve as your guide can be a bit of a nuisance; if you don't want a guide, just decline the offer firmly but politely.

If you get into the local partying scene, such as the Friday night 'jump-up' at Gros Islet, be cautious not to flash a wad of money or wear expensive jewellery, as theft is not unknown.

Hikers should keep in mind that the poisonous fer-de-lance snake favours brushy undergrowth.

## EMERGENCIES

For medical, fire and police emergencies dial ☎ 999.

## ACTIVITIES

### Beaches & Swimming

All of St Lucia's beaches are public. On the touristed north-west side of the island there's a fine white-sand beach along the causeway linking Gros Islet and Pigeon Point and nice golden sands at Choc Beach, which stretches north from the Halcyon Beach Club, and at Reduit Beach, the resort strip south of Rodney Bay.

Along the south-west coast there are numerous coves and bays, many accessible by boat only, that offer good swimming and snorkelling.

The east side of the island is less protected, with rougher water conditions.

### Diving & Snorkelling

St Lucia's rugged mountain terrain continues beneath the sea as underwater mounts, caves and drop-offs. Most of the diving takes place on the western side of the island, with some of the top sites in the south-central area.

Anse Chastanet, near Soufrière, has been designated as a marine park and boasts spectacular nearshore reefs with a wide variety of corals, sponges and reef fish; it's excellent for both diving and snorkelling.

Another favoured dive just a bit farther south is the Key Hole Pinnacles, coral-encrusted underwater mounts that rise to within a few metres of the surface.

There are a couple of wreck dives, including *Lesleen*, a 50-metre freighter that was deliberately sunk in 1986 to create an artificial reef. It now sits upright in 20 metres of water near Anse Cochon, another popular dive area.

There's also good snorkelling and diving beneath both Petit Piton and Gros Piton, the coastal mountains that loom to the south of Soufrière. In the main resort area north of Castries, Pigeon Island offers fair snorkelling.

**Dive Shops** Scuba St Lucia (☎ 452-8009) at Anse Chastanet Hotel, PO Box 7000, Soufrière, is a well-regarded five-star PADI facility. It has an introductory scuba course for US$75, a two-dive outing that combines a morning beach dive and afternoon boat dive for US$85, snorkelling trips for US$45, open-water certification courses for US$350 and referral courses for US$200. Boat transport from Castries to Anse Chastanet is available.

Dolphin Divers (☎ 451-4357, extension 127) at Marigot Bay offers one-tank dives for US$55, two-tank dives for US$65, resort courses for US$65, PADI open-water certification for US$350 and snorkelling trips for US$25. Dolphin has a branch at Rodney Bay Marina.

Buddies Scuba (☎ 452-5288), another PADI facility, is based at the Vigie Marina in Castries and has daily dives to Anse Chastanet and Anse Cochon, charging US$65 for either a two-tank dive or a resort course.

### Windsurfing
Many of the large beachfront hotels, including the St Lucian Hotel at Reduit Beach and the Anse Chastanet Hotel near Soufrière, rent windsurfing equipment. The Vieux Fort area, at the southern tip of the island, is popular with experienced windsurfers.

### Hiking
There are several trails into the mountainous interior. Most popular are the guided rainforest walks through the Edmond and Quilesse forest reserves. The Forest & Lands Department (☎ 450-2231) and the main tour agencies arrange half-day walking tours in the rainforest several days a week.

### Horse Riding
Trim's National Riding (☎ 450-8273) offers horse riding along the beach for US$25, as well as horse-drawn carriage rides around Rodney Bay Marina, Gros Islet and Pigeon Island.

### Tennis & Squash
Most of the larger hotels have tennis courts. The St Lucia Yacht Club at Reduit Beach has squash courts open to visitors for a fee.

### Golf
The Cap Estate Golf Course (☎ 450-8523), on the northern tip of the island, has a nine-hole course that can be played as 18 holes, a pro shop and a clubhouse. For 18 holes, green fees are US$20, golf clubs can be

rented for US$10 and hand-pulled trolleys cost US$4.

## HIGHLIGHTS
In the north-west, Pigeon Island makes a fine outing that combines colonial-era ruins, hiking, swimming and a nice white-sand beach. Don't miss the Castries Market, one of the largest and most colourful in the Eastern Caribbean, and while you're in town take a look at the cathedral interior and stroll around Columbus Square. The Soufrière area has fine scenery, steaming sulphur vents, a botanical garden and good diving.

## ACCOMMODATION
St Lucia has a handful of good-value, moderately priced guesthouses. Although most have only five to 10 rooms, they generally don't fill up as the guesthouses rely on independent travellers and there simply aren't that many non-package or non-yachting tourists on the island.

There are some reasonably priced mid-range hotels offering good discounts during off-peak periods and more typical rates at other times.

St Lucia also has some good, albeit pricey, upper-end offerings and some all-inclusive resorts, including Club Med, near Hewanorra Airport; Rendezvous, near the Vigie Airport; Sandals, at La Toc Bay; and Club St Lucia, in Cap Estate.

## FOOD
Standard Western fare predominates at most hotels. In contrast, local restaurants generally feature West Indian and Creole dishes – and even if you're booked into an all-inclusive hotel it's worth slipping away for at least one good local meal. St Lucia has numerous restaurants in all price ranges, with the better ones invariably featuring fresh seafood.

One thing to note is that many restaurants, including some that enjoy fine sunset views, don't begin serving dinner until 7 pm, well after the winter sun has dropped. Many of the dining spots around Rodney Bay are an exception, which makes it a good area for sunset dining.

Piton beer label

## DRINKS
Water is generally safe to drink from the tap. The island's local beer, Piton, is a decent lager that's brewed in Vieux Fort. The locally distilled Lucian Rhum, like the beer, has a logo incorporating the island's twin Piton peaks.

## ENTERTAINMENT
There's a disco at the Halcyon Beach Club, with Monday being the big party night, when entrance costs EC$25, including one drink. The St Lucian Hotel also has a disco.

On Friday nights the streets in the town of Gros Islet are blocked off, women grill food on the corners, the rum shops spill out onto the pavement and live music and partying roll into the wee hours of the morning. This long-established 'jump-up', as the partying is called, is popular with both tourists and locals but there are safety concerns, so it's best to arrive and leave by taxi, stick to the main strip and be careful with valuables.

## THINGS TO BUY
In Castries, on Bridge St near its intersection with Jeremie St, you'll find sidewalk vendors selling T-shirts and handmade dolls. Caribelle Batik, opposite the Castries post office, sells quality, locally made, batik clothing, while the nearby Sea Island Cotton

Shop also has some nice lightweight cotton clothing, although most of it is made in India.

Pointe Seraphine, the main cruise ship dock, has a duty-free shopping complex with about 20 shops selling jewellery, watches, liquor, crystal, china and other imported goods. There are also a couple of clothing shops, including Bagshaws, which sells island-made silk-screened clothing. The complex is open from 8.30 am to 5 pm weekdays, to 1 pm on Saturday, and on Sunday if cruise ships are in port.

# Getting There & Away

## AIR

St Lucia has two airports: Hewanorra International Airport in Vieux Fort at the remote southern tip of the island and Vigie Airport in Castries, near the main tourist area.

International jet flights land at Hewanorra, which has a longer runway, while most flights from within the Caribbean land at Vigie. (LIAT flights land at Vigie only, except for one noon flight from St Vincent, which stops at Hewanorra on its way to and from Vigie.)

Because of Hewanorra's inconvenient location, international visitors might want to consider taking a flight that makes a change of planes on a nearby island, such as Barbados, allowing a transfer to a smaller regional aircraft that flies to Vigie Airport. Otherwise, visitors heading to Castries can book LIAT's 11.40 am daily Hewanorra-Vigie flight or try to get a seat on one of the occasional charter flights between Hewanorra and Vigie, which costs about US$35. For more information on travelling from Hewanorra Airport to other parts of the island, see Airport Information in this section.

## Airlines

Offices for the main airlines serving St Lucia are in central Castries. The LIAT office, on Columbus Square, is open from 8 am to 4 pm Monday to Friday, to noon on Saturday. LIAT handles Air Canada ticketing. The

BWIA office, also on Columbus Square, is open from 8 am to 12.30 pm and 1.30 to 4 pm Monday to Friday.

British Airways is above Scotiabank on William Peter Blvd and American Airlines is on Micoud St, a block east of the cathedral.

The following are the airline reservation numbers on St Lucia:

| | | |
|---|---|---|
| Air Canada | – | ☎ 452-3051 |
| Air Guadeloupe | – | ☎ 452-2216 |
| Air Martinique | – | ☎ 452-2463 |
| American Airlines | – | ☎ 452-1802 or |
| | | ☎ 454-6777 |
| British Airways | – | ☎ 452-3951 |
| BWIA | – | ☎ 452-3778 |
| Eagle Air Services | – | ☎ 452-1900 |
| Helenair | – | ☎ 452-7196 |
| LIAT | – | ☎ 452-3051; |
| | | ☎ 452-2348 after hours |

### To/From the USA

American Airlines flies to each of St Lucia's airports at least once daily from San Juan, with connections to its USA flights. With a two-week advance purchase requirement, midweek fares from New York to Vigie Airport cost US$470 in the high season (25 June to 12 September and 15 December to 14 April) and US$397 the rest of the year; the fare to Hewanorra Airport is US$31 less. From Miami, all fares are US$55 less than from New York.

BWIA flies to St Lucia four times weekly direct from Miami and daily from New York via Antigua or Barbados. Rates vary with the season but are comparable to those charged by American Airlines.

### To/From Canada

Air Canada flies to St Lucia from Toronto on Sunday. A return ticket with a minimum stay of seven days and a maximum stay of 21 days costs C$579.

### To/From the UK

British Airways flies from London's Gatwick Airport to St Lucia on Thursday, Saturday and Sunday and BWIA flies from Heathrow Airport on Wednesday, Thursday and Sunday. The fare with either airline is

UK£685 with a 21-day advance purchase requirement, a minimum stay of seven days and a maximum stay of six months.

### To/From Germany
BWIA flies to St Lucia direct from Frankfurt on Monday and via Antigua on Wednesday. The fare is DM3356 for an excursion ticket with a minimum stay of 14 days and a maximum stay of three months.

### To/From South America
LIAT has flights from St Lucia to Caracas on Tuesday and Friday. The one-way fare costs US$184 and a 21-day excursion ticket is US$276.

### Within the Caribbean
LIAT has direct flights to Vigie Airport, all routes at least twice daily, from Antigua, Barbados, Dominica, Grenada, Guadeloupe, Martinique, St Vincent and Trinidad, and connecting flights from the rest of LIAT's network.

LIAT's one-way fares to St Lucia are US$132 from Trinidad, US$129 from Tobago, US$78 from Barbados, US$111 from Grenada, US$81 from Martinique, US$83 from Dominica, US$114 from Guadeloupe, US$123 from Antigua, US$82 from St Vincent and US$200 from St Thomas in the US Virgin Islands. Most fares allow up to two intermediate stopovers; the St Thomas fare, however, is a long-distance (YD) fare which allows unlimited en route stopovers.

LIAT also has excursion return fares, good for either 21 or 30 days, between St Lucia and Grenada (US$173), Martinique (US$109), Dominica (US$150), Antigua (US$229) and Barbados (US$124).

Air Martinique has daily flights from Martinique to St Lucia for US$97 return. This ticket is valid for a year and requires a minimum stay of two days.

Air Guadeloupe flies a couple of times a week from Guadeloupe to St Lucia for 695F one way.

Eagle Air Services and Helenair provide charter services throughout the Caribbean.

Note that there's a 5% tax added on to tickets purchased in St Lucia.

### Airport Information
Both Vigie and Hewanorra airports have tourist information booths, taxi stands, card and coin phones and booths for Avis, Hertz, National and a few small local car rental agencies.

**To/From Hewanorra Airport** A taxi from Vieux Fort to Castries costs about EC$120 and takes about 1½ hours. Phone ☎ 454-6136 to call a cab. If you're travelling light and in no hurry, there are inexpensive local buses from Vieux Fort to Castries, (EC$6), but they are infrequent.

**To/From Vigie Airport** Taxi fares from Vigie Airport are EC$12 to Modern Inn or Halcyon Beach Club, EC$25 to Reduit Beach, EC$30 to Rodney Bay Marina, EC$15 to Castries centre and EC$50 to Marigot.

In part because of the pressure from the taxi union, minibuses avoid Vigie Airport, so the nearest bus stop is nearly two km away, at the northern end of the runway opposite Harbour Light Inn.

### SEA
### Yacht
Customs and immigration can be cleared at Rodney Bay, Castries, Marigot Bay or Vieux Fort. Most yachties pull in at Rodney Bay, where there's a full-service marina and two customs slips marked with yellow posts opposite the customs office.

It's also easy to clear in at Marigot, where you can anchor in the inner harbour and dinghy over to the customs office. Castries Harbour is a more congested scene and yachts entering the harbour are required to go directly to the customs dock; if there's no room, anchor east of the customs buoy. At Vieux Fort, you can anchor off the big ship dock, where customs is located.

Popular anchorages around the island include Reduit Beach, the area south-east of Pigeon Point, Rodney Bay Lagoon, Marigot

Bay, Anse Chastanet, Anse Cochon and Soufrière Bay.

Yacht charters are available from First Class Yachting (☎ 452-0367), Sunsail (☎ 452-8648), Trade Wind (☎ 452-8424) and Via Carib Yacht Charters (☎ 452-9490), all at Rodney Bay Marina, and from The Moorings (☎ 453-4357) at Marigot Bay. For addresses and booking information see Yacht Charters in the introductory Getting Around chapter.

### Cruise Ship
Cruise ships dock in Castries. There are a number of berths, some on the east side of the harbour near the town centre and others at Pointe Seraphine on the north side of the harbour, where there's a duty-free shopping complex.

Wednesday and Friday are the big days for cruise ships, when three or four liners are usually docked in the harbour.

### LEAVING ST LUCIA
Air passengers leaving St Lucia must pay an EC$27 departure tax. If you're flying on LIAT there's also a EC$10 security fee.

# Getting Around

### BUS
Bus service is via privately owned minivans. This is a safe, fun and cheap way to get around and the means by which most islanders get to town, school and work. Buses are frequent on main routes (such as Castries to Gros Islet or to Marigot) during the work day but drop off quickly after the evening rush hour, so that getting a bus after about 7 pm can be challenging. Very few buses run on Sunday.

If there's no bus stop nearby, you can wave buses down en route as long as there's space for the bus to pull over. Pay the fare directly to the driver.

Sample fares are Castries to Gros Islet EC$1.50, Halcyon Beach Club to Castries

centre EC$1, Castries to Marigot EC$2, Castries to Soufrière EC$5.

### TAXI
Taxis are plentiful at the airports (see Airport Information earlier in this chapter), in Castries and in the main resort areas. Always establish the fare with the driver before you get in, doubly so if you want to do anything 'unusual', like stopping to see a view.

From your guesthouse or hotel you can ask the receptionist to call a taxi; the rates are the same as waving one down and the odds of having to squabble over the fare are much lower. To call a taxi yourself dial ☎ 452-1599 in Castries, ☎ 454-6136 in Vieux Fort.

### CAR & MOTORBIKE
#### Road Rules
On St Lucia, drive on the left. An international driver's licence is valid on the island, but if you don't have one you'll need to purchase a local licence, which can be picked up from immigration at either airport and costs EC$30. If you don't get it upon arrival, most car rental companies will either issue you a licence or take you to a nearby police station to get one.

Around the island roads vary greatly, with some sections being newly surfaced and others deeply potholed. Make sure you have a workable jack and spare tyre. Be cautious driving around Castries where many of the roads are very narrow and lined with deep rain gutters. Many of the interior and southern roads are very winding and narrow. Speed limits are generally 15 m/h in towns and 30 m/h on major roads. There are petrol stations distributed around the island.

#### Rental
Renting a car on St Lucia can be a bit confusing. As those companies operating out of the two airports generally don't offer unlimited mileage, renters should consider the base price, the number of free daily miles allowed and just how far they expect to travel.

The cheapest cars, which tend to be little Daihatsu Cuores or Nissan Marches, rent for

US$46 daily from National (☎ 452-3050) with 60 free miles and US$0.40 for each additional mile; US$60 a day from Avis (☎ 452-2046), with 100 free miles and US$0.40 for each additional mile; and US$50 a day from Hertz (☎ 451-7351) with 60 free miles and US$0.35 for each additional mile. These three international companies have offices at both airports. Renters can often get better deals with the international companies by booking (and sometimes prepaying) in advance from their home country.

One local company offering good prices with unlimited mileage is CTL Rent A Car (☎ 452-0732; fax 452-0401), which operates out of Rodney Bay Marina. Rates are US$40 a day for a Suzuki Fronte, US$45 for a Suzuki Swift and US$50 for a Mitsubishi Lancer. CTL provides free hotel pick-up.

Car rental companies offer optional collision damage waiver (CDW) for about US$12 a day, which covers theft and collision damages to the car, but the renter is still responsible for the first US$300 in damages. If the CDW is not taken, the renter is usually responsible for the first US$1200 to US$2000 in damages.

**TOURS**
Sightseeing tours by taxi cost about US$15 to US$20 an hour. A taxi tour of the Soufrière area and back to Castries generally costs about US$100, with up to four passengers.

There are several local tour companies that offer a range of land tours of the island, boat tours around St Lucia and air tours of neighbouring islands. A rainforest walking tour costs about US$35, while a round-the-island tour that includes Marigot, Soufrière, the sulphur springs and a drive up the east coast costs about US$50, lunch included. Other tours take in estate homes and plantations that are otherwise inaccessible to individual travellers.

Some of the main tour companies include Sunlink International (☎ 452-8232) at Reduit Beach; St Lucia Reps (☎ 452-3762), at the corner of Brazil and Bourbon streets, Castries; and Pitons Travel Agency (☎ 452-

1227), 3 Mongiraud St, Castries. Most larger hotels arrange tours as well.

**Boat Tours**
Day-long sails down the coast from Rodney Bay to Soufrière are very popular, with a stop at Marigot Bay, a minivan tour of Sulphur Springs and Diamond Botanical Gardens, and snorkelling at Anse Cochon or Anse Chastanet on the return trip. The sailing time between Rodney Bay and Soufrière is about two hours each way, and the tours last from about 9 am to 5 pm.

Several companies offer these sails, which can be booked directly or through tour agencies or hotels. The cost is about US$65 including hotel pick-up and lunch.

From Rodney Bay you can make the trip on the 17-metre *Endless Summer* (☎ 450-8651) catamaran or the *Brig Unicorn* (☎ 452-8232), a 43-metre-long tall ship that's a replica of a 19th-century brig. You can also sail out of Vigie Marina, on the north side of Castries, on the catamaran *Surf Queen* (☎ 452-3762).

# Castries

Castries, the island's commercial centre and capital, is a bustling port city set on a large natural harbour. The liveliest part of the city is just south-east of the port, along Jeremie St, where the colourful Castries Market spills onto the streets with scores of sidewalk-produce sellers.

The city, which was founded by the French in the 18th century, was ravaged by fire three times between 1785 and 1812 and again in 1948. Consequently most of the city's historic buildings have been lost.

One area that survived the last fire was Columbus Square, a quiet central square surrounded by a handful of 19th-century wooden buildings with gingerbread trim balconies, an attractive Victorian-style library and the imposing Cathedral of the Immaculate Conception. Incidentally, there are plans to change the name of Columbus Square to

ST LUCIA

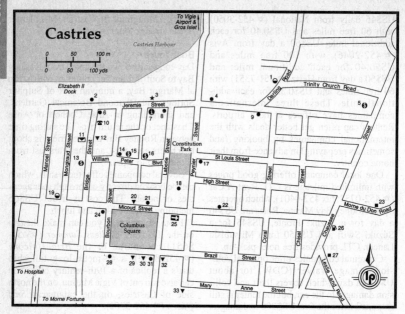

Castries

Castries Harbour

0    50    100 m
0    50    100 yds

Elizabeth II
Dock

To Vigie
Airport &
Gros Islet

Darling Road

Trinity Church Road

Jeremie Street

Manoel Street
Mongraud Street
Bridge Street
William Peter Blvd

Constitution
Park

St Louis Street

High Street

Micoud Street

Columbus
Square

Brazil Street

Mary     Anne    Street

To Hospital

To Morne Fortune

Laborie Street

Peynier Street

St Louis Street

Coral Street

Chisel Street

Chaussee

Morne du Don Road

Leslie Land Road

| PLACES TO STAY | OTHER | 16 | Royal Bank of Canada |
|---|---|---|---|

**PLACES TO STAY**

23  Chateau Blanc Guest
    House
27  Lee's Guest House

**PLACES TO EAT**

12  Paul's Place
20  Kimlan's
29  Rain
30  Buttercup Restaurant
32  White House
33  Central Bakery

**OTHER**

1   Central Bus Terminal
2   Customs
3   Port Police & Fire Station
4   Castries Market
5   Barclays Bank
6   Sea Island Cotton Shop
7   Tourist Office
8   Book Salon
9   Taxi Stand
10  Cable & Wireless
11  General Post Office
13  Barclays Bank
14  JQ's Supermarket
15  Scotia Bank & British
    Airways

16  Royal Bank of Canada
17  Town Hall
18  Court House
19  Buses to Vieux Fort &
    Soufrière
21  British High Commission
22  American Airlines
24  Library
25  Cathedral of the
    Immaculate Concep-
    tion
26  Shell Petrol Station
28  BWIA Office
31  LIAT Office

Derek Walcott Square, in honour of the St
Lucian Nobel laureate.

**Information**
**Tourist Office** The tourist office is opposite
the port police office on Jeremie St.

**Money** The Royal Bank of Canada, on
William Peter Blvd, is open from 8 am to 3
pm Monday to Thursday, to 5 pm on Friday.
There's a Scotiabank 50 metres to the west
and a Barclays Bank further west on Bridge
St.

**Post** The general post office is on Bridge St, a block south of the port. It's open Monday to Friday from 8.30 am to 4 pm.

**Telecommunications** Phone calls can be made from the Cable & Wireless office on Bridge St. For more information, see Telecommunications in the introductory section of this chapter.

**Library** The public library is open from 9 am to 6 pm Monday to Friday, to 12.30 pm on Saturday. Visitors can check out books for a refundable deposit of EC$10.

## Cathedral of the Immaculate Conception

The city's Catholic cathedral, built in 1897, is a grand, stone structure with a splendidly painted interior of trompe l'oeil columns and colourfully detailed biblical scenes. The island's patron saint, St Lucia, is portrayed directly above the altar. The church is unique both in the degree that it incorporates Caribbean and African influences and in its exceptional maintenance.

## Morne Fortune

Sitting atop the 852-metre Morne Fortune, about five km south of Castries centre, is Fort Charlotte, whose construction began under the French and was continued by the British. Because of its strategic hilltop vantage point overlooking the Castries, the fort was a source of fierce fighting between the French and British in colonial times. In recent years the fort buildings have been renovated and given a new life as the Sir Arthur College.

At the rear of the college a small obelisk monument commemorates the 27th Inniskilling Regiment's retaking of the hill from French forces in 1796. At the monument you'll also find a couple of cannons and a fairly good view of the coast north to Pigeon Point.

If you just want a nice view of the city, there's no need to venture as far as the college. The scenic lookout opposite Government House, just a km south of Castries, has a fine view of the port and capital and also gives a glimpse of the crown-topped Victorian mansion that serves as the residence of the Governor-General.

## Places to Stay – bottom end

*Lee's Guest House* is on the corner of Chaussee Rd and Leslie Land Rd at the east side of Castries. It has the ambience of a local boarding house with very basic rooms that are not terribly enticing but are relatively cheap at EC$33/66 for singles/doubles.

The 10-room *Chateau Blanc Guest House* (☎ 452-1851), Morne du Don Rd, Castries, is about a five-minute walk uphill from Courts department store in a rather poor, working-class neighbourhood. Rooms are island style and very basic, with little more than a bed and fan, but they're clean, and Alfred, the owner, is congenial. Pick one of the upstairs rooms, as the ones in the basement tend to be damp. Rates are US$14/25 for singles/doubles.

## Places to Stay – middle & top end

The new *Seaview Apartel* (☎ 450-1627), PO Box 527, Castries, has 10 very big units, all with TV, air-con, phone, bathtub, refrigerator and balcony. Although the 'sea view' is but a distant glimpse, it's still excellent value at US$50 for units with ovens, US$45 without. The location, on the east side of the airport runway, is a 10-minute bus ride from the beach. If you don't mind this, these rooms are comparable to those at beachside hotels charging triple the rate. Reception is at the Shell petrol station next door.

*Harbour Light Inn* (☎ 452-3506), City Gate, Castries, is at the intersection just north of the airport runway. While it looks quite modern from the outside, the 16 rooms are rather lacklustre, although all have TV and private bathroom. Those with air-con cost US$33/55 for singles/doubles, tax included. Those without air-con cost US$27/43 but can be a bit musty.

*Bon Appetit* (☎ 452-2757), PO Box 884, Castries, near the top of Morne Fortune, has a lovely ocean view with Martinique on the horizon. It's run by an Italian couple, Renato and Cheryl Venturi, who operate a small restaurant at the same site. There are four spotlessly clean rooms, all with double bed, shower and cable TV. The rate is US$37/41 for singles/doubles, including tax and breakfast. Credit cards are accepted.

*Green Parrot* (☎ 452-3399), PO Box 648, Castries, has 50 very nice, large rooms with air-con, cable TV, comfortable furnishings and balconies with fine hillside views. There's a pool and a good restaurant. The main disadvantage is that, like Bon Appetit, it is a bit out of the way, on the hillside of Morne Fortune, about five km from Castries. Singles/doubles cost US$68/80 in summer, US$91/110 in winter.

### Places to Eat – cheap

*Paul's Place* on Bridge St, opposite the post office, is a recommendable 2nd-floor restaurant with a nice local atmosphere. It's busiest at lunch when there's a buffet for EC$18 that includes a couple of hot dishes, rice and salad. If you're not that hungry there are also inexpensive rotis and sandwiches. At dinner you can get fish Creole or Malaysian chicken with papaya curry for EC$20 or splurge on a satay shrimp or steak flambé for double that. It's open from 9 am to 10 pm Monday to Saturday, from 6 pm on Sunday.

*Rain*, in a classic West Indian building that dates from 1885, offers balcony dining overlooking Columbus Square and is a popular lunch and dinner spot. Castries' oldest restaurant, it has a full menu that includes sandwiches, quiche and salad, pizza or chicken & chips for under EC$20 as well as more expensive hot dishes. There's also an elaborate dinner affair for EC$95. It's open from 9.15 am to 11 pm Monday to Saturday.

The *Buttercup Restaurant*, on the south side of Columbus Square, has cheerful modern decor with a dozen café-style tables. A West Indian lunch is served buffet style for EC$19, or for EC$14 if you only want a single serving. You can also get sandwiches, burgers and rotis for EC$5 to EC$8. It's open from 9 am to 5 pm Monday to Saturday.

The nearby *White House* is the best place to grab an inexpensive breakfast. For EC$5.50 you can get a generous bacon and egg sandwich served platter-style with slices of buttered French bread and lettuce and tomato garnishes. They also have other inexpensive sandwiches and rotis, as well as chicken (EC$9) or fish (EC$12) with chips. Located in an interesting older building, the restaurant's 2nd-floor dining room offers a glimpse of the cathedral. It's open weekdays from 9 am to 4 pm, Saturday until 1 pm.

*Kimlan's* is a popular 2nd-floor restaurant opposite the square. It has the ubiquitous roti as well as steamer trays with dishes such as curry fish or stew served with rice and salad for EC$10. It's open from 7 am to 11 pm Monday to Saturday.

For cheap eats on the run, you could pick up some fruit at the market and then walk over to the *Central Bakery* at the south end of Peynier St for a fresh baguette or some coconut rolls.

You can also find lots of inexpensive local food, including grilled chicken and goat stew, at the stalls around the bus terminal on Darling Rd. One of these, *Rosie's Snackette*, in a turquoise hut, serving a nice solid lunch plate for EC$9.

JQ's Supermarket on William Peter Blvd is a large, well-stocked grocery store that's open from 8 am to at least 5 pm on weekdays, to noon on Saturday.

### Places to Eat – expensive

*Jimmie's*, on the west side of the airport runway, is popular with both locals and visitors for its authentic West Indian food. Seafood is the speciality and there's a full menu of creative fresh fish dishes for around EC$40, prawn and conch for EC$50. There are also rotis, fish & chips and a few vegetarian dishes such as risotto or Florentine pancakes for around EC$15. Dining is alfresco and you might want to bring insect repellent as the mosquitoes can get a bit pesky. It's open from noon to 3 pm Monday to Saturday and from 7 to 10.30 pm daily.

For a treat, head up to the *Green Parrot Restaurant* (☎ 452-3399) for its lunch buffet, which is served from 12.30 to 3 pm Monday to Friday and costs just EC$20. Dishes vary, but usually include fish, fresh salad and local vegetables as well as coffee and dessert. If you prefer something lighter, there are sandwiches from EC$10. Dinner, also good, is a more expensive proposal, with main dishes priced from EC$35 to EC$70. Be sure to get one of the window tables to enjoy the restaurant's fine hilltop view of Castries and the north-west coast. The restaurant is in Morne Fortune, five km from Castries centre, an EC$10 taxi ride.

*Bon Appetit* (☎ 452-2757), also in Morne Fortune, is an intimate little restaurant with home-cooked food and a wonderful view. It's open from noon to 11 pm, closed on Sunday. Main dishes range from EC$40 for fish to EC$90 for freshwater crayfish, the house speciality. As there are only five tables, reservations are recommended.

*San Antoine* (☎ 452-4660), on Government House Rd, has a romantic stone and wood decor and a fine hillside setting about a km south-west of Castries centre, on the way to Morne Fortune. This restaurant, operated by an English couple, is the Castries area's most highly regarded fine-dining spot, with an extensive continental menu. There's a fixed price five-course dinner for EC$95 and a range of à la carte main courses from EC$40.

### Getting Around
**Bus & Taxi Stands** There's a taxi stand on Jeremie St, at the east side of the market. Buses to Gros Islet terminate nearby on Darling Rd, just north of Jeremie St. Buses going south to Soufrière and Vieux Fort can be picked up on the corner of Mongiraud and Micoud streets.

# Northern St Lucia

## NORTH OF CASTRIES
The Gros Islet Rd runs up the coast connecting northern Castries to Rodney Bay. This area has a number of beachside resort hotels, as well as some moderately priced guesthouses. Most of the guesthouses are on the inland side of the road but within walking distance of the beach. Choc Beach, which fronts the Halcyon Beach Club resort, is a nice sandy strip and one of the area's livelier beach scenes.

The new Gablewoods Mall, just south of the Halcyon, has a supermarket, eateries, a bank, clothing shops and a bookshop.

### Places to Stay – bottom end
The first three places listed are on Gros Islet Rd, about four km north of the airport and a 10-minute walk from Choc Beach and Gablewoods Mall.

*Modern Inn* (☎ 452-4001; fax 453-7313), PO Box 457, Vide Bouteille, Castries, is a good-value family-run hostelry with five guest rooms and a small common sitting area with cable TV, a dining table and a refrigerator. The rooms are straightforward, but clean and brightly painted and have comfortable mattresses and air-con. Rates are US$20/30 a single/double for the two smaller rooms that share a bathroom and US$35 for rooms with private bath. There are also three adjacent apartments with kitchen, cable TV and air-con for US$45 to US$50.

The 10-room *E's Serenity Lodge* (☎ 452-1987) has a quiet hilltop location five minutes' walk uphill from the Friendship Inn. There's a nice view of the coast and the inn is pleasant enough, but the rooms are spartan, essentially just a bed, fan, night table and lamp. Singles/doubles cost US$25/40 with a shared bath, US$30/50 with a private bath.

The roadside *Friendship Inn* (☎ 452-4201; in the USA ☎ (800) 742-4276) is a small concrete two-storey building with a line of motel-style rooms. The rooms are simple with two twin beds, cable TV, small kitchenette, air-con and private bathroom. Singles/doubles cost US$50/60. There's a small pool.

The *Beach Haven Hotel* (☎ 453-0065), PO Box 460, Vide Bouteille, Castries, has 10 straightforward rooms with TV, air-con and private bath that cost US$40/50 for singles/doubles in summer, US$60/70 in winter. Vigie Beach is at the rear of the hotel and there's a restaurant on site.

## Places to Stay – top end

The *Halcyon Beach Club* (☎ 452-5331; fax 452-5434; in the USA ☎ (800) 742-4276), PO Box 388, Choc Bay, Castries, is a 180-room resort hotel on a nice sandy beach a few km north of the airport. The rooms are rather standard in appearance but have air-con, phone, radio and either a patio or balcony. There's a disco, tennis courts and complimentary windsurfing and snorkelling gear, and the Castries-Gros Islet bus passes by the lobby door. Singles/doubles begin at US$95/118 in summer, US$150/170 in winter.

The *Wyndham Morgan Bay Resort* (☎ 450-2511; in the USA ☎ (800) 822-4200, in Canada ☎ (800) 631-4200) is a new 240-room hotel at the north side of Choc Bay. The rooms have either a patio or balcony, TV, air-con, a phone and a king-size or two double beds. There's a fitness centre, tennis courts, a pool, a water sports centre and three restaurants. Singles/doubles cost from US$175/270 in summer, US$250/350 in winter; add another US$40 for an ocean view.

*Windjammer Landing* (☎ 452-0913; fax 452-9454; in the USA ☎ (800) 243-1166, in the UK ☎ (800) 373742), PO Box 1504, Castries, on a quiet beach at Labrelotte Bay, is a sprawling villa-style complex with an upmarket Mediterranean appearance. Units are contemporary with beam ceilings, rattan furnishings, kitchenettes, living and dining areas, terraces, TV, VCRs and air-con bedrooms. Some have private plunge pools. There are two tennis courts, three restaurants, four pools and extensive water sports, most of which are complimentary. In winter, one-bedroom villas cost US$270, two-bedrooms are US$350 and three-bedrooms are US$495; in summer the cost is US$160/220/360 respectively. There are also weekly and all-inclusive rates.

## Places to Eat

Gablewoods Mall has a few fast-food stalls and a central dining court. Prices are a bit higher than the food warrants, but the mall is not a bad choice if you're nearby and want something quick. The eateries include *Peppino's Pizza*, with fairly good pizza priced from EC$5 for a quarter of a small cheese pizza to EC$45 for a large pizza with the works; *Miss Saigon*, with reasonably priced rotis but pricey Asian dishes; *El Burrito*, with adequate burritos for EC$10; and *Kafe Kool* for ice cream and cappuccino. The stalls are open daily from late morning to about 9 pm. There's also a sit-down restaurant, *The Patio*, which serves lunch and dinner, and a deli that sells meats and cheeses.

For a pleasant water view it's hard to beat *Chanticleer Wharf*, which sits on pilings above the water at the Halcyon Beach Club. At lunch, hamburgers, fried flying fish or omelettes with fries are under EC$20 and there's either a fish and chicken barbecue or a buffet from 12.30 to 2.30 pm for EC$25. In the evening there are a couple of light dinners for around EC$20, while full dinners, including a good grilled fish, are priced from EC$30. The only drawback is the erratic service.

The *Beach Haven Hotel* has a buffet weekdays from noon to 3 pm that includes a salad bar, soup, chicken and fish and costs EC$20. For fine dining there are upmarket dinner restaurants at the *Windjammer* and *Wyndham* resorts.

## RODNEY BAY

Rodney Bay is a large protected bay that encompasses the resort area of Reduit Beach and the village of Gros Islet. An artificial channel cuts between Reduit Beach and Gros Islet, opening to a large lagoon that's the site of the Rodney Bay Marina, the island's largest yachting port.

Rodney Bay Marina is a modern facility with a travel agency, a car rental agency, two dive shops, a swimming pool, a bookshop, card and coin phones, a chandlery, marine supply shops, a grocery store and some good eating spots – many of which are run by expatriates. There are also two banks, the Royal Bank of Canada and Barclays Bank,

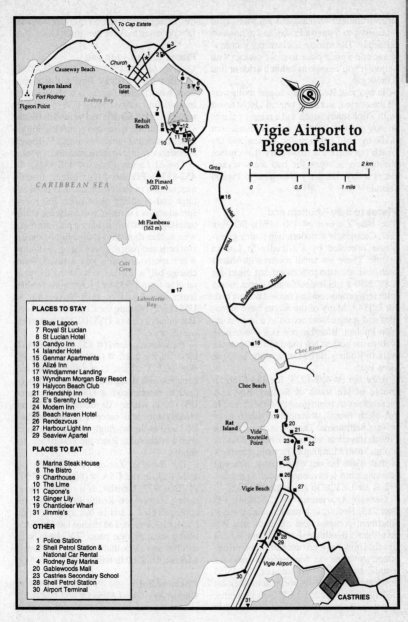

# Vigie Airport to Pigeon Island

```
0          1          2 km
0        0.5        1 mile
```

CARIBBEAN SEA

To Cap Estate

Causeway Beach

Pigeon Island
Fort Rodney
Pigeon Point

Church

Gros
Islet

Rodney Bay

Reduit
Beach

Mt Pimard
(201 m)

Mt Flambeau
(162 m)

Cuti
Cove

Labrellotte
Bay

Gros Islet Road

Bonneterre Road

Choc River

Choc Beach

Rat
Island

Vide Bouteille
Point

Vigie Beach

Vigie Airport

CASTRIES

**PLACES TO STAY**

3  Blue Lagoon
7  Royal St Lucian
8  St Lucian Hotel
13  Candyo Inn
14  Islander Hotel
15  Genmar Apartments
16  Alizé Inn
17  Windjammer Landing
18  Wyndham Morgan Bay Resort
19  Halcyon Beach Club
21  Friendship Inn
22  E's Serenity Lodge
24  Modern Inn
25  Beach Haven Hotel
26  Rendezvous
27  Harbour Light Inn
29  Seaview Apartel

**PLACES TO EAT**

5  Marina Steak House
6  The Bistro
9  Charthouse
10  The Lime
11  Capone's
12  Ginger Lily
19  Chanticleer Wharf
31  Jimmie's

**OTHER**

1  Police Station
2  Shell Petrol Station &
   National Car Rental
4  Rodney Bay Marina
20  Gablewoods Mall
23  Castries Secondary School
28  Shell Petrol Station
30  Airport Terminal

open from 8 or 8.30 am to 3 pm Monday to Thursday, to 5 pm on Friday and to noon on Saturday. The marina is a bustling yachters' scene and a great place to make contact with sailors if you're looking to hitch a ride or find a crew job.

In contrast, Reduit Beach, just south-west of the marina, is a more typical tourist resort with a fine sandy beach and a range of places to stay and eat. It's a 30-minute roundabout walk by road between the marina and the beach but there's a small ferry that crosses the lagoon between the two areas several times a day; the ferry also goes to Pigeon Island.

### Places to Stay – bottom end

The *Blue Lagoon* (☎ 450-8453), PO Box 637, Castries, is a modern two-storey guesthouse operated by a friendly St Lucian couple. There are small rooms with shared bath that are straightforward but clean for US$25/30 a single/double and larger rooms with refrigerator, ceiling fan and private bath for US$43. Many of the rooms have balconies and guests have access to a large common kitchen. Blue Lagoon is a two-minute walk to the nearest bus stand and a 10-minute walk to Rodney Bay Marina or the beach at Gros Islet.

*Alizé Inn* (☎ 452-1227; fax 453-6736), a couple of km south of Rodney Bay, is a pleasant seven-room guesthouse with simple but clean rooms, a couple of which have private bathrooms. The inn is popular with French travellers and occasionally fills with groups from Martinique. Its main drawback is that it's a bit out of the way, although catching a bus is easy enough during the day. Prices are US$26/36 for singles/doubles.

*Genmar Apartments* (☎ 452-0834), PO Box 213, Reduit, is a small suburban-style apartment complex just off Gros Islet Rd, less than 10 minutes' walk from Reduit Beach. Units have private bathroom, refrigerator, stove and fan. Single/double rates for a studio are US$30/40 in summer, US$45/55 in winter. For a one-bedroom unit, rates are US$40/50 in summer, US$50/60 in winter. To get there turn left on the first dirt road after

the Texaco petrol station and then take the first right and look for the small 'Gene' sign.

### Places to Stay – top end

*Candyo Inn* (☎ 452-0712; fax 452-0774), PO Box 386, Rodney Bay, a five-minute walk from Reduit Beach, is a pleasant new inn with four rooms costing US$75 and eight suites with kitchenette and verandah costing US$90. All are quite comfortable with air-con, phones and remote-control TV. There's a moderately priced restaurant and a pool.

The *St Lucian Hotel* (☎ 452-8351; fax 452-8331), PO Box 512, Castries, fronts a nice section of Reduit Beach. The hotel is a large and rambling place, with 260 rooms spread across a series of two and three-storey buildings. Most rooms have a pleasant decor with wicker furnishings, tiled floors, queen-size beds and patios. There are tennis courts, water sports activities and a disco. Rates change half a dozen times during the year, ranging from US$54/77 for singles/doubles from mid-April to mid-November to US$188/211 during the Christmas holidays. The January rate of US$102/125 is the best winter price.

The *Islander Hotel* (☎ 452-0255; fax 452-0958; in the USA ☎ (800) 223-9815), PO Box 907, Castries, is a rather congested complex with straightforward rooms that are hard to recommend at US$85 in summer, US$120 in winter. All rooms have air-con, refrigerators and cable TV. Add another US$5/10 in the low/high season for a room with a kitchenette. Rates are US$10 less for singles.

The *Royal St Lucian* (☎ 452-9999; fax 452-9639; in the USA ☎ (800) 255-5859), PO Box 977, Castries, is a modern three-storey complex on Reduit Beach, with the appearance of a sterile but upmarket Fort Lauderdale condo. The studios have separate sitting area, private patio, TV, room safe, minibar and rates that begin at US$194 in summer, US$260 in winter.

### Places to Eat

**Marina** *Key Largo Pizza* (☎ 452-0282) has excellent pizza cooked in an outdoor brick oven. Calzones cost EC$15 and pizzas are EC$20 to EC$45, depending on the toppings. It opens at 11.30 am in winter, 5 pm in summer, and stays open until at least 10 pm. It's closed on Monday.

The *Yacht Club*, an informal dockside restaurant, has light meals and drinks served cafeteria style. You can get sandwiches and burgers for about EC$6, fish & chips for EC$18 and a wide range of other dishes. It's open from 7 am to 11 pm daily.

The *Bread Basket* bakery sells very good breads, including whole wheat and a crispy French loaf, as well as sandwiches, muffins, Danish and other pastries. It's a popular place for a light breakfast and they make a good (though not necessarily quick) egg and bacon sandwich for EC$7. You can take your food outside and dine on the waterfront. It's open from 7.30 am to 5 pm Monday to Saturday, to 2 pm on Sunday.

*Le Marché de France* is a small market with a fair selection, including meal-size chunks of cheese, imported foods and moderately priced wines. It's open from 8.30 am to 7 pm Monday to Saturday, 9 am to 1 pm on Sunday and holidays.

*The Bistro* (☎ 452-9494), on the waterfront at Rodney Bay, is often crowded with yachters who can literally jump off their boats and into the restaurant. This popular watering hole has an extensive chalkboard menu, with items such as vegetarian lasagne for EC$25 and fish and beef dishes from EC$35 to EC$50. It's open from 5 pm daily. There's a 20% discount on food orders made before 6.30 pm.

The nearby *Marina Steak House* (☎ 452-9800) features steak and seafood and has a jazz piano bar on Friday night. Most main dishes, which include vegetables and a baked potato, cost EC$35 to EC$50. It's open from 5 pm to midnight daily except on Sunday.

**Reduit Beach** For West Indian food, *The Lime* is the place to go. It has a good-value lunch buffet from noon to 3 pm for EC$19, or you can just order a roti for EC$8. At dinner, from 6.30 to 10 pm, The Lime features fresh seafood dishes in the EC$30 to EC$45 range. It's closed on Tuesday.

*Capone's* has a takeaway counter where you can pick up inexpensive pizza and grilled chicken (there are picnic tables on the lawn) and an indoor Art Deco restaurant with Italian-style pasta, fish and meat offerings in the EC$35 to EC$50 range. Pizzas are available from 11 am to midnight and the restaurant is open from 6 pm. Both the takeaway counter and the restaurant are closed on Monday.

*Ginger Lily* offers the full range of standard Chinese dishes for EC$18 to EC$30, as well as pricier specials. It's open from noon to 2.30 pm Tuesday to Saturday and from 6 to 11 pm daily except on Monday.

*Charthouse* (☎ 452-8115) has a nice waterfront setting and has long been popular for its grilled steaks and baby back ribs; it also has chicken and fish dishes. Prices average EC$35 to EC$40; add another EC$6 for a green salad. It's open daily except Sunday from 6 pm.

The informal *Sunset Bar* at the St Lucian Hotel has open-air beach views and reasonable prices. You can get a cup of gazpacho soup for EC$5, sandwiches from EC$12 and fish kebab with Creole sauce and rice for EC$21. It's open from 12.30 to 9.45 pm daily. The hotel's *Flamingo Restaurant*, opposite the Sunset Bar, has similar offerings at lunch, moderately priced breakfasts and a more expensive à la carte dinner menu. The St Lucian's *Hummingbird* restaurant offers an unexciting and overpriced dinner buffet.

There's a small store, S K Mini Mart, near the Islander Hotel, that sells groceries, spirits and toiletries. It's open from 9 am to 7 pm Monday to Saturday.

## GROS ISLET

Gros Islet is a small fishing village of simple wooden houses with rusting tin roofs, lots of rum shops and a shore dotted with gaily painted wooden boats. If you hear a conch being blown, it's the signal that fishing boats have arrived with a catch to sell.

Though the town doesn't have any sights per se, St Joseph's Church is a formidable structure at the north side of town and there's a small market near the shore where you can often see fishermen and women mending nets. Gros Islet is also famous for its spirited Friday night jump-up (see Entertainment in the Facts for the Visitor section).

From Gros Islet, walk a couple of minutes north along the shore and you'll come to an expansive stretch of white-sand beach that curves around to Pigeon Island. You're likely to find cows lazing along the beach under shade trees, a couple of pigs milling around and only a handful of people. While the village end of the beach is a bit trashed, the beach is otherwise quite beautiful and the calm turquoise waters are inviting. There are no facilities. However, this undeveloped beach along the Pigeon Point causeway has been approved for a 300-room luxury resort, so the scene may change radically in the near future.

Most buses making the coastal drive north from Castries terminate in the centre of Gros Islet. From Rodney Bay Marina it's a 20-minute walk to the village.

### Places to Eat

*Sandees*, by the church, is a little coffee shop serving inexpensive cakes, pastries, sandwiches and rotis. It's open from 8 am to 6 pm daily except on Sunday.

For something more substantial, you could try *Coco's* or *Banana Split*, both of which specialise in seafood.

### PIGEON ISLAND NATIONAL PARK

Pigeon Island has a spicy history dating back to the 1550s when St Lucia's first French settler, Jambe de Bois ('Wooden Leg'), used the island as a base for raiding passing Spanish ships. Two centuries later British admiral George Rodney fortified Pigeon Island, using it to monitor the French fleet on Martinique. Rodney's fleet left Pigeon Island in 1782 for his most decisive military engagement, the Battle of the Saintes. With the end of hostilities between the two European rivals, the fort slipped into disuse in the

19th century, although the USA established a small signal station here during WW II.

In the 1970s a sandy causeway was constructed between Gros Islet and Pigeon Island, turning the island into a peninsula, and in 1979 Pigeon 'Island' was established as a national park.

It's a fun place to explore, with nice walking paths winding around the scattered remains of Fort Rodney, whose partially intact stone buildings create a certain ghost town effect. The grounds contain lots of tall trees, including a few big banyans, and there are fine coastal views.

As soon as you go through the entrance gate, you'll see the remains of an 1824 kitchen and officers' mess. While some people make a beeline from here to the main fortress at Fort Rodney Hill on the outer point, a walk which takes about 15 minutes, it's enjoyable to just mosey through the ruins and gradually work your way in that direction. A good route is to continue north-west from the officers' mess past some old (1782) soldiers' barracks and then loop down towards the bay where you can pick up the main path.

At the top of Fort Rodney Hill, you'll find a small but well-preserved fortress, a few rusting cannons and a spectacular view. You can see south across Rodney Bay to the gumdrop-shaped hills which dot the coast and north past Pointe du Cap to Martinique. For more views, continue north past the stone foundations of the old ridge battery to the top of 107-metre Signal Peak, about a 20-minute walk.

Pigeon Island is administered by the St Lucia National Trust and is open from 9 am to 5 pm daily. Admission costs EC$3 for foreign visitors, plus EC$1 for a map of the sites. There's a small restaurant selling sandwiches at moderate prices.

Most of the coastline around Pigeon Island is rocky, though there's a nice little sandy beach just east of the restaurant and jetty. Still, if you just want to hang out on the beach, the south side of the causeway is tops.

The walk along the causeway from Gros Islet to Pigeon Point takes about 20 minutes.

# Southern St Lucia

The main road in the southern part of the island makes a loop that can be done as a full day trip. However, many visitors simply go down the west coast from Castries to Soufrière and return the same way.

The road to Soufrière is a stunningly scenic drive, winding in and out of lush jungle valleys and up into the mountains. It goes through banana plantations and the fishing villages of Anse La Raye and Canaries and offers fine coastal and mountain vistas, including some lovely views of the Pitons as you approach Soufrière.

Choiseul, a pleasant little village south of Soufrière, is the centre of the island's handicraft industry and a nice place to pick up local basketry and pottery.

Before starting off, check road conditions, as sections of the southern loop road have recently been closed as a result of resurfacing projects.

## MARIGOT BAY

Marigot Bay is a lovely sheltered bay that's backed by green hillsides and sports a little palm-fringed beach. The inner harbour is so long and deep that an entire British fleet is said to have escaped French warships by ducking inside and covering their masts with coconut fronds. The bay was the setting for the 1967 musical *Doctor Dolittle*, starring Rex Harrison.

Marigot Bay is a popular anchorage for yachters and the site of a marina with a customs office, a small market, water, ice and fuel. The Moorings (☎ 453-4357) bases it's bareboat charters here and runs the marina facilities and hotel.

The free *Gingerbread Express*, a little pontoon boat, shuttles back and forth, connecting the two sides of the inner harbour.

### Places to Stay & Eat

Club Mariner's *Marigot Bay Resort* (☎ 451-4357; fax 453-4353; in the USA and Canada ☎ (800) 334-2435), PO Box 101, Castries, offers a variety of accommodation on both sides of the harbour. The 14 cottages on the south side are quite nice with tasteful tropical decor, rattan furniture and wraparound open-air screening; they cost US$80 in summer, US$120 in winter. There are also studios with kitchenettes at similar rates and one and two-bedroom hillside villas priced from US$95 to US$130 in summer, US$150 to US$225 in winter.

*Dolittle's Restaurant & Beach Bar* is an open-air dockside restaurant at the northwest side of the harbour. It serves three meals a day at moderate prices.

On the south side of the harbour, near the hotel lobby, is the more upscale *Rusty Anchor Restaurant & Terrace Bar*, which features fresh seafood and barbecued meats.

There are happy hours with two-for-one drinks from 5 to 6 pm at Dolittle's and from 6 to 7 pm at the Rusty Anchor.

A popular local eatery is *JJ's Restaurant & Bar* (☎ 451-4076) in the village, a 10-minute walk up the hill from the harbour. The fish Creole and chicken curry are both tasty dinner dishes that cost EC$35 and include rice, salad, vegetables and dessert. JJ's also serves lambi, shrimp and lobster, has a lighter lunch menu that includes fish or chicken with chips and throws a jump-up-style jam on Friday nights.

## SOUFRIÈRE

Founded by the French in 1746 and named after the nearby sulphur springs, the town of Soufrière has a lovely bay setting. The coastal Pitons provide a scenic backdrop to the south and the island's highest peaks rise above the rainforest just a few km inland.

Like other fishing communities along the coast, Soufrière has lots of old weathered buildings, some still adorned with delicate gingerbread trim, others little more than ramshackle shacks. There's an interesting stone Catholic church in the town centre. At the north side of the dock is the Soufrière Market, where you can buy baskets, straw hats, T-shirts and spices.

The main sights, the Sulphur Springs and Diamond Botanical Gardens, are both on the

ST LUCIA

outskirts of town and can be visited in a couple of hours.

Although most visitors are day trippers on one of the many boat or land tours that take in Soufrière, there are some interesting places to stay, including a couple of secluded retreats.

### Anse Chastanet

Soufrière's picturesque scenery is equally impressive beneath the water's surface. Anse Chastanet, a lovely sheltered bay just two km north of Soufrière, has some of the finest nearshore snorkelling and diving on St Lucia.

At the beach is a hotel, a dive shop that rents snorkelling equipment, a bar and a moderately priced restaurant that serves both simple snacks and full meals. On foot, Anse Chastanet is about a 30-minute walk from Soufrière along the coastal road that skirts the north side of Soufrière Bay.

### Sulphur Springs

The Sulphur Springs is a barren and somewhat moonscapish terrain pocked with pools of boiling mud and steaming vents. The vents release great quantities of sulphuric gases, which are responsible for the yellow mineral deposits blanketing the area. The putrid smell, reminiscent of rotten eggs, is hydrogen sulphide.

Visitors used to walk up close to the vents and peer directly into the mud ponds until a local guide leading a group of German tourists stepped through the soft earth and plunged waist-deep into boiling mud. He lived to tell the story, but everything is now viewed from the safety of overlooks.

Despite the fact that this area is promoted as a 'drive-in volcano', those expecting to peer down into a volcano will be disappointed as there's no crater. The volcanic activity is along the side of a hill; the crater itself collapsed eons ago.

Sulphur Springs is open from 9 am to 5 pm daily and admission is EC$3. Having a guide walk through with you is compulsory; although the price of the guide is theoreti-

cally included in the entrance fee, a tip will be expected.

To get there from Soufrière, go south on the Vieux Fort road, which winds uphill as it leaves town. About a five-minute drive out of Soufrière take the downhill fork to the left at the Sulphur Springs sign, from where it's a km farther to the park entrance. En route be sure not to miss the small pull-off, just south of Soufrière, which offers a picturesque view of the town.

### Diamond Botanical Gardens

The Diamond Estate's botanical gardens, waterfall and mineral baths are all at the same site and have an entrance fee of EC$5 for adults, EC$2.50 for children under 12.

Paths wind through the gardens, which are pleasant if somewhat small. Of the various tropical flowers and trees, the numerous heliconia and ginger specimens are especially lovely. At the back of the gardens a small waterfall drops down a rockface that is stained a rich orange from the warm mineral waters. The waterfall featured briefly in the movie *Superman II* as the site from which Superman plucked an orchid for Lois Lane. Swimming beneath the waterfall is not permitted.

The mineral baths have an illustrious history, dating from 1784 when they were built atop hot springs so that the troops of King Louis XVI of France could take advantage of their therapeutic effects. The baths were largely destroyed during the French Revolution, but in recent times a few have been restored and are open to visitors for an additional EC$6.50.

The Diamond Estate is one mile (1.6 km) east of Soufrière centre and the way is signposted. The grounds are open from 10 am to 5 pm daily and there's an inexpensive snack bar. The tour guides who gather at the gate are not necessary, as it's a straightforward sight to walk through on your own.

### Places to Stay

*Hummingbird Beach Resort* (☎ 454-7232), on the north side of the harbour, has 10 rooms, a pool and a view across the bay to the Pitons. Rooms are pleasantly rustic with lots of wood, two with four-poster beds and half with private bath. Standard rooms with shared bath cost US$30/55 for singles/doubles, while fancier rooms with private bath start at US$80/105.

*Home Hotel* (☎ 459-7318) on Church St, two blocks east of the dock, has been a standby for budget travellers for decades. It's a pleasant enough place, with half a dozen rooms with shared shower for US$35.

*Anse Chastanet Hotel* (☎ 454-7000; fax 454-7700; in the USA ☎ (800) 223-1108), PO Box 7000, Soufrière, on the beach at Anse Chastanet, is an appealing hideaway hotel with 48 rooms, some on the beach and others terraced up the hillside. All have a refrigerator, coffee maker, ceiling fan and natural tiled or hardwood floors; many also have open-beam ceilings and fine views of the Pitons. There's a scuba facility, tennis court and various water sports. Singles/doubles start at US$220/310 in winter, including breakfast and dinner; in summer the rates are US$90/130 without meals.

The *Ladera Resort* (☎ & fax 459-7323; in the USA and Canada ☎ (800) 841-4145), PO Box 225, Soufrière, is an exclusive resort with lots of natural wood and stone and a stunning hillside setting. There are nine suites each with a bedroom, living area and large bathroom and seven three-bedroom villas with kitchen, two bathrooms and high-beam ceilings; some have private plunge pools and all have canopy beds with mosquito nets. The west side of every unit is wall-less, open to direct views of the nearby Pitons. Double rates for suites/villas are from US$125/245 in summer, from US$260/US$400 in winter and from US$210/345 in spring and late autumn. Rates include continental breakfast and transport to and from Hewanorra Airport. The resort is on the Vieux Fort road a couple of km south of Soufrière.

### Places to Eat

The *Hummingbird* (☎ 459-7232) is the best waterfront restaurant in Soufrière and has a fine view of the Pitons. It features both French and Creole dishes, with house specialities such as freshwater crayfish, shrimp coquilles St Jacques and chateaubriand. There are also sandwiches and salads. For dessert, there's the likes of chocolate rum cake and Soufrière coffee. Main courses range from EC$25 to EC$70 and it's open daily for lunch and dinner. There's a swimming pool beside the restaurant where diners are free to take a dip.

*The Still* (☎ 459-7224) is a restaurant at the working plantation of La Perle & Ruby Estates, a km east of town and well signposted. West Indian standards such as callaloo soup, spicy pepper pot and a variety of seafood and chicken dishes are moderately priced. It's open daily for lunch only. The Still has some new apartments under construction that can be rented for US$50 to US$100 and should be worth checking out.

For expensive fine dining with an unbeatable hilltop view, there's the *Dasheene Restaurant* at the Ladera Resort, where an Austrian chef cooks up dishes such as blackened kingfish with papaya salsa, and roast lamb.

## VIEUX FORT

Vieux Fort, St Lucia's southernmost town, would be off the beaten path for most visitors if it weren't the site of the island's international airport, which is just north of the town centre. The town has a mix of older wooden buildings and newer structures and the island's second-largest port. If you're overnighting here before a flight, there are nice white-sand beaches east of town that can be explored.

There's a lighthouse atop a 223-metre hill on Moule à Chique, the island's southernmost point, which offers a nice view of the Maria Islands, St Lucia's interior mountains and, if the weather's clear, the island of St Vincent to the south.

### Places to Stay & Eat

The *Kimatari Hotel* (☎ 454-6328), PO Box 238, Vieux Fort, on New Dock Rd between

ST LUCIA

the dock and town centre, has a good inexpensive restaurant and 12 straightforward rooms that rent for US$30/40 for singles/doubles. There are also some air-con rooms and two-bedroom apartments.

The new *Skyway Inn* (☎ 454-6670; fax 454-7116), PO Box 353, Vieux Fort, on the west side of town, has 32 rooms with air-con, ceiling fan, phone and TV. Singles/doubles cost US$75/85 in summer, US$85/95 in winter. There's a bar, an open-air rooftop restaurant and a free shuttle to the beach.

*Club Med* (☎ 454-6546; fax 454-6017), PO Box 246, Vieux Fort, is on a beach one mile (1.6 km) north-east of the airport. The 256 rooms are in four-storey wings that extend from the main building. Facilities include three restaurants, eight tennis courts, a windsurfing programme and numerous complimentary water sports. Diving and horse riding cost extra. Rates, which include meals, range from US$250 to US$380 a double, depending on the season. Singles are about 25% less.

*Chak Chak*, near the airport, serves Creole-style food with an emphasis on fish, shrimp and lobster main dishes, as well as rotis and other lighter fare. It's open from 9 am to midnight, prices are moderate and credit cards are accepted.

## EAST COAST

The road up the east coast from Vieux Fort passes through a few local villages and lots of banana plantations before turning inland at the town of Dennery and making a scenic, winding cut across the mountainous rainforest to Castries.

There are two nature sanctuaries off the east coast. The Maria Islands Nature Reserve, two islands a few km east of Vieux Fort, is the only habitat of the kouwes snake, one of the world's rarest grass snakes, and the Maria Islands ground lizard. Because it's a sanctuary for terns, noddies and other sea birds, the islands are not accessible during nesting season, but can be visited at other times of the year on tours arranged by the St Lucia National Trust (☎ 452-5005).

The Frigate Islands Nature Reserve encompasses two small rocky nearshore islands that are a summer nesting site for frigatebirds. The area is also a habitat for several types of herons, a couple of the island's indigenous rare birds (the Ramier pigeon and the St Lucian oriole), boa constrictors and the more dangerous fer-de-lance. There's a small visitors' centre on the north side of Praslin Bay and tours of the area can be arranged through local tour agencies or the National Trust.

# St Martin

St Martin is one of the Eastern Caribbean's most touristed islands. It boasts lovely white-sand beaches, a wide range of places to stay, good restaurants and two quite distinct sides, one administered by the French and the other by the Dutch.

The French side is developed on a smaller scale and has a decidedly French influence in language, food and culture. The Dutch side is more commercial with large resorts, casinos and fast food chains – and precious little that's solidly Dutch. Both sides are duty free and the two island capitals, Philipsburg and Marigot, are chockablock with fashionable shops.

The island is the world's smallest land area to be shared by two countries. Despite its dual nationality, the border crossings are marked only with inconspicuous signs and there are no stops or other formalities when passing between the two sides.

While the island is rather small and quite overdeveloped in places, there are still quiet niches to explore. Its beaches are surprisingly diverse, ranging from secluded coves and naturist retreats to busy resort-front strands.

St Martin is a prime jumping-off point for trips to neighbouring islands – it's cheap and easy to get to Anguilla, St Barts and St Eustatius, some of the Eastern Caribbean's most rural and least developed destinations.

Note that the Dutch side of the island is spelled Sint Maarten and the French side is spelled St Martin, a practice followed in this chapter when referring to the different sides. When referring to the island as a whole we use the spelling St Martin.

## ORIENTATION

Marigot (the French capital) and Philipsburg (the Dutch capital) are each about a 15-minute drive from the airport, although if you happen to catch one of the four daily openings of the Simpson Bay drawbridge or hit heavy traffic it can easily take twice as long.

Driving around the island is fairly simple, as essentially one road loops around the western side of the island and another around

---

### Divvying up the Island

Local lore has it that the contentious Dutch and French colonists decided to settle their ongoing land disputes by having a Dutchman and a Frenchman stand back to back at one end of the island and then walk in opposite directions around the coastline. The island's boundary line would be established at the end of the day at whatever spot they finally met. It turned out that the Frenchman walked much faster than the Dutchman, which is why the French side of St Martin is larger than the Dutch side.

It's said the Frenchman quenched his thirst along the way with French wine, while the Dutchman quenched his with more potent Dutch gin, thus accounting for the latter's slower pace! ■

---

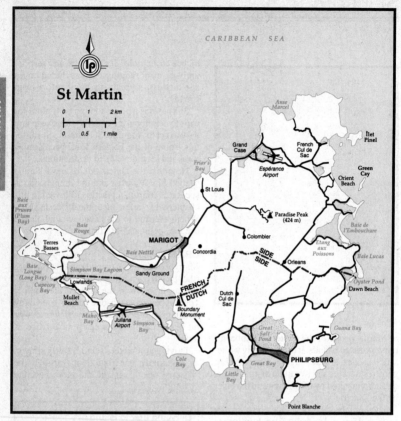

St Martin

the main part of the island. Side roads leading to beaches and resorts are generally marked.

# Facts about the Island

### HISTORY

Because of its many salt ponds, Amerindians called this island Soualiga, meaning 'Land of Salt'. According to popular belief, Columbus 'discovered' the island on 11 November 1493 and named it in honour of Bishop St

Martin of Tours. However, some historians now think the island Columbus chanced upon that day was the more southerly Nevis and that he never actually sighted St Martin. At any rate, it wasn't until 1631 that the first colonisation attempts were made, with the Dutch settling at Little Bay and the French in the Orleans area.

In 1633 the Spanish (who had claimed but not colonised the island) invaded St Martin, deporting all 128 inhabitants. The Spanish reinforced a fort that the Dutch had started and then built a second fort. In 1644 an attempt to retake the island was led by the

Dutch coloniser Peter Stuyvesant, who lost a leg to a cannonball in the fighting. While the Dutch assault was unsuccessful, four years later the Spanish reassessed their interests in the Eastern Caribbean and simply left on their own.

Both the Dutch and French hastily moved back and agreed to share the island, signing a partition agreement in 1648 which was to be repeatedly violated. During the period from 1670 to 1702 the French controlled the entire island. In 1703 the Dutch invaded from St Eustatius and then deported any French settlers who refused to leave the island.

On 11 April 1713, the Utrecht Peace Treaty returned half of the island to France. Nevertheless, St Martin continued to be batted back and forth, with the Dutch and the French each having complete control of the island for years at a time. The English also got involved, taking control in 1784 for 10 years and in 1810 for six years. In 1817 the current boundary was established and a peaceful resolution found.

In the meantime, a plantation economy was established, slaves were imported from Africa and trade flourished. The first crops were tobacco and indigo, followed by cotton, cocoa, coffee and, most importantly, sugar cane. The Dutch also harvested huge amounts of salt which was shipped to Holland for use in the herring industry. After slavery was abolished (in 1848 on the French side, 1863 on the Dutch side), the plantations declined and the island slipped into a subsistence economy.

When the Netherlands fell to the Nazis in 1940, the French took 'protective control' of the Dutch side of the island, but within two weeks France itself was under German control. An Allied occupation of the island followed and in 1943 the USA built a military airfield, now Juliana Airport. After the war the new airport, the region's largest, spurred the island's growth as a regional hub and brought on an early advent of tourism.

## GEOGRAPHY

The island is 15 km across at its widest and 13 km at its longest. The French side of the island has 54 sq km of land, the Dutch side has 34 sq km.

St Martin has an interesting topography. Its shoreline is indented with bays and coves and its coastal flats are pocketed with salt ponds. The interior is hilly, with the highest point, Paradise Peak, rising 424 metres from the centre of French St Martin.

The west side of the island is more water than land, dominated by the expansive Simpson Bay Lagoon, one of the largest landlocked bodies of water in the Caribbean.

## CLIMATE

In January the average daily high temperature is 28°C (83°F) while the low averages 22°C (72°F). In July the average daily high is 30°C (86°F) while the low averages 24°C (76°F).

The average annual rainfall is 1029 mm. The heaviest rainfall is from August to November, the lightest from February to April.

## FLORA & FAUNA

The terrain is largely green but dry, with more palms, hibiscus and cacti than ferns or forests, although there are a few thickly vegetated areas in the interior.

Herons, egrets, stilts, laughing gulls and various other shorebirds are plentiful in the brackish ponds. Frigatebirds can be spotted along the coastline, hummingbirds are common in gardens and there are colourful woodland birds in the hills. Lizards are abundant.

## GOVERNMENT

The northern part of St Martin is a sub-prefecture of Guadeloupe, which is an overseas department of France. Local control is in the hands of a sub-prefect appointed by the French government and a locally elected mayor and town council.

The southern section of the island belongs to the Netherlands Antilles, which is part of the Kingdom of the Netherlands. While regional control of the Netherlands Antilles is based in the southern Caribbean island of

ST MARTIN

Curacao, St Maarten has its own lieutenant governor who, in conjunction with an elected island council and an appointed executive council, is responsible for the island's affairs.

## ECONOMY

The island's economy is fuelled by tourism. The whole island is one big duty-free shop and while many of the goods are geared for vacationing tourists, people from throughout the Caribbean also come here to buy electronics and other high-priced items.

## POPULATION & PEOPLE

The official population is approximately 27,000 on the French side, 32,000 on the Dutch side, although it's estimated that an additional 20,000 illegal aliens also reside on the island.

The tourist boom of the past few decades has resulted in such an influx of job-seekers from elsewhere in the Caribbean that only about 20% of all residents were born on the island. Many of French St Martin's smaller restaurants and hotels are run by relatively new arrivals from mainland France.

## ARTS & CULTURE

The island culture has its roots largely in African, French and Dutch influences, though scores of more recent immigrants have added their own elements to this multicultural society.

### Dress Conventions

Topless sunbathing is customary on both sides of the island, while nude bathing is officially sanctioned only at Orient Beach on the north coast of French St Martin.

## RELIGION

The French side of the island is predominantly Catholic, while the Dutch side is more varied, with Anglican, Baptist, Jehovah's Witness, Methodist and Seventh Day Adventist churches.

## LANGUAGE

French is the official language of French St Martin but English is also widely understood. Dutch is the official language of Dutch St Maarten, although in practice English is the first language spoken on that side, Dutch the second.

On both sides, most island-born people are multilingual and can speak English, French and creole. There's also a sizeable Spanish-speaking immigrant community from the Dominican Republic.

# Facts for the Visitor

## PASSPORT & VISAS

US and Canadian citizens arriving at Juliana Airport on the Dutch side can stay up to three months with proof of citizenship. Acceptable ID includes a birth certificate with a raised seal or a voter's registration card, plus a government-approved photo ID such as a driving licence, or a passport that is not more than five years past its expiration date. Citizens of other countries entering the island on the Dutch side require a valid passport.

If entering the island on the French side, US and Canadian citizens are allowed entry for stays of up to three weeks without a passport if they have the same type of documentation listed for the Dutch side. Citizens of the EU need an official identity card, valid passport or French carte de séjour. Citizens of most other foreign countries, including Australia, need both a valid passport and a visa for France if entering the island on the French side.

A return or onward ticket is officially required of all visitors, irregardless of whether entry is made on the French or Dutch side.

While documents are checked upon arrival, beyond that immigration controls are quite lax, a situation that is partially the result of unrestricted movement between the two sides of the island.

## CUSTOMS

There are no customs checks coming into

Juliana Airport – there's not even a counter for inspecting luggage.

## MONEY
The French franc is the official legal tender on the French side and the Netherlands Antilles guilder on the Dutch side, but on both sides US dollars are widely used as well. This makes the US dollar the most convenient currency to carry as it's the only one readily accepted on both sides of the island.

On the French side, restaurants and hotels are split between posting prices in French francs or US dollars, while on the Dutch side they're virtually always posted in US dollars.

On both sides grocery stores mark goods in the local currency but generally have cash registers equipped with a key that can automatically convert the total to US dollars.

We find it useful to carry a few francs for those times when a French business gives a bad exchange rate, but most places calculate at a fair rate and it generally works out fine to simply pay in dollars.

For details on the two island currencies, including exchange rates, see the Money section in the introductory Facts for the Visitor chapter.

MasterCard and Visa credit cards are widely, though not universally, accepted around the island.

## TOURIST OFFICES
On the Dutch side, the tourist office has information booths at Juliana Airport and at Wathey Square in Philipsburg. When requesting information by mail, write to: St Maarten Tourist Bureau (☎ 22337; fax 24884), Imperial Building, Walter Nisbeth Rd, Philipsburg, St Maarten, Netherlands Antilles.

On the French side, the tourist office is at Marigot's harbourfront. The mailing address is: St Martin Tourist Office (☎ 87 57 21; fax 87 56 43), Waterfront, 97150 Marigot, St Martin, French West Indies.

### Overseas Reps
Overseas tourist offices for the French West Indies are listed under Tourist Offices in the

Facts for the Visitor section of the Martinique chapter. The overseas tourist offices for Dutch St Maarten are:

Canada
St Maarten Information Office, 243 Ellerslie Ave, Willowdale, Ontario, Canada M2N 1Y5 (☎ (416) 223-3501; fax (416) 223-6887)
USA
St Maarten Government Tourist Office, 275 Seventh Ave, 19th Floor, New York, NY 10001-6788 (☎ (212) 989-0000; fax (212) 242-0001)
Venezuela
St Maarten Information Office, Edificio EXA, Oficina 804, Avenida Libertador, Caracas (☎ (0602) 313-832)

## BUSINESS HOURS
Shop hours in Philipsburg are generally from 8 am to noon and 2 to 6 pm Monday to Saturday. In Marigot, shop hours vary but are typically from about 9 am to 12.30 pm and 3 to 7 pm Monday to Saturday. In both towns some shops open on Sunday if cruise ships are in port.

## HOLIDAYS
Public holidays on the island are:

| | | |
|---|---|---|
| *New Year's Day* | – | 1 January |
| *Queen's Day* | – | 30 April |
| *Labor Day* | – | 1 May |
| *Good Friday* | | |
| (Dutch side) | – | late March/early April |
| *Easter Sunday* | – | late March/early April |
| *Easter Monday* | – | late March/early April |
| *Ascension Thursday* | – | 40th day after Easter |
| *Pentecost Monday* | | |
| (French side) | – | eighth Monday after Easter |
| *Bastille Day* | | |
| (French side) | – | 14 July |
| *Assumption Day* | | |
| (French) | – | 15 August |
| *St Maarten Day/* | | |
| *Concordia Day* | – | 11 November |
| *Christmas Day* | – | 25 December |
| *Boxing Day* (Dutch) | – | 26 December |

## CULTURAL EVENTS
On the French side, Carnival celebrations are held during the traditional five-day Mardi Gras period which ends on Ash Wednesday. It features the selection of a Carnival Queen, costume parades, dancing and music.

ST MARTIN

On the Dutch side, which has the larger Carnival, activities usually begin the second week after Easter, with steel band competitions, jump-ups, calypso concerts, beauty contests and costume parades. Events are centred at Carnival Village on the north side of Philipsburg and last for about two weeks.

Bastille Day is celebrated with a parade, sporting events and fireworks. The 11 November holiday, called St Maarten Day by the Dutch and Concordia Day by the French, is marked by a ceremony at the Boundary Monument obelisk that notes the amicable coexistence of the two countries.

## POST

There are post offices in Philipsburg and Marigot; see those sections for more information. There's also a post office at Juliana Airport, which is open from 7.30 am to noon and 1.30 to 5 pm weekdays.

When writing to the French side, end the address with '97150 St Martin, French West Indies'. When writing to the Dutch side, end the address with 'Sint Maarten, Netherlands Antilles'.

## TELECOMMUNICATIONS

Local numbers have five digits on the Dutch side, six digits on the French side. Calls between the two sides are charged as long distance. To phone the Dutch side from the French side, dial 19-599-5 before the local number. To call the French side from the Dutch side dial 06 before the local number.

When calling the island from overseas, you must prefix local numbers with area code 590 for the French side, 599-5 for the Dutch side.

On the French side virtually all pay phones are the card phone type, while on the Dutch side card phones predominate but there are some coin phones that operate on US quarters.

For more details on phonecards and making long-distance phone calls, see Telecommunications in the introductory Facts for the Visitor chapter.

## ELECTRICITY

On the French side the voltage is 220 AC, 60 cycles, and plugs have two round prongs. On the Dutch side it's 110 volts AC, 60 cycles, and plugs have two flat prongs. Many hotels provide dual-voltage plugs for electric shavers.

## WEIGHTS & MEASURES

Islanders use the metric system.

## BOOKS & MAPS

St Martin has a couple of notable poets including Lasana M Sekou, whose works include *Born Here* (1986) and *Nativity* (1988), and Ruby Bute, whose *Golden Voices of S'Maatin* (1990) was the first published book of poetry by a St Martin woman. All the above books are published by the nonprofit island press House of Nehesi Publishers and can be found in island bookshops.

There are a number of simple maps of the island that can be picked up from tourist offices and these will probably suffice for most exploration. Otherwise, the Institut Géographique National's 4608-G Série Bleue (1:25,000) map that covers both St Martin and St Barts is a detailed topographical map and the best road map of the island – it can be picked up at bookshops around the island for 65F.

## MEDIA

There are a number of free tourist publications with information on what to do, where to eat etc that can be picked up at the airport or tourist offices. Two of the more interesting ones are *Focus* and *Discover Saint Martin/ Sint Maarten*; both magazines are in French and English.

The Dutch side's two daily newspapers, *The Chronicle* and *The Guardian*, are printed in English. On the French side, *The News* is published on Tuesday and *St Martin's Week* on Friday; both are in French and English and are distributed free.

*Le Monde*, the *International Herald-Tribune*, the *Miami Herald*, the *New York Times* and *USA Today* are available at con-

Top Left: Tower of Dutch Reformed Church, St Eustatius (NF)
Top Right: View of St Eustatius from Brimstone Hill Fortress, St Kitts (NF)
   Bottom: Sint Eustatius Museum, St Eustatius (GB)

Left: Dancers from Masquerades troupe, St Kitts (NF)
Top Right: School children, Nevis (NF)
Middle Right: Sugar cane train, St Kitts (NF)
Bottom Right: Charlestown and Nevis Peak at sunset, Nevis (NF)

venience stores and newsstands around the island.

Cable TV carries a wide range of French and North American network programmes, as well as CNN news. Most places that aren't hooked up to cable get two stations in French and two in English. The English-language Leeward Broadcasting Corporation, on channel 7, has local programming and island news.

## HEALTH
There are hospitals in Marigot (☎ 87 50 07) near Fort Louis and east of Philipsburg (☎ 31111) in the Cay Hill area.

## DANGERS & ANNOYANCES
Normal safety precautions apply. Women travellers should be cautious walking alone on deserted beaches and if hitching. Don't leave valuables in your car as break-ins, especially in remote spots, can be a problem.

## EMERGENCIES
On the Dutch side, dial ☎ 22222 for police or fire emergencies, ☎ 22111 for an ambulance. On the French side, dial ☎ 87 50 04 for the police, ☎ 87 74 14 for an ambulance.

## ACTIVITIES
### Beaches & Swimming
The island has beautiful white-sand beaches, ranging from crowded resort strands to long secluded sweeps. Most of the best and least developed beaches are on the French side. All beaches are public, although access around some of the Dutch resorts is marked with the tiniest of signs.

### Diving
The most popular diving is at Proselyte Reef, a few km south of Philipsburg, where in 1802 the British frigate HMS *Proselyte* sank in 15 metres of water. In addition to the remains of the ship, there are 10 dive sites in that area, including coral reefs with caverns.

**Dive Shops** The following dive shops are full-service facilities offering single dives for around US$45 and multi-dive packages

with prices as low as US$30 per dive. They also conduct open-water certification courses for around US$350 and accept referred students for US$200.

Lou Scuba Club (☎ 87 22 58; fax 87 92 11), at the Marine Hotel in Baie Nettlé, dives both sides of the island. Leeward Island Divers (☎ & fax 42262) at Simpson Bay Yacht Club dives off St Martin and St Barts and arranges fly/dive packages to either Saba or Statia for US$180. Trade Winds (☎ 54387) at Great Bay Marina in Philipsburg and Blue Ocean (☎ 87 66 89) at La Belle Créole on Baie Nettlé are other popular full-service dive shops.

If you're a novice and want to get a glimpse of the underwater world, Kontiki and Bikini Beach water sports huts at Orient Beach offer three-hour resort courses that include a dive at Green Cay for US$65.

### Snorkelling
There's good snorkelling at a number of places, including Baie Rouge, Dawn Beach and the islands of Green Cay, Îlet Pinel and Tintamarre off the north-east coast.

You can rent snorkelling gear at most dive shops and hotel beach huts. Most of the dive shops also offer snorkelling tours.

A few boats offer day trips to the more pristine waters around Anguilla. *Quicksilver III* (☎ 24697 or 27 33 07), a 17-metre catamaran, leaves from the ferry dock in Marigot at 9 am daily for snorkelling trips to Anguilla's Prickly Pear Cays. The cost of US$35 includes an open bar (free drinks), snorkel gear

and the St Martin departure tax. The boat returns to Marigot at about 5 pm.

## Windsurfing

Two of the island's top windsurfing spots are at Orient Bay and at the north end of Baie de l'Embouchure. At Orient Beach, the Windsurfing Club (☎ 87 40 34), run by French windsurfing champion Nathalie Simon, rents boards from US$13/42/240 an hour/day/week and has a three-hour course for beginners for US$80 and one-hour private lessons for US$44.

Sailboard rentals are also available from a number of resort water sports centres around the island, including Mullet Bay Resort, Pelican Resort on Simpson Bay, Little Bay Beach Resort and the Marine Hotel in Baie Nettlé.

The St Martin Windsurfing Association (☎ 87 93 24) has information on races and tournaments.

## Hiking

The island's most popular hike is up to Paradise Peak. The local branch of the National Parks Foundation of the Netherlands Antilles, called STINAPA, leads guided hikes one Sunday a month. Anyone is welcome to join in for a US$3 fee. For schedule information call Francois on ☎ 24454.

## Horse Riding

The OK Corral (☎ 87 40 72) at Baie Lucas, north of the Coralita Beach Hotel, has two-hour rides along the shoreline of Baie de l'Embouchure at 9 am and 3 pm daily. The cost is US$40.

Crazy Acres Riding Center (☎ 42793) at Wathey Estate on Cole Bay has a beach ride at 9 am and 2.30 pm Monday to Saturday for US$45.

## Golf

The island's only golf course is the 18-hole course at Mullet Bay. Greens fees are US$45/65 a day in summer/winter for guests, US$65/95 for non-guests.

## Other Activities

Sunfish and Hobie-Cat boats can be rented at many resort-area beaches and yacht charters can be arranged through the marinas. When the swell picks up, Mullet Bay and Orient Bay can be good for bodyboarding. Most large resort hotels have tennis courts.

Deep-sea fishing is available through Sailfish Caraibes (☎ 87 31 94) in Anse Marcel and Sodima (☎ 32120) in Philipsburg. Sailfish Caraibes organises the Marlin Open de St Martin invitational tournament held in the last week of May.

## HIGHLIGHTS

St Martin has excellent beaches. Orient Beach is a fun place with lots of activity – if you've never been ocean swimming in the nude, this is a good place to give it a try. Long Beach is great for seclusion, while Baie Rouge and the islets off the north-east coast are special places for snorkelling. Be sure to spend an evening strolling around Grand Case and dining in one of the town's fine restaurants. If you like duty-free shopping, Philipsburg's Frontstreet and central Marigot are the places to go.

## ACCOMMODATION

Almost all of the Dutch-side accommodation is between Philipsburg and Mullet Bay, with the majority of rooms being in large resorts. On the French side there's a resort cluster on Baie Nettlé but beyond that things are fairly widely dispersed and the majority of rooms are in small-scale hotels and villa-style places. Accordingly, the places on the French side tend to be more personal and friendly.

At first glance rates may appear cheaper on the Dutch side. However, the Dutch add on to their quoted rates a 5% room tax and usually a 10% to 15% service charge – and a few even tack on an additional 'energy charge'! On the French side the majority of hotels and guesthouses include tax and service in their quoted room rates, although there are a few exceptions.

## FOOD

There are numerous quality French restaurants on the island with prices that are quite moderate by Caribbean standards. Many people, regardless of where they're staying, drive to Grand Case for dinner, as it has one of the best concentrations of good eating spots. Marigot also has a number of good dining options, with the largest selection at the Port La Royale Marina.

On the Dutch side, Philipsburg has an abundance of restaurants. Fast-food eateries are plentiful along the road to the airport.

Note that some restaurants include a 15% service charge in their prices and at others you are expected to tip.

### DRINKS
There are water desalination plants on the island, but because of the high water prices many places still use catchments. The desalinated water is fine to drink from the tap, but catchment water varies in quality and should generally be treated first. Bottled water is readily available at stores for about US$1 a bottle.

Cheap Caribbean rums and French wines are plentiful and can be purchased at any grocery store. You might want to sample the local guavaberry liqueur, a sweet rum-based drink flavoured with a small cranberry-like berry, *Eugenia floribunda*, which grows on the island's hills.

### ENTERTAINMENT
The entertainment scene is centred at the Dutch-side resorts and casinos, particularly those in the Mullet Bay area. The minimum gambling and drinking age is 18. There are cinemas in Philipsburg.

The French side tends to be pretty low key, but there are a number of bars with entertainment in Marigot.

### THINGS TO BUY
St Martin is the Eastern Caribbean's top duty-free shopping spot. Philipsburg's Frontstreet is the island's most commercial strip and has the largest selection of camera and electronics shops. In both Philipsburg and Marigot, shoppers will find chic boutiques, jewellers and perfume stores carrying top-name European products. In Marigot there's a concentration of shops at the north side of Port La Royale Marina and along the adjacent Rue du Général de Gaulle. For something more local, Marigot's harbourfront market has handicrafts, T-shirts, straw hats and the like.

Duty-free alcohol is a bargain. You can pick up a bottle of Bacardi rum at shops around the island for US$5 and at the airport for about a dollar more.

## Getting There & Away

### AIR
All international flights arrive at Juliana Airport, on the Dutch side of the island. Espérance Airport, on the French side, has an airstrip only large enough to handle prop planes from nearby islands.

The following are the local reservation numbers for airlines that have scheduled flights to Juliana Airport:

| | | |
|---|---|---|
| Aeropostal | – | ☎ 54344 |
| Air Aruba | – | ☎ 54230 |
| Air Caraibes | – | ☎ 54234 |
| Air France | – | ☎ 54212 |
| Air Guadeloupe | – | ☎ 54212 or 87 53 74 |
| Air Martinique | – | ☎ 54212 |
| Air Saint-Barthelemy | – | ☎ 53151 or 87 73 46 |
| ALM | – | ☎ 54240 |
| American Airlines | – | ☎ 52040 |
| BWIA | – | ☎ 54234 |
| Continental Airlines | – | ☎ 52444 |
| Corsair | – | ☎ 87 94 07 |
| KLM | – | ☎ 54240 |
| LIAT | – | ☎ 54203 |
| Lufthansa | – | ☎ 52040 |
| Winair | – | ☎ 54230 |

### To/From the USA & Canada
Continental and American Airlines have daily nonstop flights to St Martin from New York. They sometimes engage in fare wars offering prices as cheap as US$250 return, though the more typical excursion fare is about double that from the east coast.

### To/From Europe

Air France has four flights weekly from Paris to St Martin and KLM has a couple of flights weekly from Amsterdam. Full-fare excursion tickets cost about US$2000, but travel agents can discount these fares substantially.

### Within the Caribbean

American Airlines has daily flights to St Martin from Puerto Rico which connect with their mainland USA flights. BWIA has a twice weekly flight to St Martin from Jamaica and Saturday flights from Trinidad and Barbados.

You can fly from St Martin to any of LIAT's Caribbean destinations, in most cases with same-day connections via Antigua. LIAT flights from St Martin to Anguilla cost US$26 one way, US$50 return; to Antigua, US$80 one way, US$113 for a same-day return, US$144 for a 30-day excursion with a stopover in St Kitts allowed; to St Kitts, US$60 one way, US$73 for a same-day return, US$115 for a 30-day excursion; to Montserrat, US$113 for a 21-day excursion ticket with a free stopover in Antigua.

The St Martin-based Winair flies from St Martin to St Thomas (US$68 one way, US$120 return), Tortola (US$63 one way, US$95 for a same-day return, US$118 for a 30-day excursion), St Kitts (US$54 one way, US$63 for a same-day return, US$80 for a four-day excursion) and Anguilla (US$25 one way, US$35 for a same-day return). One-way fares to Saba or Statia are US$33, to St Barts US$40; return fares are double. Flights are on Monday, Wednesday and Friday to St Thomas and Tortola and daily to all other destinations.

Air Guadeloupe flies from Juliana Airport daily to Guadeloupe (560F one way, 980F for a 21-day excursion) and from Espérance Airport to St Barts (180F one way). Air St Barts flies daily to St Barts from both Juliana (US$50 one way) and Espérance (US$41 one way) airports. Air Martinique flies daily from St Martin to Martinique for US$317 return. Air Caraibes flies once daily between St Martin and Dominica for US$125 one way, US$174 for a seven-day excursion ticket.

### Airport Information

**Juliana Airport** The island's main airport is Juliana Airport on the Dutch side of the island. There's a tourist information booth near the arrivals exit – not terribly helpful with hands-on info but nearby there's a rack of useful tourist publications and a direct-line courtesy phone to a number of hotels and guesthouses. There's a taxi stand (and rate board) just outside the arrivals exit and a line of car rental booths nearby; however, there's no regular airport bus service.

Outside the departure lounge are duty-free shops selling liquor, perfume and the like; a newsstand with international newspapers and magazines; a deli and snack shop; and a bank. There's a 2nd-floor restaurant open from noon to midnight and a more reasonably priced ground-level booth with pastries, sandwiches and drinks.

Card phones and phones that accept US quarters are spread around the airport. Netherlands Antilles phonecards are sold at the airport post office.

**Espérance Airport** This small airport, in Grand Case in French St Martin, handles flights to St Barts and Guadeloupe. The airport has a liquor store, a card phone, car rentals and a snack bar.

**To/From the Airports** A couple of taxis meet each flight arriving at Espérance Airport; if you miss them, security can call one for you. From Espérance Airport, taxis cost US$10 to either Marigot or Orient Beach. From Juliana Airport it costs US$8 to either Marigot or Philipsburg, US$16 to Grand Case and US$20 to Orient Bay.

### SEA
### To/From St Barts

The 20-metre catamaran *Eagle* (☎ 22167) and the motorsailing catamaran *Quicksilver* (☎ 24697 or 27 33 07) run from St Maarten to St Barts, leaving daily from Great Bay Marina in Philipsburg at 9 am and returning

St Martin – Getting There & Away 437

around 5 pm. The 23-metre motor catamaran *White Octopus* (☎ 24096 days, ☎ 23170 evenings) leaves for St Barts on Wednesday from Captain Oliver's Marina at Oyster Pond and daily except Wednesday and Sunday from Bobby's Marina in Philipsburg. The White Octopus accepts credit cards and charges half price for children under 12.

They all take about 90 minutes each way and charge US$50 return, which includes an open bar, snacks and use of snorkelling gear, but not the US$5 port departure tax. You can occasionally find discount coupons in the free tourist magazines that cut the rate by US$10 or so. In the low season the catamarans sometimes consolidate passengers rather than all going out half empty while in the high season additional boats often make the run. For the latest information, enquire at the marinas or check with an activities desk.

The *St Barth Express* (☎ 27 77 24) is scheduled to accommodate day trippers from St Barts. Daily except Sunday, the boat leaves Port La Royale Marina in Marigot at 3.30 pm, picks up at Bobby's Marina in Philipsburg at 4 pm and arrives in Gustavia at 5.15 pm, returning from Gustavia at 7.30 am the next day. The cost is US$35 (180F) one way, US$50 (280F) return. Children under 12 pay half price. (Note that in the past the schedule was reversed so that St Martin visitors could make a day trip to St Barts, and it may revert back.)

### To/From Anguilla

Daily ferries leave Marigot Bay for Blowing Point on Anguilla every 30 minutes from 8 am to 5.30 pm (7.30 am to 5 pm from Anguilla to St Martin). In addition, night ferries depart Marigot Bay at 7 and 10.45 pm and depart Blowing Point at 6.15 and 10 pm. The trip takes about 20 minutes.

The one-way fare is US$9 in the day, US$11 at night. From either port, as soon as you get to the dock you should sign the passenger registration list and pay the US$2 departure tax, but you pay for the ride aboard the boat.

See the Diving section in this chapter for information on snorkelling day trips from St Martin to Anguilla.

### Yacht

Yachts can clear immigration at Philipsburg and Marigot. There are marinas at Philipsburg, Marigot, Simpson Bay Lagoon, Oyster Pond and Anse Marcel and anchorages in a number of other places, including Grand Case and the islands off Orient Bay.

Landlocked Simpson Bay Lagoon is one of the best hurricane anchorages in the Eastern Caribbean. Its drawbridge entrance, at Simpson Bay on the Dutch side, opens according to a set schedule, which is listed on page 2 of the *Chronicle*; currently it's at 6 and 11 am, and 4 and 6 pm.

### Cruise Ship

St Martin is a popular cruise ship destination, largely because of the duty-free shopping. Cruise ships land passengers in Philipsburg and Marigot.

### TOURS

Irish Travel Tours (☎ 53663), Safari Building, Airport Rd, Simpson Bay, St Martin, has day trips to either (or both) St Eustatius (Statia) or Saba, which include return airfares, a sightseeing tour and lunch. Prices start at US$100 (US$70 for children under 12). Look under Tours in the Getting There & Away sections of the Saba and St Eustatius chapters for more details.

### LEAVING ST MARTIN

From Juliana Airport, there's a departure tax of US$10 (or Naf 18) for international departures and US$5 for flights to destinations in the Netherlands Antilles. They'll also except payment in French francs but the rate is a fleecing at 8F to a US dollar. There's no departure tax for children aged two and under. There are no departure taxes at all from Espérance Airport.

Try to give yourself extra time if you're flying out with LIAT, as tickets are sold at the check-in counter and at times lines can move tediously slow.

Rather absurdly, passengers who are

simply transiting at Juliana Airport are forced to clear immigration, re-check in at the airline counter, get an exemption card from the departure tax window and then finally clear security before being allowed to enter the departure lounge for their connecting flight!

# Getting Around

## BUS

There are two kinds of buses: larger public buses, which run from Philipsburg to Marigot and Marigot to Grand Case charging US$1.50, and more frequent private minivans which charge according to distance, with a top fare of about US$3. Buses have their starting and ending points marked on them, usually on the front window. The Marigot-Philipsburg bus runs between 6 am and midnight. In addition to the main Philipsburg-Marigot-Grand Case routes, there are less frequent buses to Mullet Bay and Simpson Bay. Beyond that bus service is sketchy so touring the whole island by bus is not practical.

You can flag buses down anywhere along the route, though a new government campaign intends to limit pick-ups to signposted bus stops.

## TAXI

Taxi fares are set by the government. From Marigot it costs US$8 to Philipsburg, US$10 to Grand Case and US$15 to Orient Bay. Add US$1 for each additional passenger beyond two. There's a surcharge of 25% on fares between 10 pm and midnight and 50% from midnight to 6 am. There are taxi stands at the airport, at Wathey Square in Philipsburg and near the tourist office in Marigot.

## CAR & MOTORBIKE
### Road Rules
Driving is on the right side of the road on both sides of the island, and your home driving licence is valid. Road signs and most car odometers are in km. The speed limit in built-up areas varies from 20 to 40 km/h, while outside residential areas it's 60 km/h unless otherwise posted.

### Rental
**Car** There are scores of car rental companies on the island, with the greatest abundance at Juliana Airport. If you don't have a reservation you can stroll the row of booths just outside the airport arrival lounge and compare prices. Still, you'll generally get better rates by making reservations before you arrive – all major international car rental agencies have representatives on the island. A good bet is Budget, which will pick you up anywhere on the island and has cars, when booked in advance, for around US$25 a day. Walk-in rates at Budget and most other agencies begin around US$35. Rates include unlimited km; optional CDW (collision damage waiver) costs about US$10 a day extra.

Sanaco Car Rental (☎ 87 51 21) has an office at Espérance Airport in Grand Case. Avis has an office at Great Bay Marina in Philipsburg, near the hotel.

These companies have offices at or near Juliana Airport:

| | | |
|---|---|---|
| Avis | – | ☎ 42322 |
| Budget | – | ☎ 44275 or 87 38 22 |
| Hertz | – | ☎ 54541 or 87 73 01 |
| National/Europcar | – | ☎ 44268 |
| Sunshine | – | ☎ 52684 |

**Motorbike** Motorbikes are available on the French side from Rent A Scoot (☎ 87 20 59) opposite the Hotel Laguna Beach in Baie Nettlé, and Eugene Moto Scooter Rental (☎ 87 13 97) at Le Pirate Hotel on the west end of Marigot. On the Dutch side, Honda (☎ 25712) in the Pondfill area of Philipsburg rents scooters. Rates vary with the size of the bike, starting from around US$22 a day for a 50cc scooter up to US$100 a day for a 750cc motorcycle.

## BICYCLE
Mountain Bike Caraibes (☎ 87 97 47), at the

side of the Marine Hotel in Baie Nettlé, rents mountain bikes for US$10/60 a day/week.

## HITCHING

It's fairly easy to hitch rides on the island, although it's not really advisable, particularly for women, and the usual safety precautions apply.

## TOURS

Taxi tours of the island which last about 2½ hours cost US$35 for one or two people, US$7.50 for each additional passenger.

# Marigot

Marigot, the capital and commercial centre of French St Martin, has good restaurants and some worthwhile sights. Although it is not a large town, Marigot has two commercial centres. One of them, the area around the harbourfront, has the public market, the tourist office and the dock for boats to Anguilla. The other encompasses the Port La Royale Marina, which is surrounded by a cluster of restaurants and boutiques that spill out onto bustling Rue du Général de Gaulle.

Marigot is a historic town in flux. There are still a number of older West Indian style buildings with fancy fretwork and 2nd-floor balconies, but many others have made way for more modern structures. A new land reclamation project is taking place along the harbourfront.

## Information

**Tourist Office** The tourist office, on the north side of the harbour, is open from 8.30 am to 1 pm and 2.30 to 5.30 pm.

**Money** You can avoid transaction fees and long waits by bypassing the banks and instead changing money at the storefront currency exchange booths. Inter Change on Rue du Général de Gaulle is open from 8 am to 7 pm. Change Point, near the marina, is open from 7.30 am to 6.30 pm. Both are closed on Sunday.

**Post & Telecommunications** The post office is on Rue de la Liberté. There are card phones outside the post office (where phonecards are sold) and in front of the tourist office. A lone coin phone can be found in the Marina Royale hotel lobby.

**Laundry** There are self-service laundries near the Marina Royale hotel and at the Match supermarket complex.

**Books** Maison de la Presse, opposite the post office, sells maps of St Martin, books about the Caribbean and international newspapers. The library is on Rue du Palais de Justice.

**Film** There's one-hour film processing (24 prints for 108F) at Marina Photo at Port La Royale Marina.

## Fort St Louis

Not much remains of Fort St Louis (also called Fort de Marigot) other than some partially intact stone walls and a couple of cannons, but the hilltop locale offers a fine view of Marigot and Simpson Bay Lagoon.

To get there, drive up past the hospital and park at the large cross where you'll find steps leading up to the fort – just two minutes away. If you walk up from the harbour it takes about 15 minutes.

## St Martin Archaeological Museum

This museum is small but nicely presented, with a focus on the Arawak Period. There are displays from the plantation era and period photos of Marigot as well as shell amulets, bone artefacts, arrow points and bits of pottery from the island's early Amerindian inhabitants. Interpretive plaques are in both French and English.

The museum had plans to move to a new building in 1994, but it's expected to remain on the waterfront. Opening hours are from 9 am to 1 pm and 3 to 6.30 pm Monday to Friday, and from 9 am to 1 pm on Saturday.

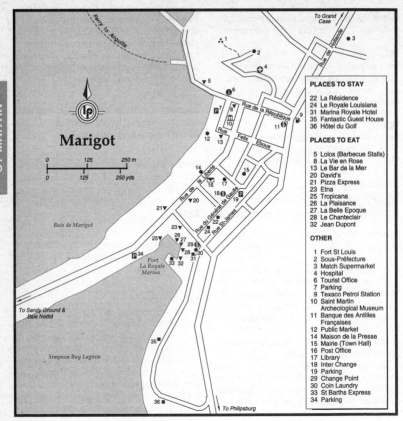

**PLACES TO STAY**

22 La Résidence
24 Le Royale Louisiana
31 Marina Royale Hotel
35 Fantastic Guest House
36 Hôtel du Golf

**PLACES TO EAT**

5 Lolos (Barbecue Stalls)
8 La Vie en Rose
13 Le Bar de la Mer
20 David's
21 Pizza Express
23 Etna
25 Tropicana
26 La Plaisance
27 La Belle Epoque
28 Le Chanteclair
32 Jean Dupont

**OTHER**

1 Fort St Louis
2 Sous-Préfecture
3 Match Supermarket
4 Hospital
6 Tourist Office
7 Parking
9 Texaco Petrol Station
10 Saint Martin Archeological Museum
11 Banque des Antilles Françaises
12 Public Market
14 Maison de la Presse
15 Mairie (Town Hall)
16 Post Office
17 Library
18 Inter Change
19 Parking
29 Change Point
30 Coin Laundry
33 St Barths Express
34 Parking

Admission is US$3 for adults and US$2 for children under 12.

**Places to Stay**

The *Fantastic Guest House* (☎ 87 71 09) is above an auto parts shop, a few minutes' walk south of the marina. There's a room with a double bed for US$42, one with two twin beds for US$52 and a larger room with a kitchenette for US$75, all with private bathroom, TV, air-con and refrigerator.

*Hôtel du Golf* (☎ 87 92 08; fax 87 83 92) has 24 small but sufficient rooms with air-con, phone and TV. However, the location, adjacent to a housing complex and office buildings, is a bit of a dud. Singles/doubles cost US$56/74 in summer, US$66/90 in winter.

The *Marina Royale* (☎ 87 52 46; fax 87 92 88), at the marina, has 62 good-sized rooms which, while not overly spiffy, have kitchenette, air-con, TV and phone; most also have a balcony. Standard rooms are US$80/90 for singles/doubles, while larger superior rooms which have a living room with a third bed cost US$90/98/115 for singles/doubles/triples, breakfast included. In the summer season you can usually negotiate a 10% discount if you're staying for a few days or longer.

The 21-room *La Résidence* (☎ 87 70 37; fax 87 90 44), in the centre of town on Rue du Général de Gaulle, is just a bit wear-worn, but adequate. Rooms are large with TV, aircon, room safe, balcony and minibar. Singles/doubles cost US$74/92 in summer, US$96/112 in winter, with breakfast included; if things are slow, the summer rate is sometimes offered in winter.

The 68-room *Le Royale Louisiana* (☎ & fax 87 86 51) on Rue du Général de Gaulle is an older in-town hotel. The rooms can be a bit dark but they have air-con, TV and phone and cost only US$45/63 for singles/doubles in summer, US$58/80 in winter, breakfast included. If you're sensitive to noise ask for a room away from the street.

### Places to Eat

**Marina** The Port La Royale Marina has a waterfront lined with restaurants offering everything from pizza and burgers to seafood and nouvelle cuisine. There's fierce competition, with some of the island's lowest menu prices and lots of chalkboard specials. The best bet is to just wander around and see what catches your fancy.

One good-value place is the small, family-run *Le Chanteclair* which has lunchtime omelettes or burgers with fries and salad for US$5 to US$7. Dinner is a full-course affair for US$19, with a wide range of standard French starters and main dishes. It's closed on Monday.

*La Belle Epoque* and *La Plaisance* are large, popular and rather conventional with varied menus that include seafood, pasta and pizza, beginning at around 45F.

The somewhat formal *Jean Dupont* has a reputation for being the finest restaurant at the marina, but it's quite a large-scale production. A more intimate choice is *Tropicana*, with good food and just eight tables. Both have classic French fare and at either dinner for two with wine will run to about US$100.

For dessert, search out *Etna*, on the street side of the marina, for delicious homemade Italian-style ice cream in tropical flavours.

**Around Town** There's a line of *lolos* (barbecue stands) between the Anguilla ferry dock and the tourist office, where you can get grilled chicken, ribs or fish with potato salad and rice and peas for US$7.

The red and white *Pizza au Feu de Bois* van, which parks opposite Le Royale Louisiana hotel in the evening, is locally popular for takeaway pizza, with prices from 25F to 50F. This little mobile pizza wagon actually has a wood-fired oven stoked up inside!

If you prefer to have pizza delivered to your door, try *Pizza Express* (☎ 87 87 72), with prices from 44F.

*Davids* on Rue de la Liberté is a lively English pub with dart boards and Fosters beer. The varied menu has pasta, meat and seafood dishes from US$10 and tops off with the house special, beef Wellington, at US$19. It's open for lunch from 11.30 am to 2.30 pm on weekdays, for dinner from 6 to 10 pm nightly and as a watering hole until midnight. There are two-for-one drinks and free bar snacks from 5 to 6.30 pm every evening and dollar beers on Sunday.

*Le Bar de la Mer*, near the harbour, draws a predominantly French-speaking crowd and is a popular spot to have a drink. It also has reasonably priced salads and pizzas, as well as a few fish and meat dishes. There's live music from 8.30 pm to 12.30 am nightly.

*La Vie en Rose* is a highly regarded French restaurant opposite the harbour. At lunch there's a sidewalk café with fish and meat dishes in the 70F to 100F range. Dinner is served in a more formal upstairs dining room that has a romantic little ocean-view balcony where parties of two are usually seated. The à la carte menu features a dozen main courses, including the likes of lobster medallions and breast of duck, all priced from 170F to 195F. It's open daily for dinner and for breakfast and lunch daily except Sunday.

Match, the large, modern supermarket on the north side of Marigot, has a pretty good deli, wine selection and bakery. It's open from 9 am to noon on Sunday, to 8 pm other days. For a bakery in the centre of town *Délifrance*, near the Mairie, is a good choice.

# Around French St Martin

## SANDY GROUND/BAIE NETTLÉ

Sandy Ground is the long, narrow, curving strip of land that extends west from Marigot, with Baie Nettlé (Nettle Bay) on one side and Simpson Bay Lagoon on the other. The first hotel went up less than a decade ago, but these days there's a strip of hotels, restaurants and small shopping centres one after the other.

In itself, Sandy Ground is not a place of any great interest – the ocean beach is marginal and not kept up and the lagoon side is a bit mucky for swimming – but it can be a convenient base if you get a good hotel deal, and some of St Martin's finest beaches are just down the road.

### Places to Stay

The best overall value of the Sandy Ground hotels is the 119-room *Marine Hôtel* (☎ 87 54 54; fax 87 92 11), BP 172, Baie Nettlé. The rooms are comfortable with ceiling fan, air-con, TV, phone, kitchenette and large balcony, some with a view across Simpson Bay Lagoon. There's a nice pool, tennis courts and a dive shop. Rates include a buffet breakfast. Standard rooms cost US$106/136 in summer/winter, US$10 less for singles and US$20 more during the Christmas holidays. In the off-season there are sometimes special deals for about US$70. Reservations can be made internationally through Resinter (in France ☎ (1) 60 77 27 27, in the USA and Canada ☎ (800) 221-4542).

Also in the moderate range is *Nettle Bay Beach Club* (☎ 87 97 04), a rather ordinary complex on the bay side with rooms from US$95/155 in summer/winter, and *Hôtel Dom* (☎ 87 04 03), immediately east of Marine Hotel, which has rooms from

US$72/87 in summer/winter, suites from US$135/163, and discounted weekly rates.

*La Belle Créole* (☎ 87 66 00; fax 87 56 66; in the USA ☎ (800) 445-8667), a Hilton hotel, is on a jut of land at the western tip of Baie Nettlé. The beach is not terribly special and the hotel's a bit sprawling, but it has the expected 1st-class amenities. Courtyard rooms cost US$165/295 in summer/winter, ocean-view rooms are US$40 more and suites start at US$310/450. The Hilton often runs special promotions that discount these rates.

### Places to Eat

*La Mouette Rieuse* (☎ 87 87 55) is a friendly waterfront restaurant with French and Creole fare. In the evenings the owner plays guitar and sings French folk songs from the '60s. There is a variety of creative salads for around US$10, while main courses begin at US$13 for kebabs or goat colombo and top off at lobster for US$22. In addition there's usually a menu of the day with wine and dessert for around US$20. It's open for dinner daily and for lunch every day except Sunday. To get there turn right opposite the stadium (at the 'Seaview Restaurant' sign) just before crossing the bridge from Marigot to Sandy Ground.

*Bach Lien*, behind the Hotel Laguna Beach, has a wide variety of Thai and Vietnamese dishes, most from 55F to 75F. You can eat in or order takeaway. It's open from 11.30 am to 1.15 pm except on Monday and daily from 6.30 to 10 pm.

*La Fayette* (☎ 87 92 89), one of the better Baie Nettlé restaurants, offers a fixed three-course meal for 94F. Otherwise à la carte main dishes range from 80F for red snapper to 110F for beef tenderloin in a green peppercorn sauce. It's on the beach at the west end of Nettle Bay Beach Club and is open for dinner from 6 pm.

*La Belle Créole* has a US$8.50 breakfast buffet that includes fresh fruit and bagels with cream cheese.

## BAIE ROUGE

Baie Rouge, a km west of Sandy Ground, has

a nice sandy strand with good snorkelling. Although this white-sand beach is just 150 metres from the main road it's delightfully free of development. For the best snorkelling swim to the right in the direction of the rocky outcrop and arch. The dirt drive leading to the beach is at a 90° turn on the road from Sandy Ground to Mullet Bay – as you have to virtually stop to negotiate the turn, it's easy to find.

## BAIE AUX PRUNES (PLUM BAY)
The remote and unspoiled Baie aux Prunes is a gently curving bay with polished shell-like grains of golden sand. The beach is popular for swimming and sunbathing and is backed by a little wood of white cedar trees with pink blossoms that attract humming-birds.

It can be reached by turning right 1.3 km south of Baie Rouge and immediately taking the signposted left fork. After two km you'll come to a T-junction; turn right and continue 200 metres, where there's a parking area and a short walkway to the beach.

## BAIE LONGUE (LONG BAY)
Long Beach, at Baie Longue, is two splendid km of seemingly endless white sand. The only development along the shoreline is the La Samanna hotel at the very southern tip. The beach is very big and well off the beaten path – a great place for long strolls and quiet sunsets. However, because it's so secluded, women walking alone should be cautious here.

You can get to Long Beach by continuing south from Baie aux Prunes or by taking the La Samanna turn-off from the main road and continuing past the hotel for a km. There's a parking area in front of a chain-link fence and a short footpath leading to the beach.

## Places to Stay
*La Samanna* (☎ 87 51 22; fax 87 87 86; in the USA ☎ (800) 854-2252) is a fine choice for a top-end hotel. This low-profile, exclusive hotel has 85 rooms, each with air-con, ceiling fan, phone, minibar and a balcony or patio that fronts the ocean. There's a pool,

tennis courts and complimentary windsurfing lessons. Rates start at US$275/440 in summer/winter and go up to US$850/1250 for a multi-terraced one-bedroom suite.

## FRIAR'S BAY
Friar's Bay, two km north of Marigot centre, is a protected cove with a nice beach. This popular local swimming spot is located just beyond the residential neighbourhood of St Louis and the road in is signposted. From noon to 4 pm you can get grilled chicken (US$2) and ribs (US$4) at *Kali's Beach Bar*, a friendly Rastafarian-style place right on the beach.

## COLOMBIER
For St Martin's version of a country drive, take the road that leads two km inland to the hamlet of Colombier. This short, pleasant side trip offers a glimpse of a rural lifestyle that has long disappeared elsewhere on the island. The scenery along the way is bucolic with stone fences, big mango trees, an old coconut-palm plantation and hillside pastures with grazing cattle.

The road to Colombier begins 350 metres north of the turn-off to Friar's Bay.

## PARADISE PEAK (PIC DU PARADIS)
Paradise Peak, the highest point on the island, offers fine vistas and good hiking opportunities. The peak is topped with a communications tower and has a rough maintenance road leading up it that doubles as a hiking track.

You can generally drive as far as the last house and then walk the final km to the top. The mountain gets more rain than the rest of the island and the woods are thick with viny trees and colourful forest birds. Ten minutes up, just before the tower, a sign to the left points the way to the best viewpoint. Take this track for about 75 metres, then veer to the right where the path branches and you'll come to a cliff with a broad view of the island's east side. You can see Orient Salt Pond and the expansive Etang aux Poissons to the east, the village of Orleans at your feet and Philipsburg to the south.

For a good view of the west side of the island, go back to the main track and walk up past the communications tower. From the rocks directly beyond you can see Marigot, Simpson Bay Lagoon and Baie Nettlé.

If you want to do more serious hiking, a network of tracks leads from the Paradise Peak area to Orient Bay, Orleans and the Dutch side of the island. Flash Media's St Martin map, available free at the tourist office, shows the trails.

The road to Paradise Peak is 500 metres north of the road to Colombier. Take the road inland for almost two km, turn left at the fork and continue a further 500 metres to the last house.

## GRAND CASE

The small beachside town of Grand Case has been dubbed 'the gourmet capital of St Martin'. The beachfront road is lined with a wonderful range of places to eat, from local lolos (barbecue stalls) to top-notch French and Italian restaurants. Some of the restaurants are open for lunch, but Grand Case is at its liveliest in the evening.

The town itself is half local, half touristy, and while there are a few colourful buildings, dining is the premier attraction. Espérance Airport, which is bordered by salt ponds that attract waterbirds, is at the east side of town.

As for the beach, Grand Case's is fine if you're staying there but it's not one of the island's top strands. Most of the beach fronting the centre of town is quite narrow, particularly at high tide, but the north side broadens out a bit and is more attractive.

### Places to Stay

*Hévéa* (☎ 87 56 85; fax 87 83 88), at the restaurant of the same name, has five good-value colonial-style rooms with air-con. In summer, singles/doubles cost from US$36/48 for standard rooms, and US$66/78 for units with kitchenettes. Winter rates are about 50% higher.

*Ma Chance Guest House* (☎ 87 50 45) consists of two simple, not overly cheerful rooms in a private home. Each has air-con

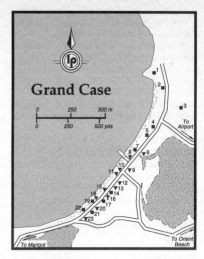

**Grand Case**

To Airport

To Orient Beach

To Marigot

**PLACES TO STAY**

1   Grand Case Beach Club
2   Flamboyant Beach Villas
3   L'Esplanade Hôtel
4   Grand Case Beach Motel
5   Les Alizés Motel
14   Ma Chance Guest House
19   Chez Martine
21   Hévéa
22   Hôtel Atlantide

**PLACES TO EAT**

6   Bye Bar Brasil
8   Talk of the Town
9   Cha Cha Cha
10   Le Fish Pot
11   Le Tastevin
12   L'Alabama
13   Les Arts Café
15   Surf Club South
18   California Pizza
19   Chez Martine
20   Jungle Café
21   Hévéa
23   Bakery

**OTHER**

7   Grand Case Superette
16   Church
17   Tony's Vegetable & Meat Market

and a refrigerator and costs US$40 for one or two people.

*Les Alizés Motel* (☎ 87 95 38) is perhaps a bit unkempt, but its nine small studios are right on the beach and each has cooking facilities and air-con. The cost is US$45/60 in summer/winter for regular units, US$50/80 for ocean views.

The *Grand Case Beach Motel* (☎ 87 87 75) is an older beachside hotel with linoleum, plastic flowers and a dated decor, but the half dozen units have fan, air-con, kitchenette and small patio. Rates are US$40 in summer and US$80 in winter, plus a 10% service charge and an additional US$5 charge to use the air-con.

*Chez Martine* (☎ 87 51 59; fax 87 87 30) has six small air-con rooms at the side of its restaurant that rent for US$56/65 for singles/doubles in summer, US$78/96 in winter.

*Flamboyant Beach Villas* (☎ 87 50 98; fax 87 81 04) is a small complex of one and two-storey buildings on the beach next to Grand Case Beach Club. Units are suitably straightforward with cottage-style furnishings, one or two bedrooms and a combined kitchen, living room and dining room. There are screened louvred windows on all sides to catch cross breezes. Summer/winter rates are US$60/96 for one-bedroom units, US$102/156 for two-bedroom units.

*Hôtel Atlantide* (☎ 87 09 80; fax 87 37 42) is a new beachside complex with half a dozen comfortably chic apartments. Units have full kitchen, living room, a big ocean-fronting balcony that serves as a dining room, TV, phone, air-con, bathtub and marble floors. Rates begin at US$85/110 in summer/winter for one-bedroom units, with the fanciest two-bedroom units topping off at US$175/220.

*Grand Case Beach Club* (☎ 87 51 87; fax 87 59 93; in the USA ☎ (800) 223-1588), on the quiet north-east end of the beach, has 74 pleasant condo-like units with air-con, full kitchen and balcony. Studios have two double beds and a small dining table, while the roomy one-bedroom units have a separate living room. Garden-view studios cost US$95 in summer, US$210 in winter and US$120 in spring and autumn. One-bed-

room units are US$110/260/155 in summer/winter/spring and autumn. There are also two-bedroom, two-bath units. Children aged 12 and under stay for free in all rooms other than the studios. There's a restaurant, pool and tennis court and rates include continental breakfast. The hotel is closed from early September to mid-October.

*L'Esplanade Hôtel*, (☎ 87 06 55; fax 87 29 15) is a new hillside hotel on the north-east edge of town. There are 24 studios and one-bedroom suites, all with kitchen, ceiling fan, air-con, TV, phone, room safe and ocean-view terrace. The one-bedroom units have a king-size bed and a living room with a sofabed and cost US$125/220 in summer/winter for doubles, plus US$25 for each additional person. Studios cost US$90/125 in summer/winter for singles, US$105/150 for doubles. There's a 10% service charge.

## Places to Eat

In the evening, a ritual of sorts takes place on the beachfront road, with restaurants placing their menus and chalkboard specials along the pavement and would-be diners strolling along the strip until they find a place that strikes their fancy.

*Talk of the Town* is the first in a line of ramshackle but very popular beachside lolos near the pier. For under US$10 you can sit at waterfront picnic tables and chow down on johnnycakes, chicken legs, spareribs and potato salad – all sold à la carte.

*Surf Club South* is a nicely funky beach bar with two-for-one drinks from 4.30 to 6 pm daily. In the morning, you can get two eggs, fries and coffee as well as other breakfast standards for US$4 to US$5 and during the day there are sandwiches and burgers at similar prices.

*California Pizza* is a pleasant place with a fine waterfront setting. It has pizzas, pastas and salads from about US$8.

A recommended spot is *L'Alabama*, a popular and friendly place serving nicely prepared French food at good prices. Tasty jumbo shrimp sautéed in pineapple marinade and a range of other offerings from chicken to lobster cost between US$11 and US$18.

Starters, salads and wine are also very reasonably priced. It's open nightly except Monday from 6 to 10.30 pm.

*Cha Cha Cha* has waitresses in traditional Creole dress and a varied menu that includes French, Mexican and Creole offerings. It has good gazpacho and black bean soups (US$5.50), while main dishes include a delicious blackened tuna dish (US$16) that's seared on the outside and sashimi-like inside. A good value early bird special between 6 and 7 pm includes soup or salad and a choice of three main courses for US$15. There's also a garden out the back with drinks and a light tapas (snack) menu. It's open for dinner only from Monday to Saturday.

Other interesting restaurants include *Bye Bar Brasil*, with traditional Brazilian food; the trendy *Les Arts Café* with Sunday night music; and *Jungle Café*, with straightforward but well-prepared food and a funky jungle ambience. Two upscale French restaurants worth a look are *Le Tastevin* and *Le Fish Pot*.

## ANSE MARCEL

Secluded Anse Marcel is a deeply indented bay with calm protected waters and a long sandy beach that's backed by French St Martin's largest resort hotel.

Anse Marcel has a flashy marina that's home base to a couple of yacht charter companies, including ATM and Nautor's Swan Charters. The marina has a few fashionable boutiques and jewellery shops, a small convenience store that sells liquor and foreign newspapers, a water sports centre and a shop that sells charts and basic yachting supplies. The port office will hold mail for boaters.

### Places to Stay

The beachfront *Le Méridien L'Habitation* (☎ 87 33 33; fax 87 30 38; in the USA ☎ (800) 543-4300) is a bustling 410-room hotel with full resort amenities and standard 1st-class rooms. Rates begin at US$169/255 in summer/winter, with breakfast included.

Recommended is the nearby *Hôtel Privilège* (☎ 87 37 37; fax 87 33 75), which has a friendly manager and a dozen roomy

units located above the marina shops. Rooms have a pleasant wood interior, TV, bathtub, queen or king-size bed, air-con and a large balcony strung with hammocks. Guests can use Le Méridien's pool and tennis courts. Studios cost US$109/142 for singles/doubles. Suites, which have a sofabed in the living room, cost US$164. A two-bedroom suite with a kitchenette costs US$193 for two people, US$254 for four. Rates include continental breakfast and are the same all year round except from 15 December to 15 January when they jump about 50%.

### Places to Eat

The best place to eat at Anse Marcel is the harbourside *La Louisiane*, which is open from 7 am to about 11 pm daily. You can get salads and omelettes for around 40F, sandwiches, burgers and pasta dishes from 45F and meat and fish dishes for about double that. The bar features a Planters punch (rum punch) for US$1 from 6 to 7.30 pm.

The standard of food at the expensive *Privilège Restaurant* is inconsistent, but it has a scenic hillside location and is a good spot for a cocktail. There's a free shuttle to the restaurant from the marina.

## FRENCH CUL-DE-SAC

French Cul-de-Sac is a small seaside community just north of Orient Bay. While there's no beach of note, local fishers run boats back and forth all day to the white sands of nearby Îlet Pinel.

### Îlet Pinel

Pinel, the most visited of the area's offshore islands, is just a km from French Cul-de-Sac. A Dutch family lives on the island and a few yachts anchor nearby, but Pinel is largely the domain of day-trippers. The island is big enough for a little exploring, you can snorkel and there are places to eat and rent water sports equipment.

It's easy to get there – simply go to the dock at road's end in French Cul-de-Sac, where you can catch a small boat to the sandy beach on Pinel's east side. The three-minute ride costs US$5 return. Boats also go to Pinel from Orient Beach.

## Places to Stay

*Jardins de Chevrise* (☎ 87 37 79; fax 87 38 03) is not the newest or spiffiest of places, but the price is fair and it's about a 10-minute walk to the beach. This two-storey complex has 29 apartment units and a pool. Singles/doubles cost US$63/66 in summer, US$96/100 in winter.

*Sunrise Hotel* (☎ 87 42 24; fax 87 39 28), Cul-de-Sac, is a cosy 10-room hotel managed by a friendly young French couple. The rooms are modern and comfortable with fully equipped kitchen, air-con, TV, phone, room safe and private terrace. There's a small pool, an ice machine, a collection of French and English books and a storage room where you can leave gear between stays. Rates are US$87/120 in the low/high season. Children under 12 are free; a third adult is US$20 more. Weekly rates are six times the daily rate.

*Hôtel Mont Vernon* (☎ 87 62 00; fax 87 37 27; in Paris ☎ 47 23 03 43) is a rambling 394-room hotel perched on a rise overlooking the northernmost end of Orient Bay. Catering to package tours, it has standard resort rooms, each with a balcony. Singles/doubles begin at US$95/125 in summer, US$180/207 in winter, breakfast included. Ocean-view rooms are about 25% higher. You can usually get substantially cheaper rates if you book the hotel as part of a package tour. There's a large pool, tennis courts, a water sports centre and a couple of restaurants.

## Places to Eat

The following places are on the village's main road. *Drew's Deli* is a Manhattan-style deli run by a friendly American from Madison, Wisconsin. This informal place has a few tables on the porch, sandwiches from US$5, salads at US$3 and hot meals such as lasagne or barbecued ribs at US$9. It's open from 11 am to 3 pm and 7 to 9.30 pm, but is closed on Friday night and all day on Saturday.

*Mark's Place* is popular for its good Creole-style food. You can get chicken colombo, conch stew or octopus stew for US$11 to US$13 and starters such as accras (cod fritters) and crab farci for under US$5. It's open for lunch from 12.30 to 2.30 pm, for dinner from 6.30 to 9.30 pm, except on Monday.

*Hoa Mai* is an Indochinese restaurant with beef, chicken and seafood main courses from 60F to 80F at lunch and dinner. Next door there's a grocery store with duty-free liquor and roast chicken to take away. The Texaco petrol station also has a mini-mart.

## ORIENT BEACH

Orient Beach is a splendid, gently curving sweep of white sand and bright turquoise waters. Clothing is optional along the entire two-km beach, although nudity is de rigueur only at the southern end where there's a naturist resort, Club Orient. A decade ago Club Orient was the only development in the area. In the past few years a handful of villa-type places have been built near the centre of the stretch but none are situated directly on the beach and all are relatively small scale.

The bay is an underwater nature reserve and the waters are usually calm and good for swimming. It's also a good spot for water sports, including windsurfing, Hobie-Cat sailing and jet skiing.

The easiest public beach access and one of St Martin's liveliest day scenes is adjacent to the north side of Club Orient. Here you'll find a bandstand with afternoon calypso and reggae music, cheap food stalls and clothing vendors selling T-shirts, swimsuits and batik pareos (sarongs). During the height of the day this strip can take on a certain carnival atmosphere attracting a few voyeurs with cameras, but for the most part it's just a mixed bag of people enjoying the beach.

## Information

There are numerous water sports centres along Orient Beach, with the largest concentration at the north side of Club Orient.

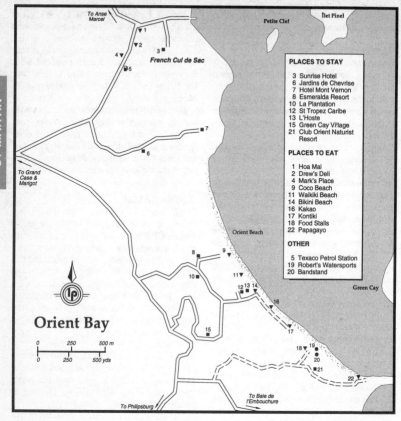

Orient Bay

```
0        250        500 m
0        250        500 yds
```

PLACES TO STAY

3  Sunrise Hotel
6  Jardins de Chevrise
7  Hotel Mont Vernon
8  Esmeralda Resort
10  La Plantation
12  St Tropez Caribe
13  L'Hoste
15  Green Cay Village
21  Club Orient Naturist
    Resort

PLACES TO EAT

1  Hoa Mai
2  Drew's Deli
4  Mark's Place
9  Coco Beach
11  Waikiki Beach
14  Bikini Beach
16  Kakao
17  Kontiki
18  Food Stalls
22  Papagayo

OTHER

5  Texaco Petrol Station
19  Robert's Watersports
20  Bandstand

Robert's Watersports, in front of the bandstand, rents snorkel sets for US$10 a day, beach chairs or umbrellas for US$5, and makes speedboat runs to Green Cay (US$8 per person return), Îlet Pinel (US$12) and Tintamarre Island (US$20).

Behind the bandstand there are showers (US$1) and restrooms (US$0.50). Taxis wait at the end of the driveway and charge US$15 (per taxi) to either Marigot or Philipsburg.

Farther north, in the quieter centre of the beach, there are five more water sports centres, one fronting each of the beachside restaurants. One of them, Bikini Water-

sports, provides a boat taxi to the offshore islands for the same price as Robert's.

**Green Cay (Caye Verte)**

Green Cay is a small islet 500 metres off Orient Beach with a nice sandy spit at its southern end and reasonably good snorkelling in the surrounding waters. The water sports centres can shuttle you over by speedboat and pick you up at a pre-arranged time. There's no shade or facilities, so consider bringing along a beach umbrella and something to drink.

Don't try to grab shade or rain cover from

the trees at the rocky end of the beach, as they're poisonous manchineel trees. The rocks are a habitat for numerous small *Anolis* lizards; the males put on an interesting show, puffing up orange sacs under their necks as a territorial warning.

## Places to Stay

*La Plantation* (☎ 87 32 04; fax 87 35 76; in the USA ☎ (800) 727-7388) is one of the area's best value places to stay. There are 14 villas of plantation-house design, each with a one-bedroom suite and two studios. All units are large and pleasant with high pitched ceiling, air-con, ceiling fan, cable TV, room safe, kitchen and private verandah facing the ocean. The studios cost US$60/75 in summer/winter for singles, US$80/105 for doubles. Suites, which have a separate living room, are US$85/115 in summer/winter for singles, US$115/145 for doubles and US$15/25 more for a third person. It's about a five-minute walk to the beach.

*St Tropez Caribe* (☎ 87 42 01; fax 87 41 69; in the USA ☎ (800) 622-7836) is a new 84-unit complex just inland from the beach. The rooms are in Mediterranean-style three-storey buildings and have a sitting area, terrace or balcony, central air-con, TV, small refrigerator, room safe and phone. All have either a king-size bed or two twins. It has a North American manager and fills predominantly with visitors from the USA. Rates are US$90 to US$110 in summer, US$120 to US$150 in winter, with the lower rates for ground-floor rooms.

*L'Hoste* (☎ 87 42 08; fax 87 39 96; in France ☎ 47 89 34 51), which has 28 units identical to those in the adjacent St Tropez Caribe, is under French management and fills primarily with Europeans. Rates are US$120 to US$135 in the low season, US$175 to US$190 in the winter.

*Club Orient Naturist Resort* (☎ 87 33 85; fax 87 33 76; in the USA ☎ (800) 742-4276) is the Eastern Caribbean's only clothing-optional resort. All activities, including dining, water sports, tennis and sailing cruises, are au naturel. The accommodation is in 62 chalets of red pine imported from Finland. They're suitably rustic with a double platform bed, sofa, desk and chair, shower, ceiling fan and a kitchenette with an oven, refrigerator, coffeemaker and toaster. Studios, which are in duplex chalets, cost from US$135/195 for doubles in summer/winter. One-bedroom units occupy a whole chalet and cost from US$165/265 in summer/winter. Single rates are about 15% cheaper.

The upscale *Esmeralda Resort* (☎ 87 36 36; fax 87 35 18) has 15 villa-style buildings,

each with a few separate rooms and suites. The rooms, which have cooking facilities, TV and safe, cost from US$165/250 in summer/ winter. The suites, which have a separate living room and kitchen area, start at US$250/350 in summer/winter. Each villa has its own pool.

*Green Cay Village* (☎ 87 38 63; fax 87 39 27) has 20 swanky new villas, each with a full kitchen, bedroom with king-size bed, a stereo CD player, cable TV with VCR and a living room that opens out to an ocean-view deck with a private swimming pool. To round it off there's free tennis and airport transfers. In summer, weekly rates are US$1450 for one-bedroom units, US$2100 for two-bedroom villas. In winter, weekly rates are US$2100/3200 respectively.

### Places to Eat

At the northern side of Club Orient there are a couple of dozen food stalls selling everything from US$1 hot dogs and beer to crêpes, ice cream and US$20 lobster lunches.

The informal open-air *Papagayo* restaurant at Club Orient has omelettes, salads, sandwiches and burgers in the US$6 to US$10 range and fish and meat dishes served with potatoes or pasta for around US$20. It's open daily for all meals.

There are five simple open-air restaurants spread along the centre of the beach that are primarily lunch spots, although a couple of them stay open for dinner. You can get lunch at any of them for US$10 to US$15. From south to north they are: *Kontiki*, which has good barbecued fish and lobster; *Kakao*, with pizza and pastas; *Bikini Beach*, with a tapas style menu but lacklustre food; *Waikiki Beach,* an American-run spot with sandwiches and seafood including a raw bar; and *Coco Beach* with more traditional French and Creole dishes.

### OYSTER POND

The Dutch/French border slices straight across Oyster Pond, a largely rural area with a growing number of small condominiums and other vacation rentals. A marina and most of the accommodation falls on the

French side, while the area's finest beach (Dawn Beach) is on the Dutch side (see the end of this chapter).

Oyster Pond is not a pond, but a bay, though it's a very protected one and its shape does resemble an oyster. For a good vantage of Oyster Pond, there's a short path leading up the cactus-studded hill on the north-east side of the bay.

Captain Oliver's Marina has 100 slips, the standard marina services, a couple of places to eat, an activities desk and a few shops and offices including those of The Moorings and the Sun Yacht Charters companies.

### Places to Stay

*Coralita Beach Hotel* (☎ 87 31 81; fax 87 31 20), BP 175, Marigot, is on Baie Lucas, the beach just north of Oyster Pond. This unpretentious two-storey hotel has the character of an old-fashioned French seaside resort. The 24 studios are mildly run-down but are large and have kitchenette, fan and a small ocean-fronting balcony. Singles/doubles cost US$60/75 in summer, US$110/135 in winter, plus 20% tax and service charge. There's a pool, a tennis court, free use of snorkel gear and a moderately priced restaurant and bar.

Good value is *Copacabana Club* (☎ 87 42 52; fax 87 39 85), a new complex with 19 comfortable condo-type units a few minutes' walk from the marina. Each has a separate bedroom, TV, phone, kitchenette and a terrace or balcony. Rates are US$75/85/100 for singles/doubles/triples in summer, US$110/120/135 in winter. Breakfast at Captain Oliver's is included, but if you prefer you can arrange with the manager, Dominique, to skip breakfast and deduct US$10 per person from the rates.

The nearby *Blue Beach Hotel* (☎ 87 33 44; fax 87 42 13), 26 Oyster Pond, has 42 small modern rooms with kitchenette, air-con, phone, TV, two twin beds or one double bed and terrace or balcony. Some rooms have ocean views at no extra cost. Singles/doubles cost US$70/85 in summer, US$85/120 in winter. There are also four larger rooms with a 2nd-floor loft for US$110/150 for up to four people. It's possible to rent a room without an ocean view on a monthly basis for US$900 plus utilities. There's a pool, bar and restaurant.

*Captain Oliver's* (☎ 87 40 26; fax 87 40 84), BP 645, Oyster Pond, a member of the Pullman chain, is at the marina. The 50 rooms have kitchenette, phone, TV, safe, air-con and balcony. There's a pool. Singles/doubles cost from US$95/105 in summer, US$168/210 in winter.

### Places to Eat

*Captain Oliver's Dinghy Dock* at the marina is a dockside snack bar with picnic tables, US$6 sandwiches, chilli dogs, croissants and Fosters on tap. Next door is Ship Shop, a small convenience store with groceries, alcohol and sundries that's open to 7 pm.

*Captain Oliver's* is a popular open-air seafront restaurant on the dock which has a daily US$10 breakfast buffet from 7 to 10 am. At lunch and dinner an avocado, lobster and shrimp salad costs US$10, while fresh seafood and meat dishes are US$16 to US$20.

*Frog's* at the Blue Beach Hotel is a pleasantly informal rooftop French restaurant with a varied chalkboard menu and a bit of a sea view. House standards include frog legs, cornish hens and grilled meats for around US$12. It's open for dinner from 6 pm to about midnight daily.

# Philipsburg

Philipsburg, Dutch St Maarten's main town, is centred on a long and narrow stretch of land that separates Great Salt Pond from Great Bay. There are some older buildings mixed among the new, but overall the town is far more commercial than quaint. Most of the action is along Frontstreet, the bayfront road, which is lined with boutiques, jewellery shops, restaurants, hotels, casinos and duty-free shops selling everything from Danish porcelain to Japanese cameras and electronics.

Wathey Square, the town centre of sorts,

has a tourist information booth, a small wharf where cruise ships dock and an old courthouse that dates from 1793. Vendors on the square sell souvenirs, drinking coconuts and fresh-squeezed sugar cane juice.

Great Bay Beach borders the entire town of Philipsburg, but the buildings lining Frontstreet face inland and it's easy to walk along the street without noticing the beach at all. Although Great Bay is not one of St Maarten's most pristine beaches, the water is calm and some people opt to swim there.

### Orientation

Four streets run east to west and numerous narrow lanes (called *steegjes)* connect them north to south. Frontstreet has one-way traffic that moves in an easterly direction and Backstreet has one-way traffic heading west. Public buses can be picked up along Backstreet. The north side of Philipsburg is sometimes referred to as Pondfill, as much of this area is reclaimed land.

### Information

**Money** There are a number of banks around Philipsburg, including Barclays Bank at Frontstreet 19 and Windward Islands Bank on Wathey Square which is open from 8.30 am to 3.30 pm Monday to Friday.

**Post** The post office, at the west end of Camille Richardson Rd, is open from 7.30 am to 5 pm Monday to Thursday, and to 4.30 pm on Friday.

**Laundry** At the Sparkling Clean Laundromat at the marina you can leave a load of clothes to be washed, dried and folded for US$7.50. It's open from 8 am to noon on Sunday, and to 6 pm other days. Alternatively, you can do it yourself at Renewed Dry Cleaners & Laundromat, opposite the marina's Texaco station, but it will cost almost as much.

### St Maarten Museum

This modest little museum at Frontstreet 119 has displays on the island's history with period photos, old bottles, a rock collection

ST MARTIN

ST MARTIN

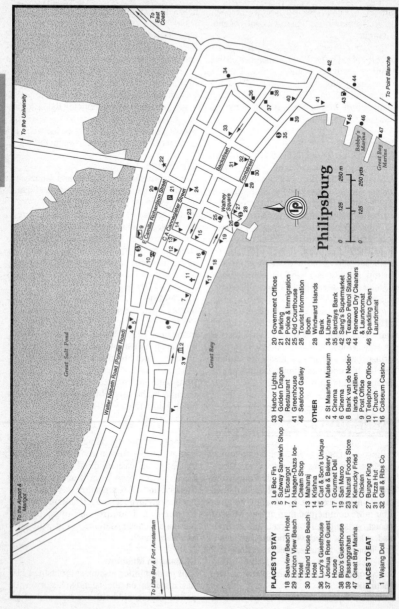

Philipsburg

To the University

Great Salt Pond

To Little Bay & Fort Amsterdam

To the Airport & Margot

Walter Nisbeth Road (Pondfill Road)

To East Coast

To Point Blanche

Great Bay

Wathey Square

Backstreet

Frontstreet

E Camille Richardson Street

C A Cannegieter Street

Bobby's Marina

Great Bay Marina

0    125    250 m
0    125    250 yds

**PLACES TO STAY**
18 Seaview Beach Hotel
29 Horizon View Beach Hotel
30 Holland House Beach Hotel
36 Lucy's Guesthouse
37 Joshua Rose Guest House
38 Bico's Guesthouse
39 Pasanggrahan
47 Great Bay Marina

**PLACES TO EAT**
1 Wajang Doll
3 Le Bec Fin
5 Subway Sandwich Shop
12 L'Escargot
13 Haagen-Dazs Ice-Cream Shop
14 Mahani
15 Krishna
17 Carl & Son's Unique Cafe & Bakery
19 Gourmet Deli
23 San Marco
24 Natural Foods Store
27 Kentucky Fried Chicken
31 Burger King
32 Pizza Hut
    Grill & Ribs Co

33 Harbor Lights
40 Golden Dragon Restaurant
41 Greenhouse
45 Seafood Galley

**OTHER**
2 St Maarten Museum
4 Cinema
6 Cinema
8 Bank van de Nederlands Antillen
9 Post Office
10 Telephone Office
11 Church
16 Coliseum Casino
20 Government Offices
21 Parking
22 Police & Immigration
25 Old Courthouse
26 Tourist Information Booth
28 Windward Islands Bank
34 Library
35 Barclays Bank
42 Sang's Supermarket
43 Texaco Petrol Station
44 Renewed Dry Cleaners & Laundromat
46 Sparkling Clean Laundromat

and similar artefacts. It's open from 10 am to 4 pm weekdays, to noon on Saturday. Admission is US$1, free for children.

### Fort Amsterdam

In 1631 the Dutch built their first Caribbean fort, Fort Amsterdam, on the peninsula separating Great Bay and Little Bay. It didn't withstand an invasion by the Spanish, who captured the fort two years later, expanding it and adding a small church.

Despite its historic significance the fort site is neglected with little remaining other than crumbling walls and a few rusting cannons. It does, however, offer a reasonably nice view across the bay to Philipsburg. To get there, drive to Little Bay and park near the Little Bay Beach Resort tennis courts. The fort is a 10-minute walk up the hill to the south.

### St Maarten Zoo & Botanical Garden

This is a very small zoo on the north side of Great Salt Pond with caged chickens, rabbits and turkeys as well as a few less domesticated creatures such as baboons and caimans. It's beneath the hillside TV satellite dishes on Arch Rd in Madame Estates. Admission is US$4 for adults, US$2 for kids. It's closed on Monday and Tuesday.

### Marina Area

Great Bay Marina and the adjoining Bobby's Marina on the south-east side of Philipsburg have a couple of restaurants, a small grocery store, car rental agencies, a dive shop and several stores with marine supplies. For information on crews wanted, boats for sale etc, check the bulletin boards at Island Water World marine store (which also sells charts) and the Great Bay Marina hotel. Boats to St Barts leave daily from the marina.

### Places to Stay

**Town Centre** *Joshua Rose Guest House* (☎ 24317; fax 30080; in the USA and Canada ☎ (800) 223-9815), PO Box 1033, Philipsburg, at Backstreet 7, is a recommendable guesthouse with friendly management. The 14 rooms are not fancy but are clean and well equipped, each with a private bathroom, air-con, phone, TV, mini-refrigerator and room safe. Standard rooms, which have one double and one twin bed, cost US$43/53 for singles/doubles in summer, US$48/68 in winter. Superiors, which are larger top-storey rooms with high ceilings and two double beds, cost US$10 more. It's US$10 extra for a child in the room.

The nearby *Lucy's Guesthouse* (☎ 22995), Backstreet 10, is quite rudimentary with small bare rooms and is overpriced at US$50. A better bet is *Bico's Guesthouse* (☎ 22294) at Backstreet 3, which has rooms in the same price range.

The *Seaview Beach Hotel* (☎ 22323; fax 24356), PO Box 65, Philipsburg, is a two-storey hotel on the beach above a casino. Rooms are small and rather straightforward with a desk and chair, air-con, TV and private bath. Rates are US$46/55 for singles/doubles in summer, US$79/99 in winter. For an ocean-view room, add US$10 in summer, US$20 in winter. Major credit cards are accepted and there's no charge for kids under 12.

*Great Bay Marina* (☎ 22167; fax 24940), PO Box 277, Philipsburg, has seven plain but adequate 2nd-floor rooms with air-con, private bathroom, small refrigerator, coffee maker, cable TV and harbourfront balcony. If you're en route to St Barts, the marina locale could be convenient as you can almost roll out of bed and onto the boat. Rates are US$50/70 in summer/winter, plus US$10 more for a third person.

The *Pasanggrahan* (☎ 23588; fax 22885), PO Box 151, Philipsburg, is a 30-room beachfront inn on Frontstreet. The restaurant and lobby are in a former governor's residence but most rooms are in undistinguished side buildings. The standard rooms, which cost US$68/114 in summer/winter, are simple and small with shared seaside balcony. Larger deluxe rooms have private balcony and cost US$88/148. All rooms have ceiling fan, air-con and private bath. In addition to the usual 5% tax and 10% service charge, there are annoying extra fees: a 5% energy charge is tacked onto every bill and there's an additional US$10 charge for each day you use the air-con. No credit cards are accepted, nor are children under 12.

The Dutch-owned *Holland House Beach Hotel* (☎ 22572; fax 24673; in the USA ☎ (800) 223-9815), PO Box 393, Philipsburg, has a central beachfront location and 54 spacious rooms. Overall they're Philipsburg's nicest, with hardwood floors, bathtub, balcony, cable TV, phone, air-con and in most cases kitchenette. Rates begin at US$80/87 for singles/doubles in summer, US$110/125 in winter. Newly renovated superior rooms are US$10 to US$20 more.

The *Horizon View Beach Hotel* (☎ 32121; fax 32123), PO Box 105, Philipsburg, on Frontstreet, is a new condo-like complex with 30 units. Studios, some with balcony, have double bed and kitchenette and cost US$90 in summer. The beachfront suites each have separate bedroom, bathtub, kitchen, large living room with plate-glass windows that provide a fine bay view and a summer rate of US$139. Rates are 35% higher in the winter. All units have air-con, cable TV and phone.

**Around Philipsburg** The *Defiance Haven Hotel* (☎ 23145; fax 22713), PO Box 933, Philipsburg, is midway between Philipsburg and Dawn Beach – a bit out of the way, but within a 10-minute drive to either if you have a car. This straightforward three-storey motel-style place is popular with vacationing Caribbean islanders. The 50 rooms have phone, TV and air-con and there's a pool. Rates are US$50/60 for singles/doubles year-round, continental breakfast included, and children under 12 stay for free.

Another inexpensive option is the 16-room *Rama Hotel* (☎ 22582; fax 22582; in the USA ☎ (800) 223-9815) in the Point Blanche area, two km south-east of Philipsburg. Studios start at US$40/45 for singles/doubles.

**Places to Eat – cheap**
*Carl & Son's Unique Cafe & Bakery* is the place to go in Philipsburg for croissants and other tempting pastries. Both a pâtisserie and

a café, it's open from 7.30 am to 11 pm but is closed on Sunday. Another early opener is *Burger King* at Wathey Square, open from 7 am to 10 pm daily.

The *Gourmet Deli*, Frontstreet 75, is a good little beachfront café that serves reasonably priced breakfasts, including croissants and egg dishes, from 8 am to noon. From 11 am to 6 pm, sandwiches, burgers, salads or a Dutch meat plate cost around US$5, while hot dishes such as curried chicken or fresh fish with rice and salad are US$6.50. It's closed on Sunday.

The *Golden Dragon Restaurant*, Frontstreet 4, has a main dining area with a wide range of Chinese standards averaging US$10 and a daily lunch special for US$7 that's served until 3 pm. There's also a takeaway window at the front of the restaurant with plate lunches from US$5 and a couple of simple tables where you can chow down.

*Krishna*, Backstreet 66, is a hole-in-the-wall eatery catering to the Indian community. The chalkboard menu is written in Hindi only and usually has half a dozen standard Indian dishes for US$5 to US$7. There's another local Indian restaurant, *Maharaj*, on the 2nd floor of the building on the opposite side of the road.

A block west on Backstreet is a *Haagen-Dazs* ice-cream shop with over 30 flavours at US$1.75 a scoop, as well as ice-cream bars, sundaes, sodas and US$1 Heineken beers. It's open daily from 11 am to 11 pm.

The *Pizza Hut* at the Old Street shopping centre has a cheap lunch special of a 'personal pan pizza' with a Pepsi for US$3 or with a Heineken for US$0.50 more.

**Places to Eat – middle**
*Harbor Lights* is an old local favourite that's recently moved to Backstreet. While it no longer has a harbour view, this personable restaurant has streetside balcony dining and good local food at honest prices. Tasty goat, fish and conch curries served with rice and beans and a small salad are US$10. The same curry flavour is found in the various rotis which range from chickpea (US$3) to lobster (US$7). The menu also includes salads, fish

& chips and Trinidad-style pilau plates. It's open for lunch and dinner.

The *Grill & Ribs Co* at the Old Street shopping centre is a popular open-air 2nd-floor eatery featuring all-you-can-eat baby back ribs for US$11. The ribs are good but if you don't want to pig out on pork a better dish is the generous chicken fajita plate for US$9. Until 4 pm, you can get burgers and grilled chicken sandwiches served with fries for US$5. It's open from 11 am to 10 pm daily. No credit cards are accepted.

*Greenhouse*, at the north end of the marina, is a lively spot best known for its happy hour from 4.30 to 7 pm, which has two-for-one drinks and free snacks. It's open weekdays from 11 to 2 am, on Saturday and Sunday from 4 pm to 1 am. At lunch, there are burgers, sandwiches, satays and gado gado for around US$6. At dinner, from 5 to 10 pm, meat and seafood dishes cost US$11 to US$16. There are pool tables, dart boards, TV screens and a DJ and dancing from 10 pm nightly.

### Places to Eat – expensive

The *Seafood Galley*, on a pier at Bobby's Marina, has a nautical New England decor and a raw bar with oysters and clams on the half shell. From 11 am to 3 pm, you can get a Spanish omelette, fishburger or roast beef sandwich with fries for US$7, salads and seafood dishes for a few dollars more. Dinner, from 6 to 10.30 pm, ranges from local catch of the day for US$13 to lobster curry for US$18. It's closed on Sunday. Take a look at the giant mullet that swarm below the pier.

For a special dinner out, *Le Bec Fin* (☎ 22976), in the same building as the museum, is an elegant French restaurant with good food and a fine sea view. Starters include melon soup, crayfish ravioli and escargot in fennel sauce. Main courses range from a catch of the day at US$16 to lobster flamed in cognac for US$31. There's usually a fixed price menu as well.

The *Wajang Doll* (☎ 22687), Frontstreet 237, is well known for its rijsttafel, a traditional Indonesian buffet. It costs US$19 for

14 dishes, US$25 for 19 dishes. It's open from 6.45 to 10 pm Monday to Saturday. Young children are not allowed.

Frontstreet has a slew of other restaurants in this price range. Two of the more atmospheric ones are *San Marco*, an Italian restaurant with waterfront dining, and *L'Escargot*, a French restaurant in a colourful 19th-century house specialising in various escargot preparations.

# Around Dutch St Maarten

## SIMPSON BAY

The Simpson Bay area is a narrow strip of land separating Simpson Bay from Simpson Bay Lagoon. A channel between the two bodies of water is spanned by a drawbridge that is raised four times a day to allow boats to pass from one side to the other.

West of the drawbridge there's a sandy beach with some moderately priced guesthouses, but it's an odd destination as the airport runway stretches the entire length, just a few hundred metres away. Despite the proximity to the airport, staying in this area is not a convenient way to avoid taxi fares or car rentals as you'd have to walk clear around the runway to get to the guesthouses, a good 20-minute haul along a busy road. On the other hand, airport noise shouldn't disturb early risers, as there are no scheduled flights between 9 pm and 7 am.

East of the drawbridge there are a couple of marinas, a clutter of bars and restaurants, and a few complexes with casinos and large hotels.

### Places to Stay

The first three places can be reached by turning south on Houtman Rd at the east end of the airport runway. Just 100 metres down Houtman Rd is *Calypso Guest House* (☎ 44233), the cheapest and closest place to the airport. Rooms, which are on the 2nd floor above a Mexican restaurant, are quite straightforward and have kitchenette, table and chairs, air-con and TV. Summer rates begin at US$50/60 for singles/doubles, winter rates at US$60/80. It's a few minutes' walk to the beach.

About 750 metres beyond is the beachfront *Mary's Boon* (☎ 54235; fax 53316), PO Box 2078, which has 12 studios with kitchenette and balcony. It has a pleasant West Indian atmosphere although it's a bit minimalist in creature comforts, with no TV or air-con. Rates are US$75 in summer, US$90 in April and November and US$150 in winter. No children under 16 are allowed and no credit cards are accepted. There's a three-day minimum stay in summer, one week in winter, and a 15% service charge.

*La Chatelaine* (☎ 54269; fax 53195), PO Box 2056, is a newer complex just before Mary's Boon. There's a pool, a nice beachside location and 17 units with kitchenette and patio. Summer/winter rates are US$75/115 for studios, US$95/$150 for one-bedroom apartments and US$135/235 for two-bedroom apartments. Rates are for up to two people; add US$20/30 in summer/winter for additional persons. No children under seven years of age are allowed.

*Pelican Resort & Casino* (☎ 42503; fax 42133; in the USA ☎ (800) 327-3286), PO Box 431, Philipsburg, is on a beach at the east side of Simpson Bay. This sprawling complex has 654 rooms, ranging from studios to two-bedroom suites, as well as restaurants, pools, tennis courts, a casino and a shopping arcade. Rooms have the standard 1st-class amenities and begin at US$115/205 in summer/winter.

### Places to Eat

*Don Carlos*, a moderately priced Mexican restaurant beneath Calypso Guest House, has tostadas or enchiladas with rice and beans for US$12 and standard breakfast fare in the US$5 to US$8 range.

On the main road is a *Pizza Hut* with a cheap lunch special, a *Grill & Ribs Co* with fairly good fajita, grilled chicken and rib plates for around U$10 and a *Burger King* open to midnight.

Immediately opposite the airport terminal is a Stop & Shop grocery store with a deli inside and a little lagoon-view café out the back. You can get salads, a cheeseburger and fries or a boneless chicken roti for US$5 to US$7 and breakfast standards for about half that price. It's open daily from 7.30 am to 8 pm (to 6.30 pm on Sunday). There's another Stop & Shop and a few restaurants at the Simpson Bay Yacht Club on the east side of the drawbridge.

### MAHO BAY & MULLET BAY

Maho Bay and Mullet Bay are adjacent resort areas along the south-west shore. Driving into the Maho Bay area is a bit like suddenly finding yourself on the central strip in Las Vegas. While little more than a block long, it's dense with multi-storey buildings housing exclusive jewellers, boutiques, art galleries, restaurants and a huge resort and casino. Parking streetside is nearly impossible; it's best to pull into the Maho Beach complex where indoor parking costs US$2 for up to 12 hours.

Maho Bay has a nice enough beach except that it's at the very end of the runway. The area is even marked with a sign warning beachgoers that 'low flying and departing aircraft blast can cause physical injury'!

Mullet Bay is dominated by a single resort, which has a golf course that fronts a fine white-sand beach. Although access to the north end of the beach is restricted by the resort, there's public parking at the south side of the golf course.

The island's main south-coast road runs straight across the golf course and consequently some killer speed bumps have been

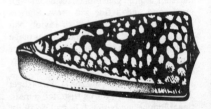

Top: Soufriére and Gros Piton, St Lucia (GB)
Bottom Left: View from Pigeon Island, St Lucia (NF)
Bottom Right: Castries market, St Lucia (NF)

Top Left: Place du Marché, Marigot, St Martin (TW)
Top Right: Fort Amsterdam, Philipsburg, St Martin (NF)
Bottom Left: Grand Case, St Martin (NF)
Bottom Right: Grand Case, St Martin (TW)

installed that are apt to bottom out many low-slung cars.

## Places to Stay

The *Maho Beach Hotel* (☎ 52115; fax 53180; in the USA ☎ (800) 223-0757) has 650 air-con rooms with private balcony that start at US$140/195 in summer/winter for singles, US$155/215 for doubles. One hotel wing faces Maho Beach, while another fronts Maho Bay's commercial strip. The hotel has pools, tennis courts, a disco and a casino.

The 600-unit *Mullet Bay Resort* (☎ 52801; fax 54281; in the USA ☎ (800) 468-5538) is a sprawling development that's large enough to have its own shuttle bus to cart guests around the grounds. There are lots of facilities including restaurants, pools, a tennis centre, a golf course and a casino. Rooms have the standard resort amenities and rates begin at US$150/240 in summer/winter; note that some of the rooms are quite a haul from the beach.

## Places to Eat

*Cheri's Cafe*, a large open-air restaurant and bar beside the Casino Royale, is one of the island's liveliest eat-and-meet spots. The varied menu includes salads, sandwiches and burgers for under US$7, grilled seafood dishes for about double that and kid's dishes for US$4. It's open from 11 am to midnight daily, with live music from 8 pm. Credit cards are not accepted.

The *West Indies Yogurt Co*, next to Cheri's, has Haagen-Dazs ice cream and Colombo frozen yoghurt.

*Trattoria Pizzeria*, a small unpretentious eatery in the alley behind Cheri's, has pastas and good-looking pizzas for about US$9 as well as cheaper sandwiches.

Nearby *La Rosa* is a popular Italian restaurant with fine candlelight dining. Pasta dishes average US$17, meat and poultry dishes US$23. It's closed on Tuesday.

Also in this area is Fountain of Health Natural Foods, which has packaged natural food items, dried fruits and vitamins. Mullet Bay Resort has several restaurants, including

*Bamboo Garden*, a formal Chinese restaurant with steep prices, ranging from US$17 for sweet and sour pork to US$45 for Peking duck.

## CUPECOY BAY

If you're looking for a beach that's quiet but not totally secluded, Cupecoy is a good choice. This pleasant white-sand beach is backed by low sandstone cliffs which are eroded in such a way that they provide a run of small semi-private coves. There's beach parking on the north side of the Ocean Club in Cupecoy.

## DAWN BEACH

Dawn Beach, on the east coast near the French/Dutch border, is a nice white-sand beach backed by a low-key resort. Swimming and snorkelling is good when the seas are calm. Snorkellers can start at the south end of the beach and follow the current, which goes north towards Oyster Pond. Snorkel gear rents at the beach hut for US$8 an hour or US$15 for four hours, kayaks for US$10 an hour. There's a shower just behind the beach hut.

To get to Dawn Beach from the French side of Oyster Pond, turn left immediately after entering the Dutch side of the island and go 1.5 km to the Dawn Beach Hotel. There's visitor parking by the hotel tennis courts – the beach is a two-minute walk away.

## Places to Stay & Eat

*Dawn Beach Hotel* (☎ 22929; fax 24421; in the USA ☎ (800) 351-5656), PO Box 389, Philipsburg, is a pleasant low-rise resort. The 155 air-con rooms have a tropical decor with rattan furnishing and pastel colours, ceiling fan, screened louvred windows, a balcony or patio, a kitchenette and TV. Summer rates start at a reasonable US$95 a double, while in winter they begin at US$200. Choicest (and most expensive) are the waterside bungalows, where you can step out your door and onto the beach. There's no charge for children aged 16 and under.

The hotel has a reasonably priced restau-

ST MARTIN

rant between the beach and pool. Lunch, from noon to 2.30 pm, includes sandwiches, burgers and salads for around US$7 and grilled fish with salad and fries for US$10. The dinner menu is varied, with prices aver-

aging US$18. There's an inexpensive children's menu and on Thursday night there's a fire-limbo dancer, steel band and barbecue. The Haagan-Dazs ice-cream shop below the restaurant is open from noon to 9 pm.

# St Vincent & the Grenadines

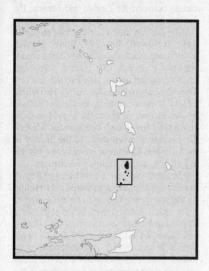

St Vincent & the Grenadines is a multi-island nation well known to wintering yachters but off the beaten path for most other visitors. The northernmost island, St Vincent, is the nation's commercial and political centre and accounts for 90% of both the land area and population. The island is lush and green, with deep valleys cultivated with bananas, coconuts and arrowroot, and a mountainous interior that peaks at La Soufrière, a 1234-metre active volcano.

The island of St Vincent remains a backwater of sorts and doesn't really cater to tourists. There are no major resort hotels, the airport is only large enough to handle inter-island aircraft and St Vincent's beaches can't compete with those in the nation's more alluring half, the southerly Grenadines. While St Vincent disappoints some visitors, others find its raw edge and rugged natural qualities refreshing.

On the other hand, the Grenadines are one of the most popular cruising grounds in the Caribbean. These small islands, which reach like stepping stones between St Vincent and Grenada, are surrounded by coral reefs and clear blue waters ideal for diving, snorkelling and boating. The islands are lightly populated and the level of development remains pleasantly low-key. Although some of the Grenadine islands like Mustique and Palm Island cater to the rich and famous, others like Bequia and Union Island are yachting havens attracting an international crowd and offering some quite reasonable places to stay and eat.

## ORIENTATION

St Vincent's airport is two km south-east of Kingstown and two km north-west of the island's main resort area at Villa. The Windward Highway runs all the way up the east coast to Fancy at the northernmost tip of the island but the Leeward Highway goes only three-quarters of the way up the west coast. If you want to tour both coasts, you have to backtrack through Kingstown.

The main Grenadine islands, with the exception of Mustique, are served by ferries from Kingstown. Bequia, Union Island, Canouan and Mustique have airports.

# Facts about the Islands

## HISTORY

When Spanish explorers first sighted St Vincent, the island was thickly settled with Carib Indians, who had driven off the earlier Arawak settlers. Heavy Carib resistance kept European colonists at bay long after most other Caribbean islands had well-established European settlements.

One of the most significant events of early foreign influence occurred in 1675, when a Dutch slave ship went down in the channel between St Vincent and neighbouring Bequia. While none of the European crew

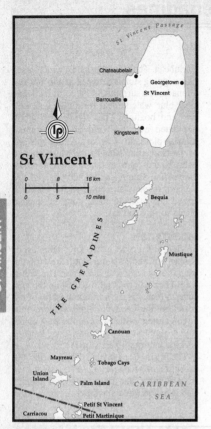

St Vincent

the first European settlement on the island in the early 1700s.

In 1783, after a century of contesting claims between the British and French, the Treaty of Paris placed St Vincent under British domain and a series of open rebellions followed. In 1795, under French instigation, Black and Yellow Caribs simultaneously swept the island, torching plantations and massacring English settlers. They joined forces on Dorsetshire Hill where Chief Chattawae of the Black Caribs, buoyed by the success of his raids, is said to have challenged the British commander Alexander Leith to a sword duel. To the dismay of his followers Chattawae quickly lost his life to Leith, an accomplished swordsman.

The following year a contingent of British troops was dispatched to the island to round up the insurgents who, with the exception of a few small bands hiding in the hills, were shipped to Roatan, an island off the coast of Honduras. In all, over 5000 Caribs were forcefully repatriated. A small number of Yellow Caribs who were not involved in the uprising were relocated at Sandy Bay to the north-eastern side of the island.

With the native opposition gone, the plantation owners briefly achieved the stability and success that had previously eluded them. In 1812, however, a major eruption of La Soufrière volcano spewed a suffocating ash over northern St Vincent, which destroyed most of the coffee and cocoa trees. The eruption also took a heavy toll on the Carib reservation at Sandy Bay.

At around the same time the British abolitionist movement was gaining political and popular favour back in London. When slavery was abolished in 1834, the plantation owners were forced to free more than 18,000 slaves. As opportunities arose, the Blacks turned away from the plantations, and planters began bringing in foreign labourers. The first to come were Portuguese from Madeira, followed later in the century by indentured servants from India. Natural disasters such as the 1898 hurricane which ravaged the cocoa trees and the 1902 eruption of La Soufrière which destroyed the sugar cane

survived, a fair number of Africans made it to shore. The shipwrecked slaves were accepted by the Caribs and allowed to marry with Carib women. Their offspring became known as Black Caribs, as distinct from the purely native Yellow Caribs. In time the two groups had their differences, especially after the Black Caribs began to increase in number.

The Caribs were generally hostile to all Europeans, but by and large they found the British, who claimed their land by royal grants, more objectionable than the French. The Caribs allowed the French to establish fields battered much of what remained of the plantation economy.

In 1969 St Vincent became a self-governing state in association with the UK and on 27 October 1979 St Vincent & the Grenadines acquired full independence as a member of the Commonwealth.

## GEOGRAPHY

St Vincent is a high island of volcanic origin; it's the northernmost point of the volcanic ridge that runs from Grenada in the south up through the Grenadine islands.

Of the 389 sq km that comprise the national boundaries of St Vincent & the Grenadines, the island of St Vincent totals 345 sq km. The other 44 sq km are spread across some 30-odd islands and cays, fewer than a dozen of which are populated. The largest of these islands are Bequia, Canouan, Mustique, Mayreau and Union Island.

The highest peak on St Vincent is La Soufrière, an active volcano that reaches an elevation of 1234 metres. On 7 May 1902 the volcano erupted violently, wreaking havoc on the island's northern region and causing an estimated 2000 deaths. A more recent eruption, on 13 April 1979, spewed a blanket of ash over much of the island and caused 20,000 people to evacuate the northern villages. Although the crop damage was substantial, no lives were lost.

The larger of the Grenadine islands are hilly, but relatively low lying, and most have no source of fresh water other than rainfall. All have beautiful white-sand beaches.

## CLIMATE

In January the average daily high temperature is 29°C (85°F) while the low averages 22°C (72°F). In July the average daily high is 30°C (86°F) while the low averages 24°C (76°F).

January to May are the driest months, with a mean relative humidity around 76%. During the rest of the year the humidity averages about 80%. In July, the wettest month, there's measurable rainfall an average of 26 days, while April, the driest month, averages six days of measurable rain-

Coconuts

fall. All these statistics are for Kingstown; the Grenadine islands to the south are drier.

## FLORA & FAUNA

The island of St Vincent has an interior of tropical rainforest and lowlands thick with coconut trees and banana estates. The Mesopotamia Valley, north-east of Kingstown, has some of the most fertile farmland and luxuriant landscapes.

The national bird is the endangered St Vincent parrot, a beautiful multi-hued Amazon parrot about 45 cm in length. The parrot lives in St Vincent's interior rainforest, as do numerous other tropical birds. The forest also provides a habitat for opossum (locally called manicou) and agouti, a short-haired rabbit-like rodent.

St Vincent has three species of snakes: the Congo snake, which coils itself around tree branches, and two terrestrial species, the black snake and the white snake. All three are harmless.

## GOVERNMENT

St Vincent & the Grenadines is an independent nation within the Commonwealth. The British monarchy is represented by a governor-general, but executive power is in the hands of the prime minister and cabinet. There is a unicameral legislature, which consists of 13 members, each elected for a five-year term. The present prime minister,

ST VINCENT

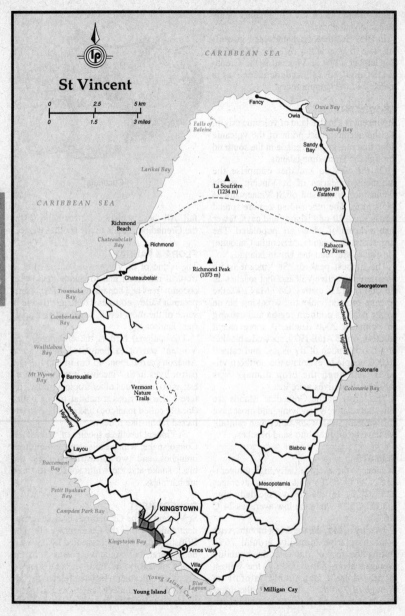

St Vincent

CARIBBEAN SEA

0   2.5   5 km
0   1.5   3 miles

Falls of
Baleine

Fancy

Owia

Owia Bay

Sandy Bay

Larikai Bay

Sandy
Bay

La Soufrière
(1234 m)

Orange Hill
Estates

CARIBBEAN SEA

Richmond
Beach

Chateaubelair
Bay

Richmond

Rabacca
Dry River

Chateaubelair

Richmond Peak
(1073 m)

Georgetown

Troumaka
Bay

Cumberland
Bay

Wallilabou
Bay

Colonarie

Mt Wynne
Bay

Barrouallie

Vermont
Nature
Trails

Colonarie Bay

Leeward
Highway

Windward
Highway

Layou

Biabou

Buccament
Bay

Petit Byahaut
Bay

Mesopotamia

Campden Park Bay

KINGSTOWN

Kingstown Bay

Arnos Vale

Villa

Young Island
Cut

Blue
Lagoon

Young Island

Milligan Cay

James (Son) Mitchell, the leader of the majority New Democratic Party, has held the office for most of the period since independence.

## ECONOMY

On St Vincent, agriculture remains the mainstay of the economy, accounting for over half of all employment. Bananas are the leading export crop, followed by arrowroot, coconuts, cocoa and spices. The government is encouraging crop diversification. Attempts to revive the sugar industry in 1981, largely to provide a domestic source for rum production, were unsuccessful and abandoned in 1985. A budding cut-flower industry of anthuriums and heliconias and an increase in small-scale vegetable farming are meeting with more success, in part due to a government land reform programme that has turned idle plantation lands into small family farms.

On the outer islands, tourism and fishing are the mainstays of the economy.

---

### Arrowroot

St Vincent is the world's leading producer of arrowroot. The plant's name is derived from its former use as an antitoxin in the treatment of wounds from poison arrows. The rhizomes of the plant yield a nutritious and highly digestible starch that's used as a thickener in gravies and other food preparations. Although less-expensive cornflour has largely replaced the use of arrowroot in the kitchen, arrowroot now has a new modern-day use as a coating on computer papers. ∎

---

## POPULATION & PEOPLE

St Vincent & the Grenadines has a population of 108,000. Over 90% live on St Vincent, with 30,000 of those in the Kingstown area. About 75% of all islanders are of pure African descent, while 15% are of mixed descent, including nearly a thousand Black Caribs. On Bequia and St Vincent there's a sizeable population of Scottish descendants, many with a noticeable Scottish brogue. Others are of English, Irish, French and Asian descent.

## ARTS & CULTURE

Reggae, calypso and steel band music are popular reflections of island culture. The main sports are cricket and European football. Some of the Grenadine islands, Bequia in particular, have long been reliant upon the sea for a living; boat building, both full-scale and models, is an island art from.

### Dress Conventions

Casual cotton clothing is suitable for almost any occasion, including dining at the more exclusive Grenadine resorts.

## RELIGION

The majority of islanders are Protestant, with Anglicanism being the largest denomination. Other religions include Methodist, Seventh Day Adventist, Baptist, Streams of Power and Baha'i. About 20% of Vincentians are Roman Catholic.

## LANGUAGE

English is the official language. Some islanders also speak a French patois.

# Facts for the Visitor

## PASSPORT & VISAS

Citizens of the USA, Canada and the UK can visit St Vincent & the Grenadines with proof of citizenship in the form of a birth certificate or voter's registration card, accompanied by an official photo ID, such as a driving licence. Citizens of other countries must be in possession of a valid passport. A return or onward ticket is required of all visitors.

## CUSTOMS

Up to a quart of wine or spirits and 200 cigarettes may be brought into the country duty free.

ST VINCENT

## MONEY

The Eastern Caribbean dollar (EC$) is the local currency; US$1 = EC$2.70.

Major credit cards, while not as widely used as on other islands, are accepted at most hotels, car rental agencies and dive shops.

A 10% service charge is added onto most restaurant bills, in which case no further tipping is necessary.

## TOURIST OFFICES
### Local Tourist Offices

The main office of the St Vincent & the Grenadines Department of Tourism (☎ 457-1502; fax 457-2880) is in Kingstown; the mailing address is PO Box 834, Kingstown, St Vincent, West Indies.

There's also a tourist information desk at St Vincent's E T Joshua Airport and branch tourist offices in Bequia and Union Island.

### Overseas Reps

Overseas offices of the St Vincent & the Grenadines Department of Tourism are:

Canada
    32 Park Rd, Toronto, Ontario N4W 2N4 (☎ (416) 924-5796)
Germany
    c/o Mr Bruno Fink, Wurmberg Str 26, D-7032 Sindelfinger (☎ 70 31 80 62 60)
UK
    10 Kensington Court, London W8 5DL, England (☎ (71) 937-6570)
USA
    801 Second Ave, 21st Floor, New York, NY 10017 (☎ (212) 687-4981 & (☎ (800) 729-1726) 6505 Cove Creek Place, Dallas, TX 75240 (☎ (214) 239-6451 & (☎ (800) 235-3029)

In Barbados, the St Vincent tourist office has an information desk (☎ 428-0961) at the airport that opens during flight times.

## BUSINESS HOURS

Shops are generally open from 8 am to 4 pm Monday to Friday and to noon on Saturday, although supermarkets often have extended hours. Most government offices are open from 8 am to noon and 1 to 4.15 pm Monday to Friday. Banks are generally open from 8 am to 1 pm Monday to Thursday, and from 8 am to 1 pm and 3 to 5 pm on Friday.

## HOLIDAYS

Public holidays are as follows:

| | |
|---|---|
| *New Year's Day* | – 1 January |
| *St Vincent & the Grenadines Day* | – 22 January |
| *Good Friday* | – late March/early April |
| *Easter Monday* | – late March/early April |
| *Labour Day* | – first Monday in May |
| *Whit Monday* | – eighth Monday after Easter |
| *Caricom Day* | – second Monday in July |
| *Carnival Tuesday* | – usually second Tuesday in mid-July |
| *August Monday* | – first Monday in August |
| *Independence Day* | – 27 October |
| *Christmas Day* | – 25 December |
| *Boxing Day* | – 26 December |

## CULTURAL EVENTS

The carnival, called Vincy Mas, is the main cultural event of the year. It usually takes place around the first two weeks of July, with a 12-day run of calypso and steel band music, colourful costume parades and lots of dancing and activities. Most of the action is centred in Kingstown.

On Bequia, there's a major regatta held over the Easter weekend.

## POST

The general post office is on Halifax St in Kingstown and there are branch post offices in larger towns and villages.

It costs EC$0.45 to airmail postcards and aerograms to other Caribbean destinations, the USA and Canada; EC$0.55 to other destinations. A letter weighing up to half an ounce costs EC$0.50 within the Caribbean, EC$0.65 to the USA and Canada, EC$0.75 to the UK and Europe, and EC$1 to Australia or New Zealand.

International mail is routed through other Caribbean nations, so mail sent to the UK takes about a week, while mail sent to other international destinations, including the USA, can easily take double that.

To write to any hotel or other business listed in this chapter, simply follow the business name with the village and/or island name. For example, the mailing address for Julie's Guest House is: Julie's Guest House, Port Elizabeth, Bequia, St Vincent & the Grenadines, West Indies.

## TELECOMMUNICATIONS

St Vincent phone numbers have seven digits. When calling from overseas add the area code 809.

Both coin and card phones can be found on the major islands. Phonecards can be purchased at Cable & Wireless offices or from vendors near the phones. It costs EC$0.25 cents to make a local call. For more information on card phones and making international calls see Telecommunications in the introductory Facts for the Visitor chapter.

## ELECTRICITY

The electric current is 220-240 volts, 50 cycles.

## WEIGHTS & MEASURES

While for the most part the imperial system is still in use, many car odometers register in km.

## BOOKS & MAPS

The best general book on the islands is *St Vincent & the Grenadines: A Plural Country* by Dana Jinkins & Jill Bobrow, Concepts Publishing, 1985, a handsome hardcover photo essay book.

The Ordnance Survey 1:50,000 scale map of St Vincent is the most detailed map available. It can be purchased at the Wayfarer Book Store, on Upper Bay St, Kingstown for EC$26.

## MEDIA

St Vincent has two island TV stations, one radio station (705 AM) and two local newspapers, *The Vincentian* and *The News*.

There are two useful publications available for free through the tourist office. The *Escape Tourist Guide* is a 100-page glossy magazine with general tourist information, lists of places to stay and eat, ads and a few feature articles. *Discover St Vincent & the*

*Grenadines* is pocket sized with a similar content.

## HEALTH

The main hospital (☎ 456-1185), a rather new 200-bed facility, is in Kingstown. There's also a hospital in Port Elizabeth on Bequia (☎ 458-3294), clinics throughout the islands and pharmacies in Kingstown and Port Elizabeth. For general information see Health in the Facts for the Visitor chapter at the start of the book.

## DANGERS & ANNOYANCES

St Vincent has its fair share of fellows who can get a bit pushy about wanting to carry your bags from the ferry or be your tour guide. If you're not interested in their services, turn them down politely but firmly.

On the Grenadines, which are far more laid-back, hassles are rare.

## EMERGENCY

Dial ☎ 999 for all fire, police and coastguard emergencies.

## ACTIVITIES
### Beaches & Swimming

There are exceptional white-sand beaches on virtually all of the Grenadine islands and some tan and black-sand beaches on St Vincent. For details on specific beaches, see the individual island sections.

### Diving & Snorkelling

There are first-rate diving spots off virtually all the islands. The waters offer excellent visibility and extensive coral reefs. Divers will find colourful sponges, soft corals, great stands of elkhorn coral, branching gorgonian and black corals, and a few sunken wrecks. There's a range of dives suitable for any level of experience, from calm, shallow dives to wall dives and drift dives. Spearfishing is prohibited.

Dive shops on four islands – Dive St Vincent, Dive Bequia, Dive Canouan and Grenadines Dive – offer a 'pick-and-mix' 10-dive package for US$420 that allows

ST VINCENT

divers to take their dives as they please from any of the four shops.

Otherwise the going rates are around US$50 for a single dive, US$90 for a two-tank dive and US$60 for a night dive.

Many dive shops also offer complete certification courses. Dive St Vincent, which is one of the islands' best regarded shops, charges US$400 and offers PADI, NAUI or CMAS accreditations. If you complete the classroom part of the programme back home, the charge is US$220 to complete the open-water certification in St Vincent.

Dive shops in St Vincent & the Grenadines include:

Dive St Vincent, PO Box 864, Young Island Dock, St Vincent (☎ 457-4714; fax 457-4948)

Dive Bequia, PO Box 16, Plantation House, Bequia (☎ 458-3504; fax 458-3886; in the USA ☎ (800) 851-3483)

Dive Canouan, Canouan Beach Hotel, Canouan (☎ 458-8648; fax 458-8875)

Grenadines Dive, Sunny Grenadines Hotel, Union Island (☎ 458-8138; fax 458-8122)

St Vincent Dive Experience, Underwater Unlimited, PO Box 1554, Blue Lagoon, Ratho Mill, St Vincent (☎ 456-9741; fax 457-2768)

Dive Anchorage, Anchorage Yacht Club, Union Island (☎ 458-8221)

Caribe Divers, Wallilabou Anchorage, St Vincent (☎ 458-7270)

Petit Byahaut, St Vincent (☎ 457-7008)

Bequia Dive Resort, Bequia Beach Club, Friendship Bay, Bequia (☎ 458-3248)

Sunsports, Gingerbread House, PO Box 1, Bequia (☎ 458-3577; fax 457-3031; in the USA (☎ (800) 535-3833)

Mustique Watersports, PO Box 349, Mustique (☎ 458-4621; fax 456-4565).

## Other Water Sports

Tradewinds blow unimpeded across the Grenadines, creating some fine conditions for windsurfing. Many resorts offer guests free use of windsurfing gear and there are huts on many of the more developed tourist beaches that rent windsurfing equipment. Some of the huts also rent out snorkelling gear, Hobie Cats and Sunfish boats. More information can be found under individual island sections.

## Hiking

The most challenging hike on St Vincent is to La Soufrière volcano. The route passes through banana estates and rainforest, up past the tree line to the barren summit where, weather permitting, hikers are rewarded with views down into the crater and over all St Vincent. The easiest access is up from the east side and even that is a hearty full-day hike of 11 km up and back. As the trailhead is a couple of km west of the Windward Highway and the nearest bus drop, the easiest way to do the hike is to join a tour. Two tour companies that arrange volcano trips are Paradise Tours (☎ 458-5545) and Sam's Taxi Tours (☎ 458-3686).

The Vermont Nature Trails are a series of short walking tracks 5.5 km inland from the Leeward Highway. See Leeward Highway later in this chapter for details.

## HIGHLIGHTS

On St Vincent be sure to visit the botanical gardens, among the finest in the Caribbean. Also fun is hopping on a minibus for a cheap local tour of the west coast; you can get off and kick around in the coastal towns, swim at a black-sand beach and finish off at a waterfall.

In the Grenadines, a day tour of the uninhabited Tobago Cays shouldn't be missed – the best jumping-off point is Union Island. For nautical character Bequia, a yachters' haunt with a history as a whaling and ship-building centre, is a special place.

## ACCOMMODATION

There are a handful of exclusive resorts on St Vincent & the Grenadines; all are of the 'barefoot' variety, situated on remote beaches and completely casual in orientation. Hotels of all categories are small – only a handful have more than a couple of dozen rooms and the largest has only 43.

In St Vincent, many hotels have the same rates all year round. The rates listed in this chapter do not include the 5% hotel tax or the 10% service charge.

There are no established camping grounds on St Vincent & the Grenadines and camping is not encouraged.

## FOOD

St Vincent has rich volcanic soil and produces most of the fruits and vegetables sold throughout the Grenadines. The sweet and juicy St Vincent orange is ripe while still green, and sells for about two to the dollar. Produce markets are found in larger towns and are the best places to pick up fruits and vegetables. Seafood is abundant, with conch, fish, shrimp, whelk and lobster making an appearance on most menus. Common West Indian foods include callaloo soup, pumpkin soup, saltfish and various breadfruit preparations.

## DRINKS

On St Vincent the tap water comes from mountain reserves and is chlorinated and safe to drink. On the Grenadines water comes from individual rain catchment systems and therefore should be boiled or treated before drinking. Bottled water is available on all the islands.

St Vincent Brewery in Kingstown not only makes the local brew, Hairoun lager, but also produces the region's Guinness stout.

## ENTERTAINMENT

In Kingstown, The Attic is a pleasant 2nd-floor jazz club in an old stone building on Melville St, open from 8 pm Monday to Saturday.

In the Villa Beach area, a nice place is Beachcombers, which has a happy hour from

Hairoun lager label

5 to 6.30 pm daily, live piano music from 8 pm on Friday and a guitarist who plays jazz, rock, blues and calypso on Saturday night.

The Young Island Resort has a cocktail party at Fort Duvernette at 6.30 pm Thursday, open to the public for US$15.

For information on entertainment in the Grenadines, see the individual island sections.

## THINGS TO BUY

In Kingstown, the St Vincent Handicrafts Centre near the university sells locally made straw bags, pottery, wooden bowls and West Indian dolls. You'll also find some attractive handicrafts at Noah's Arkade on Upper Bay St.

Bequia, Mustique and Union Island all have good boutiques and gift shops.

# Getting There & Away

## AIR

There are no international flights into St Vincent & the Grenadines. Passengers coming from overseas must fly to a neighbouring island, such as Barbados, and then

ST VINCENT

switch to a prop plane for the final leg of their journey.

LIAT (☎ 458-1821 reservations, 20458-4841 airport) has at least six daily flights to St Vincent from Barbados; the fare is US$110 one way or US$145 return on a 30-day excursion ticket. There are at least three flights daily to St Vincent from Trinidad (US$124), St Lucia (US$82) and Grenada (US$64); return fares are twice these one-way fares. Most flights to LIAT's other Caribbean destinations require routeing through one of these islands.

Airlines of Carriacou, which is affiliated with and booked through LIAT, flies from Grenada to Bequia or St Vincent for US$64 one way, US$100 return.

Mustique Airways (☎ 458-4380) has daily scheduled flights from Barbados to St Vincent (US$80), Mustique (US$85), Bequia (US$85), Canouan (US$110) and Union Island (US$110). Return fares are double these one-way fares. Flights coordinate with international flights in and out of Barbados, leaving Barbados around 3 pm in the summer and 4 pm in the winter and returning from St Vincent, Mustique, Bequia, Canouan and Union Island around noon in the summer and 1 pm in the winter.

Air Martinique (☎ 458-4528) flies daily from Martinique to St Vincent for US$245 return.

For information on flights between islands in the Grenadines, see the Getting Around section of this chapter.

### Airport Information

St Vincent's E T Joshua Airport in Arnos Vale is a modest facility with LIAT and Air Martinique desks, an exchange bureau, a small bar, a gift shop and coin and card phones. The facilities at the outer island airports are minimal.

**To/From The Airport** On St Vincent, if your luggage is very light, it's possible to get a minibus to Kingstown or Villa Beach from the main road in front of the terminal. Otherwise, taxis meet the flights.

Taxi fares from the airport are EC$20 to either Kingstown or Villa.

### SEA

The passenger/cargo boat MV *Windward* links St Vincent with Barbados, St Lucia, Trinidad and Venezuela. For details see Boat in the Getting Around chapter at the start of the book.

Information on boats between Carriacou (Grenada) and Union Island is in Getting There & Away in the Union Island section.

### Yacht

On the island of St Vincent, yachts must clear immigration and customs at either Kingstown or Wallilabou Bay.

Wallilabou has a customs officer on duty from 4 to 6pm daily, at other times it's possible to clear customs at the police station in the village of Barrouallie, immediately south of Wallilabou Bay. Many yachters prefer to clear customs here and avoid the hassles and long lines sometimes encountered in Kingstown. Moorings, night floodlights, water, ice and a postal service are all provided at Wallilabou Anchorage (☎ 458-7270).

Other popular anchorages on St Vincent include remote Petit Byahaut to the north of Kingstown and the more frequented Young Island Cut and Blue Lagoon to the south. Blue Lagoon (☎ 458-4308) has a small marina, a palm-lined bay, a 19-room hotel and the office of Barefoot Yacht Charters.

On the outer islands, there are customs and immigration offices at Admiralty Bay, Bequia; Britannia Bay, Mustique; and Clifton, Union Island. ATM Yacht Charters has a base at Union Island.

There are no port charges in St Vincent & the Grenadines. Spearfishing is prohibited.

### Cruise Ship

Cruise ships dock at the deep-water wharf in Kingstown Harbour, which is at the south side of the town centre. Some smaller cruise ships also visit some of the Grenadine islands, with Bequia, Mayreau and Union Island being the most popular destinations.

## TOURS

For information on tours to the Grenadines from Barbados, see Tours in the Getting Around section of the Barbados chapter.

## LEAVING ST VINCENT

The departure tax is EC$20.

# Getting Around

## AIR

Airlines of Carriacou island hops from Grenada to St Vincent, stopping en route at Carriacou, Union Island and Bequia. Flights depart a couple of times a day. One-way fares are US$34 from Grenada to Carriacou, US$43 from Carriacou to Union, US$19 from Union to Bequia, US$19 from Bequia to St Vincent and US$30 from Union to St Vincent.

LIAT also operates a daily flight between Grenada and St Vincent that stops en route in Carriacou and Union Island. Sector fares are the same as with Airlines of Carriacou and if you're flying between Grenada and St Vincent, one free stopover in Union or Carriacou is allowed.

Mustique Airways has two regularly scheduled flights daily between St Vincent and Bequia, leaving St Vincent at 8 am and 5 pm and leaving Bequia at 8.30 am and 5.30 pm. The fare is US$17 each way. On Sunday, flights continue on to Mustique, leaving Bequia at 8.10 am and 5.10 pm and departing from Mustique for Bequia at 8.20 am and 5.20 pm. The one-way fare between St Vincent and Mustique is US$23; between Bequia and Mustique it's US$15. In addition you can sometimes pick up an empty seat on one of the Mustique Airways charter flights that stop on Union Island; the cost is EC$45 one way from Union to either Bequia or Mustique.

Helenair, a charter airline, is experimenting with a passenger flight between Union Island and Carriacou for EC$55 one way.

## BUS

Buses on St Vincent are privately owned minivans that can cram in a good 20 people. The destinations are usually posted in the front windscreen. There's a 'conductor' on board who arranges the seating order and collects fares; you pay as you get off. Many of the buses have sound systems that blast reggae music and as long as you're not claustrophobic the buses are a good opportunity to rub shoulders with locals as well as a cheap way to travel.

Fares around Kingstown are EC$1. Fares from Kingstown are EC$1.50 to Villa, EC$2 to Layou, EC$3 to Barrouallie, EC$4 to Georgetown and EC$5 to Sandy Bay. The buses are most frequent in the morning and from mid to late afternoon when they load up with students and Kingstown commuters; however, getting a bus on a main route, such as between Villa and Kingstown, is fairly easy all day. As a general rule the farther from Kingstown you go the less frequent the buses.

There are also buses on Bequia and Union Island; see those island sections.

### Bus Station

Kingstown's central bus station, next to Little Tokyo, the city fish market, is a busy but surprisingly orderly affair. The bus stands are clearly marked – either Leeward, Windward or Kingstown, depending on the destination – and getting the right bus is fairly straightforward.

## TAXI

On St Vincent, taxis are readily available at the airport and in the greater Kingstown area. You can also have your hotel call for one, flag one down along the street or pick one up at the taxi stand on the south side of the Kingstown courthouse. For taxis on the Grenadines, see those island sections.

## CAR & MOTORBIKE
### Road Rules

Driving is on the left. A local licence must be obtained in order to drive on St Vincent; the fee is a hefty EC$40. In Kingstown, licences

ST MARTIN

can be obtained at the Traffic Branch, opposite the main police station, from 8 am to 5 pm Monday to Friday. They can also be picked up from the Licensing Authority on Halifax St, but the lines are longer and the opening hours shorter.

St Vincent roads can be narrow and a bit potholed; generally the main ones are in fairly good condition, though as a rule the farther north you go the worse they become. Be cautious, as minibus drivers commonly switch to whichever side of the road is least potholed and a few drivers have a penchant for passing with the least clearance possible.

The northernmost petrol stations on St Vincent are at Georgetown on the Windward Highway and Chateaubelair on the Leeward Highway.

### Rental

At present there are no internationally affiliated car rental agencies on St Vincent. Two local companies near the airport are Sunshine Auto Rentals (☎ 456-5380) and Unico Auto Rentals (☎ 456-5744); both have standard and 4WD vehicles and will deliver cars to your hotel. Other companies are Star Garage (☎ 456-1743) and Kim's Rentals (☎ 456-1884), both on Grenville St in Kingstown; David's Auto Clinic (☎ 456-4026), Sion Hill; Johnson's U-Drive Rental (☎ 458-4864), Arnos Vale; and Lucky Car Rental (☎ 457-1913), Kingstown.

Rentals begin at around US$40 a day for cars, US$50 for jeeps. There's often 60 to 75 free miles allowed and a fee of EC$1 for each additional mile driven.

On most of the Grenadines there are no car rentals at all (on some there are no roads!), although on a couple of the more populated islands private car rentals can be arranged through hotels at steep rates.

### BOAT

For information on the main ferry service between Bequia and Kingstown, see Getting There & Away in the Bequia section.

The mailboat MV *Snapper* carries passengers and cargo three times weekly between St Vincent, Bequia, Canouan, Mayreau and Union Island. The boat leaves St Vincent at 9.30 am on Monday, Thursday and Saturday, arriving in Union Island around 4 pm. En route it stops at Bequia, Canouan and Mayreau. On Tuesday and Friday the boat departs from Union Island early in the morning, and makes the same stopovers on the northbound route back to St Vincent. On Saturday, the boat leaves Union around 5.30 pm, usually making the return nonstop and arriving in St Vincent around 10.30 pm.

Fares from St Vincent are EC$10 to Bequia (EC$12 on weekends), EC$13 to Canouan, EC$15 to Mayreau and EC$20 to Union Island.

Although en route departure times vary depending on how long it takes to unload cargo, the sailing time between islands is one hour from St Vincent to Bequia, two hours from Bequia to Canouan, one hour from Canouan to Mayreau and 20 minutes from Mayreau to Union Island.

### TOURS

The most popular tours around St Vincent are boat rides to the Falls of Baleine (see that section under Leeward Highway) and hikes to the crater rim of the volcano (see Activities in the Facts for the Visitor section).

# Kingstown

Kingstown, the capital and commercial centre of St Vincent & the Grenadines, is a bustling city of 30,000 people.

The city centre consists of a dozen blocks that can easily be explored in a few hours. There are some appealing old cobblestone streets, brick archways and stone-block colonial buildings scattered around the centre; worth a look are the buildings lining Melville St and the churches, courthouse and police station. Still, none of these buildings is grand and overall Kingstown is more interesting for its local character than for any particular sights. It's the islanders selling their produce along Bay and Bedford streets, the crowds at the fish market and the rum

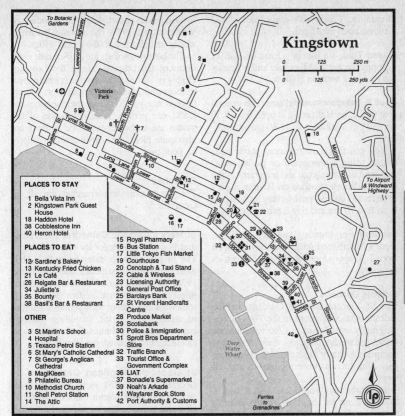

# Kingstown

**PLACES TO STAY**

1 Bella Vista Inn
2 Kingstown Park Guest
  House
18 Haddon Hotel
38 Cobblestone Inn
40 Heron Hotel

**PLACES TO EAT**

12 Sardine's Bakery
13 Kentucky Fried Chicken
21 Le Café
26 Reigate Bar & Restaurant
34 Juliette's
35 Bounty
38 Basil's Bar & Restaurant

**OTHER**

3 St Martin's School
4 Hospital
5 Texaco Petrol Station
6 St Mary's Catholic Cathedral
7 St George's Anglican
  Cathedral
8 MagiKleen
9 Philatelic Bureau
10 Methodist Church
11 Shell Petrol Station
14 The Attic

15 Royal Pharmacy
16 Bus Station
17 Little Tokyo Fish Market
19 Courthouse
20 Cenotaph & Taxi Stand
22 Cable & Wireless
23 Licensing Authority
24 General Post Office
25 Barclays Bank
27 St Vincent Handicrafts
  Centre
28 Produce Market
29 Scotiabank
30 Police & Immigration
31 Sprott Bros Department
  Store
32 Traffic Branch
33 Tourist Office &
  Government Complex
36 LIAT
37 Bonadie's Supermarket
39 Noah's Arkade
41 Wayfarer Book Store
42 Port Authority & Customs

shops at the bus terminal that give the town
its colour.

The little triangular park in front of the
courthouse, which has a cenotaph memorial
to WW I veterans, doubles as a taxi stand.
Ferries from the Grenadines arrive at the
jetty just south of the city centre. On Wednesday, when the banana boats are being loaded,
the port is abuzz with activity as trucks
loaded with stalks of bananas line the streets
to the dock.

Travellers who arrive in St Vincent by
ferry from Bequia are often rushed by a
barrage of taxi drivers and small-time hus-

tlers. This can make the first glimpse of
Kingstown a bit of a jolt, in sharp contrast to
the laid-back scenes encountered in the
Grenadines.

However, once you have passed the dock
and made your way into the heart of the city,
Kingstown takes on a much less foreboding
appearance.

## Information

**Tourist Office** The tourist office (☎ 457-
1502) is on the ground floor of the new
government building on Upper Bay St.
Opening hours are from 8.15 am to 4.15 pm

Monday to Friday; it's sometimes closed between noon and 1 pm.

**Money** There's a Barclays Bank on Halifax St, opposite the LIAT office, and a Scotiabank a block west on Halifax St.

**Post & Telecommunications** The general post office, on Halifax St, is open from 8.30 am to 3 pm weekdays, to 11.30 am on Saturday.

You can make international phone calls (either using a phonecard or paying cash) and send faxes, telexes and telegrams at the Cable & Wireless office on Halifax St. It's open from 7 am to 7 pm Monday to Saturday, from 8 to 10 am and 6 to 8 pm on Sundays.

**Laundry** For laundry and dry cleaning, there's MagiKleen on Lower Bay St, open from 7.30 am to 5 pm weekdays, to 2 pm on Saturday.

### Botanic Gardens

The St Vincent Botanic Gardens are the oldest botanical gardens in the West Indies. Originally established in 1765 to propagate spices and medicinal plants, the gardens now comprise a neatly landscaped eight-hectare park with lots of flowering bushes and tall trees.

Inside the park you'll find a small aviary that is home to about 20 of the island's remaining 500 St Vincent parrots. Most of the birds were born there, as part of a breeding programme that hopes to bring the parrot back from the brink of extinction.

Just 10 metres uphill from the aviary is a breadfruit tree that was grown from a sucker of one of the original saplings brought to the island from Tahiti in 1793 by Captain Bligh. The ill-fated captain introduced the tree, with its large starchy fruit, as an inexpensive food source for plantation slaves.

Also on the grounds is the St Vincent National Museum, which has numerous pre-Columbian stone carvings and clay works created by the island's early Amerindian settlers. The museum curator, Dr Earle Kirby, is a Canadian veterinarian-turned-local-

historian who spearheaded the founding of the museum in 1979. The museum has irregular hours; check with the tourist office.

The botanic gardens are a 10-minute walk north of the hospital, along the Leeward Highway. Although admission is free, expect to meet tour guides at the gate who will try to convince you to accept their services for US$3 per person. Although some of the guides are knowledgeable, the gardens are also quite pleasant to stroll through quietly on your own.

### Churches

The three interesting churches are all on Grenville St.

**St Mary's Catholic Cathedral** This cathedral is worth a look for its eclectic design. The original church dates from 1823, but most of the present structure was built in the 1930s by Dom Charles Verbeke, a Belgian priest. The grey-stone edifice boldly, and somewhat elaborately, incorporates a number of architectural styles, including Romanesque arches and columns, Gothic spires and an element of Moorish ornamentation.

**St George's Anglican Cathedral** St George's, circa 1820, is of late Georgian architecture. The interior has the traditional altar and stained-glass windows of a typical Anglican church but the walls are brightly painted in yellow and turquoise. There are interesting marble plaques. Look for the inscribed stone in the floor venerating the British commander Alexander Leith (1771-98). The colonel took the life of Carib chief Chattawae, only to die of 'great fatigue' following the battle.

**Methodist Church** From the outside, this church is a rather secular looking structure that could be mistaken for a warehouse. However, should you happen by when the doors are unlocked, the interior, which is full of light and colour, bears remarkably little resemblance to the exterior.

## Fort Charlotte

Fort Charlotte, on a 201-metre ridge north of the city, is a rather modest fortification, but it does provide a good view of Kingstown and of the Grenadines to the south. You can also walk through the old officers' quarters, whose walls are lined with paintings of Black Carib history that are accompanied by interesting interpretive plaques. Most of the rest of this 18th-century fort is off limits, and one area is used as a women's prison.

The fort is an hour's walk from the centre of town. If you want to go by bus, look for the red Nissan van marked 'Mad Dog' at the bus terminal; the driver can drop you off below the fort, from where it's a 10-minute uphill walk.

A taxi to the fort from the cenotaph in Kingstown centre costs EC$10. However, if you just want a quick look around, you may be able to negotiate a return trip and a 10-minute wait at the fort for EC$15.

## Places to Stay

**City Centre** The *Kingstown Park Guest House* (☎ 456-1532), PO Box 41, Kingstown, is the city's best value low-end hostelry, with friendly management and a fine hillside location. Its historic main building, which is 250 years old, served as the residence of St Vincent's first French governor. Rooms, which are simple and straightforward, are spread across three buildings and cost US$12/17 a single/double with shared bath, and US$20/23 with private bath. The main building has an atmospheric stonewall dining room where guests can get breakfast (EC$15) and a hearty home-cooked dinner (EC$20). The guesthouse is about a 10-minute walk from the city centre; take the steep footpath leading uphill opposite St Martin's School.

A few minutes' walk north-west of Kingstown Park Guest House, the *Bella Vista Inn* (☎ 457-2757) might be considered as a last resort. This private residence has six very simple island-style rooms, each with two single beds (no fan). There are a couple of shared toilets and showers in the hall. Singles/doubles cost US$15/21.

*Haddon Hotel* (☎ 456-1897; fax 456-2726), PO Box 144, Kingstown, is in a quiet location just north of the high school and only a few minutes' walk from the bustling city centre. The hotel has 18 simple air-con rooms which vary widely in size, but have private bath. Some of the rooms are a bit worn, but the staff are cheery and helpful. Posted rates are US$42/50 a single/double, but they'll sometimes let a couple of the smaller rooms go for US$26.

*Cobblestone Inn* (☎ 456-1937), PO Box 867, Kingstown, on Upper Bay St, is a charming hotel in a renovated 1814 Georgian-style warehouse of cobblestone construction. The 19 rooms have a pleasant old-world character, wooden floors, bathtub and air-con; many have cobblestone walls. The hotel, which is popular with business travellers, is both the most comfortable and most secure place to stay in the city centre. It's walking distance from the ferry dock. Singles/doubles cost US$54/70, including breakfast, all year round.

*Heron Hotel* (☎ 457-1631; fax 457-1189), PO Box 226, Kingstown, on Upper Bay St a block south of Cobblestone Inn, has 18 simple rooms with private shower, air-con and phone. You might want to avoid the streetside rooms, which can get a bit noisy. Singles/doubles cost US$40/57 year-round, breakfast included.

**Around Town** *Petit Byahaut* (☎ & fax 457-7008), Petit Byahaut Bay, is in a secluded seaside valley about five km north of Kingstown. Accommodation is in a handful of room-size tents with screened windows and one or two beds. There are hammocks, solar showers, shared restrooms and garden paths lit by kerosene lanterns. Petit Byahaut is intended for people who want a getaway holiday and don't mind paying US$125/210 a single/double to be in a simple, natural setting. Rates include three healthy meals a day and use of snorkelling equipment and sailboats. Scuba diving, which is good in this area, is available; day excursions can be arranged. The only way into the valley is by boat; a fee of US$25 per boat trip is charged to guests who stay less than three nights.

## Places to Eat – cheap

*Reigate Bar & Restaurant* on Halifax St is an airy, cheerful 2nd-floor eatery offering Kingstown's best chicken rotis – a filling lunch for a mere EC$5. Reigate also has inexpensive sandwiches, pizza and barbecued chicken. It's open from 11 am to 10 pm every day except Monday, when it closes at 5 pm.

The *Bounty* on Halifax St is an unpretentious local spot with adequate burgers, rotis, omelettes or macaroni cheese pie for EC$5 or less. Order and pay at the register and then give your receipt to the counter clerk. It's open from 8 am to 5 pm Monday to Friday, and to 1.30 pm on Saturday.

*Juliette's* is a hole-in-the-wall serving lunch to Kingstown office workers from 11.30 am on weekdays. There's one fixed meal for EC$9, which changes daily but is often fish or chicken with rice, plantains and a vegetable. It's best to come early as food is served until it's gone, commonly around 1 pm. There's a small dining area or you can order takeaway as most people do. Juliette's, which is unmarked, is on Middle St above the Family Store; enter through the alleyway and take the stairs to the 2nd floor. It's the last door on the right, next to the Youth for Christ office.

At *Kentucky Fried Chicken*, on the corner of Melville and Grenville streets, two pieces of chicken and a biscuit cost EC$7.60, or EC$10.50 with fries. It's open daily from 10 am to 11 pm (11 am to 10 pm on Sunday).

*Sardine's Bakery* on Grenville St is a good place to pick up bread and pastries, including tasty cinnamon rolls that cost a mere EC$0.50. It's open from 6 am to 5 pm weekdays, to 1 pm on Saturday.

Bonadie's Supermarket, on Egmont St, is a modern grocery store open from 8 am to 5 pm weekdays, to 6 pm on Friday, and from 7 am to 2 pm on Saturday.

If you have cooking facilities you can buy fresh fish at the new Little Toyko Fish Market (open from 7 am Monday to Saturday) next to the bus terminal on Lower Bay St and pick up fresh produce from vendors along Bedford St. At the bus terminal you'll also find rows of rum shops, popcorn stands and pavement vendors selling roasted corn on the cob and drinking coconuts for EC$1.

## Places to Eat – middle

*Le Café*, upstairs in Marcole Plaza on Halifax St, is a chic Art Deco café open daily from 9 am to 9 pm. The café offers some creative dishes, including shrimp sautéed with garlic and shallots served on rice for EC$25 and broiled fish and tomato with papaya salsa and onion rings for EC$18. A fruit platter or quiche costs EC$15 and they serve freshly ground coffee. On the ground floor of Marcole Plaza, there's another shop selling cones of Colombo frozen yoghurt for EC$2.

*Basil's Bar & Restaurant*, on Upper Bay St beneath Cobblestone Inn, has a bit of colonial character and a central location that makes it a popular business lunch locale. A burger with fries or an omelette costs EC$14, a chef's salad EC$20 and a fresh fish dish or buffet lunch EC$30. The buffet, which is served from noon to 2 pm Monday to Saturday, is small but good and usually includes a fish, chicken and beef dish as well as vegetables, salad and dessert. An offshoot of the renowned Basil's restaurant on Mustique, it's open daily from 10 am to around 10 pm.

The *Cobblestone Inn* also has a rooftop restaurant, featuring light meals in the EC$7 to EC$15 range. It's open from 7.30 am to 3 pm Monday to Saturday.

# Around St Vincent

## VILLA BEACH & INDIAN BAY

St Vincent's main 'resort' district is the Villa area, a few km south-east of Kingstown. It begins at Villa Point and runs along Indian Bay and Villa Beach, where it takes in the Young Island Cut, a narrow channel that separates the St Vincent mainland from Young Island.

The Villa area is a relatively well-to-do

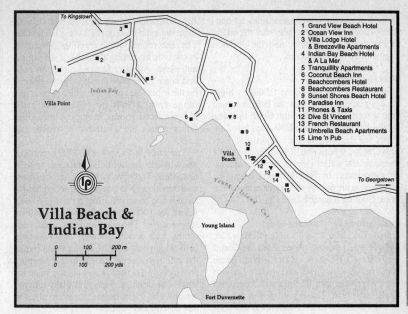

1. Grand View Beach Hotel
2. Ocean View Inn
3. Villa Lodge Hotel & Breezeville Apartments
4. Indian Bay Beach Hotel & A La Mer
5. Tranquillity Apartments
6. Coconut Beach Inn
7. Beachcombers Hotel
8. Beachcombers Restaurant
9. Sunset Shores Beach Hotel
10. Paradise Inn
11. Phones & Taxis
12. Dive St Vincent
13. French Restaurant
14. Umbrella Beach Apartments
15. Lime 'n Pub

## Villa Beach & Indian Bay

ST VINCENT

seaside suburb with about a dozen small hotels and inns. While Villa might be a fine neighbourhood to live in, it's not really the type of place most vacationers would envision when thinking of a Caribbean holiday.

The area is fairly well populated and the beaches are not terribly pristine. Indian Bay Beach, which has grainy golden sands, is generally clean enough, but Villa Beach has a couple of storm drains emptying across it and tends to get quite trashed.

Most services, including water taxis, land taxis, Dive St Vincent and the largest concentration of places to eat are near the Young Island Cut.

### Young Island

Young Island is a small privately owned island, about 200 metres off Villa Beach, that has been turned into an exclusive resort. Access is via the *African Queen*, a small ferry that the resort uses to shuttle guests and staff between Young Island and the dock at Villa Beach. At the spot where the ferry docks on Young Island there's a pleasant golden-sand beach and cleaner waters than those across the channel on St Vincent.

There's a courtesy phone line direct to the resort at the Villa Beach dock that visitors can use to request the ferry. The resort shuttles diners across to eat at its restaurant and

### Eternal View

Between Indian Bay and Villa Beach are a couple of small rocky islets, one of which has a large white cross atop it. Beneath the cross in an upright position is the body of a local landowner who once owned much of Villa's shoreline property. He requested to be laid to rest in a standing position in order to watch the sun set each day. ■

if they're not busy will sometimes let non-guests come over just to see what the island is like – but not always, and the decision seems to be made at whim.

### Fort Duvernette

Immediately south of Young Island is a high, rocky, gumdrop islet that the British turned into a fortress following the Carib uprising of the late 1790s. Some 250 steps wind up from the landing to the summit of Fort Duvernette, where you'll find the old fort's cannons and a fine view of the Grenadines. Transportation to Fort Duvernette can be arranged with one of the water taxis at the dock fronting Young Island Cut.

### Places to Stay – bottom end

*Ocean View Inn* (☎ 457-4332), PO Box 176, Villa Point, a minute's walk from the Grand View Beach Hotel, is an airy private home with five small but pleasant rooms, each with fan and private bath. The place is cheery and spotlessly clean. Tax is included in the rate of US$35/45 for singles/doubles as is a continental breakfast with fresh fruit. The manager is helpful and can arrange day tours at reasonable prices. It's a five-minute walk to Indian Bay Beach.

*Umbrella Beach Apartments* (☎ 458-4651; fax 457-4948), PO Box 530, Villa Beach, has nine simple rooms with ceiling fan, private bathroom and kitchen. Singles/doubles cost US$38/48. If you can't find anyone at the apartments go next door to the French Restaurant, which is under the same management.

*Tranquillity Apartments* (☎ & fax 458-4021), PO Box 71, Indian Bay, a bright blue building just above Indian Bay Beach, has seven studios. The rooms certainly aren't fancy but they have a full kitchen, TV, private bath and friendly family management. They also have a fine view of Young Island and the other nearshore islands. Singles/doubles cost US$40/50.

The *Coconut Beach Inn* (☎ 458-4231), PO Box 355, Indian Bay, has a pleasant beachside location in a residential neighbourhood. A bit removed from other Indian Bay hostelries, it's about a 10-minute walk from the main road or the Young Island Cut. The eight rooms, which are either in the main house or in a building alongside it, are simple and clean. All have fan and mosquito coils and some have private bath. Prices depend on the room size and the number of beds and range from US$45 to US$75, with the higher-priced rooms including breakfast. Other meals are available at reasonable prices.

The *Lime 'n Pub* (☎ 458-4227) rents out a few rooms in a building adjacent to their restaurant. There's a nice, airy one-bedroom apartment, with a separate kitchen and a large living room affording a view of Young Island for US$50 (negotiable to US$40 on longer stays). There are also two small bedrooms with private showers and two twin beds which cost US$30, but in these rooms the toilets are separated from the sleeping area by only a curtain. Rates are the same for singles or doubles. Fans and glass-louvred windows let in the breeze; there are plans to add air-con and phones.

*Paradise Inn* (☎ 457-4795), PO Box 1286, Villa Beach, has a couple of commodious two-bedroom apartments with full kitchen, living room, fan and beachfront balcony. Peeling linoleum and a slight air of neglect prevails, but the units are basically fine and the staff are friendly. There are also some very small rooms with private bath and balcony, but no cooking facilities. The rooms cost US$40/60 for a single/double and the apartments from US$60 to US$80.

*Sea Breeze Guest House* (☎ 458-4969), Arnos Vale, is about 1.5 km east of the airport, at a busy corner on the road between the airport and Villa Beach. While the location may not be ideal, the six simple guest rooms each have private bath, rates are just US$15 to US$22 and it's right on the bus route. There are common kitchen facilities and a TV room and they offer inexpensive tours of the island.

### Places to Stay – middle

*Beachcombers Hotel* (☎ 458-4283; fax 458-4385), PO Box 126, Villa Beach, on the west side of Villa Beach, is a friendly family-run operation with a dozen modern, straightforward rooms. The rooms vary a bit in size and decor: No 1 has some antique furnishings, Nos 3 and 6 are the largest, and a couple have air-con. All rooms have private bath, ceiling fan and patio, and the property has some nice old mango trees and a fine beachside location. Singles/doubles cost US$50/75, breakfast included. TVs can be rented for EC$12 a day.

*Indian Bay Beach Hotel* (☎ 458-4001; fax 457-4777), PO Box 538, Indian Bay, has 12 modern rooms, a nice beachside location and a pleasant 2nd-floor verandah with views of Bequia and Young Island. All rooms have air-con and most have a kitchenette. When making a reservation, be sure to specify that you want a kitchenette as there are a couple of smaller rooms without them which rent for the same rate: US$55/65 for singles/ doubles. There are also a few spacious two-bedroom units that cost US$80 for up to four people. The hotel is about a five-minute walk from the main road.

*Breezeville Apartments* (☎ 458-4004, fax 457-4468), PO Box 222, Villa Point, is attached to the Villa Lodge Hotel and guests have use of the hotel's pool. There are eight adequate though not cheery one-bedroom apartments with full kitchen, TV, phone, air-con and a '50s-style decor. Singles/doubles cost US$85/95 in the winter, $10 less in the summer.

If you're planning to stay awhile, you might want to consider *Ridgeview Terrace Apartments* (☎ 456-1615), PO Box 176, in Ratho Mill, just east of Villa. There are five apartments with kitchen, living room, separate air-con bedroom and balcony, which rent weekly for US$240 for one-bedroom units, US$290 for two-bedroom units. There's also a studio for US$175 a week.

### Places to Stay – top end

The *Villa Lodge Hotel* (☎ 458-4641; fax 457-4468), PO Box 1191, Indian Bay, has 10 rooms with tub, TV, air-con, mini-refrigerator and phone. There's also a pool, a breezy sitting room and a small moderately priced restaurant on site. The hotel is popular with visiting Caricom politicians and business travellers. Singles/doubles cost US$95/105.

*Sunset Shores Beach Hotel* (☎ 458-4411; fax 457-4800), PO Box 849, Villa Beach, has 31 ordinary rooms with air-con, TV, bathtub and phone. There's a pool and restaurant. The place is OK but not special for the price and the beach fronting the hotel could be kept much cleaner. Singles/doubles cost US$85/110 in the summer, US$110/130 in the winter.

The *Grand View Beach Hotel* (☎ 458-4811; fax 457-4174), PO Box 173, Villa Point, is an old hilltop plantation house on a scenic point. The rooms are large, with wooden floors, and many have fine ocean views, although the furnishings are rather simple and there's no air-con or window screens in this mosquito-hungry area. Guests have use of the hotel's health club, tennis courts and pool. The hotel is relaxed and in many ways pleasantly understated, but it's also a bit neglected and hard to recommend at US$150/210 for singles/doubles, breakfast included.

*Young Island Resort* (☎ 458-4826; fax 457-4567), PO Box 211, is an exclusive resort occupying the 10-hectare, privately owned Young Island. Accommodation is in rustic stone cottages that open to the surrounding gardens. The cottages have louvred windows, patios and al fresco showers. They are pleasantly natural, and the amenities are simple. Each room has an overhead fan and refrigerator, and the cottages are stocked daily with fresh fruit and flowers. Rates, which include breakfast and dinner, begin at US$245 in the summer for doubles, US$410 in the winter. Singles are US$90 cheaper.

### Places to Eat – cheap

The oceanfront restaurant at *Coconut Beach Inn* (☎ 458-4231) is casual and friendly and has good inexpensive food and a view of Young Island. There's a French toast or omelette breakfast with coffee for EC$13. At lunch, rotis, soup or sandwiches cost EC$8, chicken or fish & chips cost EC$13. Dinner can be arranged by reservation.

The open-air *Beachcombers Restaurant* is nicely situated above Villa Beach and has reasonably priced sandwiches, chicken rotis and conch fritters. They specialise in seafood dishes, which range from good fresh fish offerings for EC$25 to shrimp concoctions for EC$40. Bob and Sue, the Canadian-Bequian couple who run the restaurant, also make a decent pizza.

The popular *Lime 'n Pub* has pleasant open-air dining at Villa Beach. The lunch menu, available all day (from the pub after 6 pm), has rotis and sandwiches for EC$10 to EC$20, shark & chips or lasagne and salad for about EC$30. Dinner, mostly priced from EC$35 to EC$50, includes fish and shellfish dishes, curried goat, roast duckling and barbecued pork ribs. The food is generally quite good though very straightforward. It's open from 11 am to 11 pm daily.

The *Grand View Restaurant* at the Grand View Beach Hotel at Villa Point has a continental breakfast for EC$16 and a full breakfast for EC$26. At lunch there are sandwiches, salads and omelettes, most in the EC$10 to EC$25 range. Dinner is a fixed-price meal, by reservation, with a choice of two main dishes (usually meat and fish or shrimp), soup, dessert and coffee, for EC$48.

The Indian Bay Beach Hotel has open-air seaside dining at its *À La Mer* restaurant. While rotis, salads and sandwiches are reasonably priced, if you order these at dinner there's a fair chance the waiter will return from the kitchen to tell you they're out and then recommend an expensive substitute ('the lobster is good tonight'). A good alternative is the fresh fish & chips which comes with a small heap of salad and costs EC$18. Full dinners, which range from EC$32 to EC$50, are not special enough to warrant the price.

### Places to Eat – expensive

The *French Restaurant* (☎ 458-4972) at Villa Beach has a reputation for good, but expensive, French food with a West Indian accent. Starters range from EC$16 for onion soup to EC$30 for seafood salad, while main dishes like baked fish with basil sauce and duck in orange sauce average EC$45. There are also lobster dishes, such as lobster flambéed in cognac sauce. They are plucked live from the restaurant's own lobster pool. It's open daily, from 7 to 11 am for breakfast, noon to 2 pm for lunch (light snacks for around EC$15) and 7 to 9.30 pm for dinner.

For a different sort of dining experience, *Young Island Resort* (☎ 458-4826) serves up a US$35 three-course set dinner from 7.30 to 9.30 pm. On a typical evening there might be a choice of lobster, veal or chicken as a main dish, served with an appetiser, soup, salad and a simple dessert. On Tuesday and Saturday there's a US$40 buffet instead. Lunch, served from 12.30 to 2.30 pm, costs US$13. Some of the seating is outdoors under individual thatched huts, which can be quite romantic. Reservations are required for both meals.

## WINDWARD HIGHWAY

St Vincent's east coast, its windward side, is raw and rugged with a jungly interior and a surf-pounded shoreline. The Windward Highway winds up and down the east coast, passing black-sand beaches, roadside banana plantations and deep valleys thickly planted in coconut trees. Along the route are a number of small villages, an intermingling of old wooden shanties and simple cement homes.

The road is potholed here and there and is narrow in places, but by island standards it's in reasonably good condition. The final leg between Owia and Fancy is part cement and part dirt. If you're driving, allow at least an hour to get from Kingstown to Georgetown. To drive the entire 56 km from Kingstown to the end of the road at Fancy would take a good two hours each way, not including time to stop and explore.

Buses from Kingstown to Georgetown are fairly regular (except on Sunday) and cost EC$4. Continuing north from Georgetown by bus can be a bit iffy, so it's a good idea to get information from the Kingstown bus terminal before heading off.

## Georgetown

Georgetown is a fairly good-sized but rather poor town that was once the centre of the island's sugar industry. Now just a shadow of its former self, its main street is lined with cobblestone sidewalks and two-storey buildings with overhanging balconies. Once stylish, many of these buildings are now in various stages of disrepair, a few simply falling apart and abandoned.

Few tourists come this way and there really aren't any sights per se. The two churches, one Methodist and one Anglican, that sit side by side on the main street are in need of restoration, but are open to visitors.

**Places to Eat** The 2nd-storey *Footsteps Restaurant & Bar* (☎ 458-6433) above the grocery store on the main road in the centre of town is a good place for a meal. You can get breakfast for about EC$10 and a good hearty West Indian lunch or dinner for EC$15 to EC$25. The accommodating owner, Ferdie Toney, also rents out a couple of rooms.

## North of Georgetown

The farther north you go, the wilder it gets; the valleys are deeper and the villages more primitive. The active volcano La Soufrière looms inland as you continue along the road, adding a primeval element to the scenery.

About two km north of Georgetown the road goes over a hardened lava flow known as the Rabacca Dry River, a former stream that filled with lava during La Soufrière's violent 1902 eruption. The river now flows through a gravel bed buried beneath the lava. During heavy rains, however, flash floods occasionally flow above the lava, making the road crossing hazardous or impossible.

North of the dry river, a 4WD road heads inland two km through coconut and banana plantations towards **La Soufrière** and the beginning of a 5.25-km hiking trail that leads to the rim of the crater. For more information, see Activities in the Facts for the Visitor section of this chapter.

Continuing north, the Windward Highway passes through **Orange Hill Estates**, where a 1280-hectare coconut estate, once the world's largest, has been divided up and parcelled out to small farmers as part of a government land reform project. In addition to coconuts, Orange Hill produces bananas, limes, spices and vegetables.

A few km farther is **Sandy Bay**, a sizeable village that has the island's largest concentration of Black Caribs. A proud people with a turbulent history, they are distinguished from other Vincentians by their short, stocky builds and high cheekbones.

North of Sandy Bay is Owia Bay and the village of **Owia**. Turn east on the main village road at the police station to reach a salt pond on the coast. Here you'll find tidal pools protected from the crashing Atlantic by a massive stone shield. This is a popular swimming hole and there are some thatched shelters, picnic tables, a small garden and a view of St Lucia to the north. Use caution during high tide or if the waves are breaking over the rocks and watch out for yellow sea anemones which can sting. Owia also has an arrowroot mill and a couple of churches that can be visited.

True diehards can go to **Fancy**, where the road ends at St Vincent's most remote village, a rather rudimentary settlement with no electricity or phones. There's an old arrowroot mill with a rusting mill wheel that now serves as the medical clinic, a school and two simple shops selling groceries and provisions.

## LEEWARD HIGHWAY

The Leeward Highway runs north from Kingstown along St Vincent's west coast for 40 km, ending at Richmond Beach. The west coast offers some lovely scenery. Leaving Kingstown the road climbs into the mountains and then winds through the hillside and back down to deeply cut coastal valleys which open to coconut plantations, fishing villages and bays lined with black-sand beaches.

The drive from Kingstown to Richmond Beach takes about 1½ hours, not including stopping time. Just north of Kingstown, there are a few narrow sections where the shoulderless road is crumbly and a miscalculation could result in a tumble over the cliff. Otherwise the road as far as Barrouallie is in good condition, albeit narrow and winding. North beyond Barrouallie, some sections become quite potholed.

There are fairly frequent weekday buses from Kingstown to Barrouallie (45 minutes, EC$3). Buses generally don't run in the evening; plan on catching a return bus to Kingstown by 5 pm from Barrouallie to be safe. It's a 15-minute walk from the last Barrouallie bus stop to Wallilabou Bay, although the driver might be willing to take you directly to Wallilabou for a few dollars more. Generally only four buses a day (two in the morning, two in the afternoon) continue north from Barrouallie to Richmond.

### Vermont Nature Trails

About a 15-minute drive north of Kingstown, a sign along the Leeward Highway points east to the Vermont Nature Trails, 5.5 km inland from the highway. Here you'll find the Parrot Lookout Trail, a 2.75-km loop trail that passes through the south-western tip of the St Vincent Parrot Reserve. The island forestry department, with assistance from the Worldwide Fund for Nature, established the reserve in 1987 to protect the endangered St Vincent parrot, which numbers only about 500 in the wild.

The Parrot Lookout Trail climbs 150 metres in elevation into a mixed tropical rainforest of towering native hardwood trees, lush ferns, bromeliads, heliconias, abandoned cocoa trees and introduced groves of eucalyptus. The hike takes about two hours. Be prepared for wet conditions, as the forest averages more than 500 cm of rain a year, and bring insect repellent. Hikers should wear long sleeves and pants as a precaution against chiggers, which can be quite pesky along this trail.

Near the trailhead you'll find a welcome board with background information and a map. Twenty interpretive signs posted along the trail give brief descriptions of the flora and fauna encountered along the way.

The best times for parrot sightings are generally early morning and late afternoon; even if you don't spot the parrots there's a chance you'll hear their loud squawks as they move from tree to tree. Other birds sometimes seen along the trail include the rare whistling warbler, a black and white bird with eye rings that is endemic to the island, as well as brightly coloured hooded tanagers, hummingbirds, broad-winged hawks and common black hawks.

### Layou

The Leeward Highway comes out to the coast for the first time at the black sands of Buccament Bay. Shortly after that, the road curves around the coastal mountains giving a fine bird's-eye view of the fishing village of Layou, before descending down to Layou Bay. The village is colourful, a mix of simple old wooden structures and brightly painted concrete homes.

There are a scattering of petroglyphs on St Vincent's west coast. The best known are in Layou, a short walk from the river near the Bible Camp on the main road at the north end of town. However, they're on private property and if you want to see them, you'll need to arrange it with the property owner, Victor Hendrickson (☎ 458-7243), who usually charges visitors EC$5.

After Layou the road goes inland before coming back out to the coast at the north side of Mt Wynne Bay, a lovely black-sand beach backed by a broad sweep of coconut trees. Some of the tours to the Falls of Baleine stop at this undeveloped beach for picnics.

### Barrouallie

Like Layou, Barrouallie is a typical St Vincent fishing village. Barrouallie villagers are perhaps best known for their hunting of pilot whales, which are referred to as blackfish on the island.

The village has some interesting older architecture with gingerbread trim and there are petroglyphs in the yard of the Barrouallie secondary school.

### Wallilabou Bay & Falls

Wallilabou is a quiet little bay lined with a

black-sand beach and surrounded by high cliffs, complete with a picturesque little rock arch at its northern end. The waters are usually quite calm and it's possible to snorkel at the southern end of the bay.

Wallilabou is a port of entry to the island and a small flotilla of young men offering to sell provisions and run errands often row out to the yachts as they pull into the bay.

A popular little side excursion is to the Wallilabou Falls, which are some four metres high and drop into a waist-deep bathing pool. The falls are near the inland side of the main road about 1.5 km north of Wallilabou Bay; once you cross the Wallilabou River bridge, it's about a 10-minute walk.

**Places to Stay & Eat** *Wallilabou Anchorage* (☎ 458-7270; VHF 68 & 86), PO Box 851, Wallilabou, which runs the mooring facilities here, has a pleasant bayside restaurant and bar open for three meals daily. The creole fish at EC$20 is a good choice, sandwiches start at EC$6 and chicken curry or fish & chips are EC$15; avoid the fishburger, an odd minced-fish patty. A small hotel with simple seafront rooms with private bath is under construction.

### North of Wallilabou

North of Wallilabou, the next beach you come to is **Cumberland Bay**, a pretty little anchorage backed by coconut palms and lush green hills. Up on the highway is *Stephen's Hideout* (☎ 458-2325; VHF 16), a restaurant with moderately priced West Indian seafood dishes.

The road passes a few settlements, including the town of **Chateaubelair**, before ending at **Richmond Beach**. This long black-sand beach has stands of tropical almond trees and is a popular swimming and picnicking spot. Avoid swimming near the river mouth at the north side of the beach, as it can have a strong undertow.

East of Richmond is the trailhead to **Trinity Falls**, a remote triple cascade with a 12-metre drop and pools deep enough for a dip. The falls are about five km inland, on

the road beginning at the Richmond Vale Academy. With a 4WD vehicle it should be possible to drive about half of that distance and then continue to the falls on foot along a rugged hiking trail.

Also from Richmond, it's possible to hike up to the crater rim of La Soufrière. However, this trail is much rougher than the one on the windward side of the island and a local guide is necessary. The hike would take a full day.

### FALLS OF BALEINE

The 18-metre Falls of Baleine, at the isolated north-western tip of the island, is inaccessible by road but can be visited by boat from Kingstown.

The falls, which cascade down a fern-draped rock face into a wide pool deep enough for swimming, are a few minutes' walk from the beach where the boats anchor.

Most hotels and guesthouses can book tours to Baleine and a few, such as Beachcombers at Villa Beach, have their own boats. Beachcombers, and most dive-shop tours, use a speedboat which allows them to zip to the falls in about an hour.

Sailing boats are more leisurely, usually taking a couple of hours each way, and offer better odds of spotting dolphins along the way. Sea Breeze Boat Service (☎ 458-4969) has an 11-metre sloop and is the island's cheapest tour at US$25 (most other places charge about US$40). Their tour leaves at 8 am and returns at 5 pm, stopping for snorkelling en route. Bring your own lunch.

# Bequia

Just an hour's sail south of St Vincent, Bequia is the northernmost, the largest (18 sq km) and the most populated (5000 people) of St Vincent's Grenadine islands.

Bequia is a delightful place, neat, hilly and green, with lots of flowering bushes and some fine golden-sand beaches. It has a rich seafaring tradition that includes boat building, whaling and sailing. These days most of

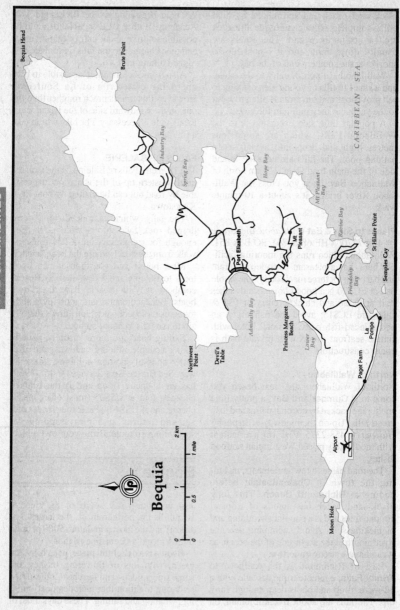

Bequia

Bequia Head

Brute Point

Industry Bay

Spring Bay

Hope Bay

Mt Pleasant Bay

CARIBBEAN SEA

Rainbow Bay

St Hilaire Point

Port Elizabeth

Mt Pleasant

Semples Cay

Friendship Bay

Admiralty Bay

Princess Margaret Beach

La Pompe

Northwest Point

Devil's Table

Lower Bay

Paget Farm

Moon Hole

Airport

0    0.5    1    2 km

0    0.5    1 mile

the boat building done on the island is on the scale of models, and over 90% of the boats pulling into the harbour are visiting yachts. The island has become the main yachting haven in the Grenadines and at the height of the season Admiralty Bay, the deep protected bay fronting the town of Port Elizabeth, is chock-a-block with yachts.

There are a number of good places to eat and several appealing guesthouses and hotels. All in all, Bequia is a fun place to add to any island-hopping itinerary.

### Activities
There's good windsurfing at Admiralty Bay, Friendship Bay and Paget Farm and for the more advanced at Industry Beach and Spring Bay. Paradise Windsurfing has rental booths at each of these sites and offers lessons at Admiralty Bay and Friendship Bay.

Sunsports (☎ 458-3577), a dive shop on the ground floor of Gingerbread Restaurant, Port Elizabeth, offers a 1½-hour snorkelling trip for US$10, rents Sunfish and arranges day sails. For information on diving, see Activities in the front of this chapter.

### PORT ELIZABETH
Port Elizabeth, the island's commercial centre, has an appealing seaside community, and is built along the curve of Admiralty Bay.

The town has an international mix of people and a fair number of the restaurants and shops are operated by expatriates – mostly yachters who came to visit and decided to stay on.

Port Elizabeth strikes a nice balance between quaintness and convenience. Many of the waterfront businesses cater to visiting boaters and offer a wide range of services, from places to pick up ice and drop off laundry to good bars and dining spots.

### Orientation
A narrow shoreline walkway at the south side of Port Elizabeth is the main access to many of the town's restaurants and other visitor businesses. The walkway begins at Barclays Bank and continues down to the Plantation House, 500 metres away. Part of

the route can be a bit precarious at high tide when waves splash up on the seawall, and it's hit-and-miss as to whether you'll be able to pass without getting your feet wet. While there's barely a beach here, this southerly section of Port Elizabeth is sometimes referred to as Belmont Beach.

Although the shoreline walkway is the main access between Belmont Beach's waterfront businesses, the hotels do have long driveways leading down into them from the Port Elizabeth-Paget Farm Rd.

### Information
**Tourist Office** The Bequia Tourist Bureau (☎ 458-3286), at the ferry dock, is open from 9 am to 12.30 pm daily, as well as from 1.30 to 4 pm every day but Saturday.

**Money** Barclays Bank, at the north end of the shoreline walkway, is open from 8 am to 1 pm Monday to Thursday and from 8 am to 1 pm and 3 to 5 pm on Friday. The Caribbean Banking Corporation, at the Bayshore Mall opposite the ferry dock, and the National Commercial Bank, a few minutes' walk to the south, both have the same hours as Barclays.

**Post & Telecommunications** The Port Elizabeth post office is opposite the ferry dock. It's open from 9 am to noon and 1 to 3 pm weekdays, 9 to 11.30 am on Saturday.

There are card and coin phones outside the tourist office.

**Bookshop** The Bequia Bookshop in Port Elizabeth is one of the best bookshops in the Eastern Caribbean. It stocks everything from charts and survey maps to yachting and travel books and guides on flora and fauna. There's also a small but select collection of West Indian literature. Credit cards are accepted.

**Laundry** The Lighthouse Service (☎ 458-3084; VHF 68), behind St Mary's Church, will do laundry for EC$20 per load. It also has hot showers for EC$5 and a few other yachters' services.

## Princess Margaret Beach

The nicest beach in the Port Elizabeth area is the Princess Margaret Beach, a secluded golden-sand beach in a natural green setting. To get there, take the shoreline walkway south past the Plantation House. From there a dirt path climbs up over a coastal hill before ending at the beach, 10 minutes away. The path, which passes agave, yucca and air plants, is a bit steep but not too strenuous and offers some nice glimpses of Admiralty Bay on the way.

## Places to Stay

*Papa Mitch* (☎ 458-3370), above the Bequia Bookshop, has a handful of spartan island-style rooms with little more than a bed with a saggy mattress and a bare light bulb hanging from the ceiling. Toilets and showers are shared. While rooms have louvred windows, the two we saw had no screens, mosquito nets or fans – so expect to either swelter or swat away the night. On the plus side the location is central and the singles/doubles rate is just US$12/19.

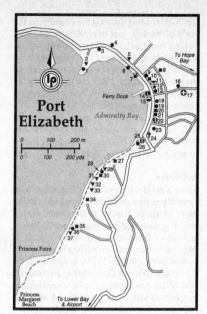

Port Elizabeth

Admiralty Bay

Princess Point

Princess Margaret Beach

To Hope Bay

To Lower Bay & Airport

Ferry Dock

| PLACES TO STAY | | OTHER | |
|---|---|---|---|
| 8 | Julie's Guest House | 1 | Bequia Marina |
| 10 | Julie's Guest House | 3 | S&W Supermarket |
| 21 | Papa Mitch | 4 | Sargeant Bros Model Boat Shop |
| 27 | Frangipani Hotel | 6 | Produce Market |
| 30 | Gingerbread Apartments | 7 | Petrol Station |
| 34 | Old Fig Tree Guest House | 9 | Knights Supermarket |
| 35 | Plantation House | 11 | Post Office |
| | | 12 | Police & Customs |
| **PLACES TO EAT** | | 13 | Bayshore Mall |
| | | 14 | Tourist Office |
| 2 | Harpoon Saloon | 15 | Bus & Taxi Stand |
| 5 | Doris Fresh Food | 16 | Library |
| 27 | Frangipani Restaurant & Bar | 17 | Hospital |
| 28 | Whaleboner | 18 | Grenadines Yachts & Equipment |
| 30 | Gingerbread Restaurant | 19 | Handy Andy's |
| 31 | Gingerbread Cafe | 20 | Bequia Bookshop |
| 32 | Maranne's Ice Cream | 22 | National Commercial Bank |
| 33 | Mac's Pizzeria & Bakeshop | 23 | Lighthouse Service |
| 37 | Coco's Grill | 24 | St Mary's Church |
| | | 25 | Barclays Bank |
| | | 26 | Shoreline Mini-Mart |
| | | 29 | Sunsports |
| | | 36 | Dive Bequia & Paradise Windsurfing |

*Julie's Guest House* (☎ 458-3304; fax 458-3812) is an old wooden boarding house that could've been torn from the pages of a Somerset Maugham novel. The 1st floor has a bar and restaurant, while the 2nd floor has simple, clean rooms with showers (cold water) and toilets that are separated from the sleeping area by a curtain. The thin wooden walls between the rooms offer no barrier to sound, so it's best to request a corner room which has only one adjoining wall. The louvred windows have no screens, but there are mosquito nets over the beds. If you prefer comfort (hot showers) to character, Julie's also has rooms in a new cement building opposite the waterfront, just a couple of minutes' walk away. Singles/doubles cost US$30/49, which includes a solid three-course West Indian dinner and a full breakfast. Credit cards are accepted.

The ageing *Old Fig Tree Guest House* (☎ 458-3201), on the waterfront, has six very basic and rather dingy rooms above the restaurant of the same name. There are no window screens or mosquito nets but there are fans. Rates are US$13/25 for singles/doubles with shared bath, US$30 for a double with private bath.

The *Frangipani Hotel* (☎ 458-3824; fax 458-3824), PO Box 1, Port Elizabeth, is a pleasant and very popular 15-room waterfront inn with its own dinghy dock. Owned by the family of the current prime minister, who was born here in room No 1, this family home was converted into an inn two decades ago. There are simple rooms on the 2nd floor of the old wooden main house as well as newer 'garden units' behind it, which have natural stone walls, private bath and sundeck. For rooms in the main house, singles/doubles cost US$25/40 in summer and US$35/50 in winter with a shared bath, US$40/60 in summer and US$50/80 in winter with a private bath. The garden units cost US$60/80 in summer, US$80/120 in winter.

The *Gingerbread Apartments* (☎ 458-3800; fax 458-3907), PO Box 1, Port Elizabeth, consists of three tidy apartments, one beneath the Gingerbread Restaurant and two behind. The units vary, but each has cooking facilities, a bathroom and a porch. The largest unit has a large living room, a main bedroom and a second smaller bedroom reached by walking through the first, which is good for families. Doubles cost US$65/90

---

## Model Boats

Bequia's shipbuilding heritage lives on through local artisans who build wooden scale models of traditional schooners and Bequian whaling boats. The boats are crafted to exact proportions, painted in traditional colours and outfitted with sails and rigging.

There are a couple of workshops opposite the waterfront on the north side of Port Elizabeth. The best known, Sargeant Bros Model Boat Shop, near the Bequia Marina, will let visitors into the workshop to watch the boats being built. The shop also does quite a custom order business, making replicas of visiting yachts for their owners. One of their best known works was a model of the royal yacht, the HMS {Britannia}, which was presented to Queen Elizabeth II during her 1985 visit.

While there are sometimes a few simpler models priced from US$100, most of the boats sell from US$400 to US$1000 and those with the finest detail cost up to US$2500. Many of the models are shipped off the island and sold to collectors. ∎

in the summer/winter. For a third person, it's US$10 for a child, US$20 for an adult. No taxes or service charges are added.

The *Plantation House* (☎ 458-3425; fax 458-3612; from the USA ☎ (800) 223-9832, from the UK ☎ (0452) 813551), PO Box 16, Belmont, has pleasant landscaped grounds dotted with peach-coloured wooden cottages. The cottages are appealingly simple, each with a ceiling fan, screened louvred windows, natural wood floors, mosquito-netted beds, a small refrigerator and a porch. There's a pool and a tennis court. The only drawback is the price: from US$210/295 for singles/doubles in the winter, US$135/180 the rest of the year, with breakfast and dinner included.

*Village Apartments* has five self-contained apartments on the Paget Farm road, a 10-minute uphill walk from the centre of Port Elizabeth. These modern units have a porch, red-tile floor and casual PVC pipe furniture. There's a studio apartment for US$140/240 a week in the summer/winter, a one-bedroom apartment for US$200/300 a week and a two-bedroom cottage for US$300/450 a week. Reservations can be made by writing to Val or George Whitney Jr (☎ 456-2960; fax 456-2344), PO Box 1621, Kingstown.

### Places to Eat

**On the Walkway** *Maranne's Ice Cream*, a little kiosk just north of Mac's Pizzeria, has good home-made ice cream, sorbet and frozen yoghurt in a variety of tropical flavours. A small cone costs a mere EC$2. It's open from 11 am to 6.30 pm daily.

*Mac's Pizzeria & Bakeshop* has porchside dining with a garden setting and a view of Admiralty Bay. Mac's is one of the most popular spots on the strip and has a full range of pizzas, from a nine-inch green olive pizza for EC$19 to a 15-inch lobster pizza for EC$75. You can also order a variety of whole wheat or pita bread sandwiches for EC$7 and a tasty appetiser of Conch MacNuggets for EC$10. Other dishes include quiche, chowder, lasagne and samosas. Don't miss the rum-raisin banana bread – a big slice

costs EC$2. It's open from 11 am to 10 pm daily.

*Frangipani Restaurant & Bar* is in the lower level of the old Mitchell house, which once served as a storeroom for the 40-metre *Gloria Colita*, the largest schooner ever built on Bequia. (The boat disappeared in 1940 and was found drifting in the Bermuda Triangle, with no trace of the crew.) Today the main anchorage for yachts fronts the Frangipani and its seaside bar is Bequia's foremost watering hole for sailors and expatriates. Until 6 pm there are sandwiches, burgers, salads and omelettes from EC$8 to EC$20 or a fresh fish dish for EC$25. At dinner there's a special three-course meal for EC$36, otherwise most main dishes are EC$30 to EC$60. It's open daily from 7.30 am to 9 pm.

The 2nd-floor *Gingerbread Restaurant* is a very popular dining spot with high ceilings, gingerbread trim and a fine harbour view. At lunch there are inexpensive sandwiches and omelettes as well as various pasta dishes from EC$10 to EC$20. Dinner features seafood dishes from EC$30 to EC$48 and on Wednesday, Friday and Sunday there's music by De Real Ting string band. Breakfast is served from 8 to 10.30 am. Happy hour, from 5 to 6 pm weekdays, usually features two rum punches for the price of one. While it makes a good choice for a dinner out, during the high season it's often necessary to make reservations early in the day.

*Gingerbread Cafe*, at the south side of the restaurant, has various cakes for EC$3 a slice and coffees, espressos and cappuccinos. It's open from 7.30 am to 6.30 pm daily. There's also a daily lunch barbecue of grilled chicken, kebabs and seafood served outdoors from noon to 3 pm.

The *Plantation House* has open-air dining on the large verandah of a reconstructed colonial-style plantation house (the original burned down in 1988). The dinner menu changes daily, but typical items are: callaloo soup for EC$10, smoked oysters for EC$15, grilled catch of the day or roast duck for EC$50 and a less expensive pasta dish. It's open from 6.30 am to 10 pm daily. Also on the Plantation House Hotel grounds is *Coco's Grill*, a lively bar which has sandwiches from EC$16, grilled fish for EC$28 and on Tuesday night live music and dancing.

Vestiges of Bequia's whaling history can be found at the *Whaleboner*, where there's a bar framed with a huge piece of whalebone and bar stools using whale vertebrae as their posts.

**Elsewhere in Port Elizabeth** The *Harpoon Saloon*, at Bequia Marina at the north side of the bay, is a large open-air restaurant and bar. The dockside grill is breezy and casual, with draught beer for EC$4, burgers with fries for EC$16 and main dishes such as ginger-marinated chicken breast or catch of the day for around EC$22. There's a jump-up here each Saturday from 9 pm, with a EC$10 cover charge.

*Julie's Guest House*, in the centre of town, has a dining room for its overnight guests that's also open to the public. A simple but wholesome West Indian dinner, served from 7.30 to 9 pm, costs EC$35 to EC$40. It's a fixed meal, often including the likes of christophene soup, green salad, chicken or fish, island vegetables, rice, dessert and coffee or tea. A breakfast of fruit, juice, coffee, and a choice of French toast, pancakes or eggs costs EC$12.50.

The Port Elizabeth produce market, just west of the pier, is the place to pick up fresh fruit and vegetables. For groceries you'll find a handful of supermarkets on the waterfront road.

*Doris Fresh Food*, opposite the produce market, has hearty whole-wheat bread baked fresh throughout the day and sold warm from the oven.

**Things to Buy**
Port Elizabeth has lots of boutiques selling attractive batik and silk-screen clothing, handpainted T-shirts, frond baskets and other island crafts. You'll also find vendors along the beach in town selling pocketbooks made from calabash gourds, printed T-shirts and a few other items.

The Bayshore Mall, opposite the ferry

dock, has a pharmacy, travel agency, and shops selling clothing, souvenirs and sundry items.

## LOWER BAY
Lower Bay is a quiet little beach community at the southern end of Admiralty Bay that's fronted by a pretty golden-sand beach and clear turquoise waters. It's one of the island's nicest beaches and has good swimming conditions.

Lower Bay has a few guesthouses, but it's a bit off the main tourist track, which adds to its appeal. This would be a fine place to hang out and play beach bum.

It's a 10 to 15-minute walk to Lower Bay from the Port Elizabeth-Paget Farm road, where you'll find the nearest bus stop. There's also a footpath leading from Princess Margaret Beach to Lower Bay.

Beware of manchineel trees that grow along some sections of Lower Bay Beach; they look like large inviting shade trees but the oils from their leaves can cause a serious rash. Some of the trees have been marked by the Bequia Sailing Club.

**Places to Stay**
The 11-room *Keegan's Guest House* (☎ 458-3530) is right across from the beach at Lower Bay. The nicest rooms are Nos 8 and 9, which are big, well appointed and share a balcony with an ocean view. All rooms have private bath, fan and comfortable beds with mosquito nets. Rooms in the older wing are smaller, but even they are good value compared to most places at Port Elizabeth. Rates, which include breakfast and a three-course dinner, are US$41/55 for singles/doubles.

The *Lower Bay Guest House* (☎ 458-3675), a minute's walk up from the beach, has eight small, basic rooms with sink, louvred windows and shared bathroom. Singles/doubles cost US$20/28.

*De Reef Apartments* (☎ 458-3484) are five new, self-contained apartments just inland from De Reef restaurant. An A-frame apartment with a loft bedroom upstairs and a kitchen, small living area and bathroom downstairs rents for US$200/280 a week in the summer/winter. Two-bedroom apartments with living/dining area and full kitchen cost US$400/500 a week. The apartments are cooled by ceiling fans and there's a housekeeping service three times a week.

## Places to Eat

*Keegan's*, opposite the beach at Lower Bay, serves breakfast (8 to 9.30 am), lunch (11 am to 2 pm) and dinner daily. At lunch you can order sandwiches for about EC$6 and chicken or fish & chips with salad for EC$18. Dinner is by reservation and usually features fresh seafood. There's a small bar.

*De Reef*, on the beach, serves meals from 10 am to 10 pm daily and has a bar that stays open later. Lunch features the likes of callaloo soup and coconut rolls for EC$8, Creole conch with rice and fried plantains for EC$24. At dinner, there's a fixed-price, three-course, West Indian meal with a choice of a couple of main dishes such as fish or baked lobster for EC$45 to EC$60.

At the east end of the beach there's *Theresa's*, a simple little concrete hut with a handful of tables that offers a dinner buffet, usually featuring West Indian dishes, for EC$42 and simple lunch-time fare from EC$10. *Dawn's Creole Garden*, on the road past Theresa's, is another small local restaurant offering West Indian food.

You can buy fresh bread at *Nando's Bake Shop*, a little village bakery open from 6 am to noon and 3 to 5 pm Monday to Saturday.

## FRIENDSHIP BAY

Friendship Bay is a deep, beautiful bay with a nice golden-sand beach and good swimming and windsurfing. The area is quiet and caters to tourists, mostly European, rather than sailors. The waterfront is only a few minutes' walk from the Port Elizabeth-Paget Farm road and it's easy to catch a shared 'dollar cab' from Port Elizabeth.

## Whaling Museum

Athneal's Private Petite Museum displays whaling paraphernalia in the home of Athneal Ollivierre, the ageing grandson of Bequia's first whaler. The trade was passed down from father to son and Athneal, now in his seventies, is the island's last harpoonist.

Because of the island's century-old whaling tradition, Bequia has been granted aboriginal whaling status by the International Whaling Foundation and has an annual quota of three whales. Athneal, still an active whaler, caught a 12-metre humpback whale in 1992, his first such catch in four years.

The museum is in La Pompe, on the inland side of the road between Friendship Bay and the airport. It can easily be identified by the whale jawbone arching above the front walkway. Admission costs US$2 and the museum is open from 10 am to 5 pm Monday to Saturday, from 9 am to 7 pm on Sunday.

## Petit Nevis

The uninhabited island of Petit Nevis, which lies about 1½ km south of Friendship Bay, is the site of a deserted whaling station, complete with a few rusting trypots (large iron kettles used for rendering blubber) and piles of whale bones. The island is a popular day anchorage with good snorkelling, though currents can be strong.

## Places to Stay

*Blue Tropic Hotel* (☎ & fax 458-3573; in Germany (☎ 70 31 8062 60), on the main road just above Friendship Bay, has 10 rather basic rooms with kitchenette, shower, ceiling fan and balcony with partial bay views. Singles/doubles cost US$46/72 in summer, US$66/92 in winter, breakfast included.

The *Bequia Beach Club* (☎ 458-3248, fax 458-3689; in Germany (☎ 70 31 8010 33), on a prime section of the beach at Friendship Bay, has 10 attractive beachside bungalows with ceiling fans, screened windows, mini-refrigerator and radio. It has a young German manager and is often fully booked with packaged tour groups from Germany. Singles/doubles cost US$80/140, including breakfast and dinner. Paradise Windsurfing and Bequia Dive operate from a beach hut here.

*Friendship Bay Hotel* (☎ 458-3222; fax 458-3840), PO Box 9, Friendship Bay, is a pleasant 27-room beachfront hotel under

Swedish management. The rooms have prints on the walls, ceiling fan and ocean-view balcony. For a prime oceanview, ask for room No 7 or 8. Singles/doubles cost US$55/70 in summer, US$95/115 in winter. There are also oceanfront rooms close to the beach but they are much pricier, and anyway none of the hotel's rooms is more than 100 metres from the water. The hotel has a tennis court, a dive shop and a jetty. Day sails to other islands can be arranged.

### Places to Eat

The *Friendship Bay Hotel* has a beach hut and bar selling burgers, sandwiches and salads for EC$12 to EC$18. There's also a more formal restaurant which has a splendid water view. Main dishes, including catch of the day, cost around EC$40 and a full meal of the day, with soup and dessert, is EC$50.

*Bequia Beach Club* has a beachside restaurant and bar with inexpensive lunchtime soup and sandwiches and more substantial continental and German fare at dinner.

### GETTING THERE & AWAY
### Air

Bequia's airport is near Paget Farm, at the south-west end of the island. Daily flights connect Bequia with St Vincent and the other Grenadine islands. For details see the Getting Around section at the beginning of this chapter.

### Sea

**Ferry** The scheduled ferry between Bequia and St Vincent is not only cheaper than flying, but may also prove more convenient. The docks are located in the centre of Kingstown and Port Elizabeth, the ferries are generally punctual and the crossing takes only one hour.

Travellers prone to seasickness should be aware that the crossing between the islands gets a bit choppy midway; it's not too bad on a calm day but at other times you might want to avoid eating a large meal before hopping on the boat. Tickets are sold on board; the fare is EC$10 during the day, EC$12 in the evenings and on weekends.

Boats leave Bequia on weekdays at 6.30

and 7.30 am, 2 and 5 pm, on Saturday at 6.30 am and 5 pm and on Sunday at 7 am and 4 pm. Departures from St Vincent are at 9 and 10.30 am, 12.30, 4.30 and 7 pm on week-days, 12.30 and 7 pm on Saturday and 9 am and 5.15 pm on Sunday.

For details on the cargo/passenger ferry MV *Snapper*, which plies between St Vincent and Union Island, see the Getting Around section at the beginning of this chapter.

**Yacht** Port Elizabeth is a port of entry for St Vincent & the Grenadines. Customs and immigration are opposite the ferry dock and open from 9 am to 3 pm. There are a couple of well-stocked chandleries in Port Elizabeth, and water, fuel, bottled gas, ice and nautical charts are readily available.

If you don't have a boat you might be able to find someone willing to take you on for shared expenses or for crew work. The Bequia Marina and the bar at Frangipani Hotel are good spots to touch base with sailors. Mac's Pizzeria has a notice board that often has a listing or two of people looking for passengers.

### GETTING AROUND

The island is small and from Port Elizabeth a lot of places are accessible on foot. It's about a 45-minute walk to three of the island's best beaches: Lower Bay, Friendship Bay or Hope Bay.

### Bus

Local transport is a system of private 'dollar cabs', which are shared taxis that will take you on short trips for EC$1, and longer trips for EC$2. The busiest route is from Port Elizabeth to Paget Farm and during the day dollar cabs are a reliable way to get around.

### Taxi

Taxis are commonly open-air pick-up trucks with bench-type seats in the tray of the truck. Taxis are generally distinguished from dollar cabs by a 'taxi service' sign and charge set fees. From Port Elizabeth it costs EC$15 to Friendship Bay, and EC$25 to the airport. There are usually a couple of taxis at the airport when the flights come in.

THE GRENADINES

### Motorbike & Bicycle

Handy Andy's (☎ 458-3722), opposite the waterfront in Port Elizabeth, rents motorbikes and bicycles.

### Tours

There are a handful of boats offering cruises throughout the Grenadines. In addition to the following, you can usually find a few options posted on the notice board at Mac's Pizzeria and listed in the tourist office.

One of the more interesting boats is the *Friendship Rose* (☎ 458-3244, ☎ 458-3255), the Bequian-built wooden schooner that until recently served as the mailboat between Bequia and St Vincent. On Tuesday and Friday, there's a day trip from Bequia to Mustique and Petit Nevis for US$50. On Thursday the boat goes to the Tobago Cays and Union Island; the cost of US$65 includes a flight back to Bequia. On Wednesday the boat goes to St Vincent, and can be booked with or without a guided land tour.

The 13-metre sailboat *Prospect of Whitby* (☎ 458-3244, VHF 68) offers a day trip to Mustique for US$50 and a trip to the Tobago Cays for US$60. The 18-metre catamaran *Passion* (☎ 458-3884) also runs similar tours.

The S/Y *Pelangi* (☎ 458-3255), a 13-metre cutter with two double guest cabins, is available for private charters. Day trips cost US$50 per person, with a minimum of four people. A three-day, two-night charter costs US$800 for two people, US$1000 for four people, including most meals and drinks.

## Mustique

Mustique, lying 12 km south-east of Bequia, is a privately owned island that has been developed into a haven for the rich and famous. Like the other Grenadines, this eight-km-long island is dry and hilly. It has a population of about 800, most of whom work either directly or indirectly for those who holiday here.

Colin Tennant, a rather eccentric Scotsman, purchased the island in 1958. In the 1960s the island was planted with about 250 acres of sea island cotton but Tennant's real intent was to turn Mustique into a retreat that would appeal to his aristocratic friends. Tennant brought the island's free-roaming sheep and cattle under control and planted coconut palms and citrus trees. In 1960 he presented Princess Margaret with, a ten-acre house lot perched between Gelliceaux Bay and Deep Bay as a wedding gift. Today there are 72 privately owned villas on the island belonging to celebrities, including the princess, Mick Jagger and David Bowie.

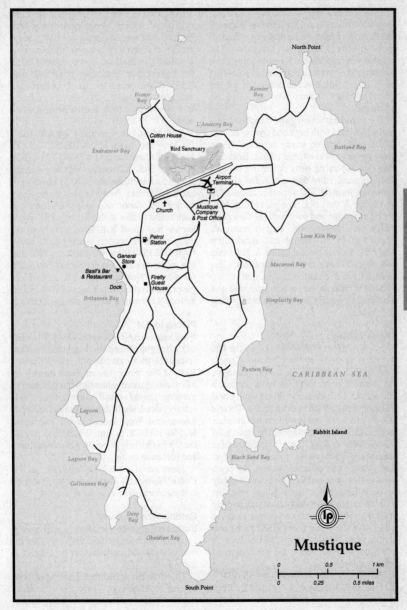

THE GRENADINES

Mustique

THE GRENADINES

Mustique has pretty much developed into the exclusive retreat that Tennant planned, although the island is now under the management of the Mustique Company. The company is responsible for everything from operating the medical clinic and desalination plant to providing accommodation for the Britannia Bay fishers who still live on Mustique.

The island has an irregular coastline that's richly indented with bays and coves, most of which harbour fine sandy beaches. While there are no towns on the island, Britannia Bay is a centre of sorts where Mustique's dock, general store and a handful of boutiques are located. The airport is about a km north-east of the dock. The post office, telephone exchange and the Mustique Company office are opposite the airport terminal. There's good swimming and snorkelling along the west coast, including at Britannia Bay. Snorkellers can enter near Basil's Bar and continue in a northerly direction.

Basil's rents water sports gear and the Mustique Company can arrange horse riding and diving.

### Places to Stay

The *Cotton House* (☎ 456-4777; in the UK ☎ (0453) 83-5801, in the USA and Canada ☎ (800) 223-1108), PO Box 349, Mustique, the island's only hotel, is built around a renovated 18th-century stone and coral warehouse once used to store cotton. There's also an old stone sugar mill on the grounds and a collection of cottages. The hotel's 24 rooms have ceiling fan, verandah and a pleasantly understated plantation decor. Guests have use of tennis courts, the pool, windsurfing gear and Sailfish boats. A sandy beach at Endeavour Bay is a few minutes' walk away. Rates for doubles, which include breakfast, afternoon tea and dinner, begin at US$325 in the autumn and US$550 the rest of the year. Singles cost US$100 less. A rental car can be added for an additional US$65 a day.

The *Firefly Guest House* (☎ 458-4621), PO Box 349, Mustique, is operated by Billy Mitchell, a Mustique resident since the early 1970s. She has four guest rooms in her cliffside house, which overlooks Britannia Bay. Each of the rooms has a private bath, refrigerator and terrace. Singles/doubles cost US$50/65 in the low season, US$65/80 in the high season, including breakfast. Add US$5 if you want air-con. Discounts are available on longer stays. Firefly is just a five-minute walk from Basil's Bar & Restaurant.

The Mustique Company (☎ 458-4621; fax 456-4565; in the UK ☎ (0628) 77-3300, in the USA and Canada ☎ (800) 223-1108), PO Box 349, Mustique, operates a rental pool which includes about 40 of Mustique's exclusive homes. As the houses are privately owned, the decor and amenities vary but each house comes with its own cook/housekeeper and about half have private swimming pools. In winter, weekly rates range from US$3500 for a two-bedroom villa that can accommodate four people to US$13,000 for a lavish five-bedroom villa. In summer the prices drop by an average of 20%. Rates include the use of a jeep or similar vehicle.

### Places to Eat

*Basil's Bar & Restaurant* (☎ 458-4621, VHF 68), a delightful open-air thatch and bamboo restaurant that extends out into Britannia Bay, is *the* place to eat (and drink) on Mustique. A more romantic setting is hard to imagine. Breakfast and lunch fare are moderately priced, while dinner features seafood, lobster and West Indian dishes averaging EC$50 to EC$75. On Wednesday night, Basil's has a lively jump-up with a steel band and barbecue buffet.

There are also poolside luncheons at the *Cotton House* and you can pick up groceries at the general store near Basil's.

### Getting There & Away

Britannia Bay is the port of entry and the only suitable anchorage for visiting yachts; immigration and customs can be cleared at the airport.

There is no scheduled passenger boat service to Mustique. There are scheduled flights from Barbados and Bequia; see

Getting There & Away and Getting Around at the beginning of this chapter. For day tours to Mustique see the Bequia and Barbados sections.

# Canouan

Canouan, midway in the Grenadine chain, is an unspoiled island of dry scrubby hills and deserted beaches. While it extends about 5.5 km, in many places this anchor-shaped island is so narrow that it can be walked across in a few minutes. There are about 700 people and at least as many goats. A large new resort development is in the planning stages for the north side of the island, so Canouan's rural nature may be about to change.

Canouan's main attraction is its beautiful sandy beaches, several of them reef protected and good for swimming and snorkelling. Other than that, you can take long walks, including one to the old stone Anglican church which sits at the site of an abandoned village that was destroyed by a hurricane in 1921.

The main anchorage is in Grand Bay, where the jetty is located, while the airport is about a km to the west. Diving can be arranged with Dive Canouan, which is based at Canouan Beach Hotel.

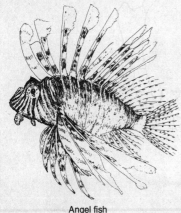

Angel fish

## Places to Stay

The *Anchor Inn Guest House* (☎ 458-8568) at Grand Bay has three straightforward rooms in the two-storey home of George and Yvonne de Roché. Singles/doubles cost US$60/74, breakfast and dinner included. It's only a few minutes' walk to the beach.

The 10-room *Crystal Sands Beach Hotel* (☎ & fax 458-8309), Grand Bay Beach, Canouan, consists of five simple duplex cottages on the beach at Grand Bay. There's a restaurant and bar. Singles/doubles cost US$80/140 all year round.

The *Villa Le Bijou* (☎ 458-8025), Friendship, Canouan, is a basic 10-room guesthouse, a 10-minute walk from the beach and main dock. The guesthouse is situated on a hillside, with a commanding view of the Grenadines from Tobago Cays to Petit St Vincent. Singles/doubles cost US$100/ 140 with breakfast and dinner included.

The 43-room, French-owned *Canouan Beach Hotel* (☎ 458-8888; fax 458-8875), PO Box 530, Canouan, is on a narrow neck of land with sea views in both directions and a nice sandy beach on the South Glossy Bay side. Rates include all meals, drinks, sports and a catamaran ride to a different Grenadine island each day. There are tennis courts, a driving range, windsurfing gear and sailing boats. Rooms are cottage style, with air-con and patio. Standard singles/doubles cost US$136/272 in the summer, US$256/340 in the winter. For reservations call ☎ 1 34 86 41 02 in France, ☎ (0813) 92-1589 in the UK or ☎ (800) 223-9815 in the USA.

## Places to Eat

The *Anchor Inn Guest House* (☎ 458-8568), south-east of the pier at Grand Bay, has West Indian meals at moderate prices.

*Villa Le Bijou* specialises in Creole-style seafood dishes. It's open daily from 8 am to 10 pm, with most main dishes ranging from EC$30 to EC$85. At dinner, reservations are required.

*Crystal Sands Beach Hotel* has dinners for EC$40 to EC$60. Main dishes include chicken, fish, conch or grilled lobster, accompanied by pigeon peas. Starters include callaloo and pumpkin soups. Reservations are advised; credit cards are not accepted.

The *Canouan Beach Hotel* serves breakfast from 7.30 to 9.30 am, lunch from 12.30 to 2 pm and dinner from 7.30 to 9 pm. The French chef serves up continental and West Indian dishes with an emphasis on seafood. There are barbecues a few times a week, a weekly steel band and a nice bar. At dinner, most main dishes are priced from EC$40 to EC$85.

## Getting There & Away

Mustique Airways has a daily flight to Canouan from Barbados. In the past Air Martinique has had a scheduled flight from Martinique to Canouan that stopped en route in St Vincent, though it seems to have been at least temporarily discontinued.

For information on the MV *Snapper*, the mailboat which connects Canouan with the other Grenadine islands, see the Getting Around section at the beginning of this chapter.

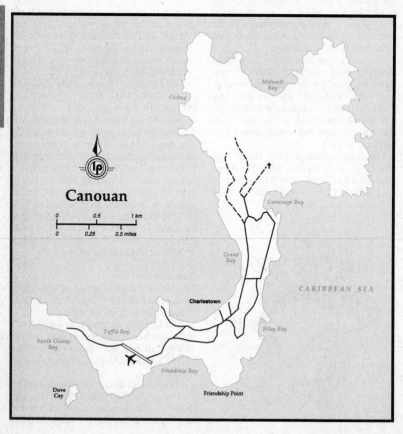

# Mayreau

Mayreau is a small island, 2.5 km in length, with a population of just 200. It has no airport and just one short road, which runs from the dock at Saline Bay, on the central west coast, up to the island's sole village.

Lying just a few km west of the Tobago Cays, Mayreau is most commonly visited on sailing cruises that combine time at the cays with a sail into Salt Whistle Bay, a deep U-shaped bay at the island's northern tip.

Salt Whistle Bay is protected from the rough Atlantic breakers by a long narrow arm, which in places is just a few metres in width. This gorgeous bay has clear waters, beautiful white sands, calm swimming conditions and a protected anchorage for visiting yachts. The small Salt Whistle Bay Club resort, which is tucked back from the beach just beyond the palms, operates a beachside restaurant and bar open to day visitors. Beware of manchineel trees, especially near the southern end of the beach.

There are no roads from Salt Whistle Bay, but a track leads south to the village, a 20-minute walk away. The footpath begins through the wooden gate at the southern end of the beach. The path is a bit eroded as it climbs uphill, but as long as it's dry it's easy to walk and simple to follow (if in doubt, bear to the right). The track passes cacti and lots of singing birds and offers some nice views near the crest. For a particularly good view, check out the hilltop stone church at the northern side of the village.

Saline Bay is where the mailboat, the MV *Snapper*, pulls in a few times a week, as does the occasional small cruise ship. It's about a five-minute uphill walk from the dock to the village centre. There's a sandy beach along Saline Bay and deserted beaches within easy walking distance on the east side of the island.

## Places to Stay

*Dennis' Hideaway* (☎ 458-8594, VHF 68), Saline Bay, has three rooms with private bath

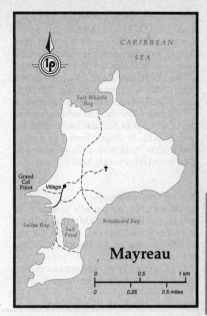

above a grocery store in the village centre. Singles/doubles cost US$35/70 year-round, breakfast included.

The *Salt Whistle Bay Club* (☎ 493-9609, VHF 16/68; in the USA ☎ (800) 263-2780) is a minimalist-style beachside resort with rather simple but spacious stone bungalows with louvred windows. The rooms vary, but all have ceiling fan and patio and most have king-size beds. The resort picks guests up at the airport in Union Island and shuttles them by boat to Mayreau, a 30-minute ride. Singles/doubles begin at US$190/280 in summer, US$280/420 in winter, including breakfast and dinner. There's a boutique that sells foreign newspapers.

## Places to Eat

*Dennis' Hideaway* is open daily from around 7 am for inexpensive breakfast and lunch fare. Sandwiches cost around EC$8. Dinners include soup and salad, with the price depending on the main dish you choose:

EC$40 for conch, EC$45 for fish, EC$50 for shrimp or EC$55 for lobster. It's also a popular spot to linger over a cold beer. Dennis, an amiable former sailor, plays the guitar on Wednesday and Saturday evenings.

The *Salt Whistle Bay Club*'s open-air restaurant offers a full breakfast from 8 to 10.30 am for EC$30. At lunch, served from noon to 2.30 pm, sandwiches and salads are priced from EC$15 to EC$25 and catch of the day costs EC$32. At dinner, from 7 to 9 pm, a three-course meal with a choice of fish or meat main courses costs EC$65.

### Getting There & Away

For information on the MV *Snapper*, the mailboat which connects Mayreau with the other Grenadine islands, see the Getting Around section at the beginning of this chapter.

The Captain Yannis catamaran tours from Union Island can drop passengers off at

Mayreau one day and pick them up the next day at no charge other than the usual cost of the day tour.

# Union Island

Union Island, the southernmost port of entry in St Vincent & the Grenadines, is high, rocky and dry. About five km in length and half that in width, the land is largely covered in thorny scrub and dotted with cacti, the consequence of decades of foraging by free-ranging goats. It has a population of 1900.

While the west side of the island reaches 305 metres at Mt Tabor, the island's most distinguished landmark is The Pinnacle, a 225-metre plug-shaped rock face that rises abruptly in the interior of the island between Clifton and Ashton, the two main villages.

Although the terrain is mildly interesting and Union Island has a couple of reasonably

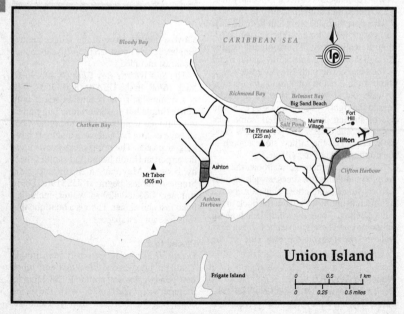

nice beaches, most visitors don't come here to see Union. Instead the island serves as a jumping-off point for cruising the uninhabited Tobago Cays and other nearby islands.

Consequently, if you wander beyond Clifton, you'll discover a decidedly local atmosphere that's virtually untouched by tourism.

## CLIFTON

Clifton is the commercial centre of the island and the site of virtually all visitor-related facilities, including the marina, airport, shops and restaurants. The town is more functional than quaint.

Clifton is at the centre of Union Island's thriving tour industry. Every morning, tour groups are flown in from Barbados, Martinique and other Caribbean islands, taken by bus to the dock in the centre of town and then by catamaran to the Tobago Cays. In the late afternoon they sail back into the bay and are bussed back to their chartered planes. While they see little of Clifton, these transiting passengers make up about half of the island's visitors. Most of the rest are yachters who use Clifton as a base for exploring the region.

## Information

The Union Island Tourist Bureau (☎ 458-8350), just south of the post office, is open from 9 am to noon and 1 to 4 pm daily.

The National Commercial Bank, the island's only bank, is open from 8 am to 1 pm Monday to Thursday, from 8 am to 1 pm and 3 to 5 pm on Friday.

The boutique at the Anchorage Yacht Club sells the *Daily Telegraph, International Herald-Tribune, Le Figaro* and *Libération*.

There are a number of gift shops around town, including Chic Unique, which has a select collection of books, some quality T-shirts and other items that could make nice souvenirs.

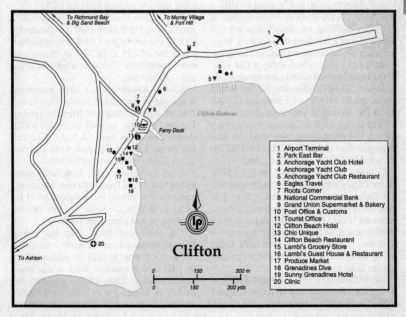

**To Richmond Bay & Big Sand Beach**
**To Murray Village & Fort Hill**

*Clifton Harbour*

Ferry Dock

**To Ashton**

**Clifton**

0    150    300 m
0    150    300 yds

1  Airport Terminal
2  Park East Bar
3  Anchorage Yacht Club Hotel
4  Anchorage Yacht Club
5  Anchorage Yacht Club Restaurant
6  Eagles Travel
7  Roots Corner
8  National Commercial Bank
9  Grand Union Supermarket & Bakery
10  Post Office & Customs
11  Tourist Office
12  Clifton Beach Hotel
13  Chic Unique
14  Clifton Beach Restaurant
15  Lambi's Grocery Store
16  Lambi's Guest House & Restaurant
17  Produce Market
18  Grenadines Dive
19  Sunny Grenadines Hotel
20  Clinic

THE GRENADINES

## Walks

There are a couple of short walks from Clifton that offer coastal views. The easiest is up to the hilltop clinic on the west side of Clifton, where there's a fair (though partially obstructed) view of the harbour.

On the east side of town, a 10-minute walk inland from the Park East bar leads to the top of a hill in Murray Village. At the crest you can get a glimpse of both sides of Union Island and a reasonable view of Clifton, Petit St Vincent and Palm Island. On the right, immediately before the last house, a half-hour walking track leads east up to Fort Hill, where there are some minor ruins and better views.

## Places to Stay

*Clifton Beach Hotel* (☎ 458-8235) is a friendly hostelry and while its rooms aren't fancy, it's the best value in town. There are 25 units in all, spread across four sites: two buildings opposite each other in the centre of Clifton, a few rooms above the nearby Grand Union Supermarket and a seaside villa a five-minute walk north of town. Rooms in the main building are straightforward and adequate and a few have ocean views, as do the units above the supermarket. The apartments in the villa, which enjoy a fine view of the neighbouring islands, are comfortable and quiet. Single/double rates for fan-cooled rooms are US$16/29 in the summer, US$20/33 in the winter. If you want air-con, add US$15 to the rate. The apartment prices vary but are not much more. The hotel can also arrange cottage rentals for US$115 to US$200 a week, US$250 to US$550 a month.

*Lambi's Guest House* (☎ 458-8549), above Lambi's grocery store and restaurant, has about a dozen basic island-style rooms, essentially just a place to sleep and shower. Rates are US$23 for a room with fan, private shower and double bed; US$16 for a room with two twin beds and shared bath. Rates are by room and up to three people can stay for the same price.

*Sunny Grenadines Hotel* (☎ 458-8327), in the centre of Clifton, has 18 rather standard rooms, each with two twin beds, but it's not the friendliest of places. Singles/doubles cost US$55/85.

The *Anchorage Yacht Club* (☎ 458-8221; fax 458-8365), on the waterfront and close to the airport, is Union Island's more upmarket option. The hotel caters to French tourists and visiting sailors. The rooms are comfortable with ocean-facing balcony, air-con and phone; rates are US$90/110 in the summer/winter. There are also rooms called 'cabanas' that are a bit bigger and nicer, and have similar amenities, but are rather steeply priced at US$170/220. All rates include continental breakfast.

## Places to Eat

There's a *bakery* in the back of the Grand Union Supermarket which opens at 8 am every morning except Sunday and is a nice place for a cheap breakfast. Get there early for warm coconut buns, slabs of banana bread and fresh coffee. The bakery also makes rotis to order for EC$4 and has vegetable pies and sausage rolls for EC$2.

The *Clifton Beach Restaurant* makes a generous triple-decker club sandwich for EC$11 and serves good fresh fish and conch meals for EC$25 to EC$30 in an open-air setting behind the Clifton Beach Hotel, at the edge of the water.

*Lambi's Restaurant* is a large waterfront restaurant in the village centre. The restaurant is named after its friendly owner, Lambert Baptiste, as well as for the conch (lambi) shells that deck the walls. At lunch and dinner there are chicken, fresh fish and conch dishes priced around EC$30.

*Roots Corner* is a small Rastafarian stand selling simple Ital food, with rice-based vegetarian dishes served in a calabash bowl for EC$7 to EC$10. Look for the tree painted red, yellow and green near the bank.

The *Anchorage Yacht Club* has a nice open-air restaurant and bar on the waterfront. Starters cost from EC$12 for callaloo soup to EC$25 for smoked fish, while main courses range from grilled chicken for EC$30 to lobster for EC$70. On Monday and Friday from 7.30 pm there's a buffet spread and a steel band for EC$100. During the afternoon the bar serves baguette sandwiches from EC$10, pastries and croissants at reasonable prices and pizza to order.

Every third building in Clifton is a grocery store, painted in bright colours and posted with names like Kash & Karry, Pay & Take and Determination Bar & Grocery. Grand Union Supermarket and Lambi's are two of the biggest markets. Virtually all produce is imported from other islands, so prices are high.

## ASHTON

Ashton is a quiet place that's backed by high hills and untouched by tourism. It can be worth a visit just to see what Union Island's more traditional West Indian half is like. There are a few older homes with weathered gingerbread trim and many brightly painted houses and shops, but no sights per se. In general people are friendlier and less hurried than in Clifton.

If you want to do some exploring, there are a few hiking tracks leading into the hills above Ashton, with one of the smoother tracks beginning at the upper road on the north-west side of the village.

### Places to Eat

There's a small family-run eatery in the home of Claire Adams, next to the Jehovah's Witness hall and post office. From Monday to Saturday she prepares a lunch of baked chicken with rice, salad and provisions and an evening barbecue with breadfruit salad. The cost of a full meal is EC$12.

There are also a few grocery stores around the village.

## RICHMOND & BELMONT BAYS

There are two remote beaches on the undeveloped northern side of the island: Belmont Bay and Richmond Bay. The two bays are separated by a point and both have turquoise waters and powdery white sands.

Big Sand, the beach at Belmont Bay, has nice views of Mayreau and the Tobago Cays, a few cows lazing in the bush, and terns and pelicans feeding in the inshore waters. Until recent government regulations stopped the excavation, Big Sand was the source of most of the sand used in construction on the island.

Richmond, while not as scenic as Big Sand, is more protected and a better beach for swimming.

From Clifton, the walk to Richmond Beach takes about 25 minutes. Start at the dirt road leading north from the bank; you'll pass the power plant after five minutes. About halfway the road skirts around a large salt pond that is rich in birdlife. Continue along the western side of the pond and in about 10 minutes you'll spot Richmond Beach on the left. To get to Big Sand Beach, take the road that comes in at the right and continue for about five minutes. From Richmond Beach it's possible to continue walking along the dirt coastal road southwesterly to Ashton, a walk of about 35 minutes.

## GETTING THERE & AWAY
### Air

LIAT, Airlines of Carriacou and Mustique Airways have regularly scheduled flights to Union Island. Details are in the Getting There & Away and Getting Around sections at the beginning of this chapter.

### Sea

Details on the MV *Snapper*, which connects Union Island with St Vincent's other main islands, are in the Getting Around section at the beginning of this chapter.

Two very small wooden sailing boats, *Wisdom* and *Jasper*, run between Ashton and Hillsborough (Carriacou) on Monday and Thursday. The boats leave from the pier near Waterfront Trading in Ashton around 7.30 am, unload their cargo in Carriacou and then return around noon. Passengers can go along for EC$10 each way, but because you're crossing into another country you should check with immigration ahead of time.

**Yacht** The port of entry is in Clifton. Customs is at the head of the main pier and immigration is at the airport. Anchorage Yacht Club (VHF 16/68), midway between

THE GRENADINES

the airport and Clifton centre, has stern-to berths for 24 boats, ice, water, fuel, showers, laundry facilities, a dry dock and a little electric minibus that can take boaters into town to buy provisions.

Other popular anchorages include Chatham Bay on Union Island's west coast and the west sides of Frigate Island and Palm Island.

### GETTING AROUND

The island is small enough to explore on foot. It's less than 10 minutes' walk from the airport to the centre of Clifton, and 30 minutes from Clifton to Ashton.

There are a few pick-up trucks with a double row of benches that serve as buses making runs between Clifton and Ashton for EC$2. Hotels will often pick you up at the airport if you have a reservation; otherwise it costs EC$10 for a taxi from the airport to Clifton centre.

### Tours

Captain Yannis (☎ 435-8451) operates three 18-metre sailboats, the catamarans *Cyclone* and *Typhoon* and the trimaran *Searose*, which account for most of the daytime

sailing business from Union Island. The crews are friendly, there's a good buffet lunch that usually includes shrimp, curried chicken, salad, cheese and wine and throughout the day there's an open bar of rum punch and beer. The itinerary usually includes a stop on Palm Island, a few hours in the Tobago Cays for lunch and snorkelling and an hour or so on Mayreau, before returning to Union Island in the late afternoon. Tours can be booked through Clifton Beach Hotel and travel agents in town. The boats generally leave Clifton around 8.30 am but the exact time depends on when the charter flights come in, as most passengers fly into Union Island to pick up the tour. The price is a bargain at EC$100.

# Other Islands

### TOBAGO CAYS

Many consider the Tobago Cays to be the crown jewels of the Grenadines. They comprise a number of small, deserted islands surrounded by coral reefs and splendidly clear turquoise waters. The islands, which are rocky and cactus studded, have tiny coves and beaches of powdery white sand.

The Tobago Cays have been set aside as a national park and measures have been taken to protect the area, including the installation of moorings and prohibitions on the taking of marine life. Perhaps the biggest danger to the cays is their popularity, as the waters can get fairly crowded with visiting yachts.

The Tobago Cays have some very good snorkelling spots although the catamaran day tours don't always take in the best sites, opting to balance the wishes of snorkellers with those who just want to sit on the beach. There are also good breezes in the cays, making for some fine windsurfing conditions.

See the Union Island section for information on day trips to the Tobago Cays.

### PALM ISLAND

Palm Island, a 10-minute boat ride south-east

of Union Island, is a small whale-shaped island that's the domain of a private resort. The beach has long been a popular anchorage with yachters and is a stopover on many day tours between Union Island and the Tobago Cays.

Spread along the sandy fringe of this 52-hectare island are two dozen cottages operated by Texan John Caldwell who took out a 99-year lease from the government back in the mid-1960s. Swamps were filled, palm trees were added to the shady casuarina trees that grow along the beach, and the island name was changed from Prune Island to the more alluring Palm Island.

At the western side of the island, where boats dock, is the picture-perfect Casuarina Beach, with sands composed of small bits of white shells and pink coral.

### Places to Stay & Eat

The *Palm Island Beach Club* (☎ & fax 458-8804; in the USA ☎ (800) 776-7256) has 24 rooms in bungalows of wood and stone, each furnished with either two twins or a king-size bed, a private bathroom and a refrigerator. Rooms are airy with screened, louvred windows, ceiling fan and sliding glass doors which open to a patio. Singles/doubles cost US$200/320 from 15 December to 31 March, US$135/210 the rest of the year. Rates include all meals, tennis, windsurfing and Sunfish boats. The Scuba Shack dive shop on the island can arrange dives for an additional charge. The resort also books a handful of villas and apartments on the island.

For day trippers there's a beachside restaurant, open daily from 8.30 am, with moderately priced sandwiches and burgers.

## PETIT ST VINCENT

Often abbreviated to PSV, Petit St Vincent is the southernmost and smallest of the islands belonging to St Vincent & the Grenadines. This 45-hectare island is fringed with white-sand beaches, coral reefs and clear waters.

The island has been developed into a single-resort 'hideaway' destination. As with Palm Island, guests must first get to Union Island. At the Union airport they're met by resort staff and taken over to PSV by motorboat, a 30-minute crossing.

While a few yachters anchor off PSV, day sails generally bypass the island and it sees less traffic than its neighbours to the north. Visiting yachts can anchor off the south-western side of the island; there's a dinghy dock just below the restaurant.

### Places to Stay

*Petit St Vincent Resort* (☎ 458-8801; fax 458-8428; in the USA ☎ (800) 654-9326) has 22 suites in stone bungalows which are spread around the island to offer maximum privacy. The bungalows have a bedroom with two queen-size beds, paddle fans, a living room with tropical decor and pleasant sundecks. There are no TVs, air-con or other unharmonious 'conveniences'. In place of a phone, each cottage has a bamboo flagpole used to 'call' for room service. A creation of US expatriate Haze Richardson, the resort is considered the ultimate retreat among the Grenadine getaway islands and it has tariffs to match. Singles/doubles cost US$340/430 in summer, US$525/680 in the winter, including meals and use of a tennis court, sailboards, Hobie Cats and Sunfish boats. Credit cards are not accepted. The resort is closed in September and October.

# Trinidad & Tobago

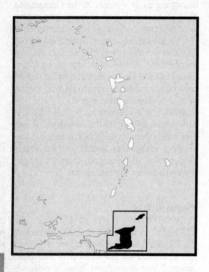

Port of Spain turns into one huge street party that attracts thousands of revellers from around the world.

The 'little sister' island of Tobago, with just 4% of the country's population and 6% of its land area, stands in sharp contrast to Trinidad. Tobago is pleasantly relaxed with good beaches, reef-protected waters and casual oceanside hotels. It too has rainforests with good birdwatching opportunities, and in addition has excellent diving and snorkelling.

There are claims that Daniel Defoe had Tobago in mind when he wrote *Robinson Crusoe*. Some visitors who trip upon Tobago these days think of it as the last undiscovered gem in the Caribbean and certainly there's much to argue in its favour.

Trinidad & Tobago is often abbreviated to T&T and Port of Spain is written POS for short – expect to see the latter on highway signs. 'Trini' is the common nickname for a native of Trinidad.

## ORIENTATION

Trinidad is a large island but few visitors tour it all. Most of Trinidad's attractions – Port of Spain, the Northern Range and the Caroni Bird Sanctuary – are in the north-west section of the island, all within an hour's drive of the airport.

Tobago's airport is in the midst of the central resort area at the south-west tip of the island and the rest of Tobago can be toured in a pleasant one-day drive.

# Facts about the Islands

## HISTORY

Known to Amerindians as Lere, 'Land of the Hummingbirds', Trinidad was sighted in 1498 by Columbus, who christened it La Isla de la Trinidad, for the Holy Trinity. The Spanish who followed in Columbus' wake enslaved many of Trinidad's Amerindian

Trinidad and Tobago are the southernmost islands in the Caribbean, a mere 11 km off the coast of Venezuela. Surprisingly there's very little South American influence – instead the country draws most strongly from its British, African and East Indian heritage.

Trinidad, the dominant partner in the twin-island nation, is the Eastern Caribbean's largest and most heavily populated island. It has a mix of urban sprawl, rainforested mountains and small farming communities.

Despite its size, Trinidad is one of the least touristed islands in the Caribbean – it doesn't have the sort of beaches that attract holiday-makers and the capital city, Port of Spain, certainly has more bustle than charm. The island does, however, offer some of the Caribbean's finest birdwatching, from flocks of scarlet ibis roosting in mangrove swamps to jungle interiors teeming with colourful forest birds. Trinidad also has the Caribbean's most festive Carnival, when

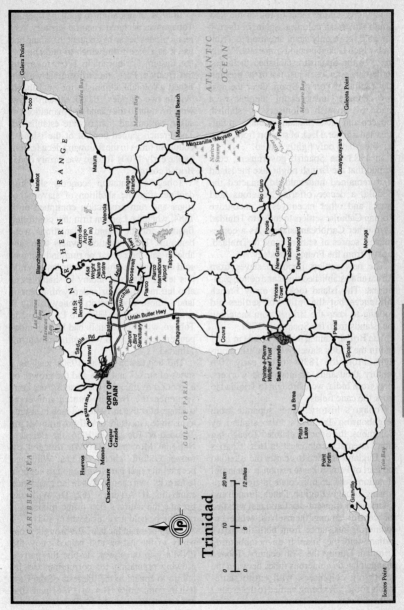

inhabitants, taking them to toil in the new South American colonies. Spain, in its rush for gold, gave only scant attention to Trinidad, which lacked precious minerals. Finally in 1592 the Spanish established their first settlement, San Josef, just east of the present-day capital of Port of Spain. Over the next two centuries unsuccessful attempts were made by Spanish colonisers to establish tobacco and cacao plantations but crop failures and a general lack of support from Spain left the island only lightly settled.

In 1783 the Spanish government, concerned that the British might take the island if it remained undeveloped, enacted the Cedula, a decree offering generous land grants and other incentives to encourage Roman Catholic settlers to move to Trinidad from other Caribbean islands. As a consequence, scores of settlers came to Trinidad, mostly from the French islands.

The new settlers imported slaves from Africa and established sugar and cotton plantations. The island took on many French influences but the influx of settlers did nothing to keep the British from snatching the islands from the Spanish in 1797.

The British banned the slave trade in 1807 and in the 1830s slavery was abolished outright. From the 1830s to the early 20th century thousands of indentured workers, most from India, were brought to Trinidad to work the cane fields.

Tobago's history stands separate from neighbouring Trinidad's. Also sighted by Columbus, the Spanish claimed Tobago but didn't attempt to colonise it. In 1628, Charles I of England decided to charter the island to the Earl of Pembroke. In response, a handful of nations took an immediate interest in colonising Tobago. English, Dutch, French and Courlanders (present-day Latvians) wrestled for control among themselves, while encountering resistance from both the native Indians and the Spanish on neighbouring Trinidad. During the 17th century, Tobago changed hands numerous times between the competing colonisers, with entire settlements sometimes being burned to the ground in the process.

In 1704, in an attempt to quell the fighting, Tobago was declared a neutral territory. As a result pirates began to frequent the island and use it as a base from which to raid ships in the Eastern Caribbean. In 1763, following the Treaty of Paris, the British finally established a colonial administration on Tobago. Within two decades 10,000 African slaves were brought to the island and plantations of sugar, cotton and indigo were established. The French gained control of the island a couple of times in the following decades, but by the early 1800s Tobago was firmly under British control.

Tobago's plantation economy slid into decline after the abolition of slavery but sugar and rum production continued until 1884, when the London firm that controlled finances for the island's plantations went bankrupt. The plantation owners were unable to sell their sugar or rum and quickly sold or abandoned most of their land. While this left Tobago's economy in shambles, it also left most of the islanders with a plot of land – those who had no money to buy it simply squatted. In 1889 the British made Tobago, which previously had its own independent legislature, a ward of neighbouring Trinidad.

The depression of the 1930s lead to a series of strikes and riots and the growth of a labour movement on the islands. As a consequence the British granted universal suffrage, effective in 1946, and took measures to institute a measure of self-government for Trinidad & Tobago. In 1956, the People's National Movement (PNM), founded by former Oxford scholar Dr Eric Williams, became the first party with enough support to form its own cabinet. When independence came on 31 August 1962, Dr Williams became the nation's first prime minister, a position he held until his death in 1981.

An oil boom in the late '70s brought prosperity to the nation and helped buoy the PNM's grip on power, despite the party's growing reputation for corruption and its failure to appeal to the interests of the East Indian community. But in 1986, with the economy suffering, the PNM was defeated

Top Left: Union Island to Carriacou boats (NF)
Top Right: Cricket on the beach, Villa Beach, St Vincent (TW)
Middle Right: Hairoun beer poster, Union Island (NF)
Bottom Left: Model boat builders, Port Elizabeth, Bequia (NF)
Bottom Right: Botanic Gardens, Kingstown, St Vincent (TW)

Top Left: Young girl at Castera Bay, Tobago (GB)
Top Right: Snorkellers at Tobago Cay (NF)
Bottom Left: Pitch Lake, Trinidad (TW)
Bottom Right: Carnival costume design, Trinidad (NF)

resoundingly by a coalition party, the National Alliance for Reconstruction (NAR). In 1989, following a period of division in the NAR, three East Indian cabinet ministers were dismissed, leading to accusations of racism in the NAR.

On 27 July 1990, members of the Jamaat al Muslimeen, a minority Muslim group led by Yasin Abu Bakr, attempted a coup. They stormed parliament and took 45 hostages, including prime minister A N R Robinson, and seized the TV station and police headquarters. Bakr demanded that Robinson resign, new elections be held within 90 days and the coup members be given amnesty.

The prime minister, who was shot in the leg after refusing to resign, was released on 31 July to receive medical attention. On 1 August the rebels surrendered after the president of the Senate, in his capacity as acting head of state, offered an amnesty to end the crisis. All in all, 30 people died and another 500 were injured in the coup attempt and concurrent street riots that broke out in the capital.

The government immediately ruled the amnesty invalid on the grounds that it was offered under duress and announced its intention to try the 114 defendants involved in the coup. A long series of appeals, including those to the Privy Council in London and the Trinidad & Tobago High Court, ruled in favour of the amnesty and against the government.

## GEOGRAPHY

Trinidad's land area is 4828 sq km and Tobago's is 300 sq km. Geographically, boot-shaped Trinidad was once part of the South American mainland. Over time a channel developed, separating Trinidad from Venezuela. The South American connection is readily visible in Trinidad's lofty Northern Range, a continuation of the Andes, and in its abundant oil and gas reserves, which are concentrated on the south-western side of the island facing oil-rich Venezuela.

The Northern Range spreads east to west, forming a scenic backdrop to Port of Spain. In the centre of the range, above Arima, lies the 941-metre Cerro del Aripo, the country's highest peak. Much of the rest of the island is given to plains, undulating hills and mangrove swamps. Trinidad's numerous rivers include the Ortoire River, which runs 50 km on its way to the south-east coast, and the 40-km Caroni River, which empties into the Caroni Swamp.

The island of Tobago, 20 km north-east of Trinidad, has a central mountain range which reaches 620 metres at its highest point. Deep fertile valleys run from the ridge down towards the coast, which is indented with bays and sandy beaches.

TRINIDAD

### Leatherback Turtles

Leatherback turtles nest on some of Trinidad's north-east beaches and on Tobago's leeward beaches. Leatherbacks are the largest species of sea turtles, some weighing more than 700 kg and reaching up to two metres in length.

The nesting season runs roughly from March to July. Between nightfall and dawn, the female leatherback crawls up on the beach, uses her flippers to dig a hole, deposits 80 to 125 rubbery white eggs, covers the hole with sand and trudges back to the sea. After two months, the hatchlings emerge from the sand, make a mad dash for the ocean and swim away. Only a few will survive to maturity; however, the females that make it will eventually return to the same beach to lay their eggs.

During the nesting season, the Grafton Beach Resort and Turtle Beach Hotel in Tobago hold nightly turtle watches on their beaches. The Pointe-à-Pierre Wildfowl Trust leads turtle watches to beaches on Trinidad.

As turtles are easily disturbed when nesting and may return to the sea prematurely if bothered, turtle watchers should remain at a distance of at least 15 metres until the turtle begins laying her eggs, be completely silent and avoid shining lights. The turtle, eggs and nest area should not be touched. ■

## CLIMATE

Because of Trinidad's southerly location, temperatures are equable year round. The average daily high temperature in Port of Spain is 31˚C (88˚F) in both January and July, while the low averages 22˚C (72˚F) in July and is only one degree cooler in January.

February to May are the driest months, with a mean relative humidity of 74%. The rest of the year the humidity ranges from 78% to 83%. June to August, the wettest months, average over 250 cm of rain and 23 rainy days each month. In contrast March sees only 34 cm of rain, with measurable precipitation on an average of nine days.

The islands are outside the central hurricane belt and generally don't experience the severe storms that hit the more northerly Caribbean islands.

## FLORA & FAUNA

Because of its proximity to the South American continent, Trinidad & Tobago has the widest variety of plant and animal life in the Eastern Caribbean. There are more than 400 species of birds, 600 species of butterflies, 50 kinds of reptiles and 100 types of mammals, including red howler monkeys, anteaters, agouti and armadillos.

Tobago has fewer species than Trinidad but parrots and other colourful tropical birds are nonetheless abundant in the mountainous interior. You can commonly spot pelicans, osprey and frigatebirds along Tobago's coast.

Plant life is equally diverse, with more

Armadillo

than 700 orchid species and 1600 other types of flowering plants. Both islands have luxuriant rainforests and Trinidad also has elfin forests, savannahs and both freshwater and brackish mangrove swamps.

## GOVERNMENT

Trinidad & Tobago is an independent republic within the Commonwealth. The nation is headed by a president, although political power is concentrated in the office of the prime minister. The legislature is comprised of a House of Representatives, whose 36 members are elected every five years by popular vote, and a Senate, whose 31 members are appointed by the president upon the advice of the prime minister and minority party leader.

Political parties are largely divided along ethnic lines, with the PNM being the predominant party of Afro-Trinidadians and the minority UNC party representing the interests of the East Indian community. The current president is Noor Mohammed Hassanali; the prime minister is Patrick Manning, head of the PNM.

Local government is divided into three municipalities, eight counties and the island of Tobago. Tobago has its own legislative assembly and since 1987 has exercised an extended measure of internal self-government in an effort to protect itself from becoming co-opted by more dominant political forces on Trinidad.

## ECONOMY

Trinidad has sizeable oil and gas reserves. Petroleum exports are the mainstay of the economy, accounting for nearly 50% of government revenue. Reliance upon world oil prices has led to uneven economic growth, however, and the government is attempting to diversify the economy.

Trinidad has deposits of asphalt, coal, iron ore and limestone. Industry includes the production of processed foods, fertilisers, cement, steel and electronics. The main agricultural products are sugar, rice, cocoa, citrus and coffee.

The country is far less reliant on tourism than other Caribbean nations, although concerted efforts are being made to develop Tobago into a resort destination. Tourism, fishing and government-related work are the main sources of employment on Tobago. Unemployment is estimated at 23%.

## POPULATION & PEOPLE

The population is 1,253,000, with just 50,300 people on Tobago and the rest on Trinidad. Trinidad has one of the most ethnically diverse populations in the Caribbean, a legacy of its colonial history. The majority are of African (43%) and East Indian (36%) ancestry. Most other islanders are of mixed ancestry, but there are also notable minorities of European, Chinese, Syrian and Lebanese people. There's also a community of a few hundred native Caribs living in the Arima area.

## ARTS & CULTURE

Carnival reaches its heights in Trinidad, which has the most elaborate costumes and festivities in all the Caribbean. Integral to Carnival is the music of the steel drum (pan), which was invented in Trinidad half a century ago using the hammered-out ends of discarded oil drums. Panyards, where steel drum bands practise in the evenings, are abundant around the capital and particularly active in the weeks preceding Carnival.

Calypso, a medium for political and social satire, has roots on Trinidad, stemming back to the days when slaves would sing in patois mocking their colonial masters. The Mighty Sparrow, long-time king of calypso, is a Trinidadian native, as are many of the Caribbean's up-and-coming calypso stars.

Trinidad has a number of internationally known writers, including V S Naipaul, Samuel Selvon and C L R James. St Lucian native Derek Walcott, the 1992 Nobel Prize winner in Literature, lived in Trinidad for much of his adult life and is an active advocate for local theatre projects.

Cricket is the most popular sport.

### Dress Conventions

Dress is casual on both Tobago and Trinidad but skimpy clothing should be restricted to the beach.

### RELIGION

Roughly a third of all islanders are Roman Catholic. Another 25% are Hindu, 15% Anglican, 13% various other Protestant denominations and 6% Muslim.

### LANGUAGE

The official language is English. Also spoken in ethnic enclaves are Hindi, creole, Spanish and Chinese.

# Facts for the Visitor

### VISAS & EMBASSIES

All visitors must have a valid passport. Visas are not needed by citizens of the USA, Canada, UK or most European countries for stays of under three months.

Visas are required by citizens of Australia, New Zealand, India, Sri Lanka, Papua New Guinea, Nigeria, Tanzania and Uganda, but not of other Commonwealth countries. In most countries, visas are obtained through the British Embassy.

### Foreign Embassies on Trinidad & Tobago

The following countries have diplomatic representation on Trinidad & Tobago:

Canada
    Huggins Building, 72-74 South Quay, Port of Spain (☎ 623-7254)
France
    Tatil Building, 11 Maraval Rd, Port of Spain (☎ 622-7446)
UK
    British High Commission, Furness House, 90 Independence Square, Port of Spain (☎ 625-2861)
USA
    15 Queen's Park West, Port of Spain (☎ 622-6371)
Venezuela
    6 Mary St, St Clair, Port of Spain (☎ 622-2468)

There are also embassies or consulates for Argentina, Barbados, Brazil, Colombia, Germany, India, Jamaica, Japan, Korea, the Netherlands, Nigeria and Peru. The yellow pages of the phone book have addresses and phone numbers.

### CUSTOMS

Visitors can bring in one quart of liquor, 200 cigarettes and gifts up to TT$50 in value without paying duty.

### MONEY

The Trinidad & Tobago dollar (TT$) is the official currency. Visa and MasterCard can be used at most moderately priced restaurants, hotels and guesthouses.

A few restaurants add a 10% service charge; for those that don't, a 10% tip is standard.

### Currency

One Trinidad & Tobago dollar equals 100 cents. Coins are in 1, 5, 25 and 50 cent denominations. Notes, which are colourfully adorned with birds, pan drums, oil rigs and the twin-tower Financial Complex, come in 1 (red), 5 (green), 10 (grey), 20 (purple) and 100 (blue) dollar denominations.

### Exchange Rates

In 1993 the Trinidad & Tobago dollar, which had been long fixed at an exchange rate of TT$4.25=US$1, was floated on the world market. The exchange rate now fluctuates; the current rate can be found on page 3 of the *Daily Express*, the country's largest newspaper. As we went to press, the exchange rate was TT$5.60=US$1.

### TOURIST OFFICES

There are tourist offices at the airports on Trinidad and Tobago, on Frederick St in Port of Spain and in central Scarborough. The airport offices tend to be the best stocked and most helpful. Be sure to pick up *Discover Trinidad & Tobago*, a useful 64-page magazine with general tourist information and ads.

When requesting information by mail,

write to: Trinidad & Tobago Tourism Development Authority (☎ 623-1932; fax 623-3848), 134 Frederick St, Port of Spain, Trinidad, West Indies.

There's a general tourist information line (☎ 623-INFO in Trinidad, 639-INFO in Tobago) open from 6 am to 10 pm.

### Overseas Reps

Overseas offices of the Trinidad & Tobago Tourism Development Authority are:

UK
    8A Hammersmith Broadway, London W6 7AL, England (☎ (081) 741-4466; fax (081) 741-1013)
USA
    25 West 43rd St, Suite 1508, New York, NY 10036 (☎ (212) 719-0540, ☎ (800) 232-0082; fax (212) 719-0988)

### BUSINESS HOURS

Government and business hours are generally from 8 am to 4 pm Monday to Friday, while most shops are open from 8 am to 5 pm weekdays, from 8 am to noon on Saturday.

Most banks are open from 9 am to 2 pm Monday to Thursday and from 9 am to noon and 3 to 5 pm on Friday.

### HOLIDAYS

Trinidad & Tobago has the following public holidays:

| | | |
|---|---|---|
| *New Year's Day* | – | 1 January |
| *Good Friday* | – | late March/early April |
| *Easter Monday* | – | late March/early April |
| *Whit Monday* | – | eighth Monday after Easter |
| *Corpus Christi* | – | ninth Thursday after Easter |
| *Labour Day* | – | 19 June |
| *Emancipation Day* | – | 1 August |
| *Independence Day* | – | 31 August |
| *Republic Day* | – | 24 September |
| *Christmas Day* | – | 25 December |
| *Boxing Day* | – | 26 December |

Carnival Monday and Carnival Tuesday are holidays in practice, with banks and most businesses closed.

### CULTURAL EVENTS

In addition to Carnival, Trinidad's main annual event, there are a number of smaller festivals. The Pan Jazz Festival, held in November, brings together pan drummers and jazz musicians for three days of concerts.

Dates for East Indian festivals vary with the lunar calendar. The biggest Hindu festival is Divali (usually in November), followed by Phagwa (usually March) and Ramleela (September or October). Muslim

---

**Carnival**

The king of all Caribbean Carnivals is unmistakably Trinidad's. Many Trinidadians prepare for Carnival with a near-consuming devotion. From New Year's Day activities swing into full gear. The *mas camps* work late into the evenings creating costumes, the panyards are full of steel band performers tuning up their rhythms and calypso music blasts through the night at pre-Carnival jams. A week before Carnival, preliminary competitions for the King and Queen contenders get underway.

Carnival festivities begin on Monday morning, two days before Ash Wednesday, with the pre-dawn J'Ouvert procession into the heart of the city. As the day proceeds, masquerade 'bands' hit the streets with members of each troupe wearing identical costumes. Tens of thousands of revellers parade and dance throughout the night and the event takes on the character of a massive street party. On Tuesday, the activities culminate with competitions for the Band of the Year and by midnight Carnival is officially over.

Most of the larger Carnival events take place at the Queen's Park Savannah in the centre of Port of Spain, including the major steel band and calypso competitions.

Information on upcoming Carnivals is available from the National Carnival Commission (☎ 623-8867), 92 Frederick St, Port of Spain. Once you're in Trinidad, dial ☎ 651-4MAS for updated events information. ■

festivals are Eid ul Fitr (usually March) and Hosay (usually July).

Tobago now has a Heritage Festival – two weeks of traditional-style festivities that begin in late July. For something quintessentially local, there's the big goat race in Tobago's Buccoo village on the Tuesday after Easter.

## POST
Postcards cost TT$1 to other Caribbean countries, TT$2 to North America, Europe, the UK and Australia. Letters up to 20 grams cost TT$1 to other Caribbean countries, TT$2.25 to the UK or USA, TT$2.50 to Europe and TT$2.75 to Canada or Australia.

When addressing mail from overseas, follow the street or box number with the town and 'Trinidad & Tobago, West Indies'.

## TELECOMMUNICATIONS
The area code is 809, which is added in front of the seven-digit local number when calling from overseas.

There are both coin and card public phones. Phonecards are sold in TT$15, TT$30 and TT$60 denominations and can be purchased at airports, shopping malls and other public places.

More information is under Telecommunications in the introductory Facts for the Visitor chapter.

## ELECTRICITY
Trinidad & Tobago has electric current of both 110 and 220 volt AC, 60 cycles. Check the voltage before plugging anything in.

## WEIGHTS & MEASURES
Trinidad & Tobago has recently converted to the metric system. Highway signs and car odometers are in km, but the small highway markers at the side of some roads still measure miles and many people give directions in miles.

## BOOKS
You can get a sense of the country's multiethnic culture by reading some of novelist V S Naipaul's books. Naipaul's *A House for Mr Biswas* creates a vivid portrait of life as an East Indian in Trinidad.

Former prime minister Eric Williams is author of *From Columbus to Castro*, one of the most authoritative histories of the Caribbean.

For bird watchers, in addition to the well-regarded *Birds of the West Indies* by James Bond, there's also Richard Ffrench's comprehensive *A Guide to the Birds of Trinidad and Tobago* and William L Murphy's 125-page *A Birder's Guide to Trinidad and Tobago*.

*The Trinidad and Tobago Field Naturalists Club Trail Guide* describes hiking trails on the islands, complete with sketch maps.

## MAPS
The best road maps of Tobago, Trinidad and Port of Spain are published by the government's Lands & Surveys Division. They are sold at the airport tourist offices for a few dollars cheaper than at island bookstores.

## MEDIA
The *Trinidad Guardian* and the *Daily Express* are the main daily newspapers, both published in the morning. There are also two smaller evening papers, the *Evening News* and *The Sun*.

The government-owned National Broadcasting Service (NBS) radio operates on 610 AM and 100 FM and there are half a dozen independent radio stations.

There's a state-sponsored TV network (channels 2 and 13) which carries a variety of programming, including CNN; AVM (channel 4), a private local network which carries US-based ABC newscasts; and CCN (channels 6 and 18), which carries CBS newscasts. All have a pretty heavy dose of US programming.

## HEALTH
On Trinidad, the general hospital (☎ 623-2951) is at 169 Charlotte St in Port of Spain and there are smaller hospitals in San Fernando and Mt Hope. On Tobago, there's a 98-bed general hospital (☎ 639-2551) at Fort King George in Scarborough.

Bhaggan's Pharmacy (☎ 627-5541) on Independence Square in Port of Spain is open until 11 pm on weekdays, 9 pm on weekends.

## DANGERS & ANNOYANCES

Theft can be a problem on both Trinidad and Tobago, so be careful with your valuables. At night avoid walking around dark areas, particularly in Port of Spain. Note that the north coast of Trinidad has a reputation for smuggling and the road to Maracas Bay sometimes has armed military roadblocks and car searches.

There are poisonous manchineel trees at some beaches on Tobago. Trinidad has venomous bushmaster, fer-de-lance and coral snakes; however, snake bites are rare. There are no poisonous snakes on Tobago.

## EMERGENCY

Dial ☎ 999 for police, ☎ 990 for fire or ambulance emergencies.

## ACTIVITIES
### Beaches & Swimming

Tobago has some fine strands on a par with many of the Caribbean's better known destinations. There are nice white-sand beaches at Store Bay and Pigeon Point and numerous protected bays around the island, some fronting small villages, others more secluded.

Trinidad is not known for its beaches. The island's singular favourite is Maracas Bay, a scenically set bay north of Port of Spain. There are also some undeveloped beaches along Trinidad's east coast but the shoreline is unprotected and water conditions are hazardous.

### Diving

Tobago has extensive coral reefs, a great diversity of marine life and some top-notch diving. The largest concentration of dive sites is around the islets off Tobago's north coast. There are drift dives off the east side of Goat Island, rocky pinnacles and an underwater canyon off St Giles Island and a manta ray feeding ground off Little Tobago. Elsewhere around Tobago, there's good diving at Arnos Vale and at Wasp Shoal off Crown Point.

**Tobago Dive Shops** Tobago Marine Sports operates out of Blue Waters Inn (☎ 660-4341; fax 660-5195) in Speyside and Crown Point Beach Hotel (☎ 639-8781; fax 639-4416). Man Friday Diving (☎ & fax 660-4676) is in Charlotteville. Dive Tobago (☎ 639-0202; fax 639-2727) is at Pigeon Point and Viking Dive (☎ 639-9202) is at Crown Point.

Single dives average US$50 with equipment included, US$40 if you bring your own gear, and there are multi-dive packages that can lower the cost a bit. PADI open-water certification courses cost US$375, resort courses around US$75. Viking Dive, a relative newcomer, sometimes undercuts these prices.

### Snorkelling

In addition to the standard Buccoo Reef tour, you can find very good snorkelling in Tobago at Pirate's Bay on the north side of Charlotteville; at Angel Reef, off Goat Island; and in Arnos Vale Bay.

### Windsurfing

On Tobago, windsurfing gear can be rented at the Turtle Beach Hotel (☎ 639-2851) for US$12 an hour and at Grafton Beach Resort (☎ 639-4008) for US$25 a day.

### Hiking

There are several hikes on Trinidad, including trails to waterfalls, but robberies and attacks on hikers are not unknown. The trail to Blue Basin Waterfall in the Northern Range should be considered unsafe unless you're on an escorted tour.

One good way to get into the wilderness is to join one of the monthly hikes, often on the last Sunday, led by the Trinidad & Tobago Field Naturalists Club (☎ 663-1334, extension 2046) or one of the frequent walks at the Asa Wright Nature Centre (☎ 667-4655; fax 667-0493).

TRINIDAD

## Birdwatching

Both Trinidad and Tobago have an abundance of birdlife and good birdwatching opportunities. There are three main birdwatching spots on Trinidad: Caroni Bird Sanctuary, Pointe-à-Pierre Wildfowl Trust and the Asa Wright Nature Centre. All are detailed in the Around Trinidad section of this chapter.

In Tobago, birdwatching activities are concentrated in the northern part of the island where there are a couple of small resorts geared for bird watchers. Little Tobago, the island off Speyside, is the most visited bird sanctuary.

## Tennis

There are tennis courts at some of the larger hotels, including the Hilton in Port of Spain and on Tobago at the Mt Irvine Bay Hotel, Crown Point Beach Hotel and the Blue Waters Inn. There are public courts (TT$5 an hour) at the Princes Building Grounds (☎ 623-1121) on Upper Frederick St in Port of Spain.

## Golf

There are 18-hole par 72 courses at the St Andrew's Golf Club (☎ 629-2314) in Maraval on Trinidad and the Mt Irvine Bay Golf Club (☎ 639-8871) on Tobago, both with golf pros, carts and club rentals. Also on Trinidad is the nine-hole Chaguaramas Public Golf Club (☎ 634-4349) in Chaguaramas and courses in Pointe-à-Pierre and La Brea.

## Other Activities

In Trinidad, the Queen's Park Savannah in Port of Spain and the Arima Race Club have horse racing 28 days a year, with the main meets around New Year's and from April to June.

The main venue for cricket is the Queen's Park Oval, a few blocks west of the Queen's Park Savannah on St Clair Ave, Port of Spain.

## HIGHLIGHTS

Trinidad has two main drawing cards: Car-

nival and birdwatching. If you're in Port of Spain in the weeks preceding Carnival, be sure to visit some of the panyards where steel bands practice in the evening and the mas camps where artists make costumes. During the scarlet ibis season, don't miss a sunset boat ride to Caroni Bird Sanctuary.

On Tobago, most people take a glass-bottom boat tour of Buccoo Reef. If you're into snorkelling, Pirate's Bay in Charlotteville and Angel Reef off Goat Island are also special places. For historic sights, Fort King George in Scarborough is the premier spot, and for white-sand beaches, Pigeon Point is a beauty.

## ACCOMMODATION

Both Trinidad and Tobago have good-value guesthouses and small hotels. If you arrive without reservations, both islands have helpful airport tourist offices that can assist in booking rooms at any price range. Finding a room in Tobago is seldom a problem, but during Carnival season hotel reservations in Trinidad should be made far in advance.

There's a 15% value-added tax (VAT) tacked onto hotel rates and a 10% service charge. Guesthouses and apartments without housekeeping service generally do not add the service charge, although there's not 100% consistency on that. Note that in many cheaper guesthouses and apartments you'll need to bring your own towel. Many, but not all, hotels allow children under 12 to stay for free; if you're travelling with children, enquire when booking.

## FOOD

Trinidad and Tobago have West Indian, Creole, Chinese and continental restaurants. East Indian influence prevails in the ubiquitous roti, a Trinidadian creation found throughout the Caribbean, and a similar fast food called doubles, a sandwich of curried chickpeas wrapped in a soft, flat bread. Curried meats and seafood are common local main dishes, often served with a side of pelau, a rice mixed with peas, meat and coconut.

Another popular Trinidadian fast food is

shark & bake. This sandwich, made with a slab of fresh shark and deep-fried bread, is the standard at informal beachside eateries. Fried flying fish & chips is another inexpensive local favourite.

Between the large East Indian population and a sizeable number of Seventh Day Adventists, vegetarian food is easy to come by on both Trinidad and Tobago.

## DRINKS
Tap water is safe to drink on Trinidad and Tobago. The Eastern Caribbean's premium beer, Carib, hails from Trinidad and the island also produces a number of rums, including Vat 19 and Royal Oak.

Carib beer label

## ENTERTAINMENT
You can find pan music in Port of Spain year round at the Amoco Renegades Pan Theatre on Charlotte St, which has steel band performances at 6 pm on Friday. In addition, there's usually a steel band playing at one of the hotels in Port of Spain and in Crown Point on weekends.

There are numerous cinemas, including five in Port of Spain and one in Tobago.

Hollywood movies are most popular, though Hong Kong kung fu and movies from India are also shown.

## THINGS TO BUY
A recording of steel band or calypso music makes a nice souvenir. You can pick up the latest tunes at Rhyner's Record Shop, which has branches at the cruise ship complex and 54 Prince St in Port of Spain and at Piarco Airport.

# Getting There & Away

Information on travelling between Trinidad and Tobago is in the introductory Getting Around section of this chapter.

## AIR
### Airlines
Most airlines have offices near Independence Square in Port of Spain. The LIAT office is on Frederick St, a few blocks south of the Queen's Park Savannah.

Airline reservation numbers in Trinidad & Tobago include:

| | |
|---|---|
| Aeropostal | – ☎ 623-6522 |
| Air Canada | – ☎ 664-4065 |
| ALM | – ☎ 625-1719 |
| American Airlines | – ☎ 664-4661 |
| British Airways | – ☎ 625-1811 |
| BWIA | – ☎ 627-2942 |
| KLM | – ☎ 625-1719 |
| LIAT | – ☎ 623-1837 on Trinidad, ☎ 639-0484 on Tobago |
| United Airlines | – ☎ 627-7000 |

### To/From the USA
American Airlines has daily flights to Trinidad direct from Miami and from New York via San Juan or Miami. The usual midweek excursion fare to Trinidad is US$383 from Miami, US$439 from New York. Tickets require a 14-day advance purchase and allow a maximum stay of 30 days.

BWIA flies daily to Trinidad nonstop from Miami and from New York's JFK Airport via Antigua or Barbados. United Airlines flies to

Trinidad daily from New York via Caracas. Both airlines have fares and restrictions similar to American Airlines'.

ALM flies to Trinidad from Miami on Monday via Curacao. An excursion ticket that allows a stay of three to 30 days and requires a seven-day advance purchase costs US$442.

### To/From Canada

Air Canada flies from Toronto nonstop to Trinidad on Friday and Saturday and via Barbados on Monday. The lowest midweek fare is C$629 in the low season, C$779 in the high season, for a seven to 22-day excursion ticket with a 14-day advance purchase requirement.

BWIA flies from Toronto to Trinidad daily except Tuesday and Wednesday, making an en-route stopover in either Antigua or Barbados. An excursion ticket for a stay of seven to 30 days, travelling on weekdays, costs C$713 in the high season, a bit less in the low season.

### To/From the UK

British Airways flies to Trinidad from London on Tuesday and Friday via Barbados. The cheapest excursion ticket, allowing a stay of seven days to six months and requiring a 21-day advance purchase, costs UK£746 from October to June and UK£860 from July to September.

BWIA flies direct to Trinidad from London five days a week, stopping en route in Antigua or Barbados, with the same fare and restrictions as British Airways.

### To/From Europe

BWIA flies from Frankfurt to Trinidad on Monday, Wednesday and Friday. The fare is DM3409 with a 14-day advance purchase and allows a stay of up to three months.

KLM has a weekly flight between Trinidad and Amsterdam. A return ticket that allows a stay of seven to 21 days costs Fls2093 in the low season, Fls2293 in the high season.

### To/From South America

United Airlines flies daily to Trinidad from Caracas for US$114 one way or US$140 for a 21-day excursion ticket. Going in the other direction, the fare from Trinidad to Caracas is US$98 one way, US$100 for a seven-day excursion ticket, US$120 for 15 days and US$160 for 21 days.

Aeropostal flies daily from Caracas to Trinidad. An excursion ticket that allows a stay of seven to 17 days costs US$191. Aeropostal's fares from Trinidad to Caracas are comparable to United's.

BWIA flies daily from Georgetown, Guyana, to Trinidad for US$156 one way, US$184 for a 30-day excursion ticket.

### Within the Caribbean

**LIAT** LIAT has nonstop flights between Trinidad and Grenada, Barbados, St Lucia and St Vincent and ongoing flights to the rest of its Caribbean network. The fare from Grenada to Trinidad is US$80 one way, US$104 return. Between Trinidad and Barbados it's US$123 one way, US$155 return. Between Trinidad and St Lucia the one-way fare is US$132.

Tobago can be included as a stopover on many flights to and from Trinidad. Flights originating on Tobago that don't have routing through Trinidad are a few dollars cheaper than those that fly via Trinidad.

LIAT also offers good-value long-distance (YD) fares between Trinidad and some of the more distant Caribbean islands. Unlike regular fares, the YD fares offer unlimited en route stopovers. The one-way YD fare is US$160 between Trinidad and St Kitts and US$171 between Trinidad and St Martin. In contrast, the regular one-way fare from Trinidad to St Kitts is US$265, to St Martin US$285.

**BWIA** BWIA has recently reduced fares from Trinidad, its home port, by about 20%. There are daily flights from Trinidad to Barbados for US$105 one way or US$91 for a seven-day excursion; to Grenada for US$78 one way, US$89 for a seven-day excursion; to Antigua for US$199 one way, US$198 for a seven-day excursion; to St Lucia for US$112 one way, US$141 for a 30-day excursion.

Generally the seven-day excursion tickets can only be bought in Trinidad; the one-way Trinidad-Barbados ticket is US$123 if purchased outside Trinidad.

**British Airways** British Airways has two flights a week between Trinidad and Barbados. An excursion ticket between the two islands that's valid for up to a year costs US$107.

**ALM** ALM flies between Trinidad and Curacao on Monday and Thursday. Excursion tickets in either direction cost US$276 for a stay of up to eight days, US$316 for a stay of up to 21 days.

### Airport Information
**Trinidad** Trinidad's only airport, the Piarco International Airport, is 23 km east of Port of Spain. There's a tourist office; duty free shops selling alcohol, watches and perfume; car rental booths; and a money exchange office open from 6 am to 10 pm daily. Between immigration and customs there are courtesy phones with a direct line to a number of hotels and guesthouses. The airport has a simple café near the domestic departure gate and a more substantial upstairs restaurant.

**Tobago** Tobago's Crown Point International Airport is a small airport with courtesy phones to hotels and car rental agents, a boutique and gift shop, a snack shop, a tourist information booth and a bank with limited hours. Pay the departure tax on the 2nd floor.

**To/From the Airport** Getting a taxi from Trinidad's Piarco Airport is not a problem; drivers will even slip by customs and into the arrival area to meet you. From the airport to Port of Spain it's TT$85, to Maraval

TT$100. For more information on taxis, see the following Getting Around section.

From 5 am to 11 pm there's an hourly bus that runs between the airport and Port of Spain. Boarding is at the shed near the car rental parking lot; buy tickets (TT$1.50) in advance at the airport left-luggage service. From Port of Spain, get the bus from the South Quay bus terminal.

For information on taxis and buses from Tobago's Crown Point Airport, see the Tobago Getting Around section at the end of this chapter.

### SEA
Windward Lines Limited has a reasonably priced passenger/cargo boat that connects Trinidad with St Lucia, Barbados, St Vincent and Guiria, Venezuela. Information is in the introductory Getting Around chapter.

### Yacht
Trinidad and Tobago are well beyond the main sweep of Caribbean islands frequented by yachters, but Trinidad does have some boating facilities in the Carenage and Chaguaramas area.

The Trinidad & Tobago Yacht Club (☎ 637-4260), Bayshore, has 50 berths, water, electricity and a restaurant. Trinity Yacht Facilities (☎ 634-4303; fax 627-0391), PO Box 3163, Carenage, Chaguaramas Bay, has an outhaul and storage facility.

### Cruise Ship
Cruise ships dock at the south side of Port of Spain, where there's a large cruise ship complex. It contains a customs hall, a few souvenir and clothing shops, car rental agencies, taxis, a small bookshop and a couple of local eateries. There's a more modest cruise ship facility in Scarborough on Tobago.

### LEAVING TRINIDAD & TOBAGO
There's a TT$75 departure tax, which must be paid in local currency. There's no tax when flying between Trinidad and Tobago.

TRINIDAD

# Getting Around

Information on getting around Tobago is at the end of the Tobago section of this chapter.

## AIR

Air Caribbean (☎ 669-2500 in Trinidad, ☎ 639-8238 in Tobago) is the main carrier between Tobago and Trinidad, with numerous daily flights making the 15-minute jaunt between the islands.

LIAT also has a daily flight and BWIA, which has scaled back most of its service between the two islands, has a few flights a week. All charge US$20 one way, US$40 return; children under 13 pay half price.

## BUS

Trinidad has two kinds of public buses. The ordinary service, which uses blue and white buses, is not terribly reliable and is most common in the mornings when it takes children to school and vendors to town.

The express buses, on the other hand, are quite reliable and offer a quick weekday service between Trinidad's largest cities in air-conditioned red, black and white buses. You must buy tickets before boarding from a kiosk or shop near the bus terminal.

From Port of Spain, express buses run to San Fernando (TT$5) via the highway and to Arima (TT$3) via the priority bus route, leaving from Broadway near Kentucky Fried Chicken; buy tickets at nearby Bhaggan's Pharmacy.

## TAXI
### Regular Taxi

Regular taxis, locally called tourist taxis, are available at the airport, the cruise ship complex and hotels. Taxis are unmetered but rates are established by the government; hotel desks or the airport tourist office have a list of fares. From Port of Spain to Maracas Beach the fare is TT$120. There's a 50% surcharge after 9 pm. To call for a taxi dial ☎ 624-3560 or ☎ 622-5588 in Port of Spain.

### Route Taxi

The predominant mode of transportation within Port of Spain is the route taxi. One type is a shared taxi which travels on a prescribed route around the city and charges TT$2 to TT$3 to drop you anywhere along the way.

The other and more common type of route taxi is the maxi-taxi, a minivan that operates a regular bus route within a specific zone. Maxi-taxis operating within the Port of Spain district have yellow stripes. Those operating on the east coast have red stripes; on the south coast, green stripes; in the San Fernando area, brown stripes. Fees vary with the distance; from Port of Spain centre it costs TT$1.50 to Maraval, TT$3 to Chaguaramas, Arima or Maracas Bay (the latter service is infrequent), TT$5 to San Fernando. If you're going to a Maraval guesthouse that's a little off the main road, maxi-taxis can usually drop you off at the door if you pay a double fare.

In Port of Spain, many route taxis leave from the Independence Square area. Route taxis to Maraval leave from the corner of Duke and Henry streets; those heading east leave from the corner of Independence Square South and Charlotte St; those to St Ann's (Normandie hotel, Alicia's House) leave from the south side of Woodford Square; and those to the west side of the city leave from the corner of Park and St Vincent streets.

Outside the city centre route taxis can be hailed down along the route. All taxis, including route taxis, can be identified by the 'H' on the licence plate.

## CAR & MOTORBIKE
### Road Rules

Driving is on the left. A home driving licence from the USA, Canada, UK, France or Germany or an International Driving Permit is valid on Trinidad & Tobago for stays of up to three months.

All petrol stations are National (NP), a state-owned network. Petrol is at a fixed price of TT$1.96 a litre throughout Trinidad & Tobago.

TRINIDAD

### Rental

There are a number of small car rental companies on Trinidad. Prices are generally high, averaging about US$70 a day with insurance and unlimited km. If you're renting from an agency not located at the airport, office hours can be quite erratic even on weekdays.

AR Auto Rentals, which has offices at both the airport (☎ 669-2277) and the cruise ship complex (☎ 624-8687), has relatively good rates, beginning at around US$50 a day with insurance; weekly rates are six times the daily rate.

Other companies with offices at the airport include Singh's Auto Rentals (☎ 664-5417), Kalloo's Auto Rentals (☎ 669-5673) and Himraj Taxi and Rental Services (☎ 669-8294).

### HITCHING

Hitching is common among islanders, especially with children who hitch to and from school and with workers trying to get home at night. It is not necessarily a safe mode of transport for foreign visitors.

As for picking up hitchhikers, be aware that young men will sometimes try to hitch a ride near major tourist sights, not so much for the ride as for the opportunity to tout their services as a guide.

### BOAT

Ferries run daily between Port of Spain in Trinidad and Scarborough in Tobago. The journey takes about five hours and costs TT$30 one way, half price for children aged three to 12, free for those under the age of three. Cabins are available for TT$80. Schedules vary; for current information call the Port Authority (☎ 625-3055 on Trinidad, ☎ 639-2417 on Tobago).

### TOURS

You can arrange island tours with individual taxi drivers. For an all-day round-the-island tour, drivers will generally ask about US$160, though you should be able to negotiate that down by about 25%.

Trinidad & Tobago Sightseeing Tours (☎ 628-1051), 12 Western Main Rd, St James, Port of Spain, offers a seven-hour circle-island tour, a 5½-hour north-coast/Asa Wright Nature Centre tour and a 5½-hour Pitch Lake/Pointe-à-Pierre Wild-fowl Trust tour, each for US$45 per person.

Other tour companies in Port of Spain include Legacy Tours (☎ 623-0150), 7 Wrightson Rd; The Travel Centre (☎ 623-5096), 44 Edward St; and Travel Trinidad & Tobago (☎ 625-2201), 69 Independence Square.

## Port of Spain

Port of Spain, the country's capital and commercial centre, is a bustling metropolitan hub of approximately 300,000 people. It's not a tourist city – the handful of hotels are geared for business travellers and the attractions are few in number.

The centre has a mingling of modern office buildings, old corrugated tin stalls and 19th-century colonial buildings – some worth a look, although few are must-see sights.

The south end of Frederick St is the central shopping area, vibrant and congested, with both labyrinthine pedestrian arcades and air-conditioned indoor malls. Along the street, vendors hawk fruit and jewellery between police patrols. The activity spills down to Independence Square – not a square at all, but rather two long streets bordering a central parking lot. At Independence Square you can pick up a route taxi and find travel agents, banks and cheap eats.

Strolling around Port of Spain in the day you're apt to be approached by panhandlers, some with engaging stories, and at night it's simply not safe to walk in many areas. Still Port of Spain is not an unfriendly city and it can be interesting poking around.

Many visitors to the capital stay at the quieter north end of the city, where most of the hotels are located, or in Maraval, a rather cushy suburb a couple of km farther north, which has some guesthouses.

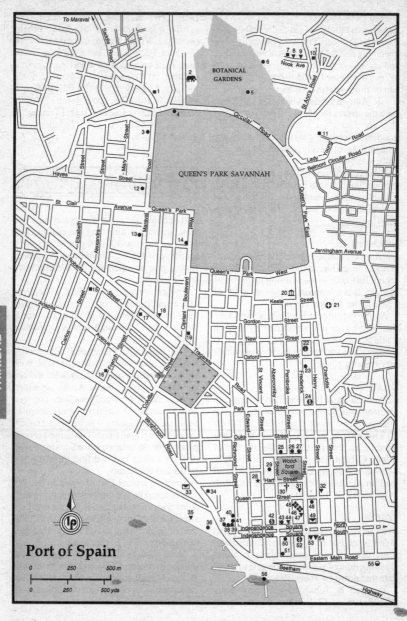

# Port of Spain

To Maraval

BOTANICAL
GARDENS

7  8  9      10
Nook Ave

6

2

1

5

4

Circular    Road

3

11

Lady    Young

Road

QUEEN'S PARK SAVANNAH

Belmont Circular Road

Hayes

St Clair    Avenue

12

Queen's    Park    West

Queen's    Park    East

13

14

Jerningham Avenue

Queen's    Park    West

15

20

Keate    Street

21

Ariapita    Avenue

17

18

Gordon    Street

New    Street

19

Oxford    Street

22

16

23

24

25  26  27

Park    Street

Duke    Street

29

Woodford
Square

32

28

Hart    Street

33

34

30    Street

31

45

Queen    Street

48

35

40

49

36

37    41

42    43 44

Independence    47

46

Square

38 39

Independence    Square

50

52

53    54

51

Beetham

55

56

Eastern Main Road

Highway

0        250        500 m

0        250        500 yds

TRINIDAD

**PLACES TO STAY**

| | |
|---|---|
| 1 | Kapok Hotel |
| 7 | Normandie |
| 10 | Alicia's House |
| 11 | Trinidad Hilton |
| 15 | Kestours Sports Villa |
| 16 | Five Star Guest House |
| 17 | La Calypso |
| 19 | YWCA |
| 34 | Holiday Inn |

**PLACES TO EAT**

| | |
|---|---|
| 1 | Tiki Village & Cafe Savanna |
| 8 | La Fantasie |
| 9 | Solimar |
| 11 | Terrace Garden Restaurant & La Boucan |
| 18 | Monsoon |
| 31 | Pizza Boys & Burger Boys |
| 32 | Kentucky Fried Chicken |
| 34 | Garden Restaurant & La Ronde |
| 35 | Breakfast Shed |
| 44 | Vie de France |
| 47 | Dairy Bar |
| 53 | Kentucky Fried Chicken |
| 54 | Mario's Pizzeria |

**OTHER**

| | |
|---|---|
| 2 | Emperor Valley Zoo |
| 3 | White Hall |
| 4 | Rock Gardens |
| 5 | President's House |
| 6 | Prime Minister's Residence |
| 12 | Queen's Royal College |
| 13 | French Embassy |
| 14 | US Embassy |
| 20 | National Museum & Art Gallery |
| 21 | General Hospital |
| 22 | Tourist Office |
| 23 | LIAT |
| 24 | Banks |
| 25 | Hall of Justice |
| 26 | Public Library |
| 27 | City Hall |
| 28 | Police Station |
| 29 | Red House (Parliament) |
| 30 | Holy Trinity Cathedral |
| 33 | General Post Office |
| 36 | Cruise Ship Complex |
| 37 | Air Canada |
| 38 | British Airways |
| 39 | British High Commission |
| 40 | KLM |
| 41 | Constellation Tours |
| 42 | Citibank |
| 43 | Supermarket |
| 45 | Town Centre Mall |
| 46 | Colsort Mall |
| 48 | Trinidad Book World |
| 49 | Branch Post Office |
| 50 | American Airlines |
| 51 | Canadian Embassy |
| 52 | Banks |
| 55 | South Quay Bus Terminal |
| 56 | Ferries to Tobago |

**TRINIDAD**

## Information

**Tourist Office** The tourist office, 134 Frederick St, is open from 8 am to 4 pm Monday to Friday.

**Money** Citibank on Independence Square North changes travellers' cheques free of fees and is open Monday to Thursday from 9 am to 2 pm and on Friday from 9 am to noon and 3 to 5 pm. The Bank of Commerce, next to Citibank, opens at 8 am. There are also banks along Frederick and Park streets.

**Post** The general post office, on Wrightson Rd opposite the Holiday Inn, is open Monday to Friday from 7 am to 5 pm. Poste restante, at the Enquiry window, is open from 8 am to 4 pm.

**Laundry** At the Shoppes of Maraval, on Saddle Rd in Maraval, there's a laundry where you can drop off a load of clothes to be washed and dried for US$5.

**Bookshops** You can get maps and books on the region at Trinidad Book World (RIK Services), 73 Queen St, and the nearby Metropolitan Book Suppliers, upstairs in the Colsort Mall on Frederick St.

**Travel Agents** If you need a travel agent, Constellation Tours (☎ 623-9269), 1 Richmond St, is helpful and has up-to-date information on the latest discount fares and excursion deals to the neighbouring islands.

## National Museum & Art Gallery

The National Museum & Art Gallery is in a classic, colonial building at the corner of Frederick and Keate streets. There are simple displays on rocks, fossils, shells, colonial agriculture and oil exploration; a room full of Carnival costumes; and paintings by 19th-century Trinidadian artist Michel Jean Cazabon.

The presentation is a bit lacking, but the museum is free. It's open from 10 am to 6 pm Tuesday to Saturday and you'll have to check your bags at the door.

### Woodford Square

Woodford Square is a public park with benches, pigeons, gospel preachers and a fair number of people just hanging out. Surrounding the park are some interesting buildings, including Red House, the imposing red parliament building constructed in 1906 in Renaissance style; the contemporary steel-and-concrete Hall of Justice; and the old public library. Behind Red House is the shell of the police station burned in the 1990 coup attempt; one little corner at the end of Hart St is still used by the police.

### Holy Trinity Cathedral

This majestic Anglican church, at the south side of Woodford Square, dates from 1818, seats 1200 and has a Gothic design. Its impressive ceiling is supported by an elaborate system of mahogany beams, whose design is said to have been modelled on London's Westminster Hall. There are also stained-glass windows that open to the breeze and a marble monument to Sir Ralph Woodford, the British governor responsible for the church's construction.

### Queen's Park Savannah

The city is crowned by the Queen's Park Savannah, once part of a sugar plantation and now a public park with a race track. Largely an expansive grassy field, the park itself is not particularly interesting but there are some sights along its perimeter. In the park's north-west corner there's a small rock garden with a lily pond and benches. The road circling the park has one-way traffic, flowing in a clockwise direction.

### Magnificent Seven

Along the west side of the Queen's Park Savannah is the Magnificent Seven, a line of seven fancy colonial buildings constructed in the late 19th and early 20th centuries. From south to north, they are the Queen's Royal Cottage, of German Renaissance design; Hayes Court, the Anglican bishop's residence; two private homes; the Catholic archbishop's residence; stately White Hall, the prime minister's office; and Stollmeyer's Castle, built to resemble a Scottish castle complete with turrets.

### Emperor Valley Zoo

Just north of Queen's Park Savannah is the Emperor Valley Zoo, which has local creatures, including ocelots, monkeys, scarlet ibis, red brocket deer and various snakes, as well as a few large exotics, such as tigers and lions. The park is open from 9.30 am to 5.30 pm daily. Admission is TT$3 for adults, TT$1.50 for children aged three to 12.

### Botanical Gardens

East of the zoo are the botanical gardens, which date from 1820 and have grand trees and nice strolling paths (not safe after dark). The President's House, a mansion originally built as the governor's residence in 1875, is adjacent to the gardens, as is the prime minister's residence.

### City Views

The Hilton hotel offers a rather good view of the city. If you want a higher perch you could drive up to Fort George, the site of a former British signal station, four km north-west of the city at the end of Fort George Rd.

### Places to Stay – bottom end

**Town Centre** The *YWCA* (☎ 627-6388), 8 Cipriani Blvd, a couple of blocks south of Queen's Park Savannah, is central and has simple double rooms for women only at US$15 per person.

*Kestours Sports Villa* (☎ 628-4028; fax 628-3792), 58 Carlos St, caters to touring cricket and cycling teams but is open to individual travellers on a space-available basis. It has friendly staff and a bit of a youth hostel atmosphere with a shared kitchen and a large sitting room with TV. The 10 rooms are basic but have air-con and private bathroom and at US$17/30 for singles/doubles are the best value of the central guesthouses.

*La Calypso* (☎ 622-4077), 46 French St, has 12 rooms, a few with rusting air-conditioners. Rooms are small and run-down and the staff are indifferent. Singles/doubles cost US$18/26 with shared bath, US$20/38 with private bath.

The *Five Star Guest House* (☎ & fax 623-4006), 7 French St, has 16 basic but clean rooms, each with a sink in the room and bathrooms in the hall, for US$20/30 for singles/doubles. There are also a couple of rooms with air-con, TV and private bath but at US$40/50 they are not on a par with rooms in similarly priced guesthouses on the north side of the city.

*Alicia's House* (☎ 623-2802; fax 623-8560), 7 Coblentz Gardens, is a new 14-room guesthouse in a residential neighbourhood north of the Hilton, about a 10-minute walk from Queen's Park Savannah. Rooms have ceiling fan, air-con, phone, TV and private bathroom with tub. There's a little pool and jacuzzi out the back and overall the place is quite nice, if not as personable as the smaller family-run guesthouses. Singles/doubles start from US$25/40; breakfast is US$5 per person more.

### Places to Stay – top end

**Town Centre** The *Kapok Hotel* (☎ 622-6441; fax 622-9677), 16 Cotton Hill, a business hotel at the south end of Saddle Rd, has 71 rooms that are pleasantly decorated with rattan furnishings, and have satellite TV, phone and air-con. Singles/doubles cost US$67/79 with or without a kitchenette. There's a pool, restaurant, free parking and a computer room.

The 54-room *Normandie* hotel (☎ 624-1811), 10 Nook Ave, has a pleasantly old-fashioned style. The rooms are nice, if a bit pricey, and most face a central courtyard and pool. Standard rooms have air-con and

phone, while the superior rooms also have TV and a bit more space. Singles/doubles cost US$60/70 for standard rooms, US$70/80 for superior rooms and US$85/95 for loft rooms.

The recently renovated *Holiday Inn* (☎ 625-3366; fax 625-4166; in the USA ☎ (800) 465-4329) on Wrightson Rd has a central city location opposite the cruise ship complex. It has 235 comfortably large and modern rooms with balcony and the standard amenities, including cable TV with HBO (movie channel). There's a pool, exercise room, a couple of on-site restaurants and free parking. There are sometimes walk-in specials for US$79 a double; otherwise, standard rooms with either a king-size or two double beds cost US$95.

The 394-room *Trinidad Hilton* (☎ 624-3211; fax 624-4485), PO Box 442, Lady Young Rd, is Trinidad's largest and most upmarket hotel. It has a hillside location with a sweeping city view across the Queen's Park Savannah. The hotel is swank with lots of glass, a huge pool and a couple of restaurants. Rooms are large and modern and most have a balcony with a good view. Singles/doubles begin at US$135/150.

If you have some dire need to be close to the airport, the 58-room *Bel Air International Airport Hotel* (☎ 664-4771; fax 664-4771) is half a km from the terminal. Rooms are basic and not very cheery, but they do have air-con, phones, two twin beds and private bath. There's a restaurant, a pool and free transport to and from the airport. Singles/doubles begin at US$55/68.

### Places to Stay

**Maraval** *Monique's Guest House* (☎ 628-3334; ☎ 622-3232), 114 Saddle Rd, Maraval, has 11 large, pleasant rooms with either two twin or two double beds, private bath, air-con, phone and radio. Singles/doubles/triples cost US$40/45/50. At Carnival time, there's a five-night rate of US$450 for either singles or doubles. One room has some facilities for the disabled. There's a common TV room and a dining room. This modern guesthouse is right on Saddle Rd, three km north of Queen's Park Savannah.

*Carnetta's House* (☎ 628-2732; fax 628-7717), 28 Scotland Terrace, Maraval, consists of five comfortable rooms in the home of Winston and Carnetta Borrell. The upstairs unit is the largest, although all are quite suitable, very clean and have private bath, air-con and phone. Singles/doubles cost US$40/45, US$10 more for a room with a kitchenette. The guesthouse is in a quiet neighbourhood off Saddle Rd, not far from Monique's. Breakfast (US$5), inexpensive sandwiches and cold drinks are available. Winston, a military reserve commander and former tourist board director, enjoys helping guests plan their daily outings.

The 16-room *Tropical Hotel* (☎ 622-5815; fax 628-3174), 6 Rookery Nook, Maraval, is a handsome colonial-style stone building in an upscale neighbourhood, one km north of the Savannah. Rooms are straightforward but large and comfortable enough, each with private bath, air-con and phone. Singles/doubles cost US$40/50; there's a three-day minimum stay. The hotel has a pool and restaurant and is within walking distance of other places to eat.

The 68-unit *Royal Palm Suite Hotel* (☎ 628-6042), 7 Saddle Rd, Maraval, is at the rear of a shopping centre, half a km north of Kentucky Fried Chicken. This is a modern, if somewhat impersonal place, with large, ordinary suites with a queen bed, kitchen and dining area for US$75/82 for singles/doubles. There are also some rooms without kitchens for US$65/72. Unlike most other hotels, rates are the same at Carnival time.

### Places to Eat – cheap

Pick-up trucks piled high with chilled drinking coconuts (TT$2) can be found along the road that circles the Queen's Park Savannah and near the south end of Frederick St. There's a supermarket on Independence Square North.

For Western fast food there are a couple of *Kentucky Fried Chicken* restaurants on the south side of the city, one on Henry St and another two blocks to the south-west on Independence Square.

*Vie de France*, a bakery on Independence Square, makes good takeaway rotis (TT$4 to TT$8), fish pies and pastries. There are a number of similar bakeries around the city, including another on the same block.

Town Centre Mall, 20 Frederick St, has a neat 2nd-floor food court with about a dozen fast-food stalls encircling a central dining area. *D'Bocas* is quite popular for salads and local food *Lisa's Indian Cuisine* cooks good Indian rotis to order. Other choices range from Chinese and Creole to tacos and burgers. You can easily get a hearty lunch for under TT$15. The food court is open from 7 am to 6 pm weekdays, until 4 pm on Saturday. The basement of the nearby Colsort Mall also has some simple, inexpensive eateries.

At 27 Frederick St are the adjacent *Pizza Boys* and *Burger Boys* which have burgers, reasonable pizzas, fish & chips and vegetarian sandwiches. Pizza prices range from TT$9 for a small cheese pizza to TT$31 for a large pizza with two toppings.

The *Dairy Bar*, also on Frederick St, has Colombo frozen yoghurt (TT$5), ice cream, salads and sandwiches.

*Singho Restaurant*, at the Long Circular Mall on the west side of the city, has good Chinese food in a slightly upmarket setting, with the usual fish, beef and chicken dishes priced from TT$15 to TT$25. There's a TT$60 Chinese buffet on Wednesday nights. It's open from 11 am to 11 pm daily.

Also in the Long Circular Mall is *Mario's Pizzeria*, a cheery Trinidadian chain restaurant with good, moderately priced pizzas.

Several places around Port of Spain, including Mario's, Pizza Boys and Kentucky Fried Chicken, will deliver food to your guesthouse or hotel.

The *Breakfast Shed*, literally a shed at the west side of the cruise ship complex, is a good place to rub shoulders with locals. A big meal of Trinidadian food, including fish, dasheen (taro), plantains and rice, costs TT$15 and is served from 10.30 am to 3 pm. It's best to arrive before 2 pm as the food sometimes runs out early. There's also a TT$10 fish breakfast from 6 am. It's closed on Sunday.

Also at the cruise ship complex is the open-air *Coconut Village*, a popular drinking hole for ship crews. From 11 am to 2 pm weekdays it has a good-value set lunch for TT$15.

For a solid, good-value meal, *Monsoon*, on the corner of Tragarete Rd and Picton St, has Indian food which is served from steamer trays but kept fresh, particularly at mealtimes. The most common meal includes a choice of three vegetables plus curried potatoes, shrimp or chicken, either wrapped in a dhal roti or served on a plate with rice, for TT$16. Wash it down with a homemade sorrel drink. The food is quite good and the dining room pleasant enough, although you can also order takeaway. It's open from 11 am to 10 pm Monday to Saturday.

### Places to Eat – expensive

*Tiki Village*, on the top floor of the Kapok Hotel, has a city view and a buffet lunch for TT$32 Monday to Thursday, TT$40 on Friday. At dinner there's a varied Chinese menu, with fish and meat dishes priced from TT$30 to TT$40 and a number of combination plates in the same range. While the restaurant is popular, the food is rather average. At lunch on weekends there's a dim sum menu.

Also at the Kapok Hotel is the *Cafe Savanna*, which has good callaloo soup, sandwiches with salad and fries for around TT$25 at lunch and the usual array of seafood and meat dinner dishes from TT$40 to TT$70.

*La Fantasie* at the side of the Normandie hotel features 'nouvelle Creole' cuisine in its brightly painted dining room or al fresco on the terrace. There's a soup-to-dessert business lunch on weekdays for TT$39 and reasonably priced sandwiches, pasta dishes and salads. At dinner there's an à la carte menu with starters such as callaloo soup and crab backs from TT$8 to TT$15 and a range of meat and seafood main dishes priced from

TT$40 to TT$80. It's open from noon to 2 pm and from 6 to 9.45 pm.

*Solimar* (☎ 624-6267), 6 Nook Ave, near the Normandie hotel, is an interesting restaurant run by Englishman Joe Brown, a well-travelled former chef for the Hilton chain. The restaurant features a changing menu of international foods, priced from TT$50 to TT$100, which on any given night might include Korean, Indian, Hawaiian and Italian dishes. There are also seafood pasta or Oriental noodle dishes, served with a salad, for under TT$40. It's open for dinner from 6.30 pm Tuesday to Saturday.

The *Garden Restaurant* at the Holiday Inn makes a generous chef's salad with fresh vegetables and large chunks of chicken, ham and cheese for TT$28. The varied menu also includes fish of the day or barbecued chicken with salad and fries for TT$40. On Sunday nights there's a buffet that includes filet mignon, shish kebab, grilled fish, various salads, fresh fruit and a dessert table for TT$94. The Holiday Inn also has a revolving rooftop restaurant, *La Ronde*, serving upmarket French and West Indian food accompanied by a 360° city view.

The Trinidad Hilton's *Terrace Garden Restaurant* has an OK but not special buffet breakfast with fruit, muffins, croissants, omelettes etc for TT$42. There's better fare at the weekday lunch buffet for TT$61 in the hotel's *La Boucan* restaurant, which has a nice view.

### Places to Eat

**Maraval** *Chaconia Inn*, 106 Saddle Rd, within walking distance of Monique's Guest House and Carnetta's House, serves meals from 6 am to 11.30 pm daily and has a bar open to 2 am for drinks. Sandwiches cost from TT$10 to TT$20.

*Michael's* (☎ 628-0445), 143 Long Circular Rd, has good Italian food in a rather elegant setting of hardwood floors and high-back chairs. Starters include such standards as minestrone soup, Caesar's salad and mussels marinara. Pasta main dishes are priced around TT$40, while chicken, shrimp, filet mignon and lobster main dishes range from TT$45 to TT$95. It's open for dinner only, from 6 to 10.30 pm Monday to Saturday.

# Around Trinidad

## MARACAS BAY

Maracas Bay, Trinidad's most popular beach, makes a nice outing from Port of Spain. Not only is the beach quite lovely but the views along the way make for a very scenic drive, just 40 minutes from the capital. The North Coast Rd, which begins north of Maraval, climbs up over the mountains through a lush tropical forest of tall trees, ferns and bamboo. When you reach the north coast there's a stunning cliffside view before the road descends to the coast.

Maracas Bay has a broad sandy beach, a small fishing hamlet at one side and a backdrop of verdant mountains. The waters can be flat in the summer, but at other times the bay usually has good waves for bodysurfing. There's a lifeguard station, changing rooms and chunky concrete picnic shelters. On weekends the beach gets pretty crowded but the rest of the week it can feel almost deserted.

**Tyrico Bay**, just east of Maracas Bay, is quieter and less commercial but also very trashed. **Las Cuevas**, eight km east of Maracas Bay, is a pretty U-shaped bay with surfing at its west end and calmer conditions at its centre. It has a nice brown-sand beach and changing rooms.

From Las Cuevas it's possible to continue over the mountains to Arima but it's a long, lonely road. You'll save time by going back to Port of Spain and taking the highway to Arima.

### Places to Eat

There are a dozen brightly painted stalls selling shark & bake opposite the beach. Best is *Vilma*, who cooks both the bake (fried bread) and shark to order (TT$5). Aloo pie (potato puff) and soft drinks cost TT$2.

If you want a sit-down meal, there's *Uncle Sam's Beach Bar* a few hundred metres west of the beach, next to the petrol station.

## CHAGUARAMAS

Chaguaramas, on the north-western end of the island, was the site of a major US military installation during WW II and now has a small golf course and a few other minor sights. It's about a 30-minute drive from the capital.

**Gasper Grande**, an island at the south side of Chaguaramas Bay, has some bathing spots and a cave with stalactites and stalagmites that can be toured from 9 am to 3 pm daily (TT$5). Boats to the island can be arranged at the Island Homeowners' jetty on the west side of Chaguaramas; expect to pay about TT$25 per person.

### Places to Eat

A good place to get a reasonably priced seafood meal or just have a drink is *Anchorage* on Point Gourde Rd, which has a nice atmosphere and a waterfront location.

## MT ST BENEDICT

On the hillside north of Tunapuna there's a Benedictine monastery with a secluded guesthouse and a pleasant wooded setting. The monastery itself isn't a major sight; the area is of most interest to people who want to stay or eat at the guesthouse.

There are also some trails in the thickly wooded hills behind the monastery, which are a habitat for hawks, owls and numerous colourful forest birds, as well as the occasional monkey. One of the more popular hikes is the hour-long trek up to the fire tower, which is visible from the monastery.

To get there from Tunapuna, take St John's Rd north 3.3 km from Eastern Main Rd. During the day there's a bus service to the monastery roughly every 30 minutes from the corner of Eastern Main Rd and St John's Rd.

### Places to Stay & Eat

*Mt St Benedict (Pax) Guest House* (☎ 662-4084; fax 662-5286), Tunapuna, is an old house owned by the monastery. This pleasantly relaxed place is booked largely by bird watchers. There are 15 spartan rooms with teak floorboards, two single beds, washbasins and fine views. Bathrooms are shared. Singles/doubles cost US$50/100, including breakfast and dinner. As there is going to be a change of management, however, the rates may change. There's a large sitting room and a wonderful view of the Caroni Plains stretched out below.

Non-guests can get a full breakfast for TT$15 and a simple lunch for TT$25. If it's not busy you might be able to just show up, but officially you need to call ahead for reservations.

## ASA WRIGHT NATURE CENTRE

The Asa Wright Nature Centre is a former cocoa and coffee plantation that has been turned into an 80-hectare nature reserve. Located amidst the rainforest in the Northern Range, the centre has attracted naturalists from around the world since it was founded in 1967. There's a lodge catering to naturalist tour groups, a research station for biologists and a series of hiking trails on the property.

More than 100 bird species inhabit the area, including blue-crowned motmots, chestnut woodpeckers, palm tanagers, channel-billed toucans, hummingbirds and white-bearded manakins. The sanctuary encompasses Dunston Cave, a gorge that is home to a breeding colony of the elusive nocturnal guacharo, or oilbird.

Birdwatching tours along the centre's trails are given at 10.30 am and 1.30 pm, last about 1½ hours and cost US$6; reservations should be made at least 24 hours in advance. A variety of seminars and field trips are also offered, most geared for people staying at the centre's lodge.

Asa Wright Nature Centre is about a 1½-hour drive from Port of Spain. At Arima, head north on Blanchisseuse Rd for 12 km, turning left into the centre after the 7½ mile marker.

### Places to Stay & Eat

The *Asa Wright Nature Centre and Lodge* (☎ 667-4655; fax 667-0493; in the USA and Canada ☎ (800) 426-7781), PO Box 4710, Arima, has 23 double rooms, some in the weathered main house and others in cottages, all quite spartan but with private bath. Singles/doubles cost US$106/160 in summer, US$139/210 in winter, including three meals a day, tax and service charge. Airport transfers can be arranged for US$40 per person return.

Non-guests can eat at the lodge, but reservations need to be made 48 hours in advance.

## EAST COAST

Trinidad's east coast is wild and rural, a mix of lonely beaches with rough Atlantic waters, mangrove swamps and coconut plantations. The east coast is most logically included in a circle-island drive, a pleasant enough day outing but certainly not a must-do excursion – in fact, you may not encounter another tourist along the entire route.

To get to the east coast from Port of Spain, head east on the Churchill Roosevelt Highway (avoid the Eastern Main Rd between Port of Spain and Arima, a horribly congested route). At Waller Field the highway will merge with the Eastern Main Rd and highway signs will guide you through the town of Sangre Grande and south to Manzanilla.

The Manzanilla Mayaro Rd, which runs along the east coast, is narrow but only carries light traffic. Save for the occasional pothole and some precarious-looking wooden bridges, the road is in reasonably good condition. There are free-roaming cows and water buffaloes and you can easily spot vultures, egrets and herons along the way. In places, coconut palms and orange heliconia line the roadside.

The main east-coast beach, **Manzanilla Beach**, has brown sand, palm trees and white beach morning glory. The winds are often strong and the waters tempestuous. You can get snacks and drinks at Junior's, a beach bar next to the parking lot.

The road continues south, skirting a freshwater swamp much of the way, and crosses the meandering **Nariva River** a couple of times.

TRINIDAD

After crossing the **Ortoire River**, Trinidad's longest river, there are a couple of small settlements with simple wooden houses on stilts and then you'll reach the town of **Pierreville**, where a sign points west to San Fernando, 56 km away.

## SOUTH-CENTRAL TRINIDAD

The south-central part of Trinidad is heavily populated, largely by the descendants of East Indians brought to the island to work the plantations after the abolition of slavery. In time the labourers came to own much of the land. The towns now have a decidedly Indian appearance, from the style of the homes to the roadside temples and mosques.

The countryside is tame with undulating hills and is planted with citrus, coffee, cocoa and bananas. In **Rio Claro**, there's a Muslim mosque, a couple of bakeries, a central produce market and a Hindu temple along the main road. The road deteriorates, becoming bumpy as you continue west from Rio Claro, but it's not a problem if you drive slowly.

If you're curious you can check out **Devil's Woodyard**, one of the island's dozen 'mud volcano' sites where small mounds of mud have built up as a result of gases released from the earth. Hindustan Rd, a narrow cane road, leads 3.5 km south from the highway to Devil's Woodyard; the turnoff is signposted about 1.5 km west of New Grant.

The highway continues to **Princes Town**, a large town in the centre of sugar cane country. Traffic in the town can be a bit confusing but as long as you end up continuing west on either the northerly Naparima Rd or the southerly Manahambre Rd, you'll get to San Fernando.

## SAN FERNANDO

San Fernando, Trinidad's second-largest city, is the centre of the island's gas and oil industries. The centre of the town is dominated by San Fernando Hill, a spot once sacred to the Amerindians. The hill is rather oddly shaped, a consequence of earlier excavations that have now been halted.

There is a golf course west of the city, but San Fernando has little of interest for tourists and most of those who see the city are just passing through on their way to Pitch Lake, 15 km to the south.

### Places to Eat

There are roti stands, including *Karamath's Roti Shop* at 157 Coffee St and *Steve's Roti Shop* on Independence Ave, a pizzeria and small food mart in the town centre.

For a sit-down lunch, *Soong's Great Wall*, at 97 Circular Rd on the east side of San Fernando Hill, is a popular spot with à la carte Chinese dishes priced around TT$20 and a lunch buffet that includes a simple salad bar for TT$49.

## PITCH LAKE

Pitch Lake is perhaps Trinidad's greatest oddity. This 40-hectare lake of tar is 90 metres deep at the centre, where hot bitumen is continually replenished from a subterranean fault. The lake is the world's single largest supply of natural bitumen and as much as 300 tonnes is extracted daily.

The surface of Pitch Lake has a wrinkled elephant-like skin which is hard enough to walk across in many places. However, as the site is essentially a huge field of tar, resembling a parking lot, many people find it anticlimactic after a two-hour drive from Port of Spain.

Pitch Lake is on the west side of the highway, just south of La Brea. It's possible

---

**Pitch Lake**

According to legend, Pitch Lake was once the site of a wealthy Chiman Indian village. The village was surrounded by gardens and orchards which attracted flocks of birds. The Chiman angered the gods by capturing the sacred hummingbirds that flew into the gardens. One night, as the villagers slept, their homes sank beneath the earth and in their place a barren sea of tar appeared. From that moment forward, Pitch Lake was known as the entrance to the underworld. ■

to get an express bus or maxi-taxi from Port of Spain to San Fernando and from there a maxi-taxi onward to Pitch Lake.

Expect to be met by young men who will want to be your guide. The tourist office once tried to organise the guides and set fees but it was unsuccessful, so you'll have to negotiate on your own. You can avoid haggling with individual guides by arranging a tour through the Lake Asphalt Company (☎ 648-7555), which is next to Pitch Lake and open from 7 am to 4 pm Monday to Friday.

## CARONI BIRD SANCTUARY

Caroni Bird Sanctuary is the roosting site for thousands of scarlet ibis, the national bird of Trinidad & Tobago. At sunset the birds fly in to roost in the swamp's mangroves, giving the trees the appearance of being abloom with brilliant scarlet blossoms. Even if you're not an avid bird watcher, the sight of the ibis flying over the swamp, glowing an almost fluorescent red in the final rays of the evening sun, is a treat not to be missed.

Long, flat-bottomed motorboats that can hold about 30 passengers pass slowly through the swamp's channels. En route the guide points out various flora and fauna – a boa constrictor sleeping on a tree branch and the mudskipper fish that cruise alligator-like with their beady eyes above the water. The boat then stops deep in the midst of the swamp for a good vantage point under the flight path of the ibis. To avoid disturbing the birds, the boats keep a fair distance from the roosting sites, so a pair of binoculars is recommended although you can still see the birds with your naked eye. You can also expect to see lots of herons and egrets, predominant among the swamp's 150 bird species.

Note that ibis roosting at Caroni is seasonal and from March to July very few ibis are sighted.

Boats leave between 4 and 4.15 pm daily. Reservations are recommended but if you just show up it's usually not a problem. The price seems to be a bit arbitrary – if you call in advance you should be able to get a reservation for TT$30, but otherwise expect to pay TT$40 – either way it's a bargain!

Nanan Tours (☎ 645-1305) does a good, reliable tour. The other major tour operator is David Ramsahai (☎ 663-2207).

The sanctuary is off the Uriah Butler Highway, 14 km south of Port of Spain. Turn at the highway sign for Caroni Bird Sanctuary and park at the LPG gas plant opposite the boat dock. If you don't have your own vehicle, tour companies such as Trinidad & Tobago Sightseeing Tours (☎ 628-1051) combine bus transportation from Port of Spain with the swamp tour for US$28. Although it's possible to get dropped off by a southbound route taxi, it would be problematic on the return as you'd have to walk out to the highway and try to wave down a fast-moving vehicle in the dark – you'd certainly be better off arranging in advance for a taxi.

If your main interest is photography, the light is more favourable in the morning. Morning tours, which leave around 4.30 am, can be arranged through Nanan Tours.

## POINTE-À-PIERRE WILDFOWL TRUST

The Pointe-à-Pierre Wildfowl Trust (☎ 637-5145, ☎ 662-4040) is a special place. Despite being in the midst of the island's sprawling oil refinery, this wetland sanctuary has a rich abundance of birdlife in a highly concentrated (26-hectare) area. There are about 90 species of birds, both wild and in cages, including endangered waterfowl, colourful songbirds and ibis, heron and other wading birds. Trails edge a lake and lead into the woods and in a 20-minute stroll of the grounds you can easily spot a few dozen bird species.

A non-profit organisation, the trust is a centre for breeding endangered species and has programmes in environmental education. The visitors' centre has small exhibits and a gift shop.

To visit, you should make reservations a day or two in advance, as the staff like to stagger the number of visitors. Without a reservation you're not likely to get past the guard at the oil refinery entrance. Hours are

9 am to 5 pm Monday to Friday and 10 am to 6 pm on weekends. The entrance fee is TT$3 for adults, TT$2 for children under 12.

Enter the trust through the Trintoc Oil Refinery gate, on the east side of the Old Southern Main Rd between San Fernando and Pointe-à-Pierre. It's about two km from the gate to the sanctuary.

# Tobago

Tobago is a delightfully relaxed and un-spoiled island with much to offer travellers. There are good beaches, pristine snorkelling and diving spots, excellent bird watching opportunities and just enough tourism to make visiting Tobago easy, yet not so much that the island feels over touristed.

Most of the white-sand beaches and tourist activities are centred in the south, starting in Crown Point at the south-west tip of the island and running along a string of bays up to Arnos Vale. The lowlands that predominate in the south extend to Tobago's only large town, Scarborough.

The coast north from Scarborough is dotted with small fishing villages, while the interior is ruggedly mountainous with thick rainforest. This area is a habitat for parrots and other tropical birds and is being pro-moted for ecotourism, with most activities centred in the northern villages of Speyside and Charlotteville. The nearby uninhabited islets of Little Tobago, Goat Island and St Giles Island are nature reserves abundant in both bird and marine life.

For information on diving and other water sports see Activities in the Facts for the Visitor section of this chapter.

Tobago has long attracted holiday-makers from Trinidad but remained a sleeper as far as foreign visitors were concerned until the late 1980s, when BWIA started offering direct flights to Tobago from Stockholm, Zurich and Frankfurt. Enough new tourists arrived that many islanders built small guest-houses and apartment hotels in anticipation of future tourism growth.

The European routes didn't turn a profit for the airline, however, and BWIA was forced to drop them in 1993. As a result Tobago, modest as its tourism development remains, has quite a bit of overcapacity with lots of rooms renting for much cheaper rates than originally intended. Even the handful of expensive resort hotels in the Mt Irvine area have been offering slashed prices in the midst of the winter season. While the lull lasts, Tobago is certainly one of the most overlooked and best value destinations in the Caribbean.

## CROWN POINT

Tobago's Crown Point Airport is literally in the middle of the island's main resort area – hotels, restaurants and the beach are all within a few minutes' walk of the terminal.

Crown Point has a good range of reason-ably priced accommodation and attracts a younger crowd than most Caribbean destina-tions, with visitors fairly evenly divided between Europeans, North Americans and Trinidadians.

**Store Bay**, the body of water at the west side of Crown Point, has white sands, a lifeguard and good year-round swimming. Store Bay is a centre of activity of sorts – there are a few vendors selling souvenirs and the occasional hawker pushing glass-bottom boat tours of Buccoo Reef – but overall the scene is relaxed and casual.

The remains of the small coastal **Fort Milford**, built by the British in 1777, is along the road a five-minute walk south-west of Store Bay. The area has been turned into a small park and there's still a bit of the old fort walls and half a dozen cannons.

**Pigeon Point**, 1.5 km north of Store Bay, is a lovely palm-fringed beach with powdery white sands and clear aqua waters. The entrance is on Milford Rd Extension. You can walk in for free along the beach or come in along the road for TT$10 (TT$5 for chil-dren) and have access to the facilities, which include changing rooms and thatched shel-ters. There's a small restaurant and a water sports rental booth.

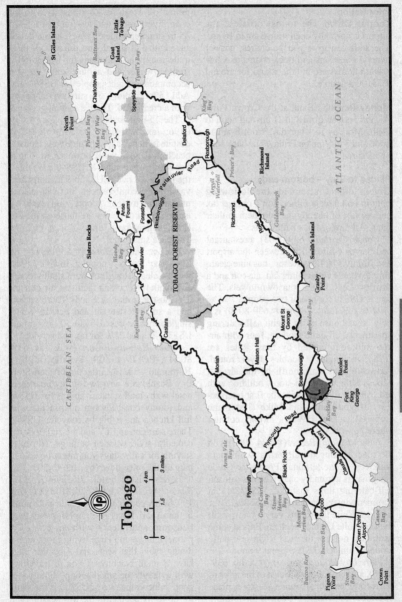

## Information

**Tourist Office** The tourist office at the airport is normally open from 6 am to 10 pm. The staff can give you brochures, answer general questions and book rooms in a few private homes around the island for around TT$100 a double.

**Money** Republic Bank at the Crown Point Airport is open from 8 to 11 am and noon to 2 pm Monday to Thursday, from 8 am to noon and 3 to 5 pm on Friday. The bank sells phonecards.

## Places to Stay – bottom end

Unless otherwise noted, the following bottom-end hotels either don't charge tax and service or already include them in their rates. All have private bathrooms.

*Woods' Castle* (☎ 639-0803), a restaurant and bar on Milford Rd between the airport and Jimmy's Holiday Resort, has nine clean, simple rooms with ceiling fan, air-con and a firm mattress. Bring your own towels. The rate is US$30 for one or two people.

*Mike's Holiday Resort* (☎ 639-8050) is a new guesthouse with eight self-catering apartments, all quite modern, four with air-con and four cooled by fans. Rates are US$35 for singles or doubles all year round. A two-minute walk north of the airport, Mike's is the white two-storey building with red trim off to the right at the first intersection. If you can't find Mike (last name Roberts), ask at BWIA's airport counter where he works.

*Jetway Holiday Resort* (☎ 624-4900) is on the road fronting the airport, a two-minute walk east of the terminal. Proprietor Clyde Chapman is a friendly chap who has a dozen self-catering units that cost US$35/45 in summer/winter for doubles, US$20/25 for singles. While the rooms vary a bit, overall they are quite simple but clean. Expect some aeroplane noise – the first flight is usually around 7 am and the last about 9 pm.

*Store Bay Holiday Resort* (☎ & fax 639-8810), a five-minute walk east of the airport, is a recommendable 15-unit two-storey place operated by Wilfred Best, a hospitable

retired oil executive. Apartments with kitchen, living room and air-con cost US$25/35 in summer/winter. There's also a deluxe suite with a small balcony, tub and TV that's quite roomy and pleasant for US$36/50 in summer/winter and a huge suite that can accommodate eight people for US$90/100. Add 15% tax, plus a 5% surcharge if paying with a credit card. There's a small pool.

The 15-unit *Arthur's by the Sea* (☎ 639-0196; fax 639-4122) on Milford Rd is, despite its name, a five-minute walk from the beach. It is good value however, as long as the walk-in rate stays at US$40 a double – the published rate is US$60. The units have various bed combinations, but can accommodate up to four people, and each has air-con. Best of the lot are those on the 2nd floor, which have high wooden ceilings. There's a small pool.

*Golden Thistle Hotel* (☎ 639-8521), off Store Bay Rd, is a popular, low-key place with 26 clean, straightforward studio rooms, each with full cooking facilities, air-con and TV; most have king-size beds. There's a pool and a small restaurant and bar. In winter singles/doubles cost US$40/50, in summer US$35/40, plus 25% for tax and service.

*James Holiday Resort* (☎ & fax 639-8084), PO Box 109, Scarborough, a 10-minute walk from the airport and Store Bay Beach, is a new two-storey apartment hotel with small standard rooms for US$45 and roomy one-bedroom apartments with full kitchen and a big balcony for US$52. There's air-con and TV and the 2nd floor has cathedral-style wooden ceilings. If you're staying for a few days you might be able to bargain the price down by 10% to 20%.

James' sister hotel, *Jimmy's Holiday Resort* (☎ 639-8292; fax 639-3100), PO Box 109, Scarborough, is a 10-minute walk north of the airport. It has 18 straightforward two-bedroom apartments with air-con, TV, phone, kitchen and large living room with a dining table that seats six. Upstairs units have a small balcony. If you're travelling with a family or small group, Jimmy's is good value as the rate of US$60 is the same for up to six people. In the low season (late

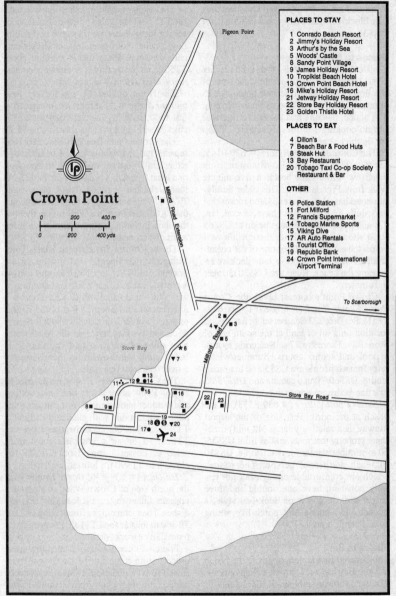

**Crown Point**

Pigeon Point

**PLACES TO STAY**

1  Conrado Beach Resort
2  Jimmy's Holiday Resort
3  Arthur's by the Sea
5  Woods' Castle
8  Sandy Point Village
9  James Holiday Resort
10 Tropikist Beach Hotel
13 Crown Point Beach Hotel
16 Mike's Holiday Resort
21 Jetway Holiday Resort
22 Store Bay Holiday Resort
23 Golden Thistle Hotel

**PLACES TO EAT**

4  Dillon's
7  Beach Bar & Food Huts
8  Steak Hut
13 Bay Restaurant
20 Tobago Taxi Co-op Society
   Restaurant & Bar

**OTHER**

6  Police Station
11 Fort Milford
12 Francis Supermarket
14 Tobago Marine Sports
15 Viking Dive
17 AR Auto Rentals
18 Tourist Office
19 Republic Bank
24 Crown Point International
   Airport Terminal

Milford Road Extension

To Scarborough

Milford Road

Store Bay

Store Bay Road

TOBAGO

April to June, September and October) they can block off one bedroom and rent it for US$36.

### Places to Stay – top end

*Tropikist Beach Hotel* (☎ 639-8512; fax 639-1110), about a 10-minute walk west of the airport, is a modern seaside hotel with 25 comfortable rooms. Rooms have air-con, TV, phone, balcony and a small refrigerator but no cooking facilities. Rates are US$60 for doubles year-round.

The *Conrado Beach Resort* (☎ 639-0145; fax 639-0755), Milford Rd extension, is on a narrow white-sand beach a five-minute walk from Pigeon Point. This older family-run hotel has 31 nicely renovated rooms that vary quite a bit in size but have air-con, fan, TV and phone. Winter rates begin at US$65 for a room facing inland, though it's well worth the extra US$10 for one of the ocean-front rooms that sport a sun deck over-looking the beach. Rates are US$20 cheaper in summer.

Crown Point's biggest hotel, the *Crown Point Beach Hotel* (☎ 639-8781; fax 639-8731), PO Box 223 Scarborough, has a good location on a jut of land at the south end of Store Bay. There are 77 self-catering rooms, a pool and tennis courts. Summer/winter rates for two people are US$50/60 in a small studio, US$60/70 in a cabana and US$75/85 in a one-bedroom apartment.

*Sandy Point Village* (☎ 639-8533), on the beach at the north-west side of the airport runway, is a relatively large (42-unit) time-share property that rents studios from US$35/60 in summer/winter for two people, US$10 for each additional person. The rooms, which are comfortable enough but not terribly polished, have one double and three single beds in a sort of bunk-bed style, a kitchen, TV, phone and porch-like sitting area. There's a pool.

### Places to Eat

The covered picnic area opposite the beach at Store Bay has a few simple eating options. The outdoor bar sells shark, flying fish or chicken served with chips for TT$15, as well as sandwiches including a hot shark & bake for TT$7. There's also a line of small sheds selling local dishes such as crab and dumplings, pelau with goat, macaroni pie and callaloo soup. Plate meals average about TT$20, but the quality is not terribly consistent – *Miss Trim* is the best bet.

The *Tobago Taxi Co-op Society Restaurant & Bar* at the airport has inexpensive fast food, such as shark & bake for TT$7, chicken with chips or cheeseburgers for TT$9.

The Crown Point Beach Hotel's *Bay Restaurant* has reasonably priced breakfasts – either a full Western breakfast with fresh fruit or a local flying fish breakfast for TT$25. At lunch, chicken or flying fish & chips costs TT$18, while sandwiches begin at about half that. At dinner there's a West Indian meal of the day, including soup, a choice of three main dishes, dessert and coffee for TT$80.

The beachfront *Steak Hut* at Sandy Point Village has continental and full breakfasts priced from TT$15 to TT$27. From 11 am to 4 pm you can get flying fish or hamburgers with chips and salad for TT$22. There's a different set dinner nightly for around TT$65 or you can order à la carte for about the same price. On Wednesday night the Muskateers play old-time calypso and the dinner is Indian curry, while on Friday there's usually a steel band and free rum.

The *Conrado Beach Resort*, on the road to Pigeon Point, has a lovely beachside setting and outdoor patio dining. You can get standard breakfast fare with juice and coffee for TT$30 and lunchtime sandwiches for under TT$20. At dinner a complete meal from salad to dessert range from TT$65 for chicken to TT$90 for lobster.

*Dillon's*, (☎ 639-8765) near Jimmy's on the north side of Crown Point, is a popular upscale dinner restaurant featuring seafood dishes. The menu ranges from flying fish for TT$60 to lobster for TT$135. It's open from 6 pm daily except Monday.

Francis Supermarket is a medium-sized grocery store at the side of the Crown Point Beach Hotel and there's a small, reasonably priced mini-mart open from 7 am to 11 pm daily at Jimmy's Holiday Resort.

## BUCCOO

Buccoo is a small village that's only lightly touristed. The brown-sand beach at Buccoo Bay doesn't compete with the white sands at Store Bay, but Buccoo's offshore waters are lovely.

### Buccoo Reef Tours

A handful of glass-bottom boats provide tours of the extensive fringing reef between Buccoo and Pigeon Point. The boats pass over the reef, much of which is just a metre or two beneath the surface, stop for snorkelling and end with a swim in the Nylon Pool, a calm shallow area with a sandy bottom and clear turquoise waters.

Johnson & Sons (☎ 639-8519) does a nice tour. Unlike most boats that go out at 11 am every day, Johnson goes out when the tide is low (and the snorkelling best), leaving between 9 am and 2.30 pm. Meet at the end of the pier at Buccoo Beach. If you're an avid snorkeller, let Johnson know beforehand and he can stop at some deeper spots with pristine coral, otherwise the tours generally stick to shallower waters. Tours last about 3½ hours and cost TT$30.

There are also boats to Buccoo Reef leaving from Store Bay and Pigeon Point for the same price.

### Places to Stay

Buccoo has a few word-of-mouth guesthouses offering simple rooms at cheap prices. A good-value place is *Aunty Flo's* (☎ 639-9192), Battery St, the third house on the right up the hill from the glass-bottom boat dock. 'Aunty Flo' has five simple but clean rooms, with a shower and toilet separated from the rest of the bedroom by a plastic shower curtain. Rates are TT$50 per person without meals, TT$70 with breakfast and dinner, the latter usually comprising fresh fish, a speciality of Aunty Flo's, who runs a food shack down by the beach.

You could also try *Miller's Guesthouse* (☎ 639-0368), the two-storey white cement house with blue trim which is immediately above the glassbottom boats.

### Places to Eat

There are a few food stalls near the beach serving bake and fish (TT$7) and other simple fare. There are also a couple of small cafés, *Joy's* and *Vicky's*, on the main road just east of the beach, serving inexpensive local food. Joy's is open for three meals a day, Vicky's for lunch and dinner.

There's respectable takeaway pizza, from 3 to 9.30 pm daily, at *Teaside Pizza* in a residential neighbourhood 200 metres north of the beach. Prices start at TT$20 for a small cheese pizza.

*La Tartaruga* (☎ 639-0940), opposite the beach, has good authentic Italian food at moderate prices. It's open for lunch from noon to 2 pm and for dinner from 7 to 11 pm Tuesday to Saturday.

## MT IRVINE TO GREAT COURLAND BAY

The stretch of coastline from Mt Irvine to Great Courland Bay is a rather exclusive area with the island's only golf course and three resort hotels, each on a separate bay: Mt Irvine Bay Hotel on Mt Irvine Bay, Grafton Beach Resort on Stone Haven Bay and Turtle Beach Hotel on Great Courland Bay.

There's a roadside public beach, **Mt Irvine Beach**, 200 metres north of the Mt Irvine Bay Hotel, with sheltered picnic tables and a beach bar selling rotis, sandwiches and other simple fare. The beach can have some good surfing conditions over a mix of sand and rocks.

On a rocky hill at the north side of Stone Haven Bay is **Fort Bennett**. Little remains of the fort other than a couple of cannons, but there's a good view of the coast from this site. The turn-off is clearly marked and the fort is only about 500 metres west of the main road.

### Places to Stay

The *Old Grange Inn* (☎ 639-0275), PO Box 297, Scarborough, is less than a km east of Buccoo, opposite the south end of the golf course. This small 15-unit lodge is a bit off the road and beyond the sound of traffic. The standard rooms are large with high wooden ceilings, air-con, ceiling fan and private bath and are good value at US$30/35 for singles/

TOBAGO

doubles. There are also newly refurbished superior rooms which have TV and phone and cost US$50/60. Breakfast and dinner can be added for another US$25 per person.

At the Buccoo Junction, adjacent to the Old Grange Inn, is the *Golf View Apartments* (☎ 639-0979), PO Box 354, Scarborough, which has a dozen straightforward self-catering apartments that rent for US$35 to US$55 year-round.

The *Mount Irvine Bay Hotel* (☎ 639-8871; fax 639-8800), PO Box 222, Scarborough, is a 105-room resort between Mt Irvine Bay and the hotel's 18-hole golf course. Hotel rooms in the two-storey main building have air-con, a balcony and standard resort amenities. Singles/doubles cost US$130/150 in summer, US$205/215 in winter. There are also roomier cottages (no cooking facilities) that cost US$275 in summer, US$360 in winter. The resort has tennis courts, a pool and a beach.

The *Grafton Beach Resort* (☎ 639-0191; fax 639-0030), Black Rock, is a modern upmarket hotel with a pleasant beachside location. The 112 rooms have air-con, ceiling fan, TV, minibar, a patio or balcony and, in most cases, two queen beds. There are squash courts, a pool and complimentary use of kayaks, catamarans, surfboards and windsurfing gear. The standard rate is US$215, however the hotel has recently been luring visitors from Trinidad with a special rate of US$67 on direct bookings for an ocean-view room – certainly a top bargain if it's still being offered.

The *Turtle Beach Hotel* (☎ 639-2851; fax 639-1495; in the UK ☎ (01) 589-0144), PO Box 201, Scarborough, is Tobago's largest hotel with 125 rooms in two and three-storey buildings along a long curving beach. The rooms are not as upmarket as the area's other two resorts, but they have an ocean-fronting balcony, air-con, phone and radio. Rates for one or two people are US$68 in summer, US$92 in January, US$162 around Christmas and US$120 for the rest of winter.

### Places to Eat

The *Papillon Restaurant* (☎ 639-0275) at

the Old Grange Inn, owned and operated by Swiss chef Jakob Straessle, has food that's both better and cheaper than at neighbouring resort restaurants. You can dine in the air-conditioned dining room or al fresco on the patio. There's a complete dinner of the day, from soup to dessert, for TT$60. On the regular menu, main courses include a veg-etarian platter for TT$45, a recommendable baby shark marinated in lime and rum for TT$50 and lobster thermidor or bœuf Chez Jacques for TT$95, all with soupe du jour (or callaloo soup on request), rice and salad.

The *Sugar Mill Restaurant* (☎ 639-8871) at the Mt Irvine Bay Hotel is an open-air poolside restaurant that incorporates the ruins of an old sugar mill. There's a daily fixed-price dinner (reservations required) that includes a starter, soup, salad, a choice of a seafood or meat main course, dessert and coffee for US$30; however, the food is not particularly distinguished. At lunch there are moderately priced salads, sandwiches and hot dishes.

The restaurant at the *Turtle Beach Hotel* has overpriced breakfast fare, pizza and burgers at lunch for around TT$35 and a Sunday lunch buffet for TT$55. On Saturday evenings there's a steel band and barbecue buffet for TT$145. Most other nights, steak and seafood main courses are priced from TT$75.

The *Grafton Beach Resort* has a beach bar that sells snacks, a moderately priced seafood restaurant and an expensive ocean-view dinner restaurant.

## PLYMOUTH

Plymouth, the largest town on the west coast, is not a major destination but does have a few sights clustered along its west side. Just opposite the tourist information booth (open from 8 am to 6 pm) on Shelbourne St is the **Mystery Tombstone** of Betty Stiven, who died in 1783, presumably during childbirth. Her tombstone reads rather cryptically: 'She was a mother without knowing it, and a wife, without letting her husband know it, except by her kind indulgences to him'.

**Fort James**, 200 metres west of the

tourist booth, is a small hilltop coastal fort overlooking Great Courland Bay. This British-built fortification, which dates from 1768, remains largely intact, with four of its cannons still mounted.

Coming back from Fort James, turn right after the tourist booth and continue 150 metres to reach the **Great Courland Bay Monument**, an odd concrete creation honouring the early Courlander colonists who settled the area in the 17th century.

### Places to Stay & Eat

*Cocrico Inn* (☎ 639-2961; fax 639-6565), PO Box 287, on Commissioner St in the centre of Plymouth, has 16 straightforward rooms, all with air-con and private showers. Upstairs units have a small balcony and there's a nice little pool on the grounds. The rooms are not intended as a place to hang out and are rather smallish but clean. Singles/doubles cost US$40/45 in summer, US$50/60 in winter, plus US$6 for one of the two units with kitchenettes. It's within walking distance of the beach and a 10-minute drive to Mt Irvine or Buccoo Bay.

Cocrico Inn has a reasonably priced restaurant open for three meals a day. A full breakfast, or a lunch of flying fish and chips, crab and dumplings or oil down with breadfruit, are all priced around TT$25. Dinner ranges from chicken or fresh fish of the day for TT$45 to lobster tail for TT$89, and there are a few moderately priced wines. You can also get inexpensive sandwiches any time of the day.

The *Arnos Vale Hotel* (☎ 639-2881; fax 639-4629), PO Box 208, Scarborough, on secluded Arnos Vale Bay, two km north of Plymouth, is a pleasant hotel in a jungle-like setting that caters largely to Italian tourists. The 30 rooms, which slope down the hillside in cottages and small two-storey blocks, have tile or wooden floors, wicker furnishings and air-con. There's a pool and an expensive seaside restaurant (breakfast US$15, lunch or dinner US$40) with Creole and Italian fare. The small bay has a sandy beach and good swimming and snorkelling.

Singles/doubles cost US$100/140 in summer, US$120/180 in winter.

## SCARBOROUGH

Scarborough, the island's administrative centre, is a bustling little city with one-way streets and congested traffic. There are some simple wooden homes on stilts along the side streets and a few older buildings in the centre but the town's character is largely commercial. Other than visiting Fort King George on the east side of town, which is quite interesting, there's not much else to see or do.

The botanical gardens, between the highway and town centre, are little more than a public park with a few identified trees and are only worth a stop if you're passing by. The sign 'Botanic Gardens Layby' marks the turn-off at the side of the highway.

Docks for cruise ships, the Trinidad ferries and visiting yachts are in a row, along with the customs office, in the town centre. The public market is a few minutes' walk to the north, up Wilson Rd. The bus terminal is immediately north-east of the market, at the corner of Post Office St and Greenside Rd.

### Information

The Royal Bank is on the corner of Main and Bacolet streets. Tobago's central post office is north of the market on Post Office St. The tourist office (☎ 639-2125), open from 8 am to 4 pm weekdays, is just east of the post office.

The Cotton House on Bacolet St, 1.5 km south of Main St, has good T-shirts and fine cotton clothing. It's open from 8 am to 5 pm weekdays, to noon on Saturday.

### Fort King George

Fort King George sits on a hill at the end of Fort St, a km from Main St. This British-built fort is the only substantial colonial fortification remaining in Tobago and is well worth a visit for both its historic significance and its fine coastal view. There's no admission charge to enter the fort grounds.

In 1781, two years after the fort's construction, the French captured Tobago and held it until 1793, when the British retook the

**TOBAGO**

island. In 1790, in the midst of the French Revolution, the French soldiers stationed at this fort mutinied, killing their officers. In the melee that followed Scarborough, known to the French as Port Louis, was burned to the ground.

Cannons line the fort's old stone walls and a number of the historic buildings have been restored. The old hospital building now contains a fine arts centre with changing exhibits of island art. Another building contains a small museum (TT$3) with displays on Amerindian artefacts and Tobago's colonial history. The old powder magazine houses the Surprise tea shop, where you can get tea, juices and pastries from 10 am Tuesday to Friday. The shop also sells locally made handicrafts.

The lighthouse at the fort has a lead crystal Fresnel lens that can throw a beam 50 km out to sea using just a 3000-watt light. If you have a keen interest in these impressive prismatic lenses that have been decommissioned just about everywhere else in the world the friendly lightkeeper will probably be quite willing to give you a quick tour.

### Places to Stay

*Sandy's Bed & Breakfast* (☎ 639-2737), at the back of the Blue Crab Restaurant, Robinson St, consists of two rooms in the home of Ken and Alison Sardinha, the amiable couple who operate the restaurant. The rooms are set off a bit for privacy and are pleasantly simple like those of an old-fashioned inn, with pine-wood floors, ceiling fan and private bath. One room has a bit of a bay view, both can have a TV on request and rates include breakfast. It's walking distance to the bus terminal and Fort King George. Singles/ doubles cost US$30/55.

*Della Mira Guest House* (☎ 639-2531), PO Box 203, Scarborough, is on Bacolet St, on the quiet south side of town, about a km from the centre. The 14 rooms are simple and wearworn. Best are the six ocean-facing rooms, which have air-con and a nice view across the bay. The inland-facing rooms are quite basic, with ceiling fans, cement floors and the shower and toilet separated from the

rest of the room by a simple shower curtain. There's a pool and an adjacent nightclub. Singles/doubles cost US$25/31 in the standard rooms, US$35/45 in the ocean-facing rooms.

### Places to Eat

*East Ocean Restaurant*, on Milford Rd one km west of the cruise ship dock, is a small, unpretentious restaurant with a full menu of inexpensive Chinese dishes. There are also combination plates for TT$20. You can eat in or order takeaway. It's open from 11 am to 11 pm Monday to Saturday, 4 to 10 pm on Sunday.

The *Blue Crab Restaurant*, on the east side of town on the corner of Main and Robinson streets, is a family-run restaurant with a pleasant al fresco setting and good upmarket West Indian food. The menu changes daily. At lunch there's a choice of a few main dishes such as Creole chicken or flying fish served with rice and island vegetables for TT$32, while average dinner prices are double that. Vegetarian meals are available. Lunch is served from 11 am to 3 pm; dinner, which is by reservation, is served from 7 pm. It's closed on Saturday.

*Rouselle's*, a km south of the town centre on Bacolet St, is a popular bar and restaurant open for dinner Monday to Saturday. Dinners range from chicken for TT$65 to lobster dishes for TT$145.

The *Old Donkey Cart House*, in a colonial house 750 metres beyond Rouselle's, has outdoor dining in a garden setting. At dinner there are dishes such as spicy pasta for TT$45, fresh fish for TT$60 and tenderloin for a few dollars more. At lunch, from noon to 3 pm weekdays, you can get sandwiches for about TT$20. The restaurant has an extensive selection of German wines.

### WINDWARD RD

Just east of Scarborough, the landscape quickly turns mountainous and rural. The Windward Rd, which connects Scarborough with Speyside, winds in and out from the coast, passing scattered villages, jungly valleys and the occasional brown-sand beach. The farther east you go the more ruggedly beautiful the scenery becomes. Although much of the road is quite narrow and curving, it's easily driveable in a standard vehicle. If you were to drive straight through from Scarborough to Speyside it'd take about 1½ hours.

Eight km east of Scarborough is Granby Point, a jut of land separating Barbados Bay from Pinfold Bay. In 1764 the British established a temporary capital on the east side of Barbados Bay and built **Fort Granby** at the tip of the point. It's only a couple of minutes' walk from the parking lot to the old fort site, but little remains other than the gravestone of the soldier James Clark, who died in 1772. There are a couple of hilltop picnic tables, a view of nearby Smith's Island, a brown-sand beach, changing rooms and the Dry Dock restaurant, which has inexpensive hot dogs, barbecued chicken and fish & chips.

The **Argyll Waterfall**, triple-tiered falls on the Argyll River, is at the north side of the Windward Rd just west of Roxborough. Guides wait along the side of the road and charge TT$15 to TT$20 to lead visitors to the falls, about a 20-minute hike away. **Roxborough** itself is a sizeable village with a post office, a petrol station and a few stores where you can pick up snacks.

Five km east of Roxborough, **King's Bay** is a deep and pretty bay with powdery dark sands and beach facilities. Inland from the bay a sign points to King's Bay Waterfall; however, the falls have been greatly diminished by recent damming. After King's Bay the road winds and twists its way over the mountains to Speyside.

### Places to Stay & Eat

*Richmond Great House* (☎ 660-4467), Belle Garden, is a small inn occupying a restored plantation house at the edge of the rainforest. The inn has five simply furnished rooms with private bath that cost US$55/65 for singles/doubles in summer, US$65/75 in winter, breakfast included. There's a pool and hilltop views. Owner Hollis Lynch is an African history teacher at New York's Colombia University and some of the common rooms are decorated with African crafts.

Non-guests can come up for breakfast (TT$25), lunch (TT$50, noon to 3 pm) and dinner (TT$75, 6.30 to 9 pm); reservations are preferred. The inn is 150 metres north of the main road, 750 metres after entering the village of Richmond; the turn-off is marked.

Forestry ranger Hubert 'Renson' Jack is opening the new *Stella Flora Nature Retreat* (☎ 660-5175), a four-room guesthouse in the rainforest, a couple of km north-east of Roxborough in the Delaford area. Renson, who leads nature tours, intends to charge about US$50 a double with breakfast.

### SPEYSIDE

Speyside is a small fishing village fronting Tyrrel's Bay and the jumping-off point for excursions to the uninhabited island of Little Tobago, a bird sanctuary two km offshore. There are beach facilities and a small fruit and vegetable market at the south end of the beach where the Windward Rd makes its first contact with the bay.

Tyrrel's Bay has protected inshore waters and some reef areas good enough for snorkelling. Be more careful if swimming around the offshore islands as there is a ferocious current between Goat Island and Little Tobago.

### Places to Stay

Canadian Peter Rickwood, a former journalist for the *Toronto Star*, and his wife, Donna Yawching, operate the new four-room *Speyside Inn* (☎ & fax 660-4852), Windward Rd, opposite Jemma's restaurant. The three upstairs rooms are pleasant with high ceilings, red-tile floors and private bath; French doors lead to small balconies with nice breezes and a good sea view across Goat Island to Little Tobago. Singles/doubles cost US$55/65 with breakfast. There's also a downstairs self-catering unit for US$50 and Peter plans to add a few more rooms.

The *Blue Waters Inn* (☎ 660-4341; fax 660-5195; from the USA ☎ (800) 742-4276), Batteaux Bay, caters largely to naturalists and divers. The 28-room hotel is

TOBAGO

secluded on its own little brown-sand cove about a km north of Speyside. You can take walks into the rainforest behind the hotel and there's a dive shop and tennis court on site. Rooms are in contemporary cottages and small two-storey buildings. Standard rooms have either two double beds or one king-size bed, private bath and ceiling fans and cost US$48/56 for singles/doubles in summer, US$80/90 in winter. There is also a handful of self-catering units priced from US$72 in summer, US$123 in winter, which can sleep a family of four.

### Places to Eat

*Jemma's* (☎ 660-4066), in the centre of Tyrrel's Bay on Windward Rd, is a simple seaside restaurant that serves excellent local food, including grilled fish, shrimp, lamb and vegetarian dishes. You can get a good solid lunch for TT$25, dinner for TT$35, served in the open-air treehouse out the back. It's open for breakfast, lunch and dinner daily except Saturday, and closes at 6 pm on Friday unless there are dinner reservations.

The beachfront restaurant at *Blue Waters Inn* also has good food. From 8 to 10 am there's a continental breakfast for TT$19 or a full breakfast for TT$37. From noon to 2 pm, there are sandwiches, burgers and a fruit plate from TT$15 to TT$35. A complete dinner, with a choice of a few main dishes that usually includes fresh fish, costs TT$95, while a vegetarian meal costs TT$60.

### LITTLE TOBAGO

Little Tobago, also known as Bird of Paradise Island, has an interesting history. In 1909 Englishman Sir William Ingram imported about 50 greater birds of paradise from the Aru Islands, off New Guinea, and established a sanctuary on Little Tobago to protect the bird, which was in danger of becoming extinct. Hurricane Flora devastated the habitat in 1963 and the bird of paradise hasn't been sighted on Little Tobago for more than a decade.

Little Tobago, now managed by the government, remains an important sea bird sanctuary nonetheless. Red-billed tropic-birds, red-footed and brown boobies, Audubon shearwaters, brown noddies, sooty terns and bridled terns are some of the species found on the island.

This hilly, arid island, which averages about 1.5 km in width, has a network of trails. Be sure to bring something to drink as there are no facilities. A caretaker goes over in the daytime.

### Getting There & Away

One way to get to Little Tobago is to simply go down to the public beach where there are usually a couple of boats waiting to take passengers over to the island, a crossing that takes about 15 minutes. The rate is commonly TT$30 per person, sometimes including a land tour, though it's all a bit negotiable.

You can get a more in-depth tour by making advance arrangements with one of three naturalist guides who are very knowledgeable about island ecology: Renson Jack (☎ 660-5175), Pat Turpin (☎ 660-4327) and David Rooks (☎ 639-4276).

In addition, there's *Fear Not*, a glass-bottom boat used for snorkelling tours of the islands, which is usually anchored in front of Jemma's restaurant; ask for Roberts. Jemma's is a bit of a hangout and a good place to meet with people.

### CHARLOTTEVILLE

It's four scenic, winding km over the mountains from Speyside to Charlotteville. At the summit, before the road snakes down to Charlotteville, a marked gravel road leads north to Flagstaff Hill. Taking this rough side road for just a few hundred metres will provide some fine jungle views and a chance of seeing, or at least hearing, a flock of parrots.

Charlotteville is a delightful little fishing village. Sleepy, secluded and with an earthy simplicity, it has the appearance of some long forgotten outpost. In the winter, the hillsides behind the village are bright with the orange blossoms of immortelle trees, which were introduced from Martinique in colonial times to shade cocoa trees.

TOBAGO

Man of War Bay, the large horseshoe-shaped bay that fronts the village, is lined with a palm-studded brown-sand beach and offers good swimming. There's excellent snorkelling at Pirate's Bay, a 10-minute walk across the point at the north side of Charlotteville, and good snorkelling around Booby Island just south of the village.

If you're up for more exploring, take a walk out to the site of the old Fort Campbelton, on the west side of the bay, which offers a good coastal view, or take a more substantial hike up Flagstaff Hill.

Visitors to Charlotteville are largely limited to divers, snorkellers and bird watchers, and there's a Danish-run dive shop, Man Friday Diving, in the village.

---

### Pirate's Bay

Pirate's Bay derives its name from the secluded haven it provided to marauding buccaneers who established a base here three centuries ago. The island proved ripe grounds for piracy after rival colonial powers, tired of battling over Tobago, declared it a 'no-man's land'. As a consequence, Tobago became a centre for attacks on both treasure-laden Spanish ships sailing from South America and British ships in the Grenadines. It's rumoured that there's still buried treasure around Pirate's Bay.

Today the bay is a feeding grounds for frigatebirds, a sort of pirate in their own right – the birds feed themselves by snatching food in mid-air from terns and gulls. ■

---

### Places to Stay

There are a number of small unofficial guesthouses in Charlotteville, most found by word of mouth, and there's seldom a problem getting a room.

A good choice is *Belle-Air Cottages*, on the hill at the north end of town, 100 metres beyond the start of Pirates' Bay Rd. This new two-storey building has five straightforward bedrooms, each with two beds and a dresser. Bathrooms are in the hall and there's access to a kitchen, sitting room and washing machine. The rate is TT$50 per person in a downstairs room, TT$60 per person upstairs where there's carpeting and a balcony. There's no phone – if no-one's around, ask for Margaret at the house across the street.

*Man-O-War Bay Cottages* (☎ 660-4327; fax 660-4328), Charlotteville Estate, is on the beach about a five-minute walk south of the village. The grounds are like a little botanical garden with lots of ferns, trees and flowering plants. There are six simple cottages with private baths, kitchens and screened louvred windows that open to the breeze and the sound of the surf. A one-bedroom unit with a double bed costs from US$45, two bedrooms with four beds cost from US$55, three bedrooms with six beds US$85 and the four-bedroom cottage with 10 beds is US$130. The cottages are owned by Pat Turpin, who leads naturalist tours around Tobago, and consequently a fair number of 'ecotourists' stay here.

### Places to Eat

*Pheb's Ville View Restaurant*, opposite the library, is a wonderful little open-air restaurant with five tables overlooking the village and some of the finest homemade food on Tobago. A full West Indian lunch plate costs TT$20. Dinner, which includes soup, costs TT$25. Portions are very generous and there's usually a choice of vegetarian, chicken or fish as a main course. Wash it down with a mixed fresh fruit drink for TT$3. It's open from noon to 9 pm Monday to Saturday.

There are also small stores in town where you can pick up provisions.

### TOBAGO FOREST RESERVE

The Roxborough Parlatuvier Rd, which crosses the island from Roxborough to Bloody Bay, is a bit narrow and curving but it is newly paved and one of the best roads on the island. It's a nice 30-minute jungle drive, completely undeveloped, with pretty valley and mountain views.

The road passes through the Tobago Forest Reserve, which was established in 1765, making it the oldest forest reserve in

TOBAGO

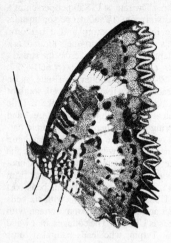

the Caribbean. There are a number of trailheads leading off the main road where you could make a jaunt into the rainforest.

There's excellent birdwatching in this area and it's not uncommon to hear squawking parrots and see hummingbirds, motmots, cocricos, woodpeckers and trogons.

Three-quarters of the way across is a roadside forestry hut with a scenic view of Bloody Bay and the offshore Sisters Rocks. From there it's just a five-minute ride down to Bloody Bay, which takes its name from a fierce battle that occurred here between the Dutch, French and British in the 1600s.

Once you reach Bloody Bay it's about an hour's drive south to Plymouth. There are a couple of nice beaches and villages along the way, unhurried places with kids playing cricket in the road. Just west of Bloody Bay is Parlatuvier, a tiny fishing village on a strikingly beautiful circular bay. Castara, farther south, is a pleasant bayside village with a good bathing beach right in town.

## GETTING THERE & AWAY

There are ferry and air services between Tobago and Port of Spain. Information on both is under the Getting Around section at the beginning of this chapter.

## GETTING AROUND
### Bus

There's a bus service between Crown Point Airport (buy tickets at the airport kiosk) and Scarborough for TT$0.75 every half-hour from 6.30 am to around 8 pm.

From Scarborough there's a much less frequent bus to Charlotteville that costs TT$2. Generally on weekdays one bus leaves Scarborough at 10 am and another at noon and a bus returns from Charlotteville at 4 pm, but verify this first with a driver or the tourist office. Buses from Scarborough to Plymouth or Mt Irvine cost TT$0.75.

### Taxi

Taxis are available at Crown Point Airport and charge TT$20 to hotels around Crown Point, TT$40 to Scarborough, TT$50 to Mt Irvine or Buccoo and about TT$200 to Charlotteville.

**Route Taxi** In addition to buses there are also route taxis, identified by the letter, H, on their plates, that charge TT$5 from Crown Point to Scarborough and TT$10 from Scarborough to Charlotteville.

### Car & Motorbike

There are a few scattered petrol stations around the island, but it's wisest to fill up before doing extensive touring, as hours can be random and stations occasionally run out of petrol. The most distant station, the one in Charlotteville, is closed on Sunday.

AR Auto Rentals (☎ 639-0644), at the side of the airport, rents mokes (Nissan Marchs modified by having their tops cut away) and small cars for TT$167 a day with collision damage waiver insurance and VAT included. The mokes are sometimes discounted by 20%. AR is open from 6.30 am to 8.30 pm daily. Although renting a moke on Tobago can be fun, mokes leave you quite open to the rays of the sun and to a good drenching during a downpour...and then there are the young men hitching rides who will commonly try to wave you down on the road and simply hop into the open side, whether you want company or not.

You can also rent cars through Singh's Auto Rentals (☎ 639-0191) at the Grafton Beach Resort, George's Auto Rentals (☎ 639-8295), Jordan's Car Rental (☎ 639-1032) and through most of the hotels and guesthouses. Prices generally range from TT$160 to TT$210 a day plus CDW of about TT$30.

There are a couple of places that rent motor scooters for about TT$70 a day; check at Tropikist (☎ 639-8512) and the Golden Thistle Hotel (☎ 639-8521).

# Glossary

**agouti** – a short-haired rabbit-like rodent with short ears, which has a fondness for sugar cane and looks a bit like a guinea pig with elevated feet

**biguine** – also spelt beguine, this Afro-French dance music with a bolero rhythm originated in Martinique in the 1930s

**calypso** – a popular Caribbean music that's essential to Carnival
**Carnival** – the major Caribbean festival that originated as a pre-Lenten festivity but is now observed at various times throughout the year on different islands
**chattel houses** – a type of simple wooden dwelling placed upon cement or stone blocks so it can be easily moved; often erected on rented land
**creole** – in terms of people, creole refers to a person of mixed Black and European ancestry; in terms of language, creole refers to local pidgin that's predominantly a combination of French and African; in terms of food, creole is characterised by spicy, full-flavoured sauces and a heavy use of green peppers and onions

**dasheen** – a type of taro; the leaves are known as callaloo and cooked much like spinach or turnip leaves, the starchy tuberous root is boiled and eaten like a potato
**dolphin** – both a marine mammal found in Caribbean waters and name given to a common type of white-meat fish (also called mahimahi); the two are not related and 'dolphin' on any menu always refers to the fish

**Ital** – a natural style of vegetarian cooking practised by Rastafarians

**jump-ups** – a type of night-time street party that usually involves dancing and plenty of rum drinking

**lime** – also limin'; to hang out, relax
**lolo** – a pavement barbecue stand where meat is grilled and sold

**mairie** – the name for town hall in the French West Indies
**manicou** – the opossum, a small marsupial
**manchineel** – a common tree on Eastern Caribbean beaches whose sap can cause a skin rash
**mas camps** – 'mas' as in masquerade, these are the workshops where artists create Carnival costumes

**obeah** – a belief system related to black magic

**panyards** – the places where steel pan bands practise their music in the months leading up to Carnival
**pareo** – a type of wrap skirt that's commonly sold on beaches in the Caribbean
**pitt** – in the French West Indies, an arena where cockfights take place
**Planters punch** or **Planteur punch** – a rum punch mixing rum and fruit juice

**sorrel juice** – a lightly tart, bright-red drink rich in Vitamin C that's made from the flowers of the sorrel plant
**souse** – a dish made out of a pickled pig's head and belly, spices and a few vegetables

**zouk** – popular French West Indies music that draws from the biguine, bebop-like cadence and other French Caribbean folk forms.

# Index

# PLANET TALK
*Lonely Planet's FREE quarterly newsletter*

We love hearing from you and think you'd like to hear from us.

**When**...is the right time to see reindeer in Finland?
**Where**...can you hear the best palm-wine music in Ghana?
**How**...do you get from Asunción to Areguá by steam train?
**What**...is the best way to see India?

For the answer to these and many other questions read PLANET TALK.

*Every issue is packed with up-to-date travel news and advice including:*

* *a letter from Lonely Planet founders Tony and Maureen Wheeler*
* *travel diary from a Lonely Planet author - find out what it's really like out on the road*
* *feature article on an important and topical travel issue*
* *a selection of recent letters from our readers*
* *the latest travel news from all over the world*
* *details on Lonely Planet's new and forthcoming releases*

*To join our mailing list contact any Lonely Planet office (address below).*

## LONELY PLANET PUBLICATIONS
**Australia:** PO Box 617, Hawthorn 3122, Victoria (tel: 03-819 1877)
**USA:** Embarcadero West, 155 Filbert St, Suite 251, Oakland, CA 94607 (tel: 510-893 8555)
TOLL FREE: (800) 275-8555
**UK:** 10 Barley Mow Passage, Chiswick, London W4 4PH (tel: 081-742 3161)
**France:** 71 bis rue du Cardinal Lemoine – 75005 Paris (tel: 1-46 34 00 58)

*Also available: Lonely Planet T-shirts. 100% heavyweight cotton (S, M, L, XL)*

# Guides to the Americas

### Alaska – a travel survival kit
Jim DuFresne has travelled extensively through Alaska by foot, road, rail, barge and kayak, and tells how to make the most of one of the world's great wilderness areas.

### Argentina, Uruguay & Paraguay – a travel survival kit
This guide gives independent travellers all the essential information on three of South America's lesser-known countries. Discover some of South America's most spectacular natural attractions in Argentina; friendly people and beautiful handicrafts in Paraguay; and Uruguay's wonderful beaches.

### Baja California – a travel survival kit
For centuries, Mexico's Baja peninsula – with its beautiful coastline, raucous border towns and crumbling Spanish missions – has been a land of escapes and escapades. This book describes how and where to escape in Baja.

### Bolivia – a travel survival kit
From lonely villages in the Andes to ancient ruined cities and the spectacular city of La Paz, Bolivia is a magnificent blend of everything that inspires travellers. Discover safe and intriguing travel options in this comprehensive guide.

### Brazil – a travel survival kit
From the mad passion of Carnival to the Amazon – home of the richest ecosystem on earth – Brazil is a country of mythical proportions. This guide has all the essential travel information.

### Canada – a travel survival kit
This comprehensive guidebook has all the facts on the USA's huge neighbour – the Rocky Mountains, Niagara Falls, ultramodern Toronto, remote villages in Nova Scotia, and much more.

### Central America on a shoestring
Practical information on travel in Belize, Guatemala, Costa Rica, Honduras, El Salvador, Nicaragua and Panama. A team of experienced Lonely Planet authors reveals the secrets of this culturally rich, geographically diverse and breathtakingly beautiful region.

### Chile & Easter Island – a travel survival kit
Travel in Chile is easy and safe, with possibilities as varied as the countryside. This guide also gives detailed coverage of Chile's Pacific outpost, mysterious Easter Island.

### Colombia – a travel survival kit
Colombia is a land of myths – from the ancient legends of El Dorado to the modern tales of Gabriel Garcia Marquez. The reality is beauty and violence, wealth and poverty, tradition and change. This guide shows how to travel independently and safely in this exotic country.

### Costa Rica – a travel survival kit
Sun-drenched beaches, steamy jungles, smoking volcanoes, rugged mountains and dazzling birds and animals – Costa Rica has it all.

### Ecuador & the Galápagos Islands – a travel survival kit
Ecuador offers a wide variety of travel experiences, from the high cordilleras to the Amazon plains – and 600 miles west, the fascinating Galápagos Islands. Everything you need to know about travelling around this enchanting country.

### Guatemala, Belize & Yucatán: La Ruta Maya – a travel survival kit
Climb a volcano, explore the colourful highland villages or laze your time away on coral islands and Caribbean beaches. The lands of the Maya offer a fascinating journey into the past which will enhance appreciation of their dynamic contemporary cultures. An award winning guide to this exotic fregion.

### Hawaii – a travel survival kit
Share in the delights of this island paradise – and avoid its high prices – both on and off the beaten track. Full details on Hawaii's best-known attractions, plus plenty of uncrowded sights and activities.

### Mexico – a travel survival kit
A unique blend of Indian and Spanish culture, fascinating history, and hospitable people, make Mexico a travellers' paradise.

### Peru – a travel survival kit
The lost city of Machu Picchu, the Andean altiplano and the magnificent Amazon rainforests are just some of Peru's many attractions. All the travel facts you'll need can be found in this comprehensive guide.

### South America on a shoestring
This practical guide provides concise information for budget travellers and covers South America from the Darien Gap to Tierra del Fuego.

### Trekking in the Patagonian Andes
The first detailed guide to this region gives complete information on 28 walks, and lists a number of other possibilities extending from the Araucanía and Lake District regions of Argentina and Chile to the remote icy tip of South America in Tierra del Fuego.

### Also available:
**Brazilian** phrasebook, **Latin American Spanish** phrasebook and **Quechua** phrasebook.

# Lonely Planet Guidebooks

Lonely Planet guidebooks cover every accessible part of Asia as well as Australia, the Pacific, South America, Africa, the Middle East, Europe and parts of North America. There are five series: *travel survival kits*, covering a country for a range of budgets; *shoestring guides* with compact information for low-budget travel in a major region; *walking guides*; *city guides* and *phrasebooks*.

# Mail Order

Lonely Planet guidebooks are distributed worldwide. They are also available by mail order from Lonely Planet, so if you have difficulty finding a title please write to us. US and Canadian residents should write to Embarcadero West, 155 Filbert St, Suite 251, Oakland CA 94607, USA; European residents should write to 10 Barley Mow Passage, Chiswick, London W4 4PH; and residents of other countries to PO Box 617, Hawthorn, Victoria 3122, Australia.

## Indian Subcontinent
Bangladesh
India
Hindi/Urdu phrasebook
Trekking in the Indian Himalaya
Karakoram Highway
Kashmir, Ladakh & Zanskar
Nepal
Trekking in the Nepal Himalaya
Nepali phrasebook
Pakistan
Sri Lanka
Sri Lanka phrasebook

## Africa
Africa on a shoestring
Central Africa
East Africa
Trekking in East Africa
Kenya
Swahili phrasebook
Morocco, Algeria & Tunisia
Arabic (Moroccan) phrasebook
South Africa, Lesotho & Swaziland
Zimbabwe, Botswana & Namibia
West Africa

## Central America & the Caribbean
Baja California
Central America on a shoestring
Costa Rica
Eastern Caribbean
Guatemala, Belize & Yucatán: La Ruta Maya
Mexico

## North America
Alaska
Canada
Hawaii

## Europe
Baltic States & Kaliningrad
Dublin city guide
Eastern Europe on a shoestring
Eastern Europe phrasebook
Finland
France
Greece
Hungary
Iceland, Greenland & the Faroe Islands
Ireland
Italy
Mediterranean Europe on a shoestring
Mediterranean Europe phrasebook
Poland
Scandinavian & Baltic Europe on a shoestring
Scandinavian Europe phrasebook
Switzerland
Trekking in Spain
Trekking in Greece
USSR
Russian phrasebook
Western Europe on a shoestring
Western Europe phrasebook

## South America
Argentina, Uruguay & Paraguay
Bolivia
Brazil
Brazilian phrasebook
Chile & Easter Island
Colombia
Ecuador & the Galápagos Islands
Latin American Spanish phrasebook
Peru
Quechua phrasebook
South America on a shoestring
Trekking in the Patagonian Andes

## The Lonely Planet Story

Lonely Planet published its first book in 1973 in response to the numerous 'How did you do it?' questions Maureen and Tony Wheeler were asked after driving, bussing, hitching, sailing and railing their way from England to Australia.

Written at a kitchen table and hand collated, trimmed and stapled, *Across Asia on the Cheap* became an instant local bestseller, inspiring thoughts of another book.

Eighteen months in South-East Asia resulted in their second guide, *South-East Asia on a shoestring*, which they put together in a backstreet Chinese hotel in Singapore in 1975. The 'yellow bible' as it quickly became known to backpackers around the world, soon became *the* guide to the region. It has sold well over half a million copies and is now in its 7th edition, still retaining its familiar yellow cover.

Today there are over 130 Lonely Planet titles in print – books that have that same adventurous approach to travel as those early guides; books that 'assume you know how to get your luggage off the carousel' as one reviewer put it.

Although Lonely Planet initially specialised in guides to Asia, they now cover most regions of the world, including the Pacific, South America, Africa, the Middle East and Europe. The list of *walking guides* and *phrasebooks* (for 'unusual' languages such as Quechua, Swahili, Nepali and Egyptian Arabic) is also growing rapidly.

The emphasis continues to be on travel for independent travellers. Tony and Maureen still travel for several months of each year and play an active part in the writing, updating and quality control of Lonely Planet's guides.

They have been joined by over 50 authors, 60 staff – mainly editors, cartographers & designers – at our office in Melbourne, Australia, at our US office in Oakland, California and at our European office in Paris; another five at our office in London handle sales for Britain, Europe and Africa. Travellers themselves also make a valuable contribution to the guides through the feedback we receive in thousands of letters each year.

The people at Lonely Planet strongly believe that travellers can make a positive contribution to the countries they visit, both through their appreciation of the countries' culture, wildlife and natural features, and through the money they spend. In addition, the company makes a direct contribution to the countries and regions it covers. Since 1986 a percentage of the income from each book has been donated to ventures such as famine relief in Africa; aid projects in India; agricultural projects in Central America; Greenpeace's efforts to halt French nuclear testing in the Pacific and Amnesty International. In 1994 $100,000 was donated to such causes.

Lonely Planet's basic travel philosophy is summed up in Tony Wheeler's comment, 'Don't worry about whether your trip will work out. Just go!'.